D0955411

The Scarecrow Author Bibliographies

1. John Steinbeck (Tetsumaro Hayashi). 1973.
2. Joseph Conrad (Theodore G. Ehrsam). 1969.
3. Arthur Miller (Tetsumaro Hayashi). 2d ed. 1976.
4. Katherine Anne Porter (Waldrip & Bauer). 1969.
5. Philip Freneau (Philip M. Marsh). 1970.
6. Robert Greene (Tetsumaro Hayashi). 1971.
7. Benjamin Disraeli (R. W. Stewart). 1972.
8. John Berryman (Richard W. Kelly). 1972.
9. William Dean Howells (Vito J. Brenni). 1973.
10. Jean Anouilh (Kathleen W. Kelly). 1973.
11. E. M. Forster (Alfred Borrello). 1973.
12. The Marquis de Sade (E. Pierre Chanover). 1973.
13. Alain Robbe-Grillet (Dale W. Frazier). 1973.
14. Northrop Frye (Robert D. Denham). 1974.
15. Federico García Lorca (Laurenti & Siracusa). 1974.
16. Ben Jonson (Brock & Welsh). 1974.
17. Four French Dramatists: Eugène Brieux, François de Curel, Emile Fabre, Paul Hervieu (Edmund F. Santa Vicca). 1974.
18. Ralph Waldo Ellison (Jacqueline Covo). 1974.
19. Philip Roth (Bernard F. Rodgers, Jr.). 1974.
20. Norman Mailer (Laura Adams). 1974.
21. Sir John Betjeman (Margaret Stapleton). 1974.
22. Elie Wiesel (Molly Abramowitz). 1974.
23. Paul Laurence Dunbar (Eugene W. Metcalf, Jr.). 1975.
24. Henry James (Beatrice Ricks). 1975.
25. Robert Frost (Lentricchia & Lentricchia). 1976.
26. Sherwood Anderson (Douglas G. Rogers). 1976.
27. Iris Murdoch and Muriel Spark (Tominaga & Schneider-meyer). 1976.
28. John Ruskin (Kirk H. Beetz). 1976.
29. Georges Simenon (Trudee Young). 1976.
30. George Gordon, Lord Byron (Oscar José Santucho). 1976.
31. John Barth (Richard Vine). 1977.
32. John Hawkes (Carol A. Hryciw). 1977.
33. William Everson (Bartlett & Campo). 1977.
34. May Sarton (Lenora Blouin). 1978.
35. Wilkie Collins (Kirk H. Beetz). 1978.
36. Sylvia Plath (Lane & Stevens). 1978.
37. E. B. White (A. J. Anderson). 1978.
38. Henry Miller (Lawrence J. Shifreen). 1978.

HENRY MILLER:
A Bibliography of Secondary Sources

by

LAWRENCE J. SHIFREEN

Scarecrow Author Bibliographies, No. 38

The Scarecrow Press, Inc.

Metuchen, N.J. & London

1979

Library of Congress Cataloging in Publication Data

Shifreen, Lawrence J   1948-
    Henry Miller : a bibliography of secondary sources.

    (Scarecrow author bibliographies ; no. 38)
    Includes indexes.
    1.   Miller, Henry, 1891-   --Bibliography.
Z8574. 93. S5   [PS3525. I5454]   016. 818'5'209   78-12518
ISBN 0-8108-1171-5

For My Parents
William and Minnie Shifreen

TABLE OF CONTENTS

v

HENRY MILLER: AN INTRODUCTION

    Although there have been several other Henry Miller bibli-
ographies, Bern Porter's Henry Miller: A Chronology and Bibliography, Thomas H. Moore's Bibliography of Henry Miller, Esta
Lou Riley's Henry Miller: An Informal Bibliography 1924-1960, and
Maxine Renkin's A Bibliography of Henry Miller 1945-1961, this bibliography was written in the attempt to include a broader scope of
Miller commentary and criticism than had previously been available
and to help the critic, scholar, and Miller reader focus upon materials relevant to his reading or research.   Therefore, I have included all items dealing with Miller scholarship.   Whenever there
was any doubt about the contribution of any item towards Miller
criticism, I have included it with the supposition that it may be of
use to the Miller scholar.   This study is the fifth attempt at a
Miller bibliography and follows the previous studies only so far as
it is chronological.   The difference comes in that it is much more
inclusive than any previous Miller study and that it is the first fully
annotated study of Miller's work.

    Miller criticism did not begin in 1925 with the publication of
Henry Miller's first work, Mezzotints, but waited ten years for the
Obelisk Press to print Tropic of Cancer.   Soon after this book was
published, such major writers as Blaise Cendrars and Montgomery
Belgion wrote glowing reviews, seeing Tropic as either an expression of despair or as a monumental study of the debasement of human life.[1] Raymond Queneau, in his review of Cancer and Black
Spring, praised Miller by comparing his heroes with those of Joyce
in Ulysses.[2] Whether these critics were attuned to Miller and understood his "point" was insignificant, for they were contributing to
Miller scholarship by reviewing the most sexually graphic novel to
appear in English in the 1930's.

Those who came closest to understanding Miller's narrator's struggle against the debased world were his friends, Lawrence Durrell and Anaïs Nin, two members of the Villa Seurat Circle. In an August 1935 letter to Miller, Durrell calls Tropic of Cancer the only important work of the twentieth century:

> I have just read Tropic of Cancer again and feel I'd like to write you a line about it. It strikes me as being the only really man-sized piece of work which this century can really boast of. ... It really gets down on paper the blood and bowels of our time. I love to see the canons of oblique and pretty emotion mopped up; to see every whim-wham and bagatelle of your contemporaries from Eliot to Joyce dunged under. God give us young men the guts to plant the daisies on top and finish the job.
>
> Tropic is something they've been trying to do since the war. It's the final copy of all those feeble, smudgy drafts--Chatterley, Ulysses, Tarr, etc. It not only goes back, but (which none of them have done) goes forward as well.
>
> It finds the way out of the latrines at last. Funny that no one should have thought of slipping out via the pan during a flush, instead of crowding the door. I salute Tropic as the copy-book for my generation.[3]

Durrell makes it clear that Miller's writing goes beyond the usual emotional romanticism found in literature and reaches a reality that can only be experienced by voyaging through the debasement of the gutters. In this "latrine" of life, one must get beyond the gentlemanly pose of hiding sex and excrement behind the door. One must move from urinating in private to immersing oneself in one's own feces "during the flush" and, from there, to escaping the mundane life by attaining freedom and vitality.

Tropic of Cancer is, as Anaïs Nin called it, a book which will restore our appetite for the fundamental realities. This appraisal comes from her "Preface" to Tropic published in 1934. In this work she makes it clear that the book begins with bitterness but through its "pure flux," one sees man's movement and hunger for life: "This book brings with it a wind that blows down the dead and hollow trees whose roots are withered and lost in the barren soil of our times. This book goes to the roots and digs under, digs for subterranean springs."[4] A journey toward rebirth is seen in

Miller's digging on, in search of freedom and newness, to the point
where he can physically and psychologically reject his surface society and become a true individual.

These two reviews were printed on the Continent yet were
never published in America. In fact, it was not until 1938, four
years after the publication of Tropic of Cancer, that an American
magazine chose to review Miller's work. And with the publication
of Edmund Wilson's favorable review of Cancer, and his damnation
of Puritan America, in "Twilight of the Expatriates," most American
critics still had not read Tropic of Cancer and knew nothing about
its author. This, in spite of the fact that Miller's The Cosmological Eye had already been published in the United States. [5] There
were occasional reviewers, like Paul Rosenfeld[6], who saw Miller's
prose as elevated and affirmative, providing a spiritual celebration
of life in the tradition of D. H. Lawrence and Hart Crane. Men
like Rosenfeld, Herbert Read, and Wallace Fowlie would be instru-
mental in placing Miller's work before the public. Their differences
of opinion would also allow Miller readers to see some of the many
different ways to view Henry Miller's work.

Yet most reviewers and critics were stymied by the ban that
the United States Government placed on the importation of Tropic of
Cancer into America, a restriction that went so far as to refuse
any American publisher the right to print the book in this country,
because of its explicitly sexual nature. The ban was so strictly en-
forced that customs officials were ordered to seize any copies they
found people attempting to smuggle into the country. The reason
given for these undemocratic restraints was that Miller's book was
"filthy." By labeling him a "pornographer," America branded one
of its greatest authors and refused him the right to free expression.
So, while Black Spring, Tropic of Capricorn, Max and the White
Phagocytes, Aller Retour New York, Money and How It Gets That
Way, What Are You Going to Do About Alf?, and the trilogy The
Rosy Crucifixion were being published throughout Europe, American
officials refused to see that an "obscene" book could be of value to
readers and would only permit edited stories by Miller to appear in
print in the United States.

This American fear of the Tropics, Black Spring, The Rosy
Crucifixion, Quiet Days in Clichy, and The World of Sex kept Miller
off the market until 1963 when the United States Supreme Court
ruled that Miller's writing was not pornographic but was of merit.
This ruling allowed Grove Press to quickly publish the above eight
books. It also provided the publisher with the publicity needed to
sell Miller's books. The court trials, having run from 1961 to
1963 and culminating with the Supreme Court's verdict, gave Miller
much more notoriety than he needed or wanted. The type of public
notice the book received never really explored the man's writings.
When E. R. Hutchison's Tropic of Cancer on Trial [A126] and when
Charles Rembar's The End of Obscenity [A129] both conclude in
1968 that Miller is not obscene, they concur with judicial decisions
that negate the fact that Miller is, in reality, "obscene." The major problem with studies and judicial decisions of this nature stems
from their inability to see morality and beauty in a literature they
call pornographic. For, when they judge Miller's writing as neither
pornographic nor obscene, they fail to come to terms with the sexual
aspects of his writing that Miller has never attempted to hide.

To understand Miller's conception of obscenity and its distinction from pornography, one must turn to a Playboy interview
with Bernard Wolfe in which Miller worked quite hard to establish
distinctions between pornography and obscenity: "I can be said to
have written obscene things, but I don't think of myself as a pornographer. There's a big difference between obscenity and pornography. Pornography is a titillating thing, the other is cleans-
ing...."7 By this statement, Miller makes it clear that in his mind
pornography differs from obscenity; the distinction lies in his feeling
that obscenity cleanses and renews while pornography merely arouses.
What Miller means by this remark is that obscenity in his work is
used for a purpose, while pornography is merely sex for its own
sake. Thus obscenity affords Miller the opportunity to openly and
honestly express himself: "The obscene would be forthright, and
pornography would be the roundabout. I believe in saying the truth,
coming out with it cold, shocking if necessary, not disguising it."8

It is evident from this definition that Miller sees obscenity as a method, not an end in itself. His stress in his definition is upon the idea of openness and, thus, if we are to come to terms with Miller's obscenity, we must view it in this context. His need to expose all aspects of the self and society indicates that Miller is acting as the practicing psychologist of America, satirizing his culture's mores.

Miller's need to damn a culture that had slighted him since the twenties was seen by many critics. Men like Harry Levin, Mark Schorer, and Harry T. Moore all testified at the Boston Tropic trial and attempted to show the court that Tropic of Cancer was a valuable literary chronicle, for each saw the book as true to life.[9] Each saw Miller's writing working to create a new morality that would help to change America. This analysis of Miller's writing and the Tropic trials throughout the United States did much to help end the ignorance about Henry Miller, as critics finally began to feel free to review his writing.

Yet, these appraisals of his canon were either lauding or damning and seemed to forget that middle ground could be found on which to approach Miller's work. In one vein, Harry T. Moore called Miller's Tropic narrator a "descendent of Dostoevsky's 'Underground Man'," who travels from a state of psychosis to wholeness. An anonymous review in Life Magazine called the work "an explosive Whitmanesque masterpiece," while Harold C. Gardiner, in an essay entitled "Publishing Disgrace--Critical Shame," considered Tropic to be "the product of a filthy mind."[10] These opposing views actually helped to create two contexts within which to view Miller's novels. Yet critics must now expand these short reviews to help readers to better view Miller's relationship to Whitman and to Dostoevsky or to see him as a distributor of filth. Thus, the sixties proved to be an era that truly began Miller scholarship, labeling him either a "genius" or a "pornographer." Yet, this two-dimensional way of viewing Miller was only the first step in seeing his ties to his culture and his relationship to many different types of writers--humanists, naturalists, romantics, transcendentalists, surrealists, biographers, and new journalists.

During the 1960's a great number of books about Miller were written. The best of these, Annette Baxter's Henry Miller Expatriate [A19], William Gordon's The Mind and Art of Henry Miller [A44], Ihab Hassan's The Literature of Silence: Henry Miller and Samuel Beckett [A45], George Wickes' Henry Miller and the Critics [A36], and Kingsley Widmer's Henry Miller [A37], view Miller through extended studies of the Tropics, Black Spring, and The Rosy Crucifixion. These five critical works provide an excellent starting place for scholarship on Miller.

Yet, one may use these studies to obtain overviews only on Miller's most noted and important works. The Miller scholar needs then to go beyond these to the 130 or so other books and pamphlets written by Henry Miller, including such important works as The Colossus of Maroussi, Sunday After the War, Aller Retour New York, Scenario, Money and How It Gets That Way, What Are You Going to Do About Alf?, Max and the White Phagocytes, The Wisdom of the Heart, Hamlet (two volumes of correspondence), Semblance of a Devoted Past, Murder the Murderer, and many others. To produce more than an isolated period study of Miller's writing, one must discover Miller's beginnings and should begin by reading his first writings--Mezzotints, Gliding into the Everglades, "The Crazy Cock," and "The World of D. H. Lawrence." To read merely the Tropics, Black Spring, and The Rosy Crucifixion and assume that one has a working knowledge of Miller is to miss the bulk of his writing.

Those who waited another ten years to evaluate Miller also advanced Miller scholarship. The first important criticism of the seventies was found in Edward Mitchell's Henry Miller: Three Decades of Criticism [A62], which provides a synthesis of Miller criticism of the preceding thirty years. The Mitchell book is a continuation of the collection of critical essays on Miller that began in 1944 with Bern Porter's The Happy Rock [A3] and which continued into the sixties in George Wickes' Henry Miller and the Critics [A36] (1963). The most important study of the seventies, Norman

Mailer's Genius and Lust: A Journey Through the Major Writings
of Henry Miller [A73], contains a brilliant essay on Miller. The
rest of the book consists of a collection of Miller's best writing as
chosen by Mailer (a follow-up to Lawrence Durrell's 1959 collection).
And, much like Durrell's in his attempt to bring Miller before the
public, Mailer's basic belief is that Miller's value as an author
needs to be restated, for he feels that the American public has a
limited knowledge of Miller and can see little more in his writing
than sex. However, Mailer gets beyond this one-dimensional view
of Miller, seeing him as a "protean man" of the twentieth century.

What needs to be done is for critics to begin where Mailer
left off, to work toward providing a more complete and thorough
overview to the writings by and about Henry Miller. As Norman
Mailer suggests, to do this one must understand the basic difference
between Miller and his contemporaries:

> The difference between Hemingway and Miller is that Hem-
> ingway set out ... to grow into Jake Barnes and locked
> himself for better and worse ... into that character who
> embodied the spirit of an age. Whereas Miller ... chose
> to go in the opposite direction. He proceeded to move
> away from the first Henry Miller he had created. He was
> not a character but a soul--he would be various. 11

By using the word "various," Mailer perceives the basis of Miller's
writing. It is his protean change, his growth and development,
which frightens a reading public that does not know how to deal with
change, a public that can only accept consistent authors like Hemingway and Fitzgerald:

> Henry Miller, however, exists in the same relation to
> legend as antimatter shows to matter. His life is anti-
> pathetic to the idea of legend itself. Where he is com-
> plex, he is too complex--we do not feel the resonance of
> slowly dissolving mystery but the madness of too many
> knots; where he is simple, he is not attractive--his air
> is harsh. 12

Because Miller is varied and because his words are too hard to digest, one comes to realize that the attempt to critically isolate a
work of his, or a moment in his life, only affords one a quick
glimpse of a many-sided man whose life and writings are as varied

as those of the greatest American authors, Melville and Faulkner.

To actually understand him, one must realize Miller's relationship to transcendentalism, to dadaism, to surrealism, astrology, naturalism, philosophy, psychology, and all the other conceptual frameworks found in his writing.   After viewing his ties to these movements, one must leave the realm of constancy and view a man in flux whose interests change, for example, from naturalism in the Mezzotints to serious self-liberation in Tropic of Cancer.   One must realize that the two Tropics present different tones, the first, a serious novel of rebirth in Paris during the 1930's, and, the second, a humorous sketch that satirically mocks New York of the 1920's. The Miller reader must come to see the differences between these works and Miller's second trilogy, and, within The Rosy Crucifixion, he must realize that Sexus was written by a man who has different outlooks from the author of Nexus and Plexus.   All of these works about the same era have totally different perspectives, a change that becomes most apparent when one reads the earlier Miller of Quiet Days in Clichy and the Miller of 1976 in Book of Friends.   In each of the two novels, Miller writes about the same two decades, yet his perspective changes again and again as he continues to ask fundamental questions about himself and his world.

NOTES

[1]Blaise Cendrars, "Un Ecrivain americain nous est né," Orbes, Summer 1935, 9-10; and Montgomery Belgion, "French Chronicle," Criterion, XV (October 1935), 83-96.

[2]Raymond Queneau, "Tropic of Cancer; Black Spring," La Nouvelle Revue Française, XXV (December 1, 1936), 1083-4.

[3]Lawrence Durrell and Henry Miller, Lawrence Durrell and Henry Miller: A Private Correspondence (New York: E. P. Dutton, 1964), p. 4.

[4]Anaïs Nin, "Preface," in Henry Miller, Tropic of Cancer (New York: Grove Press, 1961), p. xxxiii.

[5]Edmund Wilson, "Twilight of the Expatriates," New Republic, XCIV (March 9, 1938), 140.

[6]Paul Rosenfeld, "The Traditions and Henry Miller," Nation,

CXLIX (November 4, 1939), 502-503.

[7]Henry Miller, "Playboy Interview: Henry Miller," Playboy,
II (September 1964), 78.

[8]George Wickes, "Henry Miller," Writers at Work: The Paris
Review Interviews (New York: Viking Press, 1963), p. 183.

[9]"Miller Book Just True to Life, Prof Claims," Boston Globe,
CLXXX (September 27, 1961), 2.

[10]Harry T. Moore, "From Under the Counter to Front Shelf,"
New York Times, CX (June 18, 1961), VII 5; "Books: Tropic of
Cancer," Life, L (June 23, 1961), 25; Harold C. Gardiner, "Pub-
lishing Disgrace--Critical Shame: Tropic of Cancer," America, CV
(July 1, 1961), 490.

[11]Norman Mailer, "Henry Miller: Genius and Lust, Narcissism," American Review, XXIV (April 1976), p. 2.

[12]Ibid.

ABOUT THE BIBLIOGRAPHY

It is to the need to expand the knowledge about Henry Miller that my two studies, a primary works bibliography of Miller to be published by Black Sparrow Press and this secondary source bibliography, are aimed. It is my hope that the two will be considered together and that they will provide information to further Miller scholarship; their chronological arrangement serves the ends of biography. To expand the field of Miller scholarship, I felt that it would be necessary, by way of appropriate annotations, to note all events relating to the author, from the unknown Paris Tropic trials of the 1940's to the chatty society pieces talking about Miller's relationship with Hoki in 1971. By presenting as many facts as possible, I have hoped to make this study less biased and more multidimensional.

The overall purpose of this bibliography is to enable readers to view more objectively a man who has been a primary source of social criticism of America for the past fifty years, both through his own writing and through influencing such important authors as Ezra Pound, William Carlos Williams, Jack Kerouac, Norman Mailer, William Burroughs, Anaïs Nin, Lawrence Durrell, Allen Ginsberg, Thomas Pynchon, and many others. His influence has helped shape two decades of American history. His importance is emphasized by the realization that he helped change the sexual mores of America through the publication of Tropic of Cancer. He was also the father of the "Beat Generation" and founder of a literature of cultural debasement since advocated by Mailer, Burroughs, Donleavy, and Pynchon.

This bibliography of works about Henry Miller is primarily aimed at the scholar and student rather than the bibliographer. I have attempted to standardize the entries in a clear and simple form.

All works are listed chronologically and all are annotated. Section A includes books about Henry Miller. Section B contains chapters of books, prefaces, and introductions either fully devoted to him or in which important statements about Miller occur. The third section, C, is composed of important books in which Miller is mentioned significantly. Section D lists dissertations on Miller. And finally, Section E concerns itself with articles and reviews on Miller and his writing. (The annex to Section E cites works for which no date is available, and is arranged alphabetically.) The annotations in each section have been kept as short as possible yet provide essential information; still, these notes are not substitutes for the sources themselves.

There is no language limitation; the entries cover all known articles about Miller in all languages.

Two indexes have also been provided to aid the reader in finding the materials he wishes as quickly as possible. The first consists of a listing of authors, co-authors, editors, compilers, and translators of works on Miller. The other index lists titles of Henry Miller's books, as they are mentioned throughout the text and is especially helpful in using the E section of the bibliography. To better see the scope of Miller's work, my introductory essay provides a starting point, as it lists the major works by and about Miller.

My concern was the (impossible) attempt to find and annotate "all" works about Henry Miller. With this in mind, this bibliography, compiled over the past six years, begins with the origins of Miller criticism in the mid-thirties and extends to the summer of 1977.

ACKNOWLEDGMENTS

I wish to thank the following libraries: the Rare Book Room at the Library of Congress, the University of Minnesota, the University of Maryland, the University of California, Berkeley, and the University of California, Santa Barbara. Persons and staffs deserving special thanks include David V. Koch, Special Collections librarian, and his staff at Southern Illinois University, Carbondale; Ellen S. Dunlop and her staff of the Special Collections Division at the University of Texas, Austin; and Joan S. C. Crane, curator of American Literature Collections, and her staff at the University of Virginia.

Special thanks must be given to Brooke Whiting and his remarkable staff of the Special Collections Division of the University of California at Los Angeles and to the Honorable J. Rives Childs and Flavia Reed Owen of Randolph-Macon College for their invaluable help in providing me with both materials and insights to better understand Henry Miller.

Appreciation also goes to Noel Young of Capra Press and to John Martin of Black Sparrow Press for their assistance in this project, and to New Directions and Grove Press for their aid in tracing Miller materials.

Thanks also to Douglas Messerli for help and to Scarecrow Press for undertaking this project. Especially, I wish to thank Jackson R. Bryer for supporting this work, for helping to proofread, and for his invaluable ideas.

Finally I want to express special gratitude to my wife, Rebecca Hebb Shifreen, for her patience and support in typing and proofreading the manuscript of this book.

Lawrence J. Shifreen
August 1977-February 1978

BOOKS ABOUT HENRY MILLER

A1   Moore, Nicholas. <u>Henry Miller</u>. London: Opus Press, 1943.
      Miller is portrayed as a man in love with life, for he has
      learned to accept his existence. This stance on life is
      based on Walt Whitman's philosophy and is found in <u>Tropic
      of Cancer</u>, <u>Black Spring</u>, and <u>The Colossus of Maroussi</u>.

A2   Thoma, Richard. <u>Letter to Henry Miller</u>. Big Sur, Calif.:
      n.p., 1944.
      A letter written for a book about Henry Miller that was
      never published. This letter was later published as a
      pamphlet presenting a Freudian interpretation of Miller's
      work.

A3   Porter, Bern, ed. <u>The Happy Rock: A Book About Henry
      Miller</u>. Berkeley, Calif.: Bern Porter, 1945.
      A series of essays on Miller: Lawrence Durrell's "The
      Happy Rock," Emil Schnellock's "Just a Brooklyn Boy,"
      Wambly Bald's "La Vie de Bohème," Jean Helion's "Un
      Coup de chapeau," Richard Osborn's "No. 2 Rue Auguste
      Bartholdi," Michael Fraenkel's "The Genius of <u>The Tropic
      of Cancer</u>," Alfred Perlès's "Henry Miller in Villa Seurat,"
      Thomas Gilbert's "Rocanadour," Paul Rosenfeld's "Hellen-
      ism," Ossip Zadkine's "Tropic of Miller," Abraham Ratt-
      ner's "H. M. and I See America," Knud Merrild's "All
      the Animals in the Zoo," Henry Miller's "Miscellaneous
      Notes," Gilbert Neiman's "No Rubbish, No Albatrosses,"
      William Carlos Williams's "To the Dean," Philip Laman-
      tia's "To You Henry Miller of the Orchestra, the Mirror,
      the Revolver and of the Stars," George Leite's "Jupiter
      Exalted," Wallace Fowlie's "Shadow of Doom," Bern
      Porter's "Cosmic Sight," Osbert Sitwell's "Cable from
      Renishaw Hall," Herbert Faulkner West's "Camerado,"
      Parker Tyler, James Laughlin, and Roy Finch's "Three
      Americans," Hugo Manning, Claude Houghton, and Fred-
      erick Carter's "British Notes," Kenneth Patchen's "Tribute
      and Protest," Henry Miller's "Holograph Announcement,"
      Rudolph Gilbert's "Between Two Worlds," Paul Weiss's
      "Art and Henry Miller," Reginald Moore's "Miller's Im-
      pact Upon an English Writer," George Leite's "The Autoch-
      thon," Nicholas Moore's "Henry Miller in England," and
      Bern Porter's "Chronology and Bibliography."

A4   Porter, Bern.   Henry Miller: A Chronology and Bibliography.
     Berkeley, Calif.: Bern Porter, 1945.
         Porter's "Chronology" covers Miller's birth in 1891
         through 1944. The "Bibliography" is unannotated and con-
         sists of "Books and Brochures by Henry Miller," "Con-
         tributions by Henry Miller to Newspapers and Periodicals,"
         "Books Containing Original Material by Henry Miller,"
         "Articles and Reviews on Henry Miller in Books and Peri-
         odicals," and "Supplementary Notes."

A5   Fraenkel, Michael.   The Genius of the Tropic of Cancer.
     Berkeley, Calif.: Bern Porter, 1946.
         Miller is described as a man living in a world of chaos,
         yet a man who found himself.   Fraenkel looks at his first
         novel, "Crazy Cock," as a work in which Miller attempted
         to write according to American prose rules, yet still wrote
         like the author of Tropic of Cancer.

A6   Read, Herbert.   What England's Leading Critic Thinks About
     America's Most Extraordinary Writer.   New York: n.p.,
     1946.
         Miller viewed as an artist questing for reality, not litera-
         ture: "What makes Miller distinctive among modern writ-
         ers is his ability to combine the aesthetic and prophetic
         functions" (p. 1).

A7   Baradinsky, Oscar, ed.   Of, By and About Henry Miller.
     New York: Alicat Bookshop Press, 1947.
         Articles on Miller include Nicola Chiarmonte's "The Re-
         turn of Henry Miller," Paul Rosenfeld's "The Traditions
         and Henry Miller," Herbert Read's "Views and Reviews:
         Henry Miller," Wallace Fowlie's "Shadow of Doom."
         Articles by Miller include "Let Us Be Content with Three
         Little New-Born Elephants," "The Novels of Albert Cos-
         sery," "Another Bright Messenger," and "Anderson the
         Storyteller."

A8   Fraenkel, Michael.   Défense du Tropique du cancer avec des
     inédits de Miller.   Paris: Revue Variété, 1947.
         Miller began writing at a time of world chaos, yet, much
         like Bergson, he brought an ordered wholeness to his
         world.   This unity began in "Crazy Cock" and continued
         into Tropic of Cancer.   (In French.)

A9   Nin, Anaïs.   Preface to Henry Miller's "Tropic of Cancer."
     New York: Lawrence R. Maxwell, 1947.
         Nin calls Miller's Tropic an exploration of humanity: "The
         humiliations and defeats, given with a primitive honesty,
         end not in frustration, despair, or futility, but in hunger,
         an ecstatic, devouring hunger--for more life" (pp. 4-5).

A10 Villa, Georges.   Miller et l'amour.   Paris: Editions Corrêa,
     1947.

Miller's love is founded, not on the sweet feminine enchantment of Aphrodite but on the strength of Zeus, a caring father who loves his fellow men. (In French.)

A11 Bibliography of Henry Miller's Works in Chronological Order. Welwyn Garden City, England: Alcuin Press, 1955.
An anonymously produced, 12-page, unannotated bibliography of Miller's work, consisting of "Books," "Brochures and Pamphlets," "Miscellaneous Special Items," "Books and Brochures about Henry Miller," "Prefaces to Other Authors' Books," "A few books in which there are Essays about Henry Miller," and "Books with Essays by Henry Miller."

A12 Perlès, Alfred. My Friend Henry Miller. London: Neville Spearman, 1955.
A biography of Miller's life dating from his arrival in Paris, through Quiet Days in Clichy, and ending with Sunday After the War. Written much like a history, it describes Paris after the First World War and his first impressions on meeting Miller. The book ends with their reunion in Big Sur, Calif., with Perlès beckoning to Miller to give up the American life of disease for "the freshwater spring" that Paris offered.

A13 Nin, Anaïs. Preface to Tropic of Cancer. Paris: Obelisk Press, 1957.
Nin feels that Tropic is an exploration of humanity: "The humiliations and defeats, given with a primitive honesty, end not in frustration, ... but in hunger ... for more life" (p. 2).

A14 Rohde, Peter P. Henry Miller: Pornograf eller Profet? Kobenhavn: Hans Reitzel Forlag, 1957.
An eight-page book that deals with Miller as pornographer. (In Danish.)

A15 Schatz, Bezalel. 12 Illustrations to Henry Miller. Jerusalem: Turim Press, 1957.
Portfolio of 12 drawings, one a portrait of Henry Miller. Illustrations of Miller's work include: "Mademoiselle Claude," "Reunion in Brooklyn," "Via Dieppe-Newhaven," "The Tailor Shop," "A Room with a View," "The Colossus of Maroussi," "Peace! It's Wonderful!," "Into the Night Life," "Fragment from the Rosy Crucifixion," "Astrological Fricassee," and "Jazz Interlude."

A16 Durrell, Lawrence; Alfred Perlès; and Henry Miller. Art and Outrage. London: Putnam, 1959.
Series of letters between Lawrence Durrell, Alfred Perlès and Henry Miller. All of the intercourse concerns Miller's work, its greatness and its rejection. Durrell tells Perlès: "Miller is the greatest example of American genius since

Whitman," yet his books are banned in the United States (p. 8).

A17 Perlès, Alfred. Reunion in Big Sur: A Letter to Henry Miller in Reply to His Reunion in Barcelona. Northwood, England: Scorpion Press, 1959.
On March 16, 1959, Alfred Perlès wrote Miller a letter concerning their life together at Big Sur. Perlès calls it "a wonderful paradise," but one that is not Miller's home (p. 37). He tells Miller that home for them is in Europe, as he beckons Miller to return home.

A18 Omarr, Sidney. Henry Miller: His World of Urania. London: Villiers Publications, 1960.
A study of astrology in relationship to Miller's literary output. Astrology is seen governing all of Miller's work from Tropic of Cancer (1934) through The Time of the Assassins (1956).

A19 Baxter, Annette Kar. Henry Miller, Expatriate. Pittsburgh: University of Pittsburgh Press, 1961.
This book deals with Miller's need to alienate himself from the American scene, for he could not accept the evils of the modern industrial world which works to restrict the freedom of the individual.

A20 Moore, Thomas H. Bibliography of Henry Miller. Minneapolis: Henry Miller Literary Society, 1961.
This bibliography consists of "Books by Henry Miller," "Contributions to Periodicals (1945-1961)," "Contributions to Books (1945-1961)," "Recordings by Henry Miller," "Books About Henry Miller," "Books Containing Chapters on Henry Miller," "Doctoral Dissertations on Henry Miller," "Previous Bibliographies of Henry Miller," "Contributions by Henry Miller to Newspapers and Periodicals (1924-1944) from Bern Porter's Miller Bibliography (1945)." This work deals with Miller material to 1961 and is unannotated.

A21 Riley, Esta Lou. Henry Miller: An Informal Bibliography 1924-1960. Hays, Kansas: Fort Hays State College, 1961.
An unannotated bibliography broken down into seven parts: a brief introduction, "The Writings of Henry Miller," "The Writings About Henry Miller" (in chronological order), an appendix, an index to books, brochures, pamphlets, and miscellaneous items by Miller, periodicals to which Miller has contributed, and an index to authors and editors writing about Miller.

A22 Schmiele, Walter. Henry Miller in Selbstzeugnissen und Bilddokumenten. Hamburg: Rowohlt, 1961.
A biography of Miller's life beginning with his birth in the Yorkville part of Brooklyn, N.Y., his movement to

Paris and the Villa Seurat, and finally to Big Sur, Calif. (In German.)

A23 Vandenbergh, John. Kleine Biografie van Henry Miller. Rotterdam: Ad. Donker, 1961.
Sketchy biography of Miller's life from 1891 to 1960. Also includes a limited, unannotated, primary source bibliography of Miller. (In Dutch.)

A24 White, Emil. Henry Miller: Between Heaven and Hell. Big Sur, Calif.: Published by Emil White, 1961.
Consists of: Emil White's "Introduction," Judge Louis Goodman's "The 'Tropics'," Trygve Hirsch's "Attorney Trygve Hirsch to Henry Miller," Henry Miller's "First Reply to Trygve Hirsch from Henry Miller," Henry Miller's "Defense of the Freedom to Read," L. Yakovlev's "Literature of Decay," Lord Chief Justice Wold and Judge Thrap's "The Trial of 'Sexus' in the Supreme Court of Norway," Peter P. Rohde's "Henry Miller, Pornographer or Prophet," and Albert Maillet's "Henry Miller, Superman and Prophet."

A25 Anonymous. The Art of Henry Miller. New York: Crown Publishers, 1961.

A26 Childs, James Rives. The Rewards of Book Collecting. Ashland, Va.: Randolph-Macon College, 1962.
Childs describes his first experience reading Miller and calls him a major author.

A27 Gelre, Henk Van. Henry Miller Legende en Waarheid. Tielt/Den Haag, The Netherlands: Lannov, 1962.
Miller's world consists of journeys through both Paris and America, as seen in both Tropics, Black Spring, The Rosy Crucifixion, The Cosmological Eye, and The Air-Conditioned Nightmare. (In Dutch.)

A28 Moore, John G. The Latitude and Longitude of Henry Miller. Pasadena, Calif.: Marathon Press, 1962.
A critical evaluation of Miller's work in poetic form, reflecting the beauty of Miller's writing, while chastising America for censoring a major writer.

A29 Okumura, Osamu. Henry Miller: An Introduction. Tokyo: Gakuin University, 1962.
Miller is compared to D. H. Lawrence because of his anti-machine, anti-societal nature. But where Lawrence tries to turn the consciousness into the unconsciousness, Miller strives for greater awareness.

A30 Renkin, Maxine. A Bibliography of Henry Miller 1945-1961. Denver: Alan Swallow, 1962.
An unannotated bibliography of primary and secondary

sources covering the years 1945 to 1961. There are
three sections: "Books and Brochures by Henry Miller,"
"Contributions to Books and Periodicals by Henry Miller," and "Books About Henry Miller and Articles and
Reviews on Miller in Books and Periodicals."

A31 Riva, Valerio, ed. Prefazione ai Tropici. Milan: Giangi-
acomo Feltrinelli Editore, 1962.
        Contains: Henry Miller's "My Life as an Echo," "The
        World of Sex," "Obscenity and the Law of Reflection";
        Donovan Bess's "Miller's 'Tropic' Trial"; Karl Shapiro's
        "The Greatest Living Author"; George Orwell's "Inside
        the Whale"; Herbert Read's "Henry Miller"; Paul Rosen-
        feld's "The Traditions and Henry Miller"; Mario Praz's
        "Civiltà in sfacelo"; Michael Fraenkel's "The Genius of
        the Tropic of Cancer"; Kenneth Rexroth's "The Reality
        of Henry Miller"; Edvardo Sanguineti's "Henry Miller:
        una poetica barocca." (In Italian and English.)

A32 Haan, Jacques Den. Milleriana. Amsterdam: De Bezige
Bij, 1963.
        A biography and a series of letters that ends with praise
        for Miller. (In Dutch.)

A33 Hawkins, Tim. Eve the Common Muse of Henry Miller &
Lawrence Durrell. San Francisco: Ahab Press, 1963.
        A study of women in both the lives and works of Miller
        and Durrell from a Jungian psychological sense.

A34 Okumura, Osamu. Henry Miller and the Self-Liberation
Problem. Tokyo: Aoyama Tahuin University, 1963.
        Reprint from the Aoyama Journal of General Education,
        No. IV, 1963, p. 21-40.

A35 Wickes, George, ed. Lawrence Durrell--Henry Miller: A
Private Correspondence. New York: E. P. Dutton, 1963.
        Wickes discusses the shortcomings of his study on Dur-
        rell and Miller: "The complete Durrell-Miller corres-
        pondence is half a dozen scholarly annotated volumes ..."
        (p. xi). Since Wickes was unable to compile the entire
        correspondence because neither Durrell nor Miller
        wanted it done, the reader is presented with an edited,
        corrected, and changed single volume of letters which
        begin in August 1935 and continue to October 31, 1959.

A36 Wickes, George, ed. Henry Miller and the Critics. Carbondale: Southern Illinois University Press, 1963.
        Contains the following: Cendrars' "Un Ecrivain améri-
        cain Nous est né," Durrell's "Studies in Genius," Gertz's
        "Henry Miller and the Law," Hoffman's "The Booster,"
        Huxley's "Statement for the Los Angeles Trial," Kauff-
        mann's "An Old Shocker Comes Home," Levin's "Com-
        monwealth of Massachusetts...," Lowenfels' "A Note on

Tropic of Cancer," Moore's "From Under the Counter to
Front Shelf," Moore's "Preface," Muller's "The World
of Henry Miller," Orwell's "Inside the Whale," Perlès'
"My Friend Henry Miller," Powell's "The Miller of Big
Sur," Putnam's "Henry Miller in Montparnasse," Rahv's
"Sketches in Criticism," Read's "Henry Miller," Rexroth's "The Reality of Henry Miller," Schorer's "Commonwealth of Massachusetts...," Wickes' "Introduction,"
Wickes' "1930-1940," Wickes' "1940-1960," Wickes'
"1961 and After," Widmer's "The Rebel-Buffoon," Wilson's "Twilight of the Expatriates."

A37 Widmer, Kingsley. Henry Miller. New York: Twayne Publishers, 1963.
A thorough analysis of Miller's work. The first chapter
deals with Tropic of Cancer. From there, Widmer
bunches Miller's novels, analyzing all of Miller's writing in "The American Abroad," delving into his autobiographical romances in "The Brooklyn Passion," discussing his American feelings in "The Outsider Abroad," and
exploring Miller's views on literature, religion, and
morals in the final chapter, "The Rebel Buffoon." It is
a rather unsympathetic study, and one, at times, won-
ders whether Widmer understands Miller.

A38 Moore, Thomas H., ed. Henry Miller on Writing. New
York: New Directions, 1964.
Moore talks about Miller's writing in four sections: The
first is entitled "The 'Literary' Writer," where Miller is
viewed perfecting his style through imitating various
writers he admired. The second section, "Finding His
Own Voice," is a study of Miller's search within himself
to find his own method of expression. Part three, "The
Author at Work," attempts to depict Miller's methods for
preparing his books. The final section, "Writing and Obscenity," contains the most important writings of Miller
on the subject of obscenity and its relationship to the
artist.

A39 Okumura, Osamu. Henry Miller and Transcendentalism.
Tokyo: Aoyama Gakuin University, 1964.
Miller's work is placed in the transcendental spirit and
compared to Emerson, Thoreau, and Whitman.

A40 Porter, Bern. What Henry Miller Said and Why It Is Important. Pasadena, Calif.: Marathon Press, 1964.
Porter views Miller's work as realistic writing, not
pornography. He feels that "sex is everywhere," so it
cannot be hidden or dismissed (p. 14). Sex is only
natural: "Henry Miller treats sex for its own sake;
neither apologizes nor glorifies its expression" (p. 20).

A41 Temple, F(rédéric) J(acques). Henry Miller. Paris:

Editions Universitaires, 1965.
It is impossible to categorize Miller, for he is on a
scale with Thoreau, Melville, Whitman, and Faulkner.
(In French.)

A42   Wickes, George. Henry Miller. Minneapolis: University of
Minnesota Press, 1966.
"Henry Miller is likely to outlast a great many writers
who at the moment seem more important" (p. 5). With
this remark, Wickes begins one of the most positive,
praising reviews of Miller and his work. He talks about
Miller's anarchy which is derived from his individualism,
his satire, his love of sex and art. He is seen as one
of the most important writers of his time and "the best
surrealist writer America has produced" (p. 43).

A43   Dick, Kenneth C. Henry Miller: Colossus of One. Netherlands: Alberts-Sittard, 1967.
Miller is seen as both a masochist and a literary saint,
in this fine study of Miller's life and his relationships.

A44   Gordon, William A. The Mind and Art of Henry Miller.
Baton Rouge: Louisiana State University Press, 1967.
Gordon's study places Miller in the tradition of such
Romantics as Keats, Wordsworth, and Blake. Tropic
of Capricorn is based upon Miller's interest in European
and American Romantic philosophy.

A45   Hassan, Ihab. The Literature of Silence: Henry Miller and
Samuel Beckett. New York: Alfred A. Knopf, 1967.
Miller's work is seen by Hassan as "a chaotic world
constantly on the verge of transformation" (p. 8). This
change comes about through his therapeutic use of autobiography. This is accomplished by his writing, which
permits him to struggle and free himself from such
social conventions as "truth" and "right and wrong."
In his two trilogies, The Rosy Crucifixion and the one
containing the two Tropics and Black Spring, Miller
condemns social escapism: "The literature of flight,
of escapism, of a neurosis is so brilliant that it almost
makes one doubt the efficacy of health" (p. 29). Miller feels that this dream world avoids the realities of
death and rebirth and opts for the unspoken world of
anti-literature.

A46   Okumura, Osamu. Miller et le moi authentique. Brussels:
n.p., 1967.
Miller is compared to Emerson, Whitman, Thoreau,
and Lawrence. He is seen as a naturalist, transcendentalist, and existentialist. (In French.)

A47   Borba, Hermilo Filho. Henry Miller. Rio de Janeiro:
José Alvaro, 1968.

Contains: "Sob o signo da crucificação," "Misticismo e
anarquismo," "Mona," "Os agitados tempos de Paris,"
"O clown," "Os Trópicos...," "A Grécia," "Merda para
os mil dólares semanais," "A Crucifacação," "De forma
à cor," "Opiniões sôbre Henry Miller," "Cronologia,"
"Notas," and "Bibliografia." (In Portuguese.)

A48   Childs, J(ames) Rives. Collector's Quest: The Correspon-
      dence of Henry Miller and J. Rives Childs, 1947-1965.
      Charlottsville: University Press of Virginia, 1968.
      A correspondence in which Childs writes of his admira-
      tion for Miller's work, and Miller helps Childs to locate
      his books and expand his collection.

A49   Filho, Hermilo Borba. Henry Miller. Rio de Janeiro:
      José Alvaro Editôra, 1968.
      A piece of South American criticism that sees Miller as
      one of the most important authors today. It contains
      both a biography and essays praising Miller and his work
      from such critics as Perlès, Durrell, Powell, Rexroth,
      Nin, and others. (In Portuguese.)

A50   Gordon, William A. Writer & Critic: A Correspondence
      with Henry Miller. Baton Rouge: Louisiana State University
      Press, 1968.
      Exchange of letters between Gordon and Miller. It con-
      sists of 15 letters, eight by Miller concerning Gordon's
      criticism of Miller entitled The Mind and Art of Henry
      Miller. Especially important is the introduction in which
      Gordon views Miller as a Romantic, a man who has
      achieved a unity with himself and a community with the
      world. He calls Miller's movement both pacifistic and
      individualistic.

A51   Hutchison, E. R. Tropic of Cancer on Trial: A Case His-
      tory of Censorship. New York: Grove Press, 1968.
      A study of the trials of Tropic of Cancer in Wisconsin:
      "Wisconsin makes an excellent example of how censors
      can threaten even a liberal state" (p. x). The book al-
      so peers at the author of Tropic and his publisher,
      Grove Press.

A52   Rembar, Charles. The End of Obscenity: The Trials of
      Lady Chatterly, Tropic of Cancer and Fanny Hill. New
      York: Random House, 1968; London: Andre Deutsch, 1969.
      The United States Government tried to stop the publica-
      tion of Tropic of Cancer: "The ultimate question was
      whether the writing was lustful--that is, whether it ex-
      cited a sexual response" (p. 4). The result of the
      Tropic trial was that the book had literary value and
      could not be prohibited from sale in the United States.

A53   Granlid, Hans O. Henry Millers Motsägelser. Stockholm:

Bo Cavefors Bokförlag, 1969.
Granlid's The Contradictions of Henry Miller discusses
Miller's faith, hope, and ultimate concern for mankind.
To Miller, life is a miracle.   (In Swedish.)

A 54   Ueno, Kai.   Man of Earth.   Iwate, Japan: Kodosha, 1969.
Ueno calls Miller a man who has all the elements of life
--earth, air, fire, and water--in him.

A 55   Nascimento, Esdras Do.   O mundo de Henry Miller.   Rio de
Janeiro: Gráfica Record Editôra, 1969.
The World of Henry Miller contains: Cavalcante's "Henry
Miller," Nascimento's "Introducão," Carpeaux's "Litera-
tura ou pornografia," Miller and Durrell's "Sexus em
discussão," Nascimento's "A profissão de escritor,"
Okumura's "O milagre da vida sem Deus," Brassai's
"Cour Miller," Miller's "Definicão informal de princípi-
os," Henk van Gelre's "A linguagem da vida," Olinto's
"O caminho da insubmissão," Denat's "De Montaigne a
Miller," Mucciolo's "O metodo e a linguagem," Miller's
"A literatura não existe," Durrell's "O sôpro do dragão,"
Bose's "Visita a Big Sur," Nin's "Diário íntimo," Del-
teil's "Um cavaleiro em busca do graal," Gertz's "Meu
cliente Henry Miller," Ruuth's "Pacific Palisades,"
Wulff's "Miller, segundo os astrólogos," Miller's
"Quanto custa a glória," Nascimento's "Tábua crono-
lógica."   (In Portuguese.)

A 56   Schmiele, Walter.   Henry Miller.   Paris: Editions Buchet/
Chastel, 1969.
Biography of Miller's life.   (In French.)

A 57   Arfini, Alfredo.   Juzgo a Miller: delirante pornógrafo im-
portente.   Rosario, Argentina: Librería y Editorial Ruiz,
1970.
Miller is called a virtuoso of North American literature.
(In Spanish.)

A 58   Belmont, Georges.   Entretiens de Paris.   Paris: Editions
Stock, 1970.
An interview in French in which Belmont questions Miller
as to his importance on the literary scene.   (In French.)

A 59   Belmont, Georges.   Face to Face with Henry Miller.   London: Sidgwick & Jackson, 1970.
Miller talks about his life's movement back to youth:
"I came to youth late in life" (p. 1).   This takes place
in a conversation with Georges Belmont.

A 60   Nelson, Jane A.   Form and Image in the Fiction of Henry
Miller.   Detroit: Wayne State University Press, 1970.
A Jungian analysis of the archetypal processes and
images found in the individualism of Henry Miller.   The

archetypal female is the author's major concern, as she
forgets all other themes and discusses only the female
in Miller's writing. There she finds a barrier between
female-male interaction.

A61 Ueno, K. Tropiques en voyageur. Iwate, Japan: Kodosha,
     1970.
     First major study covering the entire Miller canon,
     written in Japanese.

A62 Mitchell, Edward B. Henry Miller: Three Decades of Criti-
     cism. New York: New York University Press, 1971.
     Mitchell distinguishes Miller's views about life from
     those of the existentialist: "While Miller would agree
     that man is at present alienated from reality, he repudi-
     ates the premise that cosmological alienation is a neces-
     sary condition of man's existence" (p. xvii). He sees
     man's alienation as "human" rather than "cosmological"
     because his mode of living has been chosen by man, not
     by the universe.

A63 Manning, Hugo. The It and the Odyssey of Henry Miller.
     London: Enitharman Press, 1972.
     Discussion of Miller as a fluid stylist: "Miller is equal-
     ly at ease with various styles of expression--the descrip-
     tive, the incantatory, the satirical ..." (p. 7). His
     themes are seen as based on the conflict between good
     and evil.

A64 Robitaille, Gérald. Le Père Miller: Essai indiscret sur
     Henry Miller. Paris: Eric Losfeld, 1972.
     As the title implies, Miller is seen as a literary "fath-
     er," a prime mover of the novel. Noted is the effect
     he had on Alfred Perlès, Lawrence Durrell, and Anaïs
     Nin. (In French.)

A65 Durrell, Lawrence. The Happy Rock. London: Village
     Press, 1973.
     Miller towers over his contemporaries, Hemingway, Dos
     Passos, and Faulkner, because he has discovered a
     state of life the others have missed.

A66 Gertz, Elmer. Henry Miller Exhibit. Carbondale: Southern
     Illinois University, 1973.
     A catalogue of books, letters, pictures, paintings, and
     memorabilia that appear in Gertz's collection of Henry
     Miller.

A67 Perlès, Alfred. Henry Miller in Villa Seurat. London:
     Village Press, 1973.
     Perlès' discussion of life with Miller in Villa Seurat.

A68 Schnellock, Emil. Just a Brooklyn Boy. London: Village

Press, 1973.
Schnellock looks back on the times when he and Miller
would paint in his New York studio.

A69   Langmann, Jacqueline.   Henry Miller et son destin.   Paris:
Editions Stock, 1974.
A study of Miller's opinions on life, love, sex, the
family, writing, solitude, marriage, and the world.   (In
French.)

A70   Snyder, Robert.   This Is Henry, Henry Miller from Brooklyn.
Los Angeles: Nash Pub. Co., 1974.
A scrapbook of conversations and photographs from
Snyder's film, "The Henry Miller Odyssey."   The book
also offers a chronology of Miller's life.

A71   Brassaï, Gyula H.   Henry Miller grandeur nature.   Paris:
Gallimard, 1975.
Study of Miller's Paris life by his longtime friend,
Brassaï.   It contains: "A la terrasse du 'Dôme',"
"Paris en 1930," "Hôtel des Terrasses," "Un Dévoreur
de livres," "Anaïs," "Exil à Dijon," "Correcteur de
nuit," "L'Expérience de Clichy," "June," "Villa Seurat,"
"Vérité et dramatisation," "L'Autobiographie...," "La
Voix," "Le Délicieux Coquin," "Amitiés parisiennes,"
"Voyage à New York," "Anaïs s'éloigne," "Apparition de
Larry," "L'Astrologue," and "Adieux à la France."   (In
French.)

A72   Tsutsui, Masaaki.   Henry Miller To Sono Sekai.   Tokyo:
Nanundo, 1975.
Henry Miller and His World.   (In Japanese.)

A73   Mailer, Norman.   Genius and Lust: A Journey Through the
Major Writings of Henry Miller.   New York: Grove Press,
1976.
Mailer edits a collection of Miller's writings from Tropic
of Cancer, Black Spring, Tropic of Capricorn, Sexus,
The Colossus of Maroussi, The Air-Conditioned Nightmare, Sunday After the War, Big Sur and the Oranges
of Hieronymus Bosch, Plexus, and Nexus.   Mailer includes essays preceding each section: "Foreword,"
"Status," "Genius," "Crazy Cock," "Narcissism," "Surrealism," "Grease," "Henry the First," "Domestic
Misery," "Portraits," and a "Chronology of Miller's
Life."

A74   Picca, Giuseppe.   Invito alla lettura di Henry Miller.   Milan: U. Mursia, 1976.
Study of Miller's work and life that also includes criticism and a short bibliography.   The books studied include: the Tropics, Black Spring, The Colossus of
Maroussi, The Air-Conditioned Nightmare, The Rosy
Crucifixion, and Big Sur.   (In Italian.)

B

CHAPTERS, PREFACES & INTRODUCTIONS
ABOUT MILLER*

B1   Nin, Anaïs. "Preface." In Henry Miller, Tropic of Cancer.
      Paris: Obelisk Press, 1934; pp. 7-10.
      Nin calls Tropic of Cancer an exploration of humanity:
      "The humiliations and defeats, given with a primitive
      honesty, end not in frustration, despair, or futility, but
      in hunger, an ecstatic, devouring hunger--for more life"
      (p. 8).

B2   Laughlin, James. "Preface: New Directions." In James
      Laughlin, ed., New Directions in Prose & Poetry 1936.
      Norfolk, Conn.: New Directions, 1936; p. xii.
      One of the many devices that Miller uses in his writing
      is surrealism.

B3   Laughlin, James. "Notes on Contributors." In James
      Laughlin, ed., New Directions in Prose & Poetry 1937.
      Norfolk, Conn.: New Directions, 1937; p. ix.
      Miller's Max and the White Phagocytes is scheduled to
      be his first work published in the United States.

B4   Laughlin, James. "Editor's Note." In James Laughlin, ed.,
      New Directions in Prose & Poetry 1939. Norfolk, Conn.:
      New Directions, 1939; pp. 292-294.
      Laughlin recalls Miller's remark "that the future of cre-
      ative prose literature lies with the human document"
      (p. 292).

B5   Laughlin, James. "Notes on Contributors." In James
      Laughlin, ed., New Directions in Prose & Poetry 1939.
      Norfolk, Conn.: New Directions, 1939; p. x.
      Tropic of Capricorn shows that Miller's greatness that
      began with Tropic of Cancer will continue.

B6   Lundkvist, Artur. "Henry Miller och Myten om den Ska-
      pande Doden." In Artur Lundkvist, Ikarus' Flykt.

      *Four undated works are given at the end of Part B.

13

Stockholm: Albert Bonniers Forlag, 1939; pp. 223-242, 277-279.
> Both Miller's writing and his movement from America to Europe are seen as transcendent. (In Swedish.)

B7   Laughlin, James. "Notes on Contributors." In James Laughlin, ed., New Directions in Prose & Poetry 1940. Norfolk, Conn.: New Directions, 1940; p. xi.
> It is noted that Orwell's study "Inside the Whale" is the first major study of Miller by another author.

B8   Laughlin, James. "Preface." In James Laughlin, ed., New Directions in Prose & Poetry 1940. Norfolk, Conn.: New Directions, 1940; pp. xv-xvi.
> Laughlin battles those who say that there is no form in Miller's writing. He feels that Miller's novels are "dithyrambic" and are built on rise and fall, and ebb and flow of energy in the human body.

B9   Orwell, George. "Inside the Whale." In George Orwell, Inside the Whale and Other Essays. London: Victor Gollancz, 1940; pp. 129-188.
> Miller's understanding of humanity is admired by Orwell who sees Miller as an explorer of everyday emotions. The people of Tropic of Cancer act and talk with the coarseness of real life: "He is exploring different states of consciousness, dream, reverie, drunkenness, etc. ..." (p. 136). But Miller is traveling further than exploration, for he is moving to an acceptance of life in the tradition of Walt Whitman.

B10   Orwell, George. "Inside the Whale." In James Laughlin, ed., New Directions in Prose & Poetry 1940. Norfolk, Conn.: New Directions, 1940; pp. 205-246.
> Orwell sees Miller as a man obsessed with the exploration of real life, a study no other author has attempted.

B11/12 Laughlin, James. "Re: Henry Miller." In Henry Miller, The Wisdom of the Heart. Norfolk, Conn.: New Directions, 1941.
> Introductory praise to Miller for his brilliant book of essays and short stories.

B13   Moore, Reginald. "Facing the Future." In Reginald Moore, ed., Modern Reading. London: Wells Gardner, Darton, 1944.
> It is noted that Miller, in his study on D. H. Lawrence, speaks in favor of the evolution of the individual, a process that occurs through "the wisdom of the heart."

B14   Porter, Bern. "Profile of Henry Miller." In Bern Porter, Bird Cape with California Mountain. N.p., 1944.
> A portrait of Miller.

B15 Baker, Denys Val. "Introduction." In Denys Val Baker, ed.,
Voyage: An Anthology of Selected Stories. London: Sylvan
Press, 1945; pp. ix-x.
Miller's story, "The Fourteenth Ward," is a chapter of
his novel, Black Spring, that was not published in Eng-
land in 1945 and could only be read in this small excerpt.

B16 Bald, Wambly. "La Vie de Bohème." In The Happy Rock
[A3]; pp. 25-27.
Bald recreates a typical meeting with the novelist Miller,
a man often found walking the streets of Paris. Noted
is the fact that Miller wanders in quest of words to
write and food to eat--"a wonderful life" to Miller
(p. 27).

B17 Carter, Frederick. "British Notes." In The Happy Rock
[A3]; pp. 122-123.
Miller is seen as a more positive novelist than D. H.
Lawrence, an author who tends to affirm life through ex-
periencing the natural.

B18 Durrell, Lawrence. "The Happy Rock." In The Happy Rock
[A3]; pp. 1-6.
Miller towers over his contemporaries Hemingway, Dos
Passos, and Faulkner, because he "has crossed the di-
viding line between art and Kitsch once and for all"
(p. 1). Durrell calls Tropic an autobiography, chaos
(for that is real life), a study of physical and psychological human behavior, and an Eastern philosophy.

B19 Finch, Roy. "Three Americans." In The Happy Rock [A3];
pp. 116-118.
Miller is viewed as an existentialist: "In Henry Miller's
work I find this personal concern and commitment, this
effort at self-growth and fulfillment, this unwillingness to
accept or palm off anything which is not really his own"
(p. 116). Miller's books become dialects of himself.

B20 Fluchère, Henri. "Le Lyrisme de Henry Miller." In Henry
Miller, Tropique du Cancer. Paris: Editions Denoël, 1945;
pp. 7-17.
Miller's writing is called joyous, divine, lyrical. It ab-
hors formality. Miller writes autobiography that is
based on his own liberation from American society, a
culture that is engulfed by a deadly cancerous disease.
(In French.)

B21 Fowlie, Wallace. "Shadow of Doom." In The Happy Rock
[A3]; pp. 102-107.
Miller is depicted as a seer and a prophet, an ancestor
to Rimbaud. For, like his predecessor, "he always begins with chaos and moves toward order" (p. 37). This
movement achieves a spiritual order that is not reached

by any other twentieth-century author.   See B22.

B22   Fowlie, Wallace.   "Shadow of Doom: An Essay on Henry
Miller."   In Reginald Moore, ed., Modern Reading.   London:
Wells Gardner, Darton, 1945; pp. 204-211.
Miller is considered a prophet who has achieved a spiri-
tualism unlike any other twentieth-century writer.   See
B21.

B23   Fraenkel, Michael.   "The Genius of The Tropic of Cancer."
In The Happy Rock [A3]; pp. 38-56.
Miller lives in a world of chaos yet has created an
ordered existence for himself.   For he has used the
"death theme" to create a positive, thriving individualism.

B24   Gilbert, Rudolph.   "Between Two Worlds."   In The Happy
Rock [A3]; pp. 126-132.
In this time of trouble, Miller tends to affirm life
through a "rediscovery of the Doctrine of the Heart"
(p. 128).   He bypasses individualism and stands in the
real world.

B25   Gilbert, Thomas R.   "Rocan adour."   In The Happy Rock
[A3]; pp. 62-63.
Miller is considered unexciting, yet his work is dynamic.

B26   Hélion, Jean.   "Un Coup de chapeau."   In The Happy Rock
[A3]; p. 26.
A sketch of Miller wearing a hat.

B27   Houghton, Claud.   "British Notes."   In The Happy Rock
[A3]; pp. 121-122.
A look at the apocalyptic aspect of Miller's Wisdom of
the Heart.

B28   Lamantia, Philip.   "To You Henry Miller of the Orchestra
the Mirror the Revolver and of the Stars."   In The Happy
Rock [A3]; pp. 98-100.
Poem describing Miller as a questor for love.

B29   Laughlin, James.   "Three Americans."   In The Happy Rock
[A3]; pp. 114-116.
Laughlin sees Miller as a man ahead of his time.   He
feels that it is impossible to assess his writing because
the right critical terms do not exist.   He certainly feels
that Miller is not a pornographer because the intent of
Tropic is to bring reality to literature.

B30   Leite, George.   "The Autochthon."   In The Happy Rock
[A3]; pp. 140-146.
Miller is a man who has subjected himself to so many
realities that he has become objective, an openness that
is clearly demonstrated in Tropic of Cancer, Black

Spring, and Tropic of Capricorn.

B31 Leite, George. "Jupiter Exalted." In The Happy Rock
[A3]; p. 101.
Miller is a creative force in the midst of hostility.

B32 Manning, Hugo. "British Notes." In The Happy Rock [A3];
pp. 119-121.
Miller is a saintly prophet who accurately depicts life in
both the Old and New Worlds. He writes of the paradox
between these two lands.

B33 Merrild, Knud. "All the Animals in the Zoo." In The Happy Rock [A3]; pp. 77-88.
Miller is an autobiographical writer who is both gentle
and brilliant.

B34 Moore, Nicholas. "Henry Miller in England." In The Happy
Rock [A3]; pp. 147-151.
Miller has had little effect on England because most of
his work has not been published there. In fact, the only
book of his published in that country is The Colossus of
Maroussi, a book that English critics think is merely a
travel guide to Greece. In England, Miller is never explored; he is dismissed as mad. This over-simplifica-
tion is abhorred by Moore who feels that people must begin to explore and understand Miller's reality.

B35 Moore, Nicholas. "Introductory Note." In Nicholas Moore,
ed., The PL Book of Modern American Short Stories. London: Editions Poetry, 1945; pp. 5-7.
Miller is viewed as a figure of potential and importance
to American letters.

B36 Moore, Reginald. "Miller's Impact Upon an English Writer."
In The Happy Rock [A3]; pp. 136-139.
Miller's writing is based on aloneness and individualism
and reaches a synthesis through his protagonist's learning to cope with reality.

B37 Neiman, Gilbert. "No Rubbish, No Albatrosses." In The
Happy Rock [A3]; pp. 89-96.
Miller is a writer who uses love to convey his thoughts.

B38 Osborn, Richard G. "No. 2 Rue Auguste Bartholdi." In
The Happy Rock [A3]; pp. 28-37.
Noted is the intensity of Miller's life: "Though he was
only in his late thirties, he has lived more intensely,
suffered more, than perhaps a hundred ordinary men do
in the span of a lifetime" (p. 28).

B39 Patchen, Kenneth. "Tribute and Protest." In The Happy
Rock [A3]; p. 124.

Miller is a great writer and a fine human being, yet there exists no good criticism on his writing.

B40 Perlès, Alfred. "Henry Miller in Villa Seurat." In The Happy Rock [A3]; pp. 57-61.
Perlès discusses Miller's qualities, saying that he instills life into everyone; Tropic depicts this vitality.

B41 Porter, Bern. "Chronology and Bibliography." In The Happy Rock [A3]; pp. 152-156.
The major events in Miller's life are presented from 1891-1945. Also included is a listing of Miller's novels.

B42 Porter, Bern. "Cosmic Sight." In The Happy Rock [A3]; p. 106.
Abstract drawing of Miller.

B43 Rattner, Abraham. "H. M. and I See America." In The Happy Rock [A3]; pp. 73-76.
This poem is a fragment from Rattner's account of his voyage across America with Henry Miller. For the full account see When We Were Together by Rattner and Miller's The Air-Conditioned Nightmare.

B44 Rosenfeld, Paul. "Hellenism." In The Happy Rock [A3]; pp. 64-72.
A review of the Hellenism found in Miller's Greek travel epic, The Colossus of Maroussi, a voyage into the self.

B45 Schnellock, Emil. "Just a Brooklyn Boy." In The Happy Rock [A3]; pp. 7-24.
Schnellock recalls his first meetings with Miller, their times together in the 50th Street Studio. Mixed with his memories are comparisons of Miller's two Tropics, Black Spring, The Colossus of Maroussi, and The Plight of the Creative Artist in the United States of America.

B46 Stillwell, Osbert. "Cable from Renishaw Hall." In The Happy Rock [A3]; p. 108.
A cable where Stillwell notes his displeasure at being prevented from writing about Miller, a man he considers to be unique, energetic, and visionary in his prose.

B47 Tyler, Parker. "Three Americans." In The Happy Rock [A3]; pp. 113-114.
"The author of Tropic of Cancer and The Cosmological Eye and his correspondence on Hamlet has an irresistible determination to populate literature with pieces of himself, and to consider this process ... a way of 'becoming whole,' of achieving complete existence" (p. 113).

B48 Weiss, Paul. "Art and Henry Miller." In The Happy Rock [A3]; pp. 133-135.

Miller's life is an attempt to capture innocence and is a quest for reality.

B49 West, Herbert Faulkner. "Camerado." In The Happy Rock [A3]; pp. 109-112.
Miller is unique: "Miller is an original. He is absolutely unique; he is elemental, primal, primitive" (p. 109). He is seen in the anti-intellectual tradition, an individual and a romantic.

B50 Williams, William Carlos. "To the Dean." In The Happy Rock [A3]; p. 97.
In this poem Williams talks about the depth of Miller's mind and the way it travels endlessly.

B51 Zadkine, Ossip. "Tropic of Miller." In The Happy Rock [A3]; p. 71.
Abstract drawing of a monument to be erected to Miller in Washington Square, New York, and Place St. Germain de Pré, Paris.

B52 Abailard, Pierre. "A Elle." In Henry Miller, Tropique du Capricorne. Paris: Editions des Chêne, 1946; pp. 13-15.
Miller deals with the human passions and sentiments in Tropic of Capricorn. (In French.)

B53 Jonsson, Thorsten Georg. "Henry Millers Amerika." In Thorsten Georg Jonsson, Sidov av Amerika: Intryck och Resonemang. Stockholm: Albert Bonniers Förlag, 1946; pp. 246-254.
Miller has rejected a sick society as seen in the two Tropics and The Air-Conditioned Nightmare. He is a prophet who, like Whitman, preaches about social evils. (In Swedish.)

B54 Laughlin, James. "Notes on Contributors." In James Laughlin, ed., New Directions in Prose & Poetry 1946. Norfolk, Conn.: New Directions, 1946; p. xii.
Miller's The Air-Conditioned Nightmare is a journey through the United States.

B55 Martin, E(rnest) W(illiam) L(unn). "Introduction." In E. W. L. Martin, The New Spirit. London: Dennis Dobson, 1946; pp. 7-13.
Miller is a prophet concerned with men, not with politics.

B56 Moore, Reginald. "Foreword." In Reginald Moore, ed., Selected Writing. London: Nicholson & Watson, 1946; pp. 3-4.
Notation about Miller's "Anderson the Storyteller."

B57 Perlès, Alfred. "Aller Sans Retour London." In Alfred

Perlès, Round Trip. London: Dennis Dobson, 1946; pp. 9-57.
Account of a voyage to London as recorded in a letter to
Miller.

B58   "Preface," by the editors.   In Henry Miller, Tropique du
Capricorne. Paris: Editions des Chêne, 1946; pp. 7-11.
Miller talks about a sick America which he is trying to
change.   (In French.)

B59   Brodin, Pierre.   "Henry Miller."   In Pierre Brodin, ed.,
Les Ecrivains américains du vingtième siècle. Paris: Horizons de France, 1947; pp. 131-149.
Miller is an expatriate who prefers Paris and freedom to
the United States.   He is in the romantic tradition of
such expatriates as Washington Irving, Fenimore Cooper,
Henry James, and Ernest Hemingway.   (In French.)

B60   Chiaromonte, Nicola.   "The Return of Henry Miller."   In
Of, By, and About Henry Miller [A7]; pp. 6-10.
Miller's work is neither hateful nor revolutionary but
shows pity and human modesty.

B61   Dopagne, Jacques.   "Au Lecteur."   In Défense du Tropique
du cancer avec des inédits de Miller [A8]; pp. 7-9.
Fraenkel defends Miller by placing him in the tradition
of Emerson and Whitman.

B62   Fauchery, Pierre.   "Une Epopée du sexe: Le Feuilleton
hebdomadaire. "   In Of, By, and About Henry Miller [A7];
pp. 40-43.
Miller is not the scandalous being that Americans have
created.   He is in the school of Céline, having a religious fervor, a purity, and a romanticism.   (In French.)

B63   Fowlie, Wallace.   "Shadow of Doom: An Essay on Henry
Miller. "   In Of, By, and About Henry Miller [A7]; pp. 18-24.
Miller is a prophet in the tradition of Rimbaud.   See
B21, B22.

B64   Laughlin, James.   "Notes on Contributors. "   In James
Laughlin, ed., Spearhead: 10 Years Experimental Writing
in America. New York: New Directions Books, 1947;
pp. 592-594.
A short biography of Miller's life.

B65   Read, Herbert.   "Views and Reviews: Henry Miller. "   In
Of, By, and About Henry Miller [A7]; pp. 14-17.
Miller's writing is seen as "a prolonged insult, a gob of
spit in the face of Art ... " (p. 14).   Miller strips away
art in his search for reality.

B66   Rosenfeld, Paul.   "The Traditions and Henry Miller. "   In
Of, By, and About Henry Miller [A7]; pp. 10-14.

Miller is in the tradition of D. H. Lawrence and Hart
Crane, displaying a spiritual celebration of life. His
prose is elevated, and this affirmative force has made
American literature freer.

B67   West, Herbert Faulkner. "The Strange Case of Henry Mill-
      er. " In Herbert Faulkner West, ed. , The Mind on the Wing:
      A Book for Readers and Collectors. New York: Coward-
      McCann, 1947; pp. 115-138.
            Miller is the most talked about writer in American liter-
      ature in the middle of the 1940's: "Henry Miller, now
      that Joyce and Lawrence are dead, is without much ques-
      tion the most controversial writer in English" (p. 115).
      This might well be because Miller is creating a new
      form of art, for instead of creating characters, Miller
      realizes himself.

B68   Beutel, Gottfried. "Henry Miller--Ein Essay. " In Wuze-
      Almanach 1948. Schwäbisch Hall, West Germany: Hans O.
      Lange, 1948; pp. 41-45.
            Miller's belief in freedom and life is explored in Ob-
      scenity and the Law of Reflexion, The World of Sex,
      Maurizius Forever, Tropic of Cancer, Tropic of Capri-
      corn, and Sunday After the War. (In German.)

B69   Corle, Edwin. "About Henry Miller. " In Henry Miller,
      The Smile at the Foot of the Ladder. New York: Duell,
      Sloan & Pearce, 1948; pp. 19-38.
            Tropic of Cancer is not an obscene book. Obscenity is
      found in the Puritan hang-ups of America.

B70   Fraenkel, Michael. "Letter to Henry Miller. " In Bastard
      Death [C14]; pp. 9-24.
            Bastard Death is attributed to Miller's inspiration, for
      Miller, through his Tropics, led Fraenkel to look into
      both past and future to see reality.

B71   Monicelli, Giorgio. "Nota. " In George Orwell, Domenica
      dopo la guerra. Verona, Italy: Arnoldo Mondadori Editore,
      1948; pp. 1-4.
            Miller's importance comes from his belief in life. (In
      Italian.)

B72   Monicelli, Giorgio. "Nota. " In Henry Miller, Il Colosso di
      Maroussi. Verona, Italy: Arnoldo Mondadori Editore, 1948;
      pp. 1-6.
            Miller is not obscene but is a moral writer, as can be
      seen from his Colossus of Maroussi. (In Italian.)

B73   Orwell, George. "Nel ventre della balena. " In George
      Orwell, Domenica dopo la Guerra. Verona, Italy: Arnoldo
      Mondadori Editore, 1948; pp. 5-57.
            Giorgio Monicelli translates Orwell's "Inside the Whale, "

in which Orwell calls Miller a first-rate author of importance. (In Italian.) See B9.

B74 Laughlin, James. "Notes on Contributors. " In James
Laughlin, ed. , New Directions in Prose & Poetry 1949. Norfolk, Conn. : New Directions, 1949; pp. 13-14.
After many years of living in France, Miller has again
come back to the United States.

B75 Mondadori, Arnoldo. "Nota. " In Henry Miller, Max e i
fagociti bianchi. Verona, Italy: Arnoldo Mondadori Editore,
1949; pp. ix-xii.
Discussion of the greatness of the bohemian romantic
rebel, Miller. (In Italian.)

B76 Rahv, Philip. "Henry Miller. " In Philip Rahv, Image and
Idea. Norfolk, Conn. : New Directions, 1949; pp. 144-150.
Rahv sees contradiction in both the person and the author
named Henry Miller.

B77 Rosati, Salvatore. "Introduzione. " In Henry Miller, Max e
i fagociti bianchi. Verona, Italy: Arnoldo Mondadori Editore,
1949; pp. xiii-xxviii.
Miller's realism is compared with Dreiser's Sister Carrie
and D. H. Lawrence's writing. (In Italian.)

B78 Vandenbergh, John. "Voorwoord. " In John Vandenbergh, De
Wijsheid van het Hart. Netherlands: De Driehoek-'s Grave-
land, 1949; pp. 9-14.
A biography of Miller. (In Dutch.)

B79 Dubois, Pierre Hubert. "Henry Miller en de Mythe van het
Moment. " Een Houding in de Tijd. Amsterdam: J. M.
Meulenhoff, 1950; pp. 50-63.
Miller lives for and experiences the "now" in both
Tropics. He is a moral man obsessed with living life
and not turning to an immoral dependency on the machine.
(In Dutch.)

B80 Laughlin, James. "Notes on Contributors. " In James
Laughlin, ed. , New Directions in Prose & Poetry 1950.
Norfolk, Conn. : New Directions, 1950; pp. xiii-xiv.
Miller is at present working on The Books In My Life
and Plexus.

B81 Wyss, Dieter. "Henry Miller. " In Dieter Wyss, Der Sur-
realismus: Eine Einführung und Deutung surrealistischer
Literatur und Malerei. Heidelberg, West Germany: Verlag
Lambert Schneider, 1950; pp. 55-60.
Miller is one of the modern giants of literature. His
surrealism readily appears as his mind jumps from
scene to scene. (In German.)

B82 Cendrars, Blaise. "Appendice." In Henry Miller, Blaise
Cendrars. Paris: Editions Denoël, 1951; pp. lxxi-lxxii.
Cendrars praises Miller for his realism, a truth found
in the hunger and the vomit of the Paris streets. (In
French.)

B83 Shapiro, Karl (Jay). "Dylan Thomas." In Karl Shapiro, In
Defense of Ignorance. New York: Random House, 1952;
pp. 171-186.
Dylan Thomas's primitive fertility rites are all "mixed
up with Henry Miller, Freud, and American street
slang" (p. 179). Thus it seems that Miller was a force
that shaped Thomas's writing.

B84 Shapiro, Karl (Jay). "The First White Aboriginal." In Karl
Shapiro, In Defense of Ignorance. New York: Random
House, 1952; pp. 187-204.
Conventional literature tries to "exterminate its Whit-
mans, its Blakes, its Lawrences, its Henry Millers"
(p. 203).

B85 Shapiro, Karl (Jay). "The Greatest Living Author." In Karl
Shapiro, In Defense of Ignorance. New York: Random
House, 1952; pp. 313-338.
Miller's goal in Tropic is not to be nice but to write
about truth, a reality that lies in the self, the individual:
"He can know only the fifty feet or so in his immediate
vicinity; within that radius he is a man responsible for
himself and his fellows; beyond that he is powerless."

B86 Wilson, Edmund. "Twilight of the Expatriates." In Edmund
Wilson, The Shores of Light: A Literary Chronicle of the
Twenties and Thirties. New York: Farrar, Straus and
Young, 1952; pp. 705-710.
Wilson feels that Tropic of Cancer should have been re-
viewed in America and accepted into this country.

B87 Nin, Anaïs. "Vorwort." In Henry Miller, Wendekreis des
Krebses. Hamburg: Rowohlt, 1953; pp. 7-10.
Kurt Wagenseil translates Nin's "Preface" to Tropic of
Cancer into German. See B1.

B88 Queneau, Raymond. "Henry Miller." In Raymond Queneau,
Les Ecrivains célèbres. Paris: Lucien Mazenoid, 1953;
p. 270.
Biography of Miller through 1952. (In French.)

B89 Rohde, Peter P. "Forord." In Henry Miller, Krebsens
Venderkreds. Copenhagen: Casper Nielsens Forlag, 1953;
pp. 5-12.
Miller's Tropic of Cancer is seen in the tradition of
Knud Hamsun's Sult. (In Danish.)

B90   Harding, Walter.   "Preface."   In Walter Harding, ed.,
      Thoreau: A Century of Criticism.   Dallas: Southern Metho-
      dist University Press, 1954; pp. vii-viii.
      Mentions Miller's preface to Thoreau entitled "Preface to
      Three Essays by Henry David Thoreau."

B91   Orwell, George.   "Inside the Whale."   In George Orwell, A
      Collection of Essays.   Garden City, New York: Doubleday,
      1954; pp. 215-256.
      Orwell's famous essay praising Henry Miller.   See B9,
      B73.

B92   Powell, Lawrence Clark.   "Return to France."   In Lawrence
      Clark Powell, The Alchemy of Books.   Los Angeles: Ward
      Ritchie Press, 1954; pp. 213-226.
      Powell discusses his return to France just before Armis-
      tice Day of 1918.   He notes that he stood on a bridge
      with Rimbaud, Rabelais, and Henry Miller.

B93   "Företal," by the publishers.   In Henry Miller, Kräftans
      Vändkrets.   Stockholm: Central Press, 1955; pp. 5-6.
      Tropic of Cancer is not merely a book about sex; it is a
      work of literary merit.   (In Swedish.)

B94   Laughlin, James.   "Editor's Note."   In James Laughlin, ed.,
      New Directions in Prose & Poetry 1955.   Norfolk, Conn.:
      New Directions, 1955; p. 11.
      Laughlin credits himself with getting Miller into print in
      America.

B95   Moricand, Conrad.   "Les Cinquante Rames du navire Argo."
      In Conrad Moricand, Les Cinquante Rames du navire Argo.
      Montpellier, France: Licorne, 1955; p. 5.
      Miller is thanked in this preface.   (In French.)

B96   Rexroth, Kenneth.   "Introduction."   In Henry Miller, Nights
      of Love and Laughter.   New York: New American Library of
      World Literature, 1955; pp. 7-16.
      Miller is considered to be one of the most widely read
      writers along with Jack London, Fenimore Cooper, and
      William Faulkner.

B97   Queneau, Raymond.   "Henry Miller."   In Raymond Queneau,
      Pour une bibliothèque idéale.   Paris: Gallimard, 1956;
      pp. 223-227.
      A biography of Miller's life and a look at 99 of his favo-
      rite books.   (In French.)

B98   Wilson, Edmund.   "Twilight of the Expatriates."   In Edmund
      Wilson, A Literary Chronicle: 1920-1950.   Garden City,
      New York: Doubleday, 1956; pp. 211-216.
      This is Wilson's 1938 chastisement of the American lite-
      rary critics who all failed to deal with Miller's Tropic

of Cancer. He sees the book to be of historical importance: "It is the epitaph for the whole generation of
American writers and artists that migrated to Paris
after the war" (p. 212). Also contained in this volume
is Miller's reply to Wilson's review which damns the
critics and the United States. See B68.

B99   "Henry Miller." In The American Academy of Arts and
        Letters and the National Institute of Arts and Letters. New
        York: Academy Museum, 1957; p. 6.
            Miller's writing is displayed for he has been admitted
        to the Institute.

B100   Laughlin, James. "Notes on Contributors." In James
        Laughlin, ed., New Directions in Prose & Poetry 1957.
        Norfolk, Conn.: New Directions, 1957; p. 262.
            Miller came to be elected to the National Institute of
        Arts and Letters later that year.

B101   "Poetic Background." In American Writing Today: Its In-
        dependence and Vigor. New York: New York University
        Press, 1957; p. 19.
            Miller is a bohemian who moved from the Left Bank of
        the Seine to California.

B102   Read, Sir Herbert Edward. "Henry Miller." In Herbert
        Read, The Tenth Muse. Freeport, N.Y.: Books for Li-
        braries Press, 1957; pp. 250-255.
            Read sees Miller as one of the most significant artists
        of our time. Yet, he realizes that Miller is not a
        novelist "in the ordinary sense of the word," for his
        work is "a prolonged insult, a gob of spit in the face
        of art" (p. 251). Miller is a man concerned with his
        environment, with naturalism and the prophetic.

B103   Williams, William Carlos. "To the Dean." In James
        Laughlin, ed., New Directions in Prose & Poetry 1957.
        Norfolk, Conn.: New Directions, 1957; pp. iv, 40.
            A poem where Williams views Miller as a man living
        on three different levels simultaneously. See B50.

B104   Heiney, Donald. "Henry Miller." In Donald Heiney, Re-
        cent American Literature. Woodbury, N.Y.: Barron's Edu-
        cational Series, 1958; pp. 125-128.
            Brief biography and descriptive account of Miller's ma-
        jor works. Miller is viewed as a rebel against sexual
        taboos and social rules. He certainly stands "against
        Puritanism, the sterility, and the 'respectability'" that
        forms the basis for American society.

B105   "Induction of Newly Elected Members of the Institute." In
        American Academy of Arts and Letters and the National
        Institute of Arts and Letters. New York: Academy Museum,

1958; pp. 164-166.
Miller's induction into The Academy of Arts and Letters.
Of Miller, it is noted: "His boldness of approach and
intense curiosity concerning man and nature are un-
equalled in the prose literature of our time" (p. 165).

B106   Mauriac, Claude.   "Henry Miller."   In Claude Mauriac, La
Littérature contemporaine.   Paris: Editions Albin Michel,
1958; pp. 49-59, 257.
A Devil in Paradise is reviewed with Miller appearing
an honest, straightforward man.   (In French.)

B107   Mauriac, Claude.   "Henry Miller."   In Claude Mauriac,
The New Literature.   New York: George Braziller, 1958;
pp. 51-59.
Mauriac calls Miller's literature personal therapy:
"Henry Miller is one of those who owe their health to
their works" (p. 51).   Offered are examples from
Tropic of Cancer, Tropic of Capricorn, Sexus, and A
Devil in Paradise, all of which show Miller's evolution
and his gaining of awareness and health.   See B106.

B108   Omarr, Sidney.   "A Great Writer Talks about Astrology."
In Sidney Omarr, 1958 Guidebook to Astrology.   Los Angeles: Trend Books, 1958; p. 116.
Omarr calls Miller's writing astrology and calls it the
literature of the future.

B109   Parmelee, Maurice.   "An Introduction."   In Henry Miller,
Pornography and Obscenity: Handbook for Censors.   Michigan City, Ind.:   Fridtjof-Karla Publications, 1958; pp. 30-
32.
If sex were free in America, there would be no need to
deal with obscenity.

B110   Durrell, Lawrence.   "Introduction."   In Henry Miller, The
Henry Miller Reader.   Norfolk, Conn.:   New Directions
Books, 1959; pp. ix-xi.
Praise of Miller's brilliance by his friend and critic,
Durrell.   Durrell feels that someday the world will
have to come to terms with Miller: "His work, re-
garded in its totality is simply one of the great liberat-
ing confessions of our age ..." (p. ix).

B111   Kranaki, Mimika.   "Conversation with Henry Miller."   In
Mimika Kranaki, Greece.   London: Edward Hulton, 1959;
pp. 77-90.
A criticism of Miller's The Colossus of Maroussi which
sees Miller's love of light and poverty as superficial.

B112   Kronhausen, Phyllis and Eberhard Kronhausen.   "Henry
Miller--Apostle of the Gory Detail."   In Pornography and
the Law: The Psychology of Erotic Realism and Pornography.

New York: Ballantine Books, 1959; pp. 145-150.
Miller is viewed as a realistic writer, not a pornographer.

B113   Mailer, Norman. "The White Negro." In Norman Mailer,
Advertisements for Myself. New York: G. P. Putnam's
Sons, 1959; pp. 337-358.
Mailer sees Miller as one of the major intellectual
shapers of our age. See C29.

B114   Nin, Anaïs. "Prefacio." In Henry Miller, Trópico de
Cáncer. Buenos Aires: Santiago Rueda Editor, 1959;
pp. 9-11.
Nin's "Preface" to Tropic of Cancer. See B1, B87.

B115   Powell, Lawrence Clark. "Introduction." In Henry Miller,
The Intimate Henry Miller. New York: New American Library, 1959; pp. vii-xii.
Powell talks about his first meeting with Henry Miller
at UCLA and the transformation in Miller's life "from
Brooklyn intellectual to Paris bohemian to world celebrity" (p. ix).

B116   Ray, David. "Introduction." In The Chicago Review Anthology. Chicago: University of Chicago Press, 1959;
pp. 12-16.
Contains Miller's essay, "Literature as a Dead Duck."

B117   Rexroth, Kenneth. "Introduction." In Kenneth Rexroth,
Birds in the Bush. New York: New Directions Books,
1959; pp. vi-x.
Rexroth allies himself with Miller, Patchen, and Lawrence.

B118   Rexroth, Kenneth. "Kenneth Patchen, Naturalist of the
Public Nightmare." In Kenneth Rexroth, Birds in the Bush.
New York: New Directions Books, 1959; pp. 94-105.
Miller is one of the few representatives of a world
movement of anti-literature.

B119   Rexroth, Kenneth. "The Reality of Henry Miller." In
Kenneth Rexroth, Birds in the Bush. New York: New
Directions Books, 1959; pp. 154-167.
Miller is a writer of and for the real people, not a
religious fanatic. His reality is seen by Rexroth in
his encounters in parks and brothels.

B120   Rexroth, Kenneth. "Samuel Beckett and the Importance of
Waiting." In Kenneth Rexroth, Birds in the Bush. New
York: New Directions Books, 1959; pp. 75-85.
Samuel Beckett's writing is called an indictment of industrial and commercial civilization in the tradition of
Lawrence, Celine, and Miller.

B121   Durrell, Lawrence. "Preface." In Lawrence Durrell, The
       Black Book. New York: E. P. Dutton, 1960; pp. 13-15.
       Durrell notes Miller's influence on his work: "The
       reader will discern the influence of Tropic of Cancer in
       many passages of The Black Book.

B122   May, James Boyer. "Preface." In Sidney Omarr, Henry
       Miller: His World of Urania. London: Villiers Publica-
       tions, Ltd., 1960; pp. 9-11.
       One must get beyond the vulgar to understand Miller's
       complexity.

B123   Shapiro, Karl. "The First White Aboriginal." In Karl
       Shapiro, Start with the Sun. Lincoln: University of Ne-
       braska Press, 1960; pp. 57-70.
       The power of Whitman is continued in the writings of
       Henry Miller. See B84.

B124   Shapiro, Karl. "The Greatest Living Patagonian." In Karl
       Shapiro, Start with the Sun. Lincoln: University of Ne-
       braska Press, 1960; pp. 193-205.
       Miller is an author that critics cannot write about, a
       social reformer in the tradition of Whitman.

B125   Slote, Bernice. "The Whitman Tradition." In Karl Shapiro,
       Start with the Sun. Lincoln: University of Nebraska Press,
       1960; pp. 3-11.
       Miller is called a writer in the tradition of Whitman.

B126   Sykes, Gerald. "Introduction." In Lawrence Durrell, The
       Black Book. New York: E. P. Dutton, 1960; pp. 7-10.
       Sykes notes that Durrell's writing does not convey the
       zest one finds in the words of Rabelais, Joyce, or
       Henry Miller, "whose bawdily hilarious Tropic of Can-
       cer has a welcome liberating effect on Durrell" (p. 9).

B127   Denat, Antoine. "Henry Miller clown, barocco, mistico,
       e vincitore." In Henry Miller, Il meglio di Henry Miller.
       Milan: Longanesi & Co., 1961; pp. 11-54.
       Adriana Pellegrini translates Denat's article on Miller
       that sees him as mystic, clown, and artist of the ba-
       roque. (In Italian.)

B128   Goodman, Judge Louis. "Opinion Rendered by District
       Judge Louis Goodman, Sept. 17, 1951, Concerning the Im-
       portation into the United States of Miller's 'Tropics'." In
       Henry Miller--Between Heaven and Hell [A24]; pp. 6-8.
       A California District Court ruling considering Tropic of
       Cancer and Tropic of Capricorn obscene. It is based
       on the precedent of Judge Woolsey's opinion in United
       States v. One Book Called "Ulysses."

B129   Hirsch, Trygve. "Attorney Trygve Hirsch to Henry Miller."

In Henry Miller--Between Heaven and Hell [A24]; pp. 9-10.
A letter to Miller from a Norwegian attorney involved
in a court case concerning Sexus in Norway: "I would
be very grateful if you for the sake of the ... case we
fight would give me your personal view ..." (p. 10).

B130   Maillet, Albert. "Henry Miller, Superman and Prophet."
In Henry Miller--Between Heaven and Hell [A24]; pp. 59-85.
Miller's Tropic of Cancer combines Dostoevsky, Blake,
and Nietzsche. Miller, himself, is a literary giant who
has gained his individualism from Emerson and his belief in life from Whitman.

B131   Miller, Eve. "Terrace chez Durrell." In Alfred Perlès,
My Friend Lawrence Durrell: An Intimate Memoir on the
Author of the Alexandrian Quartet. Middlesex, England:
Scorpion Press, 1961; p. 17.
A drawing of Miller, Durrell, and Perlès on Durrell's
terrace.

B132/3 Nin, Anaïs. "Preface." In Henry Miller, Tropic of
Cancer. New York: Grove Press, 1961; pp. xxxi-xxxiii.
Tropic of Cancer is a book that leads us to rediscover
reality. It sees life as a flow, flux, and rotation of
events: "This book goes to the roots and digs under,
digs for subterranean springs" (p. xxxiii). See B1.

B134   Parkinson, Thomas Francis. "Phenomenon or Generation."
In Thomas F. Parkinson, A Casebook on the Beat. New
York: Thomas Y. Crowell, 1961; pp. 276-290.
Miller is considered to be a well-known figure of Amer-
ican letters.

B135   Piovene, Guido. "Prefazione." In Henry Miller, Arte e
Oltraggio. Milan: Feltrinelli, 1961; pp. ix-xviii.
The writing of Miller, Perlès, and Durrell are seen as
moralistic, sentimental, and honest. (In Italian.)

B136   Rexroth, Kenneth. "Disengagement: The Art of the Beat
Generation." In Thomas F. Parkinson, A Casebook on the
Beat. New York: Thomas Y. Crowell, 1961; pp. 179-193.
Miller is one of the few "Beat" writers who has gained
renown.

B137   Rexroth, Kenneth. "The Influence of French Poetry on
America." In Kenneth Rexroth, Assays. Norfolk, Conn.:
New Directions Books, 1961; pp. 143-174.
Rexroth talks about the return of the expatriates to the
United States. He notes that the one exception is Henry
Miller, who neither believes in politics nor had the
money to return.

B138   Rexroth, Kenneth. "Lawrence Durrell." In Kenneth

Rexroth, Assays.   Norfolk, Conn.:   New Directions Books,
1961; pp. 118-130.
   Rexroth satirizes the Miller-Durrell relationship.   He
   says that they are loyal friends, so loyal that Durrell
   edited an anthology "presenting poor Henry as a thinker; it would seem that Durrell really believes Miller
   thinks" (p. 124).

B139   Rohde, Peter P.   "Henry Miller: 'Pornographer or
       Prophet'?" In Henry Miller--Between Heaven and Hell
       [A24]; pp. 49-58.
          Testimony at the Norway trial of Sexus showing this
          book's anti-sexual stance, and an analysis that shows
          Miller to be an equalitarian.

B140   Shapiro, Karl.   "The Greatest Living Author."   In Henry
       Miller, Tropic of Cancer.   New York: Grove Press, 1961;
       pp. v-xxx.
          See B85.

B141   Thrap, Judge.   "'Sexus' in the Supreme Court of Norway."
       In Henry Miller--Between Heaven and Hell [A24]; pp. 41-48.
          Thrap calls Sexus a fine literary statement: 'It would
          perhaps be more correct to say that Miller undertakes
          a searching self-examination" (p. 46).   He praises the
          work's merit and feels that Miller's book should be ac-
          quitted.

B142   Tosi, Guy.   "Cendrars et Henry Miller."   In Hommage à
       Blaise Cendrars.   Rome: Editions de Luca, 1961; pp. 23-
       24.
          Tosi talks about the beginning of the Cendrars-Miller
          friendship and correspondence which began when Cen-
          drars wrote Miller a letter praising Tropic of Cancer
          in 1935.   (In Italian.)

B143   White, Emil.   "Introduction."   In Henry Miller--Between
       Heaven and Hell [A24]; pp. 4-5.
          Collection of articles edited by White with an "Introduc-
          tion" by White that considers Miller to be "the greatest
          living author."

B144   Wold, Lord Chief Justice.   "'Sexus' in the Supreme Court
       of Norway."   In Henry Miller--Between Heaven and Hell
       [A24]; pp. 39-41.
          Sexus is offensive and obscene, it violates the criminal
          code of defamation and is illegal.

B145   Yakovlev, L.   "Literature of Decay."   In Henry Miller--
       Between Heaven and Hell [A24]; pp. 27-38.
          "One of the most typical representatives of the corrupt
          literature of imperialism is Henry Miller, a 'writer'
          whom the bourgeois critics have been praising to the

skies" (p. 28). Yakovlev looks at Tropic of Cancer, calls it Miller's only autobiography, and condemns the individualistic nature of the hero, in this Communist oriented, political article.

B146   Bess, Donovan. "Cronaca di un processo. " In Prefazione ai Tropici [A31]; pp. 21-65.

B147   Bode, Carl. "A Guide to Alexandria. " In The World of Lawrence Durrell [C46]; pp. 205-221.
        Miller and T. S. Eliot had major effects on Durrell.

B148   Brassaï. "Mein Freund Hans Reichel. " In Brassaï, Lawrence Durrell, and Henry Miller, Hans Reichel 1892-1958. Paris: Editions Jean Bucher, 1962; pp. 87-95.
        Reichel loved Miller's work. He held both Tropic of Cancer and The Cosmological Eye as sacred. (In German.) See B149.

B149   Brassaï. "Mon Ami Hans Reichel. " In Brassaï, Lawrence Durrell, and Henry Miller, Hans Reichel 1892-1958. Paris: Editions Jean Bucher, 1962; pp. 39-50.
        Reichel loved both Tropic of Cancer and The Cosmological Eye. (In French.) See B148.

B150   Brombert, Victor. "Lawrence Durrell and His French Reputation. " In The World of Lawrence Durrell [C46]; pp. 169-183.
        "It was above all the encounter, in Paris, with Henry Miller ... that made of Durrell a naturalized Parisian" (p. 170).

B151   Carruth, Hayden. "Nought for the Old Bitch. " In The World of Lawrence Durrell [C46]; pp. 117-128.
        Durrell's life and work changed for the better after influence from Henry Miller.

B152   Delteil, Joseph. "Henry Miller (Fussin). " In Henry Miller, et al., Joseph Delteil. London: St. Albert's Press, 1962; pp. 37-39.
        Miller is a modern romantic in the tradition of Cervantes, philosopher of Zen, free man, man of paradox.

B153   Dobrée, Bonamy. "Durrell's Alexandrian Series. " In The World of Lawrence Durrell [C46]; pp. 184-204.
        Miller's views on sex influenced Durrell immensely: "Durrell supports his flauntingly frank exposition of completely amoral sexual life, already amply covered in his Henry Millerish The Black Book ... " (p. 196).

B154   Durrell, Lawrence. "Hans Reichel. " In Brassaï, Lawrence Durrell, and Henry Miller, Hans Reichel 1892-1958. Paris: Editions Jean Bucher, 1962; pp. 8-10.

Reichel is an opposite to Miller. (In French.)

B155 Durrell, Lawrence. "Hans Reichel. " In Brassaï, Law-
rence Durrell, and Henry Miller, Hans Reichel 1892-1958.
Paris: Editions Jean Bucher, 1962; pp. 81-82.
Durrell sees Reichel as opposite to Miller, for where
Miller draws his world from human beings, Reichel
creates his from the non-human.

B156 Durrell, Lawrence. "Hans Reichel. " In Brassaï, Lawrence Durrell, and Henry Miller, Hans Reichel 1892-1958.
Paris: Editions Jean Bucher, 1962; pp. 85-86.
The Kölner Staatsanzeiger translates Durrell's article
on Reichel where he sees Reichel and Miller to be ex-
treme opposites. (In German.) See B154, B155.

B157 Durrell, Lawrence. "Letters from Lawrence Durrell. "
In The World of Lawrence Durrell [C46]; pp. 222-239.
Durrell's letter to Jean Fanchette on June 5, 1958,
where he mentions his attempt to do a Henry Miller
anthology. He also mentions seeing Miller and the fact
that Miller's Nexus has been finished.

B158 Elliott, George P. "The Other Side of the Story. " In The
World of Lawrence Durrell [C46]; pp. 87-94.
Durrell has gained much of his philosophy from read-
ing Henry Miller.

B159 Fraenkel, Michael. "Genesi del Tropico del cancro. "
Prefazione ai Tropici [A31]; pp. 185-223.
Translation of Michael Fraenkel's "The Genius of The
Tropic of Cancer. " (In Italian.)

B160 Green, Martin. "Lawrence Durrell: A Minority Report. "
In The World of Lawrence Durrell [C46]; pp. 129-145.
Miller's books create a vanished world. Durrell entered this Paris world in the 1930's with its revolutionary literary forces like Miller and Djuna Barnes.

B161 "Lawrence Durrell Answers a Few Questions. " In The
World of Lawrence Durrell [C46]; pp. 156-160.
Durrell feels that the most important American writer
he knows is Henry Miller.

B162 Mailer, Norman. "The White Negro. " In Perspectives on
Modern Literature. Elmsford, N.Y. : Row, Paterson,
1962; pp. 219-237.
See C29.

B163 Moore, Harry T. "Durrell's Black Book. " In The World
of Lawrence Durrell [C46]; pp. 100-102.
Miller's stylistic influence on Durrell is seen in The
Black Book.

B164/5   Moore, Harry T.   "Introduction. "   In <u>The World of Law</u>-
         <u>rence Durrell</u> [C46]; pp. ix-xix.
         Miller was the first man to speak out for Durrell and
         help to make him famous.

B166   Orwell, George.   'Nel ventre della balena. "   In <u>Prefazione</u>
         <u>ai Tropici</u> [A31]; pp. 101-156.
         Valerio Riva translates Orwell's "Inside the Whale" in-
         to Italian.

B167   Perlès, Alfred.   "Epilogue. "   In <u>My Friend Henry Miller</u>
         [A12]; pp. 185-189.
         Perlès talks about the things that have occurred during
         the seven years separating the first publication of <u>My</u>
         <u>Friend Henry Miller</u> and the Belmont edition.

B168   Praz, Mario.   "Civiltà in sfacelo. "   In <u>Prefazione ai</u>
         <u>Tropici</u> [A31]; pp. 177-184.

B169   Read, Herbert.   "Estetica e profezia. "   In <u>Prefazione ai</u>
         <u>Tropici</u> [A31]; pp. 157-165.
         Valerio Riva translates Read's "Henry Miller" into
         Italian.

B170   Reino, Herbert.   "Henry Miller. "   In Henry Miller, <u>Plexus;</u>
         <u>Roman</u>.   Hamburg: Bertelsmann Lesering, 1962; pp. <u>541-</u>
         <u>542</u>.
         A brief biography of Miller.   (In German.)

B171   Rexroth, Kenneth.   "La realtà di Henry Miller. "   In <u>Pre</u>-
         <u>fazione ai Tropici</u> [A31]; pp. 225-242.
         Italian translation of Rexroth's "The Reality of Henry
         Miller. "

B172   Rosenfeld, Paul.   "Miller e la tradizione. "   In <u>Prefazione</u>
         <u>ai Tropici</u> [A31]; pp. 167-175.
         Italian translation of Paul Rosenfeld's "The Tradition
         and Henry Miller. "

B173   Sanguineti, Edoardo.   "Miller: Una Poetica Borocca. "   In
         <u>Prefazione ai Tropici</u> [A31]; pp. 243-263.
         Miller is viewed as a poet.   (In Italian.)

B174   Sewell, Brocard.   "Foreword. "   In Henry Miller, et al. ,
         <u>Joseph Delteil</u>.   London: St. Albert's Press, 1962; pp. 1-2.
         Miller generously contributed an article to this book
         entitled "Joseph Delteil and François d'Assise. "

B175   Sewell, Brocard.   "Joseph Delteil's 'Jesus II'. "   In Henry
         Miller, et al. , <u>Joseph Delteil</u>.   London: St. Albert's
         Press, 1962; pp. 7-16.
         Miller sees Delteil's work coming "from a silence as
         deep and mysterious as that of the forest" (p. 7).

B176 Shapiro, Karl. "Il più grande autore vivente. " Prefazione
      ai Tropici [A31]; pp. 67-99.
          Italian translation of Shapiro's "The Greatest Living
      Author. "

B177 Steiner, George. "Lawrence Durrell: The Baroque Novel. "
      In The World of Lawrence Durrell [C46]; pp. 13-23.
          Durrell is considered a "minor disciple of Henry Mill-
      er" (p. 13).

B178 Sykes, Gerald. "One Vote for the Sun. " In The World of
      Lawrence Durrell [C46]; pp. 146-155.
          Miller was the chief mentor of Durrell, for it was his
      "deep distaste for Puritanism" that he instilled in his
      younger friend.

B179 Temple, F. J. "La Tuilerie de Massane. " In Henry
      Miller, et al. , Joseph Delteil. London: St. Albert's
      Press, 1962; pp. 27-28.
          Temple mentions a starving poet named Miller.

B180 Wain, John. "Along the Tightrope. " In Perspectives on
      Modern Literature. Elmsford, N.Y. : Row, Paterson,
      1962; pp. 204-219.
          "The world is only the mirror of ourselves. If it's
      something to make one puke, why then puke, me lads,
      it's your own sick mugs you're looking at!" (p. 204).
      What Miller is getting at is the fact that we decide
      what literature is all about through subjective interpre-
      tation.

B181 Wolton, G. E. "A Letter to Lawrence Durrell. " In The
      World of Lawrence Durrell [C46]; pp. 103-111.
          Miller is one of the few American writers to get be-
      yond copulation and rape and understand women: "He,
      like the trickster, using an irony and subtlety which we
      dub obscene, seems to be trying to bring us to our
      senses" (p. 109).

B182 Brooks, Van Wyck. "Introduction. " In Malcolm Cowley,
      ed. , Writers At Work: Paris Review Interviews: Se-
      cond Series. New York: Viking Press, 1963; pp. 1-6.
          In discussing Miller, Brooks notes that he is an indi-
      vidual who is "against groups and sets and sects and
      cults and isms... " (p. 2). He is an alien being,
      whether in Paris or Big Sur, for he feels that the
      world with its politics is rotten.

B183 Cendrars, Blaise. "Un Ecrivain américain nous est Né. "
      Henry Miller and the Critics [A36]; pp. 23-24.
          Cendrars salutes Miller for his realism, his ability to
      write "a good down-to-earth" novel. He feels that
      hunger and vomit are real and considers Miller power-

ful to have captured these feelings in portraying Paris.

B184   Durrell, Lawrence. "Studies in Genius: Henry Miller."
       In Henry Miller and the Critics [A36]; pp. 86-107.
           Durrell sees Miller's work as "germination." He sees
           the life that Miller portrays coming from an intellectual
           conglomerate of Bergson, Spengler, Freud, and Hindu
           and Chinese religion.

B185   Gertz, Elmer. "Henry Miller and the Law." In Henry
       Miller and the Critics [A36]; pp. 177-186.
           Discussion of Miller's war against institutionalized so-
           ciety, and his movement to an anarchistic stance like
           that of Emma Goldman and Frank Harris: "Being him-
           self, being natural, being truthful, meant being at war
           with the law and the upholders of the legal order ..."
           (p. 179).

B186   Hoffman, Frederick J. "The Booster." In Henry Miller
       and the Critics [A36]; pp. 20-22.
           Miller's philosophy is one that sees the world as an
           enormous womb: "This philosophy of life as darkness
           and desire for death ... is derived in large from
           psycho-medical researches into the unconscious" (p. 21).

B187   Huxley, Aldous. "Statement for the Los Angeles Trial."
       In Henry Miller and the Critics [A36]; pp. 175-176.
           Tropic is called a revulsion of sex. It becomes ex-
           tremely unattractive and can lead one to revert to
           Puritanism.

B188   Kauffmann, Stanley. "An Old Shocker Comes Home." In
       Henry Miller and the Critics [A36]; pp. 154-160.
           Miller is called dishonest, an inferior Whitman, and a
           sketchy writer, and his book Tropic of Cancer is
           called second rate.

B189   Levin, Harry. "Commonwealth of Massachusetts vs. Tropic
       of Cancer." In Henry Miller and the Critics [A36]; pp. 168-
       174.
           Levin's court statement sees Tropic of Cancer as a
           valuable social statement that discusses American
           disease and sterility: "... The symbol of the crab
           represents a certain erosion, a sickness, certainly, of
           modern society" (p. 168).

B190   Lowenfels, Walter. "A Note on Tropic of Cancer--Paris
       1931." In Henry Miller and the Critics [A36]; pp. 16-19.
           A review of Tropic of Cancer that reflects the anti-
           literary position that Miller holds, as it depicts him
           striving for and attaining real life in his writing.

B191   Mitchell, Julian, and Gene Andrewski. "Lawrence Durrell."

In Malcolm Cowley, ed. , Writers at Work: Paris Review
Interviews. New York: Viking Press, 1963; pp. 257-282.
Discussion of Durrell's first meeting with Miller.

B192   Moore, Harry T.   "From under the Counter to Front Shelf."
In Henry Miller and the Critics [A36]; pp. 149-153.
Discussion of the first-person narrative technique of
Tropic of Cancer: "The Miller man, here and in later
books, is in effect the descendent of Dostoevsky's Underground Man ... and of Rilke's Malte Laurids Brigge..."
(p. 150).   This first person approach to writing provides both self-exposure and liberation.

B193   Moore, Harry T.   "Preface. " In Henry Miller and the
Critics [A36]; pp. v-ix.
Biography of Miller's hardships publishing his work,
beginning is 1932 and moving through the publication of
Tropic of Cancer.   The major thesis is that Miller is
affirmative, even in the face of disaster.

B194/5 Muller, Herbert J.   "The World of Henry Miller. " In
Henry Miller and the Critics [A36]; pp. 44-51.
The revolt against intellect is explored in Tropic of
Capricorn.   Here, Miller criticizes the perversions of
reality such as "intellect, science, society, civiliza-
tion ... art and literature" (p. 48).

B196   Orwell, George.   "Inside the Whale. " In Henry Miller and
the Critics [A36]; pp. 31-43.
See B9.

B197   Perlès, Alfred.   "My Friend Henry Miller--Paris 1930. "
In Henry Miller and the Critics [A36]; pp. 3-10.
Perlès looks at Miller's need to purge himself and to
reveal his past.

B198   Powell, Lawrence Clark.   "The Miller of Big Sur. " In
Henry Miller and the Critics [A36]; pp. 56-62.
Powell recounts his first meeting with Miller and re-
members having asked him to construct a list of books
he found to be important.   From this conversation came
The Books in My Life.

B199   Putnam, Samuel.   "Henry Miller in Montparnasse. " In
Henry Miller and the Critics [A36]; pp. 11-15.
Discussion of Miller's years as a proofreader on the
Paris edition of the Chicago Tribune.   At this time,
the Miller story, "Mademoiselle Claude, " was published
and shocked the Americans who read it.

B200   Rahv, Philip.   "Sketches in Criticism: Henry Miller. " In
Henry Miller and the Critics [A36]; pp. 77-85.
A criticism of Miller's later work while praising such

early pieces as The Colossus of Maroussi, Tropic of
Cancer, Black Spring, and Tropic of Capricorn.   The
use of sex in these novels conveys "a sense of cultural
and social disorder, to communicate a nihilistic outlook, and ... an insatiable naturalistic curiosity" (p.
84).   Thus Miller goes beyond merely physical relief,
using sex to display man's mechanistic and fallen nature.

B201   Read, Herbert.   "Henry Miller."   In Henry Miller and the
Critics [A36]; pp. 111-118.
   Miller's writing is not literature.   Much of it is autobiography, and much concerns a naturalistic relationship between man and his environment.

B202   Rexroth, Kenneth.   "The Reality of Henry Miller."   In
Henry Miller and the Critics [A36]; pp. 119-131.
   Miller is seen as a popular writer of the people.

B203   Rohde, Peter P.   "Forord."   In Henry Miller, Krebsens
Venderkreds.   Copenhagen: Hans Reitzel, 1963; pp. 5-10.
   Foreword to Tropic of Cancer in Danish.

B204   Schorer, Mark.   "Commonwealth of Massachusetts vs.
Tropic of Cancer."   In Henry Miller and the Critics [A36];
pp. 161-167.
   Schorer's court statement in defense of Tropic of Cancer is recounted.   He consideres the book to have a
form of life uncaptured in American literature.

B205   Wasserstrom, William.   "Advancing on Chaos: Henry
Miller."   In William Wasserstrom, The Time of the Dial.
Syracuse, N.Y.: Syracuse University Press, 1963;
pp. 133-160.
   Miller is viewed as an isolated individual in quest of a
utopia.   Yet Miller's change to pessimism leads to a
book dealing with the blackest self, a self that may be
evil, yet a being who truly experiences life.

B206   Wickes, George.   "Henry Miller."   In Malcolm Cowley, ed., Writers at Work: Paris Review Interviews.
New York: Viking Press, 1963; pp. 165-191.
   First a biography of Miller's life and work is presented.
Then the interview between Miller and Wickes takes
place.   They begin by discussing Miller's writing style,
then the mechanics of writing, and then the literature.
Miller describes the plight of the artist in America who
is forced to compromise himself to become successful.

B207   Wickes, George.   "Introduction."   In Henry Miller and the
Critics [A36]; pp. xvii-xviii.
   An attempt to dispel the popular belief that Miller has
been shunned by American and British critics for the
past three decades.   However, he has not enjoyed a

"balanced critical appraisal" (p. xvii).

B208 Wickes, George. "Introduction." In Lawrence Durrell and Henry Miller, Lawrence Durrell and Henry Miller: A Private Correspondence. London: Faber & Faber Ltd., 1963; pp. xi-xv.
Wickes traces the lives of two great men of letters, their friendship, and their successes in this first British edition of the Miller-Durrell correspondence.

B209 Wickes, George. "1930-1940: Henry Miller in Paris." In Henry Miller and the Critics [A36]; pp. 1-2.
Analysis of the first four pieces in Wickes's collection, all of which attempt "to give some sense of those early years in Paris when Miller was struggling to find himself as a writer" (p. 1).

B210 Wickes, George. "1940-1960: Henry Miller in America." In Henry Miller and the Critics [A36]; pp. 53-55.
In 1940 war forced Miller to return to the United States and allowed him to tour America and write The Air-Conditioned Nightmare, a book about his journey across the continent. During this period Miller's writing was explored by such critics as Lawrence Clark Powell, Walker Winslow, Philip Rahv, Cyril Connolly, Lawrence Durrell, Herbert Read, Kenneth Rexroth, and Kingsley Widmer.

B211 Wickes, George. "1961 and After: Tropic of Cancer in America." In Henry Miller and the Critics [A36]; pp. 147-148.
Review of the reaction to the publishing of Tropic of Cancer in the United States in 1961. Noted is a favorable revue by Harry T. Moore, a reserved outlook by Stanley Kauffmann, and trial statements by Huxley, Gertz, Schorer, Levin, and a comment by Miller, himself.

B212 Widmer, Kingsley. "The Rebel-Buffoon: Henry Miller's Legacy." In Henry Miller and the Critics [A36]; pp. 132-146.
Miller rebels against his past, himself, and the America of his frustration by establishing a series of mock-identities.

B213 Wilson, Edmund. "Twilight of the Expatriates." In Henry Miller and the Critics [A36]; pp. 25-30.
"Expatriate Mr. Miller certainly is ... the spokesman, par excellence, for the Left Bank ..." (p. 26). His novel, Tropic of Cancer, is viewed by Wilson as the most honest statement about Paris in many years.

B214 Brandt, Jørgen Gustava. "Forord." In Henry Miller, Sort

Var. Copenhagen: M. Reitzel, 1964; pp. 9-12.
Brandt sees Black Spring as a most important work for
Miller, for he gained a greater control of language, increased his humor, became a great story teller, and
created a modern romance. (In Danish.)

B215 Ethridge, James M. "Henry Miller." In James Ethridge,
ed., Contemporary Authors: A Bio-Bibliographical Guide to
Current Authors and Their Works. Detroit: Gale Research
Company, 1964; pp. 340-342.
A brief biography of Miller's life, his work, and the
opinions of others about him. Listed in chronological
order are all of his novels from Tropic of Cancer
(1934) to Henry Miller on Writing (1964). He is considered an autobiographical novelist, compared to Whitman, and labelled a mystic.

B216 Moore, John G. "Prefatory Note." In What Henry Miller
Said and Why It Is Important [A40]; pp. 9-11.
"Like nature, Miller and most other artists accept the
variations of Love--Eros, Sex, Fornication, and
Agape ... " (p. 11).

B217 Moore, Thomas H. "Preface." In Henry Miller, Henry
Miller on Writing. New York: New Directions, 1964;
p. ix.
Moore edits passages taken from all of Miller's work.

B218 Ponce, Juan Garcia. "Radiografía de Henry Miller." In
Henry Miller, Primavera Negra. Buenos Aires: S. Rueda,
1964; pp. 7-21.
Like Dostoevsky, Miller is a unified writer whose first
work proved his importance. (In Spanish.)

B219 Rothenborg, Jørgen. "Forord." In Henry Miller, Myrd
Morderen. Copenhagen: Hans Reitzel, 1964; pp. 5-6.
Murder the Murderer is seen as a work dealing with
the positive merits of sex. (In Danish.)

B220 Gertz, Elmer. "The Battle for Literary Freedom." In A
Handful of Clients [C60]; pp. 229-303.
Gertz studies Tropic of Cancer and sees the book as
wrongly suppressed.

B221 Gertz, Elmer. "An Obscenity Trial." In A Handful of
Clients [C60]; pp. 229-303.
The Chicago Tropic trial is recreated and explored by
Gertz.

B222 Kershaw, Alister, and Frederic-Jacques Temple. "Notes
on the Contributors." In Alister Kershaw and Frederic-
Jacques Temple, eds., Richard Aldington; An Intimate Portrait. Carbondale: Southern Illinois University Press,

1965; pp. xiii-xix.
A brief biography of Miller from 1891-1963.

B223 Moore, Harry T. "Richard Aldington." In Alister Kershaw and Frederic-Jacques Temple, eds., Richard Aldington; An Intimate Portrait. Carbondale: Southern Illinois
University Press, 1965; pp. 80-105.
Noted is the friendship between Miller and Durrell.

B224 Stuhlmann, Gunther. "Editor's Note." In Henry Miller,
Henry Miller Letters to Anaïs Nin. New York: G. P.
Putnam's Sons, 1965; pp. v-xxvi.
Miller's letters to Nin cover fifteen years, from 1931-
1946; "These years were perhaps the most important in
Miller's life, the most fruitful in his career as a writ-
er, and the most derisive in his development as a
man" (p. v).

B225 Thien, Pham Cong. "The Ontological Background of the
Present War in Vietnam (An Open Letter to Henry Miller)."
In Pham Cong Thien, Dialogue. Saigon: La Boi, 1965;
pp. 73-86.
Letter to Miller discussing the basis of the War in
Vietnam.

B226 Brandon, William. "Blaise Cendrars: An Interview and
Selected Writing." In George A. Plimpton, ed., The Paris
Review. New York: Doubleday and Co., 1966; pp. 105-107.
See B228; this is the interview. In 1935 Cendrars dis-
covered Miller and wrote the first article on Tropic of
Cancer.

B227 Brophy, Brigid. "Henry Miller." In Brigid Brophy, Don't
Never Forget: Collected Views and Reviews. New York:
Holt, Rinehart and Winston, 1966; pp. 231-238.
Brophy sees Miller as a very repetitive writer because
Sexus is much the same as Tropic of Cancer. (He
never notices that these two works are autobiographical
and therefore should be alike.) He says that Miller
deals only with externals.

B228 Cendrars, Blaise. "Blaise Cendrars: An Interview and
Selected Writing." In George A. Plimpton, ed., The Paris
Review. New York: Doubleday and Co., 1966; pp. 108-132.
See B226; this is the selected writing. Cendrars calls
Miller a gay and joyous companion.

B229 Debenedetti, Giacomo. "Nota Introduttiva." In Henry
Miller, Il tempo degli assassini. Milan: Sugar Editore,
1966; pp. i-iv.
Miller illuminates the character of Rimbaud in The
Time of the Assassins. (In Italian.)

B230 Durrell, Lawrence. "Introduction." In Henry Miller,
Order and Chaos Chez Hans Reichel. Tucson, Ariz.: Lou-
jon Press, 1966; pp. 7-12.
Durrell talks about the happiness of Miller and his
circle in 1937 and 1938 after the publication of the two
Tropics and Black Spring.

B231 Friedman, Alan. "The Pitching of Love's Mansion in the
Tropics of Henry Miller." In Seven Contemporary Authors
[C68]; pp. 23-48.

B232 Ibrasa. "Prologo da editôra." In Henry Miller, Tropico
de Cancer. São Paulo, Brazil: Ibrasa, 1966; pp. vii-xii.
Tropic of Cancer is considered a real work of merit, a
serious piece of writing that places Miller in the tradition of Joyce and Lawrence. (In Portuguese.)

B233 Marcuse, Ludwig. "Los Angeles 1962: The Most Obscene
Writer in World Literature." In Ludwig Marcuse, Obscene:
The History of an Indignation. London: MacGibbon & Kee,
1966; pp. 255-299.
Miller is a writer who has carried the flesh to disgusting lengths: "With the man Henry Miller and with his
work the obscene has reached a new stage in its development" (p. 257).

B234 Stuhlmann, Gunther. "Introduction." In Anaïs Nin, The
Diary of Anaïs Nin: 1931-1934. New York: Harcourt,
Brace & World, 1966; pp. v-xii.
In Criterion in 1937, Miller noted that Nin's Diary
would take its place beside the world's greatest letters.

B235 Tavares, Vitor Silva. "Prefacio." In Henry Miller, O
sorriso aos pes da escada. Barcelos, Portugal: Editôra
Ulisseia, 1966; pp. 7-18.
Miller's literature is alive, covering the boundaries of
both comedy and tragedy. (In Portuguese.)

B236 Whithead, Thomas B. "Introduction." In Seven Contemporary Authors [C68]; pp. vii-xv.
Miller is an affirmative writer who finds hope in the
midst of despair.

B237 Durrell, Lawrence. "Foreword." In The Mind and Art of
Henry Miller [A44]; pp. vii-ix.
Durrell discusses Miller's statement that his books
"are not about sex but about self-liberation" (p. vii).

B238 Fogle, Richard Harter. "Preface." In The Mind and Art
of Henry Miller [A44]; pp. xi-xv.
Henry Miller fits none of the recognized patterns of
contemporary American fiction. He is one of "the
greatest romantics of them all" (p. xiii).

B239   French, Warren. "General Introduction. " In The Thirties
       [C71]; pp. 1-3.
       French feels that Frederick J. Hoffmann puts the stereo-
       typed image of Henry Miller into a wholly new light.

B240   French, Warren. "The Thirties--Fiction. " In The Thirties
       [C71]; pp. 5-10.
       Miller's fantasies of Bohemian sexual prowess, as found
       in the two Tropics, lead him to the position of defender
       and patron saint of the Beat Generation.

B241   Halperen, Max. "Ezra Pound: Poet Priest, Poet-Propa-
       gandist. " In The Thirties [C71]; pp. 123-131.
       Miller wrote and dedicated a burlesque pamphlet to
       Pound called Money and How It Gets That Way.

B242   Hoffman, Frederick J. "Henry Miller, Defender of
       the Marginal Life. " In The Thirties [C71]; pp. 73-80.
       A short biography of Miller where it is stated that he
       believed in sex, the individual, and fullness of life. In
       his works, Miller suggests "that the majority of men
       are obtuse and dull, greedy and opportunistic: that they
       have the sensitivity of the artist and the clown. . . " (p. 77).

B243   Honda, Yasunari. "Henry Miller. " In Yasunari Honda,
       Henry Miller. Tokyo: Hirosaki College, 1967; pp. 57-62.
       Miller is compared to Henry James, William Faulkner,
       and Ernest Hemingway. (In Japanese.)

B244   Honda, Yasunari. "Henry Miller's America. " In Ya-
       sunari Honda, Henry Miller. Tokyo: Hirosaki College,
       1967; pp. 88-103.
       America is seen in Miller's eyes as a cesspool. (In
       Japanese.)

B245   Olinto, Antonio. "Introdução: Henry Miller, moralista in-
       submisso. " In Henry Miller, Sexus. Rio de Janeiro:
       Gráfica Record Editôra, 1967; pp. v-viii.
       Miller is a moral writer. (In Portuguese.)

B246   Praz, Mario. "Prefazione. " In Henry Miller, Tropico del
       Cancro. Milan: Feltrinelli, 1967; pp. 9-13.
       Miller is a person striving for independence in Tropic
       of Cancer. (In Italian.)

B247   Stuhlmann, Gunther. "Preface. " In The Diary of Anaïs
       Nin: 1934-1939 [C72]; pp. v-ix.
       In November 1934, two months after the publication of
       Tropic of Cancer, Miller and Nin were going separate
       ways. He would remain in Paris, while she ventured
       to the United States.

B248   Gertz, Elmer. "Foreword. " In Tropic of Cancer on Trial

[A51]; pp. vii-viii.
The Tropic of Cancer Case changed the climate of
American literature.

B249 Hayniess, Hugh. "Chief? Crook-of-the-Month Squad Reporting." In Evergreen Review Reader, 1957-1967: A Ten-
Year Anthology. New York: Grove Press, 1968; p. 530.
A cartoon showing a policeman with a smoking gun hold-
ing a handcuffed, bullet-riddled copy of Tropic of Cancer. The policeman wears the appropriate label, "Official Literary Censor."

B250 Hollo, Anselm. "A Warrant Is Out for the Arrest of Henry
Miller." In Evergreen Review Reader, 1957-1967: A Ten-
Year Anthology. New York: Grove Press, 1968; p. 538.
A poem mocking the attack on Henry Miller. It de-
picts a man running from the law, a being who is truly
alive, as he ventures over rooftops and through alleys.

B251 Lage, Carlos. "Introdução." In Henry Miller, Sexo em
Clichy. Rio de Janeiro: Gráfica Record Editôra, 1968;
pp. 7-12.
A brief biography of Miller's life, followed by a defense of Miller's work saying that he is not pornographic but is a writer in the tradition of Joyce and Lawrence. (In Portuguese.)

B252 Mailer, Norman. "Foreword." In The End of Obscenity
[A52]; pp. vii-xi.
Miller is involved in the fight against obscenity.

B253 Miller, Tony. "Statt eines Vorworts." In Henry Miller,
Stille Tage in Clichy: Roman. Hamburg: Rowohlt, 1968;
pp. 9-11.
Kurt Wagenseil translates Miller's son's article calling
Quiet Days in Clichy a humorous book about Paris
prior to World War II. (In German.)

B254 Olinto, Antonio. "Rimbaud, Miller e o caminho de insubmissão." In Henry Miller, O tempo dos assassinos. Rio
de Janeiro: Gráfica Record Editôra, 1968; pp. 11-22.
Miller, as a young painter, has a lot to learn, yet, as
a writer, he is an expert at describing individuals like
Rimbaud. (In Portuguese.)

B255 Orwell, George. "Letters to James Laughlin." In George
Orwell, The Collected Essays, Journalism and Letters of
George Orwell: My Country Right or Left 1940-1943,
Volume II. New York: Harcourt, Brace & World, Inc.,
1968; pp. 33-34.
Orwell gives Laughlin permission to reprint "Inside the
Whale."

B256   Rein, Mark W.   "Vorbemerkung des Übersetzers. "   In
Anaïs Nin, <u>Brief An Anaïs Nin.</u>   Hamburg: Rowohlt, 1968;
pp. 31-32.
The letters from Miller to Nin are called authentic,
spontaneous outpourings of emotion.   (In German.)

B257   Schneider, Duane.   "Prefatory Note. "   In Anaïs Nin, <u>Unpub-</u>
<u>lished Selections From the Diary.</u>   Athens, Ohio: Duane
Schneider Press, 1968; p. ix.
Schneider's intention was to present a coherent <u>Diary</u>
that focused on Miller and Dr. Rene Allendy.

B258   Shapiro, Karl.   "A Defense of Bad Poetry. "   In Karl Shapiro, <u>To Abolish Children and Other Essays.</u>   Chicago:
Quadrangle Books, 1968; pp. 63-81.
Shapiro talks about the sense that Miller's obscenity
makes: "It makes a new kind of sense.   ...   He has
changed the content of the novel by ignoring the morality of social forms" (p. 77).

B259   Shapiro, Karl.   "A Malebolge of Fourteen Hundred Books. "
In Karl Shapiro, <u>To Abolish Children and Other Essays.</u>
Chicago: Quadrangle Books, 1968; pp. 169-288.
Shapiro notes that Miller provides a deeper understanding of America in <u>The Air-Conditioned Nightmare.</u>   He
deals with failure, conditioning, and the loss of humanity.   But Miller feels that man can overcome this
misery: "To Miller, misery is merely a matter of
bad luck; he can shrug it off" (p. 241).   His ability to
get beyond failure allows him to endure in spite of the
fact that so much of his work has been misunderstood,
persecuted, and rejected.

B260   Shapiro, Karl.   "The Decolonization of American Literature. "   In Karl Shapiro, <u>To Abolish Children and Other Es-</u>
<u>says.</u>   Chicago: Quadrangle Books, 1968; pp. 25-44.
Both Miller and Faulkner see American literature as
rootless because there is no relation between the American and the land.

B261   Shapiro, Karl.   "Is Poetry an American Art?"   In Karl
Shapiro, <u>To Abolish Children and Other Essays.</u>   Chicago:
Quadrangle Books, 1968; pp. 45-62.
Shapiro sees many of the volumes of American poetry
as useless because nobody reads them.   Listed are
Miller's <u>The Rosy Crucifixion,</u> Twain's <u>Huckleberry</u>
<u>Finn,</u> Bellow's <u>Henderson the Rain King,</u> etc.

B262   Wood, Richard Clement.   "Editor's Note. "   In <u>Collector's</u>
<u>Quest</u> [A48]; pp. v-vi.
A publication of all available letters exchanged by
Miller and Childs.   Personal comments have been de-
leted.

B263 Wood, Richard Clement. "Introduction." In Collector's
Quest [A48]; pp xi-xv.
Wood praises Miller's generous nature for correspond-
ing with Childs and developing a friendship.

B264 "About a Book Named Tropic." In Evergreen Review Reader, 1957-1967: A Ten-Year Anthology. New York: Grove
Press, 1968; pp. 531-532.
On September 26, 1961, in Suffolk Superior Court in
Boston, Mass., a trial against Miller's Tropic took
place. It was appropriately entitled Edward J. McCormack, Jr., Attorney General vs. A Book Named "Tropic
of Cancer." Prof. Harry T. Moore, a witness for the
defense, felt that Tropic was of high literary merit.

B265 "Henry Miller." In Evergreen Review Reader, 1957-1967:
A Ten-Year Anthology. New York: Grove Press, 1968;
p. 789.
Brief autobiography of Miller's life that notes that
Miller divides his time between writing and painting
and that he was in the landmark decision against censorship.

B266 "Henry Miller Exhibition." In Henry Miller, Henry Miller
Exhibition of Watercolors. Tokyo: Art Life Association, 1968.
Booklet of Miller's paintings exhibited in Tokyo where
Miller talks about his love for art while calling him-
self an amateur. (In Japanese.)

B267 Belmont, Georges. "Indications au lecteur." In Henry
Miller and Georges Belmont, Henry Miller Entretiens de
Paris avec Georges Belmont. Paris: Editions Stock, 1969;
pp. ix-x.
Miller is seen as a powerful life force. (In French.)

B268 Bose, Buddhadeva. "Visita a Big Sur." In O mundo de
Henry Miller [A55]; pp. 155-162.
Visit to Big Sur to celebrate Miller's birthday. (In
Portuguese.)

B269 Brassaï. "Com Miller, em Cannes." In O mundo de
Henry Miller [A55]; pp. 87-91.
Conversation at the 1960 Cannes Film Festival with
Miller. (In Portuguese.)

B270 Carpeaux, Otto Maria. "Literatura ou pornografia?" In
O mundo de Henry Miller [A55]; pp. 31-37.
Miller an apostle of liberty not a pornographer. (In
Portuguese.)

B271 Cavalcante, Hermenegildo de Sá. "Henry Miller--o velho
poder jovem." In O mundo de Henry Miller [A55]; pp. 9-
15.

Miller's literary place in the future. (In Portuguese.)

B272 Delteil, Joseph. "Um cavaleiro em busca do graal." In
O mundo de Henry Miller [A55]; pp. 181-183.
Miller a man in search of life. (In Portuguese.)

B273 Denat, Antoine. "De Montaigne a Miller." In O mundo de
Henry Miller [A55]; pp. 131-139.
Miller compared to Montaigne. (In Portuguese.)

B274 Durrell, Lawrence. "O sôpro do dragão." In O mundo de
Henry Miller [A55]; pp. 149-151.
Miller a conscious autobiographer. (In Portuguese.)

B275 Dury, David. "Sex Goes Public." In Alexander Klein, ed.,
Natural Enemies: Youth and the Clash of Generations. New
York: J. B. Lippencott, 1969; pp. 391-400.
An interview with Miller in which he voices his love for
sex while showing his anger at the fact that sex has become such a public spectacle: "This constant harping
on sex all the time is so immature..." (p. 391). He
goes so far as to view the American response to sex
as an adolescent rebellion.

B276 Gelre, Henk van. "A linguagem da vida." In O mundo de
Henry Miller [A55]; pp. 109-117.
Miller not a disciplined writer. (In Portuguese.)

B277 Gertz, Elmer. "Meu cliente Henry Miller." In O mundo
de Henry Miller [A55]; pp. 185-189.
Discusses a relationship with Miller during 1961 Tropic
trial. (In Portuguese.)

B278 Mucciolo, Genaro. "O método e a linguagem." In O
mundo de Henry Miller [A55]; pp. 141-143.
Tropic of Cancer an unconventional book about survival.
(In Portuguese.)

B279 Nascimento, Esdras do. "A profissão de escritor." In
O mundo de Henry Miller [A55]; pp. 51-76.
A look at the response to Plexus and Nexus in Brazil.
(In Portuguese.)

B280 Nascimento, Esdras do. "Introdução--a morte do bele-
trismo." In O mundo de Henry Miller [A55]; pp. 17-27.
Miller's novels are protests against society and involve
social violence. (In Portuguese.)

B281 Nascimento, Esdras do. "Tábua cronológica." In O mundo
de Henry Miller [A55]; pp. 207-270.
Chronology and bibliography of Miller. (In Portuguese.)

B282 Nin, Anaïs. "Diário íntimo." In O mundo de Henry Miller

[A55]; pp. 163-179.
Selections from Nin's Diary, volume I. (In Portuguese.)

B283 Okumara, Osamu. "O milagre da vida sem Deus." In O
mundo de Henry Miller [A55]; pp. 79-86.
Miller seen as a transcendentalist in tradition of Emerson. (In Portuguese.)

B284 Olinto, Antonio. "O caminho da insubmissão." In O mundo
de Henry Miller [A55]; pp. 119-129.
Miller a poet of reality. (In Portuguese.)

B285 Rahv, Philip. 'Henry Miller." In Philip Rahv, Literature
and the Sixth Sense. Boston: Houghton Mifflin Co., 1969;
pp. 88-94.
Miller's two Tropics and Black Spring make him the
artist hero who dominates literature by making his
world come alive.

B286 Ruuth, Marianne. "Pacific Palisades." In O mundo de
Henry Miller [A55]; pp. 191-194.
Visit to Miller's home. (In Portuguese.)

B287 Stuhlmann, Gunther. "Preface." In The Diary of Anaïs
Nin: 1939-1944 [C84]; pp. v-xiv.
Nin's view of city life was different from Miller's con-
ception. She was brought up in a world of art, while
Miller developed in a materialistic, immigrant society.

B288 Vidal, Gore. "Notes on Pornography." In Reflections
Upon a Sinking Ship [C86]; pp. 85-99.
Miller's sexual experiences are not truly edifying.

B289 Vidal, Gore. "The Sexus of Henry Miller." In Reflections
Upon a Sinking Ship [C86]; pp. 111-117.
Miller's autobiographical writing is seen by Vidal as
the effort of an egotist: "Right off, it must be noted
that only a total egotist could have written a book
which has no subject other then Henry Miller in all his
sweet monotony" (p. 118).

B290 Wulff, Wilhelm Th. H. "Miller, segundo os astrólogos."
In O mundo de Henry Miller [A55]; pp. 195-200.
Miller the astrologer viewed. (In Portuguese.)

B291 Childs, J(ames) Rives. "Introduction." In Tropiques en
Voyageur [A61]; pp. i-v.
Ambassador Childs talks about his first consciousness,
the experience of Miller that came in 1939 with his
reading of Tropic of Cancer, Black Spring, and Max
and the White Phagocytes.

B292 Fraenkel, Michael. "Note on Death." In The Life of

Fraenkel's Death [C92]; pp. 7-10.
Fraenkel and Miller would sit for hours and discuss
The Weather Paper (1932) and their joint effort, Hamlet.

B293   French, Warren.   "The Age of Salinger."   In The Fifties
[C89]; p. 17.
Miller is one of the originators of the "Beat" move-
ment: "Older writers like Henry Miller and Kenneth
Patchen became patron saints of the new movement..."
(p. 17).

B294   Geismar, Maxwell.   "The Shifting Illusion: Dream and
Fact." In American Dreams, American Nightmares [C93];
pp. 45-57.
Writers like Miller undercut the illusion of an ideal
America by depicting its nightmarish aspects: "Miller's
view ... of all modern, progressive, scientific, and
industrial life, is basically hopeless if not desperate"
(p. 55).

B295   Hassan, Ihab.   "Focus on Norman Mailer's Why Are We in
Vietnam?" In American Dreams, American Nightmares
[C93]; pp. 197-203.
Mailer's use of obscenity is in the tradition of Miller:
"Obscenity seeks 'to awaken, to usher in a sense of
reality' " (p. 198).

B296   Littlejohn, David.   "The Anti-Realists (1963)." In Interruptions [C91]; pp. 17-33.
Miller is grouped along with Djuna Barnes, Malcolm
Lowery, and Nathaniel West in the second generation
of modern anti-realists.

B297   Littlejohn, David.   "Foreword." In Interruptions [C91];
pp. vii-viii.
Littlejohn's 1967 essay on The Rosy Crucifixion takes
issue with his 1962 criticism of Tropic.

B298   Littlejohn, David.   "Henry Miller and Lawrence Durrell
(1963)." In Interruptions [C91]; pp. 73-81.
The Miller-Durrell correspondence is seen as a misunderstanding on both parts.   Miller never moves in
his conception of writing and Durrell cannot realize or
accept this fact.

B299   Littlejohn, David.   "The Permanence of Durrell (1963)."
In Interruptions [C91]; pp. 82-90.
Durrell has an ability to laugh at himself that Miller
does not possess.

B300   Littlejohn, David.   "Sexus, Nexus and Plexus (1967)." In
Interruptions [C91]; pp. 45-72.
Miller's trilogy shows his movement from confinement

to freedom, found in transcending the Christian world
and finding an existence where one merges himself with
the All to gain a fuller identity.

B301   Littlejohn, David.   "The Tropics of Miller (1962)."   In
        Interruptions [C91]; pp. 37-44.
            Miller's novels are autobiographies of individualism that
            show the merits of uninvolvement.

B302   Lowenfels, Walter.   "Fraenkel's Money Dies."   In The Life
        of Fraenkel's Death [C92]; pp. 16-19.
            Discussion of the Miller-Fraenkel debate found in Ham-
            let.

B303   Lowenfels, Walter.   "Last Conversation with Fraenkel."
        In The Life of Fraenkel's Death [C92]; pp. 22-25.
            In the Paris Days from 1927-1934 only Fraenkel, Miller,
            and Lowenfels discussed the topic of death. All three
            of them were "dead" when Miller wrote Black Spring
            and the Tropics.

B304   Lowenfels, Walter.   "Postscript for Lillian." In The Life of
        Fraenkel's Death [C92]; pp. 28-29.
            Fraenkel befriended Miller when Miller needed money,
            a room, and food. Their joint creation, Hamlet, is
            seen springing from Fraenkel's ability to get beyond
            the self, not from Miller's self-centered nature.

B305   Lowenfels, Walter, and Howard McCord.   "Correspondence."
        In The Life of Fraenkel's Death [C92]; pp. 32-67.
            A series of letters about Fraenkel beginning on May 18,
            1964, and ending on April 7, 1967, where Lowenfels
            claims that Fraenkel's death theme is the key to
            Miller's genius.

B306   McCord, Howard.   "The Death of the World."   In The Life
        of Fraenkel's Death [C92]; pp. 70-87.
            "Miller himself is not inclined to give credit to the in-
            tellectual stimulation Fraenkel provided him, and men-
            tions none of Fraenkel's works in ... The Books in My
            Life" (p. 70).

B307   McCord, Howard.   "Who is Fraenkel?: A Biographical and
        Bibliographical Sketch."   In The Life of Fraenkel's Death
        [C92]; pp. 5-7.
            Both Fraenkel and Miller believed that the West was
            dead, a topic they discussed in Hamlet. "Much of
            Miller's work of that period is pervaded by the death
            theme..." (p. 6).

B308   Madden, David.   "Introduction."   In American Dreams,
        American Nightmares [C93]; pp. xv-xlii.
            One of the bitterest views of America is expressed by

the self-exiled Miller in his autobiographical novels.

B309   Rexroth, Kenneth. "D. H. Lawrence: The Other Face of
the Coin. " In Kenneth Rexroth, With Eye and Ear. New
York: Herder and Herder, 1970; pp. 34-39.
Lawrence is compared to Miller who is the Lawrence
of the mid-twentieth century.

B310   Rexroth, Kenneth. "Disengagement: The Art of the Beat
Generation. " In Kenneth Rexroth, The Alternative Society:
Essays from the Other World. New York: Herder and
Herder, 1970; pp. 1-16.
Miller is one of the highbrow writers working today, a
man misunderstood in a mindless California world.

B311   Rexroth, Kenneth. "Henry Miller: The Iconoclast as
Everyman's Friend. " In Kenneth Rexroth With Eye and
Ear. New York: Herder and Herder, 1970; pp. 187-191.
Criticism of Miller for becoming dated. Rexroth feels
that any man who lives with millionaires cannot write
or understand social criticism.

B312   Rexroth, Kenneth. "The Prayer Mat of Flesh. " In Kenneth Rexroth, With Eye and Ear. New York: Herder and
Herder, 1970; pp. 106-108.
Miller is unaware that he has created one of the fun-
niest lines of American literature as he opens his tale
of the Cosmodemonological Telegraph Agency: 'There
was great sexual confusion in New York that summer'
(p. 107). Through this line, Miller reveals the nakedness of his characters who humorously stand before
his readers.

B313   Rexroth, Kenneth. "The Second Post-War, the Second
Interbellum, the Permanent War Generation. " In Kenneth
Rexroth, The Alternative Society: Essays from the Other
World. New York: Herder and Herder, 1970; pp. 97-123.
Miller influenced the "Beat Generation" so much that
once Ginsberg and Kerouac hitchhiked to meet him.

B314   Rowan, John. "Jack Kerouac. " In John Rowan, For Jack
Kerouac. Cardiff, Wales: John Jones Cardiff, 1970; pp.
11-15.
Kerouac's writing style and concepts came from Henry
Miller and Kenneth Patchen.

B315   Schwartz, Delmore. "French Taste in American Writing. "
In Delmore Schwartz, Selected Essays of Delmore Schwartz.
Chicago: University of Chicago Press, 1970; pp. 391-398.
R. L. Bruckbecker in the New York Times Book Re-
view for July 31, 1955, cites Miller's The Air-Condi-
tioned Nightmare as a novel chastising America.

B316 Schwartz, Delmore. "The Writing of Edmund Wilson." In
Delmore Schwartz, Selected Essays of Delmore Schwartz.
Chicago: University of Chicago Press, 1970; pp. 360-373.
Wilson has a tender weakness for Henry Miller, "an
author who merely turns Celine upside-down with a
stale optimism" (p. 372).

B317 Slotnikoff, Will. "The Existentialist Ordeal of Michael
Fraenkel." In The Life of Fraenkel's Death [C92]; pp. 10-
13.
Miller feels that the ideas for Hamlet were manifested
in Bastard Death, a work where the protagonist accepts
madness, an escape from the world of disease that his
culture offers him.

B318 Solotaroff, Theodore. "'All That Cellar-Deep Jazz': Hen-
ry Miller and Seymour Krim." In The Red Hot Vacuum
[C96]; pp. 22-36.
Miller is seen as an asocial man who is also an artist.
The asocial Miller is seen as self-indulgent, while the
artist is called ridiculous.

B319 Solotaroff, Theodore. "Herbert Selby's Kicks." In The
Red Hot Vacuum [C96]; pp. 165-170.
Tropic of Cancer is no longer a bold, shocking book.

B320 Solotaroff, Theodore. "Ship of Fools: Anatomy of a Best-
Seller." In The Red Hot Vacuum [C96]; pp. 103-121.
Miller's fiction is called "newfangled" and "noxious."

B321 Solotaroff, Theodore. "The Spirit of Isaac Rosenfeld." In
Theodore Solotaroff, The Red Hot Vacuum [C96]; pp. 3-21.
Little synthesis is found in the writing of Miller.

B322 Temple, F. J. "Un Mot du traducteur." In Henry Miller,
Les Temps des assassins: Essai sur Rimbaud. Paris:
Pierre Jean Oswald, 1970; p. 5.
Miller discovers the true Rimbaud. (In French.)

B323 Trachtenberg, Alan. "'History on the Side': Henry Miller's American Dream." In American Dreams, American
Nightmares [C96]; pp. 136-148.
Miller's major works are seen displaying contempt for
modern America and are his attempt to purge himself
of the American disease: "Like James, Dreiser, and
Fitzgerald, Miller assails the American dream of permanent wealth and happiness as the automatic reward
of individual effort and excellence of character; he joins
in the attack on the dream as a hoax and a fraud" (p.
139). But unlike other writers, Miller has a moral vision and a hope for the individual outside the bounds of
society.

B324   Widmer, Kingsley. "The Beat in the Rise of the Populist
        Culture." In The Fifties [C89]; pp. 155-173.
            Widmer notes that "the literary role of the Beat was in
            good part a recognizable variation on the anti-academic
            one that runs from Walt Whitman through Henry Miller"
            (pp. 157-158).

B325   Coleman, John. "The Critic of Popular Culture." In John
        Coleman, The World of George Orwell. New York: Simon
        and Schuster, 1971; pp. 101-110.
            Orwell respected Miller and his form of writing.

B326   Finkelstein, Sidney. "Alienation and Rebellion to Nowhere:
        Existentialism and Alienation in American Literature." In
        Henry Miller [A62]; pp. 121-128.
            Miller is a "direct link between the two generations of
            'disillusion,' that which followed the First World War
            and that which followed the Second..." (p. 121). He
            creates a protective distance between the self and hu-
            manity, a shield that protects him from man's inhu-
            manity.

B327   Fowlie, Wallace. "Shadow of Doom: An Essay on Henry
        Miller." In Henry Miller [A62]; pp. 35-42.

B328   Friedman, Alan. "The Pitching of Love's Mansion in the
        Tropics of Henry Miller." In Henry Miller [A62]; pp. 129-
        153.
            Miller is a critic of American disease who distances
            himself so far from the U.S. that he is cut off from
            this world.

B329   Gordon, William. "The Art of Miller: The Mind and Art
        of Henry Miller." In Henry Miller [A62]; pp. 173-184.
            Miller as an autobiographical novelist: "The key to
            autobiographical form is the search for individual
            identity..." (p. 173).

B330   Highet, Gilbert. "The Adventurous Traveler." In Explor-
        ations [C100]; pp. 10-19.
            Miller, in The Colossus of Maroussi, fails to compre-
            hend a passing greeting that Lawrence Durrell makes.

B331   Highet, Gilbert. "Miller's Tropics." In Explorations
        [C100]; pp. 209-215.
            The two Tropics are seen as non-stop monologues going
            on in Miller's head.

B332   Hoffman, Frederick J. "Further Interpretations." In
        Henry Miller [A62]; pp. 43-50.
            The anti-intellectualism of Miller is allied with no
            school of art, psychology, or history. However, he
            does believe in going beneath the surface of the mind,

truly questioning and exploring the roots of the self.

B333   Huxley, Aldous.   "Death and the Baroque."   In Henry
        Miller [A62]; pp. 51-62.
        "Nothing is more desolating then a thorough knowledge
        of the private self" (p. 59).   Huxley begins here in his
        exploration of the mysticism and baroque art of Tropic
        of Cancer.

B334   Kermode, Frank.   "Henry Miller and John Betzeman:
        Puzzles and Epiphanies."   In Henry Miller [A62]; pp. 85-
        95.
        Miller's anti-literature is written in a very literary
        manner.

B335   Lee, Alwyn.   "Henry Miller--The Pathology of Isolation."
        Henry Miller [A62]; pp. 67-76.
        Considers Miller a total proletarian who does not be-
        lieve in property.   His rootlessness leads him to see
        America as an Air-Conditioned Nightmare.

B336   Littlejohn, David.   "The Tropics of Miller."   In Henry
        Miller [A62]; pp. 103-111.
        All of Miller's work is autobiographical, and his life
        story is viewed from the stance of total detachment
        from society.   For he sees society as a death trap
        and aspires to attain a precivilized state.

B337   Mayne, Richard.   "A Note on Orwell's Paris."   In Miriam
        Gross, ed., The World of George Orwell.   New York:
        Simon and Schuster, 1971; pp. 39-45.
        Admiration of Miller's ability to bring the thinker down
        to earth.

B338   Mitchell, Edward B.   "Artists and Artists: The Aesthetics
        of Henry Miller."   In Henry Miller [A62]; pp. 155-172.
        Miller, like Plato, strives for a Utopia where artists
        rule: "The creative individual accepts the laws of being
        with his realization of the 'organic relatedness, the
        wholeness, the oneness of life'" (p. 161).

B339   Mitchell, Edward B.   "The Fifties."   In Henry Miller
        [A62]; pp. 63-65.
        Mitchell glances at three Miller essays written in the
        fifties.   Alwyn Lee's essay, "Henry Miller--The Path-
        ology of Isolation," sees Miller's stance of total isola-
        tion an impossibility.   Karl Shapiro's "The Greatest
        Living Author" deals with Miller's cosmic consciousness.
        Frank Kermode sees no sound understanding between
        Miller and his critics.

B340   Mitchell, Edward B.   "The Forties."   In Henry Miller
        [A62]; pp. 1-5.

Summary of five essays from the 1940's on Miller:
Orwell's "Inside the Whale" sees Miller as trying to
bring the spoken word into writing; Rahv's essay sees
Miller as an isolated individual; Wallace Fowlie sees
Miller as prophet and seer; Hoffman views Miller in a
Freudian sense; Huxley sees Miller as mythic artist.

B341   Mitchell, Edward B.   "Introduction." In Henry Miller
[A62]; pp. xiii-xviii.
Miller deals with the pilgrimage of the artist from the
social acceptance of fate to an awareness of the
strength of the individual.

B342   Mitchell, Edward B.   "The Sixties." In Henry Miller
[A62]; pp. 97-101.
Miller is seen as totally detached from society by
David Littlejohn, as writer of the grotesque by Kingsley
Widmer, as existentialist by Sidney Finkelstein, as
poet and seer by Mitchell, and as explorer of the sub-
conscious by William Gordon.

B343   Orwell, George.   "Inside the Whale." In Henry Miller
[A62]; pp. 7-25.
See B9.

B344   Perlès, Alfred.   "Epilogue to Alf Letter." In Henry Miller,
What Are You Going to Do About Alf.   London: Turret
Books, 1971; pp. 27-29.
Miller's naive nature is discussed; he thought that he
could make money on this book.

B345   Pryce-Jones, David.   "Orwell's Reputation." In Miriam
Gross, ed., The World of George Orwell.   New York:
Simon and Schuster, 1971; pp. 143-152.
Miller was angered at "Inside the Whale" and retorted
in the Paris Review Interview of 1962.

B346   Rahv, Philip.   "Henry Miller: Image and Idea." In Henry
Miller [A62]; pp. 27-34.
Miller sees the depravity of this world and welcomes
its collapse.   His nihilistic stance is especially apparent in his appraisal of sex as a dry, machine-like
fornication.

B347   Shapiro, Karl.   "The Greatest Living Author: In Defense
of Ignorance." In Henry Miller [A62]; pp. 77-84.
See B85.

B348   Smith, Bradley.   "Introduction." In Henry Miller, My Life
and Times.   New York: Gemini Smith, Inc., 1971; pp. 5-
7.
Conversation that led to My Life and Times.

B349   Stuhlmann, Gunther.   "Preface."   In The Diary of Anaïs
       Nin: 1944-1947 [C103]; pp. vii-xi.
       Nin's contact with the unknown expatriate, Henry Miller,
       mentioned.

B350   Wain, John.   "In the Thirties."   In Miriam Gross, ed.,
       The World of George Orwell.   New York: Simon and Schu-
       ster, 1971; pp. 75-90.
       Orwell praises Miller for making a successful descent
       into real poverty and writing about this actuality.

B351   Widmer, Kingsley.   "The Legacy of Henry Miller."   In Henry
       Miller [A62]; pp. 113-119.
       Miller is a writer of the grotesque who contributed to
       the Beat writers of the fifties and the rebels of the
       sixties.

B352   Bald, Wambly.   "The Sweet Madness of Montparnasse."
       In Hugh Ford, ed., The Left Bank Revisited: Selections
       from the Paris Tribune 1917-1934.   University Park:
       Pennsylvania State University Press, 1972; pp. 284-289.
       Miller looked toward tomorrow, as he labored in soli-
       tude and poverty on Tropic of Cancer.

B353   Chiaromonte, Nicola.   "Sunday After the War."   In The
       Critic as Artist [C106]; pp. 59-64.
       Review of Sunday After the War where Miller is called
       an autobiographical writer who deals with the natural,
       or real world.

B354   Ford, Hugh.   "Introduction."   In Hugh Ford, ed., The Left
       Bank Revisited: Selections from the Paris Tribune 1917-
       1934.   University Park: Pennsylvania State University
       Press, 1972; pp. 4-5.
       Miller was jobless and living in depravity when he
       wrote "Mademoiselle Claude."

B355   Ford, Hugh.   "A Paris Tribune Who's Who."   In Hugh
       Ford, ed., The Left Bank Revisited: Selections from the
       Paris Tribune 1917-1934.   University Park: Pennsylvania
       State University Press, 1972; pp. 319-320.
       Miller was the Tribune's most famous proofreader.

B356   Ford, Hugh.   "The Place: Montparnasse Described."   In
       Hugh Ford, ed., The Left Bank Revisited: Selections from
       the Paris Tribune 1917-1934.   University Park: Pennsyl-
       vania State University Press, 1972; p. 13.
       Two Tribune articles attributed to Alfred Perlès,
       "Paris in Ut-Mineur" and "Gobelins Tapestries," were
       actually written by Miller.

B357   Ford, Hugh.   "Wambly Bald Meets Henry Miller."   In
       Hugh Ford, ed., The Left Bank Revisited: Selections from

the Paris Tribune 1917-1934.   University Park: Pennsylvania State University Press, 1972; pp. 142-144.
Miller's code is to live life, not let it pass him by.

B358   Frantz, Ralph Jules.   "Recollections." In Hugh Ford, ed.,
The Left Bank Revisited: Selections from the Paris Tribune
1917-1934.   University Park: Pennsylvania State University
Press, 1972; p. 312.
Miller is the most successful proofreader on the Paris
Tribune.

B359   Kauffmann, Stanley. "Tropic of Cancer." In The Critic as
Artist [C106]; pp. 211-216.
Review of Tropic of Cancer calling it an autobiography:
"The book is a fierce celebration of his enlightened
freedom, which is to say his acceptance of real re-
sponsibilities instead of merely respectable ones" (p.
212).

B360   Mailer, Norman. "An Appreciation of Henry Miller." In
Norman Mailer, Existential Errands.   Boston: Little,
Brown, 1972: pp. 262-263.
Admiration of Miller, the man, and his work: "And in
fact I admire not only his work, which I do, enormous-
ly (his influence has been profound on a good half of all
living American writers), but I admire his personality"
(p. 262).

B361   Vidal, Gore. "The Fourth Diary of Anaïs Nin." In
Homage to Daniel Shays [C109]; pp. 403-409.
Nin helped to launch Miller's career through faith and
support.

B362   Vidal, Gore. "Pornography." In Homage to Daniel Shays
[C109]; pp. 219-233.
Miller's books have been underground favorites for
years.

B363   Vidal, Gore. "The Sexus of Henry Miller." In Homage to
Daniel Shays [C109]; pp. 197-203.
See B289.

B364   Vidal, Gore. "Woman's Liberation Meets Miller-Mailer-
Manson Man." In Homage to Daniel Shays [C109]; pp. 389-402.
A progression from Miller to Mailer to Manson sees
women at best as breeders of children and at worst as
objects to be humiliated.

B365   Wain, John. "Naked Lunch." In The Critic as Artist
[C106]; pp. 351-357.
Miller is an affirmative writer who has traveled a step
beyond Burroughs, through his belief in freedom and
his love of life.

B366 Gertz, Elmer. "Henry Miller a Pioneer of Free Expression." In Henry Miller Exhibit [A66]; pp. 3-4.
Gertz talks about Miller's self-expression, a quality he
found by defending Tropic in the 1961 trial in Chicago.

B367 Jason, Philip K. "Foreword." In Anaïs Nin, Anaïs Nin
Reader. Chicago: Swallow Press, 1973; p. 7.
Miller was interested in D. H. Lawrence and Otto
Rank.

B368 Nin, Anaïs. "Preface to Tropic of Cancer." In Anaïs Nin,
Anaïs Nin Reader. Chicago: Swallow Press, 1973; pp. 277-279.
See B1.

B369 Diehl, Digby. "Henry Miller." In Digby Diehl, Supertalk.
Garden City, N. Y. : Doubleday, 1974; pp. 2-14.
Interview with Miller where he talks about the many
sides of the self.

B370 Grigson, Geoffrey. "Shoal to the Stanchless Flux, or, The Worst
of Henry Miller." In Geoffrey Grigson, The Contrary View.
Totowa, N. J. : Rowman and Littlefield, 1974; pp. 34-38.

B371 McCarthy, H. T. "Henry Miller's Democratic Vistas." In
H. T. McCarthy, The Expatriate Perspective: American
Novelists and the Idea of America. Rutherford, N. J. :
Fairleigh Dickinson University Press, 1974; pp. 156-172.

B372 Stuhlmann, Gunther. "Preface." In The Diary of Anaïs
Nin: 1947-1955 [C117]; pp. vii-ix.
Nin seen as a catalyst for Miller.

B372a Young, Noel. "Foreword." In Henry Miller, Reflections
on the Maurizius Case: A Humble Appraisal of a Great
Book. Santa Barbara, Calif. : Capra Press, 1974.
Noel Young looks at Miller's obsession with the
East.

B373 Connolly, Cyril. "George Orwell: 1." In The Evening
Colonnade [C121]; pp. 335-339.
Miller a better journalist than Orwell.

B374 Connolly, Cyril. "George Orwell: 3." In The Evening
Colonnade [C121]; pp. 343-349.
Mentions Orwell's review of Tropic.

B375 Connolly, Cyril. "Henry Miller." In The Evening Colonnade [C121]; pp. 293-295.
Review of Tropic in which Connolly calls it overdone
and juvenile.

B376 Connolly, Cyril. "Little Magazines." In The Evening

Colonnade [C121]; pp. 375-386.
Miller edits The Booster.

B377   Connolly, Cyril. "The Modern Movement. " In The Evening Colonnade [C121]; pp. 197-201.
Miller mentioned.

B378   Connolly, Cyril. "Norman Mailer. " In The Evening Colonnade [C121]; pp. 358-360.
Narcissus found in Miller.

B379   Connolly, Cyril. "Thomas Wolfe. " In The Evening Colonnade [C121]; pp. 277-280.
Miller an egotist.

B380   May, Charles E. "Explorations in the Realm of Sex. " In
Michael T. Marsden, ed. , Proceedings of the Fifth National
Convention of the Popular Culture Association. Bowling
Green, Ohio: Popular Culture Press, 1975.

B381   Shapiro, Karl. "American Poet?" In The Poetry Wreck
[C124]; pp. 323-352.
Shapiro has glowing praise for Miller.

B382   Shapiro, Karl. "Dylan Thomas. " In The Poetry Wreck
[C124]; pp. 139-155.
Thomas uses Miller's style.

B383   Shapiro, Karl. "Foreword. " In The Poetry Wreck [C124];
pp. xv-xvii.
Antics of Miller mentioned.

B384/5   Shapiro, Karl. "The Greatest Living Patagonian. " In
The Poetry Wreck [C124]; pp. 175-200.
Miller not a writer; he's a talker, a prophet, a Pata-
gonian.

B386   Lewis, Felice Flannery, ed. "Tropic of Cancer on Trial:
The Correspondence of Henry Miller and Elmer Gertz. " In
Matthew J. Bruccoli and C. E. Frazer Clark, Jr. , eds. ,
Pages: The World of Books, Writers, and Writing. Detroit, Mich. : Gale Research Company, 1976; pp. 297-
303.
A portion of the Miller-Gertz correspondence dealing
with the Tropic of Cancer trial in Chicago in 1961.   It
contains seven Miller letters.

B387   Durand, Robert. "Foreword. " In Henry Miller, Gliding
into the Everglades. Lake Oswego, Ore. : Lost Pleiade
Press, 1977; pp. 7-8.
Historical account of the essay "Gliding into the Everglades" that sees Miller in 1928 just beginning to produce.

B388   Nin, Anaïs.   "Preface."   Delta of Venus.   New York: Har-
       court Brace Jovanovich, 1977; pp. ix-xvii.
       Nin talks about Miller's rebellion against erotic writing.

UNDATED WORKS

B389   Haan, J(acques) D(en).   "Inleiding."   In Henry Miller, Het
       Heelal van de Dood: Een Studie over Lawrence, Proust en
       Joyce.   Netherlands: Verteling van J[acques] D[en] H[aan],
       19--; pp. 5-6.
       Brief biography noting that the first Miller biography ap-
       peared in American Abroad in 1932.

B390   Laporte, Paul M.   "Picasso's Portrait of the Artist."   In
       n. w.   Hollywood, Calif. : Imaculate Heart College, n. d. ;
       pp. 296-319.
       A quote by Miller talking about fear.

B391   Okumura, Osamu.   "Preface."   In Henry Miller, The Smile
       at the Foot of the Ladder.   Tokyo: Charles E. Tuttle Co.,
       n. d.
       Miller looks at society's problems, and from them
       achieves an existential state.   (In French.)

B392   Okumura, Osamu.   "Preface."   In Henry Miller, The Smile
       at the Foot of the Ladder.   Tokyo: Hokuseido Press, n. d. ;
       pp. iii-iv.
       Miller is an existentialist in the tradition of Emerson
       and Thoreau who presents brilliant descriptions of life
       and sex.   (In French.)

C

BOOKS WITH SIGNIFICANT
REFERENCES TO MILLER

C1   Neagroe, Peter. Americans Abroad: An Anthology. The
Hague: Sevire Press, 1932.
    The first hardcover appearance of Miller's "Mademoiselle
Claude" is in this volume.

C2   Kazin, Alfred. On Native Grounds: An Interpretation of
Modern American Prose Literature. Cornwall, N.Y.: Cornwall Press, 1942; pp. 466-467.
    Miller is viewed as a part of a new school of "sensibil-
ity" in the contemporary American novel. His difference
from other novelists lies in his outrage at society's ability to undermine the individual artist.

C3   Woodford, Jack. Why Write a Novel? New York: Murray
and Gee, 1943; pp. 155-156.
    Miller writes some of the most superb prose of our time,
but because he does not bend to the wishes of publishers,
he is not in print in the United States.

C4   Frank, Erich. Philosophical Truth and Religious Understanding. New York: Oxford University Press, 1944.
    The Fletcher Lectures at Bryn Mawr College in 1943,
both quote and mention Miller several times in the notes.

C5   Gilbert, Rudolph. Four Living Poets. Santa Barbara,
Calif.: Unicorn Press, 1944; p. 1.
    Book is presented to Miller who Gilbert considers to be
the major poetry influence on his book.

C6   Manning, Hugo. Smile Ichabod; A War Poem. London:
Hugo Manning, 1944.

C7   Peyre, Henri. Writers and Critics: A Study of Misunderstanding. Ithaca, N.Y.: Cornell University Press, 1944;
pp. 184, 280.
    Miller charted new ground in describing bodily functions.

C8   Hoffman, Frederick J. Freudianism and the Literary Mind.

Baton Rouge: Louisiana State University Press, 1945; pp.
279, 299-305.
Miller wished to destroy civilization and move inward into the unconscious to find peace.

C9   Nin, Anaïs. Realism and Reality. New York: Alicat Book
Shop Press, 1946; pp. 5-6.
Miller praises Nin's Diary, calling it one of the major
contributions to letters ever written.

C10 Perlès, Alfred. Round Trip. London: Dennis Dobson, 1946.
Perlès's answer to Aller Retour New York takes the form
of a letter which is an account of Perlès's voyage to London.

C10a Spiller, Robert E. ; Willard Thorp; Thomas H. Johnson; Henry Seidel Canby; and Richard M. Ludwig. Literary History
of the United States: History. New York: Macmillan,
1946; p. 1414.
The freedom of the "Beat Movement" saw its beginnings
in such authors as Henry Miller.

C11 Fowlie, Wallace. The Clown's Grail: A Study of Love in Its
Literary Expression. London: Dennis Dobson, 1947; p. 145.
Miller is one of the few males to make art personal. He
is compared to such sensitive writers as Emily Dickinson
and Djuna Barnes.

C12 Fraenkel, Michael. The Day Face and the Night Face. New
York: Irving Stettner, 1947.
Fraenkel's novel, Bastard Death, begins with a letter to
Miller where Fraenkel explains and justifies his stance
on life.

C13 Putnam, Samuel. Paris Was Our Mistress: Memoirs of a
Lost & Found Generation. Carbondale: Southern Illinois
University Press, 1947; pp. 107, 112-116, 156, 230-232, 252.
A look at Miller's Bohemian days in Paris while publish-
ing "Mademoiselle Claude" and Tropic of Cancer. This
work also notes Perlès's influence on Miller and their
Parisian night life together.

C14 Fraenkel, Michael. Bastard Death: An Autobiography of an
Idea. New York: Carrefour, 1948.
Fraenkel's letter to Miller calls Bastard Death Miller's
creation and thanks him for the idea.

C15 Williams, William Carlos. The Autobiography of William
Carlos Williams. New York: New Directions, 1948.
It is noted that Miller left Paris, married, and lived
with his wife and children near Carmel, Calif.

C16 Fowlie, Wallace. Age of Surrealism. New York: Swallow

Press, 1950; pp. 184-187.
Capricorn, Black Spring, and The Angel Is My Water
Mark are compared to surreal art.

C17 Brassaï. Brassaï. Paris: Editions Neuf, 1952; pp. 62, 78.
Photograph of Miller and some background on "The Eye
of Paris." (In French.)

C18 Bruckberger, Raymond Leopold. One Sky to Share. New
York: P. J. Kennedy & Sons, 1952; pp. 136-140.
Discusses visit to Miller's home in Big Sur at Blaise
Cendrars' request.

C19 Häggqvist, Arne Robert. Obehagliga Författare. Stockholm:
Ars Forlag, 1953; pp. 101-105.
Miller is viewed as an existentialist. (In Swedish.)

C20 Hopkinson, Tom. George Orwell. Essex, England: Long-
mans, Green & Co., 1953; p. 24.
Mentioned is Orwell's essay on Henry Miller, "Inside
the Whale."

C21 Atkins, John. George Orwell. London: John Calder, 1954.
Orwell praises Tropic of Cancer.

C22 Bowden, Harry. Bufano. San Francisco, Calif.: Bern
Porter, 1954.
Portfolio of seven mounted photos, the first of Bufano
and Miller. Included are words by Miller concerning his
appreciation of Bufano.

C23 Häggqvist, Arne Robert. Blandat Sällskap. Stockholm:
Ars Forlag, 1954; pp. 198-203.
A section on pornography where Miller is seen as a lite-
rary master, not a pornographer. He is called a realist
who shows the truly debased nature of our world. (In
Swedish.)

C24 Kiki. The Education of a French Model. New York:
Bridgehead Books, 1954; p. 61.
Miller's involvement in a night club in Paris is explored.

C25 Ferlinghetti, Lawrence. A Coney Island of the Mind. New
York: New Directions, 1955; p. 8.
Ferlinghetti states that the title of his volume is taken
from Miller's Into the Night Life, a world where all is
"a kind of circus of the soul" (p. 8).

C26 B., J. T. Authors as Illustrators 1849-1955. San Francisco: Stanford University Libraries, 1956; p. 32.
Miller is called a fine illustrator of his own prose.

C27 Dickson, Edward Pratt. The Shadows of Desire. Denver:

Big Mountain Press, 1956; pp. 12, 32, 44, 46-47.
Dickson's work contains quotes from Sunday After the
War and The Books in My Life.

C28   Hoffman, Frederick John.   Further Interpretations in Freudi-
anism and the Literary Mind.   Baton Rouge: Louisiana State
University Press, 1957; pp. 277-308.
See C8.

C29   Mailer, Norman.   The White Negro.   San Francisco: City
Lights Books, 1957; p. 3.
Miller considered one of the intellectual shapers of our
age.

C30   Thomas, Caitlin.   Leftover Life to Kill.   London: Putnam
& Son, 1957; p. 211.
Reference is made to Miller and to Tropic of Cancer.

C31   Levin, Harry.   The Power of Blackness: Hawthorne Poe
Melville.   New York: Alfred A. Knopf, 1958; p. 230.
Orwell's essay on Miller, "Inside the Whale," is seen
as a return to pre-natal bliss, a womb made for an
adult.

C32   Alinari, Josefina Martínez.   Noches de Amor y Alegría.
Buenos Aires: Santiago Rueda, 1959; pp. 7-9.
A brief biography of Miller and the statement that he is
one of the greatest American writers.   (In Spanish.)

C33   Humphrey, Robert.   Stream of Consciousness in the Modern
Novel.   Berkeley: University of California Press, 1959;
p. 99.
Miller's belief in his protagonist's self-awareness mentioned.

C34   Knoll, Robert E.   Robert McAlmon Expatriate Publisher and
Writer.   Lincoln: University of Nebraska Press, 1959;
p. 70.
A book called Americans Abroad edited by Peter Neagroe
contains a short story by Miller.

C35   Kronhausen, Phyllis, and Eberhard Kronhausen.   Pornography
and the Law: The Psychology of Erotic Realism and Pornography.   New York: Ballantine Books, 1959; pp. 145-150.
Chapter on Miller called "Henry Miller--Apostle of the
Gory Detail" that discusses Miller's realism.

C36   Rieff, Philip.   Freud: The Mind of the Moralist.   Garden
City, N.Y.: Doubleday, 1959; p. 100.
Henry Miller and D. H. Lawrence are seen as modern
prophets of the irrational.

C37   Powell, Lawrence Clark.   Books in My Baggage: Adventures

in Reading and Collecting.   New York: World Pub. Co.,
1960; pp. 81, 148-153, 169.
Powell relives his first meetings with Miller in Paris,
at UCLA, and at Big Sur.

C38   Thorp, Willard.   American Writing in the Twentieth Century.
Cambridge, Mass.:   Harvard University Press, 1960.
The story of writing in California from Norris and Lon-
don to Henry Miller and "Howl" has yet to be written.
Thorp feels that Miller and the other American rebels
have much to contribute to literature.

C39   Boorstin, Daniel J.   The Image: A Guide to Pseudo-Events
in America.   New York: Harper & Row, 1961; p. 129.
Henry Miller, James Joyce, and William Faulkner explored the inner world of eroticism, obscenity, blas-
phemy, symbolism, stream of consciousness, and introspection that could not be viewed on the movie screen.

C40   Booth, Wayne C.   The Rhetoric of Fiction.   Chicago: University of Chicago Press, 1961; pp. 367, 371.
Edmund Wilson over-interprets Miller's Tropic.

C41   Frohock, Wilbur M.   Strangers to this Ground: Cultural Di-
versity in Contemporary American Writing.   Dallas: Southern
Methodist University Press, 1961; p. 146.
Miller's writing is equated to Christian devotion.

C42   Hassan, Ihab H.   Radical Innocence: Studies in the Contemporary American Novel.   Princeton, N.J.:   Princeton
University Press, 1961.
Miller's work is seen as both ideal and utopian, an in-
spiration to the Beat Generation: "What makes Miller's
vision finally relevant to the Beat sensibility is its postu-
late of a future state in which the two warring elements
of Beat, the saintly and the criminal, can be reconciled
... to the human condition at large" (pp. 89-90).   This
fundamental oneness comes from Eastern philosophy and
is a major concept in Miller's writing.

C43   Perlès, Alfred.   My Friend Lawrence Durrell: An Intimate
Memoir on the Author of the Alexandrian Quartet.   Middle-
sex, England: Scorpion Press, 1961.
Durrell's friendship with Miller began soon after he read
Tropic of Cancer, a book that totally reshaped Durrell's
mind and was the forerunner of his Black Book.

C44   Hoffman, Frederick J.   Marginal Manners: The Variants of
Bohemia.   Elmsford, N.Y.:   Row, Peterson, 1962; pp. 8,
10.
Miller is considered an old Bohemian, a man who has
survived earlier decades and remained pure.   He is a
transitional figure who has used his strong sense of

identity to survive.

C45   International Writer's Conference.   Edinburgh, Scotland:
        n.p., 1962.
        Two brief speeches by Miller and one concerning his
        work by Colin McInnes.   Miller's discussion concerns
        simplicity in writing.

C46   Moore, Harry T.   The World of Lawrence Durrell.   Carbon-
        dale: Southern Illinois University Press, 1962.
        Miller is discussed in the following articles: Bode's "A
        Guide to Alexandria," Brombert's "Lawrence Durrell and
        His French Reputation," Carruth's "Nought for the Old
        Bitch," Dobrée's "Durrell's Alexandrian Series," Dur-
        rell's "Letters from Lawrence Durrell," Elliot's "The
        Other Side of the Story," Green's "Lawrence Durrell,"
        Moore's "Lawrence Durrell's Black Book," Moore's "In-
        troduction," Steiner's "Lawrence Durrell," Sykes's "One
        Vote for the Sun," Wolton's "A Letter to Lawrence Dur-
        rell," and "Lawrence Durrell Answers a Few Questions."
        See II B150, B151, B152, B154, B159, B160, B162,
        B164, B165, B179, B180, B183, B184.

C47   Ginzburg, Ralph.   Les "Enfers."   Paris: Jean-Jacques
        Pauvert, 1963; pp. 173-176.
        It is suggested that Miller's Tropic of Capricorn pro-
        vides an important portrayal of the debased state of
        America.   (In French.)

C48   Porter, Bern.   I've Left.   Pasadena, Calif.: Marathon
        Press, 1963; p. 9.
        Porter feels that for straight prose no one can write like
        Miller.

C49   Ekirch, Arthur A., ed.   Voices in Dissent: An Anthology of
        Individualist Thought in the United States.   New York: Cita-
        del Press, 1964; pp. 323-332.
        Biography of Miller's life followed by a passage from
        Remember to Remember.

C50   Fiedler, Leslie A.   Waiting for the End.   New York: Stein
        and Day, 1964.
        The importance of Tropic of Cancer (1934) and Tropic of
        Capricorn (1939) as Depression novels is seen by Fiedler
        to produce erotic daydreams and freedom from a social
        structure that leads to revolution.   Fiedler considers
        Miller to be "the first important ... anti-tragic writer
        in America" (p. 42).

C51   Hoffman, Frederick J.   The Mortal No: Death and the
        Modern Imagination.   Princeton, N.J.: Princeton University
        Press, 1964; p. 491.
        A discussion of Miller's love for and belief in the

individual, a need to passionately maintain the self and
enjoy life.

C52   Powell, Lawrence Clark.   The Little Package: Pages on
Literature and Landscape from a Traveling Bookman's Life.
New York: World Pub. Co. , 1964; pp. 19, 108.
Powell notes that Tropic of Cancer is banned in the
United States while Lolita is not.   He calls this peculiar
and feels that Miller should be accepted in this country
because he has produced one of the sixty best books
written.

C53   Ray, Man.   Autoportrait.   Paris: Robert Laffont, 1964; pp.
312-313.
In Man Ray's Self-Portrait, he talks about encountering
Miller both in Paris and Hollywood and of Miller's home
at Big Sur.   (In French.)

C54   Wagner, James E.   The Fellowship of Prayer.   Boston,
Mass. : Pilgrim Press, 1964; pp. 13, 15, 33, 55, 96.
Quotes from Miller in this religious book of prayer.

C55   Evans, Oliver.   Carson McCullers: Her Life and Work.
London: Peter Owen, 1965; p. 83.
Miller says McCullers' diary will take its place beside
the "revelations of St. Augustine, Petronius, Abelard,
Rousseau, Proust ... " (p. 83).

C56   Fowlie, Wallace.   The Clown's Grail: A Study of Love in
Its Literary Expression.   Bloomington: Indiana University
Press, 1965; p. 145.
Miller one of the few male artists able to "participate
in consecration and sublimation. "

C57   Fowlie, Wallace.   Love in Literature: Studies in Symbolic
Expression.   Bloomington: Indiana University Press, 1965;
p. 145.
See C56.

C58   Freund, Gisèle, and V. B. Carleton.   James Joyce in Paris:
His Final Years.   London: Cassell & Company, 1965.
Miller never knew nor ever met Joyce, "but of course
he influenced [Miller's] writing. "

C59   Gertz, Elmer.   Censored Books and Their Right to Live.
Lawrence: University of Kansas Libraries, 1965.
Gertz looks at the Tropic obscenity cases throughout the
United States and considers them absurd.

C60   Gertz, Elmer.   A Handful of Clients.   Chicago: Follett Pub.
Co. , 1965; pp. xiv, 141, 229-303.
Gertz based two chapters of his book, "The Battle for
Literary Freedom" and "An Obscenity Trial, " on Miller's

Tropic of Cancer.

C61 Trachtenberg, Alan. Brooklyn Bridge: Fact and Symbol.
New York: Oxford University Press, 1965; pp. 160-161.
Miller saw the Brooklyn Bridge as a private experience,
a means to release himself from his culture. The
Bridge carried him away from the chaos of New York,
as he noted in Tropic of Capricorn, Black Spring, and
The Cosmological Eye.

C62 Vonnegut, Kurt. God Bless You, Mr. Rosewater: or,
Pearls Before Swine. New York: Dell Pub. Co., 1965;
pp. 111-113.
Mentions Miller's Tropic of Cancer and quotes from it.

C63 Weigel, John A. Lawrence Durrell. New York: Twayne
Publishers, 1965.
Miller was the motivating force in Durrell's life.
"...Durrell announced that he was the first writer to be
fertilized by Henry Miller" (p. 21). Thus Durrell's
Black Book was shaped by his reading and correspondences
with Miller.

C64 Hahn, Emily. Romantic Rebels: An Informal History of Bo-
hemianism in America. Boston: Houghton Mifflin Company,
1966; pp. 270-271.
An interview with Miller where he stresses the fact that
he is a writer, not a politician. It ends with the start-
ling thought that Miller may be the only true Bohemian
writer in the entire expatriate movement.

C65 Mailer, Norman. Cannibals and Christians. New York:
Delta Books, 1966; pp. xi, 99.
Mailer mentions the importance of writers like D. H.
Lawrence, Ernest Hemingway, and Henry Miller when he
calls Tropic of Cancer the first book to come close to
showing the reality of America.

C66 Nin, Anaïs. The Diary of Anaïs Nin, 1931-1934. New York:
Harcourt, Brace & World, 1966.
In Volume I of her Diary, Nin discusses both the power
of Miller's writing and his effect on her as a man. She
describes Miller's love for the natural and his realism.
To her, Henry's work is a process of growth.

C67 Slotnikoff, Will. The First Time I Live. Washington, D.C.:
Manchester Lane Editions, 1966; pp. 15-78.
Discussed is a friendship with Miller, a man who provides others with life. Included is a 13-letter exchange
between Miller and Slotnikoff.

C68 Whithead, Thomas B. Seven Contemporary Authors: Essays
on Cozzens, Miller, West, Golding, Heller, Albee, and

Powers. Austin: University of Texas Press, 1966; pp. vii-
xv, 23-48.
Miller is viewed as an affirmative writer who finds his
hope in despair.

C69 Woodcock, George. The Crystal Spirit: A Study of George
Orwell. Boston: Little, Brown, 1966; pp. 178-180, 194,
232, 243, 300, 325-328.
Orwell did not understand Miller and felt compelled to
write "Inside the Whale" in the attempt to understand
him better. Orwell felt that Miller was much like Joyce
in his ability to give life, meaning, and interest to the
commonplace. It was Miller's optimism that intrigued
Orwell most of all.

C70 Fortunatus, Kawegere. Shamba la Wanyama: Masimulizi ya
George Orwell. Nairobi, Kenya: East African Publishing
House, 1967.
Miller is mentioned in reference to "Inside the Whale."

C71 French, Warren. The Thirties: Fiction, Poetry, Drama.
Deland, Fla.: Everett Edwards, 1967; pp. 3, 8, 73-80, 129.
Miller's fantasies of Bohemian sexual prowess, found in
Tropic of Cancer and Tropic of Capricorn, led him to
the position of defender and patron saint of the "Beat
Generation."

C72 Nin, Anaïs. The Diary of Anaïs Nin: 1934-1939. New
York: Harcourt, Brace & World, 1967.
Nin talks about Miller's difficult time getting Tropic of
Cancer published because of his rebellion against compromise. Yet, the overriding quality that Nin sees is
Miller's loneliness: "Henry could be a real man if he
were alive and not a writing machine. Writing about
sex, blind to all but sex, writing about a maniac about
sex" (p. 256).

C73 Peyre, Henri. The Failure of Criticism. Ithaca, N.Y.:
Cornell University Press, 1967; pp. 192, 284, 337.
Some vulgar authors like Miller are actually great and
must be accepted.

C74 Sertoli, Giuseppe. Lawrence Durrell. Milan: U. Mursia &
Co., 1967.
Durrell's influence at the hands of Miller is discussed.
(In Italian.)

C75 Calder, Jenni. Chronicles of Consciousness: A Study of
George Orwell and Arthur Koestler. Pittsburgh: University
of Pittsburgh Press, 1968; pp. 166-168, 261.
Orwell praises Miller for his ability to portray everyday
experiences and to reveal the inner workings of the mind
in spite of his lack of concern for society and politics.

C76   Evans, Oliver. Anaïs Nin. Carbondale: Southern Illinois
      University Press, 1968.
      Noted is Miller's interest in "dream-writing."

C77   Fleishman, Stanley. Selected Obscenity Cases. Los Ange-
      les: Blackstone Book Co., 1968; pp. 68-71.
      Tropic trials throughout the United States mentioned.

C78   Gibson, Arthur. The Faith of the Atheist. New York:
      Harper & Row, Publishers, 1968.
      Contains excerpts from Nexus, Sexus, Plexus, and Re-
      member to Remember.

C79   Hartshorne, Thomas L. The Distorted Image: Changing
      Conceptions of the American Character Since Turner. Cleve-
      land, Ohio: Press of Case Western Reserve University,
      1968; p. 174.
      Hartshorne borrows Miller's concept that America is an
      "Air-Conditioned Nightmare."

C80   Nin, Anaïs. The Novel of the Future. New York:
      Macmillan, 1968; pp. 2, 16, 35.
      Miller is considered a surrealist who conveys the con-
      cept of flight from naturalism.

C81   Nin, Anaïs. Unpublished Sections from the Diary. Athens,
      Ohio: Duane Schneider Press, 1968.
      Nin discusses the relationship between Miller and his
      wife, June: "June tells me it is Henry who sees ugli-
      ness and creates ugliness ..." (pp. 4-5). Nin feels that
      June fails to understand Henry and shows this when she
      depicts Tropic of Cancer as Miller's autobiography, the
      story of a man who has been humiliated and buffeted.

C82   Wulfsberg, Frederik. George Orwell. Omslay, Norway:
      Elmer Rodin, 1968; pp. 113-114.
      Orwell enjoyed Miller's Tropic of Cancer and wrote
      about it in his essay, "Inside the Whale." (In Nor-
      wegian.)

C83   Durrell, Lawrence. Spirit of Place: Letters and Essays on
      Travel. New York: E. P. Dutton & Co., 1969.
      Durrell shows his appreciation and respect for Miller
      and his work when he applauds Tropic of Cancer, calling
      it "as large as anything as yet written in the novel line"
      (p. 35).

C84   Nin, Anaïs. The Diary of Anaïs Nin: 1939-1944. New
      York: Harcourt, Brace & World, 1969.
      In Volume III of her Diary, Nin notes that Miller has be-
      gun his odyssey on America. She discusses his plunge
      into American writing with Tropic of Capricorn and The
      Air-Conditioned Nightmare.

C85   Ueno, K.   Golden Temple in Japan.   Tokyo: Tomei Shoji,
      1969.
      Miller is quoted twice, first from The Colossus of
      Maroussi.   (In Japanese.)

C86   Vidal, Gore.   Reflections Upon a Sinking Ship.   Boston:
      Little, Brown, 1969; pp. 85-99, 111-117.
      Two chapters on Miller: "Notes on Pornography" and
      "The Sexus of Henry Miller."

C87   Wickes, George.   Americans in Paris.   Garden City, N.Y.:
      Doubleday, 1969; pp. 8-9, 237-276.
      Biographical account of Miller's need to leave America:
      "He had come to Europe to get away from America and
      to find a way of life that could answer his psychic
      needs" (p. 240).   It deals with his life in Paris, begin-
      ning with a man down and out, moving to his success
      after writing Tropic, and talking about his friendship
      with Fraenkel, Perlès, and Nin.

C88   Fraser, G. S.   Lawrence Durrell.   Essex, England: Long-
      man Group, 1970.
      A look at Miller's influence on Durrell.   The Black Book
      was "inspired both in its freedom of form and its erotic
      frankness by Tropic of Cancer" (p. 28).

C89   French, Warren.   The Fifties: Fiction, Poetry, Drama.
      Deland, Fla.: Everett Edwards, 1970; pp. 15, 17, 157-160,
      171.
      Older writers like Miller have become patron saints for
      the Beat movement.

C90   Friedman, Alan Warren.   Lawrence Durrell and the Alexan-
      dria Quartet: Art for Love's Sake.   Norman: University of
      Oklahoma Press, 1970.
      Miller's dislike of The Alexandria Quartet stems from
      the fact that the characters are not alive.

C91   Littlejohn, David.   Interruptions.   New York: Grossman,
      1970; pp. vii, 17-33, 37-44, 45-72, 73-81, 82-90.
      Littlejohn sees Miller's novels as being autobiographical,
      individualistic, and distant.

C92   Lowenfels, Walter, and Howard McCord.   The Life of Fraen-
      kel's Death: A Biographical Inquest?   Pullman: Washington
      State University Press, 1970.

C93   Madden, David.   American Dreams, American Nightmares.
      Carbondale: Southern Illinois University Press, 1970; pp.
      xxxii, 45-57, 136-148, 197-203.
      Madden sees Miller as a bitter, self-exiled man whose
      writing shows no positive feeling nor optimism.

C94   Millett, Kate. Sexual Politics. Garden City, N.Y. :
       Doubleday, 1970; pp. 294-313.
           An essay on Miller is included; he is seen as a mis-
       understood American writer trying to explain the Amer-
       ican sexual neurosis. Millett goes from this point to
       the idea that Miller is a blatant sexist; she shows an
       inability to understand Miller's individualism and belief
       in self-liberation.

C95   Schneider, Duane. An Interview with Anaïs Nin. Athens,
       Ohio: Duane Schneider Press, 1970; pp. 3, 7-8, 24-25, 29.
           Nin discusses the Paris literary community that con-
       sisted of herself, Durrell, and Miller.

C96   Solotaroff, Theodore. The Red Hot Vacuum: And Other
       Pieces on the Writings of the Sixties. New York: Athen-
       eum, 1970; pp. 3-36, 103-121, 165-170.
           Two major points are stressed in viewing Miller: The
       first is that he is an "asocial man," and the second is
       that he is an artist.

C97   Ueno, K. The Woman in B Minor. Tokyo: Kodosha,
       1970.
           Discussion of Miller's attraction to Japanese women,
       especially in Geisha. (In Japanese.)

C98   Widmer, Eleanor. Freedom and Culture: Literary Censor-
       ship in the 70's. Belmont, Calif.: Wadsworth Pub. Co.,
       1970.
           The Department of Justice felt that Tropic of Cancer
       was not obscene. Yet, this advice did little to prevent
       trials against the book on both the state and city levels.

C99   Grossman, Manuel L. Dada: Paradox, Mystification and
       Ambiguity in European Literature. New York: Bobbs-
       Merrill, 1971; pp. 153-154.
           "Although not as directly affected as the surrealists,
       other writers, such as the expatriate American novelist
       Henry Miller, who lived on the fringes of both the Dada
       and Surrealist movements, also felt the impact of Dada.
       In 'An Open Letter to Surrealists Everywhere,' which
       was part of his The Cosmological Eye, Miller testified
       to the influence of both movements on his work" (p.
       153).

C100   Highet, Gilbert. Explorations. New York: Oxford Univer-
       sity Press, 1971; pp. 16-17, 209-215.
           Miller's two Tropics are seen as non-stop monologues
       going on in the author's head.

C101   Hinz, Evelyn J. The Mirror and the Garden: Realism and
       Reality in the Writing of Anaïs Nin. Columbus: Ohio State
       University Libraries Publication Committee, 1971.

Miller views Nin's Diary as an incredible confessional, where he is portrayed as the major figure.

C102   Mailer, Norman. The Prisoner of Sex. New York: New American Library, 1971.
A defense of Miller that annihilates the sexist arguments of Kate Millett who only sees Miller's work as oppressive: "Millett obviously had not wished to weaken her indictment by qualifying the force of the shove--that was where she once again lost Miller. His work dances on the line of his dialectic. But Millett hates every evidence of the dialectic. She has ... a totally masculine mind" (p. 88). What Mailer feels is the fact that readers like Millett miss the artistic style and the anti-technological themes that Miller discusses. They merely categorize him as a sexist and dismiss all of the value and meaning found in the art of Henry Miller.

C103   Nin, Anaïs. The Diary of Anaïs Nin: 1944-1947. New York: Harcourt Brace Jovanovich, 1971.
Nin disagrees with those who make Miller a moralist or a saint: "The value of Henry Miller is not at all in spiritual or moral qualities, but in his shattering of Puritan crystallizations. He was a liberating force" (p. 66). Thus, Miller provided America and its literature with a new form of freedom.

C104   Bowles, Paul. Without Stopping: An Autobiography. New York: G. P. Putnam's Sons, 1972; p. 211.
Bowles's wife, Jane, noted that on returning home from the Champs-Elysees at 3:00 a.m., she often saw Henry Miller.

C105   Duberman, Martin. Black Mountain: An Exploration in Community. New York: E. P. Dutton & Co., 1972; pp. 104, 382-383.
Miller stopped at the Black Mountain School on his trip across America, depicted in The Air-Conditioned Nightmare.

C106   Harrison, Gilbert A. The Critic as Artist: Essays on Books 1920-1970. New York: Liveright, 1972; pp. 59-64, 211-216, 353-356.
Contains Nicola Chiaromonte's "Sunday after the War," Stanley Kauffmann's "Tropic of Cancer," and John Wain's "Naked Lunch."

C107   Nin, Anaïs. Paris Revisited. Santa Barbara, Calif.: Capra Press, 1972.
Nin remembers that Miller would sit and eat a fine meal and then run to his room to write about the experience.

C108   Rougé, Robert. L'Inquiétude religieuse dans le roman
américain moderne. Paris: L'universite de Haute-Bretagne,
1972.
Miller is considered to be a man aspiring to find a God.

C109   Vidal, Gore. Homage to Daniel Shays: Collected Essays
1952-1972. New York: Random House, 1972; pp. 197-203,
221-222, 224, 389-402, 404-405, 408.
Vidal looks at Miller in his articles "The Fourth Diary
of Anaïs Nin," "Pornography," "The Sexus of Henry
Miller," and "Woman's Liberation Meets Miller-Mailer-
Manson Man."

C110   Brooks, Cleanth; R. W. B. Lewis; and Robert Penn Warren.
American Literature: The Makers and the Making, Vol. II.
New York: St. Martin's Press, 1973; pp. 365, 2237-2250.
Miller is considered a monument of expatriate Paris
and in that role an anarchist of sexual morality and so-
cial stability. Passages from Tropic of Cancer, a
"Biographical Chart," and a brief bibliography are pre-
sented.

C111   Charters, Ann. Kerouac. San Francisco: Straight Arrow
Books, 1973; p. 194.
Kerouac's novel, The Subterraneans, is compared favor-
ably to Miller's writing.

C112   Harms, Valerie, ed. Celebration! With Anaïs Nin.
Riverside, Conn.: Magic Circle Press, 1973.
Miller is mentioned in this record of a weekend dia-
logue at Wainwright House, Rye, N.Y., in April 1972.

C113   Kalechofsky, Roberta. George Orwell. New York: Fred-
erick Ungar, 1973; pp. 9, 86.
The character George "Fatty" Bowling of Coming Up for
Air grew out of Orwell's enthusiasm for Joyce's
Ulysses and Henry Miller's Tropic of Cancer.

C114   Pells, Richard H. Radical Visions and American Dreams:
Culture and Social Thought in the Depression Years. New
York: Harper and Row, 1973; pp. 202, 343-344.
Miller represents withdrawal, for he left society for a
world of individualism.

C115   Durrell, Lawrence, and Marc Alyn. The Big Supposer.
New York: Grove Press, 1974; pp. 11, 37, 45-54.
Miller seen as a multifaceted character.

C116   Gertz, Elmer. To Life. New York: McGraw-Hill, 1974.
A chapter is devoted to Miller's views on free expression.

C117   Nin, Anaïs. The Diary of Anaïs Nin: 1947-1955. New

York: Harcourt Brace Jovanovich, 1974.
In Volume V of her Diary, Nin views Miller as a surrealist who introduced destructive elements into Nin's
life. He also engendered enthusiasm through his writing.

C118 Nin, Anaïs. A Photographic Supplement to the Diary of
Anaïs Nin. New York: Harcourt Brace Jovanovich, 1974.
Five photographs of and one water color by Miller are
found in this volume.

C119 Slade, Joseph W. Thomas Pynchon. New York: Warner
Communications, 1974; pp. 32-33.
The sinister 20th century is called "the time of the
assassins" by Miller.

C120 Carr, Virginia Spencer. The Lonely Hunter: A Biography
of Carson McCullers. Garden City, N.Y.: Doubleday,
1975; p. 209.
"Perhaps Carson's best-known fan at the time ... was
novelist Henry Miller."

C121 Connolly, Cyril. The Evening Colonnade. New York:
Harcourt Brace Jovanovich, 1975; pp. 197-201, 277-280,
293-295, 335-339, 343-349, 358-360, 375-386.
Miller seen as a juvenile writer.

C122 Falk, Randolph. Bufano. Millbrae, Calif.: Celestial Arts,
1975; p. 37.
Photograph of Miller and Benny Bufano.

C123 Ford, Hugh. Published in Paris: American and British
Writers, Printers and Publishers in Paris, 1920-1939.
New York: Macmillan, 1975; pp. 159-160.
Miller was the best-known proofreader to work for the
Paris Tribune.

C124 Shapiro, Karl. The Poetry Wreck: Selected Essays 1950-
1975. New York: Random House, 1975; pp. xv-xvii, 143-
155, 175-200.
Miller's contribution to prose poetry is considered vital
by Shapiro, who sees his writing creating a new trend
in the American novel.

C125 Nin, Anaïs. In Favor of the Sensitive Man and Other Essays. New York: Harcourt Brace Jovanovich, 1976; pp. 4-
5, 7, 20-21.
Nin speaks of getting beyond the sensuality of Miller
who makes an "honest assertion of desire."

D

DISSERTATIONS

D1   Nicholson, Homer K. , Jr. "O Altitudo: A Comparison of the Writing of Walt Whitman, D. H. Lawrence, and Henry Miller." Vanderbilt University, 1957.
Comparative study that sees the three authors as dissatisfied with the established literary mode, as seeking interpersonal relationships, as prophets, and as antiintellectual writers.

D2   Baxter, Annette Kar. "Parts of the Mosaic: Henry Miller as Expatriate." Brown University, 1958.
Exploration of the relationship between expatriate Miller and his native land. The study is done chronologically, taking the reader from New York to Paris and back to the U.S. Dealt with is Miller's anger at American society because of its falseness and evil.

D3   Bedford, Richard Colbert. "The Apocalastasis of Henry Miller." State University of Iowa, 1960.
Study of Miller's continuous changes in thought, seen in four periods: 1930-1939 "Temperamental, Tropical, and Topical Paris Expatriation," 1939-1949 "Cosmos, Colossus, and Clown--Return to America," 1949-1953 "Le Temps Perdu, Restatement and Expansion," and 1954-1959 "Big Sur Realist, Reconciliation and Resolution." The entire process shows Miller's metamorphosis and his acceptance of the cosmos.

D4   Gordon, William Alexander. "Henry Miller and the Romantic Tradition." Tulane University, 1963.
Study of Miller's belief that for man to be reborn, he must return to the primeval chaos where life had its beginnings, as seen in Cancer. Capricorn describes Miller's movement outward into the cosmos to discover the unity of the individual with all things.

D5   Cockcroft, George Powers. "The Two Henry Millers." Columbia University, 1964.
Miller seen as man divided between romantic, idealistic aspirations and the awareness of the sordidness and

75

failure in his own life.

D6   Mitchell, Edward Bell.   "Henry Miller: The Artist as Seer."
University of Connecticut, 1964.
Paper dealing with Miller's relationship to the romantic,
transcendental tradition and his closeness to zen.   The
central concept of Miller's vision--reality, awakening,
acceptance, the whole man--is explored in Chapter II.

D7   Hutchison, Earl Ray, Sr.   "Henry Miller and Tropic of Cancer; From Paris to Wisconsin--On the Censorship Trail."
University of Wisconsin, 1966.
Work concerned with obscenity, Tropic of Cancer, and
the trial in Milwaukee in 1962 followed by the Wisconsin
and U.S. Supreme Courts decisions concerning the nature
of this book.

D8   Nelson, Jane Armstrong.   "Form and Image in the Fiction of
Henry Miller."   University of Michigan, 1966.
Examination of the forms of fiction that appear in Mill-
er's writing.   Of special concern is tying Miller to
Jung's analysis of archetypes and the exploration of Mill-
er's attempt to find the meaning of the self.

D9   Jackson, Paul Russell.   "Henry Miller: The Autobiographical Romances."   Columbia University, 1967.
Exploration of the dichotomy between what Miller saw in
his works and what his critics perceived.   The synthesis
to his writing seen in Just Wild About Harry.

D10 Daugherty, Francis Leo.   "Henry Miller and the Heterocosm:
The General and Applied Literary Theory of an American
Neo-Romantic."   East Texas State University, 1970.
Correlation of the writings by Miller and the criticism
on this author that sees all his work as autobiographical.

D11 Hogue, Herbert Peter.   "The Anarchic Mystique of Five
American Fictions."   University of Washington, 1971.
Study of Cancer's belief in natural impulses overcoming
the conventional: "The anarchist spirit, the rejection of
'creeds and principles,' and the cultivation of radical independence are all important ... " (p. 22).

D12 Lewis, Leon Henry.   "Equatorial Introspection: A Critical
Study of Henry Miller."   State University of New York at
Buffalo, 1971.
Miller seen as American writer rebelling against his
cultural landscape: "Miller began to write in a condition
of nakedness, the protective promise of the American
Dream stripped away ... " (p. 25).   He faces reality,
sees that society has facades, and decides to seek a real
unity beyond the world of actors.   (But the rebellion ends
with Nexus; for with this work Miller accepts defeat.)

D13 Rankine-Galloway, Honora F. "The Impact of the 1961
Tropic of Cancer Publication on the American Literary Community." University of Pennsylvania, 1973.
By judging Tropic a work of "redeeming social importance," the critics saw the emergence of a new obscenity
code and were able to participate in this literary change
through courtroom involvement.

D14 Stone, Douglas. "Henry Miller and the Villa Seurat Circle,
1930 to 1940." University of California, Irvine, 1973.
A look at the circle of writers living in the Villa Seurat
of Paris. Besides Miller, the group consisted of
Michael Fraenkel, Walter Lowenfels, Anaïs Nin, Lawrence Durrell, and Alfred Perlès. Each of these artists
are looked at both as individuals and as products of a
literary community.

D15 Sarracino, Carmine Thomas. "Henry Miller, Spiritual Anarchist." University of Michigan, 1974.
Miller moves from political anarchism in his early work
to a stance that concerns his own development as man
and artist.

D16 Mathieu, Bertrand Marcel. "Orpheus in Brooklyn: Orphic
and Rimbaudian Ideals in the Writing of Henry Miller."
University of Arizona, 1975.
The Colossus of Maroussi best dramatizes Miller's obsession with the Orphic myth of descent and rebirth.

D17 Greenblatt, Howard Bruce. "Studies in Self-Portraiture:
Essays on Rousseau, Joyce, Proust, Miller, Céline."
Brandeis University, 1976.
Miller writes about the self through transposing his indi-
vidual quest for artistic expression into a mythical ad-
venture.

E

ARTICLES & REVIEWS ON MILLER*

E1   Bald, Wambly. "La Vie de Bohème," Chicago Tribune
     (Paris), October 14, 1931, 4.
     Miller viewed as a man who wanders in quest of words
     to write and food to eat.

E2   "Notes on Henry Miller's Works," Obelisk Notes and News,
     Winter 1935.
     Discusses Tropic of Cancer and its importance.

E3   Cendrars, Blaise. "Un Ecrivain americain nous est né,"
     Orbes, Summer 1935, 9-10.
     First review of Tropic of Cancer, seeing it as a great
     and important novel. (In French.)

E4   Belgion, Montgomery. "French Chronicle," Criterion, XV
     (October 1935), 83-96.
     First English review of Tropic of Cancer, seeing it as
     an expression of despair and disgust at human life.

E5   Perlès, Alfred. "On Goethe," T'ien Hsia Monthly, October
     1935, 281-290.
     Letter to Miller where Perlès discusses the phenomenon
     of Goethe's writing which is based on conscience and de-
     sires a united Germany.

E6   Fraenkel, Michael. "Bastard Death," n.p., October 21,
     1935.
     Letter to Miller concerning a living death.

E7   "Notes on Henry Miller's Works," Obelisk Notes and News,
     Spring 1936.
     Discusses Black Spring.

E8   "Black Spring," The Booster, August 1936.
     Review of Miller's second novel.

---

*The reviews are largely of books by Miller, though included also
are reviews of works about him.

E9   Queneau, Raymond. "Tropic of Cancer; Black Spring," La
Nouvelle Revue Française, XXV (December 1, 1936), 1083-
1084.
      Miller's contemporary heroes are compared to those of
      Joyce's Ulysses. (In French.)

E10   West, Herbert Faulkner. "Hanover Browsing," Dartmouth
Alumni, XXIX (January 1937), 8-9, 72.
      Miller is original, experimental, primitive--a writer
      with an anti-intellectual and romantic approach to litera-
      ture in Aller Retour New York.

E11   "The Prince and Hamlet," New English Weekly, X (January
14, 1937), 271-273.
      Miller says that Englishmen have always been slaves.

E12   Antonini, Giacomo. "Een Ontmoeting met Henry Miller,"
Kroniek van Hedendaagsche Kunst en Kultuur, II (February
1937), 126-127.
      A meeting with Miller before Tropic was accepted for
      publication by the Obelisk Press. (In Dutch.)

E13   Lundkvist, Artur. "Böcker från Väster," Bonniers Litterära
Magazin, VI (October 1937), 650-652.
      Review of Tropic of Cancer and Black Spring. (In
      Swedish.)

E14   "Reviews," New English Weekly, XI (October 7, 1937), 437-
438.
      Miller sees literature as a process of death and regene-
      ration.

E15   Nin, Anaïs. "A Boost for Black Spring," The Booster, II
(November 1937), 27.
      Review of Black Spring that sees it existing on many dif-
      ferent levels simultaneously: "Beneath the furry human
      warmth of certain pages lies a non-human purpose.
      There is in this book cruelty, cannibalism, worship and
      riotous joy. It is life lived on all levels ..." (p. 27).

E16   Durrell, Lawrence. "A Hymn to the Pycnik for Henry Miller," n.p., 1938, 4.
      Poem with seven verses dedicated to Miller.

E17   Wilson, Edmund. "Twilight of the Expatriates," New Republic, XCIV (March 9, 1938), 140.
      Wilson feels that Tropic of Cancer should have been re-
      viewed in and admitted into the United States.

E18   Prideaux, Tom. "Verse and Prose: 1937," Partisan Review, V (June 1938), 60-62.
      James Laughlin edited Miller's "Walking Up and Down in
      China" and felt that he had lost Miller's control of

language.

E19 "The Black Book," Time, XXXII (November 21, 1938), 69-70.
Durrell's writing is compared to Miller's.

E20 "Dithyrambic Sex," Time, XXXII (November 21, 1938), 69.
New Directions plans to publish Tropic in the United
States.

E21 Durrell, Lawrence. "Hamlet, Prince of China," Delta,
Christmas 1938, 38-45.
Letter to Miller regarding Hamlet.

E22 Lundkvist, Artur. "Henry Miller och Myten om den Skapande
Döden," Ikarus Flykt, 1939, 281.
Critique of Rimbaud, Joyce, Faulkner, and Miller. (In
Swedish.)

E23 Durrell, Lawrence. "News from Paris," New English Weekly, XIV (January 26, 1939), 241.
Durrell calls Max and the White Phagocytes a work describing the fall of our civilization.

E24 Perlès, Alfred. "Goethe: A Letter to Henry Miller," Purpose, XI (January-March 1939), 17-25.
See E4.

E25 "Money and How It Gets That Way," New English Weekly,
XIV (February 1939).
Review of Miller's Money and How It Gets That Way.

E26 "Mention," T'ien Hsia Monthly, November 1939, 435.

E27 Rosenfeld, Paul. "The Traditions and Henry Miller," Nation,
CXLIX (November 4, 1939), 502-503.
Miller's prose is elevated and affirmative, providing a
spiritual celebration of life in the tradition of D. H.
Lawrence and Hart Crane.

E28 Lewis, Jay. "The Cosmological Eye," Norfolk [Va.] Ledger
Dispatch, November 15, 1939.
Review of The Cosmological Eye.

E29 Fadiman, Clifton. "Books," New Yorker, VIII (November
18, 1939), 89.
Miller's Cosmological Eye is a contrasting work depicting both life's horrors and Miller's tendency to play
God.

E30 "Miller," Publisher's Weekly, CXXXVI (November 18, 1939),
1935.
Description of The Cosmological Eye.

E31   "Books of the Week Led by Discourse on Politicians," Birm-
ingham News, XXVIII (November 19, 1939), 7.
Miller's Cosmological Eye is called more modern than
Freud and more brutal than prostitution.

E32   "Among Today's Books," New York Sun, CVII (November 21,
1939), 9.
Cosmological Eye mentioned.

E33   "Books Out Today," New York Herald Tribune, XCIX (November 21, 1939), 23.
Cosmological Eye mentioned.

E34   Thompson, Ralph.   "Books of the Times," New York Times,
L (November 21, 1939), 21.
Miller's Cosmological Eye is called self-indulgent, ec-
centric fireworks.

E35   "One Reviewer Goes Provincial about Miller," Hartford
[Conn.] Times, XCIX (November 25, 1939), 7.
Review of The Cosmological Eye calling it obscene and
vulgar.

E36   "On Miller's Hill," New York Times, LXXXIX (November 26,
1939), 39.
Poem calling Miller's work the literature of decay.

E37   Pinckard, H. R.   "Expatriate Makes Debut in America,"
Huntington [W. Va.] Herald Advertiser, November 26, 1939.
Review of The Cosmological Eye.

E38   C., P. A.   "The Cosmological Eye," New Haven Journal-
Courier, CLXXIII (November 27, 1939), 6.
Miller called a new and rising star in this review of The
Cosmological Eye, where he is compared with Joyce,
Lawrence, Hemingway.

E39   Birney, Earle.   "Scoff Law," Canadian Forum, XIX (December 1939), 293.
Review of The Cosmological Eye where Miller is called
as great as Joyce for his portrayal of "Jabberwhorl
Cronstadt," an English poet living in Paris.

E40   Blake, Groverman.   "The Cosmological Eye and Tropic of
Cancer," Cincinnati Times-Star, December 1, 1939.
Review of The Cosmological Eye and Tropic of Cancer.

E41   Buchalter, Helen.   "Books of the Week," Washington Daily
News, XIX (December 1, 1939), 40.
Cosmological Eye called entertaining.

E42   Hansen, Harry.   "Book Marks for Today," New York World-
Telegram, LXXII (December 1, 1939), 33.

Cosmological Eye mentioned as a new publication.

E43   Berry, Lee. "This World of Books," Toledo Blade, December 2, 1939, 5.
Review of Cosmological Eye calling book dull yet eccentric.

E44   Deutsch, Babette. "Vagabond Poet-Rebel," New York Herald Tribune, XVI (December 3, 1939), 30.
In The Cosmological Eye, Miller speaks of the artist's duty to seek out reality.

E45   Fleming, Partee. "The Cosmological Eye," Nashville Morning Tennessean, December 3, 1939.
Review of Cosmological Eye.

E46   Peters, Richard. "Says Book Is Over His Head but He Likes It," Cleveland Press, December 4, 1939, 21.
Favorable review of Cosmological Eye that feels all of Miller's work should be published in the United States.

E47   "Mention," Chicago Tribune, December 6, 1939.
Cosmological Eye noted.

E48   Walker, Lillian. "From Fair to Maudlin," Nashville Banner, LXIV (December 6, 1939), 8.
Review of Cosmological Eye that sees the book as merely ordinary and views Miller as self-centered.

E49   Berry, Lee. "This World of Books," Pittsburgh Post-Gazette, XIII (December 9, 1939), 6.
Review of Cosmological Eye where Miller is called a literary eccentric.

E50   "The Cosmological Eye," Columbia Missourian, December 9, 1939.
Review of Cosmological Eye.

E51   "Book Brevities: The Cosmological Eye," Seattle Post Intelligencer, CXVII (December 10, 1939), C7.
Cosmological Eye presents a man who respects little in the twentieth century.

E52   L., R. M. "The Cosmological Eye," Chattanooga Times, LXX (December 10, 1939), 5.
Considers Cosmological Eye to be of little importance.

E53   MacMillan, Eleanor T. "Autobiographies Tell Tale of How History is Made," Portland Oregon Journal, XXXVI (December 10, 1939), 7.
Review of The Cosmological Eye where Miller is considered a genius, yet it is suggested that he concern himself less with the current and popular.

E54   Holmes, John.   "Fourth Issue of Advanced Annual Contains Selections from Samuel Greenberg's Poems," Boston Transcript, CX (December 13, 1939), 13.
      United States will not print Tropic of Capricorn.

E55   "Mention," Cincinnati Times-Star, December 15, 1939.
      Note about Miller's new novel, Cosmological Eye.

E56   Fitts, Dudley.   "More Miller," Saturday Review, XXI (December 16, 1939), 12.
      Review of Cosmological Eye where Miller is viewed as an artist of first rank, a satirist of Swiftian power and master of words.

E57   "Mention," Chicago Times, December 17, 1939.
      Review of Cosmological Eye.

E58   "Mention," Worcester Telegram, December 17, 1939.
      Notes publication of Cosmological Eye.

E59   Nicholas, Louis.   "Shades of the Left Bank," Philadelphia Record, December 17, 1939, 13.
      Miller could be the greatest force in literature says Nicholas in review of Cosmological Eye.

E60   Webster, Harvey Curtis.   "Image-Breaker," Louisville Courier-Journal, CLXX (December 17, 1939), 15.
      Miller considered the greatest stylist since Joyce in this review of Cosmological Eye.

E61   Cameron, May.   " 'Cosmological Eye' Uncovers a Genius," New York Post, XVI (December 19, 1939), 10.
      Cosmological Eye seen as a great and important work by an author with a different philosophy.

E62   Millstein, Gilbert.   "Sees Miller's Art Confusing Melange," Philadelphia Inquirer Public Ledger, December 20, 1939, 19.
      Review of The Cosmological Eye that fails to understand Miller.

E63   "Cosmological Eye," San Francisco Argonaut, December 22, 1939.
      Review of The Cosmological Eye.

E64   "Mention," Altoona (Pa.) Mirror, December 22, 1939.

E65   "Mention," Evansville (Ill.) Press, December 22, 1939.

E66   Chappel, John O.   "Samples of Henry Miller," Cincinnati Enquirer, XCIX (December 23, 1939), 5.
      Sees The Cosmological Eye as an important series of articles, stories, essays, etc., by an important American author.

E67   Lane, Robert Frederick.   "Naturalism: The Cosmological
      Eye," Omaha World-Herald, LV (December 24, 1939), 7C.
      Review of The Cosmological Eye that calls Miller a
      naturalist.

E68   S., W. T.   "Cities, Cosmologies and Sundries," Providence
      Journal, LX (December 24, 1939), 6.
      Review of The Cosmological Eye that calls Miller extra-
      ordinary and a powerful writer.

E69   "Talking & Doing," Time, XXXVI (December 25, 1939), 54-
      55.
      Both Tropics are considered to possess extraordinary
      documentary power.

E70   Bower, Helen C.   "On Greater Reality," Detroit Free Press,
      CIX (December 31, 1939), 12.
      The Cosmological Eye is the tale of a boy looking at the
      universe.

E71   "Cosmological Eye," Springfield (Ohio) News, December 31,
      1939.
      Review of The Cosmological Eye.

E72   "Mention," Pueblo (Colorado) Star Journal, December 31,
      1939.

E73   Laughlin, James.   "Note on Henry Miller," We Moderns,
      1940, 50.

E74   O'Brien, Howard V.   "The Cosmological Eye," Dayton Jour-
      nal, January 4, 1940.
      Review of The Cosmological Eye.

E75   March, Michael.   "The Cosmological Eye and Hamlet,"
      Brooklyn Citizen, January 5, 1940.
      Reviews of both The Cosmological Eye and Hamlet.

E76   "Mention," San Francisco News, January 6, 1940.

E77   MacNeill, Ben Dixon.   "Literary Hash," Raleigh News-
      Observer, CL (January 7, 1940), 5.
      Review of The Cosmological Eye where reviewer cannot
      discern what the book is about.

E78   Hawkins, Frank.   "The Cosmological Eye," Macon Telegraph,
      January 8, 1940.
      Discussion on The Cosmological Eye.

E79   Thompson, Dustan.   "Little Boy Blue," New Republic, CII
      (January 8, 1940), 61.
      Miller called the most extraordinary writer of his time
      in this review of The Cosmological Eye.

E80 Rhodes, Arthur. "Cosmological Eye Egotist's Thrust at the
World," Brooklyn Eagle, XCIX (January 11, 1940), 24.
    Miller seen in a world of his own in his self-centered
    work entitled The Cosmological Eye.

E81 "Erratic Mystic," Springfield (Mass.) Union & Republican,
January 14, 1940.
    Miller viewed as a mystic in a review of The Cosmologi-
    cal Eye.

E82 West, Herbert Faulkner. "Hanover Browsing," Dartmouth
Alumni, XXXII (February 1940), 21-22.
    Fraenkel emphasized in this review of Hamlet, a work
    where Miller calls our time schizophrenic.

E83 "New Directions Finds a Market for Neglected Authors,"
Publisher's Weekly, CXXXVII (March 23, 1940), 1220-1222.
    New Directions is interested in publishing Miller.

E84 Clark, Eleanor. "Images of Revolt," Partisan Review, VII
(March-April 1940), 160-163.
    In The Cosmological Eye, Miller battles for the inner
    man, the true being found behind the facade of civiliza-
    tion.

E85 Paludan, Jacob. "Korniken," Politiken, August 3, 1940.
    Review of The Cosmological Eye.   (In Danish.)

E86 Muller, Herbert J. "The World of Henry Miller," Kenyon
Review, II (Summer 1940), 312-318.
    The revolt against intellect is explored in Miller's
    Tropic of Capricorn. He criticizes the perversions of
    reality such as "intellect, science, society, civilization,
    ... art and literature" (pp. 315-316).

E87 Crews, J. C. "Cosmological Eye," Motive, I (August-
October 1940).
    Miller called the spiritual heir of Lawrence, a master
    of the English language.

E88 Rosenfeld, Paul. "Hamlet Is Not Enough," Nation, CLI
(September 7, 1940), 198.
    Miller is a story-teller but not one of the inner sympa-
    thetic vision of Sherwood Anderson.

E89 Smith, Winifred. "Henry Miller and Michael Fraenkel,"
Books Abroad, XIV (Fall 1940), 440-441.
    Discussion of death in life, the American schizophrenia.

E90 Symmes, Robert. "An Embryo for God: 'The Tropic of
Capricorn'," Experimental Review, I (November 1940), 78-80.
    Miller moves toward an inner reality in Capricorn by
    becoming naked.

E91 Levin, Harry. "If We Had Some Eggs," New Republic, CIII (December 30, 1940), 905-906.
Miller sees Hamlet as a fraud.

E92 "Hamlet," Experimental Review, II (1941).
Review of Miller's Hamlet.

E93 Rahv, Philip. "The Artist as Desperado," New Republic, CIV (April 21, 1941), 557-559.
Miller is the artist hero depicting the real life of the streets in his three autobiographical novels, the two Tropics and Black Spring.

E94 Orwell, George. "English Writing in Total War," New Republic, CV (July 14, 1941), 57-58.
Miller's Tropic called the only expatriate book of any value.

E95 Rosenfeld, Paul. "We Want Fortinbras," Nation, CLIII (August 16, 1941), 146.
Miller is called alive, while Fraenkel is seen as melancholy in the life-death struggle found in Hamlet.

E96 "A Major Event for September," The Colt [San Francisco], September 1941, 2.
Miller's The Colossus of Maroussi is seen as an excellent travelogue of Greece.

E97 Montgomery, Neil. "Views and Reviews: Correspondence on Hamlet," New English Weekly, XIX (September 18, 1941), 211-212.
Review of Hamlet where Miller and Fraenkel discuss schizophrenia, the split personality of modern man.

E98 Sylander, Gordon. "A Yangtse Yankee," Diogenes, I (Autumn 1941), 91-93.
In Hamlet, Miller is viewed as a man with two absolutes, a mental and a material, which blend together and create a void.

E99 Powell, Lawrence Clark. "Letters of Talented Pair Portray 'Europe on Eve'," Los Angeles Times, LXI (December 14, 1941), 10.
In both The Colossus of Maroussi and Hamlet, Miller portrays Europe on the eve of World War II.

E100 Fadiman, Clifton. "The Wisdom of the Heart," New Yorker, XVII (December 27, 1941), 60.
Review of this collection of Miller stories calling him original and a mystic.

E101 Barker, George. "Henry Miller Revivalist," Nation, CLIV (January 3, 1942), 17-18.

The Colossus of Maroussi and other Miller books are
called religious confessions.

E102   Deutsch, Babette. "The Malady of Modern Man," New York
Herald-Tribune, XVIII (January 11, 1942), 16.
    In both The Colossus of Maroussi and The Wisdom of
the Heart, Miller is a man divided against himself in
his study of cosmic schizophrenia.

E103   Rahv, Philip. "Spellbinder in Greece," New Republic, CVI
(January 12, 1942), 59-60.
    Miller's style is personal in his depiction of Greece.

E104   Kaplan, H. J. "The Colossus of Maroussi," Partisan Review, IX (January-February 1942), 85-86.
    Miller's confusion between art and self-expression is
exhibited in The Colossus of Maroussi.

E105   West, Herbert Faulkner. "Hanover Browsing," Dartmouth
Alumni, XXXIV (February 1942), 16.
    Miller appears as a man of genius as he gives his
reader a feeling of Greece in The Colossus of Maroussi.

E106   Fitts, Dudley. "Experiments in Life and Death," Accent,
II (Winter 1942), 112-115.
    Review of Hamlet dealing with death and rebirth.

E107   Politis, M. J. "In Understanding of Greece," New York
Times, XCI (March 29, 1942), VI 24.
    The Colossus of Maroussi is called Miller's biography
of Katsimbalis.

E108   Lazarus, H. P. "The Ego at Large," Partisan Review,
IX (May-June 1942), 264-267.
    Miller's confession, The Wisdom of the Heart, is a
boring work where Miller is infatuated with himself.

E109   Roskolenko, Harry. "Henry Miller," Accent, III (Autumn
1942), 63-64.
    Both The Wisdom of the Heart and The Colossus of
Maroussi are Miller against the world.

E110   "The Colossus of Maroussi," News Review, XIV (November
5, 1942).
    Favorable review of The Colossus of Maroussi.

E111   Orwell, George. "The End of Henry Miller," London
Tribune, December 4, 1942, 18-19.

E112   Ailes, Edgar H. "Letter to Cyril Connolly," Detroit, December 29, 1942.
    Deals with Miller's "Soiree in Hollywood."

E113   Matthews, Kenneth. "Three Visions of Greece," Spectator,
        January 15, 1943, 60.
        Miller's Colossus of Maroussi is called a shallow book.

E114   "A Grecian Rhapsody," Great Britain and the East, LIX
        (January 23, 1943), 14.
        Chastising of Miller for The Colossus of Maroussi,
        feeling that Miller knows little about Greece other than
        superficial comparisons with the United States.

E115   Nicolareizis, D. "The Colossus of Maroussi," Horizon,
        VII (March 1943), 210-213.
        Review of The Colossus of Maroussi that views the
        work as autobiographical and obsessed with magic.
        The reviewer feels that it is a pity that Miller knows
        so little about Greece. (In French.)

E116   "Mention," Balzac Bulletin, May 1943.

E117   Nicolareizis, D. "The Colossus of Maroussi," Athene, IV
        (June 1943), 62-63.
        See D113.

E118   Pittendrigh, Ken. "Man Alive," Angry Penguins, Septem-
        ber 1943, 19-21.
        An appreciation of the life and vitality of Miller's writ-
        ing.

E119   Lerman, Leo. "Before Band Wagons," Vogue, October 1,
        1943, 80, 140.
        Photograph of Miller and excerpt from The Colossus of
        Maroussi. Miller is called a great writer who uses
        both autobiographical and interpretative styles of writing.

E120   "Mention," Kingdom Come, IV (Autumn 1943), 2.

E121   Teece, Harry. "Enquire Within Upon Everything," Kingdom
        Come, IV (Autumn 1943), 13-18.

E122   "Our Point of View," Modern Mystic and Monthly Science
        Review, November 1943, 3.

E123   "From the New Republic Mail Bag," New Republic, CIX
        (November 8, 1943), 656.
        Miller likes to paint but feels that he is not a painter,
        and suggests that his work is of little value.

E124   "Public Notice," New Republic, CIX (November 8, 1943).
        · Miller talks about the poverty of the creative artist in
        America and asks for food, clothing, painting supplies,
        and contributions.

E125   "One of the Greatest Living Writers," Town and Country,

XCVIII (December 1943), 147.
> Noted is the fact that Miller has turned from writing to watercolors.

E126   M., A.   "Surrealist's Act Proves Difficult to Evaluate," Los Angeles Times, LXIII (December 12, 1943), 6.
> Miller's art is based on his whims.

E127   "Life by Mail Order," Time, XLII (December 13, 1943), 55.
> Article about Miller's appeal for charity in the New Republic. It notes that at present he is working on The Air-Conditioned Nightmare.

E128   "Public Notice," Time, XLII (December 13, 1943).
> See E124.

E129   S., A. G.   "Mr. Miller and His Conscience," New Republic, CIX (December 20, 1943), 888.
> Poem about Miller's inability to be published in the U.S.

E130   Moore, Reginald.   "The Creative Life--Keyserling," World Review, Christmas 1943, 41-43.
> Views the Miller-John Cowper Powys relationship.

E131   Gilbert, Thomas R.   "Rocamadour," Hemispheres, I (Fall-Winter 1943-1944), 35-43.
> Miller found unexciting, yet his work is dynamic, for he writes vital, living books about the Paris world he knows so well.

E132   Goll, Yvan.   "Histoire de Parmenia l'Havanaise," Circle, I (1944), 17-18.
> Poem dedicated to Henry Miller who brings life to all he sees and touches.   (In French.)

E133   Williams, William Carlos.   "To the Dean," Circle, I (1944), [unnumbered].
> Poem of 24 lines paying tribute to Henry Miller.

E134   Woodcock, George.   "Life More Abundant," Jazz Music, January 1944, 81-82.
> Miller offers man a better way to live through a personal form of self-expression.

E135   Hampson, John.   "Fiction," Spectator, January 14, 1944, 40.
> The new generation of writers of the 30's consisted of Miller, Saroyan, and Farrell.

E136   Anand, Mulk Raj.   "The Novel and Henry Miller," London Tribune, January 21, 1944, 18.

E137   Herring, Robert.   "Editorial Comments," Life and Letters

Today, XL (January-March 1944), 151-155.
Miller considered to be an artist and a prophet ahead
of his time.

E138   West, Herbert Faulkner.   "Hanover Browsing," Dartmouth
Alumni, XXXVI (February 1944), 12.
Thomas Wolfe is seen by Miller to be a genius.

E139   Linderman, Verne.   "Writer Turned Painter Finds America
Barren," Santa Barbara News Press, February 6, 1944.
Photograph of Miller and his water color "Tante Melia."

E140   D'Azevedo, Warren.   "Henry Miller and the Fifth Freedom,"
New Republic, CX (February 14, 1944), 212-213.
Rebuttal of Miller's December 6, "Another Open Letter."
He is called a lamenter, a cry baby.   But the problem
of Miller's art is glossed over because there is nothing
Mr. D'Azevedo can see to remedy it.

E141   "Meet Mr. Miller," Tomorrow, IV (April 1944), 244.
Miller's writing shows his disgust with Western civilization.

E142   Alexander, Irene.   "Henry Miller Makes Home in Big Sur
Country," Carmel Pine Cone-Cymbal, April 14, 1944, 12.
Notes Miller's move to Big Sur, California.

E143   Perlès, Alfred.   "Henry Miller in Villa Seurat (An Incom-
plete Portrait), Life and Letters Today, XLI (April-June
1944), 148-156.
Perlès talks about the Villa Seurat in Paris where he
and Miller lived and of Miller's love to talk and drink.

E144   Leite, George.   "To Henry Miller," Circle, I (May 1944),
[unnumbered].
Poem celebrating Miller.

E145   Loman, Stanley.   "I Am Quite Interested," Yale Literary
Magazine, CX (Spring 1944), 14.
Miller seen as one of the keenest analysts of our time.

E146   Stanford, Derek.   "The Wisdom of the Heart," Oasis,
Spring 1944, 24.
Positive viewing of Miller and his book, The Wisdom
of the Heart.

E147   Lovejoy, Ritch.   "Henry Miller Is Working Here," Monterey Peninsula Herald, June 10, 1944.

E148   "Literary," Times Literary Supplement, XLIII (June 24,
1944), 311.
Miller's work on Lawrence is intense and intellectual.

E149   Adams, J. Donald. "The Shape of Books to Come," Tomorrow, V (July 1944), 27.
Miller's writing seen as influential.

E150   "Freedom," Tomorrow, V (July 1944), 27.
Miller's writing displays independence from the norm.

E151   Wolfson, Victor. "Mr. Tyler's Hallucination," Nation,
CLIX (July 8, 1944), 50-51.
Miller considers Parker Tyler's Hollywood Hallucination
beyond anything he had ever hoped to write about Hollywood.

E152   "The Editor's Guest Book," Harper's Bazaar, LXXVIII
(August 1944), 1.
Miller called a complex expressionist of era and place.

E153   Kreiselman, Mariam. "Books," Mademoiselle, XIX (August 1944), 231, 319-321, 329.
Miller's writing is a fertile emotional flow; all forms
of order are missing from his Tropic.

E154   Sheets, Kermit. "Pilgrimage to Henry Miller," Illiterati,
III (Summer 1944).
An account of a visit with Henry Miller at Beverly
Glen, 1943.

E155   Stevens, Wil. "Editor's Note," Interim, I (Summer 1944),
2.
Miller's writing knows no geographical boundaries.

E156   Porter, Bern. "Letter to Gabene," Leaves Fall, II (September 1944), 79-80.
Discussion of Miller's drawing "Alf in Ibiza," the
frontispiece to What Are You Going to Do About Alf?

E157   "Surrealism and Superrealism," Times Literary Supplement,
XLIII (September 2, 1944), 428.
Miller's Tropic of Capricorn called supernaturalistic.

E158   P., G. "Unusual Book Is Sunday after the War," Ogden
(Utah) Standard-Examiner, September 14, 1944.
Review of Sunday after the War.

E159   Spindel, Max. "Pessimistic Intellectual," Philadelphia Inquirer, CCXXXI (September 17, 1944), 9.
Review of Sunday after the War that calls Miller truthful and entertaining.

E160   Sherman, John K. "Bilious Genius Looks at Our Civilization," Minneapolis Morning Tribune, LXXVIII (September 22,
1944), 4.
Miller enraged because America has lost her vitality

in this review of Sunday after the War.

E161   R., C. E.   "Book Review: Sunday after the War," New
Haven Journal-Courier, CLXXVIII (September 23, 1944), 10.
Review of Sunday after the War where Miller is called
a writer with an " 'air gunner' and original style exploring the defects in America. "

E162   Wilson, Edmund.   "Sunday after the War," New Yorker,
XX (October 21, 1944), 87-91.
Miller stands outside the reality of World War II in
Sunday after the War.

E163   Fowlie, Wallace.   "Shadow of Doom: An Essay on Henry
Miller," Accent, V (Autumn 1944), 49-53.
Miller seen as a prophet in the tradition of Lawrence
and Rimbaud whose violent speech announces the doom
to come.   He believes that man's only hope is to love
and accept his world.

E164   Marshall, Margaret.   "Notes by the Way," Nation, CLIX
(November 4, 1944), 562.
Sunday after the War is a vital book about real life in
the tradition of Tropic of Cancer.

E165   "A Brilliant and Controversial Figure," Town & Country,
XCIX (December 1944), 114-115, 131.
Picture of Miller.   The caption says he is not honored
enough in America.

E166   Foff, Arthur.   "Sunday after the War," San Francisco
Chronicle, CLIX (December 3, 1944), 2.
Review of Sunday after the War that sees Miller concerned with anti-materialism, individualism, and mysti-
cism.

E167   Chiaromonte, Nicola.   "The Return of Henry Miller," New
Republic, III (December 4, 1944), 751-754.
Miller's work shows feelings of pity and human understanding for one's fellow men, as he becomes one with
other human beings.

E168   Kristol, Irving.   "Genius in a Surreal World," New Leader,
December 9, 1944.
Review of Sunday after the War that calls Miller the
heir to Lawrence and explores the themes these two
authors have in common.

E169   Read, Herbert.   "Views and Reviews: Henry Miller," New
English Weekly, December 28, 1944, 93.
Miller strips away art in his quest for reality, as he
spits at and insults formalized art.

E170   Fluchère, Henri. "Le Lyrisme de Henry Miller," Cahiers
        du Sud, XXXII (1945), 729-736.
             Miller's Tropic is called a poetic work.   (In French.)

E171   Leite, George. "The Autochthon," Angry Penguins, 1945,
        137-140.
             Miller is a being who has tapped all sources to experi-
        ence the all.

E172   Merrild, Knud. "A Holiday in Paint," Circle, I (1945), 39.
             Merrild praises his long time friend, Henry Miller.

E173   Kahn, Albert E. "Odyssey of a Stool-Pigeon," New Cur-
        rents, III (January 1945), 3-4, 26.
             Miller is called a fascist, an anti-Semite, a propa-
        gandist, a labor spy, and a Nazi by this pro-Jewish
        magazine.

E174   Lingel, Fred. "Oh Me Oh Mighty," Leaves Fall, III (Janu-
        ary 1945), 94-96.

E175   Pauling, C. G. "More Books of the Week," Commonweal,
        XLI (January 5, 1945), 306-307.
             Miller's short story, "Reunion in Brooklyn," shows the
        painful gutter reality of James T. Farrell, yet it also
        possesses an emotion that Farrell is unable to reach.

E176   Kahn, Albert E. "Odyssey of a 'New Leader' Hero," Daily
        Worker, January 15, 1945, 11.

E177   Manning, Hugo. "Apropos Henry Miller," The Wind and the
        Rain, II (Winter 1945), 166-168.
             Miller needs freedom and support and can find neither
        in our society.

E178   Neiman, Gilbert. "No Rubbish, No Albatrosses: Henry
        Miller," Rocky Mountain Review, IX (Winter 1945), 69-76.
             Miller is a perceptive human being: "Here is a person
        who grasped, who kept the infant in himself alive..."
        (p. 70).

E179   Lord, Russell. "Henry Miller," Harvard Wake, I (June
        1945), 13-16.
             Miller is a critic of life itself who bases his stance on
        the freedom of the individual to experience.

E180   Etiemble, Valeurs. "Lettres étrangeres," Valeurs, July
        1945, 91-93.
             Review of The Colossus of Maroussi that calls the book
        poetic and says that it transcends the literature of de-
        generacy that Miller usually writes.   (In French.)

E181   Powell, Lawrence Clark. "We Moderns," Scop, I (Summer

1945), 5-6.
Miller is called one of the greatest writers of our time,
yet his two greatest works, Tropic of Cancer and Tropic
of Capricorn, are not published in the United States.

E182 Powell, Lawrence Clark. "We Moderns," Wilson Library
Bulletin, XX (November 1945), 218-219.
See E181.

E183 Shorey, Katherine. "Henry Miller: Air-Conditioned Nightmare," Library Journal, LXX (December 1, 1945), 1134.
The Air-Conditioned Nightmare is Miller's attempt to
reorient himself with America, yet it comes off too
self-centered, as Miller's ego overcomes any possible
union.

E184 "Aphrodite Ascending," Time, XLVI (December 24, 1945),
104-108.
Miller's conception of America as a sterile world is
honest and stark in this review of The Air-Conditioned
Nightmare and The Happy Rock.

E185 Wilson, Edmund. "Air-Conditioned Nightmare," New Yorker, XXI (December 29, 1945), 62-66.
The Air-Conditioned Nightmare is one of Miller's best
books to appear in the United States, as it presents a
truthful picture of America and Miller.

E186 Gray, James. "Henry Miller Proves Anew Low Level of
Skill and Mind," Minneapolis Tribune, December 30, 1945.

E187 Haurigot, Paul. "Joyeuse Oraison funèbre," Documents,
1946.
Tropic of Cancer is a book about eroticism and freedom.
(In French.)

E188 "Henry Miller Work Displayed," Claremont Eagle, 1946, 5.
Twenty-one Miller watercolors are on display at the
Carpenter Galleries.

E189 Read, Herbert. "What England's Leading Critic Thinks
About America's Most Extraordinary Writer," New English
Weekly, XXVIII (1946).
Miller seen as an artist questing for reality not literature: "What makes Miller distinctive among modern
writers is his ability to combine the aesthetic and
prophetic functions."

E190 "Poésie 46," Times Literary Supplement, XLV (January 5,
1946), 10.
In Poésie 46, No. 35, Pierre Seghers translates work
by Miller.

E191   De Voto, Bernard.   "Mr. Miller's Chthonian Nightmare,"
New York Times XCV (January 25, 1946), VI 12.
Miller's Air-Conditioned Nightmare seen as tolerably read-
able stuff loaded with fantasy and few glimpses at reality.

E192   Jackson, Joseph Henry.   "Bookman's Notebook," San Francisco Chronicle, CLXII (January 25, 1946), 12.
Miller's Air-Conditioned Nightmare is seen as a mixture between good and bad Miller. He's at his best
when discussing the arts and at his worst in depicting
what is wrong with America.

E193   Wylie, Philip.   "Run for Your Lives!" Saturday Review,
XXIX (February 16, 1946), 20-22.
Review of The Air-Conditioned Nightmare that depicts
the ugliness, poverty, money mania, and violence that
Miller sees in America.

E194   Wheeler, Dinsmore.   "[Review of] The Air-Conditioned
Nightmare," New Mexico Quarterly, XVI (Winter 1946),
510-511.
Miller's belief in freedom and fraternity leads him to
social analysis couched in comic fantasy, castigation,
and individualism.

E195   Haan, Jacques Den.   "Enhele Notities over Henry Miller,"
Litterair Paspoort, I (March 1946), 10.
A biography of Miller that introduces him and his work
and which goes on to compare him to Hemingway.   (In
Dutch.)

E196   Hughes, Warren.   "The Soul of Anaesthesia," Index, I
(March 1946), 2-6.
Review of The Air-Conditioned Nightmare which agrees
with Miller that America is a rich country of narrow
sighted people.

E197   "The World of Henry Miller," News Review, XVIII (March
7, 1946), 27.
Miller's Cosmological Eye is called tough and alive.

E198   Morgan, Charles.   "The Nursery Floor," Sunday London
Times, March 10, 1946, 3.
The Cosmological Eye meets praise for it contains a
superior essay by Miller on D. H. Lawrence and a fine
play, 'Scenario. "

E199   Click, Nathan.   "A Brilliant Story Teller," New Leader,
March 30, 1946.
Review of The Air-Conditioned Nightmare that sees
Miller as a brilliant social critic and a fine preacher
who understands America and the plight of its artists.

E200 Fauchery, Pierre. "Une Epopée du sexe: Le Feuilleton hebdomadaire. " Action, April 1946.
Article in French dismissing Miller from the scandalous image Americans have created. For he is described as having a religious fervour, a purity, and a romanticism. (In French.)

E201 Ormsby, Roscoe L. "From the Faculty Scrapbooks, " Berea Alumnus, XVI (April 1946), 203-204, 206.
Miller's Air-Conditioned Nightmare is praised for its belief that psychology cannot use reason and science to solve all problems, for those of emotion come from the heart and have nothing to do with the rational.

E202 Saint Jean, Robert de. "Generation of Vipers, " Fontaine, VII (May 1946), 858-861.
The metaphor of the snake is used to depict Miller and his Air-Conditioned Nightmare. (In French.)

E203 "Traductions, " Bulletin Hebdhmadaire des Informations Culturelles, May 22, 1946.
Translation of Miller's two Tropics into French would be welcomed. (In French.)

E204 Buhet, Gil. "La Vie littéraire, " Diogéne, May 24, 1946.
Miller's Black Spring an important American novel. (In French.)

E205 "Courrier des lettres, " Diogéne, May 31, 1946.
Announcement that the celebrated author of Black Spring has finished Tropic of Capricorn. (In French.)

E206 Charensol, Georges. "Les Lettres, " Chronique de France, May-June, 1946, 43.
A sense of death and the anti-hero appear in Tropic of Cancer. (In French.)

E207 Steiner, Jacqueline. "The Air-Conditioned Nightmare, " Foreground, I (Spring-Summer 1946), 189-190.
Review of The Air-Conditioned Nightmare that states that Miller does not hate America like most expatriates. He feels shocked at the degenerate nature he has seen in this country.

E208 "Les G. I. de Paris réduisent au chômage une linotypiste dévotée, " Biblio, June 1946.
American soldiers are buying Miller's Tropic of Cancer. (In French.)

E209 "Pentraits: Henry Miller, " What's Doing, I (June 1946), 13, 33-35.
The story about Miller's growing up in Brooklyn.

E210 "Livres recurs," Paris-Cinéma, June 4, 1946.
Miller's Tropic of Cancer is mentioned. (In French.)

E211 Musard, François. "Tropique du Capricorne," L'Etoile du
Soir, June 6, 1946.
Miller viewed as a miserable bohemian nihilist. (In
French.)

E212 "La Semaine d'un parisien," Le Littéraire, June 15, 1946.
Death is a theme crucial to the writing of Miller,
Faulkner, and Caldwell. (In French.)

E213 Sylvien, Jean. "Un Poéte," Syndicalisme, June 15, 1946.
Miller is an anarchist. (In French.)

E214 "Les Lecteurs jugent," Action, June 21, 1946.
Miller is a naturalist, a revolutionary, and an optimistic writer. (In French.)

E215 "Miller," Bibliographie de la France. CXXXV (June 21-28,
1946).
Miller's first two books, Tropic of Cancer and Black
Spring, are discussed. (In French.)

E216 "Miller," La Gazette des Lettres, June 22, 1946.
Tropic of Capricorn viewed as a brutal existence in a
modern world. (In French.)

E217 Valincourt. "L'Ennui par l'ordure," Paroles Française,
June 22, 1946.
Miller's horrible treatment of his fellow man is chas-
tised. (In French.)

E218 Saint Hely, Marc. "Littérature Estrangere," Rolet, June
27, 1946.
Steinbeck, Hemingway, and Miller are romantic Americans with a sense of hope. (In French.)

E219 "Annexuns existentialistes," Poésie 46, XVII (June-July
1946).
Miller faces comparison to Sartre, for both men are
considered existentialists. (In French.)

E220 Blanzat, Jean. "Les Lettres," Le Monde Français, III
(July 1946), 490-493.
Miller mentioned along with Hawthorne, for both are
concerned with imagined and actual reality. (In French.)

E221 Mead, William. "[Review of] The Air-Conditioned Nightmare," Briarcliff Quarterly, III (July 1946), 148-149.
Miller's Air-Conditioned Nightmare is an attempt to depict the brutality of American society.

E222   "L'Existentialisme va-t-il être cause d'une nouvelle 'affaire
       Baudelaire'?" Quatre et Trois, July 4, 1946.
           Miller's quest for freedom is compared to Baudelaire's.
           (In French.)

E223   L., P. "Henri Miller," Le Clou, July 4, 1946.
           Tropic is a book where Miller is concerned with his
           phallus. (In French.)

E224   Peschmann, H. "The World of Henry Miller," New English
       Weekly, XXIX (July 11, 1946), 130-131.
           Miller's primitive power and ego remained one with
           D. H. Lawrence and John Cowper Powys. He believes
           in both physical and psychological aliveness.

E225   Fowlie, Wallace. "Henry Miller, prophète américain,"
       Les Arts et les Lettres, I (July 12, 1946).
           Miller's writing concerns a prophesy of love that comes
           from the heart. (In French.)

E226   Lassaigne, Jacques. "La Critique littéraire," Les Arts et
       les Lettres, I (July 12, 1946).
           Miller's Tropics display his feelings about life. He
           faces comparison to Dostoevsky in his outlook. (In
           French.)

E227   "Oer," Le Monde, July 13, 1946.
           Miller's Tropic of Capricorn called burlesque. (In
           French.)

E228   Morelle, Paul. "Et pan dans le Miller," Franc-Tiréur,
       July 17, 1946.
           Miller seen as a sensationalist in his writing. (In
           French.)

E229   Chaulot, Paul. "La Presse et les lettres," La Gazette des
       Lettres, July 20, 1946.
           Miller's use of monologue is much like Zola's. (In
           French.)

E230   Ambriere, Francis. "Littérature américaine," La Rataille,
       July 24, 1946.
           Black Spring is a very important book about America
           by an American. (In French.)

E231   Astre, G. A. "William Saroyan: L'Audacieux Jeune
       Homme au trapèze volant," Fraternité, July 25, 1946.
           Saroyan's sense of life and passion is compared to
           Miller's. (In French.)

E232   Gandon, Yves. "Le Cas Miller," Minerve, July 26, 1946.
           Miller called a sexual spirit. (In French.)

E233   Guérin, Raymond.   "Kaputt de Curzio Malaparte," Juin,
        July 30, 1946.
            Miller, Lawrence, and Gorki all see life's greatness.
            (In French.)

E234   Morel, Henriette.   "Misère de New-York," Résistance,
        July 30, 1946.
            Miller and Nathanael West both capture the baseness
            and poverty of life in New York.   (In French.)

E235   Loewell, Pierre.   "John Dos Passos, Henry Miller, Aldous
        Huxley," L'Aurore, July 31, 1946.
            Miller seems as profound as Joyce, as vio-
            lent as Faulkner, and as open as Lawrence.   (In
            French.)

E236   D., P.   "La Revue des revues," Action, August 2, 1946.
            Miller mentioned in a Kafka review.   (In French.)

E237   "Lettres ... et le néant," Le Crochet, August 2, 1946.
            Miller's sense of romance is scandalous.   (In French.)

E238   "Souvenirs d'enfance," Question du Jour, August 3, 1946.
            Miller's Tropic of Capricorn viewed as exciting.   (In
            French.)

E239   Gallet, G. H.   "Climats torrides," V, August 4, 1946.
            Miller's two books dealing with temperature zones are
            revolutionary and brutal.   (In French.)

E240   "De quelques lectures...," Ce Soir, August 4-5, 1946.
            Miller viewed as a dreamer, not a realist.   (In French.)

E241   Ricaumont, Jacques de.   "L'Esprit des revues," Juin,
        August 6, 1946.
            Miller considered original.   (In French.)

E242   Parrot, Louis.   "De Faulkner à Henry Miller," Lettres
        Françaises, VI (August 9, 1946), 5.
            Both Faulkner and Miller are romantics, yet both can
            be cynical.   (In French.)

E243   Texeier, Jean.   "Impérialismes," Libération-Soir, August
        10, 1946.
            Miller considered absurd because his sense of individu-
            alism fails to see history.   (In French.)

E244   Noel, Maurice.   "Les Lettres et les arts," Les Dernières
        Dépêches, August 12, 1946.
            Miller's literature is called sexual.   (In French.)

E245   Dominique.   "Le Voleur d'étincelles," Cavalcade, August
        15, 1946.

Maurice Nadeau interviewed Miller.   (In French.)

E246   Laville, Victor.   "Pourquoi...," Le Tigre, August 16, 1946.
Cartoon of two children reading Tropic.   (In French.)

E247   Bay, André.   "Domaine étranger," La Gazette des Lettres,
August 17, 1946.
Miller's books deal with such spectacle as prostitution.
(In French.)

E248   "Miller for Ever," Une Semaine dans le Monde, August 17,
1946.
Miller a pessimist.   (In French.)

E249   Berger, Pierre.   "Instantanés Claude de Fréminville,"
Nouvelles Littéraires, (August 22, 1946), 5.
A feeling of certainty appears in both the literature of
Huxley and Miller.   (In French.)

E250   Bassac, Léonce.   "Lettres ... et le néant," Le Crochet,
August 23, 1946.
Miller exposes too much to society, and in this uncomfortable position, society feels that its only recourse is
to punish Miller.   (In French.)

E251   "Petit Panorama de la seurom thèatrale," n.p., August 31,
1946.
Miller writes in a period of transition.   (In French.)

E252   Goff, Lloyde Lozes.   "[Review of] Why Abstract?" New
Mexico Quarterly Review, XVI (Summer 1946), 235-237.
Miller's essay on Hiler is seen as worthless because
the critic feels that Miller knows little about painting.

E253   Shapiro, Harvey.   "Review of Rimbaud," Yale Poetry Review, II (Summer 1946), 31-32.
Positive review of Miller's essay on Rimbaud.

E254   Bataille, George.   "L'Inculpation d'Henry Miller," Critique,
I (August-September 1946), 380-384.
Miller, Joyce, and D. H. Lawrence are viewed as
literary greats, not pornographers.   (In French.)

E255   "[Henry Miller]," Le Livre et Ses Amis, September 1946.
Miller's Tropic of Capricorn uses violence to restore
society to the world from which she has fallen.   (In
French.)

E256   L., Y.   "Les Romans étrangers: Henry Miller, l'homme
de la conversation," Paru, September 1946, 43-50.
Miller's Tropics and Black Spring are called the literature of prophecy.   (In French.)

E257 Maulnier, Thierry. "Feuilleton Littéraire," La Revue des
Hommes et Mondes, September 1946, 190-202.
Miller rejects literature in Cancer and Capricorn.
What he desires is real feeling and real experience.
(In French.)

E258 "Les Revues: L'Arche," Paru, September 1946, 116.
Miller mentioned. (In French.)

E259 "Les Revues: Critique," Paru, September 1946, 120.
Miller has the morality of a sociologist. (In French.)

E260 "Les Revues: Le Magasin du spectacle," Paru, September
1946, 117.
Miller's "Scenario" considered a great play. (In
French.)

E261 Albert-Hesse, Jane. "La Fosse aux indiens," Franc-
Tireur, September 1-2, 1946.
Miller called an exhibitionist. (In French.)

E262 Henriot, Emile. "Notre Littérature vue de loin," Le Monde,
September 5, 1946.
Miller's brand of literature seems to be a mixture of
reality and history. (In French.)

E263 Magny, Claude-Edmonde. "La Critique des livres," Cavalcade, September 5, 1946.
It is difficult to judge whether Miller is a serious author or a contaminator of literature. (In French.)

E264 Forestier. "Poursuits contre les éditeurs française d'Henry Miller," Combat, September 6, 1946.
Miller's publishers are being sued. (In French.)

E265 Sidvine. "Patriotisme," Arts, September 6, 1946.
Miller, who makes revelations in Cancer and Capri-
corn and seems like the Bible, is actually an idiot.
(In French.)

E266 "Courrier," Résistance, September 7, 1946.
The two Tropics are about Miller's life. (In French.)

E267 "Literary Monsters," S.W.S., September 7, 1946.
Miller's work is a new bible of liberation and revolution. (In French.)

E268 Z. "Cette Bonne Blague des bonnes moeurs," L'Aurore,
September 7, 1946.
Moral action is being taken against Miller and his fil-
thy book, Tropic of Cancer. (In French.)

E269 Descaves, Pierre. "Les Livres tels qu'ils sont," Tel Quel,

September 10, 1946.
Miller is viewed as a man who moves contrary to society.   (In French.)

E270   M., P.   "Les Revues," Les Etoiles, September 10, 1946.
Miller is an author concerned with solitude.   (In
French.)

E271   Riollet, Marius.   "Littérature...," Le Dauphiné Libéré,
September 11, 1946.
Miller called shocking.   (In French.)

E272   Magot Solitaire, Le.   "Promenade chez le libraire," Carrefour, September 12, 1946.
Miller has become a best selling author.   (In French.)

E273   Perry, Jacques.   "Faut-il interdire Miller?" Carrefour,
September 12, 1946.
Miller is viewed as outrageous but honest by the dozen
critics who defend him in this article.   (In French.)

E274   "Les Bons Apôtres," Le Libertaire, September 13, 1946.
The complaint against Miller is that he is corrupting
the masses.   (In French.)

E275   Desanti, Dominique.   "Un Cartel français vent brûler Henry
Miller," Action, September 13, 1946.
A French Court will decide the merits of Miller's work
in the Tropic of Cancer trial.   (In French.)

E276   Duca, Lo.   "Céline 'Made in America': Le Cas Henry
Miller," Le Monde Illustré, September 14, 1946, 1030.
Miller is viewed as a genius and a lyricist in the tra-
dition of Céline.   (In French.)

E277   "Tropique du Cancer," L'Argus des Industries du Livre,
September 15, 1946.
Miller's first book is called work of genius, honest,
and cynical; Miller himself is compared to Rabelais.
(In French.)

E278   "Précédent," L'Etoile du Soir, September 15-16, 1946.
Miller's editors compare their case to that of Flaubert.
(In French.)

E279   Le Farfadet.   "Au coin du bois sacre," Tel Quel, Septem-
ber 17, 1946.
French justice allows the publication of Miller's work.
(In French.)

E280   "Ingénuité," La République du Centre, September 17, 1946.
Miller is persecuted unfairly, for his writing has much
merit.   (In French.)

E281   "Les Gammes de 'l'Enchanteur'," Le Parisien Libéré,
       September 18, 1946.
       Miller's writing called exciting.   (In French.)

E282   "Courrier littéraire," Concorde, September 19, 1946.
       French justice will decide the merits of Henry Miller
       as a writer.   (In French.)

E283   Riollet, Maruis.   "[Au retour]," Le Dauphiné Libéré,
       September 19, 1946.
       Tropic called mediocre.   (In French.)

E284   Sans, Julien.   "Retour de Tartuffe," Climats, September
       19, 1946.
       Miller should be free to express himself in spite of the
       vengeance demanded by unthinking people.   (In French.)

E285   Slocombe, George.   "Reviews of New Books in Europe,"
       Herald Tribune (Paris), LIX (September 19, 1946), 5.
       Miller's Tropic is viewed as the latest in French
       realism, yet it also contains the humor and insanity
       of the Marx Brothers.

E286   "[Traqués]," Le Dauphiné Libéré, September 19, 1946.
       The American critic, Wallace Fowlie, sees Miller as
       an extremely important writer.   (In French.)

E287   Fontain, André.   "Le Tigre au palais," Le Tigre, Septem-
       ber 20, 1946.
       Miller moves in circles like a maelstrom.   (In French.)

E288   M., L.   "Simples Rectifications," Lettres Françaises, VI
       (September 20, 1946), 2.
       Miller has been found offensive by the Soviets.   (In
       French.)

E289   "Pour ... et contre," Arts, September 20, 1946.
       Miller provides the best example of literary freedom
       and its creative success.   (In French.)

E290   "Stratégie littéraire," Franc-Tireur, September 20, 1946.
       Miller's writing follows the tradition of Gogol.   (In
       French.)

E291   Bouzinac, Roger.   "Henry Miller pour ses ouvrages,"
       L'Espoir, September 21, 1946.
       In the literary world, Miller is as base as they come.
       (In French.)

E292   "Bonne Presse," Juin, September 24, 1946.
       A look into the erotic world of Miller.   (In French.)

E293   "De Franz Kafka à Henry Miller," Lyon Libre, September

24, 1946.
Miller's writing is called as brutal as Kafka's, yet it
still shows literary merit.   (In French.)

E294   "L'Ere des grands procès littéraires," Dernière Heure,
September 24, 1946.
Miller believes in pursuit of happiness and other basic
freedoms.   (In French.)

E295   "L'Horizon littéraire," Spectateur, September 24, 1946.
Miller has as much right to depict social ills as Kafka.
(In French.)

E296   "Mieux vaut tard qui jamais," Tel Quel, September 24,
1946.
Miller has to be a man of patience for waiting so long
to have his novels read and accepted.   (In French.)

E297   Bassac, Léonce.   "Un Roman historique," France d'Abord,
September 25, 1946.
Miller's works are not history but fabrications.   (In
French.)

E298   Fboret, B. L.   "De la poésie du désespoir au drame espagnol," Cité-Soir, VI (September 25, 1946).
Miller is grouped with Faulkner and Hemingway as outstanding examples of American literature.   (In French.)

E299   Lalou, René.   "Liberté et responsabilité de l'écrivain,"
Le Populaire, September 25, 1946.
The freedom to write should exist for Miller, yet he
should not have abused the trust of humanity.   (In
French.)

E300   Petit, Henri.   "Juges, auteurs et public," Le Parisien
Libéré, September 25, 1946.
Miller's writing compared to Rabelais, Joyce, and Law-
rence.   (In French.)

E301   "Au pied de la lettre," Cavalcade, September 26, 1946.
Discussion of the case against Miller's book as obscene
literature.   (In French.)

E302   Bory, Jean-Louis.   "Faut-il brûler Miller?" Gavroche,
September 26, 1946.
Both sides are presented in the Paris trial of Tropic
of Cancer.   (In French.)

E303   "Musardises," La France au Combat, September 26, 1946.
Tropic of Cancer and Tropic of Capricorn are seen in
the scandalous tradition of Lady Chatterly.   (In French.)

E304   R., M.   "Paru," L'Avenir de l'Ouest, September 26, 1946.

Miller interviewed in <u>Paru</u>, No. 26.   (In French.)

E305   "Dans son numéro, " <u>Arts</u>, September 27, 1946.
Miller is seen as a pornographic writer.   (In French.)

E306   Pleure, Jean Qui.   "Le 'Gros Bouquin', " <u>Le Canari</u>, September 27, 1946.
Miller considered a pornographic writer.   (In French.)

E307   B. , E.   "Où sont les ciseaux?"   <u>La Gazette des Lettres</u>,
September 28, 1946.
Miller has been the object of attacks.   (In French.)

E308   Launay, P. J.   "Les Lettres, " <u>Libération</u>, III (September ·
28, 1946).
Miller 's first three works are mentioned, and he is
called a genius.   (In French.)

E309   "Baudelaire acquitté, " <u>Libération-Soir</u>, September 29-30,
1946.
Moralists deplore the writing of Henry Miller.   (In
French.)

E310   Kendrick, Alexander.   "Paris Buries a Philosophy, Hails
Quads, " <u>Chicago Sun</u>, V (September 30, 1946), 8.
Miller considered one of France's best selling authors.

E311   "Du haut de mon mirador, " <u>L'Unique</u>, October 1946.
Social and moral action is being taken against the publishers of <u>Black Spring</u> and <u>Tropic of Cancer</u> for obscenity found in the literature.   (In French.)

E312   "Justice, ou les Miller de la vertu, " <u>Fontaine</u>, VII (October 1946), 493.
The French press has been against Miller on social and
moral grounds.   (In French.)

E313   Bottemer, A.   "Pariser Bilderbogen, " <u>Le Républicain du
Haut-Rhin</u>, October 1, 1946.
Story of Miller's suit and trial in Paris, France.   (In
German.)

E314   "A la revue 'Arts et lettres', " <u>La République du Centre</u>,
October 1, 1946.
Wallace Fowlie has done a study of Miller.   (In French.)

E315   "Au fil de la plume..., " <u>Carrefour</u>, October 3, 1946.
Miller and Baudelaire both believe in reform.   (In
French.)

E316   "Les Livres, " <u>Le Tigre Montpellier</u>, October 4, 1946.
Miller and Sartre are compared as surrealists.   (In
French.)

E317 Nadeau, Maurice. "Vague de pudeur," Combat, October 4,
       1946.
       Miller's literature is expressionistic. The only ques-
       tion is how much is a man free to say. (In French.)

E318 "La Vie des lettres," Résistance, October 4, 1946.
       Author Henry Miller distances himself from society in
       his two Tropics. (In French.)

E319 "Un Espoir pour Henry Miller?" Nord-Eclair, October 5,
       1946.
       Miller's works are of social and moral outrage. (In
       French.)

E320 "Livres, couronnes et tapis vert," Le Littéraire, October
       5, 1946.
       Miller is being indicted on moral grounds. (In French.)

E321 "Le Président de la 16e chambre correctionnelle va deri
       si Miller attente aux bonnes moeurs," Samedi-Soir, Octo-
       ber 5, 1946.
       Miller's language in the two Tropics is one of constant
       sexual reference. (In French.)

E322 Breffort, A. "La Revue de l'actualité," Paris-Matin,
       October 6-7, 1946.
       Sartre lectures on Miller. (In French.)

E323 "Autodafés," Le Progrès, October 7, 1946.
       Miller and Kafka both depict the futility of life. (In
       French.)

E324 Magnaud, J. A. "Un 'Montparno' Américain accusé d'im-
       moralité...," Résistance, October 8, 1946.
       Miller has been accused of immorality in his two
       Tropics because the two books are said to endanger the
       morals of the public. (In French.)

E325 Caillet, Gérard. "L'Affaire Miller," Opéra, October 9,
       1946.
       America is intolerant of Miller, who uses obscenity
       and violence to undermine society. He does not speak
       of the apocalypse but deals pessimistically with his
       world. (In French.)

E326 Magnaud, J. A. "Faut-il condammer Miller et brûler ses
       oeuvres?" Résistance, October 9, 1946.
       Miller is viewed as a unique and honest author. (In
       French.)

E327 Margerit, Robert. "La Vie littéraire," Le Populaire du
       Centre, October 9, 1946.
       Miller's Tropic of Capricorn is seen as a book about

the moment and about obscenity. (In French.)

E328 Vert, Chartreux. "Après Lawrence et Faulkner...,"
Libération-Soir, October 9, 1946.
Miller's literature is the literature of responsibility.
(In French.)

E329 Bouvier, Emile. "Littérature ou pas?" Midi Libre, October 10, 1946.
Miller is viewed as an egotist projecting his literature
of nihilism and sex upon the world. (In French.)

E330 "Briefuisseling," Vooruit, October 10, 1946.
At the Academy of Arts and Letters, Wallace Fowlie
spoke out in favor of the American author, Henry Miller. (In Dutch.)

E331 "[Henry Miller]," L'Echo, October 10, 1946.
Miller and his work are seen as an outrage. (In
French.)

E332 Dheur, Gabriel. "Pornographes et moralistes," Temps
Présent, October 11, 1946.
Miller's literature disturbs the French because of its
obscenity. (In French.)

E333 "Pour et...," Arts, October 11, 1946.
Miller has developed into an excellent writer. (In
French.)

E334 C., P. "Dú sommaire des revues," La Gazette des Lettres,
October 12, 1946.
Wallace Fowlie sees Miller as a visionary, yet a seer
of pessimism. (In French.)

E335 C., P. "Panorama des revues," La Gazette des Lettres,
October 12, 1946.
Miller has collaborated on an anthology. (In French.)

E336 Chaulot, Paul. "Dú sommaire des revues," La Gazette
des Lettres, October 12, 1946.
Fernand Tourret has done a study of Henry Miller.
(In French.)

E337 Taillis, Hélène. "Don Juan est moins dangereux," Ici Paris,
October 13, 1946.
Miller called a brutal writer. (In French.)

E338 A., O. N. "2 Books May Lead to Court Test," Daily Mail,
October 15, 1946, 5.
Miller's books are contrary to French public morality.

E339 R., M. "L'Amérique à travers ses livres," La République

Moderne, October 15, 1946, 23.
Tropic of Cancer is a book about social progress and
how it conflicts with the spiritual.   (In French.)

E340   Ulmann, André.   "Sur la littérature américaine," Les
Etoiles, October 15, 1946.
Miller cannot write by distancing himself from his sub-
ject.   (In French.)

E341   Verdot, Guy.   "Avec une haire d'en avoir deux," Franc-
Tireur, October 16, 1946.
Miller's heroes are anti-heroes.   (In French.)

E342   Bay, André.   "Raymond Guerin l'apprenti," Carrefour,
October 17, 1946.
Guerin views Miller as a lyricist and a romantic.   (In
French.)

E343   "Dix Conseils," Forces Françaises, October 17, 1946.
The ironic is a fundamental theme in the writing of
Sartre and Miller.   (In French.)

E344   Soro.   "La Petite Puck à Paris," Carrefour, October 17,
1946.
Miller called a contaminator in a cartoon depicting his
work.   (In French.)

E345   Pierhal, Armand.   "Un Céline américain: Henry Miller,"
Temps Présent, October 18, 1946.
Miller has outraged tradition and morality and religion
by playing Jesus.   (In French.)

E346   "Et dire qu'on a condamné...," Nouvelles Littéraires,
October 24, 1946.
Miller's Tropic stands with other great books that were
condemned.   (In French.)

E347   Megret, Christian.   "Pour tout dire, ne dites pas tout,"
Carrefour, October 24, 1946.
Persecuting Miller is an indignant action.   (In French.)

E348   Slocombe, George.   "Reviews of New Books in Europe,"
Herald Tribune (Paris), LIX (October 24, 1946), 5.
Tropic of Cancer is seen as a great book with Dantesque
horror.   The experiences of poverty, hunger, cold,
filth, and debasement all show the level to which man
has fallen.   The humor is savage and grotesque, as
Miller depicts his own loneliness and perversion on the
streets of Paris.

E349   "Au fil des lettres," La Marseillaise, October 24-30, 1946.
Frenchmen are outraged at Miller for his obscenity.
(In French.)

E350   "La Vie des lettres," Lettres Françaises, October 25, 1946.
　　　　Miller's Air-Conditioned Nightmare says much about France. (In French.)

E351   "Contre-attaque de Miller," Le Littéraire, October 26, 1946. "Obscenity and the Law of Reflection" is Miller's counterattack against society. (In French.)

E352   Les Editions du Chêne. "L'Affaire Henry Miller," La Gazette des Lettres, October 26, 1946.
　　　　Miller's three novels, Tropic of Cancer, Black Spring, and Tropic of Capricorn, are said to contaminate the public, while his publishers feel that he carries on the tradition established by Proust, Lawrence, and Joyce. (In French.)

E353   'Des realities toutes crues," Sachez Tout!, October 26, 1946.
　　　　Miller is seen as an author carrying a devil's barb in one hand and displaying the grace of a saint with the other. (In French.)

E354   Bo, Carlo. "Come se la pornografia," Corriere Lombardo, October 27, 1946.
　　　　The Miller case involves the publication of the two Tropics in France, a subject discussed by Bo. (In Italian.)

E355   "Un Juge d'instruction français inculpe l'écrivain américaine Miller d'attentat aux moeurs," Franc-Soir, October 27, 1946.
　　　　The two sides of the Tropic case are presented with Miller's faction winning over Parker's; some of Miller's works, e.g., Max and the White Phagocytes and The Colossus of Maroussi, use no obscenity yet criticize society much like the two Tropics. (In French.)

E356   Glaer. "Come i Francesi verdone gli Italiani," La Tribuna del Popolo, October 29, 1946.
　　　　Miller banned in England, the United States, and maybe, soon, in France. (In Italian.)

E357   "Le Livre du jour," Combat, October 30, 1946.
　　　　Miller's "Obscenity and the Law of Reflection" offers him the opportunity to answer a hostile society. (In French.)

E358   "Courrier littéraire," Concorde, October 31, 1946.
　　　　Tropic seen lacking a sense of moral justice. (In French.)

E359   "Les Mauvais Livres," Qui?, October 31, 1946.

Tropic of Capricorn viewed as a menace to society.
(In French.)

E360   Paraf, Pierre. "Dialogue sur l'immoralité littéraire," Le
Parisien Libéré, October 31, 1946.
Miller's literature is viewed as contaminating.   (In
French.)

E361   "[Le Savetier]," Nouvelles Littéraires, October 31, 1946.
Moral and civil action against Miller has no validity
when one reads his "Obscenity and the Law of Reflection."   (In French.)

E362   "Le Tambour de ville," Gavroche, October 31, 1946.
Mentioned is the fact that moral action is being taken
against Miller.   (In French.)

E363   "Chronique l'homme de poutre," Poésie 46, XVII (October-
November 1946), 156-160.
The pseudo-justice afforded Miller in France is viewed
as grotesque for a country that prides itself on freedom.   (In French.)

E364   Theobald, John.   "[Review of] New Directions 9: An Annual Exhibition Gallery of Divergent Literary Trends," New
Mexico Quarterly Review, XVI (Autumn 1946), 365-369.
Like Patchen, Miller is a forceful writer who craves
anarchy, yet desires an anarchy that is a radiant positive Utopia.

E365   B., G.   "Littéraire et beaux-arts," Critique, November
1946, 565-566.
Miller's opinion of what constitutes good literature is
restated by Albert Cossery.   (In French.)

E366   Jaray, Gabriel Louis.   "Déracinés spirituels y aux Etats-
Unis et en France," France Amérique, XXXVII (November
1946), 607-611.
Freudianism is seen in Miller's writing.   (In French.)

E367   Rossi, Peaci.   "Novità dalla Francia," Presso la Casa
Editrice Bompiani, November 1946.
Miller's Tropics are being sued for obscenity.   (In
Italian.)

E368   Saint Jean, Robert de.   "Aperçus de littérature americaine,"
Fontaine, VII (November 1946), 657-660.
Coindreau says that he will translate Miller.   (In
French.)

E369   Ambrière, Francis.   "Porquoi j'ai voté contre la révision
du procès Baudelaire," Combat, November 1, 1946.
Miller writes in the tradition of Baudelaire.   (In French.)

E370   "[Les Editeurs]," Le Tigre, November 1, 1946.
        French publishers are outraged that they are not being
        permitted to translate the Tropics.   (In French.)

E371   "Le Procès Miller: aura-t-il lieu?" Combat, November 1,
        1946.
        Miller and his editor are subject to social action as de-
        creed by a French court on July 30, 1939, for their
        attempt to translate his writing into French.   (In French.)

E372   Thermonier, Henry.   "Déclin de l' 'esprit' français?"
        Lettres Françaises, VI (November 1, 1946), 4.
        Miller's humor is compared to Mark Twain's.   (In
        French.)

E373   V., J.   "Les Revues," Lettres Françaises, VI (November
        1, 1946), 5.
        Miller is viewed as a visionary who has produced frag-
        ments of The Rosy Crucifixion.   (In French.)

E374   Blanzat, Jean.   "Les Romans de la semaine," Le Litté-
        raire, November 2, 1946.
        Miller seen as a romantic in his writing.   (In French.)

E375   Potier, Jacques.   "L'Affaire du 'Corbeau'," L'Etoile du
        Soir, November 2, 1946.
        Miller's writing is viewed as interesting but brutal.
        (In French.)

E376   "Plumes Plumes...," Ploum-Ploum, November 5, 1946.
        Miller compared to the existentialist, Sartre.   (In
        French.)

E377   Bardi, Giovanni.   "Imoralisti attaccano gli editori sorri-
        dono," Courriere Lombardo, November 6, 1946.
        Miller is being sued by Daniel Parker for obscenity in
        .his three novels, the two Tropics and Black Spring.
        (In Italian.)

E378   Christophe, Robert.   "La Croisade de la morale con-
        tinue...," Tour a Tour, November 6, 1946.
        Miller viewed as an angelic writer.   (In French.)

E379   Margerit, Robert.   "La Vie littéraire," Populaire du
        Centre, November 6, 1946.
        The pursuit of justice in the Miller trial continues.
        (In French.)

E380   "Un Débat sur l'auteur des 'Tropiques'," France-Soir,
        November 7, 1946.
        Miller will debate the issue of morality in Tropic with
        his accusor, Daniel Parker.   (In French.)

E381 "[Dieu Merci]," Dernières Nouvelles, November 7, 1946.
The judges are attempting to condemn Miller on the
pretext of pornography. (In French.)

E382 Mousson, Yves. "Henry Miller sera-t-il condamné pour
outrage aux bonnes moeurs?" L'Ordre, November 7, 1946.
Moralists are trying to stop the translation of the
Tropics and Black Spring into French because of the
sexual nature of the three books. (In French.)

E383 Texeier, Jean. "Gare aux 'bonnes moeurs'," Gavroche,
November 7, 1946, 1-2.
Miller condemned for being outrageous and violent. (In
French.)

E384 "Courrier de lettres," Arts, November 8, 1946.
Moral and social action has been taken by Daniel Park-
er against Miller and his novel, Tropic of Cancer. (In
French.)

E385 Loewel, Pierre. "De l'obscène à l'art," Aux Ecoutes,
November 8, 1946.
Miller is obscene. (In French.)

E386 Mury, Gilberti. "La Singularité d'être américain," Tribune
des Nations, November 8, 1946.
Miller called a savage writer denouncing the social order because of his belief in individual freedom. (In
French.)

E387 Parrot, Louis. "Histoires sans fin," Lettres Françaises,
VI (November 8, 1946), 5.
Miller's sense of writing is extremely traditional, for
he follows the Russians--Dostoevsky, Gorki, and Gogol.
(In French.)

E388 "Retour de Tortufe," Action, November 8, 1946.
Miller is condemned by a hypocritical French public
that wants its freedom but will not let him have his
rights. (In French.)

E389 "La Semaine littéraire," Combat, November 8, 1946.
The Society of Arts and Letters condemns the writing
of Miller. (In French.)

E390 Sept, Les. "Les Lettres," Libération, III (November 8,
1946), 2.
Miller attends the Paris trial of his novel, Tropic.
(In French.)

E391 Smoular, Alfred. "Une Lettre de Smoular," Arts, November 8, 1946.
Miller and his portrayal of prostitutes considered

outrageous. (In French.)

E392 "Un Architecte puritain," Samedi-Soir, November 9, 1946.
Miller is detested by traditionalists. (In French.)

E393 Guth, Paul. "Raymond Guérin," La Gazette des Lettres,
November 9, 1946.
Miller is seen as organistic. (In French.)

E394 Panurge. "Pour ce que rire...," Midi, November 10, 1946.
Miller, Lawrence, Sartre, and Céline all apologize for
the faults of society. (In French.)

E395 "Jean Filou, prêtre," Combat, November 11, 1946.
Miller's "Obscenity and the Law of Reflection" shows
his stance for the freedom of the writer. (In French.)

E396 "Au Club du faubourg: Défense des libertés," L'Ordre,
November 12, 1946.
Miller fights for the freedom to write. (In French.)

E397 Ondine. "[Controverse sur Miller]," Ploum-Ploum, November 12, 1946.
The ideal way to view Tropic of Cancer is as graceful,
but it is a brutal book. (In French.)

E398 "Vague de pudeur," Midi-Soir, November 12, 1946.
Miller writes both spiritual and spirited novels. (In
French.)

E399 Bellus, Jean. "Il s'agit tout de même de prendre une
décision au sujet de cet Henri Miller...," La Bataille,
November 13, 1946.
Cartoon of four old women chatting about Miller. (In
French.)

E400 Disrasy, Lione. "De l'obscénité," Tel Quel, November 13,
1946.
A debate goes on over the morality of Miller's first
three novels. (In French.)

E401 "Echos et Nouvelles," France Libre, November 13, 1946.
Miller's trial involves the freedom to write as one
wishes. (In French.)

E402 "... Et du Renaudot," Tel Quel, November 13, 1946.
Miller is moving toward a new literature. (In French.)

E403 Laroche, Pierre. "Le Ciseau qui marche," Le Canard
Enchaîné, November 13, 1946.
Parker intends to see that the French courts undermine
Miller. (In French.)

E403a "La Semaine de poil de carotte," Le Bataille, November 13, 1946.
   Miller is the author of an infernal book about machines. (In French.)

E404   "L'Affaire Miller," Cavalcade, November 14, 1946.
   The Miller case involves the question of whether Tropic of Cancer is immoral or is Miller in the tradition of Gide, Proust, Joyce, and Lawrence. (In French.)

E405   "De Baudelaire à Miller," Fantasia, November 14, 1946.
   Miller's novels considered fine, humanistic works. (In French.)

E406   Blanchas, G. "Les Livres," Paris-Actualités, November 14, 1946.
   Miller critics, Armond Hoog, Maurice Nadeau, and Robert Kempf see Tropic of Capricorn as an extremely moral book. (In French.)

E407   "Defense des libertés," Coté Desfosses, November 14, 1946.
   The Miller case involves the freedom to write as one wishes. (In French.)

E408   Dominique. "Le Voleur d'étincelles," Cavalcade, November 14, 1946.
   Miller sees American life as scandalous. (In French.)

E409   Nadeau, Maurice. "Deux Mondes," Gavroche, November 14, 1946.
   Miller depicts the lives of his fellow American compatriots. (In French.)

E410/11 Sans, Julien. "Révision du procès Baudelaire?" Climats, November 14, 1946.
   Will the French Courts go back on the freedom granted in the Baudelaire case in the Miller trial? (In French.)

E412   "L'Affaire Lemarchand au Club du Faubourg," Arts, November 15, 1946.
   Miller is an offense to liberty. (In French.)

E413   D., J. "[Henry Miller]," L'Argus des Industries du Livre, November 15, 1946.
   Miller believes in the basic freedoms. (In French.)

E414   Gouzy, Jean-Pierre. "A propos de Henri Miller," La République Moderne, November 15, 1946.
   Miller's Tropics are seen as perverse, erotic, and obscene expressions, and he is compared to Hitler, Marx, and Lenin. (In French.)

E415   "Les Livres de Henri Miller," La France Nouvelle,

November 15, 1946.
Miller is seen caught between a hungry publisher and a
morally indignant society.   (In French.)

E416   Loiselet, Pierre.   "Pour le plaisir," La Dépêche de Paris,
November 15, 1946.
Miller is viewed as an independent human being and an
experimenter in his writing.   (In French.)

E417   "Un Miller danois," Combat, November 15, 1946.
Miller viewed as revolutionizing literature.   (In French.)

E418   Nonuma, A.   "Révolte des esprits," Le Libertaire, November 15, 1946.
The Miller critics are hypocrites who want their freedom but will not allow Miller his independence.   (In
French.)

E419   "Pour et ... contre," Arts, November 15, 1946.
The metaphor of Saint George and the dragon is used to
show the absurdity of justice in the Miller trial.   (In
French.)

E420   "La Radio," Question du Jour, November 15, 1946.
Miller does not have the artistic style to be compared
to Flaubert and Baudelaire.   (In French.)

E421   Saint-Come.   "Goncourt 1946," Paroles Françaises, November 15, 1946.
Miller is a man of desire and strength.   (In French.)

E422   "Au Club de Faubourg," Coté Desfosses, November 15-17,
1946.
Miller should be free to write as he wishes.   (In
French.)

E423   "Aux quatre vents," Le Littéraire, November 16, 1946.
Miller considered to be the most obscene writer.   (In
French.)

E424   "Les Poursuites judiciaire à propos du 'Tropique du Capricorne'," L'Aurore, November 16-17, 1946.
Miller has outraged society.   (In French.)

E425   "French Assail U.S. Books: Moral League Sues Publisher
of Henry Miller Novels," New York Times, XCVI (November 17, 1946), 47.
On November 16, 1946, the French League for Social
and Moral Action brought suit against two Paris publishing firms, Editions du Chêne and Editions de Noël,
to prevent further printing of the novels Tropic of Cancer and Tropic of Capricorn by Henry Miller.

E426   "Il est interdit de crier: 'Franco au poteau'," France Dimanche, November 17, 1946, 1-2.
      Miller writes about freedom in his two Tropics.   (In French.)

E427   "L'Affaire Miller," L'Ordre, November 17-18, 1946.
      The interrogation of the editor of Tropic of Capricorn yielded the fact that Miller has written a fine book and should be allowed the freedom to sell it.   (In French.)

E428   "Autour de 'Tropique du Capricorne'," Le Figaro, November 17-18, 1946.
      Tropic of Capricorn has outraged the French public. (In French.)

E429   "L'Editeur de Miller devant le juge d'instruction," Le Paris Libéré, November 17-18, 1946.
      The French editor of Miller's Tropics went contrary to Court orders.   (In French.)

E430   "Un Editeur et un traducteur de Henry Miller chez le juge d'instruction," Combat, November 17-18, 1946.
      Mr. Bergougnon, a French editor, wishes to personally publish Tropic of Capricorn.   (In French.)

E431   "L'Editeur et le traducteur de Miller ont été interrogés," Le Populaire, November 17-18, 1946.
      The editor and the translator of Tropic of Capricorn were interrogated by the French Court in the Tropic trial.   (In French.)

E432   "Miller sera-t-il expurgé?" Libération, November 17-18, 1946.
      Miller is the man who is charged with attempting to undermine society.   (In French.)

E433   "Les Ouevres d'Henry Miller en jugement," La République Varoise, November 17-18, 1946.
      The editor of Capricorn feels the book has merit.   (In French.)

E434   "Les Romans d'Henri Miller provoquent des poursuites judiciaires," Sud-Est Cannes, November 17-18, 1946.
      Miller's books called pornography in Tropic trial.   (In French.)

E435   " 'Tropique du Capricorne' d'Henry Miller," Nice-Matin, November 17-18, 1946.
      Miller faces charges of producing and attempting to distribute pornography.   (In French.)

E436   "Des romans d'Henry Miller," Victoire, November 18, 1946.

Tropic called pornography. (In French.)

E437 "Des romans d'Henry Miller provoquent des poursuites judiciaires," La Presse Cherbourgeoise, November 18, 1946.
The translator of Tropic of Capricorn called it a work
of merit. (In French.)

E438 "Des romans d'Henry Miller provoquent des poursuites judiciaires," La République du Centre Orléans, November 18,
1946.
There is talk about publishing Capricorn in French.
(In French.)

E439 Gouin, Th. "Lettre de Paris," Le Nouvelle République,
November 18, 1946.
Miller's two Tropics considered to be a disease. (In
French.)

E440 "Les Livres d'Henry Miller provoquent des poursuites judiciaires," Le Progrès, November 18, 1946.
Miller charged with producing pornography. (In French.)

E441 "A propos d' 'Ambre'," La République du Centre, November
19, 1946.
Miller discourages people in their outlook on life. (In
French.)

E442 C., H. "Une Lettre doit savior que...," Midi Libre, November 19, 1946.
Society fails to understand Miller's obscenity and his
purpose. (In French.)

E443 Dheur, Gabriel. "Pornographes et moralistes," Le Con-
nerie, November 19, 1946.
Miller criticized for his inability to use intellectual hy-
giene in his language. (In French.)

E444 Girodias, M. "The Case of Henry Miller," Herald Tribune
(Paris), LIX (November 19, 1946), 2.
The importance of the Miller trial is that it concerns
the future recognition of Miller's writing.

E445 Loiselet, Pierre. "Littérature immonde," Liberte, November 19, 1946.
Miller viewed as a scandalous, egotistical man who
will write anything to offend. (In French.)

E446 M., G. "Faut-il brûler Miller?" Le Havre Libre, No-
vember 19, 1946.
The question still remains, is Tropic pornography?
(In French.)

E447 Nemo. "L'Ultime atome," La Tribune de Saône & Loire,

November 19, 1946.
Miller's work shows brutality and scandal.   (In French.)

E448   "Les Poursuites contre les oeuvres d'Henry Miller," Le
Monde, November 19, 1946.
Miller editors charged with immoral behavior.   (In
French.)

E449   "Une Troisième Plainte," Paris-Presse, November 19, 1946.
Miller charged with outraging the French public.   (In
French.)

E450   "Les Conferences du Circle laïque," L'Echo Républicain,
November 20, 1946.
Miller touring France.   (In French.)

E451   Feller, Jean.   "De Baudelaire à Miller," Le Populaire du
Centre, November 20, 1946.
The literary freedom that Baudelaire gained should also
be granted to Miller.   (In French.)

E452   "Miller's 'Black Spring' Facing Anti-Vice Suit," Herald
Tribune (Paris), LIX (November 20, 1946), 1.
Suit has been filed against Black Spring.

E453   "Une Nouvelle Plainte contre l'écrivain Miller," Le Monde,
November 20, 1946.
The outraged French populace wants justice in the
Miller trial.   (In French.)

E454   "Les Poursuites judiciaires contre deux romans d'Henry
Miller," Courrier Français du Sud-Ouest, November 20,
1946.
Miller charged with social and moral impropriety.   (In
French.)

E455   "Au fil de la plume...," Carrefour, November 21, 1946.
Maurice Nadeau sees the importance of Miller's writing.   (In French.)

E456   "Au pied de la lettre," Cavalcade, November 21, 1946.
Miller is called an outrage to society.   (In French.)

E457   Chadourne, Paul.   "Le Romancier américain MacCoy pose
cette question...," Quatre et Trois, November 21, 1946.
Miller a unique and original man who faces reality.
(In French.)

E458   "[Henry Miller]," Vooruit, November 21, 1946.
Miller compared to the Russian greats--Gogol, Gorki,
and Dostoevsky.   (In Dutch.)

E459   Marcenae, Jean.   "Comme un vent chargé de lavande...,"

La Marseillaise, November 21, 1946.
The Tropics carry the reader to bizarre places; his mind is forced to deal with issues usually ignored. (In French.)

E460   P., A.   "Paris Play Protest," Daily Mail, November 21, 1946.
The French are out to stop the publication of Miller's Tropic.

E461   Piechaud, Louis.   "Vers la 'réhabilitation'," L'Epoque, November 21, 1946.
Miller's work is his attempt to rehabilitate society. (In French.)

E462   "Réflexes et réflexions," Franc-Tireur, November 21, 1946.
Miller writes well.   (In French.)

E463   Rocher, Pierre.   "Le Capricorne," Nice-Matin, November 21, 1946.
Miller is being pressured by the Committee for Social and Moral Action to ban publication of Tropic of Capricorn.   (In French.)

E464   Sans, Julien.   "Le Temps de l'invective," Climats, November 21, 1946.
Miller accused of crimes against society.   (In French.)

E465   "La Schunanette," L'Etoile de Soir, November 21, 1946.
Miller contaminates justice through his writing. (In French.)

E466   "Details," Aux Ecoutes, November 22, 1946.
Miller outraged at being treated as a criminal.   (In French.)

E467   Fauchery, Pierre.   "Deux Apprentissages," Action, November 22, 1946.
Miller admired for his ability to accurately assess the world.   (In French.)

E468   Remond, Gilles.   "Tropiques," Le Tigre, November 22, 1946.
Miller pictured as the second atomic bomb, contaminating the world.   (In French.)

E469   "Carnet des lettres et des arts," La République, November 23, 1946.
The writings of Miller and Sartre are detestable.   (In French.)

E470   "Comment on écrit l'histoire," La Gazette des Lettres, November 23, 1946.

Miller sees the importance of history in his writing.
(In French.)

E471   "La Ligue contre le vice attaque 'Le Printemps noir' d'Henry Miller," Samedi-Soir, November 23, 1946.
The League Against Vice has indicted Tropic of Capricorn and Black Spring as pornography.   (In French.)

E472   "Pasteurisation de la littérature," Sachez Tout!, November 23, 1946.
Miller's Capricorn called a romantic novel.   (In French.)

E473   Schmidt, Albert-Marie.   "L'Esprit et les lettres," Reforme, November 23, 1946.
Miller's autobiographies are the scandalous and violent adventures of a pervert.   (In French.)

E474   Morel, Henriette.   "Les Hommes oubliés de Dieu," Résistance, November 26, 1946.
Albert Cossery has compared Miller to the great Russians--Gorki, Gogol, and Dostoevsky.   (In French.)

E475   "Ecoutez sur la Chaîne nationale," Paris-Loisirs, November 27-December 3, 1946.
Parker takes action against Miller's obscenity.   (In French.)

E476   Aldebert, Max.   "Les Revues," La Nef, December 1946, 148-149.
Difficult to say whether Miller is obscene or not.   (In French.)

E477   Armand, E.   "L'Affaire Miller," L'Unique, December 1946, 81-82.
To defend morality and religion, Miller is being persecuted.   (In French.)

E478   "Les Lettres et les tribunaux," Paru, December 1946.
Miller's editors are being sued.   (In French.)

E479   Santon, And.   "On acheve bien les chevaux...," Masses Neuilly, December 1946.
The capitalist civilization has produced romantic literature like the novels of Henry Miller.   (In French.)

E480   "Editorial," L'Argus des Industries du Livre, December 1, 1946.
Moral action against Miller and his books has angered his editors.   (In French.)

E481   "Fontaine," Avenir de Cannes et du Sud-Est, December 1-2, 1946.
"Obscenity and the Law of Reflection" discusses what freedom means to an American.   (In French.)

E482   "Sommaire," L'Ordre, December 1-2, 1946.
        Fontaine, No. 55 has printed Miller's "Obscenity and the
        Law of Reflection." (In French.)

E483   Delpech, Jeanine. "Enquête chez les lecteurs," Juin, De-
        cember 3, 1946.
        Cancer compared to the writings of Balzac. (In French.)

E484   "Horizon littéraire," Spectateur, December 3, 1946.
        Miller a socially conscious and moral man. (In French.)

E485   Houches, Jean de. "Tempêtes à venir," La Voix de l'Ouest
        Rennes, December 3, 1946.
        Miller viewed as a satirist. (In French.)

E486   "Pureté soviétique," Tel Quel, December 3, 1946.
        Miller's Tropics are rejected in the USSR because of
        their strong individualistic stance. (In French.)

E487   Bil. "Tropique du Cancer," Ici Paris, December 3-10,
        1946.
        Cartoon of a man operated on. What comes from with-
        in is a copy of Tropic of Cancer. (In French.)

E488   Achard, Paul. "Un Auteur dramatique critique...," La
        France Combat, December 5, 1946.
        Zola influenced the writing of Tropic of Capricorn. (In
        French.)

E489   "Arts et Lettres," Bulletin Hebdomadaire des Informations
        Culturelles, December 5, 1946.
        Wallace Fowlie sees Miller as a prophet and the suc-
        cessor to Rimbaud. (In French.)

E490   "Au Pied la lettre," Cavalcade, December 5, 1946.
        Miller both an historical and a poetic novelist. (In
        French.)

E491   Giron, Roger. "Regards sur la littérature américaine,"
        Paysage, December 5, 1946.
        Miller's romantic writing a success. (In French.)

E492   "Le March noir de la prophétie," Concorde, December 5,
        1946.
        Miller attempts to communicate through his literature.
        (In French.)

E493   Minne, Richard. "Offemsief van het Puritanisme," Vooruit,
        December 5, 1946.
        Puritan values may stop France from publishing Miller.
        (In Dutch.)

E494   Sans, Julien. "L'Affaire Miller," Cimes, December 5,
        1946.

Miller's writing follows the pattern of Celine.   (In French.)

E495   "Fontaine," Temps Présent, December 6, 1946.
Miller defended himself against the obscenity charges by reading from "Obscenity and the Law of Reflection." (In French.)

E496   Demee, Paul.   "Carte blanche," Radio-46, December 8, 1946.
Miller a great writer who gets beyond pornography. (In French.)

E497   Hofstra, J. W.   "Parijsche Kunst Brief," De Spectator, December 8, 1946.
The Tropic scandal is the biggest thing since Lady Chatterley.   (In Dutch.)

E498   Kemp, Robert.   "Va-t-on rétablir la censure?" La Bataille, December 11, 1946, 1-2.
The good Christians have chosen to censure the work of Miller, an excellent American writer who uses the romantic and the obscene to get his message across.   (In French.)

E499   "Une Enquête de 'Carrefour' sur l'art dirigé," Carrefour, December 12, 1946.
Respect the freedom of Miller and let him continue to write about freedom and humanism.   (In French.)

E500   Loewel, Pierre.   "Encore les obscènes," L'Ordre, December 12, 1946.
Miller called a prophet.   (In French.)

E501   Texeier, Jean.   "Le Militant perverti," Gavroche, December 12, 1946.
Miller depicts a troubled world of violence.   (In French.)

E502   "La Vie des lettres," Lettres Françaises, VI (December 13, 1946), 4.
Miller's "The Universe of Death" is an important essay on Lawrence.   (In French.)

E503   Floreuce, J.   "L'Ecrasé," Une Semaine dans le Monde, December 14, 1946.
Miller's art is disordered.   (In French.)

E504   Plisnier, Charles.   "Romans noirs et quelques autres," Aube, December 14, 1946.
Miller's feelings of discontent about his society were influenced by Zola, who felt the same way years before. (In French.)

E505   Sergent, Alain. "Exigeons un littérature rénovée," La République Moderne, December 15, 1946, 28.
Miller's editors have a law suit pending. (In French.)

E506   "Une Nouvelle 'Affaire Miller'," Paris-Presse, December 17, 1946.
In his Memoirs of Hecate County, Edmund Wilson calls Miller scandalous. (In French.)

E507   "Littérature," La Bataille, December 18, 1946.
Miller's Cancer is being sold under the counter in this cartoon. (In French.)

E508   "Les Revues," Courrier Français du Sud-Ouest, December 18, 1946.
Miller has written an article in defense of himself. (In French.)

E509   "Bonne publicité," Nouvelles Littéraires, December 19, 1946.
The question of obscenity occurs in Miller's writing. (In French.)

E510   Newton, Douglas. "A Note on Henry Miller," New English Weekly, XXX (December 19, 1946), 98-99.
Miller is viewed as a realist who accepts life, whether for "good" or "evil."

E511   "Pan!" Gavroche, December 19, 1946.
What is Miller trying to do in Tropic? (In French.)

E512   Soriano, Marc. "Encore Miller," Gavroche, December 19, 1946.
Tropic of Capricorn is viewed by critics as an existential novel about life. (In French.)

E513   Morellet. "L'Immoralité littéraire et la compétence judiciaire," Paroles Françaises, December 20, 1946.
Capricorn is a work about the geography of the self. (In French.)

E514   "Plus foit que Miller...," Alger Républicain, December 20, 1946.
Miller's Tropics express romance. (In French.)

E515   Daumiere, René. "Le Carrefour des anges," L'Etoile du Soir, December 24, 1946.
Miller's lyricism is suggested. (In French.)

E516   Kanters, Robert. "Le Cahier des lettres," Spectateur, December 24, 1946.
Miller a conspirator against society. (In French.)

E517   O.   "Dans 'Mehtoub'," Le Grelot, December 24, 1946.
       Miller is a fine writer deserving respect.   (In French.)

E518   "Littérature," Paroles Françaises, December 25, 1946.
       The two Tropics are expressions of life.   (In French.)

E519   McMullen, Roy.   "The Tropics of Henry Miller," Herald
       Tribune (Paris), LIX (December 25, 1946), 4.
       Miller's trial involves the issue of liberation.

E520   "Morale et candeur," Le Monde, December 25, 1946.
       Miller's literature has outraged moralists who are now
       suing him.   (In French.)

E521   Bernoville, Gaetan.   "Philosophie et football," L'Epoque,
       December 26, 1946.
       "Obscene"--that is the word used to describe Miller's
       two Tropics.   (In French.)

E522   Braibant, Charles.   "Lettres belles lettres," Le Populaire,
       December 26, 1946.
       Miller is a sociologist and a revolutionary.   (In French.)

E523   Malric, Albert.   "Allo ... Henry Miller!?" Concorde, De-
       cember 26, 1946.
       A cartoon of Miller having sex while receiving a call
       from another woman.   (In French.)

E524   "A qu'ils pensent de la marche des affaires," L'Aurore,
       December 27, 1946.
       Miller seen as having an affair with a Kathleen Wind-
       sor.   (In French.)

E525   Barkan, Raymond.   "M. Daniel Parker part pour la croi-
       sade," Lettres Françaises, VI (December 27, 1946), 8.
       Parker feels Miller is working to undermine morality
       and respect.   (In French.)

E526   "Les Livres reçus," Arts, December 27, 1946.
       Miller spoke about obscenity in fiction.   (In French.)

E527   D., A.   "Obscénité cinique," L'Humanité, December 28, 1946.
       Miller called obscene.   (In French.)

E528   "Danmark," Cahiers du Sud, December 28, 1946.
       Miller's writing has been called scandalous in Denmark.
       (In French.)

E529   "Un Démission à propos des poursuites contre les ouvrages
       de Henry Miller," Combat, December 28, 1946.
       The suit against the French translators of Henry Miller
       goes on.   (In French.)

E530   "Les Livres du jour," L'Ordre, December 28, 1946.
　　　　Suit against Miller's Capricorn continues.   (In French.)

E531   "M. Chastel démissionne de la Commission de censure," Le
　　　　Populaire, December 28, 1946.
　　　　　Guy Chastel will speak about immorality in the Tropics.
　　　　(In French.)

E532   "Voici les écrivains millionaires en revenus," Samedi-Soir,
　　　　December 28, 1946.
　　　　　Tropic called a study of individual life.   (In French.)

E533   Tessier, Carmen.   "Louis Jouvet veut monter la piece
　　　　d'un voleur que ose dire son nom: Jean Genét," France-
　　　　Soir, December 29, 1946.
　　　　　Miller's conception of life is impossible.   (In French.)

E534   "La Pensée," Le Patriote, December 30, 1946.
　　　　Poésie 46 contains an article of criticism on Miller.
　　　　(In French.)

E535   "Hollywood-Cancans," Cinémonde, December 31, 1946.
　　　　Mentioned is Miller's divorce from his first wife.   (In
　　　　French.)

E536   Narcejae, Thomas.   "Chroniques: Les Idées et les hommes,"
　　　　Horizons, No. 8, 1947, 51-58.
　　　　Miller is seen as a romantic.   (In French.)

E537   Dam, René.   "Faire jeux des cartes," L'Age Nouveau,
　　　　January 1947, 85-87.
　　　　Miller viewed as a two-sided person.   (In French.)

E538   L., G.   "Journal a plusieurs voix," Esprit, January 1947,
　　　　170.
　　　　　Miller's literature concerns the theme of morality.   (In
　　　　French.)

E539   "On s'étonne de lire," Paru, January 1947.
　　　　　An apology for misunderstanding Miller, an author con-
　　　　cerned with freedom.   (In French.)

E540   Riverain, Jean.   "Les Arts," Le Monde Français, January
　　　　1947, 157-160.
　　　　　Miller's Tropic faces comparison to French painting.
　　　　(In French.)

E541   "Thas," Le Goelan Parame, January 1947.
　　　　　Miller's sense of justice is seen in this look at his
　　　　work, "Obscenity and the Law of Reflection."   (In French.)

E542   "Littérature et épicerie," Vendre, January 1, 1947.
　　　　　Tropic an important book.   (In French.)

E543   Saint-Come. "Confusion, désordre, incohérence," Paroles
       Françaises, January 1, 1947.
              Miller viewed as an exhibitionist, for the protagonist of
       Tropic of Capricorn is considered to be Miller, not a
       fictional character. (In French.)

E544   Lancers, Pierre. "Le Seul juge," Paysage, January 2, 1947.
       The judge will play critic and actually decide the merits
       of Miller's Tropics. (In French.)

E545   Magot Solitaire, Le. "Sorel (Cécile)," Carrefour, January
       2, 1947.
              Miller's sense of language mentioned. (In French.)

E546   "A New York on se bat pour Maurice Chevalier," Le Phare
       Quotidien, January 2-3, 1947.
              A theatre in New York was named after Miller. (In
       French.)

E547   Derain, Lucie. "La Montée du puritanisme," Le Film
       Français, January 3, 1947.
              Parker and the others who base their stance on social
       propriety are suing Miller. (In French.)

E548   Desternes, Jean. "Que pensez-vous de la littérature
       américaine?" Combat, January 3, 1947.
              American literature dealing with the theme of the jour-
       ney goes from Cooper to Miller's Tropic of Capricorn.
       (In French.)

E549   F., P. "Sur le chantier des lettres," Action, January 3, 1947.
              Miller viewed as an author of literary merit. (In
       French.)

E550   Brisville, Jean-Claude. "Chronique des romans," La
       Gazette des Lettres, January 4, 1947.
              Miller is compared to the Russian authors, Gorki,
       Gogol, and Dostoevsky. (In French.)

E551   Collinet, Marcel. "Tropique et apprenti," Yacht, January
       4, 1947.
              Miller concerned with the issue of obscenity. (In French.)

E552   "On ne prête qu'aux riches," La Gazette des Lettres,
       January 4, 1947.
              The character Boris of Tropic of Cancer fame is men-
       tioned. (In French.)

E553   "Du côté des revues," La Croix, January 5, 1947.
              Miller's stance outrages society. (In French.)

E554   M., A. "Les Lettres," Sud-Ouest, January 6, 1947.
       The success of Miller's Tropic is noted. (In French.)

E555   Desternes, Jean.   "Que pensez-vous de la littérature
américaine?"   Combat, January 7, 1947.
   Strong ground for comparison exists in the literature of
   Miller and the work of Céline.   (In French.)

E556   S., N.   "Les Pardiesses de plume dous le roman de Colette
à Jules Romains," Ici Paris, January 7, 1947.
   Miller uses his pen to produce obscenity.   (In French.)

E557   "Flaubert interdit en Italie," La Dépêche de Paris, January
8, 1947.
   Miller mentioned in passing.   (In French.)

E558   Lefevre, Frederic.   "Vive la poésie!"   Libération-Soir,
January 8, 1947.
   Miller viewed as one of the few sincere and truly great
   writers.   (In French.)

E559   "Les Revues," Le Courrier de l'Etudiant, January 8, 1947.
   Miller compared to Joyce and Proust.   (In French.)

E560   d'Aubarede, Gabriel.   "Un Homme très simple, très en-
joué: Paul Valéry inconnu," Gavroche, January 9, 1947.
   Tropic of Cancer is Miller's statement about liberty.
   (In French.)

E561   Sans, Julien.   "Un Ecole d'Alger?"   Climats, January 9,
1947.
   It is absurd to compare Miller to the great Céline.   (In
   French.)

E562   "Dans le goût espagnol," Climats, January 9, 1947.
   Miller will soon be translated into Spanish.   (In
   French.)

E563   "Prokofiev et Chostakovitch," La Marseillaise Chateauroux,
January 9, 1947.
   Parker continues to try to block publication of Tropic
   of Capricorn.   (In French.)

E564   "La Vie littéraire en 1946," Quatre et Trois, January 9,
1947.
   Miller has outraged America.   (In French.)

E565   Mury, Gilbert.   "Décors et realité," Lettres Françaises,
January 10, 1947.
   A savagery exists in the writing of Henry Miller.   (In
   French.)

E566   T., H.   "J'Irai cracher sur vos tombes," Lettres Fran-
çaises, January 10, 1947.
   Miller's major concern is with the life-death struggle.
   (In French.)

E567   Flanner, Janet.   "Letter from Paris," New Yorker, XXII
(January 11, 1947), 58-63.
Tropic of Cancer is a fine book that has attained new
literary heights.   (In French.)

E568   "La Production industrielle et la fils d'un pasteur vant-ils
être poursuivis du fait d'Henry Miller," Samedi-Soir, January 11, 1947.
Miller's works are not understood by the critics who
damn him.   (In French.)

E569   "Que faut-il penser de l'affaire Miller?"   Courrier Fran-
çais du Sud-Ouest, January 11-12, 1947.
Miller's outrages come from his vividly displaying sex.
(In French.)

E570   "Les Idées," L'Indépendant, January 13, 1947.
Anger caused by the writing of Henry Miller.   (In
French.)

E571   Brenner, F.   "Quelques Livres récents," Normandie, January 14, 1947.
Miller is not in the same world as Gogol, Dostoevsky,
or Gorki.   (In French.)

E572   B., H.   "Les Livres," Le Nouvelle République, January 15,
1947.
Miller is an example of life in one's literature.   (In
French.)

E573   "Divertissements," Claudine, January 15, 1947.
Miller concerned with history.   (In French.)

E574   "A Paris et ailleurs," Nouvelles Littéraires, January 16,
1947, 4.
Miller's Tropic called a work of academic merit.   (In
French.)

E575   "Au fil de la plume...," Carrefour, January 16, 1947.
Announcement of the publication of Miller's Rosy Crucifixion.   (In French.)

E576   Daumiere, René.   "Biefaisant humour," L'Etoile du Soir,
January 16, 1947.
Discussion of Miller's humor.   (In French.)

E577   "Le Pudibond M. Parker attaque la presse," Point de Vue,
January 16, 1947.
Parker accused the press of conspiring with Miller's
editors.   (In French.)

E578   "Si M. Daniel Parker," Fantasia, January 16, 1947.
Parker does not want Miller's work translated into

French.   (In Italian.)

E579   "Au Sommaire, " Arts, January 17, 1947.
Miller's Rosy Crucifixion mentioned.   (In French.)

E580   "En Bref, " Combat, January 17, 1947.
Mentioned is Miller's trilogy, The Rosy Crucifixion.
(In French.)

E581   "Et le best-seller, " Aux Ecoutes, January 17, 1947.
Miller one of the best selling authors in France.   (In French.)

E582   Loewel, Pierre.   "De l'affaire Henry Miller à l'aventure
de Robert Desnos, " L'Ordre, January 18, 1947.
The principles of freedom and love provide the basis
for Miller's stance in his writing.   (In French.)

E583   "Un Comité de défense Henry Miller, " Le Littéraire, January 18, 1947.
A defense of Miller based on the need for and merits
of journalistic literature.   (In French.)

E584   Favarelli, Max.   "Maurice Garçon son épée d'académicien
tout neuve, " Paris-Presse, January 19-20, 1947.
Garçon defends Tropic of Capricorn in court, seeing it
as a realistic piece of literature.   (In French.)

E585   "Un Comité de défense Henry Miller, " Lyon Libre, January
21, 1947.
The Committee for the Defense of Henry Miller consists of critics believing in literary freedom.   (In French.)

E586   Beydts, Louis.   "Musique de ballets, " Opéra, January 22,
1947.
Capricorn deals with justice and reads like jazz.   (In French.)

E587   "[Le 'Cartel d'action sociale et morale'], " Bulletin Hebdomadaire des Informations Culturelles, January 22, 1947.
The Committee of Moral and Social Action Against
Miller has led to the formation of a counter party of
critics for Miller.   (In French.)

E588   Olavach, Gabriel.   "J. P. Sartre le respectueux, " La
Vache Enragée, January 22, 1947.
Sartre sees Miller as a true existentialist.   (In French.)

E589   Osorio, Paulo.   "De vieux visages de l'amour, " Echos de
France, January 22, 1947.
Miller's writing deals with humanity.   (In French.)

E590   "A tous vents," Concorde, January 23, 1947.
       Miller's writing shows a sense of responsibility to so-
       ciety.   (In French.)

E591   Delcourt, F.   "Jean-Pierre Dorian, écrivain altruiste,"
       Gavroche, January 23, 1947.
       Dorian has spoken on the topic of Henry Miller.   (In
       French.)

E592   Desternes, Jean.   "Que pensez-vous de la littérature amér-
       icaine?" Combat, January 23, 1947.
       Miller's literature of individualism is important.   (In
       French.)

E593   Dumeix, Auguste.   "Le Tropique du Capricorne," Nouvelles
       Littéraires, January 23, 1947.
       Miller's apocalypse is a delusion, for he preaches de-
       struction in a war of individual against individual.   (In
       French.)

E594   Gandon, Yves.   "Le Critique des livres," Cavalcade, Janu-
       ary 23, 1947.
       The battle between Miller and the censors goes on.   (In
       French.)

E595   Pierhal, Armand.   "La Religion de l'obscène," Nouvelles
       Littéraires, January 23, 1947.
       Miller viewed as the devil's disciple as he preaches the
       religion of obscenity.   (In French.)

E596   Brown, John L.   "The Gallic Literary Scene: A Report
       from Paris," New York Times, XCVI (January 24, 1947),
       19.
       Miller's Tropics are viewed as American classics in
       France.

E597   "Courrier des lettres," Arts, January 24, 1947.
       Miller defended in court by French critics Maurice Na-
       deau and Claude-Edmonde Magny.   (In French.)

E598   Derout, René.   "Etre conformiste on ne pas etre," Paris
       Casablanca, January 24, 1947.
       Miller wants the freedom to write as he pleases.   (In
       French.)

E599   "Miller et le bras sé culier," Combat, January 24, 1947.
       Miller critics see him as a saint.   (In French.)

E600   "Rethléem à Rome," Lettres Françaises, January 24, 1947.
       Miller viewed as a prophet in France.   (In French.)

E601   Rim, Carlo.   "Quand M. Virgule lit...," Lettres Fran-
       çaises, January 24, 1947.

A cartoon of Romains, Rimbaud, Miller, and Rabelais.
(In French.)

E602   T., H.   "Le Roman américain et le public français," Ouest-
France, January 24, 1947.
Noted is Miller's sense of humor.   (In French.)

E603   Desternes, Jean.   "Que pensez-vous de la littérature
américaine?"   Combat, January 28, 1947.
Miller has produced one of the best literary minds ever
to leave America and come to France.   (In French.)

E604   "Vous allez voir le film qui a bornes de la censure morale
d'Hollywood," Cinévie, January 28, 1947.
There is hope that a film about Miller's life based on
his two Tropics will soon appear.   (In French.)

E605   "L'Arche," Bulletin Hebdomadaire des Informations Cultu-
relles, January 29, 1947.
Passages from Miller's Rosy Crucifixion appear in
L'Arche, No. 21.   (In French.)

E606   Huron, Le.   "Franc-Parler," Franc-Tireur, January 30,
1947.
Those against Miller call him immoral.   (In French.)

E607   "M. Joseph Denais," Le Monde, January 30, 1947.
Denais wrote the police asking them to do something
about the obscene Tropic of Cancer.   (In French.)

E608   "Musardises," La France au Combat, January 30, 1947.
Miller seen as a saint by those who defended him.   (In
French.)

E609   R., A.   "J. P. Bunoz," Résistance, January 30, 1947.
Miller continues with his Tropic trilogy in a new three-
volume book called The Rosy Crucifixion.   (In French.)

E610   V., J.   "L'Arche," La France au Combat, January 30,
1947.
A fragment from Miller's Rosy Crucifixion is enough to
add to the fame of Miller.   (In French.)

E611   "Convocations," Temps Présent, January 31, 1947.
Miller's trial is discussed.   (In French.)

E612   "Fâcheuses nouvelles," Arts, January 31, 1947.
Miller's sense of creativity is viewed as different from
the French.   (In French.)

E613   L., J.   "Chronique théâtrale," Arts, January 31, 1947.
Miller interviewed on the subject of obscenity in art.
(In French.)

E614   "M. Joseph Denais," Bulletin Parlementaire d'Informations, January 31, 1947.
Denais addresses a letter to the chief of police concerning the publication of the novel, Tropic of Cancer. (In French.)

E615   Thibaut, Charles. "Tumultes sur la ville," Paroles Françaises, January 31, 1947.
Miller viewed as an important author. (In French.)

E616   Quéval, Jean. "Henry Miller," Poésie, January-February 1947, 110-114.
Discussion of the Miller trial. (In French.)

E617   Bailly, René. "Aperçus de littérature américaine," Paru, February 1947, 77-82.
Coindreau defends Miller and Tropic. (In French.)

E618   "Big Sur," Harper's Bazaar, LXXXI (February 1947), 221.
Miller left the Left Bank of Paris to settle in Big Sur.

E619   d'Astorg, Bertrand. "Les Faussaires de l'obscénité," Esprit, February 1947, 337-340.
Miller's suit is coming to an end and many feel that he will be convicted. (In French.)

E620   King, Robin. "Potted Miller," New Statesman and Nation, XXXIII (February 1, 1947), 100-101.
Reviews of Henry Miller's Murder the Murderer and Sunday After the War that call Miller's autobiographical style common and uninteresting.

E621   Lambert, Jean-Clarence. "Avec Albert Cossery," La Gazette des Lettres, February 1, 1947.
Encouragement goes to Henry Miller. (In French.)

E622   Rousseaux, André. "A propos de l'affaire Henry Miller," Le Littéraire, February 1, 1947.
The most important issue in the Miller trial concerns the right of the audience to decide for itself whether or not it wishes to read Miller's three novels. (In French.)

E623   Guimet, Michel. "Marcel Cerdan," L'Etoile du Soir, February 2-3, 1947, 1-3.
Miller is seen as the champion of good literature. (In French.)

E624   Lefebvre, Henri. "Henry Miller," Liberté-Soir, February 4, 1947.
Miller's erotic literature is viewed. (In French.)

E625   "La Boite aux lettres," Opéra, February 5, 1947.

Miller is defended by many major literary critics.   (In French.)

E626   Clement, Patrice.   "Miller vu par Henri Lefebvre,"
Liberté-Soir, February 5, 1947.
It is impossible to see Miller as a mystic as he lies in his excrement.   (In French.)

E627   Mares, Roland de.   "La Grande Pénitence," Matin Anvers, February 5, 1947.
Miller wants his freedom to express himself.   (In French.)

E628   Slocombe, George.   "Revue of New Books in Europe,"
Herald Tribune (Paris), LX (February 5, 1947), 5.
Miller is the superior of both Faulkner and Hemingway.

E629   "[L'Affaire Miller]," Nouvelles Littéraires, February 6, 1947.
The battle for literary freedom goes on.   (In French.)

E630   "Courrier des lettres," Journal d'Alsace, February 6, 1947.
The life and freedom that Miller brings to his literature is being questioned.   (In French.)

E631   "La Chronique d'Aragon," L'Humanité, February 7, 1947.
Miller a romantic.   (In French.)

E632   "De Notre," Action, February 7, 1947.
Miller's name mentioned along with three other authors appearing in Poésie 46.   (In French.)

E633   Desternes, Jean.   "Que pensez-vous de la littérature américaine?" Combat, February 7, 1947.
Miller called a poet and a visionary.   (In French.)

E634   Henry, Maurice.   "Chronique millérienne," Combat, February 7, 1947.
The question of whether it is moral to stop a man from enjoying his freedom to write is discussed in a cartoon and an article dealing with Miller's persecution.   (In French.)

E635   Potier, Jacques.   "Farreleique," L'Etoile du Soir, February 7, 1947.
Miller's sense of language compared to Karl Marx and Pablo Picasso.   (In French.)

E636   "Quelques Aspects du désespoir," Sud-Ouest, February 7, 1947.
Miller is viewed as an intellect.   (In French.)

E637   Virgula.   "Niort," La Nouvelle République, February 7,

1947.
Miller has sex appeal. (In French.)

E638 "Le Club du Faubourg à Deauville," Revue des Arts et
Créations, February 8, 1947.
A look into the reasons for and needs for obscenity in
the writings of Miller and Sartre. (In French.)

E639 "L'Editeur de 'J'irai cracher sur vos tombes' se défend
d'avoir publié un roman pornographique," Samedi-Soir,
February 8, 1947.
Social and moral action is being taken against Miller.
(In French.)

E640 "Françaises Hommes et monde," Bel Abes Journal, Febru-
ary 8, 1947.
The greatness of the two Tropics is proclaimed. (In
French.)

E641 Laplayne, Jean-René. "Defense d'Henry Miller," Avenir des
Cannes et du Sud-Est Cannes, February 8, 1947.
The Miller trial has led to much questioning of just
what constitutes literature. (In French.)

E642 "Vernon Sullivan," Le Monde Illustré, February 8, 1947.
Miller is one of the United States's major pornographers. (In French.)

E643 "L'Editeur de Miller est prêt à faire 2 ans de prison,"
France-Soir, February 9, 1947.
The publishers of Miller could get two years in prison.
(In French.)

E644 O., J. L. "Ce qui," Normandie, February 10, 1947.
Miller seen in the tradition of Kafka. (In French.)

E645 Piver, Victor. "Rosamond Lehmann à Paris," France Vi-
vante, February 10, 1947.
Miller called an important American writer and compared to Faulkner and Hemingway. (In French.)

E646 "D'un livre à l'autre," Courrier de l'Ouest, February 11,
1947.
Miller calls for a social and moral sense throughout
his writing. (In French.)

E647 "Horizon littéraire," Spectateur, February 11, 1947.
Miller's Max and the White Phagocytes is a work in the
tradition of Tropic. (In French.)

E648 "Le No. 21," L'Echo du Soir, February 11, 1947.
An article where Miller is compared to Faust. (In
French.)

E649   Ambiére, Francis. "Le Français dans le monde," La
       Bataille, February 12, 1947.
       "Hopelessness" is the best word used to describe
       Miller's brand of literature. (In French.)

E650   "La Boite aux lettres," Opéra, February 12, 1947.
       Review of Max and the White Phagocytes; calls it a
       book worth reading. (In French.)

E651   Laporte, René. "Le Sabbat," Opéra, February 12, 1947.
       It is the general feeling in Paris that Miller will lose
       the suit against him. (In French.)

E652   Quéval, J. "L'Affaire Miller," Le Libre Poitou, February
       12, 1947.
       Miller defends himself against the pornography charge
       by saying that he is in the tradition of such great au-
       thors as Rimbaud, Proust, and D. H. Lawrence. (In
       French.)

E653   "Discussion passionnée," Liberté-Soir, February 13, 1947.
       Miller a realist. (In French.)

E654   Procuste. "Fresque Sociales," La Nouveau Rhine Français,
       February 13, 1947.
       Miller has a brilliant sense of psychology and uses his
       gift to analyze the roots of being. (In French.)

E655   Fournier, Louis. "Nous, Daniel Parker, Maréchal de
       France, décidons...," Lettres Françaises, February 14,
       1947.
       Parker has no right to decide what the French will and
       won't read. (In French.)

E656   Homeau, Edmund. "Courrier des lettres," Arts, February
       14, 1947.
       Review of the suit against Miller. (In French.)

E657   "M. Joseph Denais," Bulletin Municipal Official, February
       14, 1947.
       Tropic of Capricorn called obscene. (In French.)

E658   "Au bout de la nuit," La Gazette des Lettres, February 15,
       1947.
       At a Céline Conference, an American professor com-
       pared the great French author to Henry Miller. (In
       French.)

E659   "Projects d'editeurs," La Gazette des Lettres, February 15,
       1947.
       Miller's Max and the White Phagocytes is considered to
       be an example of the literature of the future. (In
       French.)

E660   Pallu, Jean. "Connais-tu le pays...," La République du
       Centre, February 17, 1947.
              The heat of South America comes out in Capricorn.   (In
       French.)

E661   "Ambiance de la vie," Ambiance, February 19, 1947.
              An announcement that Miller has arrived on the literary
       scene.   (In French.)

E662   Ravel, Sirius. "Chez le boaquiniste," La République Va-
       roise, February 19, 1947.
              Miller and his Tropics are innocent, for neither con-
       tains obscenity.   (In French.)

E663   Slocombe, George.   "Reviews of New Books in Europe,"
       Herald Tribune (Paris), LX (February 19, 1947), 5.
              Miller explores the lower depths of Paris in Tropic of
       Cancer.

E664   C., R.   "Propos d'un huron," La Dépêche des Charentes,
       February 20, 1947.
              Miller viewed as a propaganda writer.   (In French.)

E665   "M. Parker part en guerre centre les mauvais livres,"
       Point de Vue, February 20, 1947.
              A thank-you note to Parker for battling Miller.   (In
       French.)

E666   "Onz Edelijke Lectuur," Vooruit, February 20, 1947.
              The Miller trial in Paris may make Miller taboo in the
       U.S., England, and France.   (In Dutch.)

E667   Ronquier, René.   "Fossoyeurs et bâtisseurs," Le Patriot
       du Sud-Ouest, February 20, 1947.
              Miller considered to be erotic and nihilistic.   (In
       French.)

E668   Aniate, Antonio.   "Pericolo di morte per due moralisti,"
       Gazette Sera, February 21, 1947.
              The trial comes down to Miller versus Parker and the
       people of France.   (In Italian.)

E669   "Littérature noire, grise et incolore," Point de Vue, Feb-
       ruary 21, 1947.
              Miller exists as both a pornographer and a great au-
       thor.   (In French.)

E670   "Henri Lefebvre parle de Miller," Le Patriot du Sud-Ouest,
       February 24, 1947.
              Miller contaminates with his erotic literature.   (In
       French.)

E671   Barkan, Raymond.   "Le Sadisme de la littérature américaine,"

Le Petit Marocain, February 25, 1947.
Miller's writing passionate, loaded with sex, obscenity,
and pornography.   (In French.)

E672   Caillet, Jeraro.   "Nous avons lu pour Jous," Opéra, February 26, 1947.
Miller's Max and the White Phagocytes is viewed as a
scandalous novel in the tradition of the Tropics.   (In
French.)

E673   Nicollier, Jean.   "Le Cas du romancier Henry Miller,"
Gazette de Lausanne, February 28, 1947.
The idea of liberty is fine, but the violent nonconform-
ist found in Miller's literature is a detriment to others.
(In French.)

E674   "Osera-t-on condamner Miller?"   Masses, February-March
1947.
Miller is a moral man who writes honest literature.
(In French.)

E675   "The Miller Case," Now, VII (February-March 1947 or
1948), 5-6.
Miller's books have been banned in the U.S., England,
and France because he is a dynamic social critic who
uses obscenity as his means for making people conscious of themselves and their corrupt world.

E676   Rexroth, Kenneth.   "Letter from America," Now, VII
(February-March 1947 or 1948), 59-65.
Miller called a social critic who denounces "an unbe-
lievably shameless and shameful society" (p. 64).

E677   "L'Affaire Miller et la liberté de l'édition," L'Argus des
Industries du Livre, March 1947.
Miller's publisher has been brought to trial.   (In
French.)

E678   Kemp, Robert.   "Pièces au procès," Denoël Courrier,
March 1947, 1.
The censoring of Miller's work is called absurd.   (In
French.)

E679   Lefèvre, Frédéric.   "Pièces au procès," Denoël Courrier,
March 1947, 1.
Miller called a great psychological writer of prose
poetry.   (In French.)

E680   "Les Lettres et les tribunaux," Paru, March 1947.
The Miller trial will decide what the freedom to write
actually means.   (In French.)

E681   Pernau, Alexis.   "Point de vue d'un trouble-fête sur

l'affaire,'' L'Age d'or, March 1947, 94-96.
Miller's Capricorn is called scandalous because of the
language Miller uses.   (In French.)

E682/3   ''Pièces au procès,'' Denoël Courrier, March 1947, 1, 4.
Stands for and against Miller are restated by various
critics, all coming from articles previously published.
(In French.)

E684   Rousseaux, Andre.   "Pièces au procès," Denoël Courrier,
March 1947, 1.
A defense of Miller that considers him a social human
being.   (In French.)

E685   Maulnier, Thierry.   "Les Lettres l'apprenti," Concorde,
March 1, 1947.
Miller is the producer of erotic literature.   (In French.)

E686   Granzotto, Gianni.   "Più scandaloso di Lady Chatterley,"
Il Europeo, March 2, 1947.
Miller's publishers face charges of immorality.   (In
Italian.)

E687   Berys, Jose De.   "L'Apprenti," Midi-Soir, March 3, 1947.
Tropic fights a battle against Puritan values.   (In
French.)

E688   "Un Roman bon, peut-il être un bon roman?" Dernière
Heure, March 3, 1947.
Miller is concerned with law and justice like Koestler.
(In French.)

E689   "La Littérature et le bûcher," Normandie, March 4, 1947.
Tropic of Cancer places Miller in the tradition of Flaubert and Kafka.   (In French.)

E690   '[Henry Miller]," Courrier Français du Sud-Ouest, March 5,
1947.
Miller compared to Gogol.   (In French.)

E691   Gaillard, Albert.   "Bien écrire," Havre-Eclair, March 6,
1947.
Miller is a talented writer who depicts real life.   (In
French.)

E692   "Verdediging van Henry Miller," Vooruit, March 6, 1947.
The Committee for Moral and Social Action Against
Henry Miller was formed.   (In Dutch.)

E693   Mannycci, Loris.   "Due libri proibiti," Mattino d'Italia,
March 9, 1947.
The French scandal of the Miller case, and what con-
stitutes the freedom to read, continues.   (In Italian.)

E694　"Culture et vie," La Voix de l'Ouest, March 10, 1947.
　　　The debate for and against Miller goes on, with psychol-
　　　ogists taking the stand.　(In French.)

E695　"L'Affaire Miller," Tel Quel, March 11, 1947.
　　　Is Miller's work poison?　(In French.)

E696　Bouvier, Emile.　"Blaise Cendrars," Midi Libre, March
　　　11, 1947.
　　　Sincere, sentimental, and brutal are the three best
　　　words to describe Miller's writing.　(In French.)

E697　Kanters, Robert.　"Amour & littérature," Spectateur,
　　　March 11, 1947.
　　　Miller's literature is based on love.　(In French.)

E698　"Un Lettre doit savoir que...," Midi Libre, March 11,
　　　1947.
　　　Parker battles against Miller's first three novels, call-
　　　ing them immoral.　(In French.)

E699　M., J. L.　"[C'est François Mauriac]," Courrier de l'Ouest,
　　　March 11, 1947.
　　　Miller's Tropics are pornography.　(In French.)

E700　"Les Revues," Le Populaire du Centre, March 12, 1947.
　　　Miller found in Poésie 47, No. 37.　(In French.)

E701　Bercher, M. L.　"Pour ou contre le roman américain?"
　　　L'Ailsace, March 13, 1947.
　　　The concept of freedom appears in Miller's Tropics.
　　　(In French.)

E702　Rops, Daniel.　"L'Affaire Miller," La Nouvelle République,
　　　March 14, 1947.
　　　Rops feels that there is no need for limiting Miller.
　　　(In French.)

E703　Da, J.　"L'Espoir d'une grève," L'Action Vétérinaire,
　　　March 15, 1947.
　　　Miller's novels are in the Western European tradition.
　　　(In French.)

E704　"Livres, couronnes et tapis vert," Le Littéraire, March 15,
　　　1947.
　　　Parker's malice is as harmful as Miller's literary poi-
　　　son.　(In French.)

E705　Gallet, G. H.　"Attentat aux moeurs," V, March 16, 1947.
　　　The motif of life exists in all of Miller's work from
　　　Tropic to Max.　(In French.)

E706　Beauvais, Robert.　"Clandestinité flamboyante," A Matin,

March 18, 1947.
Miller's verbal wildness is controlled by style and grace. (In French.)

E707   Gautier, Jean-Jacques. "La Route au tabac," Le Figaro, March 18, 1947.
A sense of life and its disorder pervades Miller's literature. (In French.)

E708   "Max et les Phagocytes," Spectateur, March 18, 1947.
Max and the White Phagocytes has explosive violence. (In French.)

E709   "A la devanture du libraire," Le Figaro, March 19, 1947.
Miller's Max and the White Phagocytes is an important book. (In French.)

E710   "Les Revues," Le Courrier de l'Etudiant, March 19, 1947.
Miller's name mentioned in passing. (In French.)

E711   Anodin, Jules. "Les Feux du laupiste," La France au Combat, March 20, 1947.
Miller is an honorable man. (In French.)

E712   Cossery, Albert. "Les Hommes oubliés de Dieu," La France au Combat, March 20, 1947.
Miller is a man of dignity and romance. (In French.)

E713   Ondine. "Ridicoculisons!" Le Grelot, March 20, 1947.
Miller is a part of traditional literature. (In French.)

E714   "André Gide et Jean Cassou," Combat, March 21, 1947.
Both critics and writers have defended Miller as a novelist of merit. (In French.)

E715   Causton, Bernard. "In Paris Again," (London) Tribune, March 21, 1947, 700.
The Cartel of Moral and Social Action has sought to prosecute the publishers of the French translations of Miller's Tropics which they feel are contrary to good moral behavior.

E716   Nadeau, Maurice. "Du plaisant au sévère," Combat, March 21, 1947.
Miller and Lawrence are from the same school. (In French.)

E717   "Sur la planche," Combat, March 21, 1947.
Miller's Max and the White Phagocytes is a treatise on life. (In French.)

E718   "La Prison guette quatre éditeurs accusés d'attentat à la pudeur," Samedi-Soir, March 22, 1947.

Interpreting Miller depends upon who is reading Miller.
(In French.)

E719   "Le 'Cartel' contre Miller," Combat, March 23-24, 1947.
It is not what Miller or Parker wants, but what society
wishes, that will determine the outcome of the Tropic
trial.   (In French.)

E720   F., C. de.   "Les Loisirs du jour," Le Populaire, March
23-24, 1947.
Miller's work is called surrealistic and epic poetry.
(In French.)

E721   "André Gide adhére au 'Comité de defense de Henry Miller',"
Lyon Libre, March 25, 1947.
Gide supports Miller and the people who feel that Tropic
is a valuable novel.   (In French.)

E722   "M. Gérard Bauer est élu président de la Société des gens
de lettres," Combat, March 25, 1947.
Bauer wants to take social action against Miller on the
grounds of immorality.   (In French.)

E723   "Le Sublime à l'assommoir," Les Cahiers Médicaux Fran-
çais, March-April 1947, 11-13.
Miller is compared to the naturalists, Baudelaire and
Zola.   (In French.)

E724   Brady, Mildred Edy.   "The New Cult of Sex and Anarchy,"
Harper's, CXCIV (April 1947), 312-322.
Miller and other residents of Big Sur wrongly accused
of being members of sex cult based on the teachings of
Emma Goldman.

E725   "Courrier littéraire," La Réforme, April 1947.
The Miller trial is mentioned.   (In French.)

E726   "A propos des oeuvres d'Henri Miller," Gazette Médicale
de France, April 1, 1947.
It is outrageous to keep up the suit against Miller.   (In
French.)

E727   Roubaud, André.   "Les Valets de la liberté," Spectateur,
April 2, 1947.
Freedom of expression is important yet not when used
to insult people, like in Miller's Tropic.   (In French.)

E728   Rabaud, Jean.   "La Querelle de l'obscénité," Le Populaire,
April 4, 1947.
Miller's writing has a rich lyricism.   (In French.)

E729   Huron, Le.   "Franc-parler," Franc-Tireur, April 8, 1947.
The Tropic trial comes down to the question of Miller's

right to write.   (In French.)

E730   "Art," Time, XLIX (April 14, 1947), 53.
Miller's watercolors are called heavenly with their
images of female sexuality.

E731   "Landscapes into Fish," Time, XLIX (April 14, 1947), 53.
Review of Miller's art on exhibit in Monterey, Calif.:
"Miller's own watercolors are full of garbled doors,
heavenly bodies, female sex symbols, eyes, and echoes
of Paul Klee and Abraham Rattner" (p. 53).

E732   Antenaires, Les.   "L'Affaire Miller et les gens de lettres,"
Gazette de Lausanne, April 15, 1947.
The Society of Arts and Letters discusses the Miller
trial.   (In French.)

E733   Bottemer, A.   "Pariser Bilderlogen," Le Républicain du
Haut-Rhin, April 15, 1947.
The suit against Miller goes on in Paris.   (In German.)

E734   P., C.   "Romanzieri: Vergogna!" Milano Sera, April 16,
1947.
Ten years after printing Cancer, Miller faces suit in
France.   (In Italian.)

E735   "[La Société des gens de lettres]," L'Essor du Centre Ouest,
April 17, 1947.
Defense of Miller.   (In French.)

E736   "Masques et bergamasques," Combat, April 18, 1947.
Article and cartoon describing Miller's desire for freedom and the fact that he is a rude, angry man who does
not allow others their rights.   (In French.)

E737   Lania, Leo.   "Europe's Battered Muse," Saturday Review,
XXX (April 19, 1947), 9-10.
Miller's popularity has spread to France where Cancer
is being read in French.

E738   "Le Point de vue de reforme," La Réforme, April 19, 1947.
Miller's liberty means the acceptance of pornographic
standards in literature.   (In French.)

E739   Gros-Jean.   "L'Affaire Miller," La Vie Catholique Illustrée,
April 20, 1947.
Miller called an explosive pornographer.   (In French.)

E740   Hoog, Armand.   "Pour en finir avec l'affaire Miller,"
Carrefour, April 23, 1947.
Miller involved in a pornography case in court.   (In
French.)

E741   Hermite, Maurice.   "Cette Semaine...," Aux Ecoutes,
        April 25, 1947, 9.
            Tropic a book about the freedom of the individual.   (In
            French.)

E742   "Pitié pour les jeunes filles!" Combat, April 25, 1947.
            Miller's danger found in his pornography.   (In French.)

E743   Beguin, Albert.   "Jous le masque de l'atheisme," Une
        Semaine dans le Monde, April 26, 1947.
            Miller's writing contains revelations that could be ap-
            plied to our sense of history.   (In French.)

E744   Roubaud, Andre.   "Les Valets de la liberté," Spectateur,
        April 29, 1947.
            Freedom of expression--yes; Miller's pornography--no.
            (In French.)

E745   "The Mystic Cult of Sex and Necromany," California Peli-
        can, May 1947, 18-19.

E746   "Les Revues," Europe, May 1947, 127-129.
            Miller's "Universe of Death" is a unique addition to
            Lawrence scholarship.   (In French.)

E747   "Un Gentil Assassin," Nord-Soir, May 1, 1947.
            Miller must have a good publicity agent to make him
            seem so mean.   (In French.)

E748   "Plumes au vent," Gavroche, May 1, 1947.
            A committee for the defense of Henry Miller has been
            created.   (In French.)

E749   Humeau, Edmond.   "Courrier des lettres," Arts, May 2,
        1947.
            The merits of Miller are being questioned in Italy as
            well as in France.   (In French.)

E750   Sauvage, Leo.   "Miller ou Parker?" Le Populaire, May 2,
        1947.
            The arguments for both sides of the Tropic trial are
            presented.   (In French.)

E751   Sinclair, Georges.   "L'Affaire Miller," Nord-Soir, May 2-
        3, 1947.
            The court case concerning Miller's freedom of expres-
            sion goes on with Miller attempting to defend his hu-
            man rights.   (In French.)

E752   Gardien, Jacques.   "Le Dernier Scandale," Le Patriote du
        Morvan, May 3, 1947.
            Miller is called the pornographic American.   (In French.)

E753   Interim.   "En deçà du lyrisme," Concorde, May 3, 1947.
The revolutionary ideal of a new morality can be seen
in Miller's writing.   (In French.)

E754   Mosher, Clint.   "Group Establishes Cult of Hatred in Carmel Mountains," San Francisco Examiner, CLXXXVI (May
3[4?], 1947), 1, 3.
Miller is the leader of a fugitive group living in the
mountains of Big Sur that is anti-society.

E755/6   Schmidt, Albert-Marie.   "Adresse au lecteur silencieux,"
La Réforme, May 3, 1947.
Tropic of Capricorn is a spiritual expression of Miller.
(In French.)

E757   "A bon entendeur," La Seine, May 5, 1947.
Miller's writing is outrageous.   (In French.)

E758   Jaco.   "Faut-il brûler Delly?"   Le Bulletin des Lettres,
May 5, 1947.
Miller viewed as an author whose work is in the Orien-
tal tradition.   (In French.)

E759   Mosher, Clint.   "Emma Goldman Inspired Carmel Hate Cult
Chief," San Francisco Examiner, CLXXXVI (May 5, 1947),
5.
Miller credits Goldman with providing him with the
most important encounter of his life.

E760   Beauvais, Robert.   "En pleine spiritualité," Ce Matin, May
6, 1947.
Miller has a great sense of imagination.   (In French.)

E761   Mosher, Clint.   " 'Colony of Hate' Barker an Important
Figure," San Francisco Examiner, CLXXXVI (May 6, 1947),
4.

E762   Mosher, Clint.   "Carmel Shuts Its Doors to Miller Cult,"
San Francisco Examiner, CLXXXVI (May 7, 1947), 3.
The people of Carmel do not want Miller to violently
intrude into their world.

E763   Chrysale, Jr.   "Contremarque," Spectateur, May 20, 1947.
Miller is an erotic writer.   (In French.)

E764   Gannett, Lewis.   "Books and Things," Herald Tribune
(Paris), LX (May 21, 1947), 5.
Miller is viewed as an author with a philosophy of uni-
versal filth in this review of Samuel Putnam's Paris
Was Our Mistress.

E765   Traz, Robert de.   "Trois Recettes," Journal de Génève,
May 21, 1947.

Miller is viewed as an outrageous pornographer.   (In French.)

E766   Ran-Fan-Flan.   "Le Tambour de Ville," Gavroche, May 22, 1947.
Miller a success.   (In French.)

E767   "Aux écoutes," Aux Ecoutes, May 23, 1947.
Comparison of Miller and Sartre.   (In French.)

E768   Laroche, Pierre.   "Un 'Boum'," Le Pays, May 23, 1947.
Miller's writing has the effect of a bomb upon society.
(In French.)

E769   Moulin, Charles.   "Les Impressionnistes sont aussi des peintres," Tribune des Nations, May 23, 1947.
Miller a dynamic writing force.   (In French.)

E770   "On dit...," Dernière Heures Marseille, May 26, 1947.
French Academy of Literature presented an award to Miller for his brilliant portrayal of reality.   (In French.)

E771   "Au fil de la plume," Carrefour, May 28, 1947.
Angry correspondence and confrontation between Miller and Parker.   (In French.)

E772   Exbrayat, Charles.   "Quelle Liberté?" Journal du Centre Nevers, May 28, 1947.
Miller not a pornographer.   (In French.)

E773   Verdot, Guy.   "Surplus Americains," Liberté-Soir, May 28, 1947.
Miller's literature called "bubble-gum."   (In French.)

E774   Lehmann, Rene.   "La Pornographie que n'ose pas dire son nom," L'Intransigeant, May 29, 1947.
Miller a pornographer and traitor to society.   (In French.)

E775   D., P. M.   "Du nouveau sur Miller," Aux Ecoutes, May 30, 1947.
Fraenkel defends Tropic in Défense du Tropique du Cancer.   (In French.)

E776   "Edition," Le Monde, May 30, 1947.
Miller's writing humane and full of love.   (In French.)

E777   F., J.   "Témoines de la pureté," La France Catholique, May 30, 1947.
Miller and his writings are rejected.   (In French.)

E778   Macaigne, Pierre.   "Une Partie de campagne avec les amis des lettres," Figaro Littéraire, May 31, 1947.

Miller a member of the Friends of Letters.   (In French.)

E779   Aldridge, John W.   "Note," Occident, Spring 1947, 3.
Defense of Miller and the freedom found at the artist
colony in Big Sur, Calif.

E780   "[Miller]," L'Unique Orléans, June 1947.
Miller brought to justice for outraging society.   (In
French.)

E781   "Little Reviews Anthology," Mercure de France, June 1,
1947.
Miller's work appears in the Little Reviews Anthology.
(In French.)

E782   "Petit Courrier," Reflets de la Semaine, June 1, 1947.
Miller's work angers Parker.   (In French.)

E783   "Les Treize," L'Intransigeant, June 1, 1947.
Fraenkel's Défense du 'Tropic du Cancer' shows Miller's
merits.   (In French.)

E784   Le Floriste.   "Les Psychistes à l'assaut: De Saint-Ger-
main-des-Pres," Le Populaire, June 21, 1947.
Miller psychologically assaults society.   (In French.)

E785   "Tout Paris le dit...," Les Idées et les Lettres, June 21,
1947, 11.
The Miller trial is over, and Miller is free.   (In
French.)

E786   "L'Eventail," Gazette de Lausanne, June 27, 1947.
Miller compared to Sartre.   (In French.)

E787   Audouard, Jean.   "Les Liqueurs fortes...," Le Soir, June
28, 1947.
Miller's writing brutal, filled with cynicism and the
macabre.   (In French.)

E788   "Chez les éditeurs," De Word, June 28, 1947.
Miller and Kafka have advanced the literature of the
grotesque.   (In French.)

E789   Dussane.   "L'Interprétation de la tragédie," La Revue
Théâtre, June-July-August 1947, 270-277.
Miller and Sartre both in the tragic tradition.   (In
French.)

E790   L., G.   "Seigneur, préservez-moi de mes amis," Esprit,
July 1947.
Miller a noble person concerned with making a better
world.   (In French.)

E791   Las Vergnas, Raymond. "Lettres étrangères," La Revue Hommes et Mondes, July 1947, 509-513.
       Miller and Willa Cather extreme opposites in American writing. (In French.)

E792   "A propos de l'affaire Miller...," Gazette de Lausanne, July 1, 1947.
       Miller needs his freedom to produce art. (In French.)

E793   "Livres audacieux," Spectateur, July 1, 1947.
       Review of Tropic of Capricorn. (In French.)

E794   "Contre l'existentialisme R. Sébille lance l'intimitisme...," Ce Matin, July 4, 1947.
       Miller viewed as an existentialist. (In French.)

E795   Merlin, J. "L'Exposition surréaliste a réussi à me faire dormir alors que Duchamp avait échoué," L'Intransigeant, July 4, 1947.
       Miller one of the famous celebrities at the Conference of Surrealists. (In French.)

E796   "Pour que le procès Miller ait lieu son éditeur attaque," Samedi-Soir, July 5, 1947.
       Social and moral action continues against Miller. (In French.)

E797   "l'Obscène," Oran Républicain, July 16, 1947.
       Tropic seen as an American romance. (In French.)

E798   "A Paris dans l'intimité de quatre représentants de l'Union française," Cavalcade, July 17, 1947.
       Tropic a revolutionary novel. (In French.)

E799   Bedrossian, G. "From the Mailbag: Traduit de l'Améri-cain," International Herald Tribune (Paris), LX (July 20, 1947), 4.
       Miller's Capricorn a new type of language.

E800   Maury, Jean. "Dialogue en enfer," Combat, July 29, 1947.
       Miller's works enter French libraries for first time. (In French.)

E801   "Au fil de la plume," Carrefour, July 30, 1947.
       Edmund Wilson emulates Miller and praises Capricorn. (In French.)

E802   Bessaignet, Jacques. "Instinctivement," Opéra, July 30, 1947.
       Neither Miller or Céline are concerned with material-ism. (In French.)

E803   Lelong, M. H. "Une Première de Mauriac au Brésil,"

La Bataille, July 30, 1947.
  Tribute to Miller's control of language.   (In French.)

E804   Sans, Julien.   "Confessions et scandales," Climats, July
       30, 1947.
       To some, Miller's writing is a confessional.   (In
       French.)

E805   Roy, C.   "Panorama des livres: l'art du contre et la
       poésie," Europe, August 1947.
       Miller's Air-Conditioned Nightmare an autobiographical
       confession.   (In French.)

E806   Fauchery, Pierre.   "Littérature cynique," Action, August
       1, 1947.
       Miller's literature for adults, for it is the language of
       the cynic.   (In French.)

E807   Fournier, Louis.   "Un Marché noir qui demande de la
       culture: l'écumage des livres," Libération, August 1, 1947.
       Cancer is Miller's attempt to transform society.
       (In French.)

E808   Guiselys.   "Isme et Cie: La Tour de Babel des jargons
       littéraires," Ici France, August 1, 1947.
       Miller's language is jargon.   (In French.)

E809   "L'Injuste oubli," Paroles Françaises, August 1, 1947.
       On the anniversary of the death of René Bozin, Miller
       dedicated a piece to the French author.   (In French.)

E810   "L'Amour au soleil," L'Est Républicain, August 4, 1947.
       Miller's work contains both love and humanism.   (In
       French.)

E811   "Au Club du Faubourg," Tel Quel, August 5, 1947.
       Miller's literature called obscene.   (In French.)

E812   "Edmund Wilson--Henry Miller," Le Havre Libre, August
       5, 1947.
       Wilson emulates Miller for Capricorn.   (In French.)

E813   Roger-Marx, Claude.   "Bilan du surréalisme en peinture,"
       Spectateur, August 5, 1947.
       Miller's art compared to the Dutch painter, Bosch.
       (In French.)

E814   Secretain, Roger.   "La Littérature américaine," La Ré-
       publique du Centre, August 5, 1947.
       Miller one of the greats of American literature.   (In
       French.)

E815   "Au 'Club du Faubourg'," Opéra, August 7, 1947.

Miller found obscene.   (In French.)

E816   "Divers, " Tribune de Nations, August 8, 1947.
Obscenity suit against Miller continues.   (In French.)

E817   "On a remarqué, " Action, August 8, 1947.
Miller a man of protest.   (In French.)

E818   "Les Arrêts du Conseil des dix, " Figaro Littéraire,
August 9, 1947.
M. Nadeau, the Miller supporter, found morally sus-
pect.   (In French.)

E819   "La Competition Annuelle, " La Gazette des Lettres, August
9, 1947.
Miller's writing obscene.   (In French.)

E820   "Eclipse ou déclin?" Paroles Françaises, August 9, 1947.
Miller's truths are suspect.   (In French.)

E821   J. , C.   "Parmi les livres caïs, " Spectateur, August 9, 1947.
Miller writing about liberty.   (In French.)

E822   "Mme. Dépraux n'aime pas Henry Miller, " Samedi-Soir,
August 9, 1947.
Miller's literature has life and vitality.   (In French.)

E823   Les Sept.   "Histoire d'un livre, " La Gazette des Lettres,
August 9, 1947.
Miller compared to Kafka.   (In French.)

E824   "Une Opinion, " La Seine, August 11, 1947.
Miller's sincerity compared to Céline and Sartre.   (In
French.)

E825   Bernoville, Gaëtan.   "Notre littérature à vau-l'eau, "
L'Epoque, August 12, 1947.
Miller's writing controversial.   (In French.)

E826   Cajumi, Arrigo.   "Fragoletta, " Stampa, August 12, 1947.
Tropic scandalous.   (In Italian.)

E827   Hebrèard, Maurice.   "Emoi chez les 'existentialistes', "
Halls Spectacles, August 14, 1947.
Miller existential like Sartre.   (In French.)

E828   Combette, Dominique.   "Les Mamelles de Tirésias, " Le
Courrier des Arts et des Lettres, August 15, 1947.
Tropic's fantasy theme is of divine liberty.   (In French.)

E829   "Léo Poldès, Georges Delamare et le Club du Faubourg au
Casino de Deauville, " Ouest-France, August 16, 1947.
Miller an existentialist.   (In French.)

E830   Smith, Harrison. "The New Coast of Bohemia," Saturday Review, XXX (August 16, 1947).
        Miller seen as a leader in the new Bohemian movement.

E831   Sypher, Wylie. "Art as Experiment," Nation, CLXV (August 16, 1947), 188-189.
        Review of James Laughlin's New Directions 9 that explores Miller's idea of revolt.

E832   Dorian, Jean-Pierre. "Petite Suite," La Bataille, August 20, 1947.
        Miller's literary verse compared to Mozart's scores. (In French.)

E833   "Panne de Liberté," Paroles Françaises, August 22, 1947.
        Miller writes the literature of independence. (In French.)

E834   Etienne, Paul. "J'ai passé la nuit," Le Patriote de Nice et du Sud Est, August 24, 1947.
        Miller's Tropics, like the Bikini, leave little to the imagination. (In French.)

E835   "L'Ex-fonctionnaire soviétique Kravchenko bat Henry Miller au finish," Point de Vue, August 28, 1947.
        The Soviet, Kravchenko, feels that Miller's Capricorn is a plague to writing. (In French.)

E836   Chennault, Guy. "La Monde à New-York," Regards, August 29, 1947, 7-9.
        Miller discusses New York. (In French.)

E837   Billy, André. "Propos du Samedi," Figaro Littéraire, August 30, 1947.
        Louis de Robert's library has Miller's works. (In French.)

E838   "La Russie en paye plus... : De nombreuses faillités en perspectieve...," Concorde, August 30, 1947.
        Miller a contaminator of morals. (In French.)

E839   "Les U.S.A.," Midi, August 31, 1947.
        Miller's literature obscene in America, yet he's as American as Barnum. (In French.)

E840   Russell, Sanders. "The Golden Heresy," Contour Quarterly, II (September 1947), 26-30.
        Miller's anti-art stand is a radical move which allows one to live, explore, and feel life.

E841   Chivat, Paul. "À la recherche du cinéma perdu," Les Temps Modernes, October 1947.
        Miller's name mentioned. (In French.)

E842   Moore, Nicholas. "Henry Miller," Der Bogen, X (October

1947), 5-9.
Miller's writing compared to Joyce.   (In German.)

E843   Pierhal, Armand.   "Die Religion des Obszöner Bemerkun-
gen zu Henry Miller," Der Bogen, X (October 1947), 9-10.
Miller a religious writer concerned with God and heaven.
(In German.)

E844   Ricard, Hugues.   "Du maillot de bain," Afrique Magazine,
October 7, 1947.
Tropics are outside the realm of society.   (In French.)

E845   "Un Roman 'Prends-moi matelot' divise l'Australie en deux
camps," Samedi-Soir, October 11, 1947.
Miller and Lawrence are tranquil men of genius.   (In
French.)

E846   "Dans les vignes de Jésus (II)," Paroles Françaises, October 17, 1947.
Comparison between Céline and Miller.   (In French.)

E847   Rousseaux, André.   "Le Passage du Pont des Saints-Pères,"
Figaro Littéraire, October 18, 1947.
Miller compared to the Marquis de Sade.   (In French.)

E848   S., P.   "Offensive intruitiste," Paris-Presse, October 19-
20, 1947.
Miller an important author.   (In French.)

E849   "Les Livres," L'Ordre, October 21, 1947.
Miller's preface to James Hanley's novel called excellent.   (In French.)

E850   Nadeau, Maurice.   "Nouveaux 'Babbits'," Gavroche, Octo-
ber 23, 1947.
American authors of reform listed, among them Miller.
(In French.)

E851   "Les Dieux du ski au vert...," Records, October 27, 1947.
Capricorn mentioned.   (In French.)

E852   Bernoville, Gaetan.   "La Grande Pitié de l'intelligence,"
L'Epoque, October 29, 1947.
Miller's writing called "strange. "   (In French.)

E853   "[Review of] Remember to Remember," New Yorker, XXII
(November 8, 1947), 126.
Remember to Remember called an unorganized harangue
on the state of civilization in America.

E854   Maine, Harold.   "We Can Save the Mentally Sick," Saturday
Evening Post, CCXX (November 15, 1947), 20-21, 160-166.
Mentioned is Miller's concern with the stance of

individualism and personal strength being used to treat the mentally sick.

E855   Kees, Weldon. "[Review of] Remember to Remember," New York Times, XCVII (November 30, 1947), 5.
Unfavorable review that spends its time chastising Miller instead of his book, Remember to Remember.

E856   James, Edith. "A Bookman's Notebook: The Not So Jolly Miller," San Francisco Chronicle, CLXV (December 4, 1947), 16.
Remember to Remember seen as a series of Miller's remembrances about people in the U.S. and France.

E857   Freemantle, Anne. "Expatriate's End," Commonweal, XLVII (December 12, 1947), 229-230.
Review of Miller's Remember to Remember and Stein's Four in America that sees both authors concerned with communication.

E858   Andiat, Pierre. "Littérature et université," Almanach le Gazette des Lettres, 1948, 170-176.
Miller and Sartre called surrealists.   (In French.)

E859   Carat, J. "Les Périodiques littéraires," Almanach la Gazette des Lettres, 1948.
Miller mentioned.   (In French.)

E860   Ligaux, Mary. "Les Traductions," Almanach la Gazette des Lettres, 1948, 120-121.
Miller's preface to the book by Hanley praised.   (In French.)

E861   Adams, George. "Les Livres du mois," France Illustration, January 1948, 2-3.
Miller writes again.   (In French.)

E862   Miatleo, Adrian. "L'Optimisme et nous," La Tour de Feu, January 1948, 11-14.
Miller compared to Lawrence.   (In French.)

E863   Olivier. "Le Surrealisme en 1947," Paru, January 1948.
Miller's writing called surreal.   (In French.)

E864   "Janvier 1948 'Feulleton'," L'Avenir, January 1, 1948.
Miller compared to Sartre.   (In French.)

E865   S., P. "J'Irai cracher sur vos tombes," L'Aurore, January 3, 1948.
(In French.)

E866   "Madame Rastier-Caille altaque les positions de Martha Richard," France Dimanche, January 4, 1948.

Miller free to write.   (In French.)

E867   "Petits Echos," Nord-Matin, January 5-6, 1948.
Tropic again in print.   (In French.)

E868   Solesmes, Jean.   "Dévoilée," Claudine, January 7, 1948.
Capricorn back in print.   (In French.)

E869   Bassac, Leonce.   "Discussions d'augures," France-d'Abord,
January 8, 1948.
Miller's article on Céline excellent.   (In French.)

E870   "Le Courrier des Lettres frau Thoreau," Arts, January 9,
1948.
Tropics concerned with freedom.   (In French.)

E871   "Le Procès aura-t-il lieu?" La Gazette des Lettres, January 10, 1948.
Miller controversial.   (In French.)

E872   Prasteau, Jean.   "En 1948 le scandale sera bien français,"
Libération, January 12, 1948.
The Miller trial has ended, and he has won freedom.
(In French.)

E873   "[L'Affaire Miller]," La République du Centre, January 13,
1948.
Miller is being published in France again.   (In French.)

E874   "Le Cinéma français est en danger de mort," Valmy, January 13, 1948.
Film on Miller to be shown.   (In French.)

E875   "La Réserve est bien gardée et l'enfer décevant," Combat,
January 14, 1948.
Tropic free to be read by anyone.   (In French.)

E876   Sans, Julien.   "Aux âmes sensibles," Climats, January 14,
1948.
Sexual love present in all Miller work.   (In French.)

E877   Tessier, Carmen.   "Parce qu'il ne parle pas anglais,"
France-Soir, January 15, 1948.
Miller's pen free to write whatever it wishes.   (In
French.)

E878   Barkan, Raymond.   "Vérité ... et mensonge," Parallèle,
January 17, 1948.
Miller a realist and a nihilist.   (In French.)

E879   "Un Berger incestueux a fait des avenue qui étonneraient
Henri Miller," Liberté-Soir, January 17, 1948.
Miller free to write as he wishes.   (In French.)

E880   "M. Leonard veut mettre une culotte aux femmes nues,"
Samedi-Soir, January 17, 1948.
    Passages from Miller's work stolen and reprinted.   (In
French.)

E881   Audiard, Michel.   "Littérature en circuit fermé," La Bataille, January 21, 1948.
    Miller a pornographer.   (In French.)

E882   "Autobiographies," Le Libre Poitou, January 21, 1948.
    Miller's autobiographical form of writing influential.
(In French.)

E883   "Henry Miller prêche aux nudiste du Capricorne la renais-
sance par la sexualité," Carrefour, January 21, 1948.
    Miller feels that Reich has a dead concept about sex.
(In French.)

E884   "Le Scandale paie...," Avenir de Cannes et du Sud-Est,
January 21, 1948.
    Miller's trial has ended with his freedom.   (In French.)

E885   "Les Trois Derniers Scandales de Paris," Nord-Soir, January 21, 1948.
    Miller free to write as he pleases.   (In French.)

E886   Kemp, Robert.   "La Vie des Livres," Nouvelles Littéraires,
January 22, 1948.
    Brutality found in the writing of Sartre and Miller.   (In
French.)

E887   "Livres signales," L'Aurobe, January 25, 1948.
    Miller concerned with love.   (In French.)

E888   Weltheim, Jérôme de.   "Salut à Miller ... et à Bryen,"
La Tour de Feu, Winter-Spring 1948, 100-105.
    Miller called moralistic, religious, and a critic of our
society.   (In French.)

E889   Rolo, Charles J.   "Notes on the avant-garde," Tomorrow,
VII (March 1948), 55-57.
    Review of Remember to Remember where it is noted
that Miller feels most publishers try to hide genius, in
review calling Miller infantile.

E890   Fouéré, René A.   "Défense de Miller," Revue Palladienne,
March-April 1948, 17-19.
    Miller is one American with European genius, for in
Capricorn he creates a sense of being much like the
French philosopher, Bergson.   (In French.)

E891   Fraenkel, Michael.   "Letter de Michael Fraenkel," Arts
Lettres, III (June 1948), 27-32.

Letter of November 24, 1936, where Fraenkel discusses
Hamlet's lot as being the fate of present-day man.   (In
French.)

E892   Rivière, Marcus and T. Prigent.   "Note des Traducteurs,"
Arts Lettres, III (June 1948), 21.
Death in life was the theme that ran through the Miller-
Fraenkel correspondence.   (In French.)

E893   "[Review of] The Smile at the Foot of the Ladder," Kirkus,
LVI (June 1, 1948), 269.
Brief, favorable review of Smile at the Foot of the
Ladder.

E894   Poore, Charles.   "Henry Miller Sets Down a Tankard Parable," New York Times, XCVII (June 6, 1948), VII 6.
The Smile at the Foot of the Ladder reviewed as a tale
of a clown-poet in action.

E895   Jackson, J. H.   "A Bookman's Notebook: A Tale of a
Clown," San Francisco Chronicle, CLXVI (June 28, 1948),
16.
Miller's The Smile at the Foot of the Ladder is a symbolic, tragic story of a clown who is a poet at heart.

E896   Jackson, J. H.   "Last Expatriate," Time, LI (June 28,
1948), 92.
Review of The Smile at the Foot of the Ladder that sees
Miller as the last writer in a great tradition.

E897   Desmond, Art.   "The Most Wonderful Rat," Dale Harrison's
Chicago, I (July 5, 1948), 8.

E898   Lesdain, Pierre.   "Chronique des livres," Volonté, August
7, 1948, 4.
Review of The Colossus of Maroussi that depicts Miller's
unique way of traveling, his adopting the real color
of Greece.   (In French.)

E899   Glicksberg, Charles I.   "A Milder Miller," Southwest Review, XXXIII (Summer 1948), 311-314.
In Remember to Remember, Miller continues his feud
against the United States with its industrial cities and
its dehumanizing effect on life.

E900   Glicksberg, Charles I.   "Henry Miller: Individualism in
Extremis," Southwest Review, XXXIII (Summer 1948), 289-
295.
Miller is straight forward and honest: "His task as a
writer is to get as close to reality as he can, to reveal the truth as he sees it..." (p. 295).

E901   "Henry Miller Answers Quibbles and Queries at Carmel

Adult Class," Pacific Grove Tribune, September 24, 1948, 1, 4.
Miller spoke about meditation, society, and the devil.

E902   Greer, Scott.   "To Be or Not," Tiger's Eye, I (October 20, 1948), 68-69.
Review of The Smile at the Foot of the Ladder that sees this work as another Miller autobiography of little merit.

E903   Gregory, Horace.   "To Be or Not," Tiger's Eye, I (October 20, 1948), 70-71.
Review of The Smile at the Foot of the Ladder that sees Miller's protagonist as a sad clown with a smile, a dual nature where opposites present problems of identity for the self and with one's art.

E904   Hauser, Marianne.   "To Be or Not," Tiger's Eye, I (October 20, 1948), 69-70.
The Smile at the Foot of the Ladder seen as a clown's search to discover himself.

E905   Kees, Weldon.   "To Be or Not," Tiger's Eye, I (October 20, 1948), 71-72.
Kees sees The Smile at the Foot of the Ladder as dull and dry in an article that criticizes Miller while ignoring his work.

E906   "Retour de Tartufe," Action, November 8, 1948.
"Freedom" means that men like Miller are forced to conform.   (In French.)

E907   "Faut-il brûler les 'Tropiques'?" La Dépèche de Paris, November 17-18, 1948.
The individual must decide for himself whether or not to read Miller.   (In French.)

E908   Willis, Stanley.   "About California," Right Angle, II (December 1948), 4-5.
Miller and his Big Sur companions mentioned.

E909   Durrell, Lawrence.   "Henry Miller," n.p., 1949.
Essay on the importance of Miller's work.

E910   Spender, Stephen.   "Tour West ... Some Random Notes," Kirkeby Hotels Magazine, V (February 1949), 9-11, 61-62.
Spender talks about meeting Miller.

E911   Huxley, Aldous.   "Death and the Baroque," Harper's, CXCVIII (April 1949), 80-86.
Cancer called a desolate knowledge of the self and nothing more.

E912   "California Author Henry Miller," Fortnight, VI (May 27,

1949), 17.
> Miller sued by a man whom he called a girl-beating sadist.

E913   Lesdain, Pierre.   "Henry Miller," Sept Arts, XLVIII-XLIX (June 1949), 1-3.

E914   Winner, Percy.   "Outside America," New Republic, CXX (June 20, 1949), 9-10.
> Miller will be a posthumous success for his portrayal of the 1920's in Paris.   (Should be the 1930's.)

E915   Durrell, Lawrence.   "Studies in Genius: VIII--Henry Miller," Horizon, XX (July 1949), 45-61.
> Durrell sees Miller's writing as germinating; it is a creative force distinct of form.

E916   "A Treasury of Brooklyn," New Yorker, XXX (July 2, 1949), 60.
> Miller's work included in this anthology about his native Brooklyn.

E917   Kennedy, Lou.   "Of Cabbages and Kings: Henry Miller and Sweeney the Rat," This Week in Chicago, July 2, 1949, 16-17.
> Miller exhibit of books and paintings at "M the Studio for Henry Miller."

E918   Desmond, Art.   "The Most Wonderful Rat," Dale Harrison's Chicago, I (July 5, 1949), 8.
> Miller the misunderstood author of Cancer and Capricorn.

E919   Balch, Don.   "Henry Miller," UCLA Bruin, August 9, 1949.
> Miller a primitivist in his painting and writing.

E920   Lesdain, Pierre.   "Chronique des livres," Volonté, August 13, 1949, 3.
> Miller attributes his writing style to Knut Hamsun. (In French.)

E921   Cummings, Ridgeley.   "Fight Pending Over Government Attempt to Destroy Two Books," Twin Peaks Sentinel, August 26, 1949, 4.
> Federal government does not want the Tropics in the United States.

E922   Lesdain, Pierre.   "Henry Miller calomnié," Volonté, August 27, 1949, 4.
> Miller not scandalous because he has honest insights in the two Tropics.   (In French.)

E923   "Travel Can Be Broadening," Nation, CLXIX (October 1,

1949), 312.
Cancer and Capricorn have been found inside book
covers calling for Jane Eyre.

E924   Saroyan, Chesley.   "'The Rosy Crucifixion': A Review,"
Points, October-November 1949, 79-83.
Review of The Rosy Crucifixion.

E925   Victor, Alexander.   "Once Upon a Time," Carmel Spectator,
November 10, 1949, 17.
Miller an honest man whose Tropic is banned in the
U.S.

E926   Haan, Jacques den.   "A Dream of a Book," Kroniek van
Kunst en Kultuur, X (December 1949), 1-6.
An evaluation of Miller's Into the Night Life, a book
somewhere between dream and surrealism.

E927   Haan, Jacques den.   "Henry Miller's Droomboek," Kroniek
van Kunst en Kultuur, X (December 1949), 386-388.
Into the Night Life viewed as Miller's dream book.   It
contains passages from Black Spring, paintings, and
Miller's own handwriting.   (In Dutch.)

E928   Winslow, Edna Manley.   "Exhibit of Big Sur Artists at Wall
Gallery," Carmel Pine Cone-Cymbal, December 23, 1949,
11.
Miller painting at the Wall Gallery called the masterpiece of the show.

E929   "Henry Miller," Litterair Paspoort, 1950, 12-13.
(In Dutch.)

E930   Yakovlev, L.   "Literature of Decay," Soviet Literature, VI
(1950), 172-178.
Miller viewed as a raving, imperialist madman in a
review of Capricorn.

E931   Johnson, Falk.   "The Ups and Downs of 'Dirty' Words,"
American Mercury, LXX (January 1950), 85-92.
Miller's use of language called 'dirty'.

E932   Poorter, A. van Es-de.   "Henry Miller," Perspectieven, I
(January 1950), 5-11.
Miller's writing divorced from Lawrence's because of
the positive quality of his literature.   (In Danish.)

E933   Young, Kenneth.   "The Contemporary Greek Influence on
English Writers," Life and Letters, LXIV (January 1950),
53-64.
Miller's writing influenced by Greece and passages from
The Colossus of Maroussi show this.

E934 Cummings, Ridgely. "Freedom of Expression and Henry Miller," Mission Enterprise, LXXV (January 4, 1950), 1. American Civil Liberties Union fights to keep ban off of two Tropics.

E935 Cummings, Ridgely. "Freedom of Expression and Henry Miller," Coastside Comet, January 5, 1950, 4. See E934.

E936 Sharp, Marynell. "Beauford Delaney and Green Street," Art Digest, XXIV (January 15, 1950), 16. Miller calls Delaney 'amazing' in The Air-Conditioned Nightmare.

E937 "La Police saisit le dernier ouvrage d'H. Miller," Jeudi, January 26, 1950. Miller's Sexus considered a filthy book. (In French.)

E938 Falk, Albert. "L'Immoralisme chrétien de W. Blake," U-49 Revue Littéraire Mensuelle, January-February 1950, 3-17. Blake's immorality compared with Miller's. (In French.)

E939 Woon, Basil. "Everybody's Bookshelf," San Francisco News, February 8, 1950. The magazine Transition first published Miller in the U.S.

E940 Haan, Jacques den. "Henry Miller: Voor Jaap Sluiter," Podium, March 1950, 168-184. Miller influenced by André Gide. (In Danish.)

E941 Falk, Albert. "L'Immoralisme chrétien de W. Blake (part 2)," U-49, Revue Littéraire Mensuelle, March-April 1950, 63-74. Miller in the immoral tradition of Blake. (In French.)

E942 "Henry Miller," Quartier Latin, IV (March-April 1950), 1, 4. Miller's concept of freedom popular in France. (In French.)

E943 Goethem, Ray van. "Henry Miller et le scandale orches- tré," Cahiers, CCCXXXIII (April 1950), 25-27. (In French.)

E944 Woon, Basil. "Protest at Censorship," San Francisco News, April 1, 1950. Miller opposed to censorship.

E945 Lesdain, Pierre. "Les Âmes fortes," Volonté, April 9, 1950, 4. Miller a defender of man. (In French.)

E946   Dignan, Josef. "Don't Get It Right, Get It Written; A Satire in World News Coverage," Louisville Courier Journal,
CXCI (April 23, 1950), 15.
The Kansas City Milkman by Reynolds Packard indebted
to Henry Miller's Tropic of Cancer.

E947   "Bookshop Raided; Works by Henry Miller, Others Seized,"
San Francisco Chronicle, CLXX (May 9, 1950), 1.
Police raided Evans Books seizing Tropic of Capricorn.

E948   "Obscene Book Raids Jail 2," San Francisco Examiner,
CLXLII (May 10, 1950), 1.
Henry Evans and Jack Evans jailed for having copies of
Tropic of Capricorn.

E949   "The Police Are Confused About Those 'Obscene' Books,"
San Francisco Chronicle, CLXXII (May 10, 1950), 3.
Capricorn seized from the Evans's.

E950   Faure, Maurice. "Miller, ou l'amour éperdu de la vie,"
Combat, May 11, 1950, 4.
Miller's Sexus displays a happiness and a love for life.
(In French.)

E951   Falk, Albert. "Le Dernier Livre de Henry Miller," U-49
Revue Littéraire Mensuelle, May-June 1950, 81-82.
A look at Miller's writing. (In French.)

E952   Falk, Albert. "L'Immoralisme chrétien de W. Blake (part
3)," U-49, Revue Littéraire Mensuelle, May-June 1950, 67-
79.
Miller in the immoral tradition of Blake. (In French.)

E953   "Big Sur Country," Flair, I (June 1950), 26-27.
Miller the guardian of Big Sur. Mentioned are Cancer
and The Wisdom of the Heart.

E954   Staten, Verenigde. "Henry Miller," Litterair Paspoort,
June-July 1950, 12-13.
(In Dutch.)

E955   Vestdijk, S. "Henry Miller: Onkuud dat Niet Vergaan Zal,"
Algemeen Handelsblad, July 15, 1950, 5.
Miller's Tropics compared to the writing of Whitman,
Dostoevsky, Nietzsche, and Lawrence. (In Dutch.)

E956   Horton, Michael. "Mostly About People," Herald Tribune
(Paris), LXIII (July 19, 1950), 4.
Obelisk Press published Sexus of Miller's Rosy Cruci-
fixion.

E957   Lesdain, Pierre. "La Rage de vivre," Volonté, July 28,
1950.

Miller's Preface to Milton Mezzrow's and Bernard Wolfe's A Rage to Live concerns itself with life. (In French.)

E958   Chonez, Claudine. "Henry Miller: Du Pansexualisme à l'angélisme," Empedocle, II (July-August 1950), 74-80.
Death and resurrection are themes found in Miller's Tropics that lead to a transcendence in life. (In French.)

E959   "Henry Miller Novels Ruled Pornography," San Francisco Chronicle, CLXXII (September 29, 1950), 17.
Federal Judge Louis Goodman of California ruled Miller's two Tropics pornography.

E960   Beach, Clarke. "Smutty Books Bore the Censor," Washington Post, (November 26, 1950), 8B.
Cairns banned Miller's Tropics and The Rosy Crucifixion.

E961   Hornus, Jean-Michel. "J'ai rencontré Miller, un coeur pur," Le Semeur, December 1950, 102-110.
(In French.)

E962   Hermans, W. F. "Gezondheid Zonder Boosheid," Litterair Paspoort, VI (January 1951), 6-8.
The Rosy Crucifixion in tradition of Miller's earlier work, displaying a nightmarish world of grotesques. (In Dutch.)

E963   Kloppers, A. G. "Epigonen over Henry Miller," Litterair Paspoort, VI (January 1951), 9-10.
Ezra Pound's statement that Cancer is a dirty book worth reading is applicable to all of Miller's works. (In Dutch.)

E964   "Informations littéraires," Arts, January 19, 1951, 2.
Sexus to be published in France. (In French.)

E965   Falk, Albert. "Henry Miller, surhomme et Prophète," U-49, Revue Littéraire Mensuelle, January-February 1951, 59-78.
Falk recalls the first time he spoke to Miller about Capricorn and its Christian symbols. (In French.)

E966   N. , M. "Quatre Libraires de Nancy retournent devant les tribunaux," Combat, April 12, 1951, 4.
Miller an important social critic. (In French.)

E967   Hartung, Rudolf. "Eine weltohne Gesicht," Die Neue Zeitung, April 14, 1951, 19.
Miller's Tropics reviewed. (In German.)

E968   "Le 'Blaise Cendrars' d'Henry Miller," Combat, July 12,

1951.
The Cendrars-Miller friendship noted. (In French.)

E969 "Henry Miller," L'Homme Libre, July 13, 1951, 4.
Miller writes about Cendrars with affection, love, and understanding. (In French.)

E970 Judge, Jacquelyn. "Fred Lyon ... Happy Photographer,"
Modern Photography, XV (August 1951), 37-40, 100.
Miller mentioned in conjunction with his son, Tony.

E971 Slocombe, George. "Reviews of New Books in Europe,"
Herald Tribune (Paris), LXIV (August 22, 1951), 7.
Miller's Blaise Cendrars called one of the best pieces of writing Miller has done.

E972 "Author Says He Expected Books to be Ruled Obscene,"
Sacramento Bee, September 18, 1951.
Miller says that history will prove that Tropics are not obscene.

E973 "Obscene Books," San Francisco Chronicle, CLXXIV (September 18, 1951), 11.
A federal court judge ruled that Tropic was filthy and upheld a ban.

E974 Maine, Harold. "Henry Miller: Bigotry's Whipping Boy,"
Arizona Quarterly, VII (Autumn 1951), 197-208.
Miller's work seen as a quest that involves burying the self in chaos, in a world of both normalcy and insanity.

E975 Hersey, Jean. "Big Sur--Utopia, U.S.A.?" Family Circle,
XXXIX (December 1951), 38-42, 44.

E976 Rink, Peggy. "The Worlds of Henry Miller," Monterey
Herald, 1952.
Review of Miller's Books in My Life, a work about the real life experience one finds in literature.

E977 "USA--Author unter moralischer Quarantäne: Henry Miller
--Die Magie des Obzönen," Die Literatur, I (January 1952), 2.
(In German.)

E978 Lemarchand, Jacques. "La Mort d'un commis voyageur,"
Le Figaro Littéraire, February 9, 1952, 10.
The only thing Arthur and Henry Miller have in common is a last name. For Arthur is a fine playwright while Henry is a sex-oriented author. (In French.)

E979 Garcon, Maurice. "De l'aven," Le Monde, March 19, 1952, 1, 4.
Miller is a man who inhabited the streets of Paris. (In

French.)

E980   Franca, José Augusto. "Atenção para Miller, " Bicornio,
        April 1952, 16.
        (In Portuguese.)

E981   Petit, Henri. "Le Monde Du Sexe, " Le Parisien, April 15,
        1952.
        The World of Sex is Miller's confessional about his life.
        (In French.)

E982   Dumur, Guy. "Le Monde d'Henry Miller, " Combat, April
        17, 1952, 7.
        The World of Sex is a much tamer book than the
        Tropics or Black Spring. (In French.)

E983   Nicollier, Jean. "Henry Miller: Plexus, " Gazette de
        Lausanne, April 26, 1952.
        Miller's Sexus and Plexus are attempts to get beyond
        conformity to a self-oriented humanism. (In French.)

E984   "Plexus par Henry Miller, " Activités Correa, XIV (May
        1952), 1.
        The Rosy Crucifixion is called a monumental outrage
        against society because Plexus is too frank and to the
        point. (In French.)

E985   Hellens, Franz. "L'Oeuvre d'Henry Miller, " Dernière
        Heure, May 7, 1952.
        Plexus a much more spiritual novel than Sexus.   (In
        French.)

E986   Hecht, Yvon. "Henri Miller publie son oeuvre capitale, "
        Paris-Normandie, May 9, 1952.
        Plexus neither good nor scandalous yet with the same
        themes as Miller's other works, having both optimism
        and despair. (In French.)

E987   Jones, Archer. "Review of Current Books, " Point, May 10,
        1952.
        The Books in My Life shows the vital experience of
        literature and its effects on one man.

E988   Magny, Claude Edmonde. " 'Plexus' et 'Le Monde du sexe'
        ou Miller purifié, " Samedi-Soir, May 10-16, 1952.
        Review of Plexus and The World of Sex that sees Mill-
        er still exploring the question of sex that troubled him
        so much in Tropic. (In French.)

E989   Connolly, Cyril. "Out of Brooklyn, " London Sunday Times,
        (May 18, 1952), 9.
        Review of The Books in My Life as an autobiographical
        work concerned with the literature Miller loves.

E990   Connolly, Cyril. "[Review of] The Books in My Life,"
        Sun Times, (May 18, 1952), 9.
            See E989.

E991   Kemp, Robert. "Mammouths," Les Nouvelles Littéraires,
        May 22, 1952.
            Miller's use of sex in The Rosy Crucifixion reminds
        one of Baudelaire, for he is concerned with depicting
        real life. (In French.)

E992   Mayoux, J. J. "La Révolte d'Henry Miller," Combat,
        May 22, 1952, 7.
            Miller a revolutionary writer in The World of Sex.
        (In French.)

E993   Blondin, Antoine. "La Fille du tonnerre est un éclair de
        chaleur," Rivarol, May 30, 1952, 4.
            Miller mentioned in relationship to Cendrars and Kafka.
        (In French.)

E994   Peuchmaurd, Jacques. "Henry Miller: 'Plexus'," Litté-
        raire Revue les Beaux-Arts, June 4, 1952.
            Review of Plexus that sees it in the tradition of the
        Tropics. (In French.)

E995   Nadeau, Maurice. "Mort et transfiguration d'Henry Mill-
        er," Les Temps Modernes, July 1952, 131.
            A look at The Rosy Crucifixion which some see as the
        death of Miller, while others view it as his transfor-
        mation. (In French.)

E996   Connolly, Cyril. "[Review of] The Books in My Life,"
        Times Literary Supplement, LI (July 4, 1952), 434.
            Review of The Books in My Life.

E997   Baidault, Yves. "Jean Gino: Des fleurs de la solitude et
        Machiavel," Arts Spectacles, August 22-28, 1952, 1, 5.
        (In French.)

E998   Glicksburg, Charles. "Literature & Society," Arizona
        Quarterly, VIII (Summer 1952), 128-139.
            Miller's belief in nonattachment and noninvolvement in
        Tropic creates a strong sense of individualism.

E999   Rousseaux, André. " 'Plexus', d'Henry Miller," Le Figaro
        Littéraire, September 6, 1952.
            The Plexus story has been told before in Capricorn,
        yet the style of this work, the violence and poetry, is
        a new and better Miller. (In French.)

E1000   Kanters, Robert. "Henry, le bon sauvage," La Gazette
        des Lettres, September 15, 1952, 99-105.
            Miller's Plexus and The World of Sex are sure to

raise a scandal since they talk about sex openly. (In French.)

E1001 "Henry Miller," Alma Latina, October 4, 1952, 6.
The Tropics depict Miller's worlds in New York and Paris. (In Spanish.)

E1002 Salomon, Herbert J. "Henry Miller Writes of His Favorite Books," New York Post, CLI (October 5, 1952), M12.
The Books in My Life is clear, spontaneous, sincere, and original, a work where Miller talks about his life and the writers who most affected him.

E1003 Krim, Seymour. "The Netherworld of Henry Miller," Commonweal, LVII (October 24, 1952), 68-71.
Miller is viewed as a writer who believes in himself; The Books in My Life is just another example of the courage it takes to make these self-revealing personal statements.

E1004 Wainhouse, Austryn. "The Books in My Life," Points, Autumn 1952, 79-81.
Miller called impulsive in this review of The Books in My Life.

E1005 Lee, Alwyn. "Henry Miller--The Pathology of Isolation," New World Writing, November 1952, 340-347.
Lee sees Miller's life as based upon self expression, a private experience that never gets beyond the self: "Miller's isolation condemns him to be merely the historian ... of his won attitudes" (p. 346).

E1006 "Henry Miller's Bibliothèque Idéale," Antiquarian Bookman, X (November 1, 1952), 1198.
Review of The Books in My Life, a book about Miller's love for literature.

E1007 S., M. "The New Books: The Books in My Life," San Francisco Chronicle, CLXXVI (November 2, 1952), TW 24.
The Books in My Life is one man's unorthodox reaction to what he has read.

E1008 Bluefarb, Sam. "Have You Read...? Some Thoughts on Henry Miller," Info-mat, I (December 1952), 3.
Miller seen as a living reincarnation of the free and independent thinkers of Thoreau's, Emerson's, and Whitman's time. The Books in My Life is seen as a work about independence and life.

E1009 Paraz, Albert. "L'Humanité se divise en deux," Rivarol, December 20, 1952, 8.
Miller writes about journeys within one's own self to the core of one's being. (In French.)

E1010   Paraz, Albert. "Albert Paraz à propos de 'Furie pour
        une autre fois'," Rivarol, December 20-27, 1952, 1.
            Article on Céline that includes a mention and a com-
            parison with Miller. (In French.)

E1011   Sabatier, J. "Henry Miller à Paris," Samedi-Soir, Janu-
        ary 8, 1953, 2.
            Miller returns to Paris with wife, Eve, for a visit.
            (In French.)

E1012   L., J. "L'Amérique aux Indiens! éspère Henry Miller,"
        Le Figaro Littéraire, January 10, 1953, 1, 3.
            Miller left Big Sur for a trip to Paris to see old
            friends and visit favorite places. (In French.)

E1013   Queneau, Raymond. "Un Immortel vient d'arriver à
        Paris: Henry Miller," Carrefour, January 14, 1953, 9.
            Miller has come back to Paris to relive the 1930's.
            (In French.)

E1014   "Henry Miller: J'ai rencontré à Montparnasse un peintre
        de mes amis," Arts, January 16-22, 1953, 1, 6.
            Miller's Paris days are recalled as Tropic of Cancer
            is explored. (In French.)

E1015   Moore, Harry T. "A Writer's Book of Enthusiasms,"
        New York Times CII (January 18, 1953), VII 3.
            Review of The Books in My Life that sees Miller re-
            lating reading to other experiences.

E1016   Macdonald, Dwight. "Words Without End," Partisan Re-
        view, XX (January-February 1953), 126-128.
            Macdonald reviews Miller's The Books in My Life and
            feels that Miller suffers from diarrhea of the mouth.

E1017   Valence, Claude. "Points d'orgue," Le Goeland, January-
        February-March 1953, 2.
            Miller a dynamic romantic. (In French.)

E1018   Maillet, Albert. "Henry Miller--The Books in My Life,"
        Etudes Anglaises, VI (February 1953), 84.
            A review of Miller's The Books in My Life where
            Miller is chastised. (In French.)

E1019   Wiznitzer, Louis. " 'A vida e a literatura americana não
        me interessam'--diz Henry Miller," Letras e Artes, Feb-
        ruary 15, 1953, 6-7.
            An interview between Wiznitzer and Miller where they
            discuss Plexus, the merits of society, Nexus, South
            America, Paris, sex, and masculinity. (In Portu-
            guese.)

E1020   Doner, Ephraim. "Have You Read...?" Monterey Herald,

February 20, 1953.
Miller's The Books in My Life is Miller's own story.

E1021   Fiedler, Leslie A.   "Love Is Not Enough," Yale Review, XLII (March 1953), 455-460.
Miller depicted as a dawdling old lady who misses the world around him because of his self-concern in this review of The Books in My Life.

E1022   "Miller: Souvenir souvenirs," La Nouvelle Revue Française, I (March 1953), 7.
Miller's Remember to Remember attempts to examine all of America.   (In French.)

E1023   Blanc-Dufour, A.   "[Review of] Souvenir, souvenirs, par Henry Miller," Cahiers du Sud, XXXVII (May 1953), 162-163.
Review of Miller's Remember to Remember where Miller speaks of the humanism of Europe and the inhuman nature of America.   (In French.)

E1024   Braun, Benoit.   "Pages de journal d'un liseur," Synthèses, VIII (May 1953), 74.
In Remember to Remember Miller devotes whole chapters to discussions of painters and sculptors, for Miller is totally involved in the world of art.   (In French.)

E1025   Lambilliotte, Maurice.   "L'Homme se cherche à Henry Miller," Synthèses, VIII (May 1953), 5-12.
Miller called American with a European and an Oriental philosophy and a fine sense of humanism.   (In French.)

E1026   "Passion and Prejudice," Times Literary Supplement, LII (June 12, 1953), 376.
Remember to Remember called a book about American artists.

E1027   Lesdain, Pierre.   "Over Henry Miller; Een Paar Woorden," Der Meridiaan, July-August 1953, 42-44.
(In Dutch.)

E1028   Cormeau, Nelly.   "Chronique littéraire," Synthèses, VIII (August-September 1953), 75-83.
Miller depicted as a passionate American revolutionary in Remember to Remember.   (In French.)

E1029   Paumier, Raymond.   "Le Soutier de la vie," Revue de l'Econome, XIX (October 1953), 1215-1217.
Review of Remember to Remember that calls Miller an experimental writer moving patiently to a new form of self-awareness through autobiographical literature.

(In French.)

E1030   "Miller's 'Tropics' Obscene Says Court of Appeals, " American Civil Liberties Union News, XVIII (November 1953), I.
Ninth Circuit Court of Appeals in San Francisco on
October 23, 1953, banned the two Tropics on the
grounds of obscenity.

E1031   Røthenborg, Jørgen. "Den Fortabte Generations Fortabte
Søn, " Perspektiv, I (November 1953), 42-51.
Discussion of the effects of Miller and Tropic on
modern society and social criticism.   (In Danish.)

E1032   "Henry Miller: 'I Won't Buck the Tide', " Midweek, November 5, 1953.
Miller won't fight ban against his books in U.S.

E1033   Béalu, Marcel.   "Le Remuant et le stable, " Risques, VIII
(1954), 10-11.
Cendrars and Miller called two of the best poets of
the fifties.   (In French.)

E1034   Bittencourt, Renato.   "Miller, neurose e êxtase, " Revista
Branca, VI (1954), 100-105.
Miller called a revolutionary trying to save the entire
world.   (In Portuguese.)

E1035   Bittencourt, Renato.   "Miller, Neurosis and Ecstasy, " Revista Branca, VI (1954), 106-111.
Miller a rebel fighting against mass society who turns
within the self to find religious salvation.   See E1034.

E1036   Chabert, Pierre.   "L'Originalité de Blaise Cendrars, "
Risques, VIII (1954), 19-21.
Cendrars admired and was often seen with Miller.
(In French.)

E1037   Oswald, Pierre-Jean.   "O, " Risques, VIII (1954), 58-59.
The Miller-Cendrars friendship mentioned.   (In
French.)

F1038   Ragon, Michel.   "R, " Risques, VIII (1954), 63.
Cendrars's poetic style compared to Miller's.   (In
French.)

E1039   Roth, Samuel.   "An Open Letter to Henry Miller, " American Aphrodite, IV (1954), 3-4.
Roth enjoyed both Cancer and Plexus, two novels he
calls humanistic.

E1040   "Marriage of Author Revealed, " Los Angeles Times,
LXXIII (January 7, 1954), 25.
Miller marries for third time.

E1041   Clurman, Harold.   "Theatre," Nation, CLXXVIII (January
16, 1954), 57.
Henry Miller's brand of theatre mentioned.

E1042   Delteil, Joseph.   "Le Cinquième Acte," Prospectus, VI-
VII (January-February 1954), 3.
Delteil talks about the importance of Miller's "Preface"
to Haniel Long's Cabeza de Vaca.   (In French.)

E1043   Rousseaux, Andre.   " 'Le Sourire au pied de l'échelle'
d'Henry Miller," Figaro Littéraire, February 4, 1954.
Miller seen as the single most important figure in
literature today for his The Smile at the Foot of the
Ladder.   (In French.)

E1044   Haedens, Kleber.   "Le 'Numéro un' de Dos Passos est un
triste numéro," Paris-Presse, February 28-March 1, 1954,
2.
Miller's chastisement of the U.S. in The Air-Conditioned Nightmare is an objective outlook.   (In French.)

E1045   Billy, André.   "Miller condamné une fois de plus les
Etats-unis," Courrier Figaro, March 3, 1954.
Miller's Air Conditioned Nightmare and Remember to
Remember are seen as parodies on America and
Miller's retorts for banning his Tropics.   (In French.)

E1046   Schmidt, Albert-Marie.   "Entrée des clowns sauveurs,"
Réforme, March 27, 1954.
Miller's literature may be obscene but it is important.
(In French.)

E1047   Deroisin, Sophie.   "A propos du 'Cauchemar climatisé',"
Phare, April 18, 1954.
Letter to Miller asking if America is actually a life
in a cage as he depicts in The Air-Conditioned Nightmare.   (In French.)

E1048   Seidelin, Anna Sophie.   "Ikke Forargelig--uaktuel," Information, April 19, 1954, 2.
Cancer a book about individual trials that no society
can understand.   (In Danish.)

E1049   Holstein, Huno van.   "Den Berygtede Bog 'Krebsens
Vendekreds'," April 23, 1954, 2.
Cancer viewed by a Danish judge who feels the work
has literary merit and is in the tradition of Whitman.
(In Danish.)

E1050   "Reds Discover Kinsey, Call His Book 'Hash'," New York
World-Telegram and Sun, CXXI (May 19, 1954), 7.
Russia dislikes Miller and his Tropics.

E1051   "Le Dr. Kinsey est qualifié de pornographe," Le Jour,
May 20, 1954.
The success of Miller's Tropic called sexual perver-
sion by Kinsey.   (In French.)

E1052   Billy, André.   "Cauchemar climatisé par Henry Miller,"
Livres de France, V (May-June 1954), 25.
Discussion of the humor of The Air-Conditioned Night-
mare.   (In French.)

E1053   Sage, Robert.   "From Montparnasse to Monterey," Herald
Tribune (Paris), LXVII (September 10, 1954), 5.
Miller writing guidebooks about Big Sur.

E1054   Zailian, Marion.   "Irrepressible Bufano's Art Published in
New Album," Independent-Journal, November 20, 1954, M2.
Miller feels that Bufano, through his art, has dedi-
cated himself to mankind.

E1055   "Befehlsdruck und Convoyreflex," Frankfurter Allgemeine
Zeitung, Weihnachten 1955, 1.
Miller called a founder of modern literature.   (In
German.)

E1056   Okamoto, Atsushi.   "Are Henry Miller's Books Obscene?"
Mainichi, March 15, 1955, 1.
Police in Tokyo have taken actions to ban works by
Miller.

E1057   Mohn, Bent.   "Henry Millers Sex--og Dødsdans," Information, March 25, 1955, 4.
Miller's Tropics depict reality like the writing of Balzac, Zola, Flaubert, and Whitman.   (In Danish.)

E1058   Nicollier, Jean.   "Henry Miller: Dimanche après la
guerre," Gazette de Lausanne, March 26, 1955.

E1059   C., J.   "A la rôtissoire Hollywood vu par Henry Miller,"
Le Canard Enchainé, XXXVII (March 30, 1955), 4.
Miller feels the American cinema not the fine art
form it should be.   (In French.)

E1060   "A la rôtissoire Hollywood vu par Henry Miller," La
Canard Enchainé, XXXVII (March 30, 1955), 4.
Review of Miller's Sunday After the War.   (In French.)

E1061   Bullock, Wynn.   "A Day with Henry Miller," Carmel
Spectator, XII (April 29-May 6, 1955), 3-4.
Miller depicted and photographed as a quiet, intro-
spective person.

E1062   Nicollier, Jean.   "Henry Miller: Dimanche après la
guerre," Gazette de Lausanne, May 26, 1955.

Miller views life as perpetual conflict. (In French.)

E1063   Gulli, Elise.   "Art, East and West," Nippon Times, June
         10, 1955, 4.
         Miller's ability with his brush as great as with his
         pen in an exhibit of his art at Bridgestone Gallery in
         Tokyo.

E1064   Sakanishi, Shiko.   "Water Color Paintings of Henry Mill-
         er," Shûkan Asahi, June 26, 1955, 71-72.
         Famous Japanese critic sees importance in the paint-
         ings of Miller. (In Japanese.)

E1065   Fukuzawa, Ichirô.   "Gazin Henry Miller," Geijutsu Shinchô,
         VI (July 1955), 105-109.
         Miller viewed as painter by critics. (In Japanese.)

E1066   Fukuzawa, Ichirô.   "Water Paintings of Henry Miller,"
         Geijutsu Shinchô, VI (July 1955), 105-109.
         Review of Miller's art on display at the Bridgestone
         Art Gallery.

E1067   Winchell, Walter.   "Walter Winchell of New York," New
         York Daily Mirror, XXXII (July 1, 1955), 10.
         Miller's work demanded by those who know good liter-
         ature.

E1068   Winchell, Walter.   "Walter Winchell in New York and
         Hollywood," Los Angeles Herald & Express, July 4, 1955.
         Miller's works honest and are masterpieces of litera-
         ture.

E1069   Bruchberger, R. L.   "French Fiction and American Re-
         ality," New York Times, CIV (July 31, 1955), VII 1, 17.
         Miller's Air-Conditioned Nightmare a novel that chas-
         tises America.

E1070   Tokudaiju, Kimihide.   "The Literature and Paintings of
         Henry Miller," Bejutsu Techô, August 1955, 35-38.
         Miller's writing and eight of his watercolors are ex-
         plored. (In Japanese.)

E1071   Nymann, Bart.   "Op Bezoek bij Henry Miller," Litterair
         Paspoort, X (August-September 1955), 151-152, 158.
         Miller's belief in living life to the full explored in his
         Rosy Crucifixion, Colossus of Maroussi, Air-Condi-
         tioned Nightmare, and Tropic of Cancer. (In Dutch.)

E1072   Terduyn, Eric.   "Fris en Onfris," Litterair Paspoort, X
         (August-September 1955), 146-148.
         Miller's Tropic called pornography. (In Dutch.)

E1073   Katayama, Toshikiko.   "Watercolors of a Writer," Mizue,

September 1955, 46-47.
Miller a fine watercolorist.   (In Japanese.)

E1074   Perlès, Alfred.   "My Friend Henry Miller," Synthèses, X
(September 1955), 27-35.
Perlès talks about Miller's arrival in Paris, work on
the Paris Tribune, and the publication of "Mademoiselle Claude. "   (In French.)

E1075   Bücher.   "Henry Miller: Wettlauf der Ratten, " Der
Spiegel, IX (September 14, 1955), 34-35.
Miller's Rosy Crucifixion has high literary merit and
the theme of apocalypse.   (In German.)

E1076   Sahl, Hans.   "Ein genialer Dilettant, " Buch und Zeit,
October 1-2, 1955.
Review of Plexus.   (In German.)

E1077   Mennemeier, Franz Norbert.   "Vagabund Henry Miller,"
Literaturblatt, October 8, 1955, 234.
Plexus is the story of Miller vagabonding in the U.S.
(In German.)

E1078   Bérimont, Luc.   "Une Interview imaginaire," La Tour de
Feu, Autumn 1955, 58-60.
Imaginary interview where Miller shows his rebellious
nature against America in a discussion of Cancer.
(In French.)

E1079   Boujut, Pierre.   "Cinq Poémes d'accueil," La Tour de
Feu, Autumn 1955, 128-131.
Miller's art honored in five poems by Boujut.   (In
French.)

E1080   Boujut, Pierre.   "Miller quand même, " La Tour de Feu,
Autumn 1955, 86-90.
Miller's conception of love finds its basis in self-
enjoyment.   (In French.)

E1081   Bourguignon, Fred.   "A pas de loup, " La Tour de Feu,
Autumn 1955, 76-78.
Miller a writer society cannot control.   (In French.)

E1082   Breton, Jean.   "Henry-la-colère, " La Tour de Feu,
Autumn 1955, 64.
Salute to Miller, an insolent human being who believes
in disorder.   (In French.)

E1083   Brindeau, Serge.   "Je n'aime pas assez Miller," La Tour
de Feu, Autumn 1955, 80-85.
Letter to Pierre Chabert where Miller is called a
prophet who finds his message in individualism and
chaos.   (In French.)

E1084   Carmody, Francis. "Henry Miller et la jeunesse améri-
caine," La Tour de Feu, Autumn 1955, 61-63.
Absurd to call Miller obscene; Tropic a fine book.
(In French.)

E1085   Chabert, Pierre. "Le Colosse aux pieds d'argile," La
Tour de Feu, Autumn 1955, 16-28.
Miller creates optimistic art through his belief in in-
dividualism. (In French.)

E1086   Delahaye, Robert. "Un Mot seulement," La Tour de Feu,
Autumn 1955, 85.
Miller's revolution based on action and living to the
full, while Kafka and Camus see life as absurd. (In
French.)

E1087   Dereux, Philippe. "Le Combat pour la grâce," La Tour
de Feu, Autumn 1955, 38-43.
Miller fights passionately for life. (In French.)

E1088   Hennart, Marcel. "Prière du bon sauvage," La Tour de
Feu, Autumn 1955, 50-51.
Miller's hope, optimism, and innocence compared to
the idealistic concept of the noble savage. (In French.)

E1089   Hornus, Jean-Michel. "Celui par qui le scandale arrive,"
La Tour de Feu, Autumn 1955, 109-114.
Miller's sex a scandal for those who cannot face his
Tropics. (In French.)

E1090   Hornus, Jean-Michel. "Ce qu'apporte le facteur," La
Tour de Feu, Autumn 1955, 4-15.
Series of letters between Miller and Hornus beginning
in October 1951 and going to July of 1955 where
spiritualism and religion are discussed. (In French.)

E1091   Hornus, Jean-Michel. "J'ai rencontré Miller un coeur
pur," La Tour de Feu, Autumn 1955, 29-35.
Hornus talks about his trip to America and pilgrimage
to Big Sur to meet Miller, whom he calls revolutionary
and anti-American. (In French.)

E1092   Humeau, Edmond. "A beau dormir," La Tour de Feu,
Autumn 1955, 124-125.
Miller seen as an imaginary man who has given the
world a new form of art in this poem. (In French.)

E1093   Humeau, Edmond. "Pour revenir à Miller," La Tour de
Feu, Autumn 1955, 119.
Miller's philosophy changed Humeau's conception of
life. (In French.)

E1094   Humeau, Jean-Michel. "L'Invité de la vingt-cinquième

heure," La Tour de Feu, Autumn 1955, 47-49.
Miller's work expresses life and death quite well. (In French.)

E1095 Kanie, Anoma. "Poète vivant," La Tour de Feu, Autumn 1955, 46.
Miller's writing poetic, possessing the quality of a symphony of literature. (In French.)

E1096 Laude, Andre. "Poème," La Tour de Feu, Autumn 1955, 56-57.
Poem where Miller's ability to depict the human crucifixion noted. (In French.)

E1097 Laurent, Jean. "Nu abolu," La Tour de Feu, Autumn 1955, 44.
Poem where Miller is called a being in flux. (In French.)

E1098 Lévy, Yves. "Miller le messie," La Tour de Feu, Autumn 1955, 106-108.
Miller called a liberator of consciousness through the Tropics and The Rosy Crucifixion. (In French.)

E1099 Maillet, Albert. "Pour sauver la petite fille," La Tour de Feu, Autumn 1955, 95-97.
Miller seen as a disciple of Blake. (In French.)

E1100 Marissel, André. "Le Fossoyeur du puritanisme," La Tour de Feu, Autumn 1955, 91-93.
Miller acts as a psychologist and philosopher, using Plexus and The World of Sex, to change people's thinking. (In French.)

E1101 Martel, André. "La Barakamiller," La Tour de Feu, Autumn 1955, 36.
Poem praising Miller and calling his work sublime. (In French.)

E1102 Mathias, Pierre. "Je suis né de ce matin," La Tour de Feu, Autumn 1955, 126-127.
Miller honored as a creative, life giving force. (In French.)

E1103 Maurice, Robert. "Rabelais antidote à Miller," La Tour de Feu, Autumn 1955, 102-105.
The temperaments of Rabelais and Miller are contrasted. (In French.)

E1104 Minisclou. "Pas une leçon, une purge," La Tour de Feu, Autumn 1955, 45-46.
Amazing how scandal centers around Miller, a man obsessed with life. (In French.)

E1105   Mougin, Jules.   "Je vais vous dire," La Tour de Feu,
         Autumn 1955, 93.
             Poem where Miller is seen as an author who writes
             about love.   (In French.)

E1106   Salès, Michel; Henri-Simon Faure; Arthur Pétronio; Mar-
         cel Hennart; Paul Robic; Robert Prade; Grégoire; Henri
         Roser; Roger Mehl; Daniel Parker; Gaston Criel; Henri
         Rode; Marc Alyn; Louis Guillaume; Philippe Durand;
         Georges Delfin; Franz Hellens; Gilbert Lamireau; Alain
         Bouchez; Georges Linze; Jean-Louis Depierris; René Wi-
         told; Irène Jung; Jean Breton; Patrice Cauda; Germaine
         Chomayou; Robert Sabatier; and Pierre Mathias.   "Des
         hommes répondent," La Tour de Feu, Autumn 1955, 65-75.
             Panel discussion on the theme of Henry Miller.   (In
             French.)

E1107   Temple, F. J.   "Miller chez nous," La Tour de Feu,
         Autumn 1955, 52-55.
             Journal where Temple describes his first meeting with
             Miller in Big Sur.   (In French.)

E1108   Tristan, Frédérick.   "Miller ou la passion de l'esprit,"
         La Tour de Feu, Autumn 1955, 98-101.
             Miller a religious man following the teachings of
             Krishnamurti.   (In French.)

E1109   Weltheim, Jérôme de.   "Le Mirage millerien," La Tour
         de Feu, Autumn 1955, 115-118.
             Weltheim toasts Miller and his belief in life.   (In
             French.)

E1110   Rexroth, Kenneth.   "The Neglected Henry Miller," Nation,
         CLXXXI (November 5, 1955), 385-387.
             Rexroth sees Miller concerned with the real world
             through the encounters he depicts in parks, telephone
             booths, and brothels.

E1111   "Important Book by Henry Miller Is Now Released," Pen-
         sacola News-Journal, November 27, 1955, 4C.
             Nights of Love and Laughter important in viewing
             Miller's canon.

E1112   "Looking at Books," Sarasota Herald Tribune, November
         27, 1955, 18.
             Miller a gifted writer obsessed with truth.

E1113   French, Warren.   "One Newcomer, Two Classics among
         Pocketbooks Offering," n.p., December 1955.
             Nights of Love and Laughter clever but disorganized.

E1114   T., A.   "'So-Whatism' Plays into Fakers' Hands," Labors
         Day, December 2, 1955.

Nights of Love and Laughter dull and not original in cynicism.

E1115   Demarest, Donald. "Mass Market Edition Offers Banned Writer," News Weekly, December 11, 1955, 2B, 12B.
Miller genuine and original in Nights of Love and Laughter.

E1116-1120   Preston, Charles. "Paperbacks Bring Best to Readers," Brewster Record, December 29, 1955. Also in: Record, Villager, Yorktown Herald, Townsman, all December 29, 1955.
Nights of Love and Laughter a choice collection of Miller's best.

E1121   Lanier, F. N. "Henry Miller," Monterey Peninsula Herald, January 19, 1956.
Perlès's My Friend Henry Miller depicts Miller as a Bohemian beginning a cult.

E1122   Omarr, Sidney. "Henry Miller Today," Frontier, VII (February 1956), 20-21.
Miller's Nights of Love and Laughter seen as a diverse collection of stories containing one on astrology, another on a Paris prostitute, and a third on an alcoholic veteran.

E1123   Thomson, George Malcolm. "What Is the Truth about Henry Miller?" London Evening Standard, February 7, 1956, 16.
Miller seen as man of Paris in Perles's My Friend Henry Miller.

E1124   Juin, Hubert. "Henry Miller," Combat, February 23, 1956, 6.
Miller, the writer of obscene literature, is also religious and socially concerned. (In French.)

E1125   Perlès, Alfred. "Alfred Perlès raconte comment est né Hamlet de Miller et Fraenkel," Combat, February 23, 1956, 6.
Perlès talks about life and regeneration found in Hamlet. (In French.)

E1126   C., K. "The Song Has Almost Been Forgotten...," Shreveport Times, March 4, 1956, 2F.
The Time of the Assassins a study of Miller that shows his passion and self-revelation.

E1127   Fowlie, Wallace. "A Reflection of Self," New York Times, CV (March 4, 1956), 20.
Review of The Time of the Assassins calling it Miller's autobiography, not a study of Rimbaud.

E1128   Masters, R. E. L.   "Henry Miller: The Controversy
Rages On," Shreveport Times, March 4, 1956, 2F.
Miller's savage bitterness and nihilism leads to hos-
tility.

E1129   "Un Pari d'après boire," France-Observateur, March 8,
1956.
Hamlet a correspondence from 1935-1939 on the philosophy of death.   (In French.)

E1130   Breit, Harvey.   "In and Out of Books: Big Sur," New
York Times, CV (March 11, 1956), VII 8.
Miller living in and loving Big Sur in a mention about
his novel, Big Sur and the Oranges of Hieronymus
Bosch.

E1131   "The Novelist as Painter," London Times, March 12, 1956,
3.
Like Lawrence, Miller's writing and painting depicts
the spirit and flashes of life.

E1132   "Miller and Others," Art News & Review, (March 17,
1956).
Miller's watercolors have fresh brush strokes, as he
paints cubistic and expressionistic art.

E1133   Cendrars, Blaise.   "Historires sur Henry Miller," Arts,
March 21-27, 1956.
Many of the questions Miller had about life in 1935
comprise Hamlet.   (In French.)

E1134   Sommier, Gilbert.   "Sur les côtes du Pacifique," Arts,
March 21-27, 1956.
Savage magnificence found at Big Sur both in the land
and Miller.   (In French.)

E1135   "De mil ville à Miller," Liberté, March 22, 1956.
In Hamlet, Miller and Fraenkel talk about moral disillusionment.   (In French.)

E1136   Kah, Philippe.   "Le Voyage tranvers les livres," Nord
Automobile, March-April 1956, 107.
Mention of the Miller-Fraenkel correspondence.   (In
French.)

E1137   "Miller, Henry," Twentieth Century Literature, II (April
1956), 45.
A look at "The Neglected Henry Miller" by Kenneth
Rexroth.

E1138   Nadeau, Maurice.   "Un Nouveau Hamlet," Le Petit Cevenol,
April 5, 1956.
Miller and Fraenkel call their study of humanity,

Hamlet.   (In French.)

E1139   "Hamlet," Le Populaire du Centre, April 12, 1956.
Life friendships of Miller, Perlès, and Fraenkel recounted in Hamlet.   (In French.)

E1140   Nadeau, Maurice.   "Un Nouveau Hamlet," Les Informations Dieppoises, April 13, 1956.
Hamlet about the philosophy of death.   (In French.)

E1141   M., P.-G.   "Hamlet," Le Berry Républicain, April 18,
1956.
Miller's Hamlet the story of the tragedy of Shakespeare's protagonist.   (In French.)

E1142   Rousselot, Jean.   "Hamlet," Nouvelles Littéraires, April
26, 1956.
Hamlet an exchange of letters on the themes of life
and death.   (In French.)

E1143   "An American in Paris," Times Literary Supplement, LV
(April 27, 1956), 247.
Review of Perlès's My Friend Henry Miller that calls
the book a memoir.

E1144   Auclair, Georges.   "Une Querelle," L'Homme Nouveau,
May 1956, 78-82.
Hamlet deals with the problems of life and death.   (In
French.)

E1145   Venaissin, Gabriel.   "L'Age d'or de Miller," Critique,
XIV (May 1956), 387-399.
Miller great writer of a tour de force work in review
of Hamlet and Perlès's My Friend Henry Miller.

E1146   "Portrait d'Henry Miller," Terre Retrouvée, May 2, 1956.
Hamlet a look at the life of the moment in the Miller-
Fraenkel correspondence.   (In French.)

E1147   Bittner, William.   "A Kind of Genius," Nation, CLXXXII
(May 5, 1956), 455.
Review of Time of the Assassins and My Friend Henry
Miller where Miller's writing is called autobiography.

E1148   Girson, Rochelle.   "Interview," Saturday Review, XXXIX
(May 5, 1956), 15.
Interview with Miller where he discusses beginning
writing at age 33, censorship's effect in Tropic, and
the self as realist.

E1149   Halsband, Robert.   "Epitapher of the Expatriates," Saturday Review, XXXIX (May 5, 1956), 15, 47.
Reviews of My Friend Henry Miller and The Time of

the Assassins where Miller the man and writer is
called hollow.

E1150   "Mon Ami Henry Miller," La Nouvelle Gazette, May 8,
1956.
Discussion of Miller's love of life in a review of My
Friend Henry Miller.   (In French.)

E1151   Faure, Maurice.   "La Joie de vivre de Henry Miller,"
France-Observateur, May 17, 1956.
Miller's humanism draws the reader.   (In French.)

E1152   Bittner, William.   "A Kind of Genius," Nation, CLXXXII
(May 26, 1956), 455-456.
Reviews of My Friend Henry Miller and The Time of
the Assassins where Miller's understanding of time is
discussed.

E1153   "Hamlet par Henry Miller et Michael Fraenkel," Livres
de France, May-June 1956.
In 1935 the question of death bothered Miller.   (In
French.)

E1154   Bonnefoi, Geneviève.   "Deux Portraits d'Henry Miller,"
Les Lettres Nouvelles, June 1956, 919-923.
Look at the Miller-Fraenkel correspondence, called
Hamlet, where both writers attempt to explore the
roots of their being.   (In French.)

E1155   Engbery, Herald.   "To Kapetler mod Krigen," Die Presse,
June 1, 1956.
Miller seen as pacifist, sexist, and mystic.   (In
Danish.)

E1156   "Two Pal Joeys," Time, LXII (June 11, 1956), 114.
Review of My Friend Henry Miller where Miller's
meeting with Perlès, Tropic of Cancer, and The
Booster are discussed.

E1157   Wilson, Pen.   "Defending Henry Miller," New Orleans
Times-Picayune, CXX (June 11, 1956), 10.
Review of Perlès's My Friend Henry Miller which
sees Miller as America's greatest writer.

E1158   Clurman, Robert.   "In and Out of Books: Miller's Moricand," New York Times, CV (July 15, 1956), VII 8.
Review of Devil in Paradise seeing book as affirmation of Miller's unity with the world.

E1159   Zimmer, F.   "Whatever became of Joyce and Henry
Miller, anyway?" New York Times, CV (July 15, 1956),
VII 2.
Drawing of two customs officials.

E1160   Jacques-Benoist, Magdeleine. "Henry Miller et Michael
        Fraenkel: Hamlet," La Table Ronde, July-August 1956.
        Hamlet called an exchange of letters dealing with free-
        dom.   (In French.)

E1161   Brown, Lionel. "King of the Four-Letter Words," Modern
        Man, VI (August 1956), 14-18, 50-51.
        Miller writes about sex in an uninhibited way, as can
        be seen in his two Tropics.

E1162   "Sour Orange Juice," Time, LXVIII (August 13, 1956), 78-
        79.
        A Devil in Paradise tells the story of the Miller-
        Moricand relationship.

E1163   "Appreciating Rimbaud," Times Literary Supplement, LV
        (August 17, 1956), 482.
        Time of the Assassins called the 21st or 31st install-
        ment of Miller's life history and is concerned with
        life and creativity.

E1164   Bugeaunt, Georges.   "Henry Miller est de bonne com-
        pagnie," Guilde du Livre, XXI (September 1956), 356-357.
        Miller a man obsessed with the vitality of life.   (In
        French.)

E1165   Powell, Larry. "Arguments about Astrology," Manas, IX
        (September 5, 1956), 6-7.
        In A Devil in Paradise, Miller sees astrology as ir-
        relevant.

E1166   "Hoe Hurlijh om Miller te Zijn," Nieuive Rotterdamse
        Courant, September 22, 1956, 2.
        Miller returns to Paris and receives welcome as he
        visits old friends and old haunts.   (In Dutch.)

E1167   Gelre, Henk Van.   "Henry Miller over Rimbaud," De
        Maasbode, September 29, 1956, 5.
        Miller a visionary whose book on Rimbaud is one of
        first to capture the essence of the man and writer.
        (In Dutch.)

E1168   "Henry Miller," Sonderbeilage der Main-Post, October
        1956, 5.
        Biography of Miller and a look at Plexus.   (In Ger-
        man.)

E1169   Reiter, Paul J.   "Laegmand og Litteratur...," n.p.,
        October 2, 1956.
        Cancer a book about sex, not life, that shows man's
        failure as he loses control to the machine.   (In
        Danish.)

E1170   "The Time of the Assassins," <u>Listener</u>, LVI (October 18, 1956), 625.
Miller's study of Rimbaud is all mythology.

E1171   Cashen, Eric. "Etchings on White Stone," <u>Intro Bulletin</u>, October-November 1956, 2.
Miller writes the truth about our times.

E1172   Chabrol, Henri. "Anti Miller ou l'hommage à l'équilibre," <u>La Tour de Feu</u>, Autumn 1956, 152-153.
Defense of Miller's work where he is called a social moralist. (In French.)

E1173   Maitlev, Adrian. "Rappel à l'ordre psychologique simple," <u>La Tour de Feu</u>, Autumn 1956, 153.
Miller viewed as a psychologist. (In French.)

E1174   Pelieu, Claude. "La Bonne recontre," <u>La Tour de Feu</u>, Autumn 1956, 151-152.
Miller called a sexist. (In French.)

E1175   Samson, Jean-Paul. "Anti Miller tout court," <u>La Tour de Feu</u>, Autumn 1956, 153-154.
Miller's anti-literary stance seen in the tradition of D. H. Lawrence. (In French.)

E1176   T[emple], F.-J. "Vendanges chez Delteil," <u>Entretiens sur les Lettres et les Arts</u>, VII (Autumn 1956), I.
Miller depicted as a great author who called Delteil "Jesus II." (In French.)

E1177   Tristan, Frédérick. "Une Réussite," <u>La Tour de Feu</u>, Autumn 1956, 153.
Miller a writer obsessed with life. (In French.)

E1178   "Local Bibliophile Has Collection of Rare Ones," <u>Reading (Penn.) Record</u>, November 1, 1956, 14-15.
J. Elmer Quinn has collected Miller, for he realizes his importance as an author.

E1179   Schwanbom, Per. "Henry Miller Sem Ung," <u>B T Måndagen</u>, December 17, 1956.
Miller the forefather of a new literature of autobiography as seen in <u>Capricorn</u>. (In Danish.)

E1180   "Le Colosse de Maroussi," <u>Journal du Commerce et de la Marine</u>, December 29, 1956, 6.
Miller's joy and love of Greece found in <u>The Colossus of Maroussi</u>. (In French.)

E1181   "Impressions of Bruges," <u>Colorado Review</u>, I (Winter 1956-1957), 35-37.

E1182 Hirsh, Trygve. "Letter from Trygve Hirsh," Henry Miller Literary Society Newsletter, 1957, 2-3.

E1183 Rohde, Peter P. "Henry Miller--Pornographer or Prophet?" Henry Miller Literary Society Newsletter, 1957, 4-8.
Miller a writer of autobiography, an individual form that offends society.

E1184 Schwartz, Edward P. "Bulletin of Interest to Henry Miller Partisans," Henry Miller Literary Society Newsletter, 1957, 1.
Welcoming remark from Schwartz followed by an index consisting of: a "Letter from Trygve Hirsh," "Enclosure from Peter P. Rohde," "Enclosure from Johan Voght," "Henry Miller's Letter in Answer."

E1185 Voght, Johan. "Cut Out from Johan Voght's Book," Henry Miller Literary Society Newsletter, 1957, 9-15.
Banning Miller in Norway seen as absurd, for Miller's work displays the best example of the literature of tragedy and solitude of our time.

E1186 Arkush, Art. "Henry Miller's Erotica in Abstract," Art and Photography, VIII (January 1957), 9-12, 46-47.
Miller's writing and painting called a mixture of disconnected items plus Freudian symbols.

E1187 Rousseaux, André. "Best-Sellers," Le Figaro Littéraire, January 12, 1957.
Miller's A Devil in Paradise and Plexus selling well. (In French.)

E1188 "[Article about Henry Miller]," Davar Hashavu'a, January 24, 1957, 10-11, 19.
(In Hebrew.)

E1189 Blanzat, Jean. "Trop, c'est trop de Blaise Cendrars," Le Figaro Littéraire, February 1957, 10.
Miller's friendship with Cendrars mentioned. (In French.)

E1190 "[Henry Miller]," Haolam Haze, February 1, 1957.
(In Hebrew.)

E1191 "Arts Body Elects 12 New Members," New York Times, CVI (February 2, 1957), 21.
Miller among those elected to National Institute of Arts and Letters.

E1192 Levin, Meyer. "Author Henry Miller and the Arts Elite," Long Island Daily Press, (February 8, 1957).
Miller a controversial writer who does not fit into the National Institute of Arts and Letters.

E1193   Hogan, William. "Between the Lines," San Francisco
Chronicle, XCIII (February 10, 1957), 53.
Miller enters National Institute of Arts and Letters.

E1194   Billy, André. "Un Amateur de livres qui n'aime pas la
lecture," Le Figaro Littéraire, February 13, 1957, 2.
Miller's The Loves of My Life is explored favorably.
(In French.)

E1195   Labro, Philippe. "Henry Miller présente les 100 livres
qu'il aime," n.p., February 20-26, 1957.
Miller's interest and effect on literature explored, as
he is called the Julius Caesar of letters.   (In French.)

E1196   Roy, Claude. "Henry Miller et Blaise Cendrars," Le
Quotidien Républicain de Paris, February 27, 1957, 2.
Miller and Cendrars know and feel life.   (In French.)

E1197   Bertrand, Raoul. "Le Paradis de Henry Miller," La Nef,
XIV (March 1957), 53-57.
Bertrand talks about his visit to Big Sur and about
Miller's individualism.   (In French.)

E1198   Schatz, Bezalel. "My Friend Henry Miller," Jerusalem
Post, XXXIII (March 1, 1957), 8.
Miller called the most vital contemporary American
writer.

E1199   "Peintre et académician," L'Express, March 1, 1957, 28-
29.
Miller both a great writer and an exceptional painter
like Chagall.   (In French.)

E1200   "The 'Kingdom' of M. P. Shiel," London Times, March
25, 1957, 6.
Miller called a writer banned in England.

E1201   Labro, Philippe. "Un Dialogue de 'diables': Miller contre
Tericand," Journal 'Arts', March 27-April 22, 1957.
A Devil in Paradise deals with Miller's persecution at
the hands of Conrad Moricand.   (In French.)

E1202   Mauriac, Claude. "Henry Miller du côté des anges,"
Preuves, VIII (April 1957), 90-94.
A Devil in Paradise a tale where Moricand pesters
Miller.   (In French.)

E1203   Praz, Albert. "Libres propos littéraires," Defense de
l'Occident, XLII (April 1957), 56-61.
Miller's The Books in My Life provides a historical
account of Miller.   (In French.)

E1204   "M. Chepilov condamné le 'rock and roll'," Le Journal du

Soir, April 4, 1957.
The Soviet Secretary condemned Cancer as an imperialist novel. (In French.)

E1205   "Chepilov condamné le 'rock and roll'," La Nouvelle République, April 5, 1957.
See E1204.

E1206   "Eve Miller," Monterey Peninsula Herald, April 12, 1957, 19.
Mrs. Henry Miller plays the priestess role in "Caribbean Holiday."

E1207   "The Mystic Cult of Sex and Necromancy, Report on What's Doing Around Little Sur and Peppermint-by-the-Sea," California Pelican, LIII (May 1957), 18-19.
Miller called the leader of a sex cult found at Big Sur.

E1208   "The Object All Sublime," Manas, X (May 8, 1957), 1-2, 7-8.
Miller's Maurizius Forever about the freedom of the individual within society.

E1209   Miller, Ron. "Big Sur Author's Novels Banned Throughout U.S.," El Yanqui, May 10, 1957, 2.
The World of Sex explains Miller's stance.

E1210   Aften, Lørdag. "Norsk Politi Razzia Efter Romanen Sexus," Berlingske Tidende, May 12, 1957, 1-2.
Sexus causes stir in Norway and goes to court. (In Danish.)

E1211   Bert, Hr. "Dansk Miller--Udgave Beslaglagt i Norge," Politiken, May 12, 1957, 3.
Sexus goes to court in Norway with Miller and Reitzel against the state. (In Danish.)

E1212   "Henry Miller Hertil i Aften," Information, May 13, 1957.
Hans Reitzel will soon publish Nexus, third volume in The Rosy Crucifixion. (In Danish.)

E1213   Vogt, Docent Johan. "Miller og Lesef Riheten," Dagbladets Kronik, May 15, 1957.
Discussion of the ban on Sexus in Norway. (In Norwegian.)

E1214   Scratch, Walter L. "Big Sur and the Oranges of Hieronymus Bosch," Citizen-News, May 24, 1957.
Big Sur is Miller's depiction of his state of mind.

E1215   S. "Beslaglaeggelsen af 'Sexus' i Norge Stadfastet," n.p., May 27, 1957.
Miller's Sexus causes stir in Oslo. (In Norwegian.)

E1216   Neiman, Gilbert. "[Review of] Big Sur and the Oranges of Hieronymus Bosch," New Mexico Quarterly, XXVII (Spring-Summer 1957), 138-139.
　　　　Account of the ghosts, idols, and others who inhabit the world of Big Sur.

E1217   Schwartz, Edward P. "Critical Reviews," Henry Miller Literary Society Newsletter, June 1957, 3.
　　　　Noted is the fact that the Society is mentioned in Miller's preface to his Reader.

E1218   Carlbom, Arthur. "Mellow Observations from a Provocative Literary Sage," San Francisco Chronicle, XCIII (June 2, 1957), 23.
　　　　Review of Big Sur that sees Miller as an oriental man whose passiveness detaches him from life.

E1219   Smith, Harrison. "Heaven with Tattered Clouds," St. Petersburg Times, June 2, 1957.
　　　　Big Sur and the Oranges of Hieronymus Bosch a journal of Miller's years in Big Sur.

E1220   Møller, Kai Friis. "Henry Miller," Politiken, June 7, 1957.
　　　　Review of The Colossus of Maroussi that calls book a great and moving work. (In Danish.)

E1221   Rosenthal, M. L. "The Millennium of Henry Miller," Nation, CLXXXIV (June 8, 1957), 502-503.
　　　　Big Sur seen as a depiction of the Thoreauvian life in Big Sur where creative, self-reliant men endure.

E1222   Baker, Carlos. "Mr. Miller's Garden of Eden," New York Times, CVI (June 9, 1957), VII 22.
　　　　Miller's book about his home in Big Sur concerns itself with metaphors of paradise.

E1223   Foote, Robert O. "Henry Miller Likes the Big Sur Country," Independent Star News, June 9, 1957, 9.
　　　　Big Sur a paradise to Miller much like the one found in Bosch's paintings.

E1224   Getlein, Frank. "Henry Miller's Crowded Simple Life," Milwaukee Journal, LXXV (June 9, 1957), V5.
　　　　Big Sur concerns itself with Miller's perceptions about the simple life found on the California coast.

E1225   "Big Sur-Realism," Time, LXIX (June 10, 1957), 106-108.
　　　　Review of Big Sur that sees Miller's utopia as a failure in the tradition of New Harmony and Oneida, N.Y.

E1226   Baker, Carlos. "[Review of] Big Sur and the Oranges of Hieronymus Bosch," New Yorker, XXXIII (June 15, 1957),

127.
Miller's book called a potpourri of fragments of life
found in California.

E1227   Epstein, Lester.   "Miller Grinds Out Another...," Mexico City News, June 16, 1957.
Big Sur a book about the private life Miller found in
California; Bosch's orange symbolizes the delights of
paradise.

E1228   Bohm, Anton.   "Henry Miller: Fleisch und Gnosis,"
Wort und Wahrheit, XII (June-July 1957), 421-443.
Miller a realist and a moralist, as seen from such
writings as The World of Sex and Obscenity and Law
of Reflexion.   (In German.)

E1229   Dillon, R. H.   "[Review of] Big Sur and the Oranges of
Hieronymus Bosch," Library Journal, LXXXII (July 1957),
1770.
Miller's novel depicts the visitors who intrude on his
California world.

E1230   Holmes, Blanca.   "Henry Miller and Clifford Odets,"
American Astrology, XXV (July 1957), 29-31.
Miller's horoscope presented and his life traced ac-
cording to the stars.

E1231   Sordo, Enrique.   "El Coloso de Marusi," Revista de
Actualidades Artes y Letras, July 6-12, 1957.
With the translation of The Colossus of Maroussi into
Spanish, many more people can see the humanity of
Miller.   (In Spanish.)

E1232   Adams, Phoebe.   "Reader's Choice," Atlantic, CC (August
1957), 82.
Review of Big Sur that calls Miller's work about a
paradise on earth a subtle masterpiece.

E1233   Baker, George.   "Avant Garde at the Golden Gate," Satur-
day Review, XL (August 3, 1957), 10.
Miller mentioned as a founding father of the "Beat
Generation. "

E1234   Barrett, William.   "Henry Miller: Man in Quest of Life.
II. His Exuberant Reflections," Saturday Review, XL
(August 3, 1957), 9-10.
Miller's Big Sur the work of an aging sage.

E1235   Haverstick, John.   "Henry Miller: Man in Quest of Life.
I. His Turbulent Career," Saturday Review, XL (August 3,
1957), 8.
Miller's Tropic rebellious; Big Sur is true to form.

E1236   S[aal], H[ubert].   "I Am an Artist," <u>Saturday Review</u>, XL
(August 3, 1957), 18.
>   Miller's belief that the artist colony at Big Sur is the
answer to the artist's problems is absurd and overly
simplistic.

E1237   "Books and Gangsters," <u>Pravda Ukrainy</u>, August 9, 1957,
3.
>   Miller called an anti-humanistic writer.

E1238   Anspacher, Carolyn.   " 'Howl' Trial Starts--Big Crowd,"
<u>San Francisco Chronicle</u>, XCIII (August 17, 1957), 1, 4.
>   Miller a spectator at trial.

E1239   Baro, Gene.   "In Paradise, and Thinking Out Loud," <u>New
York Herald Tribune</u>, CXVII (August 18, 1957), VI 2.
>   <u>Big Sur</u> is a justification of Miller's life.

E1240   Fowlie, Wallace.   "Two American Autobiographies,"
<u>Accent</u>, XVII (Summer 1957), 188-192.
>   Review of <u>Big Sur</u> that sees it moving between the real
world and a spiritual world that culminates in a combination of the two.

E1241   Seco.   "El Coloso de Marusi," <u>El Norte de Castilla</u>,
September 1957.
>   Miller's <u>Colossus of Maroussi</u> an interesting travelog
of his journey to Greece.   (In Spanish.)

E1242   B.   " 'El Coloso de Marusi', un libro admirable de Henry
Miller," <u>Baleadej</u>, September 12, 1957.
>   Miller's <u>Colossus</u> a book about independence and glory.
(In Spanish.)

E1243   Kristensen, Tom.   "Bog for vaksne," <u>Erotic Anthology</u>,
October 1957, 7.
>   Miller viewed as pornographer and prophet.   (In
Danish.)

E1244   "Libros por correo," <u>Papeles de Son Armadans</u>, VII (October 1957), 13-14.
>   Review of <u>The Colossus of Maroussi</u> that sees Miller
as a man who can truly express his feelings.   (In
Spanish.)

E1245   Bradbury, Malcolm.   "Henry Miller: Room at the Very
Bottom," <u>Gemini</u>, I (Autumn 1957), 49-58.
>   "Miller is the American loathing America yet carry-
ing it always with him, the expatriate as permanent
outsider" (p. 58).

E1246   "Henry Miller: Der Parasit," <u>Der Spiegel</u>, XI (November
11, 1957), 46-47.

Miller a being who preys on others.   (In German.)

E1247   "Submissive and Sexless?" Newsweek, L (November 25,
1957), 119-120.
Miller's watercolors being shown at the Templeton
Gallery in New York. The display of 29 shows Miller
in the tradition of Raoul, Dufy, and Marin.

E1248   Chisholm, Hugh. "A Man-Sized World. Letter to Henry
Miller in Big Sur, California, from Hugh Chisholm in
Athens, Greece," Town and Country, CXI (December
1957), 87-89, 154-155.
Praise of The Colossus of Maroussi for its ability to
capture the universal heart of Greece.

E1249   Durrell, Lawrence. "The Shades of Dylan Thomas," Encounter, IX (December 1957), 56-59.
Durrell talks about Thomas's interest in Miller.

E1250   H-d. "Norsk Politirazzia Efter Romanen Sexus," n. p.,
December 5, 1957, 1-2.
Sexus being published in Norway.   (In Norwegian.)

E1251   "Big Sur and the Oranges of Hieronymus Bosch," Biography
and Autobiography, 1958, 45.
Miller's Big Sur the story of his finding a paradise in
Big Sur, Calif.

E1252   Moore, Bob. "A Note on Henry Miller," Alumnus, III
(1958), 1.
Miller compared to Stein and Pound because of the
controversy each evoked.

E1253   Carnahan, Ken. "Contenders for 1958 National Book
Awards," Berkeley Daily Gazette, January 11, 1958, 13.
Henry Miller Recalls and Reflects is a recorded
Miller conversation with Ben Graur.

E1254   R., A. "Des Lächeln am Kreuze Bemerkungen zum Werk
von Henry Miller," Panorama, February-March 1958, 4.
Miller's Rosy Crucifixion should be banned in the U.S.
(In German.)

E1255   Legg, Morley D. "Perceptions of a Creative Writer: An
Introduction to Henry Miller," Orgonomic Functionalism,
V (March 1958), 91-102.
Miller in the tradition of Wilhelm Reich, arousing
laughter and sex and depicting the baseness to which
man has fallen.

E1256   "Merhintöjä: Vaarallinen Henry," Parnasso, March 1958,
50.
Miller a pornographer vomiting out truth.   (In Finnish.)

E1257   Ritter, Paul.   "Book Reviews: Big Sur and the Oranges
        of Hieronymus Bosch," Orgonomic Functionalism, V
        (March 1958), 127-131.
            Miller's Big Sur shows insight and self-criticism.

E1258   Baruch, Gertrud.   "Henry Miller," Bücherei und Bildung,
        March 7, 1958.
            Review of Big Sur.   (In German.)

E1259   Kraus, Wolfgang.   "Lebensgenub in Pantoffeln," Der Tag,
        March 23, 1958.
            Review of Big Sur.   (In German.)

E1260   Wain, John.   "A Great Big Something," London Observer,
        March 23, 1958, 17.
            Big Sur deals with Miller's life at Big Sur and with
            Paradise Lost.

E1261   W. , H. L.   "Big Sur and the Oranges of Hieronymus
        Bosch," Express & Star, March 26, 1958.
            Big Sur is Miller's study of Big Sur life.

E1262   Owen, Evan.   "Henry Miller: A Happy Man," Oxford Mail,
        March 27, 1958.
            Big Sur is Miller's millennium, a dream world of the
            surrealist.

E1263   Vausittart, Peter.   "Big Sur and Elsewhere," London
        Spectator, March 28, 1958, 406.
            Big Sur depicts life in a California paradise.

E1264   Young, Kenneth.   "Henry Miller Beats the Ban," London
        Daily Telegraph, March 28, 1958, 15.
            Big Sur shows that Miller's work lies between John
            Cowper Powys's sensuality and Zen Buddhism.

E1265   "A Landscape Crowded Like a Bosch Panel," Scotsman,
        March 29, 1958, 12.
            Big Sur shows that Miller finds his earthly paradise
            in nature.

E1266   R. , M. G.   "Henry Miller Vond het Aards Paradijs," De
        Standaard, March 29, 1958, 8.
            Miller has honestly faced sex since the 1930's when
            Tropic appeared.   Now he transcends to the paradise
            of Big Sur.   (In Dutch.)

E1267   Read, Herbert.   "As the Grass Grows," New Statesman,
        LV (March 29, 1958), 410.
            Big Sur called both humorous and apocalyptic in this
            review.

E1268   Webster, Jan.   "On New Books: Big Sur and the Oranges

of Hieronymus Bosch," Publisher's Circular, CLXXII
(March 29, 1958), 440-441.
Big Sur is Miller's paradise on earth.

E1269   Priestley, J. B.   "The Tortoise Who Will End As a Lion,"
Reynolds News, March 30, 1958.
Miller ties life on the coastline to the dream of
Bosch.

E1270   Haan, Jacques Den.   "Big Sur en de Vrede van Schevenin-
gen," Litterair Paspoort, April 1958, 77-79.
Miller blends the saint and whore together in "Mademoiselle Claude" and in Big Sur.   (In Dutch.)

E1271   Moon, Eric.   "Too Hot to Handle," Books and Bookmen,
III (April 1958), 25.
Review of Big Sur calling it the autobiography of
Miller's life in the California mountains.

E1272   Morice-Kerné, A.   "La Lecture Heureuse," L'Ecole Ma-
ternelle Française, XXXV (April 1958), 4-6, 38.
Miller's The Books in My Life seen as an incredible
storehouse of literature.   (In French.)

E1273   "Books and Gangsters," Library Journal, LXXXIII (April 1,
1958), 1022-1023.
Miller called an anti-humanistic writer.

E1274   Hewitt, Douglas.   "Life on Six Levels at Once," Manchester Guardian, April 1, 1958, 4.
Big Sur provides Miller's account of life in an earthly
paradise.

E1275   "Big Sur and the Oranges of Hieronymus Bosch," Guardian-
Journal, April 3, 1958.
Miller discusses the paradise he has found in Big Sur.

E1276   Fane, Vernon.   "A Provocative Stylist," Sphere, April 5,
1958.
Big Sur an autobiography that conveys Miller's individual style.

E1277   "Paradise Regained," Economist CLXXXVII (April 5, 1958),
23.
Miller meditates about his California world he calls
paradise in Big Sur.

E1278   Thomas, Gilbert.   "Round the Shelves," Birmingham Post,
April 8, 1958.
Big Sur a book about Christian truth, as Miller ex-
presses his soul.

E1279   Jones, Mervyn.   "Sex, anarchy and Henry Miller," News

Chronicle, April 9, 1958.
Big Sur a religious expression about Miller's finding peace.

E1280   Frere, A. S. "Obscene Books," New Statesman, LV (April 12, 1958), 475.
Big Sur a fine book by an author who is anything but obscene.

E1281   Montague, John. "Cosmic Contemplations," Irish Times, April 19, 1958, 8.
Big Sur is Miller the sage on peace, love, and brotherhood.

E1282   Tyler, Froom. "Miller's Tale," South Wales Evening Post, April 19, 1958, 1.
Miller, like Bosch, finds paradise in this review of Big Sur.

E1283   Widmer, Kingsley. "Timeless Prose," Twentieth Century Literature, IV (April-July 1958), 3-7.
Miller's work called "poetic-prose."

E1284   Woodbridge, Hensley C. "Library Journal," Abstracts of English Studies, I (May 1958), 124-125.
Miller seen as anti-humanistic writer in Pravda Ukrainy, Aug. 9, 1957.

E1285   Cecil, Lord David. "The Traveller Comes Home," Times Literary Supplement, LVII (May 2, 1958), 242.
Big Sur a book about American primitivism.

E1286   Popham, Hugh. "Borborygmy," Time and Tide, XXXIX (May 3, 1958), 562.
Big Sur a book about the American wilderness Miller has found.

E1287   Démétriadès, Hélène. "Alexis Zorba: Uba et le cimetière marin," Guilde du Livre, XXIII (June 1958), 234-235.
Miller's poetic myth about Greece, The Colossus of Maroussi, mentioned. (In French.)

E1288   Parkinson, Thomas. "The Hilarity of Henry Miller," Listener, LIX (June 19, 1958), 1021-1022.
Big Sur a book about joy, prophesy, and love that Miller finds in California.

E1289   Tennant, Kylie. "Henry Miller Breaks Away from Society," Sydney Morning Herald, June 21, 1958, 18.
Big Sur a prophetic work in the tradition of Thoreau and Emerson.

E1290   "Banned Books," Books and Bookmen, III (August 1958), 3.

The Institute of Contemporary Arts mocks England's censorship of Miller who is called more human toward women then Lawrence.

E1291 "Plexus assolto revocato il sequestro," La Notte, August 1, 1958, 4.
Plexus being tried in Italy for obscenity. (In Italian.)

E1292 Grauer, Ben. "Henry Miller: A 'First Audition' of a Great American Writer," Artesian, III (Summer 1958), 12-13.
The recording of Miller by Grauer is described by Grauer as a new form of writing, not a conversation.

E1293 Pritchett, V. S. "The Beat Generation," New Statesman, LVI (September 6, 1958), 292-294.
Miller's recurrent theme is that society is evil.

E1294 "Censors Are Wrong," Minneapolis Star, LXXX (September 18, 1958), 10.
Censorship of Tropic goes against basic liberties.

E1295 "Man at Work: Emil White--Artist, Writer and Publisher," Monterey Peninsula Herald, October 18, 1958, 15.
White and Miller are pioneer settlers at Big Sur.

E1296 Seiler, Alexander J. P. "Henry Miller in Big Sur," Sonntags-Beilage, October 26, 1958, 1.
Big Sur is Miller's paradise. (In German.)

E1297 Braem, Helmut M. "Vademecum des Henry Miller," Literaturblatt, October 31, 1958.
Review of Big Sur and the Oranges of Hieronymus Bosch. (In German.)

E1298 Hanna, John G. "New Statesman," Abstracts of English Studies, I (November 1958), 345.
V. S. Prichett's "The Beat Generation" notes Miller's recurrent theme that society is evil.

E1299 "Im Anfang," Schwäb Donaui-Zeitung, November 8, 1958.
Review of Big Sur and the Oranges of Hieronymus Bosch. (In German.)

E1300 "Henry Miller," Kasseler Zeitung, November 15, 1958.
Review of Big Sur and the Oranges of Hieronymus Bosch. (In German.)

E1301 Blöcher, Gunther. "Einfuhrung in ein neues Leben," Der Tagesspiegel, November 16, 1958.
Review of Big Sur. (In German.)

E1302 "Romane und Erzählungen," Offenbach Post, November 20,

1958.
Review of Big Sur.   (In German.)

E1303   K. , R.   "Miller, " Frankfurter Neue Presse, November 22,
1958.
Review of Big Sur.   (In German.)

E1304   Kraus, Wolfgang.   "Lebensgenub in Pantoffeln, " Der Tag,
November 23, 1958.
Review of Big Sur.   (In German.)

E1305   Lennig, Walter.   "Amerika so und so, " Sonntagsblatt,
November 23, 1958.
Big Sur reviewed.   (In German.)

E1306   Lennig, Walter.   "Henry Miller, " Sonntagsblatt, November
23, 1958.
Big Sur reviewed.   (In German.)

E1307   K. , W.   "Lebensgenub in Pantoffeln, " Schwäbisches Tagblatt, November 25, 1958.
Big Sur reviewed.   (In German.)

E1308   K. , W.   "Lebensgenub in Pantoffeln, " Der Enztäler, November 26, 1958.
Review of Big Sur.   (In German.)

E1309   K. , W.   "Legensgenub in Pantoffeln, " Der Grenzer, November 26, 1958.
Review of Big Sur.   (In German.)

E1310   F. , W.   "Henry Miller, " Stuttgarter Nachrichten, November 29, 1958.
Review of Big Sur.   (In German.)

E1311   Kraus, Wolfgang.   "Legensgenub in Pantoffeln, " Lazener
Neuiste Nachrichten, November 29, 1958.
Review of Big Sur.   (In German.)

E1312   Kraus, Wolfgang.   "Lebensgenub in Pantoffeln, " Meneske,
November 29, 1958.
Review of Big Sur.   (In German.)

E1313   "Potpourri im Paradies, " Die Gegenwart, November 29,
1958.
Review of Big Sur.   (In German.)

E1314   Dixon, Daniel.   "The *†&!--1/?D**! Genius, " Pageant,
XIV (December 1958), 81-87.
Miller a controversial genius who has been misunder-
stood.

E1315   "Henry Miller, " Österreichischer Rundfunk, December

1958.
Review of Big Sur. (In German.)

E1316 E., M. "Henry Miller," Das Bücherblatt, December 4,
1958.
Review of Big Sur. (In German.)

E1317 Blocker, Gunther. "Vorzugsplatz im Paradies," Frankfurter Allgemeine, December 6, 1958.
Review of Big Sur. (In German.)

E1318 K., H. "Henry Miller in Big Sur," Beleg-Sendung, December 9, 1958.
Review of Big Sur. (In German.)

E1319 K., H. "Henry Miller in Big Sur," Darmstädter Echo,
December 9, 1958.
Review of Big Sur. (In German.)

E1320 "Für den Büchertisch," Kulturelles Wort, XX (December
10, 1958).
Big Sur reviewed. (In German.)

E1321 "Henry Miller," Bücherschiff, December 12, 1958.
Review of Big Sur. (In German.)

E1322/3 N. "Paradies ohne Kanalisation," Düsseldorfer Nachrichten, December 13, 1958.
Review of Big Sur. (In German.)

E1324 B., G. "Kalifornisches Potpourri," Deutsche Zeitung, December 17, 1958.
Review of Big Sur. (In German.)

E1325 Fukuzawa, Ichirô. "Water Paintings of Henry Miller,"
Colorado Review, III (Winter 1958-1959), 15-16.
Miller first startled the Japanese public with Sexus
and again with his painting.

E1326 "Henry Miller," Colorado Review, III (Winter 1958-1959),
12-14.
Miller pictured in old and new studios with wife, Eve.
His art displayed in three watercolors, one completed
in 1955, another in 1956, and a third in 1957.

E1327 "Henry Miller and his Watercolors," Colorado Review, III
(Winter 1958-1959), 11-16.
The importance of Miller as a painter discussed along
with the relationship of art and the man.

E1328 Perlès, Alfred. "Additions to Bibliography of Henry
Miller's Work Since Its Publication in Appendix of My
Friend Henry Miller," Colorado Review, III (Winter 1958-

1959), 14.
Lists additional work by and about Miller.

E1329   "Editorial," Sidewalk, I (1959).
Reference made to Miller and his censorship.

E1330   G., N. "Henry Miller: Big Sur," Der Fleend, 1959.
Mention of Miller's home in Big Sur. (In German.)

E1331   Kirsch, Robert R. "A Beautiful Henry Miller Book," Los
Angeles Times, 1959.
To Paint Is to Love Again viewed as Miller's best
piece of writing in the past two decades and consists
of 14 colored plates of Miller's art.

E1332   Sabatier, Robert. "Les Romans, quelques paysages ro-
manesques," Le Temps des Hommes, 1959, 87-92.
Review of Big Sur calling Miller's style romantic.
(In French.)

E1333   Seferis, George. "Les Anges sont blancs," Quarterly Review of Literature, X (1959). (In French.)

E1334   Uhlit, Helmut. "Author zwischen Mythos und Pornographie,"
Texte und Zeichen, II (January 1959), 192-202.
Miller a writer of myth and pornography. (In Ger-
man.)

E1335   Venetikos, Alexandros. "Letter from Phaestos," Wander-
lust, I (January 1959), 20-21.
Letter to Miller.

E1336   "Is Henry Miller Really a Positive Thinker?" Shreveport
Times, January 25, 1959.
Miller's The Smile at the Foot of the Ladder is both
parable and poetry.

E1337   "Le Colosse de Maroussi," Guilde du Livre, February
1959, 50-51.

E1338   Cuifboynes, Lol-Elie. "Le Colosse de Maroussi," Guilde
du Livre, XXIV (February 1959), 50-51.
Brief Miller biography and description of his journey
to Greece. (In French.)

E1339   "Henry Miller--Privat," Die Frukuunft, February 1959.
Review of Big Sur. (In German.)

E1340   Woodbridge, Hensley C. "Pageant," Abstracts of English
Studies, II (February 1959), 53.
Dixon's article conveys the idea that Miller is the
world's most controversial author.

E1341   Ferber, Christian.   "Die erbärmliche und die herrliche
Welt," Die Welt, February 14, 1959.
Review of Big Sur.   (In German.)

E1342   "Henry Miller Paradies," Badische Zeitung, February 17,
1959.
Big Sur reviewed.   (In German.)

E1343   Hühnerfeld, Paul.   "Obszönster Schriftsteller," Die Zeit,
February 20, 1959, 7.
Review of Big Sur.   (In German.)

E1344   Brenner, Jacques.   "Le Centre du Monde," Guilde du
Livre, XXIV (March 1959), 94-95.
Miller's Colossus compared to Melville's Moby Dick.
(In French.)

E1345   "Henry Miller," Gluchkeit, March 1959.
Review of Big Sur.   (In German.)

E1346   Gensecke, Hanns.   "Refugium in Kalifornien," Telegraf,
March 1, 1959.
Review of Big Sur.   (In German.)

E1347   Adler, Jack.   "Nocturne," Record, LXII (March 4, 1959).
Miller's Tropics and Rosy Crucifixion criticize American education.

E1348   Kraus, Wolfgang.   "Henry Miller--Sympathisch Normal,"
Sabslenrger Nachrichten, March 4, 1959.
Big Sur reviewed.   (In German.)

E1349   Lundemann, Reinhold.   "Gefundenes und verlorenes Paradies," Reinische Post, March 7, 1959.
A look at Big Sur.   (In German.)

E1350   S.   "Henry Miller," Die Ostsdineers, March 7, 1959.
Big Sur viewed.   (In German.)

E1351   L., H.   "Henry Millers Big Sur," Westdeutsche Allgemeine, March 11, 1959.
Review of Big Sur.   (In German.)

E1352   "Henry Miller," Les Ecrivains Américains à Paris et
Leurs Amis, VI (March 11-April 25, 1959), 108-109.
Listed are Miller's works from Cancer (1934) through
Capricorn (1946).   (In French.)

E1353   "Henry Miller," Suddeutsche Zeitung, March 15, 1959.
Review of Big Sur.   (In German.)

E1354   "Lawrence Novel to Be Reissued," New York Times,
CVIII (March 19, 1959), 30.

Miller's Tropic mentioned in article dealing with
Grove Press's publishing of Lady Chatterley's Lover.

E1355   Lewis, Anthony. "U.S. Relaxes Ban on Miller Novel,"
New York Times, CVIII (March 20, 1959), 25.
   U.S. Customs Bureau has admitted the importation of
Tropic into America.

E1356   "Miller Kommer med Kone og Barn," Dagbladet, March
23, 1959, 9.
   Miller's Norway trial and Hirsh's defense of Sexus
discussed. (In Norwegian.)

E1357   "Henry Miller übersiedelt nach Europa," Tagesonzeiger,
March 25, 1959.
   Big Sur reviewed. (In German.)

E1358   Ouellette, Fernand. "Blaise Cendrars, ou l'homme aux
deux pieds sur les pôles," Liberté 60, I (March-April
1959), 79-84.
   Mention made of the Miller-Cendrars friendship. (In
French.)

E1359   Ouellette, Fernand. "Le Boa gracile," Liberté 60, I
(March-April 1959), 97.
   Miller called a humane visionary. (In French.)

E1360   "Miller," Deutsche Rundschau, April 1959.
   Review of Big Sur. (In German.)

E1361   L., A. "Big Sur ist Henry Miller's Paradies," Der
Kurier, April 4, 1959.
   Big Sur reviewed. (In German.)

E1362   Durrell, Lawrence and Edward Mullins. "Lawrence Durrell Answers a Few Questions," Two Cities, V (April 15,
1959), 25-28.
   Interview: Durrell in sympathy with and influenced by
Miller.

E1363   Fanchette, Jean. "Notes pour une préface," Two Cities,
V (April 15, 1959), 56-60.
   Cancer called one of the two greatest books in recent
literature.

E1364/5 Fisner, Lotte H. "Un Surréaliste du cinéma experimental: Ian Hugo," Two Cities, V (April 15, 1959), 80-
83.
   Miller sees each person able to sit both inside and
outside himself while watching a movie. (In French.)

E1366   Perlès, Alfred. "Enter Jupiter Jr.," Two Cities, V
(April 15, 1959), 7-10.

Describes Miller's love and respect for Durrell and their first meeting.

E1367   Temple, Frédéric J.   "Construire un mur de pierre séche," Two Cities, V (April 15, 1959), 11-12.
The Miller circle mentioned.   (In French.)

E1368   Crandall, Steve.   "Henry Miller: Pornographer or Pioneer?" Gallant, I (May 1959), 10-12.
Miller seen as a pioneer who believes in changing the world rather than adapting to it.

E1369   Fraenkel, Michael.   "Portrait de Henry Miller," Guilde du Livre, XXIV (May 1959), 196.
Fraenkel sees Miller as a man who knows how to suffer and face life.   (In French.)

E1370   Vermeer, Roeland J.   "Henry Miller en de Stilte," Kultuur Leven, XXVI (May 1959), 291-292.
Miller a moralist who is misunderstood in the U.S.
(In Dutch.)

E1371   Perlès, Alfred.   "Portrait de Henry Miller," Guilde du Livre, XXIV (May 5, 1959), 196-197.
Miller seen as vagabond, yet a real, positive, honest life force.   (In French.)

E1372   "Ecrivain 'interdit' Miller retrouve 'le Paris de la liberté et de la passion'," Radar, May 8, 1959, 11-12.
(In French.)

E1373   "Henry Miller--besøg," Berlingske Aftenavis, May 13, 1959.
Miller visited Copenhagen with his wife Eve and saw Hans Reitzel.   (In Danish.)

E1374   Johansen, Niels Kaas.   "Den Maerkelige Mr. Miller," B.T., May 13, 1959.
Miller who was once a bum in Paris is now one of the best writers in the world, as seen through his Cosmological Eye.   (In Danish.)

E1375   E-sen.   "Nexus--Det Er Jo et Godt Ord!" Dagens Nyheder, May 14, 1959.
Reitzel will publish Nexus in Swedish and Norwegian.
(In Danish.)

E1376   "Den Amerikanske Forfatter Henry Miller," Morsø Folkeblad, May 14, 1959.
Picture of Miller and children in Copenhagen.   (In Danish.)

E1377   "Den Kendte Amerikanske Forfatter Henry Miller," Thisted Amts Tidende, May 14, 1959.

Picture of Miller in Copenhagen with children. (In Danish.)

E1378   'Henry Miller Ankommet, " Aarhus Amtstidende, May 14, 1959.
         Miller will return to Paris from Denmark. (In Danish.)

E1379   'Henry Miller Er nu i København, " Vestkysten, May 14, 1959.
         Miller in Copenhagen since leaving Paris. (In Danish.)

E1380   'Henry Miller i Danmark, " Nordsjaellands Venstreblad, May 14, 1959.
         Miller's trilogy, Sexus, Nexus, and Plexus, to be published by Hans Reitzel. (In Danish.)

E1381   'Henry Miller i København, " Fredericia Dagblad, May 14, 1959.
         Miller and children in Copenhagen. (In Danish.)

E1382   'Henry Miller i København, " Herning Folkeblad, May 14, 1959.
         Miller to meet with Reitzel. (In Danish.)

E1383   'Henry Miller i København, " Kalundborg Folkeblad, May 14, 1959.
         Picture of Miller in Copenhagen with his son and daughter. (In Danish.)

E1384   'Henry Miller i København, " Lolland-Falsters Folketidende, May 14, 1959.
         Miller in Copenhagen with children. (In Danish.)

E1385   'Henry Miller i København, " Østsjaellands Folkeblad, May 14, 1959.
         Miller and children in Copenhagen. (In Danish.)

E1386   'Henry Miller i København, " Silkeborg Avis, May 14, 1959.
         Miller and children in Copenhagen to meet with Hans Reitzel. (In Danish.)

E1387   'Henry Miller i København, " Vejle Amts Folkeblad, May 14, 1959.
         Picture of Miller and children in Copenhagen. (In Danish.)

E1388   'Henry Miller Paabesøg, " Vendsyssel Tidende, May 14, 1959.
         Photo of Miller and children in Copenhagen for meeting with Reitzel. (In Danish.)

E1389   "Miller i København: Nexus Kommer Snart, " Aktuelt, May 14, 1959.
         Sexus translated into Norwegian and Nexus into Danish. (In Danish.)

E1390   "Miller til Norge, " Aalborg Stiftstidende, May 14, 1959.
        Sixty-seven-year-old Miller in Copenhagen.   (In
        Danish.)

E1391   "Utrivlsomt, " Information, May 14, 1959.
        Miller's Nexus to appear in Swedish.   (In Danish.)

E1392   Vest.   "Portraet af en Kaetter: Henry Miller i Danmark, "
        Information, May 14, 1959.
        Miller in Denmark to make arrangements for publica-
        tion of Nexus.   (In Danish.)

E1393   "Vi Jordens Børn--Og vor Fremtid, " Ekstra Bladet, May
        14, 1959.
        More Miller to be published in Denmark.   (In Danish.)

E1394   Avislaeseren.   "Intet fraadende uhyre..., " Information,
        May 15, 1959.
        Miller's writing called neurotic.   (In Danish.)

E1395   "Henry Miller i Danmark, " Soro Amtstidende, May 15, 1959.
        Miller in Denmark to meet Reitzel.   (In Danish.)

E1396   "Henry Miller i København, " Aalborg Amtstidende, May 15,
        1959.
        Miller and children in Denmark.   (In Danish.)

E1397   "Henry Miller i København, " Frederiksborg Amts Avis,
        May 15, 1959.
        Miller and children in Denmark.   (In Danish.)

E1398   "Henry Miller i København, " Langelands Avis, May 15,
        1959.
        Miller in Denmark.   (In Danish.)

E1399   "Nexus Er paa Vej, " Viborg Stifts Forkeblad, May 15,
        1959.
        Miller has enjoyed Denmark and Paris.   (In Danish.)

E1400   Hansen, Eva Hemmer.   "Miller og Pasternak, " Aktuelt,
        May 16, 1959.
        Miller's Sexus on trial in Norway for being pornogra-
        phy.   (In Danish.)

E1401   "Henry Miller om Skaebnens Spor i Hans Liv, " Politiken,
        May 16, 1959.
        Miller a moral man idealistic enough to want para-
        dise on earth.   (In Danish.)

E1402   "Mine Bøger Staar jo Frit Fremme i Alle Bøglader, "
        Berlingske Tidende, May 16, 1959.
        Miller's fame comes from Tropic, Sexus, and Plexus,
        all well received in Denmark.   (In Danish.)

E1403   Ninka. "Henry Miller:--Moral Er et Spørgsmaal om
        Somvittighed," Dagens Nyheder, May 16, 1959.
        Miller's style like Dostoevsky's, Hamsun's, and Poe's.
        His novel Nexus to be published in Denmark.   (In
        Danish.)

E1404   Skanollikok.   "Møde med Giraffen, " Information, May 16,
        1959.
        Reitzel defends Miller's freedom to write.   (In Danish.)

E1405   Coulbourn, Keith.   "Henry Miller Belongs, " Shreveport
        Times, May 17, 1959.
        Miller linked to Rabelais.

E1406   M. , H. S.   "Henry Miller om Forskellen mellem Ameri-
        kanerne og Os, " Aalborg Stiftstidende, May 17, 1959.
        Miller dislikes American society as Nexus shows.   (In
        Danish.)

E1407   "Glad for det Social og Frie Denmark, " Frederiksborg
        Amts Avis, May 19, 1959.
        Miller enjoys Strindberg.   (In Danish.)

E1408   J. , J. -F.   "Reichel, " Cahiers du Musée de Poche, VI
        (June 1959), 30.
        Miller and Reichel were friends who wrote about the
        same Paris world.   (In French.)

E1409   "Henry Miller, " Der Atund, June 10, 1959.
        Review of Big Sur.   (In German.)

E1410   L. , S.   "Books: This Week's Gossip, " Illustrated Weekly
        of India, LXXX (June 14, 1959), 50.
        The Smile at the Foot of the Ladder a story about a
        clown who is himself, not an actor.

E1411   "Henry Miller, " Atund Post, June 21, 1959.
        Big Sur reviewed.   (In German.)

E1412   Eyerman, J. R.   "Rugged, Romantic World Apart, " Life,
        XLVII (July 6, 1959), 56-65.
        At 67, Miller seen as the patriarch of Big Sur.

E1413   Stella.   "A Dangerous Devil's Play, " Kontakt med Tiden,
        August 1959, 416-417, 437.
        A Devil in Paradise a socially conscious work com-
        bined with individualism and the astrology of Conrad
        Moricand.   (In Danish.)

E1414   "Noches de amor y de alegría, " Clarín, August 9, 1959.
        Nights of Love and Laughter called a humanistic work.
        (In Spanish.)

E1415   "Children ... and Ourselves: Unnecessary Fears," Manas,
        XII (August 19, 1959), 5.
            Miller fears the way adults take their children, mold
        them, and make them products of society at a loss of
        the self.

E1416   "Best-Seller de la semana," Correo de la Tarde, August
        31, 1959.
            Favorable review of Miller's Nights of Love and Laugh-
        ter. (In Spanish.)

E1417   Kleine, Don. "Innocence Forbidden: Henry Miller in the
        Tropics," Prairie Schooner, XXXIII (Summer 1959), 125-
        130.
            Miller writes two kinds of prose, one mystical, the
        other real. He is a dualistic being, experiencing life's
        all.

E1418   Woodbridge, Hensley C. "Lettres nouvelles," Abstracts
        of English Studies, II (September 1959), 308.
            Miller sees Perlès as a genius, Durrell as a brilliant
        handler of English, and Kerouac as America's best
        writer.

E1419   "Children ... and Ourselves: Goodbye to Blue Yonder?"
        Manas, XII (September 2, 1959), 5, 8.
            Miller sees the world closing in on its young people.

E1420   "Henry Miller," Saarland Rundfunk, September 5, 1959.
            Review of Big Sur. (In German.)

E1421   "Potpourri aus Kalifornien," Mannheimer Morgen, Septem-
        ber 25, 1959.
            Big Sur reviewed. (In German.)

E1422   F., G. P. "Die tägliche Post des Henry Miller," Der
        Mittag, September 26, 1959.
            Miller called the pornographer from Big Sur. (In
        German.)

E1423   "Two 'Tropic' Novels Named in U.S. Suit," New York
        Times, CIX (September 26, 1959), 2.
            U.S. Government once more bans Tropic.

E1424   Ouellette, Fernand. "Edgard Varèse," Liberté 59, I
        (September-October 1959), 274-275.
            Miller a friend of composer Varèse. (In French.)

E1425   "Die Henry Miller Story," Konkret, October 1959.
            Review of Miller's life and his work, Big Sur. (In
        German.)

E1426   "Noches de amor y de alegría," La Razón, October 3,

1959.
Miller's Nights of Love and Laughter presents such
themes as an absurd universe, sarcasm, and black
humor. (In Spanish.)

E1427   Lamerdin, Kurt. "Amerikanisches Potpourri," Berliner
Morgenpost, October 22, 1959.
Review of Big Sur. (In German.)

E1428   A., L. A.   "Noches de amor y alegría," Crítica, October
25, 1959.
Review of Nights of Love and Laughter with special attention on the stories, "Via Dieppe Newhaven" and
"Astrological Fricassee." (In Spanish.)

E1429   Schwartz, Edward P.   "Correspondence," Henry Miller
Literary Society Newsletter, November 1959, 3.
Henk Van Gelre writing a book about Miller.

E1430   Schwartz, Edward P.   "In Answer to Your Inquiry About
Henry Miller and the Henry Miller Literary Society,"
Henry Miller Literary Society Newsletter, November 1959,
1.
Information about the Society given to prospective mem-
bers.

E1431   Schwartz, Edward P.   "Israel Item," Henry Miller Literary Society Newsletter, November 1959, 3.
Beautiful Jewish New Year card created by Miller entitled, "Flowers of the Holy Land."

E1432   Schwartz, Edward P.   "Minneapolis," Henry Miller Lite-
rary Society Newsletter, November 1959, 3.
Items written by Miller found in Prairie Schooner,
Manus, Saturday Review of Literature, New Leader,
Rogue, New York Times, Life, etc.

E1433   Schwartz, Edward P.   "Most," Henry Miller Literary Society Newsletter, November 1959, 3.
Miller found in Kronhausen's Pornography and the Law
in chapter entitled, "Henry Miller--Apostle of the
Gory Detail."

E1434   Schwartz, Edward P.   "Note," Henry Miller Literary Society Newsletter, November 1959, 3.
Miller's letter to the Society about his trip to France
in typical Miller style.

E1435   Schwartz, Edward P.   "Paris Note," Henry Miller Lite-
rary Society Newsletter, November 1959, 3.
Both Miller's Quiet Days in Clichy and Nabokov's
Lolita suppressed in France.

E1436   Schwartz, Edward P. "Points of Information for Those
        Interested in the Work of the Henry Miller Literary So-
        ciety," Henry Miller Literary Society Newsletter, Novem-
        ber 1959, 4.
            Four items about Miller: First is election to Ameri-
            can Academy and National Institute of Arts and Letters,
            second a review of Big Sur in New Statesman, third
            Durrell's description of Miller's importance, and fourth
            is the Newsletter's attempt to provide Miller with a
            fair press.

E1437   "Henry Miller," Die Barke, November 1, 1959.
            Review of Big Sur. (In German.)

E1438   Heathman. "Heathman's Diary," n.p., November 27,
        1959.
            Perlès feels that Miller should be a better known writ-
            er so he writes Reunion in Big Sur, Art and Outrage,
            My Friend Henry Miller.

E1439   Gerstenberger, Donna. "Evergreen Review," Abstracts of
        English Studies, II (December 1959), 443.
            Discussion of Miller's "Defense of the Freedom to
            Read."

E1440   "Henry Miller," Banspiegel, December 1959.
            Review of The Colossus of Maroussi. (In German.)

E1441   "Henry Miller," Die Unnelle, December 1959.
            Review of Big Sur. (In German.)

E1442   "Durrell, Inselsucht," Der Spiegel, XIII (December 2,
        1959), 82-84.
            The Miller, Durrell, Perlès circle mentioned. (In
            German.)

E1443   "Henry Miller," Österreichischer Rundfunk, December 2,
        1959.
            Big Sur reviewed. (In German.)

E1444   Cellier, Jean. "Henry Miller a emporté de sommières et
        d'Uzés," Le Provençal, December 8, 1959, 5.
            Miller's Big Sur compared with the writings of Rabe-
            lais and Montaigne; all three are called humanists.
            (In French.)

E1445   Coleman, John. "Just Being," Spectator, December 11,
        1959.
            Miller called an author of one book in a review of
            Art and Outrage, Reunion in Barcelona, and Reunion
            in Big Sur.

E1446   M., R. E. L. " 'The Henry Miller Reader' Will Have to

Do Till Real Thing Comes Along," <u>Shreveport Times</u>, December 13, 1959.
> <u>The Henry Miller Reader</u> a fine introduction to Miller, but more of his work now desired.

E1447   Durrell, Lawrence.   "The Black Book," <u>Two Cities</u>, V (December 15, 1959), 1-22.
> Durrell credits Miller with helping him publish <u>The Black Book</u> and calls <u>Tropic</u> one of its major inspirations.

E1448   Shapiro, Karl.   "The Greatest Living Author," <u>Two Cities</u>, V (December 15, 1959), 25-44.
> Miller seen waging a war against conventional writing; <u>Tropic</u> seen as autobiographical.

E1449   May, William.   "A Miller Reader," <u>Newark News</u>, December 20, 1959, III E7.
> <u>Henry Miller Reader</u> a sampling of a philosophy that is vital.

E1450   Moore, Harry T.   "Hard-Boiled Eloquence," <u>New York Times</u>, CIX (December 20, 1959), VII 10.
> <u>Henry Miller Reader</u> called healthy and therapeutic book dealing with erotic realism, not pornography.

E1451   "Big Three," <u>Times Literary Supplement</u>, LVIII (December 25, 1959), 752.
> Review of <u>Art and Outrage</u>, a correspondence about Miller by <u>Perlès and Durrell</u>, <u>Reunion in Barcelona</u> by Miller, <u>Reunion in Big Sur</u> by Perlès.

E1452   McMurtry, Larry.   "Henry Miller Through a Hygienic Bottle," <u>Houston Post</u>, XCVIII (December 27, 1959), 11.
> <u>Henry Miller Reader</u> has strong, vigorous, and graceful prose.

E1453   Sherman, John K.   "Miller Turns Experience into Lusty, Lively Art," <u>Minneapolis Tribune</u>, XCIII (December 27, 1959), 8.
> <u>The Henry Miller Reader</u> a selection of all of Miller's work, realistic, nostalgia, passion, and sex.

E1454   "Miller Expurgated," <u>Time</u>, LXXIV (December 28, 1959), 60.
> Review of <u>Miller Reader</u> which satirizes work calling it merely sex.

E1455   Bruckberger, Father Raymond L.   "Big Sur," <u>Big Sur Guide</u>, V (1960), 2-6.
> Look at Miller's home in Big Sur and mention of the author's life there.

E1456   Gossman, Otis Jr.   "Wide Range Found in New Collection," Norfolk Virginian-Pilot, CCXXXIV (January 1, 1960).
Henry Miller Reader a work by a banned moralist.

E1457   Lea, George.   "Out from Under the Counter," Chicago
Sun-Times, XIII (January 3, 1960), III 4.
Miller Reader shows Miller's boldness of approach and
his intense curiosity concerning man and nature.

E1458   Rexroth, Kenneth.   "Miller Comes at You Like a Cave
Man," San Francisco Chronicle, XCVI (January 3, 1960),
20.
Miller Reader an introduction to a primitive naturalist.

E1459   Omarr, Sydney.   "A Collection of Henry Miller," Los
Angeles Times, LXXIX (January 4, 1960), III 5.
The first opportunity for America to read Miller ap-
pears with publication of The Henry Miller Reader.

E1460   Villa, Percy.   "Almost About Everything," Minneapolis
Spokesman, January 15, 1960.
Schwartz writes about Miller and his Reader, a book
by an erotic realist.

E1461   Walser, Paul Ludwig.   "Henry Miller und Big Sur," Der
Laudbote, January 15, 1960.
Discussion on Big Sur.   (In German.)

E1462   Ross, Orvis.   "An Old Friend Looks Back: Henry Miller
Needs Sympathy," Minneapolis Tribune, XCIII (January 24,
1960), 6.
Ross talks about his first meeting with Miller in the
1920's at a time when Miller worked hard on a piece
called "Make Beer for Man."

E1463   Elliott, Desmond.   "Genius or Rubbish?" Books and
Bookmen, V (February 1960), 17.
Cancer called a long, dull account of Miller's associ-
ation with prostitutes in Paris.

E1464   "Da Henry Miller Levede Som Maler," Information, February 2, 1960, 8.
Miller's plight as an artist seen in his need to ask
for food and clothing to survive.   (In Danish.)

E1465   Miller, George.   "Hangover!" London Daily Express,
February 4, 1960, 10.
Miller's Colossus a fine travel piece.

E1466   "Miller er Opaa Maler," Dagens Nyheder, February 4,
1960, 4.
Miller an excellent painter.   (In Danish.)

E1467 Øjet. "Haandmalet Miller," Ekstrabladet, February 4, 1960, 8.
      Miller not an amateur, as painter or writer. (In Danish.)

E1468 Belmont, Georges. "Henry Miller ou la sexualité du coeur," Arts, February 9, 1960, 1.
      Miller realizes that sex is a part of life and will not hide this actuality. (In French.)

E1469 Dudar, Helen. "Mails and Morals," New York Post, CLIX (February 9, 1960), 25.
      Miller deals with life in blunt, explicit terms.

E1470 Henry, Maurice. "Oserais-je vous demander si vous avez 'Nimbus' de Henry Miller," L'Express, February 11, 1960, 31.
      Cartoon about the world of Miller. (In French.)

E1471 L., P. "Maleren Miller og en Ung Dansk," Politiken, February 11, 1960, 10.
      Miller's painting compared to Klee and Picasso. (In Danish.)

E1472 Weber, Jean-Paul. "Entretien," L'Express, February 11, 1960, 31-32.
      Interview discussing Sexus, Plexus, and Nexus. (In French.)

E1473 Z., J. "Den Malende Henry Miller," Berlingske Tidende, February 14, 1960, 11.
      Miller books called interesting expressions of his life and his art compared to Chagall. (In Danish.)

E1474 West, Richard. "Disorganisation Man," Manchester Guardian Weekly, February 18, 1960, 11.
      Miller learns to laugh at the world and transcend society.

E1475 Sage, Robert. "From Paris to Greece with Miller," New York Herald Tribune, CXIX (February 20-21, 1960), 5.
      Miller an author who reacts with every cell of his body to feel the life of Greece in The Colossus of Maroussi.

E1476 Hoffman, Frederick J. " 'The Little Boy Himself': A Look at Henry Miller's Lusty World," Milwaukee Journal, LXXVIII (February 21, 1960), V4.
      Henry Miller Reader a book where Miller tells all, for he wants to turn the individual inside out and bring hidden thoughts from deep in his unconscious to the surface.

E1477   Elliott, Desmond. "The Ego of Henry Miller," Books and
        Bookmen, V (March 1960), 10.
        Capricorn seen as ego experience for Miller who deals
        solely with "I. "

E1478   Target, G. W. "Has Henry Miller Polluted Desmond El-
        liott?" Books and Bookmen, V (March 1960), 3.
        Target wants chance to judge Cancer without help of
        Elliott.

E1479   Nucera, Louis. "Je trouve drôle d'être membre du jury
        du festival," Le Patriote, March 5, 1960, 4.
        Miller's arrival at Cannes Film Festival seen as his
        return to the France he loves so much.   (In French.)

E1480   Courtin, M. "Brassaï," Arts, March 16, 1960.
        Miller calls Brassaï a rare, tender artist.   (In
        French.)

E1481   "Brassaï," Libération, March 17, 1960.
        Miller a friend of Brassaï's.   (In French.)

E1482   "The Colossus of Maroussi," Oxford Mail, March 24, 1960.
        Mixture of Miller and Greece in this work.

E1483   Nucera, Louis. "Henry Miller fervent de Dostoïevsky,"
        Le Patriote, March 24, 1960, 5.
        Miller has the passion of Dostoevsky.   (In French.)

E1484   Tank, K. L. "Romane, die bis heute Schmuggelware
        sind," Welt am Sonntag, March 27, 1960.
        Review of Art and Outrage.   (In German.)

E1485   Filiatrault, Jean. "Henry Miller et notre faculté de libé-
        ration," Liberté 60, II (March-April 1960), 79-83.
        It is hard to define obscene, but Miller a sincere man
        attempting to liberate himself and his world.   (In
        French.)

E1486   Huggett, Colin. "The Obscenity of Henry Miller," Books
        and Bookmen, V (April 1960), 3.
        The need for the freedom to create found in the writ-
        ing of Miller whose books are very honest, human
        documents.

E1487   Larsen, Henrik. "Henry Miller Stå Stille Som Kolibrien!"
        Perspektiv, VII (April 1960), 7-14.
        Larsen writes about visit to Big Sur and Miller.   (In
        Danish.)

E1488   Lembourn, Hans Jørgen. "Nye Bøger; Skål for Napoleon!"
        Perspektiv, VII (April 1960), 56-59.
        Miller seen as dominant, self-centered figure in a

review of Nexus. (In Danish.)

E1489 Morley, George A. "The Books in His Life," Books and Bookmen, V (April 1960), 3.
Miller's belief is that a book should be read slowly so that one can think his own thoughts.

E1490 Schwartz, Edward P. "Among the New Society Members," Henry Miller Literary Society Newsletter, April 1960, 2.
Noted is the increased concern for Henry Miller.

E1491 Schwartz, Edward P. "Articulate Author of 12 Previous Books," Henry Miller Literary Society Newsletter, April 1960, 2.
Powell's Books in My Baggage discusses Miller's work.

E1492 Schwartz, Edward P. "Bern Porter Advises the Society," Henry Miller Literary Society Newsletter, April 1960, 3.
Porter notes that he wishes to incorporate all the Miller pieces he has published into one volume.

E1493 Schwartz, Edward P. "Constant Correspondent," Henry Miller Literary Society Newsletter, April 1960, 1-2.
Henk Van Gelre intends to publish an international Miller letter.

E1494 Schwartz, Edward P. "Hakan Ljunge," Henry Miller Literary Society Newsletter, April 1960, 1.
Dagens Nyheter, Sweden's largest daily paper, had article on Miller and mentioned the Newsletter.

E1495 Schwartz, Edward P. "Members Might Be Interested," Henry Miller Literary Society Newsletter, April 1960, 1.
Correspondence between Perlès and Durrell on Miller's art has been published and is called Art and Outrage.

E1496 Schwartz, Edward P. "Most Important Item," Henry Miller Literary Society Newsletter, April 1960, 1.
Henry Miller Reader published and reviews by John Sherman in the Minneapolis Tribune and Harry T. Moore in the New York Times are favorable.

E1497 Schwartz, Edward P. "News from the Drs. Kronhausen," Henry Miller Literary Society Newsletter, April 3, 1960, 2.
The Kronhausen's book, Pornography and the Law, deals with Miller.

E1498 Schwartz, Edward P. "New York Times," Henry Miller Literary Society Newsletter, April 1960, 2-3.
New York Times Best Seller List ranks Miller Reader well; it has gained tremendous reviews.

E1499   Schwartz, Edward P.   "Note Pink Sheet," Henry Miller
        Literary Society Newsletter, April 1960, 2.
             Most friendly bookstores to Miller are Roland Bartell
        in Monterey, Frances Stelloff in New York, and Sand-
        berg' Bokhandel in Stockholm.

E1500   Schwartz, Edward P.   "Notes from Big Sur," Henry Miller
        Literary Society Newsletter, April 1960, 1.
             Miller has completed three books of water colors and
        plans a visit to Japan.

E1501   Schwartz, Edward P.   "Off the Beaten Path," Henry Mill-
        er Literary Society Newsletter, April 1960, 2.
             Miller invited to join jury for International Film Festi-
        val in Cannes, France.

E1502   Schwartz, Edward P.   "Pulitzer Prize Winner in Poetry,"
        Henry Miller Literary Society Newsletter, April 1960, 2.
             Shapiro's piece on Miller in Two Cities is masterful
        defense of Miller's work, a Miller praise that will be
        expanded in his book, In Defense of Ignorance.

E1503   Schwartz, Edward P.   "Richards Third," Henry Miller
        Literary Society Newsletter, April 1960, 3.
             Richards Third a book by Richard Liebow with a water-
        color by Miller.

E1504   Schwartz, Edward P.   "This Led to Many," Henry Miller
        Literary Society Newsletter, April 1960, 1.
             Note about the society's increased correspondence on
        Miller.

E1505   Schwartz, Edward P.   "Your Executive Board," Henry
        Miller Literary Society Newsletter, April 1960, 1.
             New members include Perlès, Nin, Durrell, and
        Reitzel.

E1506   Wright, R. O.   "Miller's Serene Innocence," Books and
        Bookmen, V (April 1960), 3.
             Freedom of expression a belief of U.S. Constitution
        and Miller.

E1507   "What Do You Think?" Books and Bookmen, V (April
        1960), 3.
             Letters about Miller.

E1508   Coleman, John.   "Landscapes with Figures," Spectator,
        April 1, 1960, 48.
             Colossus of Maroussi an account of Miller's travels to
        Greece.

E1509   Sauvage, Daniel.   "Henry Miller refait à Paris ses promé-
        nades d'il y a 30 ans," Le Figaro Littéraire, April 13,

1960, 2.
> While at Cannes, Miller returned to Paris for visit. (In French.)

E1510 O'Strit, Henning. "Liosens Stav," n.p., April 21, 1960, 4.
> Miller's "Astrological Fricassee" a story about American failure. (In Danish.)

E1511 "In Hamburg zu Gast," Hamburg Echo, April 23, 1960.

E1512 "Keine Bekenntnisse--Geschichten," Die Welt, April 23, 1960.
> Miller now in Germany. (In German.)

E1513 "In Hamburg zu Gast...," Hamburger Abendblatt, April 24, 1960.
> Miller arrives in Hamburg. (In German.)

E1514 Mandwasser, Dr. Jean. "Der Mann aus Big Sur," Hamburger Abendblatt, April 28, 1960.
> Miller in Hamburg to meet with Rowalt about publishing books. (In German.)

E1515 "Buchbesprechangen," Der Yeihbuchhändler, May 1960.
> Black Spring discussed. (In German.)

E1516 "Henry Miller: Schwarzer Frühling," Die Kultur, May 1960.
> Review of Black Spring. (In German.)

E1517 Sachett, S. J. "Kultuur Leren," Abstracts of English Studies, III (May 1960).
> Vermeer in "Henry Miller en de Stilte," sees Miller as a moralist who is misunderstood in America. (In Dutch.)

E1518 Ohff, Heinz. "Die Liebe zum Ganzen," Bremer Nachrichten, May 5, 1960.
> Miller the author and artist tours Germany. (In German.)

E1519 Zimmer, Dieter E. "Der glückliche Anarchist," Die Zeit, May 6, 1960.
> Miller, the individualist and anarchist, visits Hamburg. (In German.)

E1520 Benedick, Claude. "Henry Miller: solo pido al cine poesía," La Cultura, May 9, 1960, 1, 7.
> Miller views films at Cannes and feels arts are on decline. (In Spanish.)

E1521 Muller, Robert. "In Cannes," London Daily Mail, May

13, 1960, 16.
Interview with Miller where he claims to be anti work
and society.

E1522   "Film Award for Italy," Daily Telegram and Morning Post,
May 21, 1960, 10.
Miller a member of Cannes jury.

E1523   Fleming, Rudd.   "Wrong--But Wonderful," Washington
Post and Times-Herald, LXXXIII (May 22, 1960), E7.
Miller's belief in joy mentioned in Shapiro's In De-
fense of Ignorance.

E1524   Neumann, Harry.   "Wie tief ist der Vulkan?" Der Tag,
May 29, 1960.
Art and Outrage reviewed.   (In German.)

E1525   L., J. C.   "La Leçon d'amour de vivre dans un mazet,"
Midi Libre, May 31, 1960, 7.
Miller a nonconformist in his correspondence with
Durrell.   (In French.)

E1526   Diéguez, Manuel de.   "Chroniques: L'Univers spirituel
de Henry Miller," Esprit, XXVIII (June 1960), 1165-1174.
Miller's writing compared to the spiritualism of Dostoevsky.   (In French.)

E1527   Lombardo, Agostino.   "Italian Criticism of American
Literature," Sewanee Review, LXVIII (July 1960), 353-515.
Collection of 13 essays with one on Miller.

E1528   Moravia, Alberto.   "Two American Writers," Sewanee Re-
view, LXVIII (July 1960), 473-481.
Miller's work undermined the Puritan morality of the
U.S.

E1529   "Miller, Perlès, Durrell," Hessischer Rundfunk, July 9,
1960.
Art and Outrage reviewed.   (In German.)

E1530   "St. Paul Shows Exhibit of J. R. Sherman," Minneapolis
Tribune, XCIV (July 17, 1960), 7.
Eight Miller watercolors included in show.

E1531   Amery, Jean.   "Aus den Leben Cines Taugenichts," St.
Galler Tagblatt, July 24, 1960.
Miller a great author, all his canon explored.   (In
German.)

E1532   T., S.   "Hingegeben an die verzerrte Welt," Hamburger
Echo, July 30, 1960.
Black Spring explored.   (In German.)

E1533   Perlès, Alfred. "Our Honorary Chairman," Henry Miller
Literary Society Newsletter, August 1960, 1.
Perlès has read the French edition of Nexus, a fine
novel.

E1534   Pivano, Fernanda. "Tutto andrebbe demolito," Successo,
II (August 1960), 40-43.
Miller's Eastern philosophy seen in both writing and
painting. (In Italian.)

E1535   Schwartz, Edward P. "Back to the Local Scene," Henry
Miller Literary Society Newsletter, August 1960, 1.
Orvis Ross describes Miller's struggle to write his
first essay, "Make Beer for Man."

E1536   Schwartz, Edward P. "Between Worlds," Henry Miller
Literary Society Newsletter, August 1960, 2.
Between Worlds contains first chapter of new book by
Miller.

E1537   Schwartz, Edward P. "Dorian Book Quarterly," Henry
Miller Literary Society Newsletter, August 1960, 2.
Dorian Book Quarterly of San Francisco publicized
Miller and his society.

E1538   Schwartz, Edward P. "Ephriam Doner," Henry Miller
Literary Society Newsletter, August 1960, 2.
Libros y Discos inviting Miller to autograph party in
Mexico City.

E1539   Schwartz, Edward P. "Everyone Seems," Henry Miller
Literary Society Newsletter, August 1960, 2.
Two recordings cut by Miller in 1949 entitled Sound
Portraits, where Miller read from Black Spring and
The Colossus of Maroussi.

E1540   Schwartz, Edward P. "Finally," Henry Miller Literary
Society Newsletter, August 1960, 1.
Signet Books republished Nights of Love and Laughter
with introduction of Kenneth Rexroth.

E1541   Schwartz, Edward P. "First Public Showing," Henry
Miller Literary Society Newsletter, August 1960, 2.
Eight Miller watercolors on display at first public
showing of art collection of late John Rogers Sherman.

E1542   Schwartz, Edward P. "From the Famous," Henry Miller
Literary Society Newsletter, August 1960, 2.
Institute for Sex Research's librarian requests infor-
mation on books by Miller.

E1543   Schwartz, Edward P. "Henry Miller's Special," Henry
Miller Literary Society Newsletter, August 1960, 1.

Miller's letter, "Europe Revisited," enclosed where Miller states he will travel to Mexico, Japan, or Europe again.

E1544   Schwartz, Edward P.   "Illustrations to Henry Miller's Writing," Henry Miller Literary Society Newsletter, August 1960, 2.
Bezalel Schatz has done 12 pen and ink drawings of Miller's work.

E1545   Schwartz, Edward P.   "It's Amazing," Henry Miller Literary Society Newsletter, August 1960, 1.
Jim Brust conveys the strong effect Intimate Henry Miller had on him.

E1546   Schwartz, Edward P.   "Judson Crews," Henry Miller Literary Society Newsletter, August 1960, 2.
Judson Crews, a friend of Miller, has several out-of-print items, Echolalia and Murder the Murderer.

E1547   Schwartz, Edward P.   "Miscellaneous Special Items, Brochures and Pamphlets by Henry Miller," Henry Miller Literary Society Newsletter, August 1960, 4.
List of 19 titles beginning with What Are You Going to Do About Alf? (1935) and ends with The Waters Reglitterized (1950).

E1548   Schwartz, Edward P.   "One of Henry's Old Parisian Friends," Henry Miller Literary Society Newsletter, August 1960, 1.
Walter Lowenfels has article written in 1933 and never published reviewing first 50 pages of Tropic. It will appear in Henk Van Gelre's World Miller Review.

E1549   Schwartz, Edward P.   "Plans for Van Gelre's," Henry Miller Literary Society Newsletter, August 1960, 1.
Van Gelre's international Miller publication waits for articles from Nin, Durrell, Rattner, Perlès, and others.

E1550   Schwartz, Edward P.   "Sam L. Steinman," Henry Miller Literary Society Newsletter, August 1960, 1.
Miller considers himself in the rear of literature.

E1551   Schwartz, Edward P.   "San Quentin Prison," Henry Miller Literary Society Newsletter, August 1960, 2.
Library at San Quentin Prison received autographed copy of Miller Reader from Literary Society.

E1552   Schwartz, Edward P.   "Thanks a Million," Henry Miller Literary Society Newsletter, August 1960, 2.
Henry Miller group formed in Eastern Canada.

E1553   Schwartz, Edward P.   "Thanks to Karl Shapiro," Henry
Miller Literary Society Newsletter, August 1960, 2.
Shapiro's strongly pro-Miller essay in his In Defense
of Ignorance.

E1554   Schwartz, Edward P.   "Works by Henry Miller," Henry
Miller Literary Society Newsletter, August 1960, 4.
Listing of works by Miller from 1934 to 1959 in
chronological order, beginning with Tropic and ending
with Art and Outrage.

E1555   Fehse, Willi.   "Amerikanische Erzählungen," Stuttgarter
Nachrichten, August 6, 1960.
Miller compared to Truman Capote and Irwin Shaw.
(In German.)

E1556   Moravia, Alberto.   "Two American Writers," Sewanee Review, LXVIII (Summer 1960), 473-477.
Chaos used as theme to provide Miller with inward
movement into the self and outward journey to perceive self in terms of one's world.

E1557   Shapiro, Karl.   "A Non-New England Primer," Prairie
Schooner, XXXIV (Summer 1960), 182-183.
Miller the most vital literary critic of our time be-
cause he penetrates into the unconscious to make
things conscious to his reader in this review of The
Henry Miller Reader.

E1558   Thibant, Philippe.   "Un Avatar de Rimbaud: Henry Miller,"
Relâche, Summer 1960, 29-31.
Miller compared to Rimbaud, both passionate writers
obsessed with life.   (In French.)

E1559   Sage, Robert.   "The Best of Henry Miller's Production,"
New York Herald Tribune, CXX (September 10, 1960), 5.
The Best of Henry Miller contains portions from all
of Miller's major work.

E1560   Scott, Winfield Townley.   "With the Faults and Virtues of
Youth," New York Herald Tribune, CXX (September 18,
1960), VI 8.
Review of Durrell's Black Book where Miller's praise
and help in publishing the work are noted.

E1561   Childs, J. Rives.   "Collecting Henry Miller: Or What
Miller Means to Me," Private Library, III (October 1960),
34-37.
Childs talks about Miller's relationship to Restif de la
Bretonne and of first experiencing Miller.

E1562   "Der Dichter des Obszönen," Neue Zeit, October 1, 1960.
Black Spring reviewed.   (In German.)

E1563   Eyssen, Jurgen. "Henry Miller: Nexus," Bücherei und
         Bildung, October 13, 1960.
         Review of Nexus. (In German.)

E1564   "Henry Miller," Frankische Presse, October 13, 1960.
         Look at Black Spring. (In German.)

E1565   Lerman, Leo. "Prelude to the Quartet," Saturday Review,
         XLIII (October 29, 1960), 21.
         Miller's help in publishing Durrell's The Black Book
         is recalled.

E1566   Fink, Bob. "Bob Fink on Alfred Perlès," Henry Miller
         Literary Society Newsletter, November 1960, 4.
         Perlès thinks that the greatest man in the world is
         Miller.

E1567   Schwartz, Edward P. "Abe Rattner in 'Time'," Henry
         Miller Literary Society Newsletter, November 1960, 4.
         Miller's friend Abe Rattner appeared in Time, Septem-
         ber 26, 1960.

E1568   Schwartz, Edward P. "About Contributions," Henry Miller
         Literary Society Newsletter, November 1960, 4.
         Newsletter voluntarily supported, not by Miller.

E1569   Schwartz, Edward P. "About the Recordings," Henry
         Miller Literary Society Newsletter, November 1960, 3.
         Henry Miller readings taped in 1949 will not be re-
         recorded.

E1570   Schwartz, Edward P. "Add to Your Collection," Henry
         Miller Literary Society Newsletter, November 1960, 4.
         Judson Crews has copies of Murder the Murderer and
         Echolalia for sale.

E1571   Schwartz, Edward P. "Back to the Old Days," Henry
         Miller Literary Society Newsletter, November 1960, 4.
         Nin tells Society Miller has written over 25,000 lett-
         ers to Huntington Cairns, Harold Ross, Emil Schnel-
         lock, Anaïs Nin, Joe O'Regan, Bill Deware, Lawrence
         Durrell, Alfred Perlès, and June Miller (his ex-wife).

E1572   Schwartz, Edward P. "Bibliography in Offing," Henry
         Miller Literary Society Newsletter, November 1960, 4.
         Miller Society plans to publish up-to-date bibliography
         on Miller.

E1573   Schwartz, Edward P. "Current Book 'Info'," Henry Miller
         Literary Society Newsletter, November 1960, 1.
         Five Miller books in print: Nexus, To Paint Is to
         Love Again, Nights of Love and Laughter, Wisdom of
         the Heart, Colossus of Maroussi.

E1574   Schwartz, Edward P.   "Durrell Black Book," Henry Miller
         Literary Society Newsletter, November 1960, 4.
         Miller's support of The Black Book noted in articles
         by Leo Lerman in Saturday Review and New York
         Herald Tribune Book Review.

E1575   Schwartz, Edward P.   "Editor at Big Sur Studio," Henry
         Miller Literary Society Newsletter, November 1960, 3.
         Paul Smith, one of America's major editors, writing
         biography at Miller's home in Big Sur while Miller
         tours Europe.

E1576   Schwartz, Edward P.   "Flash from Perlès," Henry Miller
         Literary Society Newsletter, November 1960, 1.
         Perlès's My Friend Henry Miller to be translated and
         published in Germany.

E1577   Schwartz, Edward P.   "Man and Mountain," Henry Miller
         Literary Society Newsletter, November 1960, 4.
         Robert Fink describes his first meeting with Miller in
         his work, The Man and the Mountain.

E1578   Schwartz, Edward P.   "Miller on the Move," Henry Miller
         Literary Society Newsletter, November 1960, 1.
         Miller stopped in New York to visit with Ben Grauer,
         the man who recorded Henry Miller Recalls and Re-
         flects.

E1579   Schwartz, Edward P.   "Miscellaneous Items," Henry
         Miller Literary Society Newsletter, November 1960, 1.
         Miller appears in Two Cities, No. 4 (Summer 1960);
         Esprit, No. 4 (April 1960); Esprit, No. 6 (June 1960);
         Between Worlds, No. 1 (Summer 1960); Liberté 60;
         Liberté 59; and Novedades (May 8, 1960).

E1580   Schwartz, Edward P.   "Museum Reproductions," Henry
         Miller Literary Society Newsletter, November 1960, 1.
         Two Miller watercolor prints available through Mu-
         seum Reproductions.

E1581   Schwartz, Edward P.   " 'Outsider' Is New Mag," Henry
         Miller Literary Society Newsletter, November 1960, 1.
         Outsider will feature Walter Lowenfels-Henry Miller
         correspondence in first four issues.

E1582   Schwartz, Edward P.   "Plug for 'Relâche'," Henry Miller
         Literary Society Newsletter, November 1960, 1.
         Miller writes brief letter in Alfred Maillet's review,
         Relâche.

E1583   Schwartz, Edward P.   "Shuman Memorial," Henry Miller
         Literary Society Newsletter, November 1960, 4.
         Three Miller watercolors found in Shuman Collection.

E1584   Schwartz, Edward P.   "So What's Cooking?"   Henry Miller
        Literary Society Newsletter, November 1960, 4.
            Request from Jacqueline Stephens and Jeannine Green-
            lee for a recipe from Miller for a famous people's
            cookbook.

E1585   Schwartz, Edward P.   "Sydney Omarr's Latest," Henry
        Miller Literary Society Newsletter, November 1960, 1.
            Omarr's Henry Miller: His World of Urania a study
            of a man's relationship to astrology.

E1586   Schwartz, Edward P.   "Washington, D.C., Show," Henry
        Miller Literary Society Newsletter, November 1960, 1.
            Showing of 25 Miller watercolors at Collector's Studio
            in D.C. well received.

E1587   Schwartz, Edward P.   "Will See Many People," Henry
        Miller Literary Society Newsletter, November 1960, 1.
            Miller to see Durrell, Perlès, Hemingway, and
            Charles Chaplin on his European tour.

E1588   Schwartz, Edward P.   "With the Book Stores," Henry
        Miller Literary Society Newsletter, November 1960, 1.
            List of dealers who have rare Miller works.

E1589   Solotaroff, Theodore.   "The Irrational Karl Shapiro,"
        Commentary, XXX (November 1960), 445-448.
            The poetic in the writing of Miller is praised.

E1590   Steinman, Sam'l.   " 'Lady' Makes History," Henry Miller
        Literary Society Newsletter, November 1960, 3.
            London jury feels Lady Chatterley not obscene; should
            pave way for Miller.

E1591   Sancet, Jean.   "Les Agents prenaient Brassaï pour un fou
        il voulait photographier la nuit," Judi, November 3, 1960,
        30-31.
            Miller mentioned.   (In French.)

E1592   "Schwarzer Frühling," Badische Zeitung, November 13,
        1960.
            Review of Black Spring.   (In German.)

E1593   Z., D.   "Einen Fultritt," Die Zeit, November 18, 1960.
            Miller in Hamburg meeting with publisher.   (In Ger-
            man.)

E1594   Dennis, Nigel.   "New Four-Star King of Novelists," Life,
        XLIX (November 21, 1960), 96-109.
            Tropic the greatest influence on Durrell.

E1595   "The Literature of Revolt," John O'London's, November
        24, 1960.

Miller considered a writer of revolution.

E1596   Connolly, Cyril.   "The Dissenter of Big Sur," London
Times, November 27, 1960, 27.
   Best of Henry Miller bits and pieces of a great man's
work.

E1597   Thomas, Denis.   "Quick Flips," Sunday Dispatch, November 27, 1960.
   Best of Henry Miller provides shorts from this re-
vered man of letters.

E1598   Toynbee, Philip.   "Much Better Than We Thought," Observer, November 27, 1960, 28.
   Best of Henry Miller shows his mind's freedom at its
best.

E1599   West, Richard.   "Disorganisation Man," Guardian, December 2, 1960, 6.
   Miller anti society.

E1600   "Works of an 'honest vagabond'," Evening Gazette, De-
cember 2, 1960.
   Miller attempts to depict the real world in Best of
Henry Miller.

E1601   "Genius of Henry Miller," Evening Express, December 3,
1960.
   Best of Miller shows he is a moralist.

E1602   "Henry Miller's Way," Press and Journal, December 10,
1960.
   Best of Miller depicts life of this literary vagabond.

E1603   Rymer, Thomas.   "Mr. Durrell as Interpreter," Birmingham Post, December 13, 1960.
   Best of Miller only the printable best of Miller--there
is better.

E1604   "The Best of Henry Miller," Eastern Daily Press, December 16, 1960.
   Anthology of Miller now in print.

E1605   Coleman, John.   "All Gravy," Spectator, December 16,
1960, 995.
   Best of Miller shows him to be a courageous man who
sees truth.

E1606   "The Best of Henry Miller," Illustrated London News,
December 17, 1960.
   The Best of Miller shows Rebelais's influence on him.

E1607   Fane, Vernon.   "Incomparable Nijinsky," Sphere,

December 17, 1960, 498.
Best of Henry Miller shows his various moods and styles, a good piece of writing.

E1608   King, Norman. "Gay Twenties," Newcastle Journal, December 17, 1960.
Miller's Best called dull.

E1609   R., A. "A Miller's Tale," South Wales Evening Post, December 17, 1960.
The Best of Miller shows the author's individualistic stance.

E1610   "Credit Balance," Punch, December 21, 1960.
The Best of Miller leads his reader to want more.

E1611   Hugh-Jones, Sirial. "Books," Tatler, December 21, 1960.
The Best of Henry Miller impossible to read.

E1612   "The Best of Henry Miller," Guardian-Journal, December 22, 1960, 6.
Miller's Best shows vivid imagination.

E1613   "The Best of Henry Miller," John O'London's, December 22, 1960.
Miller's Best a dream sequence through peace and nightmare.

E1614   "Corn and Chaff," London Times, December 22, 1960, 11.
The Best of Miller shows a vivid writer about life who at times is shoddy.

E1615   Owen, B. Evan. "Sage of Big Sur," Oxford Mail, December 22, 1960.
Miller's many moods appear in The Best of Henry Miller.

E1616   Leslie, Andrew. "Hitting Below the Head," Guardian, December 23, 1960, 5.
The Best of Henry Miller provides emotionally charged excerpts from his life.

E1617   "Cendrars le magnifique," Paris-Presse-L'Intransigeant, December 24, 1960, 8D.
Miller wrote an excellent preface to Cendrars's work. (In French.)

E1618   Corke, Hilary. "A Real Man's Real Life," Weekly Post, December 24, 1960.
Miller lives rather than writes about his world as is apparent from the group of his experiences that comprise The Best of Miller.

E1619 Barstow, Stan. "Henry Miller Shames the Devil," York-
shire Post, December 29, 1960, 4.
The Best of Miller shows there is much feeling to
Miller's view of life.

E1620 Leslie, Andrew. "Hitting Below the Head," Manchester
Guardian, December 29, 1960, 4.
Best of Henry Miller shows his concern with vitality
and life.

E1621 Fallon, Brian. "I, Henry Miller," Irish Times, December 31, 1960, 6.
The Best of Henry Miller depicts a man ruled by his
heart.

E1622 Milner, Richard. "Diamonds on the rubbish heap,"
Western Mail, December 31, 1960.
The Best of Henry Miller a work about life.

E1623 Helmut, Gunther. "Miller," Welt und Wort," Heft 9, 1960.
Review of Black Spring. (In German.)

E1624 "Henry Miller," Die Barke, 1961.
Review of Nexus. (In German.)

E1625 Lowenfels, Walter. "Tropic of Cancer by Henry Miller:
Paris, 1933," Kulchur, 1961, 97-99.
Miller seen as spider who sucks blood of others and
creates works like Cancer.

E1626 Norris, Hoke. "Some Dreadful Books," Chicago Sun Times,
Absurd to ban Tropic.

E1627 Nielsen, Hans. "Han Tirrer Stadig USA," Jørgen Leth,
1961.
Miller's Tropics still anger Americans. (In Danish.)

E1628 Okumura, Osamu. "D. H. Lawrence the Preacher,"
Aoyama Journal of General Education [special issue], 1961,
63-84.
Lawrence is compared to Whitman and Miller. (In
Japanese.)

E1629 Wittkopt, Rudölf. "Henry Miller," Rhinozeros, III (1961),
2.
Tribute to Miller's Time of the Assassins. (In German.)

E1630 Potts, Paul. "The Tough 'Outsider' Who Just Fails to
Be Great," Daily Herald, January 3, 1961, 3.
The Best of Henry Miller lacks the vision and wide
concern of Whitman and Blake.

E1631   Sanford, Derek. "Realism and Fantasy," Daily Telegraph,
        January 6, 1961, 17.
            The Best of Henry Miller a surreal fantasy placing
            Miller with the angels.

E1632   Waterman, Jack. "This Man with a Genius for Living,"
        Evening Standard, January 10, 1961, 10.
            Best of Henry Miller an experience of life and feeling.

E1633   Bauer, Gérard. "Mort de Blaise Cendrars," Le Figaro
        Littéraire, January 23, 1961.
            Cendrars was a friend of celebrated author, Miller.
            (In French.)

E1634   "In a Nutshell," Birmingham Mail, January 25, 1961.
            Best of Miller an anthology of a banned yet venerated
            author.

E1635   Gelre, Henk Van. "Henry Miller I," Aristo-, XXIX
        (January-February 1961), 11-17.
            A look at Miller in Paris from early 30's to 1940.
            (In Dutch.)

E1636   May, James Boyer. "Henry Miller (An Individualist as
        Social Thinker)," Trace, January-March 1961, 24-31.
            Miller a man concerned with knowing the self through
            personal inner exploration. To prove this point, May
            explores Nexus, Henry Miller Reader, Time of Assas-
            sins, World of Sex, Plexus, and Air-Conditioned Night-
            mare.

E1637   "Tropical Fruit," Times Literary Supplement, LX (Febru-
        ary 3, 1961), 76.
            Best of Miller a gospel of self liberation and reconcil-
            iation by total confession.

E1638   Vigorelli, Giancarlo. "Il diavolo in salotto," Tempo,
        February 11, 1961, 61.
            Miller feels that love is most important human state.
            (In Italian.)

E1639   D., G. "Perhaps He Was Born Too Soon...," Manchester
        Evening News, February 17, 1961.
            Miller sees life and lives it.

E1640   Xirau, Ramón. "New Paperback Edition for the Author of
        the Famous 'Tropics'," News, February 19, 1961, 8.
            Wisdom of the Heart a work where Miller denies ori-
            ginal sin and feels the purpose of man is to live and
            find paradise on earth.

E1641   Poesio, Paolo Emilio. "Diventò poeta e romanziere per
        conendo le vie del mondo," Nazione Sera, February 20,

1961, 3.
    Cendrars's writing compared to Miller's.   (In Italian.)

E1642   Armitage, Merle.   "The Man Behind the Smile: Doing
Business with Henry Miller," Texas Quarterly, IV (Winter
1961), 154-161.
    Discussion of Armitage's trips to Big Sur, helping to
publish The Smile at the Foot of the Ladder, and talks
of the American dream-real conflict that offends Miller.

E1643   Kermode, Frank.   "Henry Miller and John Betjeman,"
Encounter, XVI (March 1961), 69-75.
    Review of The Best of Henry Miller that sees Miller
attempting to escape the present.

E1644   Fraser, Hugh Russell.   "The Open Mind of Henry Miller,"
Los Angeles Times, LXXX (March 8, 1961), III 5.
    Miller's words clear and his style simple, both of
which create an awareness missing from most writing.

E1643   Wilcock, Rodolfo J.   "L'Aspite spiacevole," Mondo, XIII
(March 14, 1961), 8.
    Miller imprecise thinker and irrational writer whose
skill comes from his translators.   (In Italian.)

E1644   Moore, Harry T.   "Ban for Removal," Sunday Post-Dis-
patch, March 26, 1961, 4B.
    Art and Outrage contains interesting confession by
Miller.

E1645   Praz, Mario.   "Civiltà in Safacclo," Il Tempo, Roma,
March 30, 1961, 3.
    Tropics both seen as vital and real life.   (In Italian.)

E1646   Kaufman, J. Lee.   "Commentary," Abstracts of English
Studies, IV (April 1961), 152-153.
    Solotaroff sees and praises the poetic in Miller.

E1647   McNeal, Archie L.   "ALA as Amicus Curiae," ALA Bulletin, LV (April 1961), 290.
    American Library Association feels the right to read
Tropic imperative.

E1648   Schwartz, Edward P.   "About Miller," Henry Miller Literary Society Newsletter, April 1961, 1.
    Following written on Miller: Powell's Books in My
Baggage, Riley's Henry Miller: An Informal Bibliography.

E1649   Schwartz, Edward P.   "Add to Your Collection," Henry
Miller Literary Society Newsletter, April 1961, 4.
    Judson Crews still has copies of Murder the Murderer
and Echolalia.

E1650   Schwartz, Edward P.   "Also to Be Published," Henry
Miller Literary Society Newsletter, April 1961, 1.
Emil White to publish special edition called Big Sur,
California, on Miller.

E1651   Schwartz, Edward P.   "Between Worlds Coming," Henry
Miller Literary Society Newsletter, April 1961, 3.
Second edition of Between Worlds contains Perlès
article where Miller is mentioned.

E1652   Schwartz, Edward P.   "Biography of Miller," Henry
Miller Literary Society Newsletter, April 1961, 1.
Miller one of series of authors viewed by Walter
Schmiele.

E1653   Schwartz, Edward P.   "Concerning Book Stores," Henry
Miller Literary Society Newsletter, April 1961, 4.
Society thanks book merchants who carry Miller's
work.

E1654   Schwartz, Edward P.   "Cross New Book," Henry Miller
Literary Society Newsletter, April 1961, 4.
Robert L. Cross printing The Henry Miller Circle in
Paris: 1930-1939.

E1655   Schwartz, Edward P.   "Durrell Surrenders," Henry Miller
Literary Society Newsletter, April 1961, 3.
Miller's friend Durrell is marrying.

E1656   Schwartz, Edward P.   "First Reviewer Dies," Henry
Miller Literary Society Newsletter, April 1961, 1.
Blaise Cendrars was first reviewer of Tropic in Orbes
(Summer 1935).

E1657   Schwartz, Edward P.   "Freedom and HM," Henry Miller
Literary Society Newsletter, April 1961, 4.
John Wilcock did strip for April 6 issue of Village
Voice called "Of Freedom and Henry Miller."

E1658   Schwartz, Edward P.   "God Love Doc Fink!" Henry
Miller Literary Society Newsletter, April 1961, 2.
Schwartz praises letter from Fink to Henk Van Gelre
which will appear in International Henry Miller Review.

E1659   Schwartz, Edward P.   " 'Life' Looks at Life," Henry
Miller Literary Society Newsletter, April 1961, 3.
In Life article of November 21, 1960, Durrell's
greatest influence was reading Miller's Tropic.

E1660   Schwartz, Edward P.   "Museum Reproductions," Henry
Miller Literary Society Newsletter, April 1961, 4.
Two new Miller watercolor prints available from
Museum Reproductions.

E1661   Schwartz, Edward P.   "New Book Coming," Henry Miller
         Literary Society Newsletter, April 1961, 1.
             The Art of Henry Miller combination book-record set
             to appear in June 1961.

E1662   Schwartz, Edward P.   "New Brochure," Henry Miller Lite-
         rary Society Newsletter, April 1961, 1.
             Miller published Ein Weihnachtsabend in der Villa
             Seurat in December 1960.

E1663   Schwartz, Edward P.   "New Reprints," Henry Miller Lite-
         rary Society Newsletter, April 1961, 1.
             New reprints of Miller include: World of Sex, Nexus,
             Best of Henry Miller, Art and Outrage.

E1664   Schwartz, Edward P.   "New Watercolor Book," Henry
         Miller Literary Society Newsletter, April 1961, 1.
             New Miller book of watercolors called Angel Is My
             Watermark.

E1665   Schwartz, Edward P.   "Notes from Siegferth," Henry
         Miller Literary Society Newsletter, April 1961, 3.
             Charles Siegferth has written letter to Society about
             visit to Miller.

E1666   Schwartz, Edward P.   "Notes on Bibliography," Henry
         Miller Literary Society Newsletter, April 1961, 3.
             Society notes its bibliography on Miller will appear
             shortly.

E1667   Schwartz, Edward P.   "On Water Colors," Henry Miller
         Literary Society Newsletter, April 1961, 1.
             Praise for Miller's To Paint Is to Love Again.

E1668   Schwartz, Edward P.   "Other Material by Miller," Henry
         Miller Literary Society Newsletter, April 1961, 1.
             Miller found in "First Love" in Metronome, March
             1961; in "Preface" to History of Art by Elie Faure;
             in "Preface" to Women and Goddesses.

E1669   Schwartz, Edward P.   "Outsider Due in April," Henry
         Miller Literary Society Newsletter, April 1961, 3.
             Outsider contains Miller-Lowenfels correspondence.

E1670   Schwartz, Edward P.   "Pardon the Delay," Henry Miller
         Literary Society Newsletter, April 1961, 1.
             Apology to Miller people for Newsletter not appearing
             in March.

E1671   Schwartz, Edward P.   "Reading in German," Henry Miller
         Literary Society Newsletter, April 1961, 3.
             Miller sent Literary Society poster noting Heinz Hil-
             pert's readings from Miller's work.

E1672 Schwartz, Edward P. "Recent Reprints," Henry Miller
       Literary Society Newsletter, April 1961, 1.
              Reprints of Miller's Wisdom of the Heart and Nights
       of Love and Laughter comprise entry.

E1673 Schwartz, Edward P. "Salute to Miss Steloff," Henry
       Miller Literary Society Newsletter, April 1961, 1.
              Bookseller Frances Steloff believed in Miller when
       most publishers were sceptical about his ability.

E1674 Schwartz, Edward P. "Shapiro Hurt in Crash," Henry
       Miller Literary Society Newsletter, April 1961, 1.
              Shapiro calls Miller the "world's greatest author."

E1675 Schwartz, Edward P. "Worth Reading," Henry Miller
       Literary Society Newsletter, April 1961, 4.
              Both David Loth's The Erotic in Literature and James
       Jackson Kilpatrick's The Smut Peddlers mention
       Miller.

E1676 Siegferth, Charles. "Notes from Siegferth," Henry Miller
       Literary Society Newsletter, April 1961, 3.
              Siegferth looks back on visit to Big Sur and discus-
       sions with Miller.

E1677 Solomon, David. "News from Big Sur," Henry Miller
       Literary Society Newsletter, April 1961, 3.
              Although Miller banned in U.S., his work appeared in
       Metronome.

E1678 "Tropic of Cancer," Psychiatric Quarterly, XXXV (April
       1961).
              Tropic called a book about a schizoid young man's
       life.

E1679 "Tropic of Cancer before the U.S. Supreme Court," ALA
       Bulletin, LV (April 1961), 291-298.
              Tropic's merit being discussed by U.S. Supreme Court.

E1680 Fruchter, Norman. "In Defense of Henry Miller," Time
       and Tide, XLII (April 6, 1961), 572-573.
              Miller sees life as process of continuous development
       and self-liberation and sees growth process as divine
       voyage to self-discovery in Best of Henry Miller.

E1681 Wilcock, John. "Of Freedom and Henry Miller," Village
       Voice, (April 6, 1961).
              Miller's works inject freedom into reader, as seen in
       World of Sex, Tropics, Rosy Crucifixion, Black
       Spring, Air-Conditioned Nightmare, and Colossus of
       Maroussi.

E1682 Benjamin, Philip. "Henry Miller Ban to Be Defied Here,"

New York Times, CX (April 25, 1961), 37.
 Grove Press will defy Miller ban by printing Tropic
 in U.S.

E1683   "File Film Brief vs. U.S. Customs on 'Tropic' Book,"
 Variety, CI (April 26, 1961), 3, 214.
  Motion Picture Association will file court brief to test
  right of U.S. Customs to censor Tropic of Cancer.

E1684   Gerstenberger, Donna.   "Trace," Abstracts of English
 Studies, IV (May 1961), 209.
  James May's "Henry Miller" conveys idea that Miller
  is wrong to be aligned with Beats for Miller has inner
  sense of value.

E1685   "Grove Press Will Publish Miller's 'Tropic of Cancer',"
 News, May 1, 1961, 29.
  Tropic to be published by Grove this year.

E1686   T., V. G.   "Henry Miller," Oberhessischen Presse, May
 2, 1961.
  Review of Devil in Paradise.   (In German.)

E1687   "Judge Asked to Free 'Tropic of Cancer'," New York
 Times, CX (May 10, 1961), 48.
  Federal Judge Thomas F. Murphy asked to end ban
  and clear way for Tropic in U.S.

E1688   "Miller Book Date Set," New York Times, CX (May 16,
 1961), 40.
  Grove to publish Tropic; available by June 24, at
  $7.50.

E1689   Kaye, Joseph.   "Woman Sues to Import Banned Book,"
 New York Star, May 20, 1961, 4.
  Court battle over Dorothy Upham's right to bring
  Tropic into U.S. rages.

E1690   "Miller Novel on Sale," New York Times, CX (May 20,
 1961), 21.
  Tropic released to midtown New York bookstores for
  sale.

E1691   Qutden, Martin, Jr.   "Anything Goes!" Motion Picture
 Herald, May 20, 1961.
  Motion Picture Association filed brief to allow Tropic
  to be brought into U.S.

E1692   Kaye, Joseph.   "A Look at New York," Kansas City Star,
 May 21, 1961.
  Miller mentioned.

E1693   Hobby, Diana Potest.   "Tropic of Cancer," Houston Post,

LXXVII (May 23, 1961), 16.
Grove to publish Tropic; many critics call it great.

E1694   "Author Applauds Lifting 'Tropic of Cancer' Ban," n.p.,
May 24, 1961.
Miller feels decision to publish Tropic in U.S. marks
turning point from Puritanism in America.

E1695   "Miller Hails U.S. Copy of 'Tropic of Cancer'," Tucson
Citizen, LXXXIX (May 24, 1961), 28.
Miller sees publication of Cancer in U.S. as turning
point of American literature.

E1696   "Author Terms Lifting of Ban Turning Point," San Diego
Tribune, May 25, 1961.
Miller sees decision to publish Tropic in U.S. as turn-
ing away from Puritanism.

E1697   "Miller's Book Okayed in U.S.," Fort Lauderdale News,
May 25, 1961.
U.S. Customs Department's decision to allow Tropic
in U.S. has changed literary climate of country.

E1698   Dam, Everett. "U.S. Ends Long Ban on 'Obscene' Book,"
Minneapolis News, May 27, 1961.
Miller sees decision to publish Tropic in U.S. as ma-
jor turning point in American literature.

E1699   Tanner, Tony. "Book Reviews," Cambridge Review, May
27, 1961.
Best of Henry Miller shows Miller to be a man in
quest of reality which is experienced through self-
liberation.

E1700   "The Arts: A Mixed Bag," Cleveland Press & News,
May 17, 1961, 10.
Miller pleased Tropic finally published in U.S.

E1701   "Barney Rosset," Saturday Review, XLIX (May 27, 1961), 7-8.
Rosset and Grove will publish Tropic in U.S.

E1702   "Miller's 'Tropic' Is Top Seller," Dallas Texas News,
CXII (May 28, 1961), V9.
Tropic best seller in Dallas and in U.S.

E1703   Fink, Robert. "A Letter from Robert Fink," International
Henry Miller Letter, June 1961, 3-4.
Fink praises Miller as saint in letter to Henk Van Gelre.

E1704   Fink, Robert. "A Quiet Afternoon in Miller's Front-
Yard," International Henry Miller Letter, June 1961, 16.
Photograph by Robert Fink in 1957 or 1958 showing
Miller, Edith Fink, Wallace Fowlie, Eve Miller, and
unidentified neighbor.

E1705   Fink, Robert. "Henry Miller in His Back-Yard about
1956," International Henry Miller Letter, June 1961, 13.
Photograph of Miller at Big Sur.

E1706   Kosner, Edward. "Another Journey for Henry Miller,"
Henry Miller Literary Society (Critical Review), June 1961,
4.
Miller notes that Cancer depicts things nakedly and
brutally in real life.

E1707   Lowenfels, Walter. "A Note on Henry Miller's Tropic of
Cancer," International Henry Miller Letter, June 1961,
5-6.
Miller's Tropic anti-literary because it is alive not
mere words.

E1708   Reitzel, Hans. "Tony and Henry Miller in the Garden of
Hans Reitzel," International Henry Miller Letter, June
1961, 18.
Photograph of Miller and son, Tony.

E1709   "Written Especially for Me," Bookman's Briefcase, June
1961, 1-3.
In The Books in My Life, Miller feels the books a
person reads determine his life.

E1710   McPhaul, Jack. "Critic At-Large: Is It Pornography?"
Chicago Sun-Times, XIV (June 2, 1961), II 6.
Tropic dynamite, to some art, others pornography.

E1711   " 'Cancer' Symptoms Here?" Dallas Times Herald, June
4, 1961.
Many in Dallas believe Tropic's sale will cause court
fight.

E1712   "Tropic O'Miller," New York Times, CX (June 4, 1961),
VII 8.
Miller shows no expression over change in U.S. allow-
ing Tropic.

E1713   "Greatest Living Patagonian," Time, LXXVII (June 9, 1961),
88-89.
Cancer a dirty book whose hero is a base man of gutter
who rejects Western ideas.

E1714   "Henry Miller's Novel Faces Post Office Ban," San Francisco Chronicle, XCVII (June 9, 1961), 32.
Post Office to ban Tropic from the mails.

E1715   "Hollywood," Time, LXXVII (June 9, 1961), 55.
Problem of making Cancer into a film noted.

E1716   Kirsch, Robert. "The Emergence of Henry Miller," Los

Angeles Times, LXXX (June 9, 1961), III 5.
Publishing Tropic in U.S. a step toward freedom.

E1717   "Henry Miller Novel Banned from Mails," Los Angeles
Times, LXXX (June 10, 1961), 5.
Miller's Tropic banned from mails for being obscene.

E1718   Lewis, Anthony. "Post Office Moves for Ban on Novel
'Tropic of Cancer'," New York Times, CX (June 10, 1961),
25.
On June 9, 1961, the U.S. Post Office moved to ban
Tropic from mails on grounds of obscenity.

E1719   " 'Tropic of Cancer' Banned in Mails Pending Hearing,"
New York Herald Tribune, CXXI (June 10, 1961), 5.
Tropic banned from U.S. Mail pending Court decision
on obscenity charge.

E1720   Grieg, Michael. "Getting on the Banned Wagon With
'Tropic of Cancer'," San Francisco Examiner, (June 11,
1961), H2.
Miller will finally be recognized as great author.

E1721   Maslin, Marsh. "[Henry Miller]," San Francisco Call
Bulletin, June 12, 1961.
Miller a moral man commenting on our modern soci-
ety.

E1722   Mayer, Robert. " 'Tropic' of Controversy," Newsday,
(June 12, 1961).
Miller's Tropics banned in U.S. because of supposed
obscenity.

E1723   " 'Tropic of Cancer' Scores a Victory," New York Times,
CX (June 14, 1961), 21.
U.S. Post Office drops move to ban Tropic because of
fear of losing court trial.

E1724   Kutscher, Gerdt. "Frauen und Göttinnen," Die Bücher-
Konnentare, June 15, 1961.
Review of Miller's Nights of Love and Laughter.   (In
German.)

E1725   Manville, Bill. "Saloon Society," Village Voice, (June 15,
1961).
Miller uses dirty words for effect and double meaning.

E1726   Moon, Eric. "Miller, Henry," Library Journal, LXXXVI
(June 15, 1961), 2338.
Miller has taken novel farther than any other 20th-
century American author.

E1727   Anderson, C. V. J. "Miller's Spoiled Mystery," Time,

LXXVII (June 16, 1961), 7.
Tropic called dull.

E1728   Lytton, Lyle. "[Miller and Durrell]," Time, LXXVII
(June 16, 1961), 7.
Miller and Durrell called "cocky, small-statured,
dirty-minded bad boys" (p. 7).

E1729   "Miller à New York," Continent, June 17, 1961.
Tropic being sold in U.S. after 27-year ban.   (In
French.)

E1730   Cross, Leslie. "Henry Miller Uncut: A Legendary Shocker Comes Into the Open," Milwaukee Journal, LXXIX (June
18, 1961), 6.
Tropic the story of the little people of the Paris
streets.

E1731   Hobby, Diana Poteat. "Tropic of Cancer," Houston Post,
LXXVII (June 18, 1961), 28.
Triumph of individual over art is what Miller desires.

E1732   "Long-Banned Novel," Greensboro (N.C.) News, XCIX
(June 18, 1961), D3.
Tropic went on sale today and sold out.

E1733   Moore, Harry T. "From Under the Counter to Front
Shelf," New York Times, CX (June 18, 1961), VII 5.
Review of Tropic where Miller-narrator seen as de-
scendant of Dostoevsky's "Underground Man," by going
from psychotic to whole man.

E1734   Nichols, Lewis. "In and Out of Books," New York Times,
CX (June 18, 1961), 8.
Miller Literary Society's purpose to spread word of
Miller.

E1735   Pittman, Kay. "Will 'Tropic of Cancer' Ever Be Available to U.S. Public?" Jackson Mississippi State Times,
VII (June 18, 1961), 7B.
Tropic now banned from mails, so it is questionable
whether it will ever be allowed in U.S.

E1736   Thorpe, Day. "The Question of Henry Miller," Washington Star, CIX (June 18, 1961), C5.
Look at Miller's belief that each individual must be
himself and search within the self to know self.

E1737   "Fit to Print?" Leedsburg (Va.) Commercial Ledger,
June 19, 1961.
Tropic unfit for general distribution because shocking.

E1738   K., E. "News Comments," Monterey Peninsula Herald,

June 19, 1961, 1, 4.
Miller's view of American society called ridiculous.

E1739   "Tropic of Cancer," Chapel Hill (N. C.) Weekly, June 19,
1961.
People have right to decide for selves whether or not
to read Tropic.

E1740   "Tropic Storm," Newsweek, LVII (June 19, 1961), 33.
Tropic caught between censors and those who see it
as work of high merit.

E1741   O'M., E. "The Ban Is Banished," Emporia (Kan.) Gazette, LXXI (June 20, 1961), 4.
Miller's Tropic free of ban and being distributed.

E1742   Gordon, George. "Anti 'Tropic'," n. p., June 22, 1961.
Tropic called dull.

E1743   Howard, Richard. "Miller: Naturalist of the Self,"
Morningsider, June 22, 1961.
Miller's Tropic the story of survival in a hell on
earth.

E1744   "Postal Ban Lifted on Miller's 'Tropic'," n. p., June 22,
1961.
U.S. Post Office dismissed complaint against Tropic.

E1745   Thoma, Richard.   " 'Tropic'--At Long Last," n. p., June
22, 1961.
Calls Tropic first piece of American genius.

E1746   "Books: Tropic of Cancer," Life, L (June 23, 1961), 25.
Tropic an explosive Whitmanesque masterpiece.

E1747   Walsh, Bob.   "The Battleground of Censor," n. p., June
23, 1961.
Miller style called obscene.

E1748   Brown, Ruth.   " 'Cancer' and the Cops," Saturday Review,
XLIV (June 24, 1961), 13.
Factual account of Tropic's publication by Grove
Press in paperback.

E1749   Dolbier, Maurice. "Tropic of Cancer," New York Herald
Tribune, CXXI (June 24, 1961), 9.
Miller's autobiography about his down-and-out days
in Paris.

E1750   Menn, Thorpe. "Books of the Day," Kansas City Star,
CXXIV (June 24, 1961), 7.
Tropic a romantic fantasy and affirmation of negation.

E1751   Pasley, Virginia.   "Critic's Corner," Newsday, (June 24, 1961), 21.
Tropic neither shocking nor great literature.   Anti-society slant and anti-materialism remind one of Steinbeck.

E1752   Redman, Ben Ray.   "An Artist's Education," Saturday Review, XLIV (June 24, 1961), 12.
Review of Tropic that admires Miller as man who is word master and who writes like an angel or a devil because his work lives.

E1753   Schott, Webster.   "Here's That Famous Dirty Book," Kansas City Star, CXXIV (June 24, 1961), 7.
Cancer dated, yet it possesses a vigor, a humor, and an honest, beautiful prose poetry that endures.

E1754   B., J.   "Another Banned Book Comes to Its Native Land," St. Petersburg (Fla.) Times, (June 25, 1961).
Tropic called Miller's protest against convention and culture.

E1755   "Banned Book Comes Home," Lewiston (Me.) Tribune, June 25, 1961.
Tropic to be published by Grove.

E1756   Bolton, Whitney.   " 'Tropic of Cancer' Is Criticized by Writer," Lubbock (Texas) Sun Avalanche-Journal, June 25, 1961.
Miller a fair writer but book not worth all praise it received.

E1757   Edel, Leon.   "After All the Hubbub, a Fossil," New York Herald Tribune, CXXI (June 25, 1961), 32.
Edel calls book dated.

E1758   " 'Fan Club' for Miller Has Grown," Minneapolis Tribune, XCV (June 25, 1961), 14.
Miller mentions Society in Henry Miller Reader.

E1759   Kosner, Edward.   "Another Journey for Henry Miller," New York Post, CLX (June 25, 1961), II 4.
Miller journeys to Europe at time when Tropic published in U.S.

E1760   Sherman, John K.   "Henry Miller's Novel Now Legal, But Still Not Tender," Minneapolis Tribune, XCV (June 25, 1961), 14.
Tropic broke down inhibitions, destroyed romantic notion of sex, and influenced such writers as Durrell, Algren, and Mailer.

E1761   Hyman, Stanley Edgar.   "The Innocence of Henry Miller,"

New Leader, XLIV (June 26, 1961), 22-24.
Miller's book an attempt to liberate individual.

E1762 Helms, John. "Art and Trash," Morristown Gazette, June 27, 1961.
Miller's book called poor, outdated art.

E1763 "Aus 'Nexus' und anderen Werken," Student und Gesellschaft, June 28, 1961, 7.
Review of Nexus. (In German.)

E1764 Kerkhoff, Horst. "Ein Faun av Nachmittag," Student und Gesellschaft, June 28, 1961, 6-7.
Miller has established a modern literary revolution. (In German.)

E1765 "One Suit on Novel is Dismissed Here," New York Times, CX (June 28, 1961), 40.
Action to restrain the U.S. Customs from interfering with Tropic dismissed by Federal Judge Thomas Murphy.

E1766 Forst, Don. "Three Major Book Sellers Here Won't Carry 'Tropic of Cancer'," New York Post, CLX (June 29, 1961), II 4.
Doubleday, Macy's, and Scribner's will not sell Miller novel.

E1767 Atkinson, Brooks. "Critic at Large: Henry Miller's Use of an Emerson Quotation in 'Tropic of Cancer' is Discussed," New York Times, CX (June 30, 1961), 24.
Miller destroys illusions to show reality of modern civilization and the animal-like existence one must face to be part of it.

E1768 French, Warren. "Miller, Henry," Twentieth Century Literature, VII (July 1961), 96.
Miller seen as honest author in review of J. Rives Childs's article, "Collecting Henry Miller."

E1769 Gardiner, Harold C. "Publishing Disgrace--Critical Shame: Tropic of Cancer," America, CV (July 1, 1961), 490.
Review of Tropic calling it the product of a filthy mind.

E1770 Hirshberg, Ed. "Popular Books Reissued," Tampa Times, July 1, 1961.
Tropic being reprinted in U.S.

E1771 Rexroth, Kenneth. "The Empty Zone," Nation, CXCIII (July 1, 1961), 15-16.
Review of Tropic which sees Miller as social outcast

creating dead literature.

E1772   Shaw, Fred.   "Nothing is Tomorrow in Tropic of Cancer,"
Miami News, July 2, 1961.
Civilization the cancer in Miller book.

E1773   Remington, Fred.   " 'Obscenity' Gets Bright Thoughtful
Treatment," Pittsburgh Press, LXXVIII (July 4, 1961), 44.
Debate on pros and cons of Tropic.

E1774   Shain, Percy.   "Night Watch," Boston Globe, CLXXX (July
5, 1961), 31.
Merits of Tropic discussed on T. V. show, P. M. East.

E1775   Ferber, Christian.   "Miller nehmen wie er ist...," Die
Welt, July 8, 1961.
Nexus reviewed.   (In German.)

E1776   Atkinson, Brooks.   "Smuggled No Longer," St. Louis Post
Dispatch, LXXXIII (July 9, 1961), 4F.
Miller a prophet of American doom.

E1777   "Customs Case vs. 'Tropic' Sent to Eastern District
Court," Publishers Weekly, CLXXX (July 10, 1961), 45.
Two Tropic suits in New York dismissed.

E1778   Flowers, Paul.   "The Infirmities of Age," Commonweal,
LXXIV (July 10, 1961), 382-383.
Tropic called dull, dreary book.

E1779   Kauffmann, Stanley.   "An Old Shocker Comes Home," New
Republic, CXLV (July 10, 1961), 17-19.
Tropic a fierce celebration of enlightened freedom.

E1780   "Cites Careful Choice of Books for Library," Cleveland
Press-News, July 11, 1961, D5.
Tropic in Atlanta, Georgia, library.

E1781   Bennett, Bill.   "Bored by 'Tropic'," Village Voice, (July
13, 1961).
Tropic boring, not the work Ulysses is.

E1782   "Tropic of Cancer," Islip (L. I.) Town Crier, July 13,
1961.
Miller a positive, life giving experience.

E1783   Gorn, Lester.   "Miller's 'Tropic'," San Francisco Examiner, (July 14, 1961), 33.
Miller a shocker, but he fails to shake society to its
roots.

E1784   Marcuse, Ludwig.   "Der verlorene Vater," Literatur,
July 14, 1961, 13.

Nexus appears in Germany; Tropic in U.S. (In German.)

E1785 " 'Best-Seller' Move Made," Akron Beacon Journal, July 16, 1961.
State Attorney General McCormack has probably helped Tropic sales.

E1786 Flowers, Paul. "The Infirmities of Age," Memphis Commercial Appeal, CXXII (July 16, 1961), IV 10.
Tropic called dull, dreary, and dead.

E1787 Morrison, Oliver. "What Orwell Said," New York Times, CX (July 16, 1961), VII 26.
In Orwell's "Inside the Whale," Miller called hardboiled person talking about life, not a great writer.

E1788 B., V. A. " 'Tropic' Reaches Stores," Chicago News, LXXXVI, July 17, 1961, 17.
Tropic available after 27-year ban.

E1789 "Aus dem Kulturleben," Die Welt, July 18, 1961.
Miller's work a bust. (In German.)

E1790 "Book Faces Scrutiny," Fall River (Mass.) Herald News, July 19, 1961.
Massachusetts Obscene Literature Control Commission will hold special meeting to discuss merits of Tropic.

E1791 Sohmers, Harriet. "P'town Does It Again," Village Voice, VI (July 20, 1961), 7-8.
Tropic seen as expression of truth.

E1792 "Talk on Henry Miller," Village Voice, VI (July 20, 1961), 8.
Mike Rivise will discuss Miller at N.Y. Writers Guild on July 26.

E1793 "Asks 'Tropic of Cancer' Ban," Boston Record, July 21, 1961.
Massachusetts Obscene Literature Control Committee against sale of Tropic.

E1794 Braum, R. A. "Begegnung mit Henry Miller," Sonntagsblatt Staats-Zeitung und Herald, July 21, 1961, 6c.
Look at Miller's canon. (In German.)

E1795 "City Censor in Favor of Book Ban," Lowell (Mass.) Sun, July 21, 1961.
City Censor, Joseph Vaillaneourt, upholds state obscenity decision against Tropic.

E1796 Herstatt, Cornelia. "Abenteurer der Literatur," Berlin

Bild Zeitung, July 21, 1961.
Miller's Plexus, Colossus, and Tropic viewed. (In German.)

E1797   Bennett, Bill. "Starvation Diet," Saturday Review, XLIV (July 22, 1961), 29.
Tropic not well written.

E1798   Huston, Denis N. "The Concepts," Saturday Review, XLIV (July 22, 1961), 29.
Tropic not wholesome or of merit.

E1799   Dolbier, Maurice. "Miller: Two Views," New York Herald Tribune, CXXI (July 23, 1961), VI 2.
Miller named lifetime Associate of Academy of Perigord in France while being banned in Massachusetts.

E1800   Fulmer, Daniel W. "Outrageous," New York Herald Tribune, CXXI (July 23, 1961), VI 15.
Tropic called one man's truth; Miller has First Amendment rights to proclaim it.

E1801   Knopf, Alfred A. "A Publisher Comments on Books and Authors," Toledo Blade, CXXVL (July 23, 1961), II 6.
Miller book called sheer sex and nothing more.

E1802   Nichols, Lewis. "In and Out of Books: Tropical," New York Times, CX (July 23, 1961), VII 8.
One cannot bring Tropic into U.S., but one can buy it here.

E1803   "The Tropic of Henry Miller," New York Herald Tribune, CXXI (July 23, 1961), VI 15.
People will not sell Tropic either out of fear or from sense of morality.

E1804   Wolfson, Martin. "Delicious," New York Herald Tribune, CXXI (July 23, 1961), VI 15.
Refutation of Leon Edel's review of Tropic which buries novel.

E1805   "Massachusetts Moves to Ban 'Tropic of Cancer'," Publishers' Weekly, CLXXX (July 24, 1961), 44-45.
Tropic will sell better with ban.

E1806   "What Is More Precious Than Right of Choice?" San Leandro (Calif.) News, July 24, 1961.
People must decide merits of Tropic for themselves.

E1807   "Author to Get Day in Court," North Attleboro (Mass.) Chronicle, July 25, 1961.
Author and publisher of Tropic have until August 23 to show validity of book.

E1808   " 'Banned in Boston' Has Familiar Ring Once Again, " Bath
        (Me.) News Journal, July 25, 1961.
        Grove publishers must show why book not obscene by
        August 23.

E1809   "Book Going on Trial as Obscene, Impure, " Greenfield
        Recorder-Gazette, July 25, 1961.
        Boston Superior Court Judge Donald Macaulay has
        ordered Grove Press to show why Tropic not obscene.

E1810   "Can't Even Loan Copy of 'Cancer', " Boston Traveler,
        (July 25, 1961).
        Illegal to buy or loan copy of Tropic in Massachusetts.

E1811   "Hearing Set on 'Tropic of Cancer', " Springfield (Mass.)
        Evening News, July 25, 1961.
        August 23 hearing set for Tropic.

E1812   "Judge Bans 'Tropic of Cancer', " New York Times, CX
        (July 25, 1961), 25.
        Boston Superior Court Judge Macauley ruled Tropic
        obscene, banning it in Massachusetts.

E1813   "Judge Rules Henry Miller Book Obscene, " Oakland Tri-
        bune, July 25, 1961.
        Tropic ruled obscene in Massachusetts.

E1814   "Massachusetts Court Brands 'Tropic' Obscene, " Washing-
        ton Post & Times Herald, LXXXIV (July 25, 1961), 15.
        Tropic called obscene in Massachusetts.

E1815   "Miller Book Ruled Obscene in Massachusetts, " Seattle
        Times, LXXXIV (July 25, 1961), 12.
        Miller's adventures in Paris after World War I ob-
        scene.

E1816   "Miller's Book Ruled Obscene in High Court, " Berkshire
        Eagle, July 25, 1961.
        Author and publisher of Tropic have opportunity to
        prove book not obscene.

E1817   "Publisher Must Explain Why Book is Not Obscene, "
        Attleboro (Mass.) Sun, July 25, 1961.
        Grove press has until August 23 to show why Tropic
        not obscene.

E1818   "Steps Taken to Ban 'Tropic of Cancer' in Boston, " Bath
        (Me.) Times, July 25, 1961.
        Judge Macauley ordered Grove to show why Tropic
        should not be banned.

E1819   " 'Tropic of Cancer' Banned in Massachusetts, " Bethlehem
        (Penn.) Globe-Times, July 25, 1961.

Tropic obscene in Boston.

E1820 " 'Cancer' Tabu in Massachusetts," Variety, July 26, 1961.
Cancer banned in Massachusetts.

E1821 Kane, Ann. "Hail Banning of Obscene Book in Boston,"
Boston Record, July 26, 1961.
Banning Tropic truly moral act.

E1822 "Sales Boost," Waterbury (Conn.) American, July 26, 1961.
Miller ban in Massachusetts another absurd restriction.

E1823 Derleth, August. "The Provocation of the Forbidden,"
Madison (Wisc.) Dispatch Star, July 27, 1961.
Lure of forbidden will sell Tropic.

E1824 Dudley, Bronson. "The Shout Is All," Village Voice,
(July 27, 1961).
Miller's lack of style shows his brilliance, as he
writes new form of literature.

E1825 Hoyer, Franz A. "Provozierende Maskenspiele," Der Tag,
July 30, 1961.
Nexus reviewed. (In German.)

E1826 Marcuse, Ludwig. "Der verlorene Vater," St. Galler
Tagblatt, July 30, 1961.
Tropic favorably compared to Moby Dick. (In Ger-
man.)

E1827 " 'Old Yeller' Sequel Coming," Dallas Times Herald, July
30, 1961.
Tropic cannot be distributed in Massachusetts.

E1828 "Two Years Ago," Elmira (N.Y.) Telegram, July 30,
1961.
Grove Press strikes blow for freedom of press with
Tropic publication.

E1829 "Grove Press Will Fight 'Tropic' Ban in Massachusetts,"
Publishers Weekly, CLXXX (July 31, 1961), 23.
Grove will go to court to allow Tropic sale in U.S.

E1830 "Henry Miller," Atlantic, CCVIII (August 1961), 98-99.
Tropic called a disgusting book.

E1831 Kaye, Joseph. "About Anaïs Nin," Henry Miller Literary
Society Newsletter, August 1961, 3.
Nin helped Miller when he was penniless in Paris and
also wrote a Preface for Tropic.

E1832 Moore, Harry T. "From Under the Counter to Front
Shelf," Henry Miller Literary Society Newsletter, August

1961, 1.
See E1733.

E1833   Nichols, Lewis.   "In and Out of Books," Henry Miller
Literary Society Newsletter, August 1961, 1.
See E1734.

E1834   Redman, Ben Ray.   "An Artist's Education," Henry Miller
Literary Society Newsletter, August 1961, 2.
See E1752.

E1835   Schwartz, Edward P.   "About Book Stores," Henry Miller
Literary Society Newsletter, August 1961, 2.
Since publication of American edition of Tropic many
more bookstores will carry Miller.

E1835   Schwartz, Edward P.   "About Miller," Henry Miller Literary Society Newsletter, August 1961, 4.
Bibliographical study of Miller by Esta Lou Rile delayed.

E1837   Schwartz, Edward P.   "A Little About Bibalo," Henry
Miller Literary Society Newsletter, August 1961, 2.
Bibalo writing score for The Smile at the Foot of the
Ladder.

E1838   Schwartz, Edward P.   "Also to be Published," Henry
Miller Literary Society Newsletter, August 1961, 4.
Special edition on Miller by Emile White to be pub-
lished in winter, 1961-1962.

E1839   Schwartz, Edward P.   "Among the Many," Henry Miller
Literary Society Newsletter, August 1961, 3.
Good reviews on Miller by Larry Dann in Bachelor,
September 1961 and Harold Gardiner in America, July
1, 1961.

E1840   Schwartz, Edward P.   "Available Material," Henry Miller
Literary Society Newsletter, August 1961, 3.
Watercolor reproductions by Museum Reproductions and
Illustrations to Henry Miller's Writing by Bezalel Schatz
available.

E1841   Schwartz, Edward P.   "Awards for Miller," Henry Miller
Literary Society Newsletter, August 1961, 3.
Academy du Perigord of France named Miller a life-
time Associate.

E1842   Schwartz, Edward P.   "Ben Ray Redman, The Saturday
Review," Miller Literary Society Newsletter, August 1961,
4.
Redman in Saturday Review of June 24, 1961, described Miller as one of most remarkable and most

original authors of this age.

E1843   Schwartz, Edward P.   "Book and Recording Combo, "
Henry Miller Literary Society Newsletter, August 1961, 4.
Combination book and record set to be called The Art
of Henry Miller.

E1844   Schwartz, Edward P.   "Books and Writing by Members of
Henry Miller Literary Society, " Henry Miller Literary So-
ciety Newsletter, August 1961, 4.
Robert Cross's The Henry Miller Circle in Paris; Jim
Ullyot's story on Tropic in Harvard Crimson (May 29,
1961); Collecting Henry Miller by J. Rives Childs in
PLA III (October 1960).

E1845   Schwartz, Edward P.   " 'Cancer' Tabu in Massachusetts, "
Henry Miller Literary Society Newsletter, August 1961, 3.
Judge Macauley ruled Tropic obscene, indecent, and
impure.

E1846   Schwartz, Edward P.   "Correction, " Henry Miller Literary Society Newsletter, August 1961, 3.
Barney Rosset signed Miller to American publication
of Tropic.

E1847   Schwartz, Edward P.   "Day Thorpe, Washington Star, "
Henry Miller Literary Society Newsletter, August 1961, 4.
Thorpe in Washington Star on June 18, 1961, called
Miller superb story-teller.

E1848   Schwartz, Edward P.   "Eric Moon, Library Journal, "
Henry Miller Literary Society Newsletter, August 1961, 4.
Moon in Library Journal (June 15, 1961) calls Miller
a man happy without illusions.

E1849   Schwartz, Edward P.   "First Play, " Henry Miller Lite-
rary Society Newsletter, August 1961, 4.
Miller's play, Just Wild about Harry, published by
New Directions.

E1850   Schwartz, Edward P.   "Fleeting Moment, " Henry Miller
Literary Society Newsletter, August 1961, 2.
Tom Kassis met and spoke to Miller about freedom.

E1851   Schwartz, Edward P.   "From Montana Newsman, " Henry
Miller Literary Society Newsletter, August 1961, 3.
Henry Miller Reader found in Great Falls, Mont.,
public library.

E1852   Schwartz, Edward P.   "Gerald Walker, New York Post, "
Henry Miller Literary Society Newsletter, August 1961, 4.
Walker of New York Post (June 18, 1961) called Miller
a great writer and Tropic one of few truly important
books.

E1853   Schwartz, Edward P.   "Goes on Record!" Henry Miller
        Literary Society Newsletter, August 1961, 3.
                Mary Salmon of Malibu, Calif., told library it lacked
                Miller works.

E1854   Schwartz, Edward P.   "Great Collection," Henry Miller
        Literary Society Newsletter, August 1961, 3.
                Donte Thomas has superb collection of Miller noted in
                My Friend Henry Miller and Books in My Life.

E1855   Schwartz, Edward P.   "Harry T. Moore, the New York
        Times," Henry Miller Literary Society Newsletter, August
        1961, 4.
                Moore in New York Times (June 18, 1961) calls
                Miller's protagonist a descendant of Dostoevsky's
                "Underground Man."

E1856   Schwartz, Edward P.   "Heart-Warming News," Henry
        Miller Literary Society Newsletter, August 1961, 2.
                Miss Dott Moss Burns feels Miller helped boost her
                morale.

E1857   Schwartz, Edward P.   "Henry in Hamburg," Henry Miller
        Literary Society Newsletter, August 1961, 1.
                Photograph and article about Miller's arrival in Ham-
                burg, Germany.

E1858   Schwartz, Edward P.   "John K. Sherman, Minneapolis
        Tribune," Henry Miller Literary Society Newsletter,
        August 1961, 4.
                Sherman's review of Tropic on June 25, 1961.

E1859   Schwartz, Edward P.   "Leslie Cross, Milwaukee Journal,"
        Henry Miller Literary Society Newsletter, August 1961,
        4.
                In the Milwaukee Journal (June 18, 1961) Cross calls
                Miller an anti-literary writer.

E1860   Schwartz, Edward P.   "Life Magazine," Henry Miller
        Literary Society Newsletter, August 1961, 4.
                Life Magazine on June 23, 1961, called Tropic an
                explosive, Whitmanesque masterpiece and an obscen-
                ity.

E1861   Schwartz, Edward P.   "Marsh Maslin, San Francisco Call
        Bulletin," Henry Miller Literary Society Newsletter,
        August 1961, 4.
                Marsh Maslim of the San Francisco Call Bulletin on
                June 12, 1961, called Miller a moral man commenting
                on modern society.

E1862   Schwartz, Edward P.   "Merchandising Miller," Henry
        Miller Literary Society Newsletter, August 1961, 3.

John P. Randen sends clippings on Miller ads.

E1863   Schwartz, Edward P.   "Miller's Old Friends," Henry
        Miller Literary Society Newsletter, August 1961, 3.
        Orvis Ross presented the Society with one of rarest
        Miller pieces from The Booster.

E1864   Schwartz, Edward P.   "Miscellaneous," Henry Miller Lite-
        rary Society Newsletter, August 1961, 4.
        An opera based on Smile at the Foot of the Ladder
        being composed by Antonio Bibalo; Miller-Emil Schnel-
        lock correspondence acquired by UCLA; Annette Bax-
        ter's Henry Miller, Expatriate; Walter Schmiele's
        Henry Miller; Moore's Bibliography; Perlès's My
        Friend Henry Miller.

E1865   Schwartz, Edward P.   "New Reprints," Henry Miller Lite-
        rary Society Newsletter, August 1961, 4.
        New reprints of Miller's work: Tropic (Grove); Re-
        member to Remember, Cosmological Eye, Sunday After
        the War (New Directions); Capricorn (New Directions
        Reader); Devil in Paradise (New American Library);
        Mademoiselle Claude (Scene Magazine); Smile at the
        Foot of the Ladder (John Miro); To Paint is to Love
        Again.

E1866   Schwartz, Edward P.   "News from Japan," Henry Miller
        Literary Society Newsletter, August 1961, 3.
        Yamada Houkoh, Kariya, Aichi, Japan, did graduation
        thesis on Miller.

E1867   Schwartz, Edward P.   "New Watercolor Book," Henry
        Miller Literary Society Newsletter, August 1961, 4.
        The Angel is My Watermark to be produced by Harry
        Abrams.

E1868   Schwartz, Edward P.   "New Writing," Henry Miller Lite-
        rary Society Newsletter, August 1961, 4.
        Miller in following journals: "Ein Ungebumlelte
        Fuchselbiss" in Rhinozeros No. 3 (1961); "My Life
        as an Echo," "Stand Still Like the Hummingbird," and
        "Ashihari and the Story Shunkin" in International Miller
        Letter No. 1 (June 1961); "Letters to Lowenfels" in
        Outsider; "Letter to the Editor" in Metronome (May
        1961).

E1869   Schwartz, Edward P.   "Official Bibliography," Henry
        Miller Literary Society Newsletter, August 1961, 1.
        Noted is arrival of Thomas H. Moore's Bibliography
        of Miller.

E1870   Schwartz, Edward P.   "Plugs for the Society," Henry
        Miller Literary Society Newsletter, August 1961, 1.

Society's goal to get Miller read in U.S.

E1871   Schwartz, Edward P.   "Radio-TV," Henry Miller Literary
Society Newsletter, August 1961, 4.
Interview of Miller on German television in Cologne.

E1872   Schwartz, Edward P.   "Thanks for Clips," Henry Miller
Literary Society Newsletter, August 1961, 2.
Clippings of Grove Press announcement of Cancer pub-
lication have reached Society.

E1873   Schwartz, Edward P.   " 'Tropic of Cancer' Best Seller,"
Henry Miller Literary Society Newsletter, August 1961, 1,
3.
On August 6, 1961, Tropic sixth on New York Times
Best Seller list.

E1874   Schwartz, Edward P.   "Webster Schott, Kansas City Star,"
Henry Miller Literary Society Newsletter, August 1961, 4.
Schott on June 24 called Tropic most important book
of the year.

E1875   Schwartz, Edward P.   "With the Kronhausens," Henry
Miller Literary Society Newsletter, August 1961, 2.
Kronhausens, who wrote Pornography and the Law,
plan to meet Miller in Germany.

E1876   Sherman, John K.   "Henry Miller's Novel Now Legal, But
Still Not Tender," Henry Miller Literary Society News-
letter, August 1961, 3.
See E 1760.

E1877   Falleder, Arnold.   "Critic's Function," Morningsider,
August 3, 1961.
Tropic not a good book from standpoint of traditional
literature.

E1878   "Current Borrower Last Legal Reader of Prohibited Book,"
Springfield (Mass.) Morning Union, August 4, 1961.
Forbes Library in Northampton will permit no more
circulation of banned Tropic.

E1879   R., H.   "Bildschirm," Frankfurter Rundschau, August 4,
1961.
Miller seen on German television.   (In German.)

E1880   "Book Censorship Sparks Indignation," Boston American,
(August 5, 1961).
All have right to decide Tropic's merits for them-
selves.

E1881   C., W.   "Let People Choose," Boston American, (August
5, 1961).

Let people stoop to read Tropic trash if they wish.

E1882   "Tropic of Cancer," Greensboro Record, August 5, 1961.
Grove now publishes Tropic in U.S.

E1883   Green, A. C.   "Bad Ol' Best Seller Lists," Dallas Times,
August 6, 1961.
Tropic sells well because of sex.

E1884   Harlan, Howard.   "Critic Say of Banned Book," n. p.,
August 6, 1961.
Tropic called realistic, surrealistic, and mystical.

E1885   Kirsch, Robert R.   "Miller Tales that Boston Didn't Ban,"
Los Angeles Times, LXXX (August 7, 1961), II 8.
Miller works not banned in U.S. are Cosmological Eye,
Remember to Remember, and Sunday After the War.

E1886   C., E. M.   "Still On List," Boston Traveler, August 9,
1961.
Feels people have right to read Tropic.

E1887   "Federal Order Lifts Ban on Importing 'Tropic of Cancer',"
New York Times, CX (August 11, 1961), 25.
Department of Justice removed ban on importation of
Tropic.

E1888   Russell, Francis.   "The Cult of Henry Miller," National
Review, II (August 12, 1961), 92-94.
Review of Cancer that feels work is shocking and
nothing more.

E1889   "[Tropic of Cancer]," New Yorker, XXXVII (August 12,
1961), 86.
Tropic called a literary dud.

E1890   Winchell, Walter.   "Walter Winchell's America," San
Diego Union, XCIII (August 12, 1961), 13.
Tropic based on life of eccentric New York newspaper
man in Paris named Boris.

E1891   Danforth, Ken.   "Censors, Readers Differ on 'Tropic of
Cancer'," Arkansas Gazette CXLII (August 13, 1961), 6E.
Miller's characters alive because they respond like
human beings.

E1892   Davis, Bob.   "Pornography or Masterpiece?" Santa Rosa
Press Democrat, August 13, 1961, 2-3.
American public to decide merits of Miller's Tropic
for selves.

E1893   "Banned Book Said Sold Here, Police to Check," Holyoke
(Mass.) Transcript-Telegram, August 14, 1961.

Police investigating bookstores in Holyoke for sale of Tropic.

E1894   "Change of Obscenity," Washington Post & Times Herald, LXXXIV (August 14, 1961), 10.
U.S. Justice Department allows for publication of Tropic.

E1895   "Dallas Bans Book Via New State Law," Fort Worth Evening Star-Telegram, August 16, 1961.
Dallas police use new state law to prohibit sale of Tropic.

E1896   "Dallas Police Ban 'Tropic of Cancer'," New York Post, CLX (August 16, 1961), 79.
Dallas police order bookstores to quit selling Tropic or face legal consequences.

E1897   "Dallas Police Block Sale of Miller," Houston Press, August 16, 1961.
Dallas police have ordered bookstores to stop selling Tropic.

E1898   Ewell, James. "Police Label Book Obscene," Dallas News, CXII (August 16, 1961), 1.
Dallas bookstores ordered not to sell Tropic or face police action.

E1899   Greene, A. C. "City Booksellers in Uproar Over Police 'Ban' on Novel," Dallas Times Herald (August 16, 1961), 1, 10.
Bookstore owners object to police playing censor. Feel courts must decide Tropic's fate.

E1900   Greene, A. C. "Miller's Tropic of Cancer 'Banned' by Dallas Police," Dallas Times Herald (August 16, 1961), 10.
Tropic first book ever banned in Dallas.

E1901   "No Ban on 'Tropic of Cancer' Here--DA," Fort Worth Press, August 16, 1961.
Fort Worth District Attorney Doug Crouch says Tropic of literary merit.

E1902   "Dallas Bans 'Tropic'," New York News, XLIII (August 17, 1961), 36.
New state anti-obscenity law in Dallas used by police to halt sale of Tropic.

E1903   "Dallas Booksellers Rap Police Warning on Novel," Houston Post, LXXVII (August 17, 1961), 14.
Dallas booksellers object to police stopping sale of Tropic.

E1904   F., W.   "Henry Miller," Wiesbadener Kurier, August 17,
        1961.
        Review of Nexus. (In German.)

E1905   Greene, A. C.   "Publishers Ready to Help in Fight
        Against Book Ban," Dallas Times-Herald, August 17, 1961.
        Grove Press to support anyone who will fight Tropic
        ban in Dallas.

E1906   Konnelly, T.   "Defends Legality of Action on 'Tropic',"
        Boston Herald, CCXX (August 17, 1961), 20.
        Tropic called obscene, as McCormack supported.

E1907   "Miller Book Banned," New York Times, CX (August 17,
        1961), 18.
        Dallas Police issue warning against sale of Tropic.

E1908   "Now Dallas Police Deny Banning Book," Houston Press,
        (August 17, 1961).
        Police Chief Curry says Dallas bookstores not ordered
        to remove Tropic from shelves.

E1909   "Tropic of Cancer," Renton (Wash.) News Record, August
        17, 1961.
        Tropic for first time being published in U.S.

E1910   "Tropic of Cancer," Warren (Penn.) Times-Mirror, Aug-
        ust 17, 1961.
        Tropic a boring and dirty book.

E1911   " 'Tropic of Cancer' Book Banned in Dallas," Los Angeles
        Times, LXXX (August 17, 1961), 13.
        Dallas police order bookstores to stop selling Tropic
        under state anti-obscenity law.

E1912   "U.S. Finally to Let Lawyer Read His French Books,"
        Baltimore Sun, CCXLIX (August 17, 1961), 24.
        U.S. will allow Mr. Goodman to read two Tropics.

E1913   Crume, Paul.   "Big D," Dallas News, CXII (August 18,
        1961), 1.
        If police feel Tropic dirty, they have read smut be-
        fore so book cannot damage them.

E1914   "The Dallas-Boston Axis," Long Beach Independent, August
        18, 1961.
        Censorship of Tropic compared to Hitler.

E1915   "Library Orders Henry Miller's 'Tropic of Cancer',"
        Honolulu Star-Bulletin, L (August 18, 1961), 10.
        Two copies of Tropic ordered by public library.

E1916   "Publisher to Help Fight Book Ban," Houston Press,

August 18, 1961.
Grove will help any Dallas bookstore charged with selling Tropic.

E1917   Schwartz, Edward P.   "Tropic of Cancer," Twin City Spokesman, August 18, 1961.
Miller's book a truthful, uninhibited exhibition of his life.

E1918   Shirley, Joseph A.   "Wrong Target," Dallas Times-Herald (August 18, 1961).
Any adult who reads Tropic can judge merits for himself.

E1919   Wysatta, Jean.   " 'Tropic of Cancer' a Best Seller Here, Naturally, After Ban Talk," Fort Worth News, August 18, 1961.
Tropic best seller in Fort Worth.

E1920   "Book Fight Takes on Circus Air," Dallas News, CXII (August 19, 1961), 12.
City Manager Crull tells police they have no right to decide merits of Cancer.

E1921   "What Is Obscenity?" Dallas News, CXII (August 19, 1961), IV 2.
District Attorney in Fort Worth feels Tropic does not violate new Texas pornography law, yet police continue to enforce law.

E1922   Hass, Victor P.   "From a Bookman's Notebook," Omaha World Herald, LXXVII (August 20, 1961), G20.
Tropic a book about slums and brothels.

E1923   "Miller's Classic," Trenton Times, LXXIX (August 20, 1961), 14.
Tropic a classic and Miller outstanding.

E1924   "Banned Book Returns," Urbana (Ill.) Courier, August 23, 1961.
Tropic called tiresome.

E1925   "Signs of Wet Winter," San Francisco Chronicle, XCVII (August 23, 1961), 34.
Perverse Tropic brings perverse changes of mind.

E1926   "Banned Book Right Waved," Boston Record, (August 24, 1961).
Publishers of Tropic waived right to hearing on August 23.

E1927   Crume, Paul.   "Big D," Dallas News, CXII (August 24, 1961), 1.

Public irritated at Cancer censoring.

E1928   "Police Deserve Praise," Dallas News, CXII (August 24, 1961), IV 2.
Police praise taking Tropic off shelves.

E1929   "Trial Date Slated for Miller Book," Springfield Morning Sun, August 24, 1961.
September 22 marks beginning of Tropic trial in Boston.

E1930   Braem, Helmut M. "Die Liebe ist ausgeschlossen," Saarbrücher Zeitung, August 26, 1961.
Miller's Rosy Crucifixion and Miller as artist explored. (In German.)

E1931   "Chicago Trib Drops Two 'Best Sellers'," Editor & Publisher, XCIV (August 26, 1961), 15.
Tropic one of two books dropped from Chicago Tribune's best-seller list.

E1932   "Die Liebe ist ausgeschlossen," Von neuen Buchern, August 26, 1961.
Article dealing with Sexus, Nexus, and Plexus. (In German.)

E1933   "400 Attend Rally to Protest Smut," Dallas Times-Herald, August 26, 1961.
U.S. Representative John Dowdy read from and called Tropic smut.

E1934   Shorka, Gladys. "Cautions Committee to Investigate," El Paso Times, August 26, 1961.
Tropic must be read before it can be banned in El Paso.

E1935   Beatty, Jerome, Jr. "Trade Winds," Saturday Review, XLIII (August 27, 1961), 6.
Grove's Tropic banned in Boston.

E1936   Earwood, J. W. "The Readers on Censorship," Dallas Times-Herald, August 27, 1961.
Belief that Miller does not need obscenity in Tropic.

E1937   Mitchell, Francis. "[Tropic of Cancer]," Dallas Times-Herald, August 27, 1961.
Tropic seen as piece of representative literature.

E1938   "Obscenity and Mr. Miller," Dallas Times-Herald, August 27, 1961.
Miller interview dealing with Tropic from "Obscenity and the Law of Reflection."

E1939   "Trib Censors Its Book List," Dallas News, CXII (August 27, 1961), V 11.
Cancer censored from Chicago Tribune's best-seller list.

E1940   "Dallas Sets 'De Facto' Ban on 'Tropic of Cancer'," Publishers' Weekly, CLXXVIII (August 28, 1961), 260.
Dallas following Boston's example of banning Tropic.

E1941   Greene, A. C. "Why Censorship Is Bad," Dallas Times, August 29, 1961.
People of Dallas should individually judge merits of Tropic.

E1942   Gibbons, Louis. "Miller Novel Held Great Work of Art," Dallas News, CXII (August 30, 1961), IV 1.
Tropic called great and high art.

E1943   "Other Viewpoints," Carlisle (Penn.) Sentinel, August 30, 1961.
Department of Justice allows Miller book to enter U.S.

E1944   Dann, Larry. "[Henry Miller]," Bachelor, September 1961.

E1945   Dawson, Lawrence R., Jr. "Encounter," Abstracts of English Studies, IV (September 1961), 371.
Frank Kermode sees Miller as attempting to escape the present in his article "Henry Miller and John Betjeman," Encounter, XVI (March 1961), 69-75.

E1946   Dawson, Lawrence R., Jr. "Times and Tide," Abstracts of English Studies, IV (September 1961), 421.
Miller's technical facility, his honesty, and his imagination seen in Norman Fruchter's "In Defense of Henry Miller," Time and Tide, XLII (April 6, 1961), 572-573.

E1947   Galloway, David. "Books," Night Watch, September 1961.
Miller sees world dying and his language shows frustration rather than reform.

E1948   "Justice Department Lifts Ban on 'Tropic of Cancer'," Newsletter on Intellectual Freedom, X (September 1961), 1-2.
U.S. Justice Department announced in August that two Tropics and Plexus not obscene and that ban against books would be lifted.

E1949   Milgrom, A. L. "Henry Miller and Friends," Select Magazine, IV (September 1961), 22-23.
Henry Miller Literary Society finally sees Miller in print in U.S.

E1950   Parker, Dorothy.   "Tropic of Cancer," Esquire, LVI
         (September 1961), 32-34, 42.
                 Tropic an honest but tedious book.

E1951   Webber, John.   "Mondo," Abstracts of English Studies, IV
         (September 1961), 384.
                 Rodolfo J. Wilcock's "L'aspite spiacevole" sees Miller
                 as an imprecise thinker whose skill comes from his
                 translators.

E1952   Buffer, Joe.   "Police Censorship Called Dangerous,"
         Dallas News, CXII (September 1, 1961), IV 1.
                 Censorship of Tropic or anything else dangerous.

E1953   "Banned Novel Ruling Slated," Dallas Times-Herald,
         September 1, 1961.
                 Believed that Tropic violates Texas state obscenity
                 laws.

E1954   "A Sensible Approach to a Vexing Problem," Bristol
         (Penn.) Courier, September 2, 1961.
                 Justice Department lifts ban on Tropic, a move oppo-
                 site Pennsylvania belief.

E1955   "Grossvater der Beatniks," Mannheimer Morgen, Septem-
         ber 2, 1961.
                 Miller called grandfather of Beat Generation in review
                 of Nexus.   (In German.)

E1956   "No Book Ban Says Mayor's Review Chief," El Paso Times,
         September 2, 1961.
                 El Paso takes no action to ban sale of Tropic.

E1957   "[Tropic of Cancer]," Morning Telegraph, September 2,
         1961.
                 Tropic legal outside Texas.

E1958   Ziler, Mrs. Doyle L.   "Comments on Controversial Book,"
         El Paso Times, September 2, 1961.
                 Tropic a dirty book.

E1959   Ballinger, Theodore R.   "Censorship Hits Our Basic
         Rights," Dallas News, CXII (September 3, 1961), IV 1.
                 Both Tropics are low literature, but police have no
                 right to decide what people can read.

E1960   "Best Sellers Screened," Sioux City (Iowa) Morning Journal,
         XCII (September 3, 1961), 6.
                 Chicago Tribune screened Tropic from best-seller list.

E1961   "Henry Miller," Der Stern, September 3, 1961.
                 Tropic being translated into all languages.   (In Ger-
                 man.)

E1962   Hogan, William. "Between the Lines," San Francisco
        Chronicle, XCVII (September 3, 1961), TW 27.
        Chicago Tribune bans Tropic from its best-seller list.

E1963   Knopf, Alfred A. "Censorship is Futile," Dallas News,
        CXII (September 3, 1961), IV 1.
        Censorship will not work in Tropic's case.

E1964   Manolis, Paul G. "Book Mark," Oakland Times, Septem-
        ber 3, 1961.
        Noted is Miller's right to appear on best-seller list.

E1965   Safran, Don. "Shown Biz," Dallas Times-Herald, Septem-
        ber 3, 1961.
        Noted is the enjoyment of the Miller controversy.

E1966   Tinkle, Lon. "Primer for Censors: A Few Basic Ideas,"
        Dallas News, CXII (September 3, 1961), V 7.
        Miller's use of four-letter words spirited and shows
        life in Tropic.

E1967   Washburn, Beatrice. "The Ideas of Henry Miller," Miami
        Herald, LI (September 3, 1961), 8J.
        Tropic a movement toward freedom.

E1968   Washburn, Beatrice. "Miller--Raw Color on Canvas,"
        Gary Post-Tribune, (September 3, 1961).
        Tropic called a raw book about base life.

E1969   "Women Will Be Interested," Johnson City (Tenn.) Press-
        Chronicle, September 3, 1961.
        Mayne Williams Library has Tropic.

E1970   "Silly Season in Chicago," Publishers Weekly, CLXXVIII
        (September 4, 1961), 25.
        Absurd to keep Tropic off best-seller lists.

E1971   Crume, Paul. "Big D," Dallas News, CXII (September 7,
        1961), 1.
        Each person has right to read and decide merits of
        Tropic.

E1972   Hill, Gladwin. "Milestones in Texas," New York Times,
        CX (September 8, 1961), 18.
        Tropic voluntarily removed from bookstore shelves
        pending court test.

E1973   "[Tropic of Cancer]," Watertown (N.Y.) Times, Septem-
        ber 9, 1961.
        To make up mind about Miller one must read Cosmo-
        logical Eye, Remember to Remember, and Sunday
        After the War.

E1974   Peckham, Stanley. "Spot-Cleaning Best Seller Lists Is No Panacea," <u>Denver Post</u>, LXX (September 10, 1961), 10.
Chicago Tribune takes <u>Tropic</u> off best-seller list because of obscenity.

E1975   Sazama, Joan. "Defending Censorship," <u>Dallas News</u>, CXII (September 10, 1961), IV 2.
<u>Tropic</u> called a source of disease and infection.

E1976   Gard, Wayne. "A Letter from Texas," <u>Baltimore Sun</u>, CCXLIX (September 11, 1961), 10.
Dallas, the city of tolerance, bans <u>Tropic</u>.

E1977   Gibbons, Louis. "Need for Repeal of Censorship Law," <u>Dallas News</u>, CXII (September 13, 1961), IV 3.
Protest of ban on <u>Tropic</u>.

E1978   "How to Wage War on Dirty Books," <u>Lynchburg Advance</u>, September 13, 1961.
<u>Tropic</u> only book called controversial in Chicago.

E1979   Melbourn, Richard N. "Censorship of Novels," <u>Dallas News</u>, CXII (September 14, 1961), IV 4.
Belief in right to read <u>Tropic</u>.

E1980   Wooley, James C. "Ban Shakespeare?" <u>Dallas News</u>, CXII (September 14, 1961), IV 4.
If we ban <u>Tropic</u> we might as well ban such other great literature as Shakespeare.

E1981   George, J. A. "Misguided Censorship," <u>Dallas News</u>, CXII (September 15, 1961), IV 4.
Banning of <u>Tropic</u> by police compared to Russian seizure of East Germany.

E1982   "Sexy Library Books Cited," <u>Wichita Eagle & Beacon</u>, LXXXIX (September 15, 1961), 4.
The Wichita Library has <u>Tropic</u>, which should be suppressed.

E1983   "Henry Miller Play Rejected--'Sentimental'," <u>San Francisco Chronicle</u>, XCVII (September 16, 1961), 20.
Miller's <u>Just Wild About Harry</u> rejected by London's Royal Court Theatre because too sentimental.

E1984   Gordon, Jack. "Hedy's Famed Nude Swim at Capri," <u>Fort Worth Press</u>, September 17, 1961.
<u>Tropic</u> thought to be a medical book by woman.

E1985   "Sales Notes," <u>Publishers Weekly</u>, CLXXX (September 18, 1961), 44.
<u>Tropic</u> selling well.

E1986   "Schriftsteller," Der Speigel, September 20, 1961, 87-88.
         Miller a pop artist--review of Rosy Crucifixion.   (In
         German.)

E1987   Bailey, Daryl P.   " 'Fraud' vs. 'Cancer'," Dallas News,
         CXII (September 22, 1961), IV 2.
         No need to fear Tropic.

E1988   Sibley, Celestine.   " 'Dirty' Book's Loss Isn't So Terrible,"
         Indianapolis News, XCII (September 23, 1961), 2.
         Loss of Tropic could only aid society.

E1989   Jenkins, Roy L.   "TV Editor," Dallas Times-Herald,
         September 24, 1961.
         No need to fear corrupting small children who do not
         read Tropic anyway.

E1990   Liebson, Paula.   "Just Browsing," El Paso Times, Sep-
         tember 24, 1961.
         Tropic called a dull, gushing book.

E1991   Prisendorf, Anthony.   " 'Tropic' Action Hearing is Set,"
         Hackensack Bergen Record, September 24, 1961.
         Bergen County Prosecutor, Guy W. Calissi, and nine
         police chiefs ordered to appear in U.S. District Court
         to defend reasons for banning sale of Tropic.

E1992   Turner, Cal.   " 'Tropic' Is Not Written But Said," Jack-
         son (Miss.) State Times, September 24, 1961.
         Tropic a mad, bad, happy book about real life that
         slices space and time.

E1993   " 'Tropic of Cancer,' Has Value, Says Professor," Boston
         Globe, CLXXX (September 26, 1961), 38.
         Harry T. Moore, professor of literature at Southern
         Illinois, says Tropic has literary value.

E1994   " 'Tropic of Cancer' Opinion by Kimble," Rockville Senti-
         nel, September 26, 1961.
         Police in Maryland carry out their duty in Tropic
         seizure.

E1995   Baker, Doug.   "Baker's Dozen," Portland (Ore.) Journal,
         LX (September 27, 1961), 2.
         In two weeks Tropic will be available in bookstores in
         Portland.

E1996   Featherstone, Joseph L.   "Critics Testify for 'Tropic of
         Cancer'," Harvard Crimson, September 27, 1961.
         Schorer and Moore testified to merits of Tropic in
         Boston trial.

E1997   "Miller Book Just True to Life, Prof Claims," Boston

Globe, CLXXX (September 27, 1961), 2.
    Professor Mark Schorer, chairman of English Dept. at
    University of California, Berkeley, called Tropic true
    to life.

E1998   "SIU Professor Defends 'Honest' Language in Controversial
    Book," Duquesne (Ill.) Call, September 27, 1961.
        Professor Harry T. Moore feels Miller's use of four-
    letter words an honest portrayal of life.

E1999   "[Tropic of Cancer]," Boston Traveler, September 27, 1961.
        Miller's novel about another world.

E2000   " 'Tropic of Cancer' Sex Didoes Defended," Boston Herald,
    CCXXX (September 27, 1961), 3.
        Professors Schorer and Moore spoke on literary merits
    of the masterpiece, Tropic.

E2001   Brady, Fred.   "Minister Says Most Words in 'Tropic'
    Familiar to Him," Boston Herald, CCXXXI (September 28,
    1961), 4.
        Minister defends Miller's book having words common
    to all.

E2002   "Court Hears Critic on Book Ban," Boston Traveler,
    (September 28, 1961).
        Professor Harry Levin defends Tropic.

E2003   "4-Letter Words Have Day in Court in Book Trial,"
    Boston Globe, CLXXX (September 28, 1961), 5.
        Dr. Morton Bloomfield discussed legitimacy of four-
    letter words in Boston Tropic Trial.

E2004   "Lawyer Reading 'Racy Novel' to Texas Jury," Hot Springs
    Sentinel Record, September 29, 1961.
        Defense Attorney, Cecil Morgan, threatens to read
    Tropic to jury.

E2005   Milner, Samuel.   " 'Tropic of Cancer' Trial," Morning-
    sider, September 28, 1961.
        State of Massachusetts may nullify Bill of Rights of
    the Constitution with Tropic judgment.

E2006   Denat, Antoine.   "Henry Miller: Clown Baroque, Mys-
    tique et Vainqueur," Syntheses, XVI (October 1961), 32-44.
        Miller depicted as a revolutionary like Poe, Joyce,
    and Lawrence.   (In French.)

E2007   "First Time on Canadian TV," Time, LXXVIII (October
    1961), 20.
        Review of Canadian Broadcasting Company's produc-
    tion of Miller's "The Alcoholic Veteran with the
    Washboard Cranium."

E2008   "The Henry Miller Reader," Mid Century, October 1961,
        1, 10.
        Miller Reader a sampling of Miller which contains
        passages from two Tropics, Sexus, Black Spring, Air-
        Conditioned Nightmare.

E2009   "Miller, Henry," Book Review Digest, October 1961.
        Tropic part of never-ending autobiography of Miller's
        life.

E2010   Moore, Everett T. " 'Tropic of Cancer' the First Three
        Months," ALA Bulletin, LV (October 1961), 779-780.
        Tropic tests American freedoms of expression and
        press.

E2011   Solotaroff, Theodore. " 'All That Celler Deep Jazz':
        Henry Miller and Seymour Krim," Commentary, XXXII
        (October 1961), 317-324.
        Tropic called a self-liberating novel whose author is
        a "Left Bank Mark Twain," a natural story writer who
        mixes comedy and nihilism, actuality and dreams, and
        life and death.

E2012   " 'Tropic of Cancer' Questioned," Operation LAPL, Octo-
        ber 1961, 3-4.
        Los Angeles vice squad arrested book dealer and
        charged him with knowingly selling obscene literature
        in form of Tropic.

E2013   "Miller Novel Sells Here," Corpus Christi Times, Octo-
        ber 3, 1961.
        Tropic being sold in Corpus Christi while being banned
        in San Antonio.

E2014   Taylor, Robert. "Hotter Than the Tropics!" Boston
        Herald, CCXXXI (October 4, 1961), 47.
        Tropic not that hot a book.

E2015   " 'Tropic of Cancer' Kept from Mercer Newsstands,"
        Trenton Times Advertiser, LXXIX (October 5, 1961), 3.
        Mercer County not permitting sale of Miller book.

E2016   Landry, John. "Miller Book Available in Library at
        Groton," Hartford Courant, CXXIV (October 7, 1961), 12.
        Groton, Conn., Librarian Martha H. Hagerty has
        Tropic available in library.

E2017   "Mr. Miller," New York Times, CX (October 8, 1961), 8.
        Miller passes through New York on way to Europe.

E2018   Nichols, Lewis. "In and Out of Books," New York Times,
        CX (October 8, 1961), 8.
        Miller passed through New York where his publisher,

Barney Rosset, held party for him.

E2019 "Rival 'Tropic of Cancer' Paperback Discontinued," Publishers Weekly, CLXXX (October 9, 1961), 31.
   Grove will only have hardback edition of Tropic available.

E2020 "Juries Differ Over Novel," Plainfield (N.J.) Courier-
News, October 10, 1961.
   Grand juries in Essex and Bergen counties came up
   with different results in Tropic trial.

E2021 "Librarian Rips Book Ban," Los Angeles Mirror, October
10, 1961, 1-2.
   Los Angeles City Librarian, Harold Hamill, feels
   there is no right to ban Tropic.

E2022 "SM Police Eye Miller Book Sales," Evening Outlook,
October 10, 1961, 13.
   Santa Monica Police will check copies of Tropic and
   take appropriate action.

E2023 "City Attorney Leads War Against 'Tropic of Cancer' as
Lewd Book," Los Angeles Times, LXXX (October 11,
1961), 1, 30.
   L.A. City Attorney, Roger Arnebergh issued a criminal complaint against Bradley R. Smith, a Hollywood
   bookseller, for selling Tropic.

E2024 "Dealer Charged in Smut Case," Chicago's American,
LXII (October 11, 1961), II 3.
   Robert A. Penny of Chicago arrested for selling
   Tropic.

E2025 "Jersey County Bans Sale of Miller Book," New York
Times, CX (October 11, 1961), 35.
   Copies of Tropic ordered removed from newsstands
   in Middlesex County by Prosecutor Edward J. Dolan,
   who called book vilest filth.

E2026 Kavanaugh, Reginald. "Police Seize Copies of 'Tropic of
Cancer' on Dolan Order," New Brunswick Home News,
October 11, 1961.
   Tropic removed from sales in Middlesex County, N.J.

E2027 "L.A. Labels Miller Book 'Latrine Literature'," Monterey
Peninsula Herald, October 11, 1961, 11.
   L.A. City Attorney Arnebergh called Tropic "latrine
   literature."

E2028 "New Smut Test for Miller's 'Tropic' Novel," San Francisco News-Call Bulletin, October 11, 1961.
   Court test to determine whether Bradley Smith can

sell Tropic.

E2029   "Suburb Police Act to Bar Miller Book," Chicago Sun-
Times, XIV (October 11, 1961), 4.
Police in several North and Northwest suburbs of Chi-
cago took action to remove Tropic from bookstands.

E2030   Williams, Vera. "Banned in L.A. but Miller Book Still
Available Here," Long Beach Press Telegram, October
11, 1961.
Miller's Tropic available in Long Beach library and
in bookstores.

E2031   Aunente, Jerome. "Middlesex Book Ban Is Effective,"
Newark News, October 12, 1961, 9.
Tropic not on shelves in Middlesex County.

E2032   "Ban 'Tropic of Cancer'," New York Herald Tribune,
CXXI (October 12, 1961), 23.
Tropic banned in six suburbs of Chicago.

E2033   "Controversial Novel Starts Police Action," Waterbury
American, October 12, 1961.
Tropic not banned in Boston, yet banned in Chicago
and Jersey.

E2034   "Jersey Counties Score 'Tropic'," New York Journal-
American, October 12, 1961, 14.
Morris County asks booksellers to stop selling Tropic.

E2035   Kavanaugh, Reginald. "Publisher Threatens to Sue Prosecutor," New Brunswick Home News, October 12, 1961.
Grove threatens to sue Prosecutor Dolan for interfering with sale of Tropic.

E2036   "Mass. Seeks Absolute 'Tropic of Cancer' Ban," Huntington (W. Va.) Advertiser (October 12, 1961).
Tropic sales stopped in Boston.

E2037   "Mayor Lyrical Over Culture Here," Chicago News,
LXXXVI (October 12, 1961), 3.
Major Daley promised book review of Tropic.

E2038   "Middlesex Bans 'Tropic' as 'Vilest' Book Filth," Pater-
son News, October 12, 1961.
Soft cover editions of Tropic removed from Middlesex
County, N.J., newsstands.

E2039   "'Tropic of Cancer' Called 'Latrine Literature'," Duluth
(Minn.) News-Tribune, XCII (October 12, 1961), 21.
L.A. City Attorney Arnebergh called Miller's book
latrine literature.

E2040 " 'Tropic of Cancer' Off Bookshelves in L.A. , " <u>Los Angeles Times</u>, LXXX (October 12, 1961), 28.
<u>Tropic</u> vanished from shelves since attack by city attorney.

E2041 "27-year-old Novel Causing Trouble Across Land Still, " <u>Wichita Eagle & Beacon</u>, LXXXIX (October 12, 1961), 16C.
<u>Tropic</u> not banned and causing trouble across U.S.

E2042 "Book Shocks Daley, He Orders Probe, " <u>Chicago's American</u>, LXII (October 13, 1961), 3.
Mayor Daley of Chicago shocked by <u>Tropic</u>.

E2043 "Dealers Asked to Remove Book, " <u>Bayonne Times</u>, October 13, 1961.
Bayonne, N.J. , police ask book dealers to remove <u>Tropic</u> from shelves.

E2044 Dissoff, Allen L. "County Arrests Drug Store Clerks in Bid to Ban Controversial Book, " <u>Washington Post & Times Herald</u>, LXXXIV (October 13, 1961), 1.
Montgomery County bans sale of <u>Tropic</u> and arrests four.

E2045 "Harris Staff to Determine if Miller Novel is Obscene, " <u>Baltimore Sun</u>, CCXLIX (October 13, 1961), 29.
<u>Tropic</u> being read by Maryland State's Attorney's staff to see if obscene.

E2046 "Henry Miller, " <u>Neue Mosbacher Zeitung</u>, October 13, 1961.
Review of <u>Nexus</u>. (In German.)

E2047 Mabley, Jack. "A Paperback Insult to Community, " <u>Chicago's American</u>, LXII (October 13, 1961), 3.
<u>Tropic</u> invades Chicago and called pornographic smut by critic.

E2048 Norris, Hoke. "Critic At-Large: Police Censor Book, " <u>Chicago Sun & Times</u>, XIV (October 13, 1961), 40.
Censorship of <u>Tropic</u> compared to Orwell's <u>1984</u>.

E2049 "Prosecutor Scerbo Bans 'Tropic of Cancer' Sale, " <u>Morristown Record</u>, October 13, 1961.
Morris County, N.J. , Prosecutor Frank C. Scerbo ordered <u>Tropic</u> banned from newsstands.

E2050 "Prosecutor Scerbo Bans 'Tropic of Cancer' Sale, " <u>Morristown Daily Record</u>, October 13, 1961.
<u>Tropic</u> banned from sale.

E2051 " 'Tropic of Cancer' Sales Ban Asked, " <u>New York Mirror</u>, XXXVII (October 13, 1961), 5.

All New York book sellers asked to refrain from sale of Tropic.

E2052   " 'Tropic of Cancer' Sale Cut," New York Times, CX (October 13, 1961), 39.
Frank C. Scerbo, Morris County, N.J., Prosecutor, asked book shops to stop selling Cancer.

E2053   "Calissi Men Nab Distributor, 7 Sellers of 'Banned' Book," Passaic Herald-News, October 14, 1961.
Eight arrested in Bergen County over Tropic.

E2054   "Controversial Book Seized, 7 Arrested," Elizabeth (N.J.) Journal, October 14, 1961.
Seven book sellers in Bergen County arrested for sale of Tropic.

E2055   Dessoff, Alan L.   "Alexandria Police Concerned About 'Tropic of Cancer'," Washington Post & Times Herald, LXXXIV (October 14, 1961), C1.
Alexandria Police Chief Russell A. Havves concerned about the lewd book, Tropic.

E2056   "Miller Novel Banned," Long Beach Independent, October 14, 1961.
Long Beach officials withheld library copies of Tropic pending obscenity trial.

E2057   "Plans a Suit to Ban Book," Milwaukee Journal, LXXIX (October 14, 1961), 1, 9.
District Attorney of Wisconsin to be plaintiff against Tropic.

E2058   "7 Arrested for Selling Miller Book," Perth Amboy News, October 14, 1961.
Seven arrested in Bergen County for sale of Tropic.

E2059   "Asks Falls Dealers Remove Miller Book," Akron Beacon-Journal, October 15, 1961.
Officials at Cuyahoga Falls seeking to halt spread of Cancer.

E2060   "Book Ban Talk Late; It's Gone," Milwaukee Sentinel, October 15, 1961, 3, 4.
Tropic being sold under counter.

E2061   Daniels, Edward.   "[Tropic of Cancer]," Los Angeles Times, LXXX (October 15, 1961), C5.
Police credit selves with greater insight into Tropic than courts.

E2062   "Exception to Rule," Duluth News-Tribune, XCII (October 15, 1961), 18.

Harper Bookstore in San Francisco refuses to carry Tropic.

E2063 Gannon, Olga. "Book Ban Beef Amuses Her," Los Angeles Examiner, October 15, 1961.
Feels U.S. childish for bans on Tropic.

E2064 "Henry Miller soll 'veropert' werden," Welt am Sonntag, October 15, 1961.
Miller and Nights of Love and Laughter in Germany. (In German.)

E2065 "Newark Joins 'Tropic' Ban," Newark News, October 15, 1961, 1.
Newark Police confiscate several copies of Tropic.

E2066 Williams, Nick B. "Time to Put Lid on Moral Garbage," Los Angeles Times, LXXX (October 15, 1961), C4.
Tropic's four-letter words not smut.

E2067 "The Epidemic of Nonfeasance," Hackensack Bergen Record, October 16, 1961.
New Jersey Prosecutor Calissi has seized copies of obscene Tropic.

E2068 " 'Filth' Book Ban to Start in Hudson," Union City Hudson Dispatch, October 16, 1961.

E2069 Furey, Thomas. "Sale of 'Tropic' Brings Arrests," New York World Telegram, CXXIX (October 16, 1961), 1-2.
Arrests of 10 in Bergen County, N.J., for sale of Tropic; Hudson County, N.J., bans its sale and display.

E2070 "Seven Slated for Arraignment in Miller's Novel Controversy," Hackensack Bergen Record, October 16, 1961.
Seven New Jersey merchants arrested for displaying Tropic.

E2071 "The Successful Author," Ely (Nev.) Times, October 16, 1961.
Miller will be a success for Tropic will soon be accepted throughout U.S.

E2072 "Thevos to Ask 'Tropic' Sale Ban to Minor," Paterson News, October 16, 1961.
New Jersey Prosecutor John G. Thevos said he will ask local book distributors to refuse to sell Tropic.

E2073 Weinstock, Matt. "Close Eye Kept on Censor War," Los Angeles Mirror, October 16, 1961.
Test case of Bradley R. Smith is watched to see Tropic's fate.

E2074   "Book Censorship by Industry Urged," Rockaway Times
        Union, October 17, 1961.
                Passaic County Prosecutor John G. Thevos called for
        publishing industry to set up self-censoring board for
        books like Tropic.

E2075   "Book Publishers Urged to Censor," Newark News, Octo-
        ber 17, 1961, 2.
        See D2043.

E2076   "Civil Liberties Unit Sues to Halt Ban on 'Tropic'," Chi-
        cago Sun & Times, XIV (October 17, 1961), 21.
                Superior Court in Chicago asked to permit sale of
        Tropic.

E2077   Forst, Don.   " 'Tropic' Sales Bring 15 Arrests in New
        Jersey," New York Post, CLX (October 17, 1961), 10.
                Fifteen shopkeepers in Bergen County arrested for
        selling Tropic.

E2078   Gorn, Lester.   "Censor's Howl," San Francisco Examiner,
        (October 17, 1961), 33.
                Cancer sold freely in San Francisco.

E2079   "Illegal Seizures of Books Charged," New York Times, CX
        (October 17, 1961), 36.
                American Civil Liberties Union charged Chicago po-
        lice with conspiring to ban Tropic unlawfully, while
        Passaic County, N.J., Prosecutor John G. Thevos
        moved against Tropic.

E2080   "Jersey Official Seeks Ban," New York Times, CX (Octo-
        ber 17, 1961), 36.
                Passaic County Prosecutor Thevos seeks to ban Can-
        cer.

E2081   "Jersey Seizes 16 for Displaying 'Tropic of Cancer',"
        Washington Post & Times Herald, LXXXIV (October 17,
        1961), 12.
                Sixteen bookstore owners arrested for displaying
        Tropic.

E2082   "Keuper Asks Police, Dealers to Stop Sale of Miller
        Book," Asbury Park (N.J.) Press, October 17, 1961.
                Monmouth County, N.J., Prosecutor asks to prevent
        sale of Cancer.

E2083   Koenig, Dennis.   "Proposes 'Read Before Banning',"
        Patterson (N.J.) News, October 17, 1961.
                U.S. Post Office lifted ban on Tropic so novel is
        legal everywhere.

E2084   Lasser, Michael L.   "Dolan's Taste Hit," New Brunswick

Home News, October 17, 1961.
　　Tropic not obscene and Dolan has no right to remove
it from public.

E2085　"Legal Process Starts--Is Best Selling Book Too Bad for
County Readers?" Rockville Sentinal, October 17, 1961.
　　First hearing on Tropic begins in Maryland.

E2086　Lieberson, Joseph M.　"Book-Banning," Washington Post
& Times Herald, LXXXIV (October 17, 1961), 12.
　　Since Tropic sold to adults, why have book purge?

E2087　"Miller Book Decision Set," Baltimore Sun, CCXLIX (Octo-
ber 17, 1961), 11.
　　Maryland Committee for Decency will decide merit of
Tropic.

E2088　Nadler, J.　"Censoring of 'Tropic of Cancer'," Washington Post & Times Herald, LXXXIV (October 17, 1961), 12.
　　Censoring Tropic will only help sales.

E2089　Nagy, Thomas G.　"Sees Censorship," New Brunswick
Home News, October 17, 1961.
　　Obscenity of Tropic in the narrow-mindedness of those
who read book.

E2090　"Passaic Joins Counties Banning Miller's Novel," Hackensack Bergen Record, October 17, 1961.
　　Bergen County has had 16 arrests over Tropic sales.

E2091　"Rules for 'Tropic'," Newark News, October 17, 1961, 2.
　　Attorney General Furman of New Jersey says it's no
crime to sell Tropic.

E2092　Sheehy, Marie C.　"Resents Dolan Action," New Brunswick
Home News, October 17, 1961.
　　Prosecutor Edward Dolan has no right to play God and
have Tropic seized.

E2093　"Two North Platte Men Protest Ban," Scottsbluff Star-
Herald, October 17, 1961.
　　Two members of American Civil Liberties Union say
police have no right to ban Tropic.

E1094　Weinstock, Matt.　"Close Eye Kept on Censor War," Los
Angeles Mirror, October 17, 1961.
　　Book people watching California test case of Bradley
Smith and Tropic.

E2095　"Will Discuss Paperbacks," Newark News, October 17,
1961, 2.
　　Obscenity discussed in Tropic.

E2096   "A. C. L. U. Won't Take Role," New York Times, CX (October 18, 1961), 40.
A. C. L. U. stays out of Chicago efforts to suppress Tropic.

E2097   Brodnax, Gary. "Does Obscene Literature Problem Go Deeper Than the Booksellers?" Los Angeles Times, LXXX (October 18, 1961), III 4.
Raiding bookstores no way to end Tropic controversy.

E2098   "Calissi Plans to Go Ahead in Book Trial," Hackensack Bergen Record, October 18, 1961.
Tropic goes on trial before Bergen County grand jury.

E2099   "Censors on Horseback," New York World Telegram, CXXIX (October 18, 1961), 31.
Police raids in New Jersey anything but due process of law for Tropic.

E2100   Daniels, Edward. "Letter to the Times," Los Angeles Times, LXXX (October 18, 1961), III 5.
Police think they know more about obscenity than courts in Miller controversy.

E2101   Dawson, George B. "For Local Court Test," New Brunswick Home News, October 18, 1961.
Question of whether Tropic pornography or not.

E2102   "Hudson Lifts Ban on Miller Book," Bayonne Times, October 18, 1961.
Tropic legally cleared in Hudson County, N. J.

E2103   "Jersey Prosecutor Bans 'Tropic' Despite OK by Attorney General," New York World-Telegram & Sun, CXXIX (October 18, 1961), 37.
Monmouth County goes contrary to state Attorney General on Tropic.

E2104   "Monmouth Bans Novel Despite OK by Jersey," New York World-Telegram & Sun, CXXIX (October 18, 1961), 42.
Monmouth County bans Tropic which has not been banned by State Attorney General.

E2105   "Miller's 'Tropic of Cancer' okayed for sale in Jersey," Newark Star-Ledger XLVIII (October 18, 1961), 7.
Attorney General David D. Furman of New Jersey says it's legal to sell Tropic in state.

E2106   "N. J. Attorney General Rules 'Tropic of Cancer' Sales Legal," New York Herald Tribune, CXXI (October 18, 1961), 17.
N. J. State Attorney General, David D. Furman, ruled Tropic OK for sale.

E2107   " 'Tropic' Called Artistic by Attorney General," Morris-
town Record, October 18, 1961.
Attorney General Furman says Tropic breaks no
Jersey laws.

E2108   " 'Tropic' Cases Stand Without Interference," Washington
Evening Star, CIX (October 18, 1961), B7.
Montgomery County officials arrested four men for
selling Tropic in Aspen Hill, Maryland.

E2109   " 'Tropic of Cancer' Upheld in Jersey," New York Times,
CX (October 18, 1961), 40.
Attorney General David Furman of Jersey told all 21
county prosecutors it was not a crime to sell Tropic.

E2110   "Waiting List Grows for 'Cancer'," Glendale (Calif.) News-
Press, October 18, 1961.
Controversial Tropic available at Glendale, California,
Public Library.

E2111   "Bookstores Deplore Ban," Red Bank Register, October
19, 1961.
Bookstore owners in Red Bank, N.J., feel state has
no right to ban Tropic.

E2112   " 'Cancer' Book Lingers On," Union City Hudson Dispatch,
October 19, 1961.
Tropic a conversation piece in Jersey.

E2113   "New Obscenity Law to Get Test with 'Tropic of Cancer',"
Milwaukee Journal, LXXIX (October 19, 1961), 22.
District Attorney McCauley has civil complaint against
Tropic based on obscenity.

E2114   "The Principle Aside, How About the Book?" Hackensack
Bergen Record, October 19, 1961.
Miller's Tropic not a good novel and has dated approach
to sex.

E2115   "Solution Needed in Smut Problem," Elizabeth (N.J.) Journal, October 19, 1961.
Whether Tropic dirty or not should finally be decided.

E2116   "Trial Opens Tomorrow on 'That' Book," Chicago American, LXII (October 19, 1961), 3.
Court Trial in Chicago to begin on October 20, 1961,
to decide Tropic issue.

E2117   " 'Tropic' Battle," Morristown (N.J.) Record, October 19,
1961.
Tropic storm over whether Tropic is literature or
pornography.

E2118 "Bergen Indicts 4 in 'Cancer' Sale," Union City Hudson Dispatch, October 20, 1961.
Cancer faces four indictments in Bergen County, N. J.

E2119 " 'Cancer' in Public Library," Long Beach Independent, October 20, 1961.
Library has right to have Tropic on its shelves.

E2120 Chamberlin, Charles M. "Book Purge," Washington Star, CIX (October 20, 1961), 16.
Montgomery County, Maryland, purges bookstores and confiscates copies of Cancer.

E2121 "Clerk Arrested for Selling Book by Henry Miller," St. Paul Pioneer, CXIII (October 20, 1961), 15.
Minneapolis police arrested clerk for selling Cancer.

E2122 "College Instructor Defends Banned Book," Asbury Park (N. J.) Press, October 20, 1961.
Steward Rodnon sees ban of Tropic as unrealistic and harmful to our culture.

E2123 "8 Indicted in Jersey for Sale of 'Tropic'," New York Times, CX (October 20, 1961), 30.
Bergen County Grand Jury indicted eight for sale of Tropic.

E2124 Genzanto, Conrad J. "Supports Censorship," New Brunswick Home News, October 20, 1961.
Tropic called obscene and pornographic.

E2125 Lunegaard, Bob. "Book Clerk Arrested for Selling Copy of 'Tropic of Cancer'," Minneapolis Tribune, XCV (October 20, 1961), 1, 5.
Herman Fineman arrested for selling Cancer.

E2126 "More Area Towns Ban Miller Book," Youngstown Vindicator, October 20, 1961.
Ohio and Pennsylvania banning Tropic.

E2127 Prisendorf, Anthony. "I'm Scapegoat Says Dealer," Hackensack Bergen Record, October 20, 1961.
Jack Miller feels he has been made scapegoat of County Prosecutor Guy Calissi for selling Tropic.

E2128 "Ranks Fall of Obscene Books," Passaic Herald News, October 20, 1961.
Tropic only one offensive book.

E2129 Rice, George. "An Editorial," WCCO-TV News, October 20, 1961.
Statement attempting to free Tropic for sale because it is an expolsive Whitmanesque masterpiece.

E2130 Shelley, William. "Hits Censorship," New Brunswick
       Home News, (October 20, 1961).
           Bookstore owners feel First Amendment violated in
           Tropic seizure.

E2131 Dessoff, Alan. "County Lays Library Ban on 'Tropic',"
       Washington Post, LXXXIV (October 21, 1961), 1.
           Montgomery County, Md., manager ordered libraries
           to remove Miller book from circulation.

E2132 Edgerton, Jay. "Does Paper Cover Make Book Obscene?"
       Minneapolis Star, LXXXIII (October 21, 1961), 6.
           Minneapolis police and city attorney's office have de-
           cided that Minneapolitans shall not be allowed to read
           Miller's Tropic.

E2133 "It Did Happen Here," Minneapolis Tribune, XCV (October
       21, 1961), 4.
           Noted that Minneapolis police took law into own hands,
           seizing copies of Tropic.

E2134 Jones, Jenkin Lloyd. "The Stomach-Turning Point," Tulsa
       Tribune, (October 21, 1961),
           Tropic a disgusting book.

E2135 Kellough, Lt. B. "Duty of Police," Chicago Sun & Times,
       XIV (October 21, 1961), 21.
           Right of police to carry out justice and remove Tropic.

E2136 "Legal Views Sought on 'Tropic of Cancer'," Waterbury
       American, October 21, 1961.
           Connecticut State Attorney John D. Labelle plans to
           contact other attorneys of Connecticut to take action
           against Tropic.

E2137 Marks, Alvin Jasper. "Literary Masterpiece," Chicago
       Sun & Times, XIV (October 21, 1961), 21.
           Tropic a masterpiece of stark realism.

E2138 "Police Censorship," Chicago Sun & Times, XIV (October
       21, 1961), 21.
           Police of Chicago disrupted sale of Tropic without due
           cause.

E2139 "Police Censorship," Washington Post & Times Herald,
       LXXXIV (October 21, 1961), 8.
           Tropic not a good book but Constitution allows its
           freedom.

E2140 "Should be Law Against Obscene Book," Lakewood Times,
       October 21, 1961.
           Tropic should be banned.

E2141   Ylvisaker, Bob. "Mayor Calls Parley to Discuss 'Tropic of Cancer' Issue," Minneapolis Tribune, XCV (October 21, 1961), 1, 5.
Mayor of Minneapolis will confer with experts over Tropic obscenity issue.

E2142   Ylvisaker, Bob. "Naftalin Calls Parley on Sales of Miller Book," Minneapolis Tribune, XCV (October 21, 1961), 1, 5.
Minneapolis Mayor calls meeting to clear up Tropic controversy.

E2143   "Book-Banners are At It Again," Carbondale Southern Illinoisan, October 22, 1961.
Chicago Superior Court bans Tropic.

E2144   "Censorship 'Tropic' Again," Washington Star, CIX (October 22, 1961), C3.
Efforts to suppress Tropic arose last week in three states.

E2145   "Controversial Book on Sale--But Briefly," San Angelo Standard Times, October 22, 1961.
Tropic on sale in San Angelo, Texas, for limited time.

E2146   "5 Ohio Cities Open Drive to Remove Miller Book," Louisville Courier-Journal, CCXIV (October 22, 1961), IV 7.
Tropic called filth and trash in Dayton, Akron, Cuyahoga Falls, Cleveland, and Columbus.

E2147   Moore, John G. "The Henry Miller Problem," Pasadena Independent, October 22, 1961.
Tropic divides emotions, attracts and repulses at same time.

E2148   "Police Bypass Law in Book Ban Here," Dayton News, October 22, 1961.
Dayton, Ohio, police have banned Tropic without considering the law.

E2149   Procuniar, Ruth R. "[Tropic of Cancer]," Washington Post & Times Herald, LXXXIV (October 22, 1961), E4.
Tropic provides no ill effects.

E2150   Weirich, F. C. "That Book," Washington Post & Times Herald, LXXXIV (October 22, 1961), E4.
Tropic called rotten and revolting and should be censored in Maryland.

E2151   "[Tropic of Cancer]," New York Times, CXI (October 22, 1961), VII 53.
Dayton, Ohio, bans Miller book.

E2152   "2 Arraigned for Selling 'Tropic' Novel," <u>Union Courier</u>
<u>Dispatch</u>, October 22, 1961.
　　　Two clerks selling <u>Cancer</u> in Ft. Lauderdale, Fla.,
jailed.

E2153   White, Jean M.   "County Officials Do Their Best to Fill
Henry Miller Request," <u>Washington Post</u>, LXXXIV (Octo-
ber 22, 1961), 6.
　　　Copies of <u>Tropic</u> have been removed from Montgomery
County libraries.

E2154   S., R. H.   "Cops, Councilors and 'Tropic of Cancer',"
<u>Publishers' Weekly</u>, CLXXX (October 23, 1961), 35.
　　　Local censorship drives have affected sale of <u>Tropic</u>
adversely.

E2155   " 'Tropic of Cancer' Sales Not Illegal," <u>Minneapolis Star</u>,
LXXXIII (October 23, 1961), 1.
　　　<u>Cancer</u> not obscene in eyes of law and may be sold in
Minneapolis says Milton Gershin, assistant city attorney.

E2156   "Tropic of Cancer: The Law's Hard Role," <u>Fayetteville</u>
<u>(N. C.) Observer</u>, October 23, 1961.
　　　Police caught in middle of <u>Tropic</u> scandal.

E2157   Weitzel, Tony.   "Good Paperbacks Can Get a Fair Shake,"
<u>Chicago Daily News</u>, LXXXVI (October 23, 1961), 16.
　　　<u>Tropic</u> called evil book.

E2158   Weitzel, Tony.   "Tony Weitzel: Good Paperbacks," <u>Chi</u>-
<u>cago Daily News</u>, LXXXVI (October 23, 1961), 6.
　　　<u>Tropic</u> in paperback all over Chicago.

E2159   "Wholesome Reaction," <u>Trenton Times</u>, LXXX (October
23, 1961), 10.
　　　Refreshing reaction to <u>Tropic</u> in Trenton, N.J.

E2160   "Author and Publisher of That Book File Suit," <u>Chicago's</u>
<u>American</u>, XLII (October 24, 1961), 4.
　　　Suit filed by Miller and Grove Press against state of
Illinois.

E2161   " 'Cancer' Decision," <u>Minneapolis Daily</u>, October 24, 1961.
　　　Minneapolis City Attorney says <u>Tropic</u> not obscene--
will not prosecute.

E2162   " 'Cancer' Decision," <u>Minnesota College Daily</u>, October
24, 1961.
　　　<u>Tropic</u> not obscene according to Minneapolis City Attorney.

E2163   "City Library Has Disputed Miller Novel," <u>Niagra Falls</u>

Gazette, October 24, 1961.
Tropic available at Niagra Falls Public Library.

E2164   "Court Action is Studied on Corrigan 'Tropic' Ban," Cleveland Press, October 24, 1961, 1.
Court action being considered against County Prosecutor John T. Corrigan and any police seeking to enforce his Tropic ban.

E2165   "Elizabeth Firm Joins Suit to Halt Seizure of Book," Elizabeth Journal, October 24, 1961.
Cosmo Book Distributing Company has joined Grove in federal court suit against Bergen County.

E2166   "Expert Opinion," Utica Press, October 24, 1961.
Attorney General of New Jersey sees Tropic as art.

E2167   Fuller, James C.   "To the Editor," Minneapolis Tribune, XCV (October 24, 1961), 4.
Miller a serious author who has right to publish his Tropic.

E2168   Goetz, John R.   "To the Editor," Minneapolis Tribune, XCV (October 24, 1961), 4.
Censorship of Tropic like restraints in Nazi Germany.

E2169   "Grove Press Sues Bergen D.A. Over Miller Book," New York Herald Tribune, CXXI (October 24, 1961), 25.
Grove Press files suit in federal court against Bergen County Prosecutor Guy W. Calissi for Tropic ban.

E2170   Hanna, Charles.   "City Cites Federal Decision," Minneapolis Tribune, XCV (October 24, 1961), 1, 10.
Tropic now free to be sold and read in Minneapolis.

E2171   Hearst, Joseph.   "Top U.S. Court Bars Plea on Obscenity Ban," Chicago Daily Tribune, CXX (October 24, 1961), 11.
U.S. Supreme Court refuses to review a case attacking Wisconsin's law forbidding obscene literature.

E2172   "Injunction Sought Against Book Ban," Washington Star, CIX (October 24, 1961), B1.
Two Montgomery County, Md., persons asked that Tropic be allowed to remain in library.

E2173   "Jersey Suit Seeks End to 'Tropic' Ban," New York Times, CXI (October 24, 1961), 35.
Grove Press filed suit in New Jersey District Court to halt Tropic ban.

E2174   Kahm, H. S.   "To the Editor," Minneapolis Tribune, XCV (October 24, 1961), 4.

Police censorship a real cancer, not book.

E2175   Lewis, Mrs. George. "Aid to Obscenity?" Chicago American, LXII (October 24, 1961), 6.
Wishes Tropic suppressed because it reeks of filth.

E2176   Moen, Eleanor. "To the Editor," Minneapolis Tribune, XCV (October 24, 1961), 4.
Right to sell Tropic.

E2177   "Obscenity and Over-Sensitivity," Minnesota Daily, October 24, 1961.
Miller called a pioneer in field of realism and Tropic not obscene.

E2178   "One Way to Sell a Book," Ravenna Record & Courier-Tribune, October 24, 1961.
By banning Tropic, it's only more desirable.

E2179   "Police Chiefs Sued for Ban on Book Sales," Chicago Daily Tribune, CXX (October 24, 1961), 3.
Grove sues 10 suburban Chicago Police Chiefs for ban on Tropic.

E2180   Purdie, C. E. "To the Editor," Minneapolis Tribune, XCV (October 24, 1961), 4.
Tropic called smut.

E2181   Schwartz, Edward P. "To the Editor," Minneapolis Tribune, XCV (October 24, 1961), 4.
Censorship of Miller called absurd.

E2182   Spiovano, Lex. " 'Tropic of Cancer' Praised," Baltimore Sun, CCXLIX (October 24, 1961), 18.
Tropic called poetry.

E2183   Tate, Allen. "To the Editor," Minneapolis Tribune, XCV (October 24, 1961), 4.
No right to suppress Miller's Tropic.

E2184   "10 Suburban Chiefs Sued Over Book," Chicago Sun-Times, XIV (October 24, 1961), 33.
Miller and Grove sue Tropic ban in Illinois.

E2185   " 'Tropic' Suit Asks Bar on N.J. Seizures," New York Post, CLX (October 24. 1961), 44.
Grove files suit for Tropic in Bergen County, N.J.

E2186   "Two Miller Novel Suits Are Filed," Baltimore Sun, CCXLIX (October 24, 1961), 6.
Suits filed in Chicago and Newark for banning Tropic.

E2187   "What the Law Is," Minneapolis Star, LXXXIII (October

24, 1961), 12.
Meeting called by Minneapolis Mayor Naftalin following police attack on Tropic where decision was made
to free the book.

E2188   Bartlett, Anne.   "Prohibition Era," Chicago News, LXXXVI
(October 25, 1961), 12.
Tropic ban only inspires people to want book more.

E2189   "Crumlish Studies 'Tropic,' May Prosecute Sellers,"
Philadelphia Evening Bulletin, CXV (October 25, 1961), 30.
Philadelphia District Attorney James C. Crumlish has
no plans to ban Tropic.

E2190   "Filth is Filth," Morristown Record, October 25, 1961.
Tropic called filth masked as literature.

E2191   "Leopold's Lawyer to Defend Sellers of 'Tropic of Cancer',"
Northtown News, October 25, 1961.
Elmer Gertz will defend Tropic in Chicago.

E2192   "Local Stores Take Objectionable Book Off Their Shelves,"
New Britain Herald, October 25, 1961.
In New Britain, Conn., booksellers have removed
Tropic from shelves.

E2193   "Miller Novel Banned in S.A.," San Antonio Express,
October 25, 1961.
Tropic banned in San Antonio.

E2194   "Novel Removed," Bristol (Conn.) Press, October 25,
1961.
In Dallas, the D.A. has banned sale of Tropic.

E2195   "Police Powers Rightfully Include Preventive Steps," Dayton News, October 25, 1961.
In Tropic Case, the burden of proving a crime exists
lies with state.

E2196   "San Antonio Blocks Sale of 'Cancer' Novel," Fort Worth
Evening Star Telegram, October 25, 1961.
Tropic removed from San Antonio bookstores.

E2197   " 'Tropic' Gets Stopped by a Cop in Connecticut," New
York Post, CLX (October 25, 1961), 23.
State's Attorney John D. LaBelle has given Hartford
stores until Friday to get Tropic off their shelves.

E2198   "Wisconsin Tests Obscenity Law," St. Paul Pioneer-Press,
CXI (October 25, 1961), 13.
Wisconsin's 1957 obscenity law to test Tropic sales.

E2199   Ackerman, Wendell.   "Young Merchants Score Smut, But

Disagree With 'Tropic' Ban," <u>Hackensack Bergen Record</u>,
October 26, 1961.
Miller's novel called pornography.

E2200   "A 'Tropical' Storm Is Brewing," <u>Silver Spring Record</u>,
October 26, 1961.
<u>Cancer</u> censorship without due process of law.

E2201   Ballard, John S.   "Did Not 'Ban' Book, But Warned Sale
Would Bring Prosecution," <u>Akron Beacon Journal</u>, October
26, 1961.
<u>Tropic</u> not banned in Akron but sale will bring prose-
cution.

E2202   Boyle, Thomas E.   "On Censorship," <u>Chicago Sun & Times</u>,
XIV (October 26, 1961), 43.
With so much lewdness accepted by society, why not
accept <u>Tropic</u>?

E2203   "Cancers in Book Form," <u>Paterson News</u>, October 26,
1961.
Belief that <u>Tropic</u> sale should be halted.

E2204   "Case for a Jury," <u>Cleveland Plain Dealer</u>, CXX (October
26, 1961), 43.
Jury should decide whether or not <u>Tropic</u> is obscene.

E2205   Cole, Martha.   "Sandburg Says JFK to Be 'Great President'," <u>Long Beach Independent</u>, October 26, 1961.
Sandburg calls Miller sick.

E2206   Hanna, Charles.   "City Says 'Tropic' Can be Sold,"
<u>Minneapolis Tribune</u>, XCV (October 26, 1961), 1.
<u>Tropic</u> available for sale in Minneapolis.

E2207   Margolis, Mrs. Irving, and Mrs. Ben Epstein.   "Oppose
Censorship," <u>Evanston Review</u>, October 26, 1961.
No right to censor freedom of <u>Tropic</u>.

E2208   "One Way to Increase Demand," <u>Pottstown Mercury</u>,
October 26, 1961.
Ban is one way to insure sale of <u>Tropic</u>.

E2209   "Publisher Fights Connecticut 'Tropic' Ban," <u>New York
Post</u>, CLX (October 26, 1961), 13.
Grove Press will defend any Hartford County book-
seller arrested for selling <u>Tropic</u>.

E2210/11   "San Antonio Dealers Drop Banned Novel," <u>Dallas News</u>,
CXIII (October 26, 1961), II 2.
Book dealers accept D.A. ruling against <u>Tropic</u>.

E2212   "Students Want 'Tropic' Back," <u>New Brunswick Home News</u>,

October 26, 1961.
Rutgers University Student Council demands freedom
to read Tropic.

E2213   " 'Tropic' Generates Much Heat," South River Spokesman,
October 26, 1961.
Tropic an artistic work.

E2214   "Tropic of Cancer," New Britain Herald, October 26,
1961.
Connecticut censorship standards ban Tropic.

E2215   " 'Tropic of Cancer' Ban Is Refused by Putman," Canton
Repository, October 26, 1961.
Tropic not banned in Stark County, Ohio.

E2216   "Banned Book Disappears from Pottstown Stands," Pottstown Mercury, October 27, 1961.
Tropic not available for sale.

E2217   Brewster, Even B.   "Hails Ballard's Book Ban," Akron
Beacon Journal, October 27, 1961.
Tropic should be banned as filth.

E2218   "Calissi Defends Smut Ban; 'Tropic' Ruled 'Sticky
Slime'," Passaic Herald-News, October 27, 1961.
Tropic ruled obscene by Bergen County Prosecutor in
New Jersey.

E2219   Chaney, Francis E.   "Letter," Washington Star, CIX
(October 27, 1961), 18.
Maryland confiscation of Tropic leads one to wonder
whether it's a free or police state.

E2220   Chaney, Francis E.   "Tropic of Cancer," Washington Star,
CIX (October 27, 1961), 18.
Right to read Tropic in free state.

E2221   "City Cracks Down on Smutty Books," Allentown Call,
October 27, 1961.
Pennsylvania obscenity trial over Tropic rages.

E2222   "Distributor Stops Book," Long Branch Record, October
27, 1961.
Clergy appeal in Union County, N.J., has led distributors and dealers to stop Cancer.

E2223   "Fighting For Clean Book Shelves," Bethesda Tribune,
October 27, 1961.
Tropic filth and should not be read.

E2224   "Firm bows to protests, halts 'Tropic' distribution,"
Newark Star-Ledger, XLVIII (October 27, 1961), 5.

Cosmos Publishing Company halts distribution of
Tropic.

E2225   Fosdick, George D. "Oppose Ban," Morristown Daily
Record, October 27, 1961.
Student Council of Rutgers wants Tropic free.

E2226   Hieber, L. "Tropic of Cancer," Washington Star, CIX
(October 27, 1961), 18.
Tropic called morally bad.

E2227   Larkin, Morgan C. "Book Ban Arrogant," Cleveland Press
October 27, 1961, B10.
Tropic a work of literary importance.

E2228   "Monitor Attacks Book Ruling," Elizabeth Journal, October
27, 1961.
Trenton, N.J., Roman Catholic Monitor feels that
Tropic is obscene.

E2229   "Prudent Postponement," Baltimore Evening Sun, CCXLIX
(October 27, 1961), 14.
Tropic judgment postponed.

E2230   "Publisher Acts in 'Tropic' Case," Hackensack Bergen
Record, October 27, 1961.
Grove Press sends attorney to New Jersey to defend
Tropic.

E2231   Radweseki, Clara G. " 'Sensual' Books Called Dangerous,"
Newark Star-Ledger, XLVIII (October 27, 1961), 5.
Tropic may be harmful to readers.

E2232   "Warning on Miller Book," New York Times, CX (October
27, 1961), 32.
Louisville, Ky., police chief warns against sale of
Tropic.

E2233   Wassling, Harry C. "Tropic of Cancer," Washington Star,
CIX (October 27, 1961), 18.
Right of freedom to decide whether or not to read
Tropic.

E2234   "Who Made Police the Censors for Louisville?" Louisville Times, CLV (October 27, 1961), 12.
Police have no right to censor Tropic.

E2235   "Around the State," Erie News, October 28, 1961.
American Civil Liberties Union will defend Tropic.

E2236   "Book Action Clarified," Erie News, October 28, 1961.
State of Pennsylvania will not ban Tropic.

E2237 "Book Wholesalers Cutting Off Flow of 'Tropic' to City,
       Monahan Told," Allentown Call, October 28, 1961.
       Tropic hard to find in Allentown, Pa.

E2238 " 'Cancer' Publishers Lose Court Round," Plainfield (N.J.)
       Courier-News, October 28, 1961.
       Publishers of Tropic lost court battle when federal
       judge refused to lift ban.

E2239 Hawkes, Thomas T. "To the Editor," Minneapolis Star,
       LXXXIII (October 28, 1961), 6.
       Tropic legal but trashy.

E2240 Johnsson, Gilford. "To the Editor," Minneapolis Star,
       LXXXIII (October 28, 1961), 6.
       Police action too severe with Tropic.

E2241 "Juveniles Don't Buy 'Tropic of Cancer' News Dealers
       Say," York Gazette & Daily, October 28, 1961.
       Tropic only sold to adults, so how can it ruin moral-
       ity of children?

E2242 Keve, Paul W. "Battle of the Books," Minneapolis Star,
       LXXXIII (October 28, 1961), 6.
       Tropic not just four-letter words but a well-written
       book.

E2243 Kravit, Stanley. "Ridiculous Comparison," New Bruns-
       wick News, October 28, 1961.
       Censorship of Tropic absurd.

E2244 Miller, Gene. "Sellers to Protest Book Ban," Miami
       Herald, LI (October 28, 1961), A6.
       Tropic should be legal, book sellers feel.

E2245 "No Action at State Level Planned in 'Tropic of Cancer'
       Novel Issue," Litonsville Herald, October 28, 1961.
       Attorney General, David Stahl, wants local officials
       to take action on Tropic, not state.

E2246 Palmer, Ben W. "To the Editor," Minneapolis Star,
       LXXXIII (October 28, 1961), 6.
       Police buy Tropic to get idea about book.

E2247 "Treat Literature as Booze?" Easton Express, October
       28, 1961.
       Miller's book not fit to read.

E2248 "U.S. Court Refuses to End 'Tropic' Ban," New York
       Times, CX (October 28, 1961), 19.
       Newark federal judge refused to interfere in Jersey
       Tropic ban.

E2249   "Withdraw 'Cancer' Mayor Asks Dealers," <u>Reading Times</u>,
         October 28, 1961.
             Reading Mayor appeals to bookstore to stop selling
             <u>Tropic</u>.

E2250   "Yorty's Duty," <u>Citizen-News</u>, October 28, 1961, 14.
             Yorty wants clean Los Angeles with no <u>Tropic</u>.

E2251   Backers, Clair. "Obscene Book Solution," <u>St. Paul Pio-
         neer Press</u>, CXII (October 29, 1961), III 6.
             Minnesota's ambiguous obscenity laws cause problem
             in dealing with <u>Tropic</u>.

E2252   Fain, Jim. " 'Tropic' Sells Like Hotcakes After Police
         Censorship," <u>Dayton News</u>, October 29, 1961.
             Police only help sale of book.

E2253   Howe, Richard. " 'Tropic of Cancer' Sales Spurt After
         Temporary Ban," <u>Minneapolis Tribune</u>, XCV (October 29,
         1961), III 1, 5.
             <u>Cancer</u> selling well.

E2254   "It's Wonderful," <u>Waterbury Republican</u>, October 29, 1961.
             Official Connecticut ban on <u>Tropic</u> will only help it
             sell.

E2255   Kindrick, Sam. "Banned Book Sales Skyrocket," <u>San An-
         tonio Express-News</u>, October 29, 1961.
             Banning <u>Cancer</u> only helps book sell.

E2256   McCord, Merrill. "Justice Calls High-Court Test of Con-
         troversial Books 'Intricate'," <u>Louisville Courier Journal</u>,
         CCXIV (October 29, 1961), 21.
             Supreme Court has many ways of viewing <u>Tropic</u>.

E2257   Sherman, John K. "Let's Do the Job Up Brown and
         Throw Out All Books," <u>Minneapolis Tribune</u>, XCV (Octo-
         ber 29, 1961), II 2.
             Sex found in <u>Tropic</u> not as obscene as bombs, fallout,
             poverty, disease, and ignorance.

E2258   "Speakers Condemn 'Tropic of Cancer'," <u>Ridgewood News</u>,
         October 29, 1961.
             <u>Tropic</u> called filth.

E2259   "Strange New Literary Arbiters for Louisville," <u>Louis-
         ville Courier-Journal</u>, CCXIV (October 29, 1961), IV 2.
             <u>Tropic</u> not a work of art, but there is still no reason
             to ban work.

E2260   "Book Banning Helps Filth Peddlers," <u>Bethlehem Globe-
         Times</u>, October 30, 1961.
             <u>Cancer</u> ban only increases interest of public.

E2261   Cesaletti, Mrs. R. "Mother's View on Obscenity," Passaic Herald-News, October 30, 1961.
       Tropic obscene and illegal.

E2262   Crumrine, John. "A Matter of Principle," Akron Beacon
Journal, October 30, 1961.
       Crumrine wishes to buy copy of Tropic out of protest
at being told what to read.

E2263   "Grand Jury to Be Called After 'Tropic' Arrest," Washington Star, CIX (October 30, 1961), B1.
       Montgomery County, Md., grand jury will have special
session to decide Tropic merits.

E2264   Harris, Sydney J. "Pornography Stems from the Spirit,"
Chicago Daily News, LXXXVI (October 30, 1961), 6.
       Ulysses a great book while Tropic a poor one.

E2265   Miller, Jack. "Book Ban Raises Old Issue of Censorship,"
Passaic Herald-News, October 30, 1961.
       No one has right to judge merits of Tropic.

E2266   "Miller's Tome 'Dirty', Not Illegal--Baggaley," Santa
Monica Evening Outlook, October 30, 1961.
       Tropic dirty but not in violation of state obscenity
laws says Santa Monica, Calif., deputy city attorney.

E2267   "More Problems With Filth," Monroe News, October 30,
1961.
       Monroe, Mich., mayor and police ban Tropic.

E2268   "New Novel Causes Confusion," Oil City Derrick, October
30, 1961.
       Harrisburg, Pa., Attorney General David Stahl told
police to take action if they found Tropic obscene.

E2269   Powers, Dennis. "Controversy Rages Over Miller's
'Tropic'," Oakland Tribune, October 30, 1961.
       Grove institutes legal action for Tropic in Jersey.

E2270   "Sheriff Grabs 5,693 Copies of 'Cancer'," Reading Times,
October 30, 1961.
       Amarillo, Texas, Sheriff Jim Line seized Cancer
from local stores.

E2271   "South Bend Police Confiscate Copies of Banned Book,"
Columbia City Post, October 30, 1961.
       Tropic confiscated from South Bend stores.

E2272   "Texas Sheriff Plans to Burn 5,693 Copies of Miller
Novel," Tulsa Tribune, October 30, 1961.
       Amarillo sheriff to burn Cancer.

E2273   " 'Tropic of Cancer' Seized, Banned at South Bend, " Indi-
anapolis News, XCII (October 30, 1961), 30.
Seven copies of Cancer confiscated.

E2274   Weinbaum, Robert C.   "Arbitrary Censoring Steals Rights
From Reading Public, " Dayton News, October 30, 1961.
Dayton police decide what public will read.

E2275   "Banned Book Doesn't Show, " Windsor Daily Star, October
31, 1961.
Windsor, Ont. , customs collector, Harold Beardmore
said there has been no attempt to bring Tropic into
Canada.

E2276   "Drive Started Against Novel," Providence Journal,
CXXXIII (October 31, 1961), 25.
Rhode Island Attorney General Nugent called Tropic
obscene and wants it removed from bookstores.

E2277   Greene, David M.   "Voice of the People, " Bethlehem
Globe Times, October 31, 1961.
Freedom suppressed in Bethlehem, Pa. , with Tropic
ban.

E2278   "Jury Labels 'Tropic' Criminally Obscene, " Louisville
Times.   CLX (October 31, 1961), 1, 16.
Jefferson County Grand Jury finds Tropic obscene.

E2279   "Kardy Asks Indictment of Dealer, " Rockville Sentinel,
October 31, 1961.
State's Attorney sets Tropic Court test in Maryland.

E2280   Leib, Roy A.   "Fair Editorial, " Cleveland Plain Dealer,
CXX (October 31, 1961), 12.
Right of people to read Tropic.

E2281   "Miller Book Held Obscene By Nugent, " Pawtucket Times,
October 31, 1961.
Rhode Island Attorney General Nugent read Tropic and
called it obscene.

E2282   Riordan, John.   "4 Letter Words on Fences--Freedom
Too?" Paterson News, October 31, 1961.
Tropic has filthy stench says Judge Goodman.

E2283   Seull, David.   "Tropic of Cancer, " Rockville Sentinel,
October 31, 1961.
Banning of Tropic only helps spread pornography.

E2284   "State Attorney Is No Censor, " Miami News, October 31,
1961.
Florida State Attorney Richard Gerstein will not ban
Tropic.

E2285   "Wants a Bonfire of 'Tropic' Books," Cleveland Press-
        News, October 31, 1961.
           Amarillo officials wish to burn seized Tropic.

E2286   Gardner, George. "Progressive Revelation," Rebel Review,
        (Fall 1961).
           Tropic a book about social revolution and carries meta-
        phor of death and decay for the old.

E2287   Lowenfels, Walter. "Editor, the Outsider," Outsider, I
        (Fall 1961), 64.
           Lowenfels talks about Miller's ability to write, his
        honesty, and his poverty.

E2288   Denat, Antoine. "Henry Miller: Clown baroque, mys-
        tique et vainqueur," Synthèses, XVI (November 1961), 269-
        290.
           Miller described as a gentle spirit concerned with hu-
        manity. (In French.)

E2289   Highet, Gilbert. "Henry Miller's Stream of Self-Con-
        sciousness," Horizon, IV (November 1961), 104-105.
           Highet sees Miller's need to write the Tropics to keep
        from going mad and to protect himself from the past.

E2290   Shaw, Fred. "Banned in Miami?" Miami News, Novem-
        ber 1961.
           Impossible to define Tropic's obscenity.

E2291   "Tropic of Cancer," Cincinnati Writer's Digest, November
        1961.
           Tropic called a dirty, sexist work.

E2292   Widmer, Kingsley. "Strange Artistic Sophistication of
        America," Four Quarters, XI (November 1961), 8-12.
           Miller's prose based on alienation and defiance.

E2293   "Ask Surrender of Banned Book," Windsor Daily Star,
        November 1, 1961.
           Ottawa, Ont., citizens turned over copies of Tropic
        to customs.

E2294   Baggs, Bill. "Bad, Bad, Bad," Miami News, November
        1, 1961.
           Questions the obscenity of Cancer.

E2295   "Banned Book Not on Sale in Elkhart," Elkhart Truth,
        November 1, 1961.
           Tropic not sold in Elkhart, Ind.

E2296   "Banned Novel Isn't Available at Library," Corpus Christi
        Times, November 1, 1961.
           Tropic not found in Corpus Christi, Texas Public

Library.

E2297   Berning, Cy. "Gerstein Files Suit for 'Tropic' Ban,"
        Miami Herald, LI (November 1, 1961), C1.
           State Attorney Gerstein filed injunction to stop sale of
           Tropic.

E2298   "Bookseller Denies Guilt in Sale of 'Tropic of Cancer',"
        Colton Courier, November 1, 1961.
           Los Angeles Bookseller, Bradley Smith, denies guilt
           in selling Cancer.

E2299   "Bookseller Indicted Over 'Tropic'," Washington News,
        XL (November 1, 1961), 16.
           Montgomery County Grand Jury indicted bookseller
           Samuel Yudkin for selling Cancer.

E2300   "Controversial Book No Longer on Sale Here," Lubbock
        Morn-Avalanche-Journal, November 1, 1961.
           Lubbock, Tex., book stores voluntarily removed
           copies of Cancer from shelves.

E2301   "Corry Dealers Remove Book," Erie News, November 1,
        1961.
           Tropic not available in Corry, Pa.

E2302   "Grand Jury Condemns 'Tropic', Lauds Police," Louis-
        ville Courier-Journal, CCXIV (November 1, 1961), 4.
           Louisville Grand Jury condemns Tropic.

E2303   "It's Not Censorship," Washington Star, CIX (November 1,
        1961), 22.
           Tropic obscenity issue in courts where it belongs.

E2304   Lawhorne, Cliff. " 'Tropic of Cancer' Is Banned Locally,"
        Corpus Christi Caller, November 1, 1961.
           County Attorney Franklin Smith ordered Tropic banned
           in Corpus Christi, Texas.

E2305   "Librarians Protest Ban on Tropic'," Waterbury Republi-
        can, November 1, 1961.
           Librarians protest ban of Tropic.

E2306   "Miller's Novel Banned by R.I.," New York Mirror,
        XXXVII (November 1, 1961), 9.
           Attorney General Nugent bans Tropic from sale in
           Rhode Island.

E2307   Monaghan, William E. "Excuse Booksellers," Union City
        Hudson Dispatch, November 1, 1961.
           Tropic called unaesthetic sexually.

E2308   Moore, John F. 'In Opposition to Mr. Dolan," New

Brunswick Daily Home News, November 1, 1961.
People can decide for selves about Tropic.

E2309   "Mr. Nugent's Book Ban Shortcuts the Law," Providence
Journal, CXXXIII (November 1, 1961), 19.
Attorney General Nugent issues personal injunction
against Tropic in Providence.

E2310   Page, John.   "Why Allow Any Books at All in Monroe
[Mich.]?" Toledo Blade, CXXVI (November 1, 1961), 24.
Recent ban on Tropic shows law enforcers play judge
and jury.

E2311   "Public Demand Rises for 'Tropic of Cancer'," Providence
Journal, CXXXIII (November 1, 1961), 4.
Demand for Tropic increases in Providence, Rhode
Island.

E2312   "Reviews Awaited on 'Cancer'," Dayton News, November 1,
1961.
Dayton County prosecutor waiting to finish book before
judging.

E2313   "Rhode Island Bans 'Tropic'," New York Times, CXI (November 1, 1961), 21.
Rhode Island Attorney General Nugent bans Tropic,
calling it the foulest work he ever read.

E2314   Schlotzhauer, Virginia H.   "Tropic of Cancer," Washington
Star, CIX (November 1, 1961), 22.
Banning Tropic not right in free society.

E2315   " 'Tropic of Cancer' Ban Question of Judgment," Corpus
Christi Caller, November 1, 1961.
Nueces County, Texas, Attorney Franklin Smith in-
voked state's obscenity law to censor and ban sale of
Tropic.

E2316   " 'Tropic of Cancer' Novel Difficult to Buy in City," Pawtucket Times, November 1, 1961.
Pawtucket, R.I., does not want Tropic sold.

E2317   "Asks Court Rule on Book," Providence Evening Bulletin,
November 2, 1961.
ACLU to seek test of Tropic rights in Rhode Is-
land.

E2318   "Banned Books," Corpus Christi Times, November 2,
1961.
Banning Tropic an attempt to legislate public morals.

E2319   "Book Burning Set in Jacksonville," Valdosta Times,
November 2, 1961.

Jacksonville, Fla., will burn copies of Miller's Tropic.

E2320　"Brown Seeks Court Ruling on 'Cancer'," Providence Journal, CXXXIII (November 2, 1961), 1, 12.
Brown University wants Superior Court ruling on Tropic.

E2321　"Brown University Aiming at Court Ruling on 'Tropic of Cancer'," Boston Herald, CCXXXI (November 2, 1961), 5.
Brown wants Rhode Island Court to decide if it can use book.

E2322　"Cancer and the Cure," New Canaan Advertiser, November 2, 1961.
Connecticut police have no right to remove book from shelves.

E2323　"Harrington's Pot-Pourri," Bristol Press, November 2, 1961.
Ban on Tropic only increases Connecticut sales.

E2324　Henkel, David C. "Hypocritical," Cleveland Plain Dealer, CXX (November 2, 1961), 46.
Seizure of Cancer a crime against artist and community.

E2325　"The Law and the Book," Hackensack Bergen Record, November 2, 1961.
Attempt being made to keep Bergen County clean of Tropic.

E2326　"Profs Protest," South Bend Tribune, November 2, 1961.
Bookstore owners let police confiscate Tropic in South Bend.

E2327　Rosichan, Richard H. "Public Has a Right to Read," Miami Herald, LI (November 2, 1961), A6.
Public has right to read Tropic.

E2328　"Thought Control," Winsted Citizen, November 2, 1961.
Right of public to choose in Tropic trial.

E2329　"'Tropic of Cancer' Not Distributed for Valley Sales," Harlington Valley Star, November 2, 1961.
Brownsville, Tex., will not permit sale of Tropic.

E2330　"'Tropic of Cancer' No Longer Available in Town's Stores," Ridgefield Press, November 2, 1961.
Ridgefield, Conn., stores have removed copies of Tropic.

E2331　"Tropic of Cancer's," Wall Street Journal, CLVIII (November 2, 1961), 12.

Tropic's rising legal expenses eating into publisher's profits.

E2332   "25 Stores Remove 'Tropic of Cancer' from Sales Racks," Marysville Appeal-Democrat, November 2, 1961.
Tropic voluntarily taken from shelves.

E2333   "University Seeks Ruling on Novel," Waterbury Republican, November 2, 1961.
Brown seeks court ruling on Tropic.

E2334   'World's Worst Judges," Bridgeport Herald, November 2, 1961.
Tropic suppressed throughout Connecticut.

E2335   "Book Banned in Duval Disappears in Pinellas," Jacksonville Times-Union, XCVI (November 3, 1961), 44.
Tropic disappears in St. Petersburg, Fla.

E2336   "Censorship Should Be Referred to the Courts," Louisville Courier-Journal, CCXIV (November 3, 1961), 8.
Tropic issue belongs to courts.

E2337   "Disputed Book Sold Out in New Haven," New Haven Journal-Courier, CXCV (November 3, 1961), 3.
Tropic sold out in New Haven, Conn.

E2338   Johnson, Mack.   " 'Tropic of Cancer' Found Too Hot for City Shelves," Lynchburg News, XCI (November 3, 1961), 19.
Tropic a valuable book banned in Lynchburg, Va.

E2339   Tazewell, William L.   " 'Tropic of Cancer' Not for Sale," Norfolk Virginian-Pilot, XCVI (November 3, 1961), 33.
Tidewater area of Virginia no longer permits sale of Cancer.

E2340   "Raps Split on 'Tropic'," Jersey City Jersey Journal, November 3, 1961.
Different opinions by Jersey officials regarding Tropic.

E2341   "Right to Read," Citizen News, November 3, 1961, 14.
Believes Tropic should not be read by anyone.

E2342   "Roanokers Can Buy 'That Book'," Roanoke World News, November 3, 1961.
Tropic available in Roanoke, Va.

E2343   "Tainted Literature No Problem Here," Elkhart Truth, November 3, 1961.
Book stores not selling Tropic in Elkhart, Ind.

E2344   " 'Tropic of Cancer' Ban Question of Judgment," Corpus

Christi Caller, November 3, 1961.
Ban of Tropic should be individual right.

E2345   " 'Tropic of Cancer' Encounters no Censorship Problems
Here," Reno Gazette, November 3, 1961.
Reno, Nev. sells book.

E2346   " 'Tropic of Cancer' Faces Ban from Glendale Library,"
Glendale News-Press, November 3, 1961.
Tropic banned in Glendale, Calif.

E2347   Wojtycki, M.   "Book-Snatching," Chicago Daily News,
LXXXVI (November 3, 1961), 8.
Only obscenities in Tropic are those performed by
police in removing book from shelves.

E2348   "Chester County Bans 'Tropic of Cancer'," Wilmington
Journal Every Evening, XXIX (November 4, 1961), 34.
Tropic banned in Chester County, Pa.

E2349   "Couple to Rescue of 'Tropic' Seller," San Francisco Examiner, (November 4, 1961), 3.
Young couple asks court to permit Tropic sales.

E2350   "Drawing the Line," Lynchburg News, XCI (November 4,
1961), 6.
In Lynchburg, Va., Miller book withdrawn from news-
stands--persecuted and discriminated against.

E2351   "Deny Guilt in Book Sale," Paterson News, November 4,
1961.
Four indicted in Tropic trial in Bergen County, N.J.,
plead not guilty.

E2352   K., A.   "Nurgends bluht das Wunder," Literatur, November 4, 1961.
Henry Miller Reader reviewed.   (In German.)

E2353   "Library Trustees Defy R.I. Ban on 'Tropic of Cancer',"
Boston Herald, CCXXXI (November 4, 1961), 3.
Providence Public Library continues to circulate
Tropic.

E2354   "Marin Jury Begins 'Tropic of Cancer'," San Francisco
News-Call Bulletin, November 4, 1961.
San Rafael Jury begins Tropic trial to discover book's
value.

E2355   "On Book Banning," Middletown Press, November 4, 1961.
Connecticut booksellers fight for right of people to read
Tropic.

E2356   "Plead Not Guilty in 'Tropic' Case," Union City Hudson

Dispatch, November 4, 1961.
In Hackensack pleas of innocent were entered in Tropic
case.

E2357   "Police Ban Racy Novel in Stockton," Oakland Tribune,
November 4, 1961.
Stockton, Calif., police crack down on Tropic.

E2358   "Rabbi Blasts Morality of Ban by Calissi on 'Tropic'
Novel," Hackensack Bergen Record, November 4, 1961.
Rabbi feels that some booksellers should not be ar-
rested while others get rich.

E2359   "Stockton Ban on Miller Novel," San Francisco Chronicle,
XCVII (November 4, 1961), 3.
Marin County, Calif., D.A. Roger Garety has banned
Tropic sales.

E2360   "Tropic of Cancer," Warren Tribune-Chronicle, November
4, 1961.
Because of the need for decency, Tropic has been
banned in Warren, Ohio.

E2361   Utley, Sue Taylor. "Blasts Book Ban," Louisville Courier-
Journal, CCXIV (November 4, 1961), 6.
Miller's honest expression should be freely expressed
and openly received.

E2362   "Book Studied for Obscenity," Portland Oregonian, LXXX
(November 5, 1961), 2.
Jackson County, Ore., district attorney to study
Tropic.

E2363   "City Attorney Requests Dealers to End Sales of Book
'Tropic of Cancer'," Newport News Press, November 5,
1961.
Newport News, Va., city attorney requests Tropic
removal.

E2364   Gulbeau, Edgar. "Novel Really Sells If It's Banned,"
Orange Leader, November 5, 1961.
In Texas, the Tropic ban allows the novel to sell
better.

E2365   Kray, Raymond H. "It's Not Censorship," Washington
Star, CIX (November 5, 1961), B4.
Tropic called dirty book.

E2366   M., R. "It's Not Censorship," Washington Star, CIX
(November 5, 1961), B4.
Tropic publicity has stimulated sales of this filthy
book.

E2367   Maidenburg, Ben. "Nothing Subs for Training," Akron Beacon-Journal, November 5, 1961.
Tropic called sewage, a work unworthy of being a part
of American novel tradition.

E2368   "Many Shore Libraries Shy Away from Controversial Mill-
er Books," Asbury Park Press, November 5, 1961.
Monmouth and Ocean county librarians do not have
Tropic available for readers.

E2369   Norwood, John W.   "It's Not Censorship," Washington
Star, CIX (November 5, 1961), B4.
Tropic condemns immorality and filth.

E2370   Odysshus.   "The Threat," South Bend Tribune, November
5, 1961.
Ban on Tropic absurd, not right to tell people what to
read.

E2371   Troy, George.   " 'The Tropic of Cancer' Reflects Henry
Miller's Lifelong Muting," Providence Journal, LXXVII
(November 5, 1961), W 20.
Tropic attempts to find a greater reality, a society of
humane individuals.

E2372   "Hardly Puritan, Mork Calls It Plain Dirt," Portland
Journal, LX (November 6, 1961), 2.
Tropic called filthy, obscene, and revolting.

E2373   "Library Group Protests Ban on 'Tropic of Cancer', "
Stamford Advocate, November 6, 1961.
Connecticut Library Association is pro-Tropic.

E2374   Luminello, Patrick.   " 'Tropic' Sellers Arrests Arouse
One Unitarian," Hackensack Bergen Record, November 6,
1961.
The Rev. Sheffer feels censorship of Tropic stupid.

E2375   Monagham, William F.   "Dealers are Innocent," Hackensack Bergen Record, November 6, 1961.
To arrest and prosecute book dealers not answer to
getting rid of Cancer.

E2376   Ringen, Opal.   "Tempting," South Bend Tribune, November 6, 1961.
Cancer tempting to read because of all the commotion.

E2377   "Another Step Backwards," Allentown Call, November 7,
1961.
Lehigh Valley has taken steps to ban sale of Cancer.

E2378   "Banned Book at College," Long Beach Record, November
7, 1961.

Tropic at Monmouth College, New Jersey.

E2379　"Book Banned," Norfolk Ledger-Star, November 7, 1961.
Voluntary ban on Tropic by Roanoke book dealers.

E2380　"Burn Book, City Official Shouts," Griffin (Georgia) News,
November 7, 1961.
Columbus, Ga., City Commissioner Steve Knight said
that one paragraph of Tropic warrants its banning.

E2381　Caen, Herb. "To the Barricades," San Francisco Chronicle, XCVII (November 7, 1961), 19.
Defense of Tropic claiming work is anything but filthy.

E2382　"D.A.'s OK on Seizure of 'Tropic'," San Francisco Examiner, (November 7, 1961), 3.
Santa Rosa police have right to seize copies of Tropic.

E2383　H., L. "Will the Censors Allow Life to be Reported?"
Lewiston Tribune, November 7, 1961.
Tropic about real life, a truth the censors do not
want on market.

E2384　"Henry Miller's Book Circulating in Marin," San Rafael
Independent Journal, November 7, 1961.
Tropic still circulating in Mill Valley, Sausalito, and
Marin County Public Libraries.

E2385　Hill, Arthur. "Voluntary Ban Placed on 'Tropic of Cancer'," Roanoke Times, November 7, 1961.
Roanoke police place voluntary ban on Tropic sales.

E2386　Jones, William B. "Bookseller's Opinion," Warren
Tribune-Chronicle, November 7, 1961.
What is obscene to one person not obscene to another,
like Tropic.

E2387　Knight, Arthur. "Miller Has Right to Be Heard," Petaluma Argus-Times, November 7, 1961.
Miller has right to present his view of life in Cancer.

E2388　"Lehigh D.A. Hits Book Ban," Bethlehem Globe Times,
November 7, 1961.
D.A. sees no right to ban Tropic.

E2389　" 'No Ban,' Mayor Declares," Allentown Chronicle, No-
vember 7, 1961.
Allentown, Pa., Mayor John T. Gross will not ban
Cancer.

E2390　"Novel Banned Again," Jacksonville Times-Union, XCVI
(November 7, 1961), 7.

Tropic banned in Jacksonville, Fla.

E2391   "Official Says 'Burn Best-Seller'," Cordele (Ga.) Dispatch, November 7, 1961.
Columbus, Ga., City Commissioner Steve Knight says burn Tropic.

E2392   "Only Courts, Using Valid Statutes Can Ban Publication as Obscene," North Tonawonda News, November 7, 1961.
People will decide merits of Miller book for selves.

E2393   Silvers, Louise.   "Sex Is Out in the Open," New York Post, CLX (November 7, 1961), 26.
Selling Tropic shows our loss of morals.

E2394   "To the Barricades," San Francisco Chronicle, XCVII (November 7, 1961), 19.
Cancer and all other books should not be banned.

E2395   "Trial Set in Book Sale; Attorneys Plan Fight," Washington Star, CIX (November 7, 1961), B2.
Samuel Yudkin pleads "not guilty" to charges of selling indecent book.

E2396   "Won't Ban 'Tropic of Cancer'," Allentown Call, November 7, 1961.
Lehigh D.A. says Tropic not obscene.

E2397   Zorgell, Myron E.   "Book Confiscation Seems 'High Handed'," Santa Rosa Press-Democrat, November 7, 1961.
Santa Rosa police chief plays critic, judge, and jury in banning Tropic in California.

E2398   "Banned Books," Beach Haven Times, November 8, 1961.
Increased desire for Tropic since ban.

E2399   "Book Banning in Roanoke," Roanoke Times, November 8, 1961.
Roanoke, Va., threatens to prosecute those who do not voluntarily withdraw Tropic from newsstands.

E2400   "Censorship Often Inflates Inferior Goods," Louisville Courier-Journal, CCXIV (November 8, 1961), 6.
Injunction in Montgomery County, Md., against Tropic will help sales.

E2401   "Chief Price on 'Tropic'," Dayton Journal Herald, November 8, 1961.
Chief Price allows Tropic to be withdrawn from sales.

E2402   Clark, M. I. De.   "Everybody's Say-So," Warren Tribune-Chronicle, November 8, 1961.
Right of each individual to decide merits of Tropic.

E2403   "Hagerstown Moves to Ban Miller Novel," Baltimore News-
Post, November 8, 1961, VI 6.
Hagerstown, Md., Police Chief requests Washington
County Library to remove Cancer.

E2404   Hellmuth, C. T.   "More on Mr. Miller," Washington Post,
LXXXIV (November 8, 1961), 14.
Tropic should be banned.

E2405   "Library Argues Rights to Lend Questioned Book," Boston
Herald, CCXXXI (November 8, 1961), 5.
Counsel for Providence, R.I., Public Library says
people have right to read Tropic under U.S. Constitu-
tion.

E2406   "Miller's Book Being Withdrawn," Waterbury American,
November 8, 1961.
Stockton, Calif., distributor of Tropic orders its with-
drawal.

E2407   " 'No Ban'--But 'Tropic' Goes Back," Sacramento Bee,
November 8, 1961.
Tropic not banned but sent back to publisher by book-
dealers.

E2408   "Police Here Scrutinizing Miller Novel," San Francisco
Chronicle, XCVII (November 8, 1961), 3.
San Francisco police look at Cancer.

E2409   "SRJC Students Protest Police Seizure of 'Tropic'," Santa
Rosa Press-Democrat, November 8, 1961.
Santa Rosa Junior College protests police seizures of
Tropic.

E2410   Schlotzhauer, V. H.   "More on Mr. Miller," Washington
Post, LXXXIV (November 8, 1961), 14.
Need for judicial procedure in banning Tropic.

E2411   Shapiro, Hilda.   "More on Mr. Miller," Washington Post,
LXXXIV (November 8, 1961), 14.
Yudkin has right to sell Tropic.

E2412   "Stockton's No Longer 'Tropic'-al," San Francisco Examiner, (November 8, 1961), 3.
Tropic being withdrawn from four California counties.

E2413   "A Cancer Which Must Be Removed," Clifton Leader, November 9, 1961.
Cancer called a sick book.

E2414   Brewbaker, Jon.   "Editor, Virginian-Pilot," Norfolk Virginian-Pilot, XCVI (November 9, 1961), 4.
Alarm about sale of Tropic in Tidewater area.

E2415   "Cops Shouldn't Judge," San Francisco Chronicle, XCVII
(November 9, 1961), 36.
Right to sell Tropic because of Lady Chatterley de-
cision.

E2416   Eureka. "Henboldt Ban on Miller's Novel," San Francisco
Chronicle, XCVII (November 9, 1961), 2.
San Francisco D.A. Leonard M. Conry compares
Tropic to scribbling on washroom walls.

E2417   Fleming, Howard W. "Ban Good Books," Miami Herald,
LI (November 9, 1961), 6.
Banning Tropic will only increase its popularity.

E2418   Foulke, Madeline A. "Book Censorship," Dayton Journal-
Herald, November 9, 1961.
No right of Police Chief Caylor to ban Cancer in Day-
ton.

E2419   Friedman, Albert. "A Jewish Viewpoint," American Examiner, November 9, 1961.
Cancer possesses a strange sensitivity of Jewishness.

E2420   "The Greater Evil," Salem (Va.) Times Register, November 9, 1961.
Roanoke police and attorney impose their own censorship on Tropic.

E2421   Harrison, Earl. " 'Ban' on Henry Miller Novel Scored by
Literary People," Roanoke World News, November 9, 1961.
Many Virginia literary people wish Tropic withdrawn
from sale.

E2422   Jurgensen, Mrs. Alma R. "On Censorship," Clifton
Leader, November 9, 1961.
Tropic a worthwhile work which should not be censored.

E2423   Kloss, Gerald. "Literary Censorship: An Age Old Story,"
Milwaukee Journal, LXXIX (November 9, 1961), 22.
Notice about upcoming Milwaukee Court test of Tropic
which will receive the freedoms gained by Joyce's
Ulysses and Mencken's American Mercury Magazine.

E2424   Levy, Jacques. "Junior College Students Seek Action on
Book Ban," Santa Rosa Press Democrat, November 9,
1961, 1, 8.
Students at Santa Rosa Junior College believe in
Tropic freedom.

E2425   "Pastor Criticizes Use of Censorship," Ridgewood Herald-
News, November 9, 1961.
Self-imposed censorship is only way to deal with
Tropic.

E2426 "Propaganda--or Literature?" <u>Newport News Press</u>, November 9, 1961.
　　　　Cancer obscene to Newport News City Attorney Herbert L. Nachman.

E2427 " 'Tropic of Cancer' Novel Hot Issue in Salem," <u>Salem Times Register</u>, November 9, 1961.
　　　　Salem, Va., has ban on Tropic.

E2428 Trupin, James E. "All in the Mind," <u>New York Post</u>, CLX (November 9, 1961), 42.
　　　　Cancer a humorous, satirical work.

E2429 Walter, Clyde. "No Indictment Made on Book," <u>Amarillo Globe-Times</u>, November 9, 1961.
　　　　Grand Jury in Potter County, Texas, will not indict Cancer.

E2430 Williams, Carleton. "Henry Miller Isn't Alone Around Marin in Writing Descriptively," <u>San Raphael Independent Journal</u>, November 9, 1961.
　　　　Pushina singled out for obscenity in Miller case.

E2431 "Yudkin's Attorney Plans Long Fight to Prove Miller Book Is Not Obscene," <u>Montgomery (Md.) Sentinel</u>, November 9, 1961.
　　　　Attorney for Montgomery County book dealer says Tropic not obscene.

E2432 Abbey, Robert L. "Banned Books," <u>Bethesda Tribune</u>, November 10, 1961.
　　　　Each American has the mind to judge Tropic for himself.

E2433 "Church Review Finds Beauty in Miller's Novel," <u>Grass Valley Union</u>, November 10, 1961.
　　　　Tropic called a poem in prose form.

E2434 Field, Carol. "Editor," <u>San Francisco Chronicle</u>, XCVII (November 10, 1961), 38.
　　　　Right of individual to discover value of Miller for self.

E2435 Gallagher, Patricia. "Editor," <u>San Francisco Chronicle</u>, XCVII (November 10, 1961), 22.
　　　　Individual must read Tropic and make evaluation.

E2436 "Grand Jury Must Decide If Miller Novel Is Obscene," <u>San Bernardino Sun</u>, November 10, 1961.
　　　　D.A. Price said he plans to let Sacramento Grand Jury decide Tropic obscenity issue.

E2437 "It 'Ought to Be Read'," <u>San Francisco Examiner</u>, (November 10, 1961), 8.

San Francisco Theological Seminary in San Anselmo
feels Tropic should be read as fine poetry.

E2438   Lawrence, Wes. "Breakfast Commentator," Cleveland
Plain Dealer, CXX (November 10, 1961), 22.
Tropic evaluated by individual reader.

E2439   McDonald, John. "Obscene? His Duty to Decide," San
Francisco Examiner, November 10, 1961, 1, 8.
Police Chief Hanrahan must decide whether or not
Tropic obscene.

E2440   "Miller Book Isn't Smut, Cop Says," San Francisco Chronicle, XCVII (November 10, 1961), 3.
San Francisco Police Department's assigned reader
says that Cancer is not obscene in a legal sense.

E2441   "Miller Given Good Review at Seminary," San Raphael In-
dependent Journal, November 10, 1961.
Marin County, Calif., D.A. Roger Garety branded
Tropic obscene, while book openly accepted in San
Francisco Theological Seminary.

E2442   "N.H. Court Test Set for Novel by Henry Miller," St.
Johnsbury Caledonian Record, November 10, 1961.
Tropic goes to court in Hanover, N.H.

E2443   Olsen, Paul. "Tropic of Cancer?" San Francisco Examiner, (November 10, 1961), 24.
People asked about Tropic and conflicting opinions
found.

E2444   O'Neal, Mrs. A. V. "Banned Books," Bethesda Tribune,
November 10, 1961.
Tropic must go in cleaning away filth.

E2445   Phillips, George. "The Wrath to Come," Cleveland Plain
Dealer, CXX (November 10, 1961), 22.
Society more obscene than Tropic.

E2446   Schlotzhaver, Mrs. Elbert. "Banned Books," Bethesda
Tribune, November 10, 1961.
Lack of judicial procedure in banning Tropic in Mary-
land.

E2447   "Sound Judgment on 'Tropic'," Easton Express, November
10, 1961.
D.A. Andrew Herster of Northampton County has taken
action to force ban on Tropic.

E2448   "The Tropic of Cancer," San Francisco Call-Bulletin,
November 10, 1961.
Police Captain William Hanrahan of San Francisco

reading Tropic.

E2449 " 'Tropic of Cancer' Won't Be Sold in Santa Cruz," Santa
Cruz Sentinel, November 10, 1961.
Tropic not distributed in Santa Cruz.

E2450 Becker, Jack. "Move Is Involved," Minneapolis Star,
LXXXIII (November 11, 1961), 6.
Tropic involves issue of freedom of speech.

E2451 "Book Removal Upheld," Providence Journal, CXXXIII (November 11, 1961), 2.
Montgomery County, Md. , bans Tropic.

E2452 "Bookseller Will Face a Jury," San Francisco Chronicle,
XCV (November 11, 1961), 14.
Jury trial for Samuel Yudkin arrested for selling
Tropic begins.

E2453 "Captain Hanrahan Reads a Book," San Francisco Examiner,
(November 11, 1961), 16.
Captain William Hanrahan of San Francisco police
reads Tropic to discover book's value.

E2454 Carberry, Edward. "The 'Tropic of Cancer' Case," Cincinnati Post & Times Star, November 11, 1961.
Tropic most scandalous success of year.

E2455 "City to Seek 'Tropic' Ban," Philadelphia Inquirer,
CXXXIII (November 11, 1961), 7.
Tropic banned in Philadelphia.

E2456 "Court Endorses Ban on 'Tropic' as Indecent," Washington
Star, CIX (November 11, 1961), B5.
Montgomery County, Md. , Circuit Court upheld county
action to remove Cancer from public libraries.

E2457 "Court Upholds Miller Novel Ban," San Francisco Chronicle, XCVII (November 11, 1961), 7.
Montgomery County, Md. , Circuit Court upholds Cancer ban.

E2458 "Crumlish Moves to Ban Sale of 'Tropic of Cancer',"
Philadelphia News, November 11, 1961.
D.A. Crumlish thinks Miller book obscene.

E2459 "Dealer Returns Controversial Book," San Diego Union,
XCIII (November 11, 1961), 17.
San Diego wholesaler returns 6,000 copies of Tropic
to distributor.

E2460 "Divinity Students Assail Book Ban," San Francisco
Chronicle, XCVII (November 11, 1961), 14.

San Francisco Theological Seminary calls Tropic poetry.

E2461   Irwin, Elson.   "Miller's 'Cancer' Tends Toward Literary
Heights," Santa Mara Times, November 11, 1961.
Cancer about real life with its sex and debasement.

E2462   "Judge Upholds Ban on 'Tropic'," San Francisco Examiner,
November 11, 1961, 3.
Montgomery County, Md., Circuit Court bans Tropic
because of book's "shameful and morbid interest in
sex."

E2463   "Law Makes Miller Novel Hard to Ban," San Francisco
Chronicle, XCVII (November 11, 1961), 14.
Top California legal aid says the law makes Miller's
novel difficult to ban.

E2464   "Library Still to Circulate 'Cancer' Book," Providence
Journal, CXXXIII (November 11, 1961), 1, 2.
Providence Library continues to circulate Tropic.

E2465   "Miller Book Goes Back to Merchants," Petaluma Courier,
November 11, 1961.
D.A. will not prosecute Tropic.

E2466   "Police 'Critics' Hit by UC Prof," Berkeley Gazette, No-
vember 11, 1961.
Larzer Ziff, professor of English at University of
California, Berkeley, says Tropic not pornography.

E2467   Stafford, Samuel.   "Judge Backs 'Tropic' Ban," Washington News, XLI (November 11, 1961), 5.
Montgomery County Judge Ralph Shure upheld Tropic
ban.

E2468   " 'Tropic' Bookseller Gets Offers of Aid," New York Times,
CXI (November 11, 1961), 11.
Manager of Dartmouth College Bookstore, Wilbur Good-
hue, supported by professors and clergy at Dartmouth
for his sale of Tropic.

E2469   "B.U. Can't Find Banned Book Tie," Boston Traveler,
November 12, 1961.
Tropic not being forced on English students at Boston
University.

E2470   " 'Cancer' Not in Libraries," Allentown Call-Chronicle,
November 12, 1961.
Ban on Tropic will not affect Lehigh Valley libraries
who never stocked book.

E2471   Grant, Lou.   "Book of the Month Club," Oakland Tribune,

November 12, 1961.
Police seen clubbing seller of Tropic in a cartoon.

E2472   Howerton, Jean. "Old and Popular Sport--Book Burning,"
Raleigh News & Observer, CLXLIII (November 12, 1961), 8.
In Louisville, police have read and banned Tropic.

E2473   "Newsdealer Bans 'Tropic' in Poconos," Allentown Call-
Chronicle, November 12, 1961.
Newsdealer returns 600 copies of Tropic to Grove
Press.

E2474   Ragan, Sam. "Southern Accent," Raleigh News & Observer, CLXLIII (November 12, 1961), III 5.
Absurd to protect people by removing book from
shelves.

E2475   Rexroth, Kenneth. "Why Book Burners?" San Francisco
Examiner, (November 12, 1961), II 2.
Miller a contender for Nobel Prize, so only illiterate
beings could fail to realize his value as writer.

E2476   "Santa Rosa Dealer Defies 'Tropic' Ban," San Francisco
Chronicle, XCVII (November 12, 1961), 3.
Book dealer in Sonoma County to sell Tropic despite ban.

E2477   "Tropic Bookseller Gets Offer of Aid," New York Times,
CXI (November 12, 1961), 83.
Manager of Dartmouth College Book Store aided by
college people in Tropic case.

E2478   "We Want to Protect Youth--Not Censors," Miami News,
November 12, 1961.
Literature Council wants to protect young people from
Tropic, not censor all literature.

E2479   "Baffling Decisions on Censorship," Chicago Daily News,
LXXXVI (November 13, 1961), 8.
A question about Chicago's legal right to censor
Tropic.

E2480   "Censorship Attempts Anger Readers," Miami News, November 13, 1961.
Banning Tropic makes one fear loss of basic rights
and freedoms.

E2481   Hoppe, Art. "Read Any Good Walls Lately?" San Francisco Chronicle, XCVII (November 13, 1961), 36.
San Francisco police captain no judge of Tropic.

E2482   "Pornography: D.B. Specialist," Newsweek, LVIII
(November 13, 1961), 109.
Miller a pornographer in public eye.

E2483   Scalise, Frank E.   "Vile, Corruptive, Repulsive, Obnoxious," Long Island Daily Press, November 13, 1961.
Tropic nothing but filth that will add to sex crimes.

E2484   Thomas, Ted.   "Denies Library Board's Right to Reject Book," Citizen News, November 13, 1961, 10.
People have Constitutional right to read Tropic if they wish.

E2485   Tomerlin, John.   "Disagrees," Citizen News, November 13, 1961, 10.
Each person has right to judge Cancer without help from others.

E2486   " 'Tropic of Cancer' Not Sold Here on Newsstands," Rochester Democrat & Chronicle, CXXIX (November 13, 1961), 20.
Tropic not selling in Rochester, N.Y., but library circulating book.

E2487   "Widespread Censorship of Paperback 'Tropic of Cancer'," Publishers' Weekly, CLXXX (November 13, 1961), 21.
Paperback Tropic banned across U.S. in Jersey, Connecticut, Rhode Island, Maryland, Pennsylvania, Ohio, Texas, and Canada.

E2488   "Bay State Bans 'Tropic'," New York Times, CXI (November 14, 1961), 47.
Massachusetts Superior Court Judge Lewis Goldberg called Miller novel "obscene, indecent, and impure."

E2489   "Boston Judge Bans 'Tropic'," Willimantic Chronicle, November 14, 1961.
Tropic banned in Massachusetts.

E2490   "Lynch Gives OK for Sale of 'Tropic' in SF," San Francisco News-Call Bulletin, November 14, 1961.
Tropic free and for sale in Bay Area.

E2491   "Miller Book Pulled Back," Buffalo Courier Express, November 14, 1961.
Tropic disappears from shelves of Buffalo stores.

E2492   Newell, Theron.   "An Awful Lot of Worry About a 27-Year-Old Book," San Raphael Independent Journal, November 14, 1961.
Tropic not that obscene or worth burning.

E2493   "San Francisco, Santa Clara OK Miller's Book," Oakland Tribune, November 14, 1961.
Tropic not obscene according to San Francisco police captain.

E2494   "Sales of Miller's Book Dwindle," Niagara Falls Gazette,

November 14, 1961.
Paperback copies of Tropic removed from bookstore
shelves in Buffalo.

E2495   " 'Tropic' Banned in Massachusetts," New York Herald
Tribune, CXXI (November 14, 1961), 25.
Tropic banned in Massachusetts by Superior Court
Judge Lewis Goldberg.

E2496   " 'Tropic of Cancer' Ruled Obscene," Boston Record
American, November 14, 1961.
Judge Goldberg in Suffolk Superior Court called Tropic
obscene.

E2497   "Whether 'Tropic of Cancer' Is Obscene Is Up to Court,"
San Raphael Independent Journal, November 14, 1961.
Debate in Marin County as to whether Tropic belongs
in Court.

E2498   Winward, K. Boyd. "Controversial Book Article 'Para-
doxical'," Santa Monica Times, November 14, 1961.
Sex is real so Tropic is neither a lie nor a gross
obscenity.

E2499   Barnes, R. P. "Too Much Crusading in Our City Hall,"
Roanoke World-News, November 15, 1961.
Banning Cancer shows that crusaders think they can
determine right and wrong.

E2500   "Bergna Agile Man on a Tightrope," San Jose Mercury,
November 15, 1961.
Bergna looks at Californians who helped free Tropic
and will not prosecute book.

E2501   "Board Finds 'Tropic' OK for Library," Washington Star,
CIX (November 15, 1961), B25.
Montgomery County Library Board returned Tropic to
shelves.

E2502   "BU President Probing Charge on Miller Book," Boston
Traveler, November 15, 1961.
President inquires whether professor required female
student to read Tropic.

E2503   " 'Cancer' Book Case Sent to Grand Jury," Union City
Hudson Dispatch, November 15, 1961.
Case of three Bergen County booksellers carrying
Tropic continues.

E2504   Chew, Edward W. "After Deadline," San Leandro News,
November 15, 1961.
Miller's works called Nobel Prize contenders.

E2505   Dillard, Richard H. W. "Webb's Book Ban Ignored Law,"
        Roanoke World-News, November 15, 1961.
            Under Virginia law, Webb cannot ban Tropic but he
        has.

E2506   "86 on Library's Waiting List for 'Tropic'," San Francisco
        Chronicle, XCVII (November 15, 1961), 26.
            Frisco librarian William R. Holmer says 86 waiting
        for Tropic.

E2507   Goben, Ron. " 'Tropic of Cancer' Called Boring Book,"
        Honolulu Star-Bulletin, L (November 15, 1961), 1.
            Cancer boring book.

E2508   Howerton, Jean. "Old and Popular Spirit of Book Banning
        Has Axed Bible, Too," Louisville Courier-Journal, CCXIV
        (November 15, 1961), 8.
            Tropic target of overzealous guardians of public
        morals.

E2509   Hinsen, Albrecht. "Henry Miller: Nexus," Kulturredaktion,
        November 15, 1961.
            Review of Nexus. (In German.)

E2510   Young, Wes. " 'Tropic of Cancer' Faces Ban; Liu's Aid
        Calls Book 'Filthy'," Honolulu Star-Bulletin, L (November
        15, 1961), 1, 1A.
            Tropic must be banned from public.

E2511   "A Definition Before Judgment," Boothbay Harbor Register,
        November 16, 1961.
            Tropic contains merits in this Maine article.

E2512   "Book Under Fire Allowed in Mail," San Diego Union,
        XCIII (November 16, 1961), 40.
            Tropic not on U.S. Post Office obscenity list.

E2513   "The Cops Shouldn't Judge," Roanoke Times, November 16,
        1961.
            Police know little about literature and have no right to
        tell people value of Tropic.

E2514   "D.A. Asks Court to Prohibit Sale of 'Tropic of Cancer',"
        Philadelphia Bulletin, CXV (November 16, 1961), 15.
            D.A. Office attempts to prohibit sale of Tropic.

E2515   Detro, Gene. " 'No Sale' Here," San Leandro News, No-
        vember 16, 1961.
            Tropic not handled in San Leandro, Calif.

E2516   Dunn, Mary. "More on 'Tropic'," Rockville Sentinel, No-
        vember 16, 1961.
            Tropic obscene.

E2517   "1st Amendment Elasticity," Boston Herald, CCXXXI (November 16, 1961), 34.
Massachusetts went too far stretching First Amendment in ban of Tropic.

E2518   Goldberg, Joel. "Police Here Ban Sexy Book as Obscene," Honolulu Advertiser, CVI (November 16, 1961), 1, 6.
Honolulu police arrest distributors of Tropic on obscenity charge.

E2519   Levin, Charlotte. "Lauds the Sentinel," Rockville Sentinel, November 16, 1961.
Tropic creates no ill effects for Levin.

E2520   Prettyman, William F. "Mr. Prettyman's View," Rockville Sentinel, November 16, 1961.
Tropic obscene and should be removed from shelves.

E2521   "Sacramento Not to Sell Miller Book," Oakland Tribune, November 16, 1961.
Sacramento book distributors agree not to sell Tropic.

E2522   Salamone, Charles. "For Better Living," Hackensack Bergen Record, November 16, 1961.
Tropic should be banned.

E2523   "State Keeps Hands Off 'Tropic' Book," Bethlehem Globe-Times, November 16, 1961.
Pennsylvania will leave Tropic alone.

E2524   "Tough Court Fight Forecast for Ban on Book," San Jose Mercury, November 16, 1961.
California's new anti-pornography law to give Tropic tough time in courts.

E2525   "Tropic of Tropic," San Jose News, November 16, 1961.
D.A. Louis P. Bergna refused to seize copies of Cancer.

E2526   " 'Tropic' Status Up to Court," Honolulu Advertiser, CVI (November 16, 1961), 6.
Honolulu Prosecuting Attorney John H. Peters says Tropic fate up to courts.

E2527   "Banned Book Under Investigation Here," Phoenix Gazette, November 17, 1961.
Phoenix, Arizona, police investigating Cancer.

E2528   "Bitter Legal Battle Seen on Police Book Banning," Honolulu Advertiser, CVI (November 17, 1961), 1-2.
Honolulu police ban on Tropic causes battle.

E2529   Fink, Dorothy Kruger. "Opposing Voices Speak on

Censorship," <u>Miami News</u>, November 17, 1961.
Miller's books boring and tedious so let people read
them.

E2530   Glazier, Larry. "Librarian Feels the Fire?" <u>Sunnyvale</u>
<u>Standard</u>, November 17, 1961.
Santa Clara librarian George Farrier announces ban
on Miller book.

E2531   Herke, Mr. & Mrs. William. "To the Editor," <u>Miami</u>
<u>News</u>, November 17, 1961.
America and <u>Tropic</u> both filth.

E2532   "Is 'Tropic' Art or Dirt? Not for Police to Judge," <u>Hono-</u>
<u>lulu Advertiser</u>, CVI (November 17, 1961), B2.
Police see <u>Tropic</u> as dirt, while Miller accepted by
U.S. Justice Department and Post Office.

E2533   Kinnaman, James A.   "Law and Literature," <u>Easton Ex-</u>
<u>press</u>, November 17, 1961.
<u>Tropic</u> called criminal and unchristian.

E2534   "The Smirk Counts in Book Sales," <u>San Francisco Exami-</u>
<u>ner</u>, (November 17, 1961), 34.
Test of <u>Tropic</u> as dirty book is first encounter with
California's new obscenity statutes.

E2535   " 'Tropic' Sellers Fail to Appear," <u>Hackensack Record</u>,
November 17, 1961.
Three booksellers fail to appear in Jersey Municipal
Court.

E2536   "When Critics Disagree," <u>Washington Post & Times Herald</u>,
LXXXIV (November 17, 1961), 16.
Montgomery County Library Board calls <u>Tropic</u> serious
and honest in depicting life, while Montgomery County
Circuit Judge Shure says Miller novel is dirt.

E2537   " 'Dirty' Books? Yes, to Those With Dirty Minds," <u>San</u>
<u>Leandro News</u>, November 18, 1961.
<u>Tropic</u> not bad; it is sick mind that makes book bad.

E2538   "Gerstein: Censorship More Evil Than Smut," <u>Miami</u>
<u>News</u>, November 18, 1961.
Censorship more evil than <u>Tropic</u>.

E2539   Southern, Terry. "Miller: Only the Beginning," <u>Nation</u>,
CXCIII (November 18, 1961), 399-401.
Miller a great author, yet America cannot perceive
his brilliance.

E2540   "Trial on Miller Book Postponed for One Week," <u>San</u>
<u>Rafael Independent-Journal</u>, November 18, 1961.

Jury trial in San Rafael to determine literary qualities of Tropic.

E2541   Bartley, Jim.   "Miller Held 'Provocative'," Honolulu Advertiser, CVI (November 19, 1961), 10.
Out of Tropic fiasco, many Americans will be exposed
to a great author.

E2542   "Book Burning, No Less," Washington Star Bulletin, CIX
(November 19, 1961), B5.
Honolulu police wish to burn copies of Tropic.

E2543   Evans, Dan.   "Says 'Tropic' Compels Thought," Honolulu
Advertiser, CVI (November 19, 1961), 10.
Satirical letter where Evans suggests that Tropic has
some of finest prose ever penned by an American.

E2544   Freshwater, Philip C.   "Henry Miller and Tropics,"
Sacramento Bee, November 19, 1961.
Tropic a book about the celebration of disillusionment.

E2545   Hoffenberg, Sheldon.   "Miller Book Trial Delayed to 22nd,"
Chicago Star, November 19, 1961, 3, 8.
Judge takes time to read all of Tropic, not just pas-
sages.

E2546   Jones, Will.   "How to Be Un-Bored in Twin Cities,"
Minneapolis Tribune, XCV (November 19, 1961), F3.
Read Tropic.

E2547   "Library Unit Raps Book Ban," Honolulu Advertiser, CVI
(November 19, 1961), 11.
Honolulu Library Association condemns police for ban-
ning Tropic.

E2548   "Library, University of Hawaii Won't Ban 'Tropic'," Honolulu Advertiser, CVI (November 19, 1961), 1, 4.
University of Hawaii allows students to read Tropic
despite police.

E2549   Ryseck, Walter.   "Montgomeries Ban Together," Dayton
News, November 1961.
Tropic banned in Montgomery County, Md., and Mont-
gomery County, Ohio.

E2550   Shore, Sherman.   "Miller's Tropic of Cancer," Winston
Salem (N.C.) Journal & Centinel, November 19, 1961.
Miller's language frank and uninhibited.

E2551   Speakman, Jim.   "Criticizes Censorship," Modesto Bee,
November 19, 1961.
Peril not in Tropic but in free reign of police.

E2552   "State Takes Hands Off Stand on Book Sale," Erie Times,
        November 19, 1961.
        Pennsylvania will not try Tropic on obscenity grounds.

E2553   Tackner, Mary Anne.   "Reader's Choice," Philadelphia In-
        quirer, CXXXIII (November 19, 1961), B6.
        Up to individuals about Tropic, not D.A. Crumlish.

E2554   Tinkel, Lon.   "A Report on Censorship in Texas," New
        York Herald Tribune, CXXI (November 19, 1961), VI 6,
        15.
        Dallas Police Department seizes Tropic.

E2555   "Police Bar 'Tropic of Cancer'," Pasadena Star News,
        November 20, 1961.
        Pasadena police call Tropic obscene.

E2556   "Smut Disgusts," Woodland Democrat, November 20, 1961.
        Tropic filthy and not worth reading.

E2557   " 'Tropic' Loses in Mass.; Arrest Hartford Bookseller,"
        Publishers Weekly, CLXXX (November 20, 1961), 21-22.
        Grove Press lost in Tropic trial in Boston Superior
        Court and had bookseller arrested in Hartford, Conn.,
        in Cancer fight.

E2558   Amused.   "Eavesdropping on the Vice Squad," Honolulu Ad-
        vertiser, CVI (November 21, 1961), B2.
        Assistant Chief of Police Fred Pava objects to Tropic
        four-letter words.

E2559   "Banned Book Makes List of Professor," Bakersfield Cali-
        fornian, November 21, 1961.
        Dr. Kingsley Widmer has Tropic on his recommended
        reading list.

E2560   Elders, Joanne.   "Foothill Bookstore Removes 'Tropic',"
        Palo Alto Times, November 21, 1961.
        Foothill College (Calif.) bookstore removed Tropic
        pending censorship issue.

E2561   "Not Only Beauty...," Wilton Bulletin, November 21, 1961.
        Wilton, Conn., resident believes in individual right to
        read Tropic.

E2562   "Professor Clarifies Stand on Book," San Diego Tribune,
        November 21, 1961.
        Kingsley Widmer, professor of English at San Diego
        State, calls Tropic serious and significant literature.

E2563   "Purchase of Additional Miller Books Attacked," Burbank
        Review, November 21, 1961.
        Bernard Wanek demands Burbank City Council block

library purchase of Tropic on obscenity grounds.

E2564   Scrivo, William E. "Smut Book Banned in Lorain,"
Lorain Journal, November 21, 1961.
Tropic banned by Lorain, Ohio, Mayor John C. Jawor-
ski.

E2565   Spitz, C. W. and W. G. Canright. "Thinking ... Makes
It So," Honolulu Advertiser, CVI (November 21, 1961), B2.
Tropic a satire that Honolulu police fail to understand.

E2566   Tillich, Rene S. "Did Chief Pava Read the Book?"
Honolulu Advertiser, CVI (November 21, 1961), B2.
Miller called most imaginative prose writer to appear
in years.

E2567   "Democrats Eyeing Book Ban Probe," Honolulu Star-Bulletin, L (November 22, 1961), 1, 1A.
Four Democratic lawmakers question police right to
ban Tropic.

E2568   Long-Time Reader. "Wants Police to Stick to Knitting,"
Honolulu Advertiser, CVI (November 22, 1961), B2.
Tropic should not be banned.

E2569   "New Ban on Miller Book," New York Herald Tribune,
CXXI (November 22, 1961), 23.
Philadelphia Judge banned book dealer for selling
Tropic.

E2570   Phillips, Mrs. Dorothy. "Book Ban Is 'Juvenile'," Honolulu Advertiser, CVI (November 22, 1961), B2.
Tropic needs no ban.

E2571   "Police Department's Book Ban Has Comic Overtones,"
Press, November 22, 1961, 2.
Honolulu police ban on Tropic absurd.

E2572   "Public Standards," Lorain Journal, November 22, 1961.
Tropic vulgar and obscene.

E2573   Scholik, Sue. "Says Police Are 27 Years Late," Honolulu
Advertiser, CVI (November 22, 1961), B2.
Tropic obscene in thirties, not in sixties.

E2574   "Time to Get Hopping," Detroit Free Press, CXXXI (November 23, 1961), 6.
Tropic placed with other banned books in Detroit.

E2575   " 'Tropic' Topic Finds Liu Mum," Honolulu Advertiser,
CVI (November 23, 1961), 1, 8.
Honolulu Police Chief Liu will not comment on Tropic
ban.

E2576   "Set Hearing for December 15 on Book," Chicago Daily
        News, LXXXVI (November 24, 1961), B3.
            Superior Court Judge Samuel B. Epstein will begin
            Tropic hearing on December 15.

E2577   Wagner, Jonathan M.   "Police Chief Held Not Book Re-
        viewer," San Diego Union, XCIII (November 24, 1961), B2.
            Police Chief Jarsen by branding Cancer obscene has
            put himself in disfavor in San Diego.

E2578   Williams, Carleton.   "Pershina Can Sell 'Tropic of Can-
        cer' If He Has the 'Audacity'," San Rafael Daily Independ-
        ent Journal, November 24, 1961, 14.
            Right to sell Cancer freely.

E2579   " 'Cancer' Author Fights Officials with Law Suits," Dayton
        News, November 25, 1961.
            Publisher and author of Tropic sue Cleveland officials
            for ban.

E2580   Collier, John H.   "An Excellent Book," Baltimore Afro-
        American, LXX (November 25, 1961), 4.
            Miller's Tropic bitter but excellent book about a new
            and better life.

E2581   Daschbach, J. C.   "Suit Charges Eight Ban 'Tropic', Asks
        $600,000 Each," Cleveland Plain Dealer, CXX (November
        25, 1961), 1.
            Eight law enforcement officers sued for $600,000 each
            in U.S. District Court in Cuyahoga, Ohio.

E2582   "4.8 Million Is Asked in Banning 'Tropic'," New York
        Times, CXI (November 25, 1961), 47.
            Grove and Miller sue Cleveland police for banning
            Cancer.

E2583   "$4,800,000 'Tropic' Suit to Be Aired December 4,"
        Cleveland Press, November 25, 1961, 3.
            Battle of legality of Tropic set for December 4 with
            Federal Judge James C. Connell presiding.

E2584/5 "Judge Sets Full Hearing for December 15 on 'Tropic of
        Cancer' Censorship," Chicago Sun Times, XIV (November
        25, 1961), 14.
            Full hearing on Tropic set for December 15 by Super-
            ior Court Judge Samuel H. Epstein.

E2586   "Library to Surrender Copies of 'Tropic' to Customs Offi-
        cials," Globe and Mail, November 25, 1961.
            Toronto Public Library surrendering copies of Tropic
            to customs officials.

E2587   "Philadelphia Orders Book Out of Libraries," Franklin

News-Herald, November 25, 1961.
Free Library of Philadelphia ordered to remove
Tropic from shelves.

E2588   Tobin, George. "Calls It Gibberish," Baltimore Afro-
American, LXX (November 25, 1961), 4.
Tropic says nothing.

E2589   " 'Tropic of Cancer' author fights back with law suit, "
Willoughby News-Herald, November 25, 1961.
Publisher and author of Tropic have law suit against
Cleveland law officers.

E2590   "Answers Are in Order," Honolulu Advertiser, CVI (November 26, 1961), 10.
Hawaii Police Chief Liu attempting to ban Tropic.

E2591   Boyle, Jack. "Americans Lean Slightly to Censorship, "
Long Island Press, November 26, 1961.
Americans favor censorship of Tropic.

E2592   "Court Rules 'Tropic' Dirt for Dirt's Sake," Brooklyn
Tablet, November 26, 1961.
Montgomery County, Md., court calls Tropic dirt.

E2593   Feis, Herbert. "Speaking of Books," New York Times,
CXI (November 26, 1961), VII 2.
The only reason Feis will not read Tropic is that he
has already read it.

E2594   "Arrest N. H. Bookseller for 'Tropic'," Publishers'
Weekly, CLXXX (November 27, 1961), 24-25.
Manager of Dartmouth bookstore arrested for sale of
Tropic.

E2595   Harris, Sidney. "Censorship Worse Than What It Would
Correct," Pittsburgh Post-Gazette & Sun Telegraph, XXXV
(November 27, 1961), 14.
Cancer not great book, but censorship will only spread
its mediocrity.

E2596   "Library Adamant, Keeps Copy of 'Tropic of Cancer',"
Du Bois Courier-Express, November 27, 1961.
D.A. James C. Crumlish may take action against
Free Library of Philadelphia if it fails to remove 86
copies of Tropic from circulation.

E2597   Schoen, Derek. "Library Handles 'Tropic'--With Care, "
Palo Alto Times, November 27, 1961.
Tropic available at Palo Alto Public Library.

E2598   "Who's to Decide What You May Read?" Record Search-
light, November 27, 1961.

Right for each Californian to decide for self about
Tropic.

E2599   "Council Amends Law on Obscene Literature," Danville
(Ill.) Commercial News, November 28, 1961.
Tropic unlawful in Danville, Ill.

E2600   "Eine Porträtplastik von Henry Miller," Der Tagesspiegel,
November 28, 1961.
Miller tours Germany.   (In German.)

E2601   Sharp, Dennis.   "Banned Book Is Available Here," Newark
(Ohio) Advocate & American Tribune, November 28, 1961.
Newark, Ohio, allows open sale of Tropic.

E2602   Liu, Dan.   "Chief Liu, Police Commission Defend Action
on 'Tropic of Cancer'," Honolulu Star-Bulletin, L (November 29, 1961), 1, 4.
Chief of police cites reasons for Tropic ban.

E2603   Mrstik, Richard.   " 'Obscene' Book Sold in P.C. Despite
Plea," Portchester Item, November 29, 1961.
Despite plea by Portchester, N.Y., police, Tropic
sold.

E2604   "Princeton Answers," Princetonian, November 29, 1961.
Article condemning those who wish to ban Tropic.

E2605   "Rockefeller Urged to Ban Miller Book," Long Island Star
Journal, November 29, 1961.
New York Governor Rockefeller urged to ban Tropic.

E2606   " 'Tropic' Suit Called Yule Sales Publicity," Cleveland
Plain Dealer, CXX (November 29, 1961), 22.
Akron officials feel Tropic sellers will benefit from
publicity.

E2607   "An Old Trick," Ravertown (Conn.) News Citizen, November 30, 1961.
Tropic much ado about nothing.

E2608   "Classics on the Sly," Salon Times Register, November
30, 1961.
Miller not pornography in Vermont.

E2609   Gotham, Gil.   "Spotlight on Your Stars," New Leader,
November 30, 1961.
Tropic widely publicized in New York and New Jersey.

E2610   "Hobbis's Attorney Says Police Demanded Copies of
'Tropic'," Honolulu Star-Bulletin, L (November 30, 1961),
1, 1A.
Police demanded Tropic, refusing dealer his basic

freedoms.

E2611   Murphy, Thomas E.   "Topical Tropic," Hartford Courant,
         CXXIV (November 30, 1961), 10.
             Tropic neither new nor scandalous in its ideas.

E2612   "[Tropic of Cancer]," Olean News, November 30, 1961.
             All copies sent to Olean returned to distributor.

E2613   Dann, Larry.   "Bachelor's Bookshelf," Bachelor, Decem-
         ber 1961, 4, 76.
             Miller great writer of naked, honest truth in man's
             struggle to throw off social disease and be an indi-
             vidual.

E2614   Delteil, Joseph.   "Henry Miller--A Charcoal Sketch," In-
         ternational Henry Miller Letter, December 1961, 7-8.
             Miller a paradox, for he is both learned scholar and
             innocent, newly-born primitive.

E2615   Denat, Antoine.   "Henry Miller: Barocker Clown, Mysti-
         ker und Überwinder," Der Monat, XIV (December 1961),
         27-34.
             Article praising Tropic of Cancer and Sunday After
             the War which sees Miller as clown, mystic, and
             central figure in his work.   (In German.)

E2616   Deschner, Karlheinz.   "Unscrew the Doors from Their
         Jambs!" International Henry Miller Letter, December
         1961, 9-11.
             Miller not greatest American author, "but in his vi-
             sion of the world he was perhaps more original and
             ahead of his times than all of them" (p. 10).

E2617   Gelre, Henk van.   "Henry Miller's Self-Discovery," Inter-
         national Henry Miller Letter, December 1961, 13-22.
             In Reflections on Writing, Miller feels an author can-
             not copy another's style but must realize his own.

E2618   Gonko, Robert.   " 'Tropic of Cancer' Still Hot Topic,"
         Illinois State Journal & Register, CXXXI (December 1961),
         4.
             Tropic autobiographical.

E2619   Günther, Helmut.   "Miller, Henry," Welt und Wort, De-
         cember 1961.
             Review of Nexus.   (In German.)

E2620   Rublowsky, John.   "The Long Voyage of Henry Miller,"
         Scene, VII (December 1961).
             Miller finally being read in the U.S.

E2621   Schwartz, Edward P.   "About the Opera," Henry Miller

Literary Society Newsletter, December 1961, 4.
Smile at the Foot of the Ladder, an opera by Antonio
Bibalo, recorded by Wilhelm Hansen Music Publishers.

E2622 Schwartz, Edward P. "Biblio Selling Well," Henry Miller
Literary Society Newsletter, December 1961, 1.
Moore's bibliography of Miller selling well.

E2623 Schwartz, Edward P. " 'Blue' Hawaii," Henry Miller
Literary Society Newsletter, December 1961, 3.
Police action against Tropic causes storm of com-
plaints in Honolulu.

E2624 Schwartz, Edward P. "Book Burners Harass Stores Selling 'Tropic of Cancer'," Henry Miller Literary Society
Newsletter, December 1961, 1, 3.
Unfair treatment of Tropic in Cleveland, Iowa, Boston,
etc.

E2625 Schwartz, Edward P. "Bronze Bust Available," Henry
Miller Literary Society Newsletter, December 1961, 1.
Galerie Springer in Berlin has six original casts of
Miller.

E2626 Schwartz, Edward P. "Correction," Henry Miller Literary
Society Newsletter, December 1961, 1.
Correction about original Danish translation of Nexus,
published by Hans Reitzel, Copenhagen, 1959.

E2627 Schwartz, Edward P. "Dylan Thomas on HM," Henry
Miller Literary Society Newsletter, December 1961, 4.
William White of Wayne State University has series of
letters from Dylan Thomas to Vernon Watkins and
Glyn Jones on Miller.

E2628 Schwartz, Edward P. "First Four Issues," Henry Miller
Literary Society Newsletter, December 1961, 4.
First four of Society's Newsletters on Miller impos-
sible to find.

E2629 Schwartz, Edward P. "Hidden Treasures," Henry Miller
Literary Society Newsletter, December 1961, 3.
Dr. Robert Fink, in visit to Miller, discovered old
notes on Paris and original manuscript of "Crazy Cock."

E2630 Schwartz, Edward P. "Honor 70th Birthday," Henry
Miller Literary Society Newsletter, December 1961, 3.
In honor of Miller's 70th birthday, Italian sculptor
Marino Marini did bust of Miller.

E2631 Schwartz, Edward P. "Information Wanted," Henry Miller
Literary Society Newsletter, December 1961, 3.
Kingsley Widmer looking for information on writings

by and about Miller.

E2632 Schwartz, Edward P. "Lose in Maryland," Henry Miller Literary Society Newsletter, December 1961, 3.
Bookstore operator Samuel Yudkin sentenced to six months in jail for sale of Tropic in his Rockville, Md. store.

E2633 Schwartz, Edward P. "New Articles About Henry Miller," Henry Miller Literary Society Newsletter, December 1961, 4.
Father Bruckberger's "Big Sur" in Big Sur Guide, Dorothy Parker reviews Tropic in Esquire (September 1961), Henk van Gelre's International Miller Letter (No. 2), John Rublowsky's "The Long Voyage of Henry Miller" in Scene Magazine, XVII (December 1961).

E2634 Schwartz, Edward P. "New Books About Henry Miller," Henry Miller Literary Society Newsletter, December 1961, 4.
Book on Miller written by Widmer; Henk van Gelre compiles another, while Yamada Houkoh explores Miller literature.

E2635 Schwartz, Edward P. "New Books by Henry Miller," Henry Miller Literary Society Newsletter, December 1961, 4.
Stand Still Like the Hummingbird, Just Wild about Harry, The Angel Is My Watermark, and Miller-Durrell Correspondence all new in 1961.

E2636 Schwartz, Edward P. "New Contributions to Books by Henry Miller," Henry Miller Literary Society Newsletter, December 1961, 4.
Miller contributed "Obscenity and the Law of Reflection" to Widmer's Literary Censorship and "Preface" to Maid, Madonnas, & Witches by Andreas Feininger.

E2637 Schwartz, Edward P. "New Contributions to Periodicals by Henry Miller," Henry Miller Literary Society Newsletter, December 1961, 4.
Miller wrote "Stand Still Like the Hummingbird" for Esquire, (November 1961); "Statement on Massachusetts Ban of Tropic of Cancer" for Playboy (January 1962); Interview with Wickes in Paris Review (Winter 1961-1962); "Letter to Lawrence Durrell" in Bachelor III (December 1961).

E2638 Schwartz, Edward P. "New Long-Playing Record," Henry Miller Literary Society Newsletter, December 1961, 1.
Miller's Henry Miller: Life As I See It a recording on subjects of morality, safety, prostitution, insects, and freedom.

E2639   Schwartz, Edward P.   "New Reprints by Henry Miller,"
        Henry Miller Literary Society Newsletter, December 1961,
        4.
            New reprints of The Time of the Assassins, The Air-
            Conditioned Nightmare, and Tropic of Cancer issued.

E2640   Schwartz, Edward P.   "Opera Sets for 'Smile'," Henry
        Miller Literary Society Newsletter, December 1961, 1.
            Opera set for Smile at the Foot of the Ladder de-
            signed.

E2641   Schwartz, Edward P.   "Reading by Henry Miller," Henry
        Miller Literary Society Newsletter, December 1961, 4.
            Miller to read from works in the Kongresshalle, Ber-
            lin.

E2642   Schwartz, Edward P.   "Recommended Stores," Henry
        Miller Literary Society Newsletter, December 1961, 3.
            Listing of stores that sell Miller.

E2643   Schwartz, Edward P.   "Season's Greetings," Henry Miller
        Literary Society Newsletter, December 1961, 3.
            Magazine Los Angeles mentions buying Tropic for
            Christmas gifts.

E2644   Schwartz, Edward P.   "Study Club," Henry Miller Lite-
        rary Society Newsletter, December 1961, 4.
            Mrs. McVay spoke on Miller at El Trueco Study Club,
            Walla Walla, Wash., November 15, 1961.

E2645   Schwartz, Edward P.   "Thanks for Clips," Henry Miller
        Literary Society Newsletter, December 1961, 4.
            Society wants members to send all clippings on Miller.

E2646   Schwartz, Edward P.   "Therapeutic Value," Henry Miller
        Literary Society Newsletter, December 1961, 3.
            Dr. David Morgan has written paper on therapeutic
            value of Cancer, Capricorn, and World of Sex.

E2647   Schwartz, Edward P.   "Toast to 'Nexus'," Henry Miller
        Literary Society Newsletter, December 1961, 4.
            Nexus first published in Copenhagen in 1959.

E2648   Schwartz, Edward P.   " 'Tropic of Cancer'--Choice of 3
        Book Clubs," Henry Miller Literary Society Newsletter,
        December 1961, 4.
            Tropic chosen by Marboro, Readers Subscription, and
            Arts & Letters, while Henry Miller Reader choice of
            Mid Century Book Club.

E2649   Schwartz, Edward P.   "T.V. Shows," Henry Miller Lite-
        rary Society Newsletter, December 1961, 4.
            Film reminiscences of Miller-Perlès friendship shown

on Canadian television on December 17, 1961.

E2650   Schwartz, Edward P.   "Two Sages--East & West," Henry Miller Literary Society Newsletter, December 1961, 4.
    Photograph of Miller and Confucian Sage entitled "Two Sages."

E2651   Schwartz, Edward P.   "Win in California," Henry Miller Literary Society Newsletter, December 1961, 3.
    Bookseller Franklin Pershina found not guilty by Marin County jury on December 15, 1961.   This is first jury trial involving Tropic and reaffirms freedom to read.

E2652   Sher, Lonny.   "Henry Miller," Topper, December 1961.

E2653   Simenon, Georges.   "An Unique Frescoe," International Henry Miller Letter, December 1961, 12-13.
    Simenon traces Miller's movement from obscure, unconventional behavior to his acceptance of society.

E2654   Simpson, Harry.   "Simpson Writes," Henry Miller Literary Society Newsletter, December 1961, 4.
    Miller's visit to England in August 1961 recounted.

E2655   White, Emil.   "Henry Miller and Georges Simenon, Lausanne, 1960," International Henry Miller Letter, December 1961, 12.
    Photograph of Miller and Simenon standing, talking, and smoking in Paris.

E2656   White, Emil.   "Henry Miller in Göttingen, Germany, 1960," International Henry Miller Letter, December 1961, 9.
    Photo of Miller in Germany staring at "Sappho," poster of play by Durrell.

E2657   White, William.   "Henry Miller," American Book Collector, XII (December 1961), 2-3.
    Review of Thomas H. Moore's Bibliography of Henry Miller.

E2658   "Book Burning, No Less--11," Honolulu Star-Bulletin, L (December 1, 1961), 8.
    Honolulu Police Department wishes to burn Tropic.

E2659   Frankel, Chuck.   " 'Tropic of Cancer' Still 'Filth'--Mazzei," Honolulu Star-Bulletin, L (December 1, 1961), 25.
    Irvin Mazzei brought action against Tropic.

E2660   "Providence Library Takes Strong Stand on 'Tropic of Cancer' Censorship," Library Journal, LXXXVI (December 1, 1961), 4142-4143.
    Providence Public Library circulating Cancer against

state's wish.

E2661   "Tropic of Cancer," Maryland News, December 1, 1961.
         Tropic boring.

E2662   "ACLU Rebukes Crumlish for Library Ban on 'Tropic',"
         Philadelphia Bulletin, CXV (December 2, 1961), 22.
         ACLU feels Philadelphia censorship of Tropic unfair.

E2663   "Henry Miller," Saarbrücker Allgemeine, December 2,
         1961.
         Review of Henry Miller Reader. (In German.)

E2664   "Remove 'Tropic' from Bookstands," Des Moines Register,
         (December 2, 1961), 6.
         Tropic removed from Sioux City stores.

E2665   "Book-Critic Says Miller's Tropics are Foul Things,"
         Times News, December 3, 1961.
         Gilbert Highet called Tropic foul.

E2666   Hatch, Janet. "'Tropic' Defender Ejected," Sunday News,
         December 3, 1961.
         Youth questions Republican Club president's rap of
         Tropic.

E2667   Nicolosi, John. "Clissi Says He's Upset by Incident,"
         Sunday News, December 3, 1961.
         James Stewart sees no reason for Tropic ban.,

E2668   Bergen, Bus. "Asks Injunction Against Officials to Permit
         Sale of 'Tropic' Here," Cleveland Press, December 4,
         1961, B9.
         Lawyer defending Tropic claims judge influenced wit-
         ness.

E2669   Byerly, Ken, Jr. "Tropic of Cancer," Tidewater (Va.)
         News, December 4, 1961.
         Tropic called Miller's philosophy.

E2670   Wechsler, James A. "Naughty Boy," New York Post,
         CLXI (December 4, 1961), 30.
         James Stewart understands value of Tropic more than
         adults.

E2671   "Book Sellers Testify in 'Tropic' Suppression," Middletown
         (Ohio) Journal, December 5, 1961.
         Tropic suppressed by police is book dealer's testi-
         mony in court.

E2672   Crumlish, James C., Jr. "That Book Is Still Sizzling,"
         Philadelphia Bulletin, CXX (December 5, 1961), 56.
         Tropic called obscene.

E2673   Daschbach, J. C. "Distributors Testify on 'Tropic' Sale Halt," Cleveland Plain Dealer, CXX (December 5, 1961), 13.
Six dealers say they were forced to stop selling Tropic.

E2674   G., Mrs. J. M. "More Power to Judge Vincent Carroll," Philadelphia Bulletin, CXV (December 5, 1961), 56.
Tropic called one of foulest books ever.

E2675   Guth, Robert O. "Wants People to Be Own Publishers," Philadelphia Bulletin, CXV (December 5, 1961), 56.
Freedom of press should be offered to Tropic.

E2676   "Henry Miller in Ohio Appeal," New York Times, CXI (December 5, 1961), 28.
Miller and Grove in Federal Court in Cleveland feel ban on Tropic deprives freedom of press.

E2677   Morney, Cotton. "Can't Find Censorship in the Laws," Philadelphia Bulletin, CXV (December 5, 1961), 56.
Right to read Tropic is constitutional.

E2678   Schlessinger, Albert. "Book Called Trash But Censorship--?" Philadelphia Bulletin, CXV (December 5, 1961), 56.
Tropic trash but do not censor.

E2679   "Taxpayer's Suit Seeks Release of 'Tropic of Cancer'," Philadelphia Bulletin, CXV (December 5, 1961), 2.
John V. Lovitt filed suit to have Tropic reissued to libraries.

E2680   Weirich, F. C. "Tropic Action is Endorsed," Philadelphia Bulletin, CXV (December 5, 1961), 56.
Tropic a moral root to establish a better society.

E2681   Bess, Donovan. "8 Women on 'Tropic' Jury Panel," San Francisco Chronicle, XCVII (December 6, 1961), 1, 16.
Jury to decide Tropic fate in Marin County, Calif.

E2682   "'Blue' Hawaii," Variety, December 6, 1961.
Mentions Tropic ban in Hawaii.

E2683   Byrne, Ed. "'Tropic of Cancer' Not in Shops After Brief Buying Flurry Here," Utica (N.Y.) Observer-Dispatch, December 6, 1961.
Tropic sells out in Ithaca.

E2684   Daschbach, J. C. "8 Law Officers Absolved in 'Tropic of Cancer' Suit," Cleveland Plain Dealer, CXX (December 6, 1961), 13.
U.S. District Court Judge says officers did nothing to suppress sale of Tropic.

E2685   Ferber, Christian.   "Die Weltgier des Henry Miller," Die
        Welt, December 6, 1961, 35.
                Review of Henry Miller Reader.   (In German.)

E2686   "Hundreds of Phone-Callers Laud Youth's Stand on 'Out-
        lawed' Book," Paterson Call, December 6, 1961.
                Paul Brown feels Miller should not be banned, an idea
                he stated at Republican Club.

E2687   "Judge's Ruling in 'Tropic' Suit Shocks CCLU," Cleveland
        Plain Dealer, CXX (December 6, 1961), 47.
                Cleveland Civil Liberties Union horrified over ruling
                against Tropic.

E2688   Wolfe, Mary Ellen.   "Be Your Own Censor, Professor
        Advises," Dayton Journal Herald, December 6, 1961.
                Censorship of individual in Miller case desired.

E2689   Aubel, D. P.   "Aubel Asks Freedom to Buy 'Tropic' and
        Then Decide," Ridgefield (Conn.) Press, December 7,
        1961.
                Connecticut resident wants to buy, read, and decide
                about Tropic for self.

E2690   Bednar, Bob.   "A Look at the Lively Arts," Clementon
        Record Breeze, December 7, 1961.
                Tropic belongs to the people who wish to read it.

E2691   Bess, Donovan.   "The D.A. Reads Miller," San Francisco
        Chronicle, XCVII (December 7, 1961), 1, 5.
                Marin County D.A. Roger P. Garety shocked jury with
                Cancer's four-letter words for ten minutes.

E2692   "Citizens' Group Blasts Decision on 'Cancer'," Dayton
        Journal-Herald, December 7, 1961.
                Cleveland Citizens for Freedom of the Mind accused
                Federal Judge James C. Connell of endorsing censor-
                ship.

E2693   Crawford, Mary.   "Jurors Browse in 'Tropic' on Easy
        Seats," San Francisco News-Call Bulletin, December 7,
        1961.
                Jury reads Tropic.

E2694   Cruttenden, Charles.   "Like It or Not--They Read Tropic,"
        San Francisco Examiner, December 7, 1961, 1.
                Marin County, Calif. jury reads Tropic to gain first-
                hand knowledge.

E2695   "Ein Henry Miller Lesebuch," Neue Presse, December 7,
        1961.
                Review of Henry Miller Reader.   (In German.)

E2696   Bess, Donovan. "Special Code on Obscenity for Marin
         Readers?" San Francisco Chronicle, XCVII (December 8,
         1961), 1, 13.
                Bess feels Marin County has no right to create new
                obscenity standards in Tropic trial.

E2697   Dessoff, Alan L.   "Montgomery Library Head Resigns in
         Dispute Over 'Tropic of Cancer'," Washington Post &
         Times Herald, LXXXV (December 8, 1961), B1.
                Chairman of Montgomery County Library Board reads
                Tropic, finding it disgusting.   Disagreement with other
                members leads to his resignation.

E2698   "Obscenity Censorship," Des Moines Register, December
         8, 1961, 14.
                Sioux City, Iowa, County Attorney Edward F. Samore
                said book dealers removed Tropic after his talk.

E2699   "P. T. Council Asks Book Free Choice," Portchester
         Item, December 8, 1961.
                Portchester Police ask local bookstores to remove
                Tropic from shelves.

E2700   Bess, Donovan. "Marin Trial Whets 'Tropic' Appetites,"
         San Francisco Chronicle, XCVII (December 9, 1961), 1, 4.
                Marin County D.A. denies special obscenity program.

E2701   "Teachers for Book Ban," Washington Post & Times
         Herald, LXXXV (December 9, 1961), 13.
                Teachers of Montgomery County, Md., condemn ban-
                ning Tropic.

E2702   " 'Tropic' Is State Guest--Briefly," Wilmington News,
         December 9, 1961.
                Tropic removed from State Library in Dover, Del.

E2703   "Tropic of Cancer," Tablet, December 9, 1961.
                Tropic a sewer.

E2704   Williams, Carleton.   "Judge for 'Tropic' Trial Knows Few
         Words, Too," San Raphael Independent Journal, December
         9, 1961, 1, 10.
                Judge uses obscene word in Tropic trial.

E2705   Bess, Donovan.   " 'Tropic' Luring the Non-Reader," San
         Francisco Chronicle, XCVII (December 10, 1961), 1, 15.
                Case against Tropic in Marin County only expands
                book's circulation.

E2706   "Philadelphia Colleges Ban 'Tropic'," New York Post,
         CLXI (December 11, 1961), 6.
                Tropic withdrawn from University of Pennsylvania,
                Drexel, Temple, St. Joseph's, and La Salle.

E2707   Shepard, Lyn. "R. I. Smut Probe Simmers," Christian
        Science Monitor, LIV (December 11, 1961), 10.
            No right to censor Miller's novel.

E2708   Beall, Clarkson J. "Book Banning," Washington Star,
        CIX (December 12, 1961), 12.
            Congratulations for Rabbi Friedman's defense of
            Tropic.

E2709   Bess, Donovan. "Experts Testify Book Is Obscene," San
        Francisco Chronicle, XCVII (December 12, 1961), 1, 14.
            James W. Kirchanski swore at Tropic during trial.

E2710   Cruttenden, Charles. "Profanity Lesson at Book Trial,"
        San Francisco Examiner (December 12, 1961), 1, 4.
            Profanity display shows Tropic language to be real.

E2711   "Doctor of Theology Terms 'Tropic' an Important Work,"
        Oakland Tribune, December 12, 1961.
            Tropic a book about individualism.

E2712   "Head of County Library Board Finds 'Tropic' Filthy,
        Quits," Maryland Sentinel, December 12, 1961.
            Montgomery County Library Board Chairman Frank J.
            Duane feels Tropic is filthy and disagrees with Board.

E2713   "Temple Bans Miller Novel," Philadelphia Inquirer,
        CXXXIII (December 12, 1961), 45.
            Temple University withdraws Tropic from library.

E2714   " 'Tropic' Trial," Berkeley Gazette, December 12, 1961.
            Tropic called filthy and of no redeeming value in
            Marin County trial.

E2715   Ullyot, James R. and Bruce L. Paisner. "Counsel for
        Grove Press Defends Miller's Novel," Harvard Crimson,
        (December 12, 1961).
            Counsel for Grove Press said that people do not have
            to read a book that offends them.

E2716   Williams, Carleton. "Ministry Is Mixed on Miller Book--
        Two Are Con, One Is Pro 'Tropic'," San Raphael Inde-
        pendent Journal, December 12, 1961, 1, 4.
            One man of God sees Tropic as literary masterpiece.

E2717   Bess, Donovan. "Court Shocker--Minister Reads Those
        Words," San Francisco Chronicle, XCVII (December 13,
        1961), 1, 19.
            Minister reads from Tropic, calls it a work of poetry
            and of independence.

E2718   Bess, Donovan. "Mark Schorer Speaks Out for 'Tropic',"
        San Francisco Chronicle, XCVII (December 13, 1961), 1, 12.

Mark Schorer, chairman of English Department at
University of California, sees Tropic as the struggle
of an individual in a machine-like society.

E2719   Kessler, Felix. "Cops Start Survey of 'Tropic' Sellers,"
New York World Telegram & Sun, CXXIX (December 13,
1961), B1.
New York police survey on Tropic popularity.

E2720   "Manners and Morals of Marvelous Marin," San Francisco
Chronicle, XCVII (December 13, 1961), 40.
Tropic called obscene.

E2721   "Minister Reads Those Words," San Francisco Chronicle,
XCVII (December 13, 1961), 12.
The Rev. Arnold Cure read Tropic and called it poe-
try.

E2722   "The Obscene Book," Chicago American, LXII (December
13, 1961), 26.
Tropic best-seller in Chicago.

E2723   "Publisher to Carry Ball in Court for 'Tropic' Sale,"
Philadelphia News, December 13, 1961.
Grove will defend Tropic in Pennsylvania.

E2724   "Smut Case Defense Motion Denied," Chicago Sun-Times,
XIV (December 13, 1961), 40.
Elmer Gertz, lawyer defending Tropic, contends that
judges who issued warrants for book had not read it.

E2725   " 'Tropic' Hearing Is Put Off, Ban on Novel Sale Continues," Philadelphia Bulletin CXV (December 13, 1961), 5.
Hearing on Tropic continues.

E2726   "Tropic Publisher Ousts Lawyer for Trial Here," Washington News, XLI (December 13, 1961), 5.
Defendent and lawyer in Tropic case part company over
fee.

E2727   " 'Tropic' Will Go on Trial in San Diego," San Francisco
Chronicle, XCVII (December 13, 1961), 12.
Tropic will go to court in San Diego Municipal Court.

E2728   Bess, Donovan. "Eugene Burdick Says 'Tropic' A Social
Work," San Francisco Chronicle, XCVII (December 14,
1961), 1, 16.
Professor of political science calls Tropic social work.

E2729   "Burdick vs. Marin's D.A. --Highlights of the Duel," San
Francisco Chronicle, XCVII (December 14, 1961), 16.
Doctor sees literary merit of Cancer in our sick
society.

E2730   "Obscene Book Jury Trial Due February 19," San Diego
Tribune, December 14, 1961.
    Jury trial of Tropic set for February 19.

E2731   "Put That Book on the Shelf or I'll Quit," Oakland Tribune,
December 14, 1961.
    Two members of San Mateo City Library Board pro-
    test ban on Tropic.

E2732   Dusheck, George. "Miller Calls Himself a Rebel," San
Francisco News-Call Bulletin, December 15, 1961.
    Miller rebellious and reckless.

E2733   "Federal Supports Anti-Bias Measure," Bethesda Tribune,
December 15, 1961.
    County Civic Federation of Bethesda, Md. , feels
    Tropic OK.

E2734   Kuhn, Christoph. "Henry Miller--ein grosser Aussenseiter,"
Zürcher Woche, December 15, 1961.
    Review of The Rosy Crucifixion.   (In German.)

E2735   "Moves to Strike 'Tropic' Answer," Milwaukee Sentinel,
(December 15, 1961), II 13.
    D.A. wishes to strike six of the eight pages of
    answer by Tropic publishers.

E2736   Anthony, Donald B.   "Letter," San Francisco Chronicle,
XCVII (December 16, 1961), 8.
    Obscenity found in mind, not in Tropic.

E2737   "Attorney Hails 'Tropic' Decision," San Francisco Chronicle, XCVII (December 16, 1961), 8.
    Attorney Lowenthal predicts Tropic will overturn Roth
    Decision.

E2738   Bess, Donovan.   " 'Tropic' Verdict--Bookseller--'Not
Guilty'," San Francisco Chronicle, XCVII (December 16,
1961), 1, 8.
    Marin County jury finds book dealer not guilty in
    Tropic case.

E2739   Bess, Donovan.   " 'Tropic' Case Will Go to Jury Today,"
San Francisco Chronicle, XCVII (December 16, 1961), 1,
17.
    Jury decides book's fate in Marin County, California.

E2740   Crawford, Mary. "Jury Clears 'Tropic' Seller, but...,"
San Francisco News-Call Bulletin, December 16, 1961.
    Franklin Pershina not guilty in selling Tropic.

E2741   Davies, David S.   "Knuckling Under," Philadelphia Inquirer, CXXXIII (December 16, 1961), 6.

Librarians fall from grace with Tropic.

E2742   Earle, William.   "Jurors Urge Ban on 'Tropic'," San
Francisco Examiner, December 16, 1961, 4.
Tropic should be found obscene and not sold in Marin
County.

E2743   "Juror Indicates Trial Was Followed in Press," San
Raphael Independent Journal, December 16, 1961.
Cancer juror keeps up with newspaper coverage of
trial.

E2744   "Juror William Brice Talked to Newsmen After the Verdict," San Francisco Examiner, December 16, 1961, 4.
Photograph of trial.

E2745   "Jurors' Views of Case," San Francisco Examiner, December 16, 1961, 4.
All thought Tropic a filthy book.

E2746   "Jury's Reaction to 'Tropic'," San Francisco Chronicle,
XCVII (December 16, 1961), 8.
Tropic found 'not guilty' in San Raphael.

E2747   "S. F. Group Applauds Verdict," San Francisco Examiner,
December 16, 1961, 4.
San Francisco Freedom to Read Citizens' Committee
pleased Tropic acquitted in Marin County.

E2748   Schmitt, Donald.   "Book Burners," San Francisco Chronicle, XCVII (December 16, 1961), 8.
Tropic called a great work.

E2749   "Schorer's View of the Verdict," San Francisco Examiner,
December 16, 1961, 4.
Schorer believed in common man's ability to judge
Tropic.

E2750   " 'Tropic' Dealer Acquitted," San Francisco Examiner,
December 16, 1961, 1, 4.
Jury disgusted with book but finds dealer not guilty.

E2751   "Court Must Determine: Is Theme of 'Tropic' Obscene?"
Washington Sunday Star, CIX (December 17, 1961), B4.
Chicago Judge says he does not need to read Tropic
to try book.

E2752   Duke, William.   "Jury Reading 'Cancer' on Motion of
State," Washington Star, CIX (December 18, 1961), B2.
Montgomery County, Md., jury reads book to deter-
mine status.

E2753   "Eight Suburbs Dismissed in Book Ban Suit," Chicago

Tribune, CXX (December 19, 1961), II 10.
Epstein dismisses eight municipalities in Cancer suit.

E2754   Hagen, John Milton.   "Free Speech and Miller's Book,"
San Raphael Independent Journal, December 19, 1961.
Miller's Tropic a study of free speech and other free-
doms.

E2755   Hoppe, Art.   "A Revolting Development," San Francisco
Chronicle, XCVII (December 19, 1961), 34.
Cancer does not corrupt; it's a book of literary merit.

E2756   Hoppe, Art.   "Henry Miller Really Bugs You," San Francisco Chronicle, XCVII (December 19, 1961), 34.
Tropic a fine travel book.

E2757   Maslin, Marsh.   "Some Thoughts on the 'Tropic of Cancer' Trial," San Francisco News-Call Bulletin, December
19, 1961.
Miller's work not objectionable in Tropic.

E2758   "Trial Set January 10 in ACLU Suit on 'Tropic of Cancer'," Chicago Sun & Times, XIV (December 19, 1961), 18.
Superior Court Judge Epstein sets January 10 as trial
date.

E2759   " 'Tropic of Cancer' Trial Set January 10," Chicago Sun-
Times, XIV (December 19, 1961), II 32.
Judge Epstein sets Tropic trial for January 10.

E2760   Velsey, Victoria.   "Jury's 1st Job in Obscenity Trial Is to
Read 'Tropic of Cancer'," Washington Post & Times
Herald, LXXXV (December 19, 1961), B1.
Montgomery County, Md., jury reads Tropic in at-
tempt to determine its value.

E2761   Caen, Herb.   "Pocketful of Notes: Bay City Beagle,"
San Francisco Chronicle, XCVII (December 20, 1961), 23.
Censorship of Tropic only increases sales.

E2762   "DA Lifts Shasta County Ban on 'Tropic of Cancer',"
Redding (Calif.) Record-Searchlight, December 20, 1961.
Redding, Calif., permits Tropic sale.

E2763   Velsey, Victoria.   " 'Tropic' Dealer Guilty on Maryland
Obscenity Law," Washington Post & Times Herald, LXXXV
(December 20, 1961), 3.
Bethesda book dealer found guilty in Maryland Tropic
trial.

E2764   Caen, Herb.   "Big Wide Wonderful Whirl," San Francisco
Chronicle, XCVII (December 21, 1961), 17.
Miller sending Christmas cards with a quote from

Whitman.

E2765   "Food for Thought," Washington Post & Times Herald,
         LXXXV (December 21, 1961), 18.
         Leonard T. Kardy, D.A. for Montgomery County, Md.,
         feels Tropic is important literature.

E2766   Marcuse, Ludwig. "Der alte, böse Elefant Henry Miller,"
         Die Zeit, December 21, 1961.
         Henry Miller Reader discussed. (In German.)

E2767   "Seller of 'Cancer' Sentenced," New York Times, CXI
         (December 21, 1961), 23.
         Samuel Yudkin sentenced to six months in prison for
         sale of Tropic in Montgomery County, Md.

E2768   "Sentenced Six Months for Selling Detective 'Tropic of
         Cancer'," York Gazette & Daily, December 21, 1961.
         Samuel Yudkin sentenced to six months for sale of
         Tropic.

E2769   "Tell Suburbs' Status on Ban," Chicago Sun-Times, XIV
         (December 21, 1961), II 30.
         Suburbs wait for Tropic trial to see status of book.

E2770   Velsey, Victoria. "'Tropic' Book Seller No Crusader,"
         Washington Post & Times Herald, LXXXV (December 21,
         1961), 3.
         Yudkin, the book dealer who sold Tropic, no real
         lover of book.

E2771   Zett. "Keine Angst vor Henry Miller," Westdeutsche
         Rundschau, December 21, 1961.
         Review of Henry Miller Reader. (In German.)

E2772   Come, Arnold B. "'Tropic' Witness Explains His Stand,"
         San Raphael Independent-Journal, December 22, 1961.
         Freedom for Tropic necessary.

E2773   Montague, Richard. "'Tropic' Fight Going to Maryland's
         Top Court," New York Post, CLXI (December 22, 1961),
         32.
         Yudkin appeals obscenity conviction to Maryland's
         highest court.

E2774   Ferber, Christain. "Ansturm wider Hölle und Himmel,"
         Die Welt, December 23, 1961, 5.
         Review of Big Sur and the Oranges of H. Bosch. (In
         German.)

E2775   H., T. "Auf der Seite der Engel," Mannheimes Morgen,
         December 23, 1961.
         Henry Miller Reader discussed. (In German.)

E2776   Gorn, Lester. "One Critic's Favorites from the Year's Books," San Francisco Examiner, (December 24, 1961), H2.
Tropic an attempt at a greater realism than ever before found in our literature.

E2777   Körling, Martha Christine. "Seine einzige Waffe ist das Wort," Berliner Morgenpost, December 24, 1961.
Bust of Miller created. (In German.)

E2778   Clayton, James E. "Maryland 'Tropic' Ruling Faces Test," Washington Post & Times Herald, LXXXV (December 25, 1961), B16.
Maryland's Tropic obscenity ruling differs from Customs Bureau.

E2779   Come, Arnold B. "Theologian Explains His Stand on 'Tropic'," San Francisco News-Call Bulletin, December 25, 1961.
Freedom of human spirit is major issue in Tropic case.

E2780   Collins, Jerome F. " 'Tropic of Cancer' Gets Gate," Laguna Beach South Coast News, December 26, 1961, 1-2.
Tropic banned in Laguna Beach, Calif.

E2781   Gard. "Quest," Variety, December 27, 1961.
Miller's first television airing occurs along with Alfred Perlès and Robert Whitehead.

E2782   "Henry Miller," Der Tag, December 28, 1961.
Miller watercolors viewed. (In German.)

E2783   "Henry Miller Book Booted Out by Police Action," Laguna Beach Post, December 28, 1961.
Mr. Dilley removed Tropic from sale pending Grove Press action.

E2784   "Local Chiefs Named as Co-defendants," Palisade (N.J.) Palisadian, December 28, 1961.
Suit by Grove against seizure of Tropic in New Jersey.

E2785   R., B. "Censorship Censured," Laguna Beach Post, December 28, 1961.
Horror of zealous police creating their own ban of Tropic.

E2786   Pasley, Virginia. "Critics' Corner," Newsday, December 30, 1961.
Tropic dull but should be free to read.

E2787   Gelre, Henk van. "Henry Miller--Alleen Maar Zichzelf," Nieuw Vlaams Tijdschrift, XV (1961-1962), 1191-1206.

Miller an artist attempting to find an individual mode
of expression that is unique and that allows one to perceive himself.   (In Dutch.)

E2788   Lowell, Robert.   "William Carlos Williams," Hudson Review, XIV (1961-1962), 530-536.
Lowell refers to Miller's knowledge of Williams.

E2789   Beaver, Harold.   "A Figure in the Carpet: Irony and the
American Novel," Essays and Studies, XV (1962), 101-114.
Miller depicted "mouthing his black mass of sexual re-
lease in Paris."

E2790   C., C.   "Education," Michigan Daily, 1962.
Rhode Island Attorney J. Joseph Nugent allows Brown
University to sell Tropic for educational purposes.

E2791   Hiner, James.   "For God, in Case Henry Miller Dies,"
Coastlines, V (1962), 35.
Anti-Miller poem where Hiner does not see how God
could have made a foul man like Miller.

E2792   Kirsch, Robert.   " 'Tropic' Author Talks It Over," n.p.,
1962.
Miller does not know what it feels like to be best
selling author.

E2793   "News Notes," Poetry, C (1962), 266-267.
Robert Lowell supported publication of Tropic.

E2794   Okumura, Osamu.   "Henry Miller: An Introduction,"
Aoyama Journal of General Education [Tokyo] (Special
issue), 1962, 35-50.
A look at the writing of Henry Miller.   (In Japanese.)

E2795   "Personality Parade," Jefftown Journal, 1962, 3.
Miller's friendship with convict Roger Bloom discussed.

E2796   Seaver, Richard.   "[Tropic of Capricorn]," Hudson Book
Club Bulletin, 1962.
Review of Capricorn.

E2797   Weinstock, Matt.   "So Gung Hay Fat Choy to All!" n.p.,
1962.
People testify against Tropic who are unqualified to
judge it.

E2798   Renken, Maxine.   "Bibliography of Henry Miller: 1945-
1961," Twentieth Century Literature, VII (January 1962),
180-190.
Chronological bibliography on Miller in three parts:
Part I consists of "Books and Brochures by Henry
Miller," Part II, "Contributions to Books and

Periodicals by Miller," and Part III, "Books About
Henry Miller and Articles and Reviews on Miller in
Books and Periodicals. "

E2799   "Tropic of Cancer," Wilson Library Bulletin, XXXVI (Jan-
uary 1962), 338-340.
Review of Tropic's sale problems because of bans in
California, Connecticut, Illinois, Maryland, Massachu-
setts, New Hampshire, New Jersey, New York, Ohio,
Pennsylvania, Rhode Island, Texas.

E2800   Yudkin, Vivian. "Who Will Be Next?" Washington Post
& Times Herald, LXXXV (January 3, 1962), 14.
Mrs. Yudkin calls conviction of husband loss of basic
freedom.

E2801   "Chicago Smut Law Wins First Bout in Court," Cleveland
Plain Dealer, CXXI (January 4, 1962), 8.
Chicago obscenity law is valid in Miller Tropic case.

E2802   Th. "Auf der Seite der Engel," Heidelberger Tageblatt,
January 5, 1962.
Henry Miller Reader discussed.   (In German.)

E2803   "Police Launch Crackdown on Miller's Book," Enterprise,
(January 6, 1962).
Beaumont, Texas, police stop sale of Tropic.

E2804   "Book Dealer Is Freed," New York Times, CXII (January
7, 1962), 24.
Honolulu book dealer, Charles Hobbis, free, as
Tropic set free in Hawaii.

E2805   Hoffenberg, Sheldon.   "Free Speech-Obscenity Line:
Where to Draw It!" Long Island Star, January 7, 1962.
Where does free speech end and obscenity begin?
The Tropic issue is decided differently in each state.

E2806   Hogan, William.   "Anglo-Saxon Writers," Hollywood Citizen-News, January 8, 1962.
Tropic first published by Obelisk Press in Paris.

E2807   Perlès, Alfred.   "Henry Miller's Banned Books," York-
shire Post, January 12, 1962.
Perlès surprised Americans lifted ban on Tropic, says
there is a move in England to do same, and calls
Miller a seer and man who confronts real human experience.

E2808   "Librarian Won't Ban 'Tropic'," Jamaica (N.Y.) Press,
January 14, 1962.
Queens, N.Y., head librarian won't ban Tropic.

E2809 " 'Tropic' Case May Lead to Revision of Law," Honolulu
Star-Bulletin, LI (January 14, 1962), 2.
Tropic case dismissed in Honolulu.

E2810 Bowron, Albert. " 'Tropic' in Canada," Library Journal,
LXXXVII (January 15, 1962), 184. .
Canada using search and seizure to prohibit entrance
of Tropic.

E2811 "Censorship Issues and Legal Cases," Publishers Weekly,
CLXXXI (January 15, 1962), 68-71.
Tropic cases show reversal of freedom from censor-
ship in U.S.

E2812 "Pennsylvania Libraries Disagree on 'Tropic'," Library
Journal, LXXXVII (January 15, 1962), 192-193.
Difference of opinion on Tropic in Pennsylvania li-
braries.

E2813 "Supervisors Back Librarian," Ves Free Press, January
17, 1962.
County librarian, Mrs. Chadwick, received criticism
for not stocking Cancer.

E2814 "Umstrittener genealer Henry Miller," Lübecker Nachrichten, January 20, 1962.
Discussion of Miller's Eastern philosophy. (In German.)

E2815 Marcuse, Ludwig. "Ein alter böser Elefant," Rhein-
Nechar-Zeitung, January 20-21, 1962.
Review of Henry Miller Reader. (In German.)

E2816 B., O. F. "Der unbequeme Miller," Bücherspiegel Neues
Österreich, January 21, 1962.
Henry Miller Reader discussed. (In German.)

E2817 Fink, Humbert. "Das Werk Henry Millers ist vor allem
Henry Miller selbst," Die Presse, January 21, 1962.
Miller Reader seen as self-centered work. (In Ger-
man.)

E2818 Lewis, Anthony. "The Most Recent Troubles of 'Tropic',"
New York Times, CXII (January 21, 1962), 4-5, 16, 18.
Article showing Barney Rosset of Grove Press and
Miller fighting to have Tropic sold in bookshops across
America.

E2819 Lind, Jack. "Book, Community Standards on Trial,"
Chicago Daily News, LXXXVII (January 22, 1962), 24.
Tropic case a question of community standards.

E2820 Marshall, Sam. "Pastor Finds Censorship Carries Seeds

of Tyranny, " Cleveland Plain Dealer, CXXI (January 22,
1962), 23.
    The Rev. Gordon B. McKeeman says that Tropic
should be free so people can decide merits of book for
themselves.

E2821 " 'Tropic of Cancer' Is Defended by Two Professors, "
Pottstown (Penn.) Mercury, January 23, 1962.
    Professors Carl Bode and Sculley Bradley testified to
Tropic's literary merit and social importance in Phila-
delphia trial.

E2822 " 'Tropic of Cancer' Merit Is Cited in Court, " Philadelphia
Inquirer, CXXXIII (January 23, 1962), 13.
    See E2821.

E2823 "Book Damaging, Mabley Testifies, " Chicago American,
LXII (January 24, 1962), 3.
    Mabley calls Tropic damaging to our moral character.

E2824 " 'Cancer' Lewd, Obscene Novel, Witnesses Say, " Philadelphia Inquirer, CXXXIII (January 24, 1962), 9.
    Five Philadelphia witnesses blast Tropic as obscene.

E2825 "Reading of Test-Case Book Resumed in Court, " Los
Angeles Times, LXXXI (January 24, 1962), IV 10.
    Tropic being read aloud in Los Angeles Municipal
Court to jury.

E2826 " 'Tropic of Cancer' Is Described as Obscene, " Washington (Penn.) Observer, January 24, 1962.
    In Philadelphia court, Dr. Austin Joseph App called
Tropic a pornographic work.

E2827 Bylin, James E. " 'Tropic' Branded Outhouse Scrawl, "
Los Angeles Valley Times, January 25, 1962, 1-2.
    Kates, who runs Sunset News Company, says Tropic
offends.

E2828 Bylin, James E. "UCLA Dean Says Book Not Obscene, "
North Hollywood Valley Times, January 25, 1962.
    Dr. Lawrence Clark Powell called Tropic realistic.

E2829 "Controversial Novel Assailed By Witness, " Los Angeles
Times, LXXXI (January 25, 1962), IV 15.
    Arthur J. Kates, owner-manager of Sunset News
Company, called Tropic a "diseased outhouse of a de-
mented mind. "

E2830 Bylin, James E. "UCLA Library Dean Says 'Tropic' Not
Obscene Book, " Los Angeles Valley Times, January 26,
1962, 1-2.
    Dr. Lawrence Clark Powell called the sex in Tropic

realistic and grossly boring for the purpose of turning people away from mechanical sex.

E2831   Byrne, Jim.   "Miller Novel off Shelves After 'Request'-- Not 'Ban', " Wilmington News, January 26, 1962.
Delaware Attorney General's office asked Dover book- stores to discontinue sale of Tropic.

E2832   "Educator Condemns 'Tropic of Cancer' as 'Dirty, Ob- scene', " Hollywood Citizen-News, January 26, 1962, 1.
Dr. C. C. Trillingham called Cancer filthy, obscene, and objectionable.

E2833   "Librarian Backs Novel but Won't Read from It, " Los Angeles Times, LXXXI (January 26, 1962), 26.
Powell calls Tropic important social document.

E2834   " 'Tropic of Cancer' Wins Praise From Librarian, " Holly- wood Citizen-News, January 26, 1962, 1.
Tropic called important social document by Lawrence Clark Powell.

E2835   "A Book Flops, " McKeesport News, January 27, 1962.
Tropic costly flop to U.S. publisher.

E2836   "Book 'Tropic of Cancer' Called 'Muck,' 'Filth', " Los Angeles Times, LXXXI (January 27, 1962), 8.
Dr. C. C. Trillingham, County Superintendent of Schools, and Mrs. Edith Stafford, former president of L.A. City Board of Education, called Tropic ob- scene.

E2837   Bylin, James E.   "Professor Notes 'Shock Therapy' in 'Tropic' Novel, " Los Angeles Valley Times, January 27, 1962, 2.
UCLA English Professor Blake Nevius says Miller uses shock therapy to get society to examine its stan- dards.

E2838   "Theory That Smut Spurs Crime Is Hit, " Cleveland Plain Dealer, CXXI (January 27, 1962), 10.
Charles Rembar, president of Grove Press, defended Tropic and said book does not contribute to crime.

E2839   " 'Tropic of Cancer' Novel in Another Court Fight, " Jacksonville Journal, January 27, 1962.
Tropic in Los Angeles Court fight.

E2840   " 'Tropic' Publisher Ready with Two Miller Books, " Cleveland Press, January 27, 1962, 4.
If Supreme Court allows Tropic, Grove will publish Capricorn and Black Spring.

E2841   "Educators Flunk Literary Test at 'Tropic' Obscenity
         Trial," Long Beach Independent Journal, January 30, 1962.
             Tropic denounced by Drs. Howard McDonald and Ellis
         A. Jarvis in Los Angeles trial.

E2842   " 'Tropic' Obscene, Educators Assert," Evening Outlook,
         January 30, 1962, 3.
             Tropic called obscene by Drs. McDonald and Jarvis.

E2843   "2 Educators Rap 'Tropic of Cancer'," Los Angeles Times,
         LXXXI (January 30, 1962), III 1, 3.
             Dr. Howard McDonald, president of Los Angeles State
         College, and Ellis Jarvis, superintendent of Los Ange-
         les City Schools, called Tropic obscene, morbid, and
         without saving grace.

E2844   "Bookseller Says Miller Novel Is Not Obscene," Los Ange-
         les Times, LXXXI (January 31, 1962), III 3.
             Bradley J. Smith says Tropic full of exaggeration for
         effect.

E2845   "I Know What I Like," n. p. , January 31, 1962.
             Miller book branded filth by educators who know noth-
         ing about literature.

E2846   "I Said...," Smoke Signals, February 1962, 3.
             Old librarian tells young child he cannot read Tropic
         in a cartoon.

E2847   Molin, Sven Eric.   "Commentary," Abstracts of English
         Studies, V (February 1962), 51.
             Solotaroff's " 'All That Cellar-Deep Jazz'," suggests
         time has caught up with Miller's romantic movement.

E2848   Moore, Everett T.   "Tropic of Cancer (Second Phase),"
         ALA Bulletin, LVI (February 1962), 81-84.
             Suppression of Tropic brings book to court in Minne-
         sota, Los Angeles, San Francisco, New Hampshire,
         Connecticut, Illinois, Pennsylvania, New Jersey,
         Rhode Island, Massachusetts.

E2849   Sanguineti, Edoardo.   "Henry Miller: una poetica baroc-
         ca," Il Verri, (February 1962), 26-39.
             Miller's animation and his rhythm make his writing
         poetic.   (In Italian.)

E2850   Waller, John O.   "National Review," Abstracts of English
         Studies, V (February 1962), 71.
             Francis Russell's "The Cult of Henry Miller" views
         Miller as the writer of shocking four-letter words,
         but little else.

E2851   Cummings, Ridgely.   "Civic Center Spotlight," Los Angeles

City Press, February 1, 1962.
Bradley Smith calls Tropic autobiographical study.

E2852   E., H. "Blick in neue Bücher," Weser Krorer, February
1, 1962.
Review of Miller's work, stressing the Miller Reader.
(In German.)

E2853   " 'Tropic of Cancer' Held 'Honest' by Professor," Los
Angeles Times, LXXXI (February 1, 1962), III 3.
Los Angeles State College Professor, Otto W. Fick,
called Cancer honest, humorous, and lively.

E2854   " 'Tropic' Reverses Lawyers' Role," West Los Angeles Independent, February 1, 1962, 1, 6.
Tropic read to Los Angeles jury by lawyer.

E2855   "Book Attacked by Professor," Oklahoma City Oklahoman,
LXXI (February 2, 1962), 10.
Dr. Frank Baxter says Tropic of no social value in
Los Angeles trial.

E2856   Coats, Paul. 'Some Strange Testimony Comes out of
'Tropic of Cancer' Case," Los Angeles Times, LXXXI
(February 2, 1962), III 6.
Ellis Jarvis and Dr. McDonald do not know literature.

E2857   Higginbotham, Bill. "Moral, Spiritual but Not Literary,"
Star-Free Press, February 2, 1962.
No need to read Tropic to criticize.

E2858   Malone, Mrs. Mae. " 'Cancer' Trial," Star-Free Press,
February 2, 1962.
Pleased that educators do not read Tropic.

E2859   Olson, Mrs. Earl D. 'Editor," Star-Free Press, February 2, 1962.
Miller's Tropic filth.

E2860   Scott, Marguirite C. "Cancer," Star-Free Press, February 2, 1962.
Tropic nauseating.

E2861   "Times Literary Editor Defends Miller's Novel," Los
Angeles Times, LXXXI (February 2, 1962), III 3.
Robert Kirsch says Tropic great influence on Ameri-
can writers.

E2862   Vincent, Richard F. "No Excuse for Cultural Zombies,"
Star-Free Press, February 2, 1962.
Too bad educated professors cannot see merit of
Tropic and understand Miller.

E2863   Nash, C. Knowlton.   "The Life of Crime: Helping Canadi-
        ans Get Their 'Cancer' Copies, " Financial Post, February
        3, 1962.
        Tropic smuggled into Canada.

E2864   P., A.   "Ein Henry-Miller-Lesebuch, " Des Kline Blatt,
        February 3, 1962.
        Miller Reader explored.   (In German.)

E2865   "Professor Testifies in Defense of 'Tropic', " Long Beach
        Independent, February 3, 1962.
        Dr. Charles Kaplan called Tropic an American master-
        piece.

E2866   " 'Tropic of Cancer' Is Honest, Educator Says, " Los Ange-
        les Times, LXXXI (February 3, 1962), III 3.
        Dr. Charles Kaplan calls Tropic's language honest,
        seeing Miller as American rebel seeking individualism.

E2867   Thell, Wayne.   "Henry Miller, the Myth of the Rebellious
        Puritan, " Ivory Tower, LXIII (February 5, 1962), 6-7.
        Miller writes erotic realism to celebrate the whole
        man and to undermine Puritanism.

E2868   " 'Tropic' Novel Called Deeply Religious Book, " Los Ange-
        les Times, LXXXI (February 6, 1962), 18.
        Tropic called deeply religious by Dr. Jack Hirschman
        of UCLA, who sees Miller's journey from darkness
        and despair to happiness and light.

E2869   " 'Tropic' Religious, Says Professor, " Evening Outlook,
        February 6, 1962, 6.
        Dr. Hirschman of UCLA calls Tropic religious jour-
        ney from despair to light.

E2870   "Bookseller Defends His Sale of 'Tropic', " Los Angeles
        Times, LXXXI (February 7, 1962), 27.
        Bradley R. Smith called Tropic a book of social merit.

E2871   "Ministers Add Voices to Defense of 'Tropic', " Los Ange-
        les Times, LXXXI (February 8, 1962), II 2.
        Dr. Glenn Whitlock called Tropic an angry novel, a
        man's attack against the falseness of life.

E2872   "Dr. Frank Baxter Assails 'Tropic', Calls It Obscene, "
        Los Angeles Times, LXXXI (February 9, 1962), II 1, 8.
        Baxter calls Tropic an anarchistic work against all
        values.

E2873   " 'Tropic' Obscene, Says Dr. Baxter, " Los Angeles Times,
        LXXXI (February 9, 1962), II 8.
        Tropic called purposefully obscene and shocking by
        Baxter.

E2874   Maria, Ave. "Uneducated Bookworm," National Catholic
         Weekly, February 10, 1962.
             Drawing criticizing those who do not read Tropic.

E2875   "Westwood Rabbi Calls 'Tropic' Anti-Semitic," Los Ange-
         les Times, LXXXI (February 10, 1962), III 6.
             Rabbi R. Trattner called Tropic a dangerous parable
         to Hitler's Mein Kampf.

E2876   "Baxter Calls 'Tropic' Tissue of Calculated Offense,"
         Sunday Green Sheet, February 11, 1962, 1, 10.
             Book called unhealthy by Baxter.

E2877   Cummings, Ridgely. "Baxter Blasts 'Tropic' with H-
         Bomb Outburst," Lincoln Heights Bulletin-News, February
         11, 1962, 1, 23.
             Baxter calls Tropic obscene.

E2878   "[Tropic of Cancer]," Valley State Sundial, February 13,
         1962.
             Cartoon of school teacher reading children Tropic.

E2879   " 'Tropic' a Book for Animals, Says Doctor," Los Angeles
         Times, LXXXI (February 14, 1962), 24.
             Dr. Marcus Craham called Tropic a book for canni-
         bals and animals.

E2880   "Novelist Calls 'Tropic' Frustrated Man's Work," Los
         Angeles Times, LXXXI (February 15, 1962), III 15.
             John Otis Carney called Tropic a frustrated man's
         work in the Los Angeles trial.

E2881   "Banning 'Tropic' Seen as 'Dreadful Crime'," Los Angeles
         Times, LXXXI (February 16, 1962), II 8.
             Professor Procter Thomson feels that banning Tropic
         a crime since book contains insights into human con-
         dition.

E2882   Drucker, H. M. " 'Tropic' Author Miller Defended
         Against Charge of Anti-Semitism," Los Angeles Times,
         LXXXI (February 16, 1962), II 5.
             Tropic called for independence through psychological
         revolution.

E2883   Howard, Eleanor. " 'Tropic' Author Miller Defended,"
         Los Angeles Times, LXXXI (February 16, 1962), II 5.
             Miller not anti-semitic.

E2884   "Two Professors Join in Defense of 'Tropic'," Los Ange-
         les Times, LXXXI (February 16, 1962), I 28.
             UCLA and Claremont educators said Tropic redeems
         self through honest and human insights.

E2885   Carter, Roger W.   "Tropic of Cancer," Star Free Press, February 17, 1962.
Miller should be read objectively for his fine control of language.

E2886   " 'Tropic' Called Obscene by Novelist Leon Uris," Los Angeles Times, LXXXI (February 17, 1962), III 3.
Uris called Tropic perverted and irrational babbling.

E2887   "Guilty Verdict Urged Against 'Tropic' Novel," Los Angeles Times, LXXXI (February 20, 1962), 28.
Prosecution urges verdict of guilty against Tropic because book lies beyond bounds of free speech.

E2888   Kirsch, Robert.   " 'Tropic' Author Talks It Over," Los Angeles Times, LXXXI (February 20, 1962), IV 4.
Miller does not know what it feels like to be best-selling author.

E2889   " 'Tropic' Trial Likened to Salem Witch Hunts," Los Angeles Times, LXXXI (February 21, 1962), III 15.
Defense argues that prosecution confused freedom in Los Angeles trial.

E2890   "Book Is Dirty, but Not Obscene, Judge Decides," Chicago's American, LXII (February 22, 1962), 4.
Judge Samuel Epstein ruled Tropic had vile and disgusting moments, however not obscene.

E2891   Lind, Stanley L.   "Judge Epstein Rules 'Tropic' Is Not Obscene," Chicago Daily Law Bulletin, CVIII (February 22, 1962), 1, 8.
Tropic not obscene in Chicago trial.

E2892   " 'Tropic' Honest Work, Defense Lawyer Says," Los Angeles Times, LXXXI (February 22, 1962), III 10.
Tropic called honest work of real life by defense lawyer Mark W. Tumbleson.

E2893   " 'Tropic of Cancer' Ruled Not Obscene; Sale Here OK'd," Chicago Sun-Times, XV (February 22, 1962), 26.
Superior Court Chief Justice Samuel Epstein ruled Tropic not obscene under the law.

E2894   " 'Tropic of Cancer' Wins," New York Times, CXII (February 22, 1962), 23.
Tropic wins in Chicago.

E2895   London, Mike.   " 'Tropic of Cancer.' Student Meets Controversial Author," El Yanqui, XVI (February 23, 1962), 3.
Mike London described his happiness at meeting Miller.

E2896   " 'Tropic of Cancer' Sale Convicts Book Dealer, " Los
Angeles Times, LXXXI (February 24, 1962), 1, 12.
  Bradley R. Smith convicted by Los Angeles jury of
violating new state obscenity law.

E2897   Barucca, Primo. "Henry Miller sconcertante, " Fiera
Letteraria, XVII (February 25, 1962).
  (In Italian.)

E2898   "Miller's 'Tropic' Held Obscene, " New York Times, CXI
(February 25, 1962), 38.
  Los Angeles jury returned verdict against Bradley
Smith in Tropic trial.

E2899   Owen, Humphrey. "Dr. Murphy, Portrait of a Chancellor, "
Los Angeles Times, LXXXI (February 25, 1962), 1, 16.
  Tropic a mirror of Miller's life.

E2900   " 'Tropic of Cancer' Declared Out of Bounds, " News,
February 25, 1962, 10.
  Smith found guilty and Tropic found obscene.

E2901   "A Library Fights Back, " Publishers Weekly, CLXXXI
(February 26, 1962), 33.
  Queens Borough Librarian Harold W. Tucker stood in
defense of Tropic.

E2902   "Jury Finds Miller Book Is Obscene, " Leader Herald,
February 26, 1962.
  Los Angeles jury finds Tropic obscene and sentences
Smith.

E2903   Weinstock, Matt. " 'Tropic' Trial Ends but Cancer Re-
mains, " Los Angeles Times, LXXXI (February 28, 1962),
II 6.
  Tropic loses and book ban remains.

E2904   Eskin, Stanley G. "Durrell's Themes in the Alexandria
Quartet, " Texas Quarterly, V (Winter 1962), 43-60.
  Miller's rejection of society a major influence on
Durrell's themes.

E2905   Galloway, David D. "Camels and Hummingbirds, " Trace,
XI (Winter 1962), 342-344.
  Miller concerned with conditions of modern man, his
divorce from sensation and experience.

E2906   Wickes, George. "Henry Miller at Seventy, " Claremont
Quarterly, IX (Winter 1962), 5-20.
  Excerpt from Paris Review Interviews where Miller
talks about beginning as a writer in New York and
working for Western Union.

E2907   "Library Ousts Miller Novel," n.p., March 1962.
         Tropic removed from Ventura County Library.

E2908   Sinclair, Dorothy and Frank N. Jones. "On Speaking Up,"
         ALA Bulletin, LVI (March 1962), 207.
         Courts must first decide if laws have been violated
         before police uphold them.

E2909   Langsner, Jules. "Man on a Rollercoaster," Beverly
         Hills Times, March 1, 1962.
         Tropic censorship will affect other arts in Los Ange-
         les.

E2910   Livingston, D. " 'Tropic': Of Social Value," UCLA Daily
         Bruin, March 1, 1962, 5.
         People have right to read Tropic to find out book not
         obscene.

E2911   Smith, John Justin. "You Can," Chicago Daily News,
         LXXXVII (March 1, 1962), 18.
         Judge Epstein's ruling in keeping with Supreme Court.

E2912   Hamel, Sam. "Defense Freed," Chicago New World,
         March 2, 1962, 4.
         Cartoon of Tropic being held by a snake with the
         words "moral death."

E2913   Kelly, J. M. "Great Day for Peddlers of Literary Trash,"
         Chicago New World, March 2, 1962, 4.
         Judge Epstein accused of providing Tropic filth for
         children.

E2914   Mabley, Jack. " 'That Book' to Get Shock Treatment,"
         Chicago's American, LXII (March 2, 1962), 3.
         Judge Epstein's opinion on Tropic must be fought.

E2915   Norris, Hoke. "A Guest Columnist," Chicago Sun-Times,
         XV (March 2, 1962), 40.
         Norris presents Judge Epstein's opinion on Tropic in
         Chicago trial.

E2916   Butcher, Fanny. "Illumination Cast Upon Authors and
         Their Work," Chicago Tribune, CXXI (March 4, 1962), 8.
         Durrell compared to Miller as writer.

E2917   Cromie, Robert. "The Bystander," Chicago Tribune,
         CXXI (March 4, 1962), IV 7.
         No right to censor books like Tropic.

E2918   Littlejohn, David. "The Tropics of Miller," New Repub-
         lic, CXLVI (March 5, 1962), 31-35.
         Miller's work autobiographical, dealing with individu-
         al's detachment from society.

E2919   "Tropic of Cancer Gets Clean Bill of Health," <u>Roosevelt</u>
        <u>Torch</u>, XVII (March 5, 1962), 31.
                Epstein declares <u>Tropic</u> free from pornography label
                in Chicago.

E2920   "The Right to Read," <u>Minneapolis Star</u>, LXXXIV (March 6,
        1962), 10.
                Buyers of <u>Tropic</u> have obtained injunction against Chi-
                cago police on grounds that barring book interferes
                with right to read.

E2921   Mabley, Jack. "High School Girl Speaks Out on Smut,"
        <u>Chicago's American</u>, LXII (March 7, 1962), 3.
                Girl disturbed over <u>Tropic</u> freedom.

E2922   Norris, Hoke. "Flood of Filth," <u>Chicago Sun-Times</u>, XV
        (March 7, 1962), II 14.
                Attacks Jack Mabley for wanting 1984 world of censor-
                ship in <u>Tropic</u> case.

E2923   " 'Tropic' Ruled Obscene," <u>New York Times</u>, CXI (March
        8, 1962), 15.
                In Hartford, Conn., Superior Court, bookseller Trum-
                bull Huntington was found guilty of violating state ob-
                scenity law for sale of <u>Tropic</u>.

E2924   Bloem, Don F. "Michigan Reader," <u>Chicago Sun-Times</u>,
        XV (March 13, 1962), 29.
                Agrees with Norris on <u>Tropic</u> value.

E2925   Hoffenberg, Sheldon. "Gertz, Kilgallon Still Talk About
        'Tropic' Case Future," <u>Chicago Learner Newspaper</u>, March
        13, 1962.
                Gertz says Chicago ill advised to appeal Epstein de-
                cision.

E2926   Kennedy, James A. "For Norris," <u>Chicago Sun-Times</u>,
        XV (March 13, 1962), 29.
                <u>Tropic</u> has right to civil liberties.

E2927   Lazarz, Mrs. Theodore T. "Against Norris," <u>Chicago</u>
        <u>Sun-Times</u>, XV (March 13, 1962), 29.
                Calls <u>Tropic</u> immoral.

E2928   Norris, Hoke. "From Norris," <u>Chicago Sun-Times</u>, XV
        (March 13, 1962), 29.
                Right of individual to buy or not purchase <u>Tropic</u>.

E2929   " 'Tropic of Cancer' Reading Raided," <u>Chicago Sun-Times</u>,
        XV (March 13, 1962), 4.
                A North Chicago reading of <u>Tropic</u> halted by police.

E2930   Kupcinet. "Kup's Column," <u>Chicago Sun-Times</u>, XV

(March 14, 1962), 30.
Citizens for Decent Literature took Miller out of context and ignored Judge Epstein's decision.

E2931   Molloy, Paul.   "He Questions the Merit of 'Tropic'," Chicago Sun-Times, XV (March 16, 1962), 40.
Tropic has smutty passages.

E2932   "Book Dealer Sentenced for Selling 'Tropic'," Los Angeles Times, LXXXI (March 17, 1962), III 3.
Bradley Smith sentenced to 30 days in jail for Los Angeles Tropic trial.

E2933   " 'Tropic' Seller Is Sentenced," New York Times, CXI (March 17, 1962), 52.
Bradley Smith draws 30-day jail sentence for L.A. Tropic sale.

E2934   "Appeal 'Tropic' Ruling," Chicago Star, March 18, 1962.
Chicago Appeals Judge Epstein's decision moves to Illinois Appellate Court.

E2935   Nichols, Lewis.   "In and Out of Books: Legal Department," New York Times, CXI (March 18, 1962), VII 8.
Absurd having sixty cases dealing with Tropic divided and fifty more in progress, when no one decision can be reached.

E2936   "Epstein Stays Action on His Book Decision," Chicago's American, LXII (March 22, 1962), 10.
Epstein stayed injunction against Chicago police's interfering with Tropic, a book he previously rules was not obscene.

E2937   Mabley, Jack.   "It's the Day Readers Have Their Say!" Chicago's American, LXII (March 23, 1962), 3.
Tropic will corrupt morals in U.S.

E2938   Dove, Joyce M.   "Agrees with Judge," Chicago Sun-Times, XV (March 26, 1962), 29.
Agrees with Judge Epstein's ruling on Tropic.

E2939   E., Mrs. M. H.   "The Antidote," Chicago Sun-Times, XV (March 26, 1962), 29.
If Tropic too 'dirty' one should find a 'clean' book to read.

E2940   A Reader.   "Freedom No License," Chicago Sun-Times, XV (March 26, 1962), 29.
Limit pornography like Tropic.

E2941   Rose, Don.   "Why He's Attacked," Chicago Sun-Times, XV (March 26, 1962), 29.

Miller attacked because he criticizes American standards.

E2942   "Princess Metlova to Speak on 'Tropic of Cancer' Trial,"
Los Angeles News, March 29, 1962.
Princess a witness for prosecution in L.A. Tropic
trial.

E2943   Bess, Donovan. "Miller's 'Tropic' on Trial," Evergreen
Review, VI (March-April 1962), 12-37.
Bess satirizes an America that puts Miller's literature on trial: "Henry Miller was right about us in
1931.   He is still right.   That is why we have to
keep putting him on trial: he talks about our cancer"
(p. 12).

E2944   Denet, Antoine. "Henry Miller," Perspektiv, IX (April
1962), 21-27.
On the man.   (In Danish.)

E2945   French, Warren G.   "Miller, Henry," Twentieth Century
Literature, VIII (April 1962), 58.
Comments on Armitage's "Doing Business with Henry
Miller" and Southern's "Miller: Only the Beginning."

E2946   Goldfarb, Russell M.   "Horizon," Abstracts of English
Studies, V (April 1962), 155.
Gilbert Highet sees Tropic as Miller's endless remi-
niscence.

E2947   Smith, Hubert W. "New Republic," Abstracts of English
Studies, V (April 1962), 163-164.
Stanley Kauffmann sees Tropic as fierce celebration
of enlightened freedom.

E2948   Suskind, R. R. "Henry Miller in Paris," Climax, X
(April 1962), 21-25, 71-72.
Review of Tropic that agrees with Miller that our society is not so frail that a little obscenity can wreck
it.   The article looks at Miller's personal failures
and poverty in Paris in the 1930's.

E2949   Epstein, Judge Samuel. "Judge Epstein's Opinion in
Tropic Case," Chicago Star, April 1, 1962, 10.
Entire text of Epstein's opinion on Tropic reprinted.

E2950   "Sale of Book Still Awaits Appeal," Chicago Star, April 1,
1962, 10.
Tropic still not sold in Chicago even after clearance
by Epstein.

E2951   Cohn, Marjorie. "UCLA's Part in 'Tropic' Trial," UCLA
Daily Bruin, April 4, 1962, 9.

Tropic a book with redeeming features.

E2952   Golden, Harry.   "Only in America," Arizona Daily Star,
        April 4, 1962.
            Feels Tropic got rough deal in Los Angeles trial.

E2953   "Kaplan, Religious Leaders Testify in 'Tropic' Trial,"
        UCLA Daily Bruin, April 6, 1962, 3, 16.
            Dr. Abraham Kaplan, a professor at UCLA, opposed
            censorship of Tropic.

E2954   E., H.   "Gezügelter Aussenseiter," Kölner Stadtanzeiger,
        April 13, 1962.
            Article dealing with Miller Reader.   (In German.)

E2955   Perlman, S. J.   "If It Please Your Honor," New Yorker,
        XXXVIII (April 28, 1962), 37-38.
            Parody showing injustice of events in Los Angeles
            Tropic trial.

E2956   Hutchens, John K.   "The Writer: Henry Miller: Writer
        with a Paintbrush," New York Herald Tribune, CXXII
        (April 29, 1962), VI 3.
            Look at diverse opinions about Tropic, at Miller-
            Rosset meeting, and at Miller's generosity.

E2957   Pollack, Peter.   "The Artist: Henry Miller: Writer with
        a Paintbrush," New York Herald Tribune, CXXII (April 29,
        1962), VI 3.
            Review of Henry Miller: Watercolors, Drawings, and
            His Essay, "The Angel Is My Watermark," where it
            is noted that Miller lacks both professional skill and
            artistic vision.

E2958   Durrell, Lawrence.   "Art and Life," Show, II (May 1962),
        80-84.
            Durrell contemplates a trip to America to see Miller.

E2959   Gard.   "Television Review," Henry Miller Literary So-
        ciety Newsletter, May 1962, 2.
            Review of Quest, a 30-minute film of Miller shown by
            the Canadian Broadcasting Company.

E2960   Schwartz, Edward P.   "A Chapter In Rome?"   Henry
        Miller Literary Society Newsletter, May 1962, 4.
            Samuel Steinman talks to Schwartz about organizing
            Rome Chapter of Miller Literary Society to bring
            Miller to more of the world.

E2961   Schwartz, Edward P.   "A Lecture," Henry Miller Literary
        Society Newsletter, May 1962, 4.
            Lecture entitled "Henry Miller: The Happy Rock" pre-
            sented by Dan Georgakas at Unstabled Theatre Club of

Detroit.

E2962   Schwartz, Edward P.   "A Library Fights Back," <u>Henry
        Miller Literary Society Newsletter</u>, May 1962, 3.
            Queens Borough Librarian Harold W. Tucker stood up
        against American Legion censorship group in defense
        of <u>Cancer</u>.

E2963   Schwartz, Edward P.   "Amazing Coverage of Martin Case
        in Evergreen Review," <u>Henry Miller Literary Society News-
        letter</u>, May 1962, 2.
            One of most detailed coverages of <u>Tropic</u> trial in
        <u>Evergreen Review</u>.

E2964   Schwartz, Edward P.   "Articles About Henry Miller,"
        <u>Henry Miller Literary Society Newsletter</u>, May 1962, 4.
            Articles include: Antoine Denat's "Henry Miller,
        Clown Baroque...," <u>Synthèses</u> (November 1961), <u>Der
        Monet and Perspektiv</u>; Peter Rohde's "Henry Miller...,"
        <u>Henry Miller--Between Heaven and Hell</u>; Joseph Del-
        teil's "Henry Miller--A Charcoal Sketch," <u>Internation-
        al Henry Miller Letter</u>; Karlheinz Deschner "Unscrew
        the Doors from Their Jambs," <u>International Henry
        Miller Letter</u>; Georges Simenon's "An Unique Fresco,"
        <u>International Miller Letter</u>; Henk van Gelre's "Henry
        Miller's Self-Discovery," <u>International Miller Letter</u>;
        R. R. Suskind's "Henry Miller in Paris," <u>Climax</u>
        (April 1962); Wayne Thell's "Henry Miller," <u>Ivory
        Tower</u>, February 5, 1962; Lonny Sher's "Henry
        Miller," <u>Topper</u>, December 1961; Donovan Bess's
        "Miller's <u>Tropic</u> Trial," <u>Evergreen Review</u>, March-
        April 1962; Maxine Renken's "Bibliography of Henry
        Miller" <u>20th Century Literature</u>, VII (January 1962);
        and Merle Amitage's "The Man Behind the Smile,"
        <u>Texas Quarterly</u>, winter 1961-1962.

E2965   Schwartz, Edward P.   "Biblio Passes 500-Mark," <u>Henry
        Miller Literary Society Newsletter</u>, May 1962, 1.
            Sale of <u>Miller Bibliography</u> continues to be successful.

E2966   Schwartz, Edward P.   "Books," <u>Henry Miller Literary So-
        ciety Newsletter</u>, May 1962, 4.
            New books by Miller include: Henry Miller: <u>Water-
        colors, Drawings, Essays, Stand Still Like the Hum-
        mingbird, Just Wild About Harry, Durrell-Miller Cor-
        respondence</u>.

E2967   Schwartz, Edward P.   "Books About Henry Miller,"
        <u>Henry Miller Literary Society Newsletter</u>, May 1962, 4.
            Books about Miller: Emil White's <u>Henry Miller--Be-
        tween Heaven and Hell</u> and Henk van Gelre's <u>Henry
        Miller--Legend and Truth</u>.

E2968   Schwartz, Edward P.   "Chicago Situation--Two Views,"
         Henry Miller Literary Society Newsletter, May 1962, 1.
                 Chief Justice Samuel B. Epstein of Chicago Circuit
                 Court allowed sale of Tropic.

E2969   Schwartz, Edward P.   "Contributions to Books," Henry
         Miller Literary Society Newsletter, May 1962, 4.
                 Miller contributed to: Visions of Censorship, Henry
                 Miller--Between Heaven and Hell, Stories of Scarlet
                 Women, Banned.

E2970   Schwartz, Edward P.   "Contributions to Periodicals,"
         Henry Miller Literary Society Newsletter, May 1962, 4.
                 Miller contributed to the following periodicals: "Henry
                 Miller at 70," Claremont Quarterly; "Interview with
                 Wickes," Paris Review; "Miller-Lowenfels Corres-
                 pondence," Outsider; "The Woman...," International
                 Henry Miller Letter; "An Unpublished Introduction...,"
                 International Henry Miller Letter; "Les Amours,"
                 Elle, December 15, 1961; "Ein Ungebundene Fuchsel-
                 biss," Between Worlds (Fall-Winter 1961-2); "One
                 Night in Tropic," Bachelor (March 1962); "Berthe,"
                 Tales from Topper (February 1962); "From 'New Re-
                 public' Mailbag," New Republic (November 8, 1943).

E2971   Schwartz, Edward P.   "Durrell's Travel Idea," Henry
         Miller Literary Society Newsletter, May 1962, 4.
                 In Show (May 1962), Durrell contemplates trip to
                 America with Miller.

E2972   Schwartz, Edward P.   "Exhibitions Held," Henry Miller
         Literary Society Newsletter, May 1962, 3.
                 Exhibition of Miller watercolors held at Ramon Lopez
                 Gallery, Siera Madre, Calif., from April 6-April 29.

E2973   Schwartz, Edward P.   "First Edition to UCLA," Henry
         Miller Literary Society Newsletter, May 1962, 4.
                 Orvis Ross presented first edition of Tropic to UCLA
                 Library.

E2974   Schwartz, Edward P.   "Important Symposium," Henry
         Miller Literary Society Newsletter, May 1962, 3.
                 Symposium on Miller found in Emil White's Henry
                 Miller.

E2975   Schwartz, Edward P.   "Last Call," Henry Miller Literary
         Society Newsletter, May 1962, 2.
                 M. E. Porter offers four copies of Henry Miller Mis-
                 cellanea for sale.

E2976   Schwartz, Edward P.   "Life Goes On," Henry Miller
         Literary Society Newsletter, May 1962, 3.
                 Library Journal notes that Glen Rock Republican Club

of New Jersey denounced Tropic as pornography.

E2977   Schwartz, Edward P.   "Little Man on Campus," Henry
Miller Literary Society Newsletter, May 1962, 3.
Cartoon of school teacher reading students Tropic.

E2978   Schwartz, Edward P.   "Miller Visits Bloom," Henry
Miller Literary Society Newsletter, May 1962, 2.
Article in Jefferson Journal of Missouri State Prison
describes Miller's visit to Roger Bloom, a criminal.

E2979   Schwartz, Edward P.   "New Long-Playing Record," Henry
Miller Literary Society Newsletter, May 1962, 3.
Miller's Henry Miller: Life As I See It, a conversation with Ben Grauer, a record the Literary Society
has for sale.

E2980   Schwartz, Edward P.   "Page One for H. M.," Henry Miller
Literary Society Newsletter, May 1962, 2.
New York Herald Tribune devoted page one of "Book
Section" to Miller.

E2981   Schwartz, Edward P.   "Point with Pride," Henry Miller
Literary Society Newsletter, May 1962, 1.
Miller left for Europe in March to take part in lite-
rary judging at Cape Formentor, Mallorca, Spain.

E2982   Schwartz, Edward P.   "Princeton Answers," Henry Miller
Literary Society Newsletter, May 1962, 3.
Article from Princetonian on November 29, 1961, con-
demning those who wish to bar Tropic.

E2983   Schwartz, Edward P.   "Puritans Progress: Drive Against
'Tropic of Cancer'," Henry Miller Literary Society Newsletter, May 1962, 1.
Tropic sold in Hawaii, New Hampshire, Chicago; not
sold in Los Angeles, Philadelphia.

E2984   Schwartz, Edward P.   "Recommended Stores," Henry
Miller Literary Society Newsletter, May 1962, 4.
List of stores that stock Miller's books and are friend-
ly to him.

E2985   Schwartz, Edward P.   "Reprints," Henry Miller Literary
Society Newsletter, May 1962, 4.
Reprints of Miller's The Time of the Assassins and
Tropic.

E2986   Schwartz, Edward P.   "Uneducated Bookworm," Henry
Miller Literary Society Newsletter, May 1962, 2.
Drawing from Ave Maria of National Catholic Weekly
criticizing those who do not read Miller.

E2987   Schwartz, Edward P.   "Whitman Quotation," Henry Miller
        Literary Society Newsletter, May 1962, 2.
            Herb Caen quoted Miller quoting Whitman when calling
            America a nation of lunatics.

E2988   Schwartz, Edward P.   "Who Did You Say?"   Henry Miller
        Literary Society Newsletter, May 1962, 3.
            William Hogan of the San Francisco Chronicle noted
            that Tropic outsold all other books when paperback
            and hardback figures are combined.

E2989   Schwartz, Edward P.   "Works in Progress," Henry Miller
        Literary Society Newsletter, May 1962, 4.
            Works including Miller: Kingsley Widmer's Pamphlets
            on American Writers.

E2990   Schwartz, Edward P.   "Would Be a Surprise," Henry
        Miller Literary Society Newsletter, May 1962, 3.
            Shapiro, who wrote the foreword to Tropic, will do
            reading in Minneapolis.

E2991   Schwartz, Edward P.   "[Cartoon]," Henry Miller Literary
        Society Newsletter, May 1962, 3.
            Cartoon of old librarian telling young child: "I said
            I don't give a damn who told you that you could read
            Tropic of Cancer."

E2992   Ustvedt, Yngvar.   "Introduksjon til Henry Miller," Samti-
        den, LXXI (May 1962), 297-305.
            Chronological look at Miller's life and work.   (In Nor-
            wegian.)

E2993   "Couple Cleared in Book Obscenity Case," Los Angeles
        Times, LXXXI (May 2, 1962), 20.
            Mr. and Mrs. Lawrence McGilvery arrested for sell-
            ing Tropic yet cleared because of free speech.

E2994   "2 Cleared in 'Tropic' Sale," New York Times, CXI (May
        3, 1962), 22.
            San Diego jury deliberated 12 hours before acquitting
            couple for sale of Tropic.

E2995   Kanters, Robert.   "Henry Miller: 'Monsieur Nicolas',"
        Le Figaro Littéraire, May-June 1962.
            All Miller work autobiographical.   (In French.)

E2996   Temple, F. J.   "Henry Miller: Interview," Mercure de
        France, CCCXLV (May-August 1962), 184-185.
            Interview in which Miller discusses friendship with
            Blaise Cendrars.   (In French.)

E2997   Widmer, Kingsley.   "The Literary Rebel," Centennial Re-
        view, VI (Spring 1962), 182-201.

Miller called one of archetypal American literary
rebels and father of the Beat Generation.

E2998   Green, Gael. "A Woman Looks at Beds, Bedbugs and
Henry Miller," Nugget, VII (June 1962), 39.

E2999   Leaming, Delmar. "Miller: The Wheel of Identity, Con-
clusion," Newton Daily News, June 1962.
Miller's writing is intensity which cleans our senses
and offends.

E3000   Moore, Everett T. " 'Tropic' Controversy: Not Yet Con-
cluded," ALA Bulletin, LVI (June 1962), 492-494.
Tropic case involves freedom to read. Won in Chicago, lost in Los Angeles, so we wait for Supreme
Court.

E3001   "A Fun Book," Times Literary Supplement, LXI (June 1,
1962), 384.
Review of Watercolors, Drawings, and "The Angel Is
My Watermark."

E3002   Backers, Clair. "Henry Miller Blasts 'Illusion'," St. Paul
Pioneer Press, CXIV (June 6, 1962), 15.
Miller feels Americans an unrealistic people who want
only life's best.

E3003   Burton, Vic. "Night Beat," Minneapolis Daily Herald,
June 8, 1962, 12.
Appearance of Miller in Minneapolis.

E3004   Schwartz, Edward P. "Henry Miller's Visit," Rocky
Mountain Herald, CIII (June 16, 1962), 12.
Description of Schwartz's excitement at Miller's visit
to Minneapolis.

E3005   Ciardi, John. "The Book Banners," Saturday Review,
XLV (June 23, 1962), 39.
Ciardi lists Miller with nine other authors whose work
suppressed.

E3006   " 'Tropic' Loses Wisconsin Test," New York Times, CXI
(June 23, 1962), 7.
Judge Ronald Drechsler called Tropic "repugnant to
decency" in Milwaukee Wisconsin trial.

E3007   "The Dry Pornographer," Time, LXXIX (June 29, 1962),
78.
Cutting review of Stand Still Like the Hummingbird
where Miller criticized for his style and simplistic
method of finding happiness.

E3008   "The Miracle," n.p., June 29, 1962.

Stand Still Like the Hummingbird a book about Miller's
inability to move as he watches society destroy itself.

E3009   Norris, Hoke. "Henry Miller," Chicago Sun-Times, XV
(June 29, 1962), 32.
Miller's Stand Still Like the Hummingbird the work of
a rebel concerned with freedom.

E3010   Ciardi, John. "Manner of Speaking: Tropic of Cancer,"
Saturday Review, XLV (June 30, 1962), 13.
Cancer a novel of protest and the stand of an indi-
vidual in an ugly world.

E3011   Moore, Harry T. "Portrait Gallery and Pet Gripes,"
Saturday Review, XLV (June 30, 1962), 18.
Moore applauds Miller's self-exposure, his exploration
into religion, money and love in review of Stand Still
Like the Hummingbird.

E3012   Lindgren, Sören; Mårten Ringten; and Pekka Tarkha. "Tre
röster om Miller," Nya Argys, LV (July 1, 1962), 174-
177.
On suppression of recent translation of Tropic. (In
Swedish.)

E3013   R., W. G. "Stand Still Like the Hummingbird," New York
Herald Tribune, CXXII (July 7, 1962), 10.
In Stand Still Like the Hummingbird, Miller discusses
Thoreau, Whitman, Sherwood Anderson, Kenneth
Patchen, and other artists.

E3014   Baxter, Annette K. "Random Brushstrokes, of a Radical
Optimist," New York Times, CXI (July 8, 1962), VII 6-7.
Reviews of Henry Miller: Watercolors, Drawings, and
His Essay "The Angel Is My Watermark" and Stand
Still Like the Hummingbird where his work is called
primitive, surreal, and expressionist (both painting
and writing).

E3015   Kirsch, Robert R. "Henry Miller Has Say ... No 4-
Letter Words," Los Angeles Times, LXXXI (July 8, 1962),
C16.
Stand Still Like the Hummingbird a belief in freedom
of artist to write, paint, sculpture, and create in any
way.

E3016   Gertz, Elmer. "Lawyer for 'Tropic of Cancer' Explains
Stand," Chicago Courier, July 14, 1962, 4.
Gertz believes in freedom and right of Cancer to exist.

E3017   "Massachusetts High Court Upsets Ban on 'Tropic', 4-3,"
New York Times, CXI (July 18, 1962), 26.
Massachusetts Supreme Court overturned state Tropic

ban though they found book dull, dreary, and offensive.

E3018   Goldstein, Larry.   " 'Banned' Books Aimed At Sex-Seeking
Reader," UCLA Summer Bruin, July 20, 1962, 4.
Freedom from censorship necessary to enter world of
Miller.

E3019   Interlandi.   "Below Olympus," Los Angeles Times, LXXXI
(July 22, 1962), C17.
Cartoon of old woman on beach saying to friend, "I
think Henry Miller ... designed bathing suits this
year!"

E3020   " 'Tropic' Ban Upset by Massachusetts Supreme Court,"
Publishers Weekly, CLXXXII (July 30, 1962), 30.
Massachusetts Supreme Court says Tropic defended by
First Amendment.

E3021   " 'Tropic of Capricorn' To Be Published Sept. 5," Publishers Weekly, CLXXXII (July 30, 1962), 32.
Notice of Capricorn's first appearance in America.

E3022   Norris, Hoke.   " 'Cancer' in Chicago," Evergreen Review,
VI (July-August 1962), 40-66.
"In this most Puritan, most evil, most enlightened,
most bedeviled, most entertaining, most dingy and
corrupt city" Tropic went to court, in a society based
on a dual ethic.

E3023   Childs, J. Rives.   "What Miller Means to Me," International Henry Miller Letter, August 1962, 11-14.
Childs compares Miller to Restif de la Bretonne: "I
look upon the license of language used by Restif and
Miller as a means chosen by them to express their
profound dissatisfaction with the world about them"
(p. 11).

E3024   Denat, Antoine.   "Henry Miller: Baroque Clown and
Prophet Triumphant," International Henry Miller Letter,
August 1962, 16-22.
Miller seen depicting confusion of life and many-
sidedness of the self.   He uses Bergson and his ideas
about creative evolution.

E3025   Gelre, Henk van.   "Attention!" International Henry Miller
Letter, August 1962, 3.
Daniel A. de Graaf, the Dutch Rimbaud specialist,
feels Miller is the literary giant of our time.

E3026   Graaf, Daniel A. de.   "The Rimbaldian Henry Miller,"
International Henry Miller Letter, August 1962, 4-10.
Miller compared to Rimbaud, for both changed litera-
ture.

E3027   Matarasso, H. "A Letter from H. Matarasso," International Henry Miller Letter, August 1962, 15.
Praise of Miller's evaluation of Rimbaud as a magical
being in The Time of the Assassins.

E3028   Interlandi. "Below Olympus," Minneapolis Tribune, XCVI
(August 12, 1962), W21.
See E3019.

E3029   "Radio Series Set on Henry Miller," Minneapolis Tribune,
XCVI (August 12, 1962), W21.
Announcement that Miller will be heard over KUOM
Radio.

E3030   "3 Guilty in Obscenity Case," New York Times, CXI
(August 14, 1962), 22.
Three Syracuse, N.Y., booksellers, all employees of
the Economy Book Store, found guilty of selling obscene literature.

E3031   Mottram, Eric. "Laughing Jeremiah," Spectator, August
17, 1962, 219-220.
Review of four Miller books, Tropic of Cancer,
Tropic of Capricorn, Air-Conditioned Nightmare, Colossus of Maroussi. In each, Miller rejects "cancer"
(conformity) in favor of chaos.

E3032   Ackroyd, Graham T. "The Joy of Henry Miller," Painter
and Sculptor, V (Summer 1962), 18-21.
Miller has painted since 1927 and feels he expresses
himself better in this medium than in writing.

E3033   Delteil, Joseph. "Henry Miller (fusain)," Aylesford Review, IV (Summer 1962), 278-280.
Miller a man of contradictions, a renegade, a liberated man, a saint. (In French.)

E3034   Lowenfels, Walter. "Editorial, The Outsider," Outsider,
I (Summer 1962), 74.
Same letter as Outsider, No. 1.

E3035   Sewell, M. Brocard. "Editorial," Aylesford Review, IV
(Summer 1962), 245-246.
Miller's article on Delteil in Two Cities caused Ayles-
ford Review to contact Miller.

E3036   Sewell, M. Brocard. "Joseph Delteil's 'Jesus II'," Aylesford Review, IV (Summer 1962), 251-260.
Miller finds excitement in all Delteil's books.

E3037   Gertz, Elmer. "I Meet Henry Miller," Henry Miller
Literary Society Newsletter, September 1962, 3.
Gertz, the lawyer who defended Tropic in Chicago,

finds Miller charming.

E3038   Mallory, T. O.   "Nation," Abstracts of English Studies,
         V (September 1962), 335.
                 Terry Southern balances Miller's optimism with mor-
                 bidity.

E3039   Moore, Thomas H.   "Tom Moore on Miller," Henry Miller
         Literary Society Newsletter, September 1962, 3.
                 Moore's description is a Miller self-quote from Capri-
                 corn.

E3040   Schwartz, Edward P.   "About Robert Gover," Henry Miller
         Literary Society Newsletter, September 1962, 1.
                 Miller delighted with Gover's novel, One Hundred
                 Dollar Misunderstanding.

E3041   Schwartz, Edward P.   "At ALA Sessions," Henry Miller
         Literary Society Newsletter, September 1962, 1.
                 Robert S. McClure predicted that U.S. Supreme Court
                 would free Tropic for distribution.

E3042   Schwartz, Edward P.   "Bare Facts," Henry Miller Lite-
         rary Society Newsletter, September 1962, 1.
                 Erotica from Miller that makes censors howl is noth-
                 ing compared to articles on woman's fashions.

E3043   Schwartz, Edward P.   "Book Club Choice," Henry Miller
         Literary Society Newsletter, September 1962, 1.
                 Hudson Book Club announces Capricorn as future se-
                 lection.

E3044   Schwartz, Edward P.   "Childs' Collection," Henry Miller
         Literary Society Newsletter, September 1962, 4.
                 J. Rives Childs, former U.S. ambassador, spoke on
                 Miller at Randolph-Macon College, Va.   His vast
                 Miller collection goes to College on his death.

E3045   Schwartz, Edward P.   "Ciardi Reprints from S/R," Henry
         Miller Literary Society Newsletter, September 1962, 4.
                 John Ciardi to speak on Tropic.

E3046   Schwartz, Edward P.   " 'Hamlet'--New Edition?" Henry
         Miller Literary Society Newsletter, September 1962, 3.
                 Walker-de Berry, Inc., considering reprinting Hamlet.

E3047   Schwartz, Edward P.   "He Came, He Saw, Etc.," Henry
         Miller Literary Society Newsletter, September 1962, 3.
                 Schwartz described meeting Miller for first time.

E3048   Schwartz, Edward P.   "McGilverys Cleared," Henry Miller
         Literary Society Newsletter, September 1962, 4.
                 Legal status of Tropic remains in doubt in San Diego.

E3049   Schwartz, Edward P. "New Miller Items," Henry Miller Literary Society Newsletter, September 1962, 1.
New Miller items are: Stand Still Like the Humming-bird; Tropic of Capricorn; "Paris la Nuit" Evergreen Review; Hoke Norris's "Tropic Case in Chicago" Evergreen Review; Perlès' My Friend Henry Miller; Elmer Gertz's "Test Case" Focus; Gael Greene's "A Woman Looks at Beds...," Nugget; Paris Review Interview.

E3050   Schwartz, Edward P. "Rabbi on Censorship," Henry Miller Literary Society Newsletter, September 1962, 4.
Rabbi Dudley Weinberg discussed censorship, yet never referred directly to Tropic.

E3051   Schwartz, Edward P. "Right to Read," Henry Miller Literary Society Newsletter, September 1962, 1.
Nearly 200 leading American writers and critics supported Judge Epstein's statement that Tropic was not obscene.

E3052   Schwartz, Edward P. "Search Goes On!" Henry Miller Literary Society Newsletter, September 1962, 1.
Miller Literary Society always searching for Miller items.

E3053   Schwartz, Edward P. "Sold Out in Finland," Henry Miller Literary Society Newsletter, September 1962, 4.
When Finnish authorities decided to confiscate Cancer, the bookstores had already sold out.

E3054   Schwartz, Edward P. " 'Tropic' Ban Upset by Massachusetts Court," Henry Miller Literary Society Newsletter, September 1962, 1.
Supreme Court of Massachusetts lifts state ban on Tropic.

E3055   Schwartz, Edward P. "Where Did They Go?" Henry Miller Literary Society Newsletter, September 1962, 4.
Aller Retour New York impossible to find in first edition says J. Rives Childs.

E3056   Stein, Shelly. "Minneapolis Visitor," Henry Miller Literary Society Newsletter, September 1962, 4.
Shelly Stein, sales representative of Grove Press, spoke of publication of Capricorn.

E3057   Shattuck, Robert. "A Loner's Lark Through Brooklyn," New York Times, CXI (September 2, 1962), VII 6.
Capricorn shows Miller's loner personality, his savage intellect, and his imaginary autobiography or self-journalism.

E3058   Stanley, Donald. "Miller's Second 'Tropic'," San Francisco

Examiner (September 2, 1962), H2.
Capricorn autobiographical account of Miller in New
York at Cosmodemonic Telegraph Company.

E3059   Alexander, Philippe.   "Nous autres les maudits, nous
sommes des gens très ordinaires," Candide Lettres,
September 5, 1962, 13.
Durrell, Mailer, and Miller spoke in Edinburgh.   Dur-
rell called Miller a great writer misunderstood.   (In
French.)

E3060   "A Distinguished Address," Lynchburg (Va.) News, XCVI
(September 7, 1962), A4.
Childs spoke about the merits of Miller's work.

E3061   Scruggs, Philip Lightfoot.   "Editorial," Lynchburg (Va.)
News, XCVI (September 7, 1962), 6.
James Rives Childs gave address on "The Rewards of
Book Collecting" on May 30, at Randolph-Macon Col-
lege, where he defended Miller.

E3062   "Tropic B," Time, LXXX (September 7, 1962), 80.
Capricorn a study of heart over mind or self-
consciousness.

E3063   Norris, Hoke.   "Sledgehammer and Broadsword: 'Tropic
of Capricorn'," Saturday Review, XLV (September 8,
1962), 23, 50.
Both Capricorn and Cancer exciting, funny, warm,
and nostalgic.

E3064   Kluger, Richard.   "Splattering the Puritans," New York
Herald Tribune, CXXII (September 9, 1962), VI 4.
Capricorn a fiery book against America, a nightmare
about the American dream turned sour.

E3065   "Fined for Selling Miller Book," New York Times, CXI
(September 11, 1962), 20.
In Syracuse Court, Judge Rocco Regietano fined book-
store manager for selling Tropic.

E3066   Winters, Warrington.   " 'Absolutely Crazy and Chaotic',"
Nation, CXCV (September 15, 1962), 135-136.
Miller seen as tie between Whitman and Kerouac, a
surrealistic naturalist soaked in Bergson and topped
with Dada in Capricorn.

E3067   Kirsch, Robert R.   "Why Is Everybody Mad at Henry
Miller?" Los Angeles Times, LXXXI (September 23,
1962), C1, 14.
Miller uses emotion of outrage, surprise, and recognition in Capricorn to shock reader into realizing horror of society.

E3068   Wickes, George.   "Henry Miller: The Art of Fiction
XXVIII," Paris Review, VII (Summer-Fall 1962), 129-159.
Interview with Miller where he discusses his writing
and the process he uses to create his literature.

E3069   Blond, Anthony.   "Unshockable Edinburgh," Books and
Bookmen, VII (October 1962), 26-27.
Miller heralded at Writer's Conference in Edinburgh
as major mover of literature in the 20th century by
Mary McCarthy, Lawrence Durrell, and Colin MacInnes.

E3070   Gerstenberger, Donna.   "Evergreen Review," Abstracts of
English Studies, V (October 1962), 396-397.
Tropic trials are best way to depict the cancer Miller
sees.

E3071   Link, Franz H.   "Monat," Abstracts of English Studies, V
(October 1962), 409.
Denat sees Miller as a clown concerned with flux.

E3072   Moore, Everett T.   "Massachusetts Provides First Major
Tropic Decision," ALA Bulletin, LVI (October 1962), 785-
786.
Massachusetts Supreme Court provides Tropic with
First Amendment rights and protection.

E3073   Rocher, Pierre.   "Province," Nie Metir, October 1962.
Review of Air-Conditioned Nightmare that agrees with
Miller that Americans are childish and which sup-
ports France.   (In French.)

E3074   "Miller Novel Case Taken to Appellate Court," Los Ange-
les Times, LXXXI (October 16, 1962), 18.
Tropic taken to Appellate Department of Los Angeles
Superior Court.

E3075   "Supreme Court Rejects Obscene Book Appeal," Los Angeles Times, LXXXI (October 16, 1962), 18.
U.S. Supreme Court will not hear appeals on Tropic.

E3076   O'Brien, R. A.   "Mr. What's-His-Name," Nation, CXCV
(October 20, 1962), 245.
Review of Stand Still Like the Hummingbird that calls
this collection a celebration of the individual: "He is
one with all the great American social critics and
rebels, from 'Thoreau, Whitman, Emerson' to Lewis
and Mencken ..." (p. 245).

E3077   De Witt, Gene E.   "Henry Miller's 'Unstitched Wound',"
Blue Guitar, Fall 1962, 18-21.
Key metaphor in Tropic the 'unstitched wound,' as
work gushes forth; it is a tour de force.

E3078   Evans, Oliver. "Anaïs Nin and the Discovery of Inner
Space," Prairie Schooner, XXXVI (Fall 1962), 217-231.
Miller states Nin's Diary is a monumental work.

E3079   Shapiro, Karl. "Henry Miller: Important Reprints,"
Prairie Schooner, XXXVI (Fall 1962), 287-288.
Shapiro feels one finds choice Miller in Cosmological
Eye, Sunday After the War, and Remember to Remem-
ber, for the essays in these works among the best in
the English language.

E3080   "Henry Miller Faces Arrest in Case Here," New York
Times, CXII (November 2, 1962), 39.
Warrant for Miller's arrest issued in Brooklyn Criminal Court because of Miller's failure to appear on obscenity charge.

E3081   "Henry Miller Warrant Out," New York Post, CLXI (November 2, 1962), 26.
Judge Gomez of Brooklyn Criminal Court issued warrant for Miller's arrest in New York.

E3082   Droit, Michel. "Miller et le juge de Brooklyn," Le Figaro Littéraire, November 10, 1962, 1.
Brooklyn judge wishes to arrest Miller.   (In French.)

E3083   " 'Tropic' Test Suit Reinstated," New York Times, CXII
(November 14, 1962), 52.
Rochester, N.Y., court seeks ruling on whether Tropic
obscene.

E3084   Chiew, Ooi. "The Singapore News," Variety, November
14, 1962.
Malayan police seized copies of Cancer.

E3085   "Author Evaluates Unusual Album," Jefferson Journal, December 1962, 5.
Roger Bloom, serving life sentence in prison, visited
by Miller.

E3086   "Home Town Strikes Back," Henry Miller Literary Society
Newsletter, December 1962, 5.
Satire about warrant issued for Miller's arrest in
Brooklyn.

E3087   Brassaï. "Henry Miller in Paris, 1932," International
Henry Miller Letter, December 1962, 7.
Photo of a younger Miller standing with cigarette in
hand.

E3088   Denat, Antoine. "Henry Miller: Baroque Clown and
Prophet Triumphant," International Henry Miller Letter,
December 1962, 4-11.

Miller overflows with life and defies fixed forms,
which can be seen through the metaphor of the clown.

E3089 Gelre, Henk van. "Dear Friends," International Henry
Miller Letter, December 1962, 3.
Gelre speaks about his desire to publish recollections
of one of figures of Tropic.

E3090 Robitaille, Gerald. "Cher Maître," International Henry
Miller Letter, December 1962, 12-18.
Admiration of Miller's control of words. The metaphor of the swamp used to portray the raw natural-
ness of Miller's writing.

E3091 Schwartz, Edward P. "About WC 'Shows'," Henry Miller
Literary Society Newsletter, December 1962, 2.
Requests for Miller to exhibit watercolors goes un-
heard.

E3092 Schwartz, Edward P. "Articles About H. M.," Henry
Miller Literary Society Newsletter, December 1962, 4.
Articles about Miller found in Book Review Digest,
Letters of H. L. Mencken (pp. 409-470), Bulletin of
American Library Association, LV (pp. 779-780), En-
counter XVI (pp. 69-75), Greece, the Painter and
Sculptor V (Summer 1962), Jan Valek's Henry Miller,
International Miller Letter (August 1962), Criterion I
(Summer 1962), Elmer Gertz's Handful of Cases,
Theodore Solotaroff's An Age of Enormity, Aylesford
Review (Summer 1962), Blue Guitar (Fall 1962).

E3093 Schwartz, Edward P. "Awarded to Judge," Henry Miller
Literary Society Newsletter, December 1962, 3.
1962 Intellectual Freedom Award of Illinois Library
Association presented to Samuel B. Epstein for his
ruling in favor of Tropic in Chicago.

E3094 Schwartz, Edward P. "Best on Mexico," Henry Miller
Literary Society Newsletter, December 1962, 4.
John Wilcock did great comic strip of Miller pleading
for publication of Tropic.

E3095 Schwartz, Edward P. "Books About H. M.," Henry Miller
Literary Society Newsletter, December 1962, 4.
Books about Miller published: Maxine Renken's Bibli-
ography of H. M.; Feltrinelli's Prefazione ai Tropici;
Kingsley Widmer's Henry Miller; George Wickes'
Henry Miller and the Critics; Jacques den Haan's
Milleriana; H. Bowden's Henry Miller; John G.
Moore's The Longitude and Latitude of Henry Miller.

E3096 Schwartz, Edward P. " 'Capricorn' Reviews," Henry
Miller Literary Society Newsletter, December 1962, 4.

Best reviews of Capricorn written by Robert Kirsch of
L.A. Times, Eric Moon of Library Journal, John K.
Sherman of Minneapolis Tribune, and Richard Seaver
of Hudson Book Club Bulletin.

E3097 Schwartz, Edward P. "Contributions to Books," Henry
Miller Literary Society Newsletter, December 1962, 4.
Miller contributed to the following: The World of Law,
365 Days, Prefazione ai Tropici, The World of Lawrence Durrell, Lausanne, Aylesford Review, H.M. and
the Critics, Writers at Work.

E3098 Schwartz, Edward P. "Contributions to Periodicals,"
Henry Miller Literary Society Newsletter, December 1962,
4.
Miller contributed to following periodicals: Aylesford
Review, Harper's Bazaar (October 1962), L'Herne (No-
vember 1962), Outsider, Olympia Review (November
1962), Review of English Literature IV, Mademoiselle
(January 1963).

E3099 Schwartz, Edward P. "Dear Ol' Brooklyn!" Henry Miller
Literary Society Newsletter, December 1962, 3.
Grand jury accused Miller of violating penal code
through writing obscene literature.

E3100 Schwartz, Edward P. "Don't Miss This!" Henry Miller
Literary Society Newsletter, December 1962, 3.
Lawrence Durrell and Henry Miller brings together
the personal letters from this 25-year-old correspondence.

E3101 Schwartz, Edward P. "Far East News," Henry Miller
Literary Society Newsletter, December 1962, 1.
Ooi Chiew reporting the Singapore news to Variety
noted that in Malaya police seized copies of Tropic.

E3102 Schwartz, Edward P. "From the Daily Princetonian,"
Henry Miller Literary Society Newsletter, December 1962,
2.
The Daily Princetonian on November 29, 1961, noted
that such dangers to our society as Tropic only expand
our freedom.

E3103 Schwartz, Edward P. "Henry Miller on Writing," Henry
Miller Literary Society Newsletter, December 1962, 4.
Thomas Moore editing best selections of Miller's writ-
ing.

E3104 Schwartz, Edward P. "Idea From Rome," Henry Miller
Literary Society Newsletter, December 1962, 3.
Samuel Steinman sends Miller Literary Society steady
stream of clips from European publications on Miller.

E3105   Schwartz, Edward P.   "In Memoriam," Henry Miller Lite-
        rary Society Newsletter, December 1962, 4.
                Miller penned a story called "The Story of George
                Dibbern's 'Quest'. "

E3106   Schwartz, Edward P.   "Lecture," Henry Miller Literary
        Society Newsletter, December 1962, 4.
                Cancer talk given by Elmer Gertz, lawyer who de-
                fended book.

E3107   Schwartz, Edward P.   "Librarian Says 'Yes'," Henry
        Miller Literary Society Newsletter, December 1962, 4.
                City Librarian, Harold L. Hamil, approved Tropic of
                Capricorn for inclusion in Los Angeles Library.

E3108   Schwartz, Edward P.   "Lose in Syracuse," Henry Miller
        Literary Society Newsletter, December 1962, 4.
                Manager of Economy Bookstore in Syracuse fined $150
                for selling Tropic.

E3109   Schwartz, Edward P.   "Miller at His Best," Henry Miller
        Literary Society Newsletter, December 1962, 1.
                Miller at best after satisfying meal and pleasant com-
                panionship.

E3110   Schwartz, Edward P.   "Miller on Censorship," Henry
        Miller Literary Society Newsletter, December 1962, 1.
                Miller and Durrell discussed censorship during Edin-
                burgh Conference, a discussion published by BBC.

E3111   Schwartz, Edward P.   "Miller Water-Colors," Henry
        Miller Literary Society Newsletter, December 1962, 3.
                Several original Miller watercolors and copies of The
                Happy Rock available from Mrs. M. E. Porter.

E3112   Schwartz, Edward P.   "More on 'Harry'," Henry Miller
        Literary Society Newsletter, December 1962, 3.
                Just Wild About Harry the story about a young man
                whose attraction for the ladies leads to farce as well
                as tragedy.

E3113   Schwartz, Edward P.   "Movie," Henry Miller Literary So-
        ciety Newsletter, December 1962, 4.
                Film of The Smile at the Foot of the Ladder to be
                produced by Patricia Hardesty.

E3114   Schwartz, Edward P.   " 'Naked Lunch' Reviewed," Henry
        Miller Literary Society Newsletter, December 1962, 1.
                Many reviewers compared Burroughs's Naked Lunch to
                Tropic, however critic John Wain says that Miller is
                affirmative, while Burroughs is not.

E3115   Schwartz, Edward P.   "Out of the Darkness Came Light,"

Henry Miller Literary Society Newsletter, December 1962,
3.
   Schwartz continues to discuss Miller's visit to Minneapolis.

E3116   Schwartz, Edward P.   "Poems About H. M. ," Henry Miller
Literary Society Newsletter, December 1962, 4.
   Poems about Miller include: George Seferis's "Les
Anges sont blancs," Quarterly Review of Literature,
X (1959); James Hiner's "For God, in Case Henry
Miller Dies," Coastlines (1962).

E3117   Schwartz, Edward P.   "Radio," Henry Miller Literary So-
ciety Newsletter, December 1962, 4.
   Radio programs on Miller: Jim Crockett adapting
Smile and Staff of Life into four-part reading at Uni-
versity of Idaho; Charles Seigferth's Portrait of Henry
Miller aired in San Francisco; David Sliger to discuss
Syracuse Tropic Case and Censorship.

E3118   Schwartz, Edward P.   "Radio Script Published," Henry
Miller Literary Society Newsletter, December 1962, 1.
   Radio script of University of Minnesota KUOM featur-
ing voices of Professor Alan Trachtenberg, Elmer
Gertz, and Miller published.

E3119   Schwartz, Edward P.   "Rap Book Censors," Henry Miller
Literary Society Newsletter, December 1962, 3.
   Miller attacked by National Council of Teachers of
English.

E3120   Schwartz, Edward P.   "Reprints & Translations," Henry
Miller Literary Society Newsletter, December 1962, 4.
   Cancer published in Hebrew, Finnish, Dutch, Italian;
Capricorn in Italian and Spanish; Obscenity and the Law
of Reflection in Italian; Smile at the Foot of the Lad-
der in Finnish and Czech; Air-Conditioned Nightmare
in Italian; Devil in Paradise in Italian; Henry Miller
Reader in German; Just Wild About Harry in German.

E3121   Schwartz, Edward P.   "Theses," Henry Miller Literary
Society Newsletter, December 1962, 4.
   Theses on Miller include: Ronald Kesselring's master's
thesis (Syracuse University); Edward Mitchell's Ph.D.
dissertation (University of Connecticut); Carter Burden's undergraduate thesis (Harvard); Leonard Cheev-
er's master's thesis (Trinity University); Gil Muller's
honor's thesis (University of Kentucky).

E3122   Schwartz, Edward P.   "Trinity College Scores a 'First'
with Miller Day," Henry Miller Literary Society Newsletter, December 1962, 1.
   Trinity College, Hartford, Conn. , devoted day to

Miller, his books, watercolors, recordings.

E3123   Schwartz, Edward P. "T. V. ," Henry Miller Literary Society Newsletter, December 1962, 4.
Smile at Foot of Ladder to be produced for television
in Paris.

E3124   Schwartz, Edward P. "Who'll Play Miller?" Henry Miller
Literary Society Newsletter, December 1962, 2.
Cancer to be made into film with Bernie Wolfe doing
the writing.

E3125   White, William. "Dylan Thomas on Henry Miller," International Henry Miller Letter, December 1962, 11.
Thomas likes Miller's anti-literature, however he objects to Miller's use of the old literary way to achieve
this stance.

E3126   Wain, John. "The Great Burroughs Affair," New Republic,
CXLVII (December 1, 1962), 21-23.
Review of Burroughs's Naked Lunch where Wain says
it can not be compared to Tropic: "Miller is an affirmative writer. The 'I' of Miller's writing ... is a
figure who has achieved complete liberation ... " (p.
21).

E3127   "Prizes and Awards," Publishers Weekly, CLXXXII (December 3, 1962), 28.
Judge Samuel Epstein won the 1962 Intellectual Freedom Award for his ruling on Tropic.

E3128   Rowan, Richard. "Henry Miller," Guardian, December 6,
1962, 8.
Rowan describes first meeting Miller, a happy man.

E3129   "Book News: Judge Honored," Los Angeles Times, LXXXII
(December 16, 1962), C21.
Illinois Library Association's 1962 Intellectual Freedom
Award presented to Judge Epstein for Tropic opinion.

E3130   Schumach, Murray. " 'Tropic of Cancer' Is Scheduled as
a Movie," New York Times, CXII (December 19, 1962), 4.
Tropic movie to appear.

E3131   Ames, Evelyn. "Eric Barker--Figure in a Landscape, "
Literary Review, VII (1963), 40-50.
Big Sur and Miller mentioned.

E3132   Connolly, Cyril. "Miller, the Premature Beatnik," n. p. ,
1963.
Tropic an autobiographical work about sex that is adolescent.

E3133   "Henry Miller and the Critics," Psychiatric Quarterly
         Supplement, 1963, part 2.
             Wickes's Henry Miller and the Critics described as
             Miller's adolescent revolt.

E3134   Okumura, Osamu.   'Henry Miller and the Self-Liberation
         Problem." Aoyama Journal of General Education [Tokyo],
         1963, 21-40.   (In Japanese.)
             Miller resists the conventional forms of the novel, for
             Miller "completely ignores the literary divisions of
             genre" (p. 21).   He is concerned with life itself in
             both Tropics, The Air-Conditioned Nightmare, Sexus
             and The Smile at the Foot of the Ladder.

E3135   S., C.   "The Edinburgh Drama Conference," n.p., 1963,
         20.
             Just Wild About Harry discussed.

E3136   "Salgs-succes i verrnekredsen," n.p., 1963.
             Tropic published in England.   (In Danish.)

E3137   Squirru, Rafael.   "Correspondencia Durrell-Miller," Eco
         Contemporaneo, 1963, 139-144.
             Durrell-Miller Correspondence seen as important ex-
             ample of the relationship of two of the world's great
             authors.   (In Spanish.)

E3138   Dalton, Jack P.   " 'A More Modern Instance,' Henry
         Miller's Tropic of Cancer," A Wake Newsletter, January
         1963, 8-10.
             Cancer believed to have been begun by Miller in 1924.

E3139   Durrell, Lawrence and Henry Miller.   "Lawrence Durrell
         and Henry Miller: A Private Correspondence," Made-
         moiselle, LVI (January 1963), 60-63, 103-106.
             Letters of admiration from Miller to Durrell and vice
             versa.

E3140   Fukunaga, Takahiko.   'Solace Oneself with Art: All About
         Watercolor of Henry Miller," Geijutsu Seikatsu, XVI
         (January 1963), 50-59.
             Miller's watercolors explored and viewed.   (In Japa-
             nese.)

E3141   White, William.   'H.M. in 1962: An Article About Henry
         Miller," American Book Collector, VIII (January 1963), 8-
         10.
             Look at Miller's canon to 1962, his fame, yet the poor
             quality of the criticism written of his work.

E3142   "Banned Novel to Be Published," London Times, January
         27, 1963, 23.
             Tropic to be published by John Calder.

E3143   Reinert, Otto. "Samtiden," Abstracts of English Studies,
        VI (February 1963), 79.
        Sex is Miller's primary means to self-realization.
        (In Danish.)

E3144   Riseley, Jerry B.   "No Coffee and Soup," San Fernando
        Valley Bar Bulletin, February 1963.
        Tropic viewed as violation to moral code.

E3145   Ciardi, John.   "Concrete Prose and the Cement Mind,"
        Saturday Review, XLVI (February 9, 1963), 17.
        Ciardi mocks the law process based on jargon and
        stupidity, for this process condemns Tropic.

E3146   "Supreme Court Gets Miller Novel Case," Los Angeles
        Times, LXXXII (February 14, 1963), III 14.
        Bradley R. Smith's California conviction appealed to
        U.S. Supreme Court.

E3147   Gertz, Elmer.   "Miller and Durrell ... Private Corres-
        pondence," Chicago Daily News, LXXXVIII (February 16,
        1963), P10-11.
        Review of Lawrence Durrell and Henry Miller where
        Gertz feels the understanding between the two men
        bridges all distances.

E3148   Bess, Donovan.   "Two Authors Lifted One Another by the
        Bootstraps," San Francisco Chronicle, XCIX (February 17,
        1963), TW30.
        Lawrence Durrell and Henry Miller tells of admiration
        of two authors for each other.

E3149   Leland, Gerry.   "Durrell-Miller Letters," Charlotte Ob-
        server, February 17, 1963, 5C.
        Durrell and Miller: A Private Correspondence begins
        with Durrell as pupil and later as Miller's equal for
        Alexandria Quartet.

E3150   Weinstock, Matt.   "Nailed: Bald Lie About Wambly,"
        Los Angeles Times, LXXXII (February 17, 1963), G7.
        Bald a character in Tropic.

E3151   "Tropic of Alexandria," Newsweek, LXI (February 18,
        1963), 94-95.
        Durrell-Miller Correspondence seen as a slight on
        Miller's ability to write.

E3152   Carroll, Paul.   "Is Miller Really a Puritan?" Saturday
        Review, XLVI (February 23, 1963), 29.
        Miller seen in Puritan tradition of Jonathan Edwards,
        Hawthorne, and Melville, a man looking for a state of
        purity that ended when Eve ate the apple.

E3153   Moon, Eric.   "From the Twosome, a Quartet," Saturday
Review, XLVI (February 23, 1963), 28-29.
Review of Durrell-Miller Correspondence in which Miller
is called a "steamroller" who avoids interaction.

E3154   "Cancer: One New Case & Four Old Ones," Newsletter on
Intellectual Freedom, XII (March 1963), 22.
California Supreme Court reviews four Tropic cases.

E3155   Millett, Kate.   "Henry Miller," English Literature, March
1963, 72-90.
Miller viewed as sex prophet, a mover of the "Beat
Generation," a hero above law and morality, an anarchist, an anti-materialist.

E3156   Ross, Virginia L.   "Cancer in California," Newsletter on
Intellectual Freedom, XII (March 1963), 22.
California cases involving Tropic question legal rights
of book.

E3157   "Larry & Henry," Time, LXXXI (March 1, 1963), 80.
Review of Durrell-Miller Correspondence where Dur-
rel considers Tropic to be truly great.

E3158   "Lively Letters of Miller and Durrell," St. Louis Globe
Democrat, CXI (March 2-3, 1963), 4F.
Correspondence called spontaneous.

E3159   H., B. H.   'New Play by Miller 'Routine'," Anniston
(Ala.) Star, March 3, 1963.
Just Wild About Harry typical barroom.

E3160   "Just Wild About Harry," St. Louis Globe Democrat, CXI
(March 3, 1963), 4F.
Miller play depicts love of life and of human behavior.

E3161   "Plays In Print," Sacramento Bee, March 3, 1963.
Just Wild About Harry in modern tradition of Ionesco.

E3162   "Any Outlook," Miami News, March 10, 1963.
Just Wild About Harry full of fun and bursting with
life.

E3163   T., H. F.   "Just Wild About Harry," Wilmington News
(March 11, 1963).
Just Wild About Harry could have been written by 12-
year-old.

E3164   Wright, Giles E.   "Miller Gets Tedious," Los Angeles
Herald Examiner, XCII (March 11, 1963), D2.
Black Spring shows Miller's Puritan heart.

E3165   F., G. W.   "Just Wild About Harry," Washington Star

News, CXI (March 17, 1963), C6.
Review calls Harry rotten play.

E3166   T., D. "Benefits of Henry Miller of Doubtful Value Here,"
Washington Star, CXI (March 17, 1963), C6.
Just Wild About Harry leads one to feel Miller should
stick to novels.

E3167   De Waskin, Ronald M. "New Medium of Conversation:
Tropic of Capricorn," Oracle, I (March 18, 1963), 1, 4.
Capricorn a book about alienation and self-liberation.

E3168   Hertz, Murray. "Book Banning--A Hitler Tactic," Las
Vegas Review-Journal, March 21, 1963.
Banning Tropic outright insult to American freedom.

E3169   "Tropic of Cancer: How Will the Law Treat Henry Mill-
er?" Scene, March 23, 1963, 12-15.
Tropic to be published for first time in Britain on
March 28.

E3170   Kirsch, Robert R. "The Miller-Durrell Letters," Los
Angeles Times, LXXXII (March 28, 1963), IV 4.
Durrell-Miller Correspondence consists of letters of
praise and rebuke between two literary giants.

E3171   Waiman, Donald. "More Magazines Banned in Vegas,"
Las Vegas Review Journal, March 28, 1963.
Free-for-all debate over merits of Cancer held in City
Hall.

E3172   "The Guy That Wrote Those Dirty Books," Observer Weekend Review, March 31, 1963, 24.
Miller legend, because of his books about sex and the
social criticism of him, leads many not to understand
him at all.

E3173   "Henry Miller Turns Out His First Play," Detroit News,
XC (March 31, 1963), 3G.
Just Wild About Harry for theatre of absurd.

E3174   Durrell, Lawrence. "An Exchange of Letters Between
Henry Miller and Lawrence Durrell," Paris Review, VIII
(Winter/Spring 1963), 133-159.
Durrell voices his love and amazement over Cancer.

E3175   Wickes, George. "Introduction: An Exchange of Letters
Between Henry Miller and Lawrence Durrell," Paris Review,
VIII (Winter/Spring 1963), 134.
In August 1935, Durrell read Tropic and was so taken
with book that he wrote Miller a letter which began
their friendship and correspondence.

E3176 Bloom, Lynn Z. "American Book Collector," Abstracts of English Studies, VI (April 1963), 146.
William White's "H. M. in 1962" presents a short annotated bibliography that lists writings by and about Miller.

E3177 Gerstenberger, Donna. "Evergreen Review," Abstracts of English Studies, VI (April 1963), 171.
Hoke Norris sees Tropic as valuable literature.

E3178 Gerstenberger, Donna. "Evergreen Review," Abstracts of English Studies, VI (April 1963), 171.
Harry T. Moore testified for Tropic in the Boston trial.

E3179 Watson, W. H. C. "The Fifth Horseman," Scotsman, April 1963.
Miller called an individual living in a state of chaos.

E3180 Wickes, George. "For Obscenity Against Pornography," Books and Bookmen, VIII (April 1963), 5-6, 51-54.
Wickes interviews Miller.

E3181 Allsop, Kenneth. "Frankly, I Rate Miller a Boring Foul-Mouthed Old Gasbag," Daily Mail, April 4, 1963.
Tropic called comic bragging.

E3182 "The Escape Route Leads Back to the Swamp Again," Daily Worker, April 4, 1963, 2.
Tropic a masterpiece of the uninhibited ego.

E3183 Hertz, Murray. "Murray-Go-Round," Las Vegas Review Journal, April 4, 1963.
Hertz feels that in any country where one needs a Literary Society to get one elected, there exists an oppressive government.

E3184 Lindblom, Noel. "Sell-Out for a 'Banned' Book," London Times Herald, April 4, 1963.
Tropic sold in England for first time.

E3185 "We Must Accept That the Time for Blushing Is Over...," Daily Mirror, April 4, 1963, 13.
Tropic in England changes country's whole approach to sex through base emotions.

E3186 MacInnis, Colin. "Benevolent Faun," Spectator, April 5, 1963, 437.
Miller called a prophet who seeks truth, accepts life, and refuses to allow deception.

E3187 " 'Tropic of Cancer' Sold in the Open in Britain," New York Times, CXII (April 5, 1963), 44.

John Calder published Tropic in Great Britain.

E3188   C., P. M. "The Reviewer Doesn't Get the Message,"
St. Paul Dispatch, April 6, 1963.
Just Wild About Harry avant-garde yet dead.

E3189   Brauns, Robert. "A Play by Miller," Peninsula Living,
April 7, 1963.
Just Wild About Harry not fresh or new.

E3190   Dennis, Nigel. "The Scribbling on the Wall," Sunday Telegram, April 7, 1963.
Tropic means free speech in England.

E3191   Fass, Martin. "1934 Autobiography by Miller Published
First Time in U.S.," Los Angeles Times, LXXXII (April
7, 1963), Cal 16.
Black Spring in process of attacking and destroying the
romantic in our society.

E3192   H., E. N. "Henry Miller Writes a Play," New Haven
Register, (April 7, 1963).
Just Wild About Harry the tired story of a girl re-
jected by her seducer.

E3193   Morse, Walter. "Slices of Life in Early 1900s," Chicago
Sun-Times, XVI (April 7, 1963), III 2.
Black Spring evokes real life in Brooklyn at turn of
century, while Just Wild About Harry a fraud.

E3194   Wain, John. "Henry Miller at His Boisterous Best,"
London Observer, April 7, 1963, 24.
Tropic a statement for life, adventure, and the indi-
vidual.

E3195   Young, Gavin. "The Definition of 'Dirt'," London Observer, April 7, 1963, 2.
No one nationwide attitude toward Tropic in U.S.

E3196   "Black Spring," Newsweek, LXI (April 8, 1963), 99.
Black Spring light and humorous, unlike the Tropics.

E3197   Wainwright, Arthur. "Delirium and Joy in the 'Best' of
the Early Miller Novels," Chicago Daily News, LXXXVIII
(April 10, 1963), 34.
Black Spring leaps back and forth between New York
and Paris, presenting a flight through a surrealistic
world.

E3198   Littlejohn, David. "What They Wrote and What They
Were," Reporter, XXVIII (April 11, 1963), 42-48.
Review of Durrell-Miller Correspondence where the
tragic fact is that neither man understands the other

and each has been trying to make the other into an acceptable image.

E3199 "Britain Decides Not to Seek a Ban on 'Tropic of Cancer'," New York Times, CXII (April 12, 1963), 25.
 British government not to contest publication of Tropic.

E3200 "Journey to the End of ... What?" Times Literary Supplement, LXII (April 12, 1963), 243.
 Cancer compared to Lawrence, for "Miller preaches against modern civilization and takes sex as the mainspring of vitality" (p. 243).

E3201 Kermode, Frank. "Jonah," New Statesman, April 12, 1963, 521.
 Miller a surrealist who celebrates romantic joy.

E3202 "No Action Over Miller Book," Daily Telegraph, April 13, 1963, 9.
 No action taken in Great Britain against Tropic.

E3203 " 'Tropic of Cancer' Action Refused," London Times, April 13, 1963, 4.
 See E3202.

E3204 " 'Tropic of Cancer' Summons Withdrawn," Courier, April 13, 1963.
 Summons against Tropic no longer lawful.

E3205 Henry, Maurice. "Books," Le Figaro Littéraire, April 19, 1963.
 Cartoon of police directing people to buy Tropic. (In French.)

E3206 "Ruée des Anglais sur 'Tropique du cancer'," Le Figaro Littéraire, April 19, 1963.
 Tropic sells well with no difficulty in France. (In French.)

E3207 Brown, Irby B. "The Letters of Miller, Durrell," Richmond Times-Dispatch, CXIII (April 21, 1963), L7.
 Praise of Miller-Durrell Letters.

E3208 Gold, Herbert. "A Rotating Set of Messages from a Life-Loving Stoic," New York Times, CXII (April 21, 1963), VII 5.
 Miller called fantastic autobiographical essayist for New York sketch in Black Spring.

E3209 Muggeridge, Malcolm. "Smut for the Millions," Daily Herald, April 23, 1963, 6.
 To prosecute Tropic in Britain would make this sordid work about society's sickness more of a best-seller.

E3210   "Henry Miller Play, His First, Is Slated," New York
        Times, CXII (April 25, 1963), 39.
            Just Wild About Harry avant-garde in style, full of
            love of life, and about freedom.

E3211   Zolotow, Sam. "Play's Debut Set by Henry Miller," New
        York Times, CXII (April 25, 1963), 39.
            Miller's play to be presented at Spoleto Festival in
            Italy in July.

E3212   Shrubb, Peter. "Not So Henry: The Banned Bowels of
        Henry Miller," Bulletin, April 27, 1963, 34-35.
            Review of Tropic that notes it is still banned in Aus-
            tralia and England and calls Miller a pornographer.

E3213   Taaning, Tage. "Henry og Larry," Berlingske Tidende,
        April 27, 1963.
            Review of Miller-Durrell Correspondence.   (In Danish.)

E3214   Norris, Hoke. "Censorship Revisited," Chicago Sun-
        Times, XVI (April 28, 1963), III 2.
            Black Spring a novel dealing with a juvenile Miller.

E3215   "Hearing Is Granted to 'Tropic' Seller," New York Times,
        CXII (April 30, 1963), 33.
            U.S. Supreme Court agrees to review case of Los
            Angeles bookseller Smith.

E3216   "High Court Will Hear 'Tropic of Cancer' Case," Los
        Angeles Times, LXXXII (April 30, 1963), 16.
            Bradley Smith granted hearing by U.S. Supreme Court
            on novel Tropic.

E3217   Schwartz, Edward P. "Additions to 'Henry Miller Bibli-
        ography'--May 1963," Henry Miller Literary Society News-
        letter, May 1963, 1-2.
            In May 1963, the Newsletter published additions to
            works by and about Miller.

E3218   Daniel, John. "A Pair of Loud-Speakers," Guardian,
        May 3, 1963, 8.
            Durrell-Miller Correspondence about two similar men
            who use same styles and ideas.

E3219   Holloway, David. "The Durrell-Miller Axis," London
        Daily Telegraph, May 3, 1963, 21.
            Durrell-Miller Correspondence deals with two uncon-
            ventional outsiders.

E3220   "Pen Friends," Times Literary Supplement, LXII (May 3,
        1963), 326.
            Review of Durrell-Miller Letters where "the two men
            emerge as very different, ... one realizes that its

central theme is the development of two distinct talents
and temperaments. "

E3221   Adam, Robert.   "Eyes Down for That Book," Herald, May
4, 1963, 4.
Tropic sells out in Britain in first few hours.

E3222   "Cancer All Day," Guardian, May 4, 1963, 6.
Tropic sold out in one day in London.

E3223   Hoggart, Richard.   "The Ever Interesting Tropic," Guardian, May 4, 1963, 6.
Publication of Tropic in England a study of individualism.

E3224   " 'Tropic' Is a Sell-Out on First Day," Daily Mail, May 4,
1963.
In England.

E3225   Wolfe, Clair.   "Sunday Big Day on Gallery Row," Los
Angeles Citizen News, May 4, 1963.
Miller art on display at County Museum at Hancock
Park.

E3226   Hughes, David.   "Exaltation Across Europe," Chicago Sun
Times, XVI (May 5, 1963), 23.
Durrell-Miller Correspondence shows two men absurd-
ly lauding each other.

E3227   Pryce-Jones, Alan.   "Letter-Writing a Manic Note,"
London Observer, May 5, 1963, 27.
Durrell-Miller Correspondence the praise of one man
for another beginning with Tropic and The Black Book.

E3228   "Lawyer Schoichet Probes Obscenity, 'Tropic of Cancer',"
UCLA Daily Bruin, May 7, 1963.
Attorney Nathan Schoichet talks about obscenity, cen-
sorship, and Tropic.

E3229   Benson, Paulette.   "Schoichet: Censoring May Lead to
Fear," UCLA Daily Bruin, May 8, 1963, 1, 7.
No right for government to decide what can and can-
not be read.

E3230   Kirsch, Robert R.   "Eavesdropping at a Literary Round
Table," Los Angeles Times, LXXXII (May 12, 1963),
Cal 13.
Miller's ideas during Paris Review interview on writ-
er's need for solitude and to let work flow show noth-
ing new.

E3231   Bain, C. C.   "Henry Miller," Bulletin, May 18, 1963, 28.
Refutation of Shrubb's "Not So Henry" that feels this

critic misread Tropic, which should have been seen
as a poem.

E3232   Baldwin, B.   "Henry Miller, " Bulletin, May 18, 1963, 28.
Refutes Shrubb calling Miller's description excellent.

E3233   Collins, Carol.   "Miller Writes of 'Gutter' Favorites, "
Hollywood Citizen-Herald, May 20, 1963.
Just Wild About Harry deals with eccentric skid-row
types.

E3234   "Ban on Miller's 'Tropic' Overruled in Wisconsin, " Chicago Tribune, CXVI (May 21, 1963), 5.
Wisconsin Supreme Court feels Tropic entitled to free
speech protection.

E3235   "Miller Novel OK'd for Sale in Wisconsin, " Chicago Tribune, CXVI (May 21, 1963), 5.
Wisconsin Supreme Court, in a 4-3 vote, said Tropic
entitled to protection of free speech.

E3236   " 'Tropic' Held Not Obscene, " New York Times, CXII
(May 21, 1963), 12.
Wisconsin Supreme Court ruled 4 to 3 that Tropic was
not obscene.

E3237   " 'Tropic' Upheld by Court, " Chicago Sun-Times, XVI
(May 21, 1963), 14.
Wisconsin Supreme Court says Tropic not obscene.

E3238   " 'Tropic of Cancer' Decision, " Milwaukee Journal, LXXXI
(May 22, 1963), 24.
Wisconsin Supreme Court guarantees Tropic First
Amendment freedom.

E3239   Howard, Percy.   "If Morals Are Declining--This Is Where
the Blame Lies, " London Sunday Express, May 24, 1963.
Cancer will corrupt Britain.

E3240   Pamp, Oke G.   "Word to Censors, " Chicago's American,
LXIII (May 27, 1963), 12.
Miller an honest writer who says what he feels.

E3241   Bode, Carl.   "Columbia's Carnal Bed, " American Quarterly, XV (Spring 1963), 52-64.
Bode's search for a 19th century work like Tropic.

E3242   Lowenfels, Walter.   "Editor, The Outsider, " Outsider, I
(Spring 1963), 79.
See E2287.

E3243   Gerstenberger, Donna.   "Trace, " Abstracts of English
Studies, VI (June 1963), 303.

Miller concerned with condition of modern man and
his loss of life.

E3244   Lipmanson, Don.   "Henry Miller and the Tropics," Advent,
June 1963, 42-44.
Two Tropics about "a man's possessing the courage to
defy social custom by disrobing in public" (p. 42).

E3245   Sackett, S. J.   "Nieuw Vlaams Tydschrift," Abstracts of
English Studies, VI (June 1963), 284.
Henk van Gelre sees Miller as an artist attempting to
find a mode of literary expression that is both individual and unique.

E3246   Steensma, Robert C.   "Twentieth Century Literature,"
Abstracts of English Studies, VI (June 1963), 304.
Maxine Renken has a Miller bibliography covering
1945-1961.

E3247   Thayer, C. G.   "Review of English Literature," Abstracts
of English Studies, VI (June 1963), 292.
Miller's article on Powys notes how remarkable the
latter was as writer and human being.

E3248   Rogus, David.   "Books by Henry Miller Have Beauty and
Vigor," Nashville Banner, LXXXVII (June 28, 1963), 25.
In Black Spring, Miller is lyrical, while Just Wild
About Harry deals with realism, fantasy, and trickery.

E3249   Olay, Lionel.   "Meeting with Henry," Cavalier, XIII (July
1963), 6-9, 84-87.
Cancer written because of desperation, yet during this
time Miller never became cynical.

E3250   Ross, Alan.   "Lawrence Durrell and Henry Miller: A
Private Correspondence," London Magazine, III (July 1963),
85-87.

E3251   " 'Tropic of Cancer' Upheld," New York Times, CXII
(July 3, 1963), 25.
California Supreme Court rules Tropic not hard core
pornography but "a kind of grotesque, unorthodox art
form."

E3252   "Henry Miller Play Is Given at Spoleto, Italy," New York
Times, CXII (July 5, 1963), 14.
Premiere of Miller play enthusiastic.

E3253   "Henry Miller Play Is Given at Spoleto," New Yorker,
XXXIX (July 6, 1963), 66.
Just Wild About Harry enthusiastically received.

E3254   " 'Tropic' Ban Illegal, High Court Rules," Los Angeles

Times, LXXXII (July 10, 1963), 2.
>State of California Supreme Court says Tropic not
>pornography and is legal in California.

E3255   Dales, Douglas.   " 'Tropic of Cancer' Is Ruled Obscene,"
New York Times, CXII (July 11, 1963), 31, 59.
>New York's highest court held Tropic obscene under
>New York obscenity laws.

E3256   Savory, Philip.   "Appeals Court Rules 'Tropic' Obscene,
4 to 3," New York Herald Tribune, CXIII (July 11, 1963),
19.
>Judge Scileppi of State Court of Appeals of New York
>ruled Tropic flagrantly obscene.

E3257   " 'Tropic of Cancer' Is Ruled Obscene by Court in N.Y.,"
New York Times, CXII (July 11, 1963), 27.
>N.Y. State Supreme Court held Tropic obscene, 4 to 3.

E3258   " 'Tropic of Cancer' Ruled Obscene by N.Y. Court," Los
Angeles Times, LXXXII (July 11, 1963), 4.
>Tropic called filthy by New York Supreme Court.

E3259   "A Book Banning," New York Times, CXII (July 12, 1963),
24.
>Literary men who know Tropic's merit, not judges,
>should decide value of book.

E3260   "Book Critics on the Bench," New York Post, CLXII (July
12, 1963), 34.
>Tropic protected by First Amendment.

E3261   Cooke, Alister.   " 'Tropic of Cancer' Found Obscene,"
Guardian, July 12, 1963, 11.
>New York's highest court finds Tropic obscene.

E3262   Gilroy, Harry.   " 'Fanny Hill' Book Called Obscene," New
York Times, CXII (July 12, 1963), 23.
>Mentioned is ban on Tropic by New York Court of
>Appeals.

E3263   Mabley, Jack.   "Flower Seed 'Jog' Newest Teen Thrill
Fad," Chicago's American, LXIV (July 12, 1963), 3.
>New York State Supreme Court holds Tropic obscene.

E3264   "Mr. Zeitlin and 'Tropic' Win Important Decision," UCLA
Librarian, XVI (July 12, 1963), 143-144.
>California Supreme Court says Tropic not obscene.

E3265   "Sex and Seven Judges," New York Herald Tribune, CXXIII
(July 12, 1963), 12.
>Rebuttal of four judges on New York's highest court
>that ruled Tropic obscene.

E3266   "Tropic of Corn," Time, LXXXII (July 12, 1963), 57.
        Just Wild About Harry a dull, dry dialogue.

E3267   "Tripe Topic," Newsweek, LXII (July 15, 1963), 53.
        Review of Just Wild About Harry depicts self-interested
        man and mistreats others.   It further condemns Ameri-
        cans, wars, and mass conformity.

E3268   "Wild About Harry," Variety, July 17, 1963.
        Just Wild About Harry an interesting, lively play.

E3269   "Court Ruling on 'Tropic of Cancer'," Los Angeles Times,
        LXXXII (July 21, 1963), 8.
        California Supreme Court unanimously says Tropic not
        obscene; book called surreal and autobiographical.

E3270   "Zeitlin Gets Tropic Okayed," Antiquarian Bookman, XXXII
        (July 22, 1963), 270.
        Cancer free in California, banned in New York.

E3271   Smith, Michael.   "Harry-Kiri in Umbria," Village Voice,
        July 25, 1963, 11.
        Just Wild About Harry too loose, a failure with flat,
        dull lines.

E3272   Adams, J. Donald.   "Speaking of Books," New York Times,
        CXII (July 28, 1963), VII 2.
        Fanny Hill much better than Tropic because sex in the
        former seen as positive and redeeming.

E3273   Miller, Ron S.   "Miller's Play: Is He Kidding?" Los
        Angeles Times, LXXXII (July 28, 1963), Cal 14.
        Just Wild About Harry a surreal parody about narcis-
        sistic being.

E3274   "Because Our Nation Slept," Advocate, August 1963, 4.
        U.S. degenerating when Tropic goes free.

E3275   Braun, R. A.   "Begegnung mit Henry Miller," Chick So-
        ciety Magazine, August 1963.
        (In German.)

E3276   "CCDL Petition for Rehearing Denied," Advocate, August
        1963, 4.
        Supreme Court decision providing Tropic with freedom
        stands.

E3277   "California Supreme Court Says Yes!" Advocate, August
        1963, 1.
        California Supreme Court says Tropic not pornography.

E3278   Cortum, Don.   "Editorial Comment," Advocate, August
        1963, 2-3.

Tropic should be found obscene in California.

E3279   "Freedom or License?" Advocate, August 1963, 3.
         Tropic called literary pus.

E3280   Gelre, Henk van. "A French De-luxe Edition of 'Sexus',"
         International Henry Miller Letter, August 1963, 22.
                 Mockery of new French edition of Miller's Sexus, com-
                 plete with half nude women.

E3281   Gelre, Henk van. "Antonio Bibalo's Opera," International
         Henry Miller Letter, August 1963, 10.
                 In a letter on February 19, 1963, Antonio Bibalo re-
                 ported the completion of his opera based on The Smile
                 at the Foot of the Ladder.

E3282   Gelre, Henk van. "Preface to Four Letters of Henry
         Miller to Count Keyserling," International Henry Miller
         Letter, August 1963, 11.
                 Gelre talks about the few letters that have survived
                 the correspondence between Count Keyserling and
                 Miller.

E3283   Hiler, Hilaire. "What I Remember of Henry Miller,"
         International Henry Miller Letter, August 1963, 5-10.
                 Discussion of Miller's interest in Otto Rank, Céline,
                 and D. H. Lawrence.

E3284   "Indiana Court Calls 'Tropic' Pornography," Advocate,
         August 1963, 3.
                 Jury in Indiana calls Tropic obscene.

E3285   Keyserling, Count Manfred. "Introduction to Four Letters
         of Henry Miller to Count Keyserling," International Henry
         Miller Letter, August 1963, 11-12.
                 The Count talks about his visit to Miller's flat in
                 Paris and their conversation.

E3286   "Los Angeles Jury Says No! Finds Seller Guilty," Advo-
         cate, August 1963, 1.
                 Tropic obscene and Bradley Smith guilty says Los
                 Angeles jury.

E3287   "New York Court Rules 'Tropic of Cancer' Smut," Advocate,
         August 1963, 1, 4.
                 State of New York--People v. Fritch on July 10, 1963,
                 in 4-3 decision, found Tropic pornography.

E3288   "Banned Book List Changes," Ablaik Aluntimes, August
         2, 1963.
                 Two Miller books, Quiet Days In Clichy and The
                 World of Sex have made banned booklist in Australia.

E3289   Coats, Paul. "Are the Book-Burners Throwing More Fuel on the Fires of Filth?" Los Angeles Times, LXXXII (August 2, 1963), II 6.
            Miller not pornography; book burners pornographers for they deal in filth.

E3290   Curtiss, Thomas Quinn. "Henry Miller Film--'Faithful to the Letter and the Spirit'," International Herald Tribune (August 6, 1963), 6.
            Miller immortalized in film version of Tropic.

E3291   "El hombre nuevo de América ha rebasado los esquimas tradicionales de izquierdas y derechas," La Nueva Prensa, I (August 8, 1963), 1.
            Miller's enthusiasm compared to D. H. Lawrence. (In Spanish.)

E3292   "The Subject," Los Angeles Times, LXXXII (August 18, 1963), G6.
            Miller stands in front of portrait of self made by artist.

E3293   "3 Booksellers Are Fired in 'Tropic of Cancer' Case," New York Times, CXII (August 23, 1963), 22.
            Three employees of Syracuse bookstore freed of obscenity charges stemming from sale of Tropic.

E3294   "Censorship Delays Henry Miller Play," New York Times, CXII (August 27, 1963), 27.
            Just Wild About Harry must have script cuts in abortion scene.

E3295   "Henry Miller's Play Hits British Censorship Snag," New York Times, CXII (August 27, 1963), 27.
            Just Wild About Harry must be cut to be performed in England.

E3296   "Lord Chamberlain Uneleemosynary About 'Harry'," Village Voice, August 29, 1963.
            Harry to cut abortion scenes.

E3297   Feron, James. "Miller Play Closes in Edinburgh After Its Second Performance," New York Times, CXII (August 30, 1963), 15.
            Miller play gets poor reviews as audience walks out.

E3298   "Notes on Foreign Sales," Times Literary Supplement, LXII (August 30, 1963), 664.
            Miller sells well in other countries.

E3299   Haas, Willy. "Salamander, Lemuren, Nachtmahre," n.p., August 31, 1963.
            Review of the Miller discussions of Goethe's Faust.

(In German.)

E3300   Gertz, Elmer.   "The 'Tropic of Cancer' Litigation in Illinois," Kentucky Law Journal, LI (Summer 1963), 591-610.
Gertz talks about freedom of Tropic and the Nazi tac-
tics of Chicago police.

E3301   Jones, Robert C.   "Texas Quarterly," Abstracts of English
Studies, VI (September 1963), 389.
Stanley Eskin's "Durrell's Themes in Alexandria Quartet" make reference to fact that Miller's rejection of
society was a major influence on Durrell.

E3302   Yackshaw, Robert.   "Spectator," Abstracts of English
Studies, VI (September 1963), 384.
Colin MacInnes sees Miller's chief virtues as his ac-
ceptance of life.

E3303   Braun, R. A.   "Henry Miller wieder einmal freigespro-
chen," Feuilleton, September 7, 1963.
Tropic before U.S. Supreme Court.   (In German.)

E3304   "Mr. Henry Miller's First Play at the Age of 72," London
Times, September 7, 1963, 12.
Just Wild About Harry has theme of responsibility.

E3305   Hobson, Harold.   "Henry Miller--Latter Day James Bar-
rie," San Francisco Chronicle, XCIX (September 8, 1963),
D2.
Just Wild About Harry shows Miller's lack of genius.

E3306   "Epics in Miniature," Times Literary Supplement, LXII
September 13, 1963, 688.
Miller admires H. E. Bates' Seven by Five because
of the epic nature and real feeling of this work.

E3307   "Popularity and Obscenity," Times Literary Supplement,
LXII (September 13, 1963), 689.
Miller sees many popular writers as quite good, as
H. E. Bates.

E3308   Hobson, Harold.   "Miller's 'Just Wild About Harry' Is
Just Wild," Los Angeles Times, LXXXII (September 15,
1963), Cal 12.
Harry a poor work that overuses the theme of love
makes the world go round.

E3309   "Wird Henry Miller einmal ein Klasseker?" Feuilleton,
September 21-22, 1963, 6.
Tropic restricted in U.S.   (In German.)

E3310   Wachsmann, Paul.   "Die Kunst des Lesens," Chronique
Culturelle, September 24, 1963, 1-3.

German review of The Books in My Life.

E3311   O'Shea, Michael Sean.   "The Sardi Set," Backstage, September 27, 1963.
Just Wild About Harry only Miller's first play.

E3312   Temple, F. J.   "La Correspondance Durrell-Henry Miller," Le Figaro Littéraire, XVIII (September 28, 1963), 1, 16, 18.
Durrell-Miller Correspondence a true document of the times.   (In French.)

E3313   Gregory, Harry.   "The Book Nook," Gent, October 1963.
Black Spring a poetic work where Miller's sense of humor and his depiction of nightmare blend into reality.

E3314   Schwartz, Edward P.   "Additions to Our 1961 'Henry Miller Bibliography'," Henry Miller Literary Society Newsletter, October 1963, 3-4.
In October 1963, The Newsletter published additions to Miller canon.

E3315   Schwartz, Edward P.   "Another English Note," Henry Miller Literary Society Newsletter, October 1963, 1-2.
Tropic will be translated into braille.

E3316   Schwartz, Edward P.   "Dr. Marvin Sukov," Henry Miller Literary Society Newsletter, October 1963, 2.
Dr. Marvin Sukov, Minneapolis psychiatrist, gave his entire Miller collection to University of Minnesota Library.

E3317   Schwartz, Edward P.   "Enclosed with This 'Newsletter'," Henry Miller Literary Society Newsletter, October 1963, 2.
Enclosed with the Newsletter are: Bern Porter sketch, Miller reviews from England, book list compiled by Tom Moore, advertising card on Miller bibliography.

E3318   Schwartz, Edward P.   "Henry Miller on Writing," Henry Miller Literary Society Newsletter, October 1963, 2.
Henry Miller on Writing contains many important passages on his self-education as a writer.

E3319   Schwartz, Edward P.   "How About That!" Henry Miller Literary Society Newsletter, October 1963, 1.
Schwartz comments on conflicting California Court ruling where one says that Cancer is obscene while other says it is not.

E3320   Schwartz, Edward P.   "In a Henry Miller," Henry Miller Literary Society Newsletter, October 1963, 2.

Henry Miller water color showing at Ankrun Gallery,
Los Angeles, used 50 water colors on display.

E3321   Schwartz, Edward P.   "In April the California Case,"
Henry Miller Literary Society Newsletter, October 1963, 1.
California case of Tropic involving Smith accepted for
review by U.S. Supreme Court.

E3322   Schwartz, Edward P.   "In Contrast," Henry Miller Lite-
rary Society Newsletter, October 1963, 1.
British Attorney-General will not allow publication of
Tropic in England.

E3323   Schwartz, Edward P.   "In the Meantime," Henry Miller
Literary Society Newsletter, October 1963, 1.
California Supreme Court ruled Tropic not "hard-core
pornography."

E3324   Schwartz, Edward P.   "Lord Chamberlain Uneleemosynery
About 'Harry'," Henry Miller Literary Society Newsletter,
October 1963, 2.
Deletions wanted in Harry shows how free a country
England is.

E3325   Schwartz, Edward P.   "There Have Been...," Henry
Miller Literary Society Newsletter, October 1963, 1.
Newsletter discusses court cases involving Tropic.

E3326   Schwartz, Edward P.   "Turning to New York State,"
Henry Miller Literary Society Newsletter, October 1963,
1.
Early in September 1963, the New York Supreme
Court saw no reason to ban Tropic.

E3327   Schwartz, Edward P.   "While All These," Henry Miller
Literary Society Newsletter, October 1963, 2.
Joseph Levine of Embassy Pictures plans to produce
Tropic in 1964.

E3328   Schwartz, Edward P.   "While the Illinois," Henry Miller
Literary Society Newsletter, October 1963, 1.
While Illinois Supreme Court tries Tropic, Southern
Illinois University Press publishes Henry Miller and
the Critics.

E3329   Schwartz, Edward P.   "Wisconsin's Supreme Court,"
Henry Miller Literary Society Newsletter, October 1963,
1.
On May 20, 1963, Wisconsin Supreme Court took logi-
cal path out of absurd world.

E3330   Schwartz, Edward P.   "World Premiere," Henry Miller
Literary Society Newsletter, October 1963, 2.

Miller's first play a success.

E3331   "La Correspondance Durrell-Miller," Le Figaro Littéraire, XVIII (October 5, 1963), 8, 26.
(In French.)

E3332   Letofsky, Irv.   "Henry Miller Goes Mimeograph," Minneapolis Tribune, XCVII (October 11, 1963), 38.
Letofsky notes Newsletter has accomplished purpose
of getting Miller read and accepted.

E3333   Schwartz, Edward P.   "After Last Night," Minneapolis
Tribune, XCVII (October 11, 1963), 38.
Founders of Newsletter discuss reasons for calling it
quits.   One is that Miller now known and read.

E3334   "Henry Miller: Die Kunst des Lesens," Vianonte, October
13, 1963.
Review of The Books in My Life.   (In German.)

E3335   Fiedler, Leslie A.   "An American Illusion," Manchester
Guardian Weekly, October 24, 1963.
Plexus looks at sex and freedom through eyes of noble
savage.

E3336   Mauriac, Claude.   "Deux amis: Henry Miller et Lawrence
Durrell," Le Figaro Littéraire, XVIII (October 30, 1963).
Durrell-Miller Correspondence viewed as accomplished
and revealing.

E3337   Mayoux, Jean-Jacques.   "De meilleur en Miller," Etudes
Anglaises, XVI (October-December 1963), 369-373.
Review of The Best of Henry Miller where Miller is
called a psychiatrist in the tradition of Rank, Jung,
and Freud, and is a man concerned with life's vitality
like Van Gogh.   (In French.)

E3338   Baxter, Annette K.   "An Imaginary Correspondence,"
Ararat, Autumn 1963, 29-35.
Miller and Henry James have imaginary correspondence
on the morality of the artist.

E3339   "The Tropic Myth," Times Literary Supplement, LXII (November 1, 1963), 892.
Review of Plexus where Miller's writing considered
"cliché-ridden, repetitious, and boring, and preoccu-
pied with himself to the verge of egomania" (p. 892).
Only works worth reading: Cancer and Max.

E3340   Piarier, Jacqueline.   "Henry Miller et Lawrence Durrell
publient leur correspondance," Le Monde, November 2,
1963, 9.
Critical assessment of Durrell-Miller Correspondence.

E3341 Hartwijk, Henrik. "De Landloper en de Heer," Kunst-en Geestesleven, November 2-3, 1963, 33.
  Review of Miller-Durrell Correspondence. (In Dutch.)

E3342 "Wer weiss es...," Aufbau, November 15, 1963.
  Miller seen as wise man. (In German.)

E3343 "Die Kunst des Lesens," Volksblatt, November 17, 1963.
  Review of The Books in My Life. (In German.)

E3344 Goldschmidt, Irma. "Mit der Hand geschrieben," Aufbau, November 19, 1963.

E3345/6 Gruesse, Beste. "Wer weiss es?" Aufbau, November 19, 1963.
  Miller compared to philosopher, Plato. (In German.)

E3347 "Die Kunst des Lesens--Bücher als Lebensspuren," Westdeutsche Zeitung, November 30, 1963.
  Review of The Books in My Life. (In German.)

E3348 Gaines, Ervin J. "Freedom to Read in New Hampshire," ALA Bulletin, LVII (December 1963), 1009-1010.
  New Hampshire libraries will not forbid Tropic in state.

E3349 Stuart, Lyle. "Freedom to Read & the Law," Independent, December 1963.
  Tropic obscene in New York state but not obscene in Washington and California. Obscenity not in book but in minds of viewers.

E3350 "Doner," Los Angeles Times, LXXXIII (December 5, 1963), 2.
  Miller donates paintings to Westwood Art Association.

E3351 "Henry Miller Donates Manuscripts to Art Association of Westwood," North Shore Shopper, December 5, 1963, 2.
  Miller donates hand-written manuscripts of Into the Night Life to Westwood Art Association.

E3352 Kraus, Wolfgang. "Bücher als Lebensspuren," Bonner Rundschau, December 6, 1963.
  Review of The Books in My Life. (In German.)

E3353 Mat. "Borge soviel wie möglich," Bergedorfer Zeitung, December 7, 1963.

E3354 "Squirru Delineates Role Played by Imagination," Chattanooga Times, XCIV (December 15, 1963), 12.
  Miller admired in Latin America because he speaks new language based on individual freedom.

E3355   "Wickes, George," Booklist and Subscription Book Bulletin,
         LX (December 15, 1963), 367.
         Wickes' Henry Miller and the Critics a collection of
         essays on Miller the writer.

E3356   "City Loses 'Tropic of Cancer' Fight," Los Angeles Times,
         LXXXIII (December 17, 1963), II 1, 8.
         U.S. Supreme Court frees Tropic.

E3357   Lewis, Anthony.   "Sale of 'Tropic' on Coast Stands," New
         York Times, CXIII (December 17, 1963), 28.
         California Supreme Court says Tropic cannot be banned
         as obscene.

E3358   "Supreme Court Actions," New York Times, CXIII (Decem-
         ber 17, 1963), 28.
         U.S. Supreme Court refuses to review California
         Court decision on Tropic.

E3359   Kraum, Wolfgang.   "Bücher als Lebensspuren," National-
         Zeitung Basel, December 21, 1963.
         Review of Books in My Life.   (In German.)

E3360   K., W.   "Bücher als Lebensspuren," Beleg-Sendung, De-
         cember 24, 1963.
         Review of Books In My Life.   (In German.)

E3361   Bullock, Wynn.   "Henry and Emil," Circle of Enchantment,
         X (1964), 47.
         Photograph of Miller sitting next to Emil White.

E3362   Rossi, Matti.   "Milleristeistä ja vastamilleristeistä,"
         Eteläsuomalainen, 1964, 12.
         Interest in Miller spreading to Scandinavian criticism
         of Miller.   (In Finnish.)

E3363   White, Emil.   "By Way of Introduction," Circle of En-
         chantment, X (1964), 1.
         A thank you to Miller for help with White's Big Sur
         Guide.

E3364   White, Emil.   "Editor's Comments in the Form of a
         'Letter to Henry'," Circle of Enchantment, X (1964), 48.
         White tells Miller that success can change a man.

E3365   "Die Kunst des Lesens," Beitrage zur die Industrie, Janu-
         ary 1964.
         Review of The Books in My Life.   (In German.)

E3366   Foster, Steven.   "A Critical Appraisal of Henry Miller's
         Tropic of Cancer," Twentieth Century Literature, IX
         (January 1964), 196-208.
         Foster views Miller's work as subjective biography by

comparing him to both Whitman and Melville because
Tropic possesses an apocalyptic vision. This vision
comes from exploring the inner self which Henri Bergson calls "the intuitive perception of inner duration"
which means that time and space are whole and based
on the individual's perception (p. 205).

E3367 Poe, Elizabeth. "Henry Miller on Big Sur," San Diego,
XVI (January 1964), 53, 70.
Interview where Miller talks about Big Sur and how its
land will never be spoiled.

E3368 Wiehe, R. E. "New Statesman," Abstracts of English
Studies, VII (January 1964), 29.
Frank Kermode calls Miller a surrealist who cele-
brates Romantic joy.

E3369 Guaraldi, Antonella. "Individuo e società in Henry Miller,"
Aut Aut, January-March 1964, 98-114.
Miller concerned with the struggle of the individual
against totalitarianism. (In Italian.)

E3370 "[Henry Miller]," Creative America, February 1964.
Photo of Miller.

E3371 "Priapus in Brooklyn," Times Literary Supplement, LXIII
(February 13, 1964), 121.
Review of Capricorn where his verbal flow and his
dealing with American background help make this
work superior to Cancer. Miller's diction also compared to Gertrude Stein.

E3372 "Henry Miller and the Critics," Virginia Quarterly Review,
XL (Winter 1964), p. xx.
Wickes' Henry Miller and the Critics a defense of
Miller because of attacks against him in America.

E3373 Wheeler, Dinsmore. "The Air-Conditioned Nightmare,"
New Mexico Quarterly Review, XVI (Winter 1964), 510-511.
Review of Air-Conditioned Nightmare that calls Miller
a beast undermining America.

E3374 Gertz, Elmer. "Miller Revisited," Newsletter on Intellectual Freedom, XIII (March 1964), 22-23.
Wickes' Henry Miller and the Critics views Miller as
a major novelist.

E3375 " 'Tropic' Key Issue in Wisconsin Race for Seat on Court,"
New York Times, CXIII (March 28, 1964), 17.
Cancer key issue in Wisconsin Court election campaign.

E3376 Dommergues, Pierre. "Le Dernier Roman de Jack Kerouac," Langues Mordernes, LVIII (March-April 1964), 77-

80.
Kerouac the heir to Lawrence and Miller.

E3377   Dwiggins, Don.   "Pornography: In the Eye of the Be-
holder," Connoisseur's World, I (April 1964), 15-16, 73.
Tropic has won the right to be read.

E3378   Jochum, Klaus Peter.   "Essays and Studies," Abstracts of
English Studies, VII (April 1964), 166.
The American novel has failed to achieve tradition of
ironic realism according to Harold Beaver, who sees
Miller as sentimental.

E3379   Pachoutinsky, Eugène.   "Chair et Metal," International
Henry Miller Letter, April 1964, 8-12.
Pachoutinsky talks about first meeting with Miller and
Miller's job with Herald Tribune.

E3380   Widmer, Kingsley.   "The Imaginary Jew: Henry Miller's
Testimony," International Henry Miller Letter, April 1964,
19-21.
One of the fullest and most intriguing examples of the
gentile identifying with the Jew found in Miller.

E3381   Young, Noel.   "An Uncle to Some," International Henry
Miller Letter, April 1964, 22-23.
Young discusses first meeting with Miller.

E3382   Lennon, Peter.   "Prison for the Publisher," Manchester
Guardian Weekly, April 2, 1964, 5.
Publisher Maurice Girodias sentenced to a year in
prison for publishing Miller in French.

E3383   London, John O.   "We Refuse to Review This Book," Time
and Tide, XLV (April 10, 1964), 21.
Tropic called dirty.

E3384   Laine, George.   "TV's Peyton Place Mirrors Book,"
Evening Outlook, April 18, 1964, 1, 5.
Miller discusses the way the part of Mary Anderson
in Peyton Place should be played.

E3385   Barkham, John.   "Greece Evokes Nostalgia for Aging
Henry Miller," New York World Telegram, CXXXI (April
23, 1964), 23.·
Miller's Greece an essay on poor, proud, humble
people whose lives are tied to the past.

E3386   Le Clec'h, Guy.   "Anaïs Nin, muse de Durrell et de
Miller," Figaro Littéraire, XIV (May 7-13, 1964), 18.
Interview with Anaïs Nin about her influence on the
writing of Durrell and Miller.

E3387   Valtiala, Nalle. "Det Ar Synd om Finländarna," Nya
         Pressen, May 9, 1964, 8-9.
             Miller discusses pornography, Tropic, Big Sur, Fin-
             land, sex. (In Swedish.)

E3388   Sheehan, Dave. "Miller Meets Bonaparte," Santa Monica
         Evening Outlook, May 22, 1964.
             Miller goes to French restaurant called Napoleon and
             relives Villa Seraut days.

E3389   Lowenfels, Walter. "Unpublished Preface to Tropic of
         Cancer," Massachusetts Review, V (Spring 1964), 481-491.
             Lowenfels creates fine biography of Miller, carrying
             his reader from the early, dated work to Miller's ex-
             periment of using autobiography as a novel in Tropic.
             Second half of article consists of unpublished preface
             to Tropic.

E3390   " 'Tropic of Cancer' Held Lewd," New York Times, CXIII
         (June 19, 1964), 12.
             Illinois Supreme Court ruled Tropic contained a
             "series of revolting sexual encounters."

E3391   "Court Voids Ban on 'Tropic' Book," New York Times,
         CXIII (June 23, 1964), 26.
             U.S. Supreme Court says Tropic cannot be constitu-
             tionally banned by vote of 5 to 4.

E3392   'Supreme Court Reverses Florida Ban on 'Tropic'," Pub-
         lishers Weekly, CLXXXV (June 29, 1964), 48.
             U.S. Supreme Court says Tropic not obscene.

E3393   " 'Tropic' Found Obscene in Illinois Supreme Court," Pub-
         lishers Weekly, CLXXXV (June 29, 1964), 49-50.
             Supreme Court of Illinois finds Tropic obscene.

E3394   Gelre, Henk van. "Leven Zonder Beginselen," Aristo-,
         XXXII (July 1964), 162-177.
             Progression of Miller's work from "Crazy Cock" to
             Tropic of Cancer and from there to Rosy Crucifixion
             seen. (In Dutch.)

E3395   Sherman, John K. 'Shapiro Attacks 'Established' Poetry,"
         Minneapolis Tribune, XCVIII (July 5, 1964), E8.
             Shapiro has tribute to Miller in his A Malebolge of
             1400 Books. Speaks about Miller as leader in move-
             ment to form free society.

E3396   "Illinois High Court Bows Over 'Tropic of Cancer'," New
         York Times, CXIII (July 9, 1964), 13.
             Illinois Supreme Court withdrew its ruling on Tropic
             to conform with decision by U.S. Supreme Court.

E3397   "Wordmania," Times Literary Supplement, LXIII (August 6, 1964), 683.
   Reading Nexus like listening to psychotic in manic stage.

E3398   'Spellman Assails Court Ruling on Pornography," New York Times, CXIII (August 7, 1964), 31.
   Cardinal Spellman says Supreme Court decision dealing with Cancer shows degeneracy in America.

E3399   Keeley, Edmund. "Sunday, Monday and Always," New York Herald Tribune, CXXIV (August 9, 1964), BU 1, 12.
   Miller's love for Greece is narcissistic love of peasant life.

E3400   Callua, Anton. "Venus de Milo Will 'Star' in Art Show," Los Angeles Times, LXXXIII (August 13, 1964), VII 1.
   Miller's first nude studies will be sold.

E3401   Kirsch, Robert R. "Miller Waxes Eloquent in Essays on Writing Craft," Los Angeles Times, LXXXIII (August 19, 1964), V 6.
   Review of Henry Miller on Writing where book seen as one of few truly good books on writing.

E3402   Scholes, Robert. "Return to Alexandria: Lawrence Durrell and Western Narrative Tradition," Virginia Quarterly Review, XL (Summer 1964), 411-420.
   Durrell's style in Alexandria Quartet quite different from Miller's.

E3403   Shapiro, Karl. "Henry Miller and Myself," Carleton Miscellany, V (Summer 1964), 115-135.
   Miller's writing 'beyond wall of books," as innocent depicts real life (p. 119).

E3404   Knef, Hildegard. "Die Knef über Henry Miller: Er ist mein grosser Freund," Twen, VI (September 1964), 86-88.
   Knef talks about meeting Miller and of their talks about sex and love. (In German.)

E3405   Wolfe, Bernard. "Playboy Interview: Henry Miller," Playboy, XI (September 1964), 77-90.
   Miller wishes to break down absurd barriers of our lives; calls himself criminal in eyes of society.

E3406   Yerbury, Grace D. "Of a City Beside a River: Whitman, Eliot, Thomas, Miller," Walt Whitman Review, X (September 1964), 67-73.
   Tropic called a "surrealistic prose poem, which ... attempts to sum up the spiritual contents of 2000 years of Christianity" (p. 70). Miller deals with society's dual ethic of idealism and reality, finds a unity

and becomes whole unlike Eliot.

E3407   "Nine Clergymen Score High Court," New York Times,
        CXIII (September 1, 1964), 37.
        Anger that ban on Tropic was ended by Supreme Court.

E3408   Peignot, Jérôme. "Henry Miller ou le juif manqué," La
        Nouvelle Revue Francaise, XII (September 1, 1964), 516-
        525.
        Miller's writing in tradition of Gertrude Stein--work
        between spiritual and philosophical. (In French.)

E3409   Kirsch, Robert R. "Defending Free Expression Isn't Ac-
        tually the Same as Defending What's Said," Los Angeles
        Times, LXXXIII (September 14, 1964), IV 6.
        Supreme Court Tropic decision reverses prior deci-
        sions.

E3410   Segebrecht, Wulf. "Henry Miller," Bücherei und Bildung,
        September 15, 1964.
        Books in My Life discussed. (In German.)

E3411   "Viva, Ziva!" Los Angeles Times, LXXXIII (September
        17, 1964), VII 1.
        Miller's portrait of Actress Ziva Rodan displayed.

E3412   Way, Brian. "Sex and Language," New Left Review, Sep-
        tember-October 1964, 66-80.
        In the two Tropics, Miller's obscene words are neces-
        sary.

E3413   Sandell, Tom. "Henry Millers Universum," Nya Argus,
        LVII (October 1, 1964), 242-244.
        Review of Miller's Colossus, Plexus, Tropics. (In
        Dutch.)

E3414   "Villagers' Art Exhibit Dons Parisian Garb," UCLA Daily
        Bruin, October 1, 1964.
        Original paintings of Miller on sale in Westwood Vil-
        lage.

E3415   "Lawyer Analyzes 'Law and Smut'," UCLA Daily Bruin,
        October 7, 1964.
        Roger Arnebergh, the successful prosecutor of Bradley
        Smith in 1962 Los Angeles Tropic case.

E3416   "Arnebergh Flays Latrine Literature," UCLA Daily Bruin,
        October 8, 1964.
        Arnebergh calls Tropic pornography.

E3417   "Store Windows Win Decoration Awards," Los Angeles
        Times, LXXXIII (October 8, 1964), VII 8.
        Miller book display wins award.

E3418   " 'Tropic of Cancer' Accepted--At Last--In Brooklyn,"
n. p. , October 19, 1964, 35.
Tropic case dismissed in Brooklyn, N. Y.

E3419   Wolfe, Bernard.   "Ohne unsere Fehler sind wir nullen,"
Der Spiegel, XVIII (October 21, 1964), 147-155.
See E3405.   (In German.)

E3420   Eerde, John Van.   "Aut Aut," Abstracts of English Studies,
VII (November 1964), 467.
Antonella Guaraldi feels Miller committed to individual-
ism.

E3421   Schwartz, Edward P.   "Additions to Publication List,"
Henry Miller Literary Society Newsletter, November 1964,
2.
Final list of additions to Thomas Moore's Bibliography
of Miller.

E3422   Schwartz, Edward P.   "In This Mailing," Henry Miller
Literary Society Newsletter, November 1964, 1.
Moore's Henry Miller on Writing has received excel-
lent reviews.

E3423   Schwartz, Edward P.   "Item No. 1," Henry Miller Literary Society Newsletter, November 1964, 1.
U.S. Supreme Court reversed ban on Tropic.

E3424   Schwartz, Edward P.   "Item No. 2," Henry Miller Lite-
rary Society Newsletter, November 1964, 1.
As result of Supreme Court action, both Illinois and
New York Supreme Courts reversed previous bans on
Tropic.

E3425   Schwartz, Edward P.   "Item No. 3," Henry Miller Literary Society Newsletter, November 1964, 1.
On October 2, Brooklyn Criminal Court dismissed indictment against Miller and Grove Press for issuing
obscene book.

E3426   Schwartz, Edward P.   "Item No. 4," Henry Miller Literary Society Newsletter, November 1964, 1.
Work on Tropic movie to begin in Paris in 1965.

E3427   Schwartz, Edward P.   "Item No. 5," Henry Miller Lite-
rary Society Newsletter, November 1964, 1.
Smile at Foot of Ladder, an opera by Bibalo based on
Miller story, scheduled for premiere in April 1965 in
Hamburg, Germany.

E3428   Schwartz, Edward P.   "Item No. 6," Henry Miller Literary Society Newsletter, November 1964, 1.
In late September 1964, Miller a star attraction at

Westwood Village Festival of Arts.

E3429   Schwartz, Edward P.   "Item No. 7," Henry Miller Lite-
rary Society Newsletter, November 1964, 1.
Miller chosen honorary president of "First American
Encounter of Poets" held in Mexico City in February.

E3430   Schwartz, Edward P.   "Item No. 8," Henry Miller Lite-
rary Society Newsletter, November 1964, 1.
Creative America (February 1964) includes photo of
Miller.

E3431   Kostelanetz, Richard.   "The 'Cancer' That Aims to Cure,"
New York Herald Tribune, CXXIV (November 8, 1964), VI
26.
Miller talks about being oneself in his writing.

E3432   "Connecticut Court Clears Seller of 'Tropic of Cancer',"
New York Times, CXIV (November 11, 1964), 40.
Connecticut Supreme Court of Errors, basing its decision on the U.S. Supreme Court, reversed conviction of Trumbull Huntington for sale of Tropic.

E3433   Metzger, Deena P.   "Collages," Los Angeles Free Press,
November 26, 1964, 8.
Noted that Nin wrote Preface to Tropic.

E3434   Coleman, Alexander.   "Auntie Knew the Answers," New
York Times, CXIV (November 29, 1964), VII 55.
Miller Preface to Prevelakis' The Sun of Death, de-
picts love and life found in novel.

E3435   Goyan, William.   "Bits and Images of Life," New York
Times, CXIV (November 29, 1964), VII 5, 24.
Miller the first to see Nin's importance as writer.

E3436   Mabley, Jack.   "Court Ruling to Bring New Flood of
Smut," Chicago's American, CXXXIV (November 29, 1964),
3.
Freeing Tropic by Supreme Court will bring more dirt
into society.

E3437   Magee, William H.   "New Republic," Abstracts of English
Studies, VII (December 1964), 540.
David Littlejohn sees Miller's writing as continuation
of his life.

E3438   Wieche, R. E.   "Virginia Quarterly Review," Abstracts of
English Studies, VII (December 1964), 573.
Robert Scholes sees Durrell's style as quite different
from Miller's.

E3439   Bennett, Charles G.   "City's Smut Drive Will Try Suasion,"

New York Times, CXIV (December 5, 1964), 33.
New York's anti-pornography drive calls Tropic and
two other novels obscene despite Supreme Court ruling.

E3440   "Beardsley: Dreifach bepudert," Der Spiegel, XVIII (December 23, 1964), 93-94.
Just Wild About Harry popular in Germany.   (In German.)

E3441   "Area Growth Highlights '64," Los Angeles Times, LXXXIV
(December 27, 1964), J1.
Miller paintings in Westwood Art Association's annual
auction.

E3442   Robischon, Thomas.   "A Day in Court with the Literary
Critic," Massachusetts Review, VI (Autumn-Winter 1964-5),
101-110.
Courtroom and trial of Tropic form basis for an article that describes the failure of critics Harry T.
Moore, Mark Schorer, and Harry T. Levin to express
themselves in Suffolk County Superior Court.

E3443   Beck, Theodore Toulon.   "Miller, Henry," Twentieth Century Literature, X (January 1965), 190.
Abstract of Jérôme Peignot's "Henry Miller ou le juif
manqué," where Miller offers us a drug for happiness
and life.

E3444   Gertz, Elmer.   "The Illinois Battle Over 'Tropic of Can-
cer'," Chicago Bar Record, XLVI (January 1965), 161-172.
Gertz discusses his battle in the Illinois courts to free
Tropic.

E3445   Munro, John.   "Etudes Anglaises," Abstracts of English
Studies, VIII (January 1965), 10.
Review of Durrell's The Best of Henry Miller that dis-
cusses Miller's changing concerns and his vitality.

E3446   Stamm, Ester F.   "Miller, Henry," Twentieth Century
Literature, X (January 1965), 190.
Discussion of James P. Carse's "Henry Miller and
the Morality of Art" that sees Miller's work as his-
toric.

E3447   Eerde, John Van.   "Langues Modernes," Abstracts of
English Studies, VIII (February 1965), 78.
Analysis of Pierre Dommergues's "Le Dernier Roman
de Jack Kerouac" that calls Kerouac the heir to
Lawrence and Miller.

E3448   "Henry Miller on Writing," Choice, I (February 1965), 556.
Miller called a serious writer, not a pornographer.

E3449   Tapia, Atols. "Una nueva forma de santidad," Hoy en la
         Cultura, February 1965.
             Black Spring a fine work about youth which combines
         individualism, humor, first love, and other human
         qualities. (In Spanish.)

E3450   Rohde, Peter P. "Henry Miller: Pornógrafo o profeta,"
         Eco Contemporaneo, Winter 1965, 97-103.
             All of Miller's literature primitive, autobiographical,
         sexual, offensive, yet the brutal effect of the works is
         contrived by Miller who wishes to change society. (In
         Spanish.)

E3451   "The Unsinkable Fanny Hill," Playboy, XII (March 1965),
         76-80, 140-141.
             Miller's Tropics firmly vindicated.

E3452   Meeske, Marilyn. "Memoirs of a Female Pornographer,"
         Esquire, LXIII (April 1965), 112-115.
             In Miller's work, the pornographic first merged with
         the literary and philosophical.

E3453/4 Norman, Sylva. "Claude Houghton and Texas," Aryan
         Path, XXXVI (April 1965), 173-177.
             Miller one of the few literary men to value Houghton's
         work.

E3455   Santangelo, G. A. "Miller, Henry," Twentieth Century
         Literature, XI (April 1965), 54.
             Evaluation of Lowenfels's "Unpublished Preface to
         Tropic."

E3456   Temple, Frédéric-Jacques. "Henry Miller en quôte de
         lui-même," Actuelles, April 1965, 6-7.
             Miller compared to 19th-century French philosophers,
         to a Buddhist monk, and to a primitive. (In French.)

E3457   "Henry Miller Story Is Opera in Hamburg," New York
         Times, CXIV (April 7, 1965), 37.
             Smile at Foot of Ladder well received in Hamburg,
         Germany.

E3458   Davis, Robert A. "Massachusetts Review," Abstracts of
         English Studies, VIII (May 1965), 267.
             Evaluation of Lowenfels's "Unpublished Preface to
         Tropic."

E3459   McCall, Harvey. "Henry Miller," Hi-Life, VI (May 1965),
         11-12.
             Tropic and Rosy Crucifixion viewed as methods for
         seduction.

E3460   Powell, Lawrence Clark. "Letters from the Famous and

the Faceless," New York Times, CXIV (May 1965), 5, 34-35.
>Powell discusses Miller's effect on others, viewing the letters many people write him.

E3461   Schneider, Duane B.   "New Left Review," Abstracts of English Studies, VIII (May 1965), 278.
>Brian Way's "Sex and Language" feels that obscene words are essential to writing of Miller.

E3462   Winters, Warrington.   "We Two, the World, and the Whale," Saturday Review, XLVIII (May 15, 1965), 27-28.
>Review of Miller's Letters To Anaïs Nin where reviewer discusses Miller's need for analysis and his sessions with Otto Rank.

E3463   Omarr, Sydney.   "Henry Miller: A Rebel In Repose," Los Angeles Times, LXXXIV (May 16, 1965), Cal 17.
>Letters to Anaïs Nin from 1931-1946 seen as the movement of a struggling writer to attain fame.

E3464   Stiensma, Robert C.   "Twentieth Century Literature," Abstracts of English Studies, VIII (June 1965), 354.
>Stephen Foster's appraisal of Tropic realizes that responsible criticism has passed Tropic by.

E3465   Watts, Alan.   "Sculpture by Ron Boise: The Kama Sutra Theme," Evergreen Review, IX (June 1965), 64-65.
>Miller described pushing line back in literature like Boise's sculpture.

E3466   Metzger, Deena.   "[Review of] the Letters of Henry Miller to Anaïs Nin," Los Angeles Free Press, II (June 18, 1965), 5.
>Miller seen as a man attempting to explore the self and others.

E3467   Winters, Warrington.   "Transcendentalist in the Basement," Saturday Review, XLVIII (June 19, 1965), 39.
>Review of Sexus that calls Miller "not merely our greatest American Existentialist but as nothing less than the presiding genius ... of American transcendentalism" (p. 39).

E3468   "Letters by Writers Are Given to N. Y. U. by Frances Steloff," New York Times, CXIV (June 21, 1965), 26.
>Letters from Miller, Joyce, and Katherine Ann Porter donated to New York University by Frances Steloff.

E3469   "The High Price of Zap," Time, LXXXV (June 25, 1965), 112.
>Sexus a book about a fantasy world, a comical world with a clown named Henry Miller.

E3470   Baro, Gene. "Profound Rapport," New York Times, CXIV
          (June 27, 1965), VII 5.
          Henry Miller: Letters to Anaïs Nin covers his most
          troubled period and his most creative time, and his
          struggle for recognition in the midst of poverty.

E3471   Smith, Bob. "Visitation at Walden with Thoreau and Henry
          Miller," n.p., July 10, 1965.
          Miller existed in Paris but did not find life's essence
          there.

E3472   Vidal, Gore. "Oh, Henry," New York Herald Tribune,
          CXXV (August 1, 1965), BW 1, 10.
          Vidal reviews Sexus and Miller calling the novel poor
          and the author an egotist.

E3473   Sansom, Clive. "Accumulation," New York Times, CXIV
          (August 8, 1965), VII 19.
          Sees no point in UCLA Miller Collection having letter
          to Miller.

E3474   Wickes, George. "Ecstasy Is Lacking," New York Times,
          CXIV (August 8, 1965), VII 5, 28.
          Quiet Days in Clichy, The World of Sex, Sexus,
          Plexus, and Nexus represent over half of Miller's
          writing from 1940-1960. All deal with his life during
          the twenties when trying to discover himself.

E3475   Girodias, Maurice. "Pornography," Twentieth Century,
          CLXXIV (Summer 1965), 24-29.
          Girodias talks about meeting Miller and reading Tropic
          and having trouble reconciling the human and the
          clownish persons in both the work and the man.

E3476   Kostelanetz, Richard. "Pornography," Twentieth Century,
          CLXXIV (Summer 1965), 5-10.
          Miller described as author who inflames and rips at
          structures.

E3477   Snee, Don. "Pornography," Twentieth Century, CLXXIV
          (Summer 1965), 12-14.
          Miller freed himself from Puritanism and found a
          place of openness and truth.

E3478   Phillipson, John S. "Esquire," Abstracts of English
          Studies, VIII (September 1965), 377.
          Marilyn Meeske notes that in Henry Miller's work the
          pornographic first merged with the literary and philo-
          sophic.

E3479   Kostelanetz, Richard. "From Nightmare to Serendipity:
          A Retrospective Look at William Burroughs," Twentieth
          Century Literature, XI (October 1965), 123-130.

Burroughs's novels lack the affirmation of life that Miller's offer.

E3480   Rule, Henry B. "Walt Whitman Review," Abstracts of English Studies, VIII (October 1965), 475.
Grace Yerbury suggests that Whitman's "Crossing Brooklyn Ferry" anticipates the setting, techniques, and themes of Miller's Tropic.

E3481   Richler, Mordecai. "The Miller's Tale," Spectator, October 8, 1965, 451.
Review of Black Spring, Letters to Anaïs Nin, Henry Miller: Selected Prose I, The Air-Conditioned Nightmare that sees Miller as risque.

E3482   Nye, Robert. "A Cosmogonic Baby," Scotsman, October 23, 1965, 2.
Black Spring written from eyes of child who knows joy and horror.

E3483   Capouya, Emile. "Henry Miller," Salmagundi, I (Fall 1965), 81-87.
"It may be that his work will serve chiefly to give lesser writers self-confidence and freedom, partly because it states in the strongest terms the artist's modern autonomy" (p. 81).

E3484   Kitaif, Theodore. "Becoming Oneself," Prairie Schooner, XXXIX (Fall 1965), 270-273.
Review of Bern Porter's I've Left where the Porter-Miller friendship is mentioned.

E3485   "Henry Miller: Quiet Days in Clichy," Choice, II (November 1965), 581.
Nostalgia about former days in Paris.

E3486   "Henry Miller: The Rosy Crucifixion," Choice, II (November 1965), 581.
Trilogy about Miller's struggle to find himself and become a writer.

E3487   "Henry Miller: The World of Sex," Choice, II (November 1965), 647.
"A short, finely written autobiographical-philosophical statement of Miller's ideas on the subject of sex."

E3488   Raes, Hugo. "Struasvogeltje Spelen: De Evolutie van de Erotische Literatuur," Vlaamse Gids, XLIX (November 1965), 693-706.
A look at Tropic's effect on erotic literature.   (In Dutch.)

E3489   Steiner, George. "Arts pose le question," Arts, November

10-16, 1965, 3-6.
Importance of Tropic freeing literature from the censor noted.   (In French.)

E3490   Austin, Alex.   "The Real Henry Miller," Gentleman, V
(December 1965), 52-54, 59.
Miller concerned with exploring the self; he looks in
self's mirror and becomes naked.

E3491   "Henry Miller and the Critics," English Association, December 1965.
Wickes' Henry Miller and the Critics balances critical
opinions of Miller with 21 different opinions.

E3492   "Flowers of the Miller Mill," Times Literary Supplement,
LXIV (December 16, 1965), 1177.
Miller goes beyond sex: "Miller's writing has a
centre [which] is not sex but the search for a lyrico-
religious state in which the beauty and the horror of
life are fused ... " (p. 1177).

E3493   Bedford, Richard.   "Full of the Old Harry," East-West
Review, II (Winter 1965-6), 115-123.
Critical evaluation of Just Wild About Harry which
sees the play as another of Miller's life-giving forces.

E3494   "Big Sur," Camera Mainichi, II (1966), 12-13, 44-50.
Look at Miller's Big Sur.   (In Japanese.)

E3495   Gresset, Michel.   "Les Rites matinaux de John Cowper
Powys," Cahiers du Sud, LIII (1966), 85-89.
Powys' account of daily events compared to Miller's.

E3496   Ueno, K.   "Born Out of a Wound," New Bound, I (1966),
26-47.
Essay about Miller's birth in a sterile America and
his movement and flowering in Paris.   (In Japanese.)

E3497   Rode, Alex.   "Henry Miller: The Novelist as Liberator,"
Américas, XVIII (January 1966), 41-43.
Because Miller is open and honest, he faces rejection
in America, a country that does not accept truthful
standards of life.

E3498   Gowland, Peter.   "Novelist Henry Miller: 'I Prefer to
Carry the Image in My Mind, Even if It Becomes Slightly
Blurred in Time... ," Photography, LVIII (March 1966),
66-67, 100.
Miller talks about photography: "I feel that when a
celebrity is being photographed he should be surrounded
by his atmosphere.   The picture should reflect the
ambiance and thought of the person" (p. 100).

E3499   Kermode, Frank. "Henry Miller and John Betjeman,"
        Encounter, XVI (March 1966), 69-75.
                Critics and Miller fail to see eye-to-eye when talking
                about "measure" and "form": "Miller's strength lies
                in his ability to depose intellect, to frighten away
                measure" (p. 74).

E3500   Mathison, Paul. "Henry Miller: Veteran Hero of Sexual
        Revolution--Paints!" Los Angeles Free Press, III (March
        11, 1966), 1.
                Miller leads a sexual revolution in U.S., for his paint-
                ings and writing are both spontaneous, not traditional
                in the American sense.

E3501   Seldis, Henry J. "More to Miller than Meets the Eye,"
        Los Angeles Times, LXXXV (March 14, 1966), IV 1, 12.
                Miller's watercolors called joyous and exuberant, free
                of anger and frustration. He echoes Klee's magic and
                Marin's transformation of nature.

E3502   Bart, Peter. "A Second Career for Henry Miller," New
        York Times, CXV (March 23, 1966), 40.
                Miller interested in painting not writing, as his paint-
                ings are shown at Westwood Art Association.

E3503   Geismar, Maxwell. "Henry Miller: Last of the Giants,"
        Minority of One, VIII (April 1966), 20-21.
                Review of The Rosy Crucifixion which is seen as more
                crafted than Miller's first trilogy. It compares Miller
                to the "divine innocence" of Melville and the radical
                social criticism of Dreiser.

E3504   "People," Time, LXXXVII (April 1, 1966), 40.
                Miller gives up writing and the sexual revolution for
                painting.

E3505   "Exhibit to Travel," Los Angeles Times, LXXXV (April
        7, 1966), VIII 16.
                Miller exhibit to leave Westwood Art Association and
                go on tour.

E3506   Flatley, Guy. "Time of the Oscar," New York Times,
        CXV (April 17, 1966), X 25.
                Miller feels the camera incapable of establishing itself
                as art because it dominates and silences the artist.

E3507   "GPO Employee Writes 'Novel'," n.p., April 21, 1966.
                Miller writes Preface to Will Slotnikoff's The First
                Time I Live, a book which concerns itself with letters
                to and by Miller.

E3508   Dury, David. "Sex Goes Public: A Talk with Henry
        Miller," Esquire, LXV (May 1966), 118-121, 170-172.

Interview with Miller where he voices anger at America's obsession with sex because it is so one-dimensional: "One is bored with making such a tremendous issue of [sex]" (p. 118).

E3509   Ruuth, Marianne. "Sällsamt nöte: Olle Länsberg Hemma Hos Henry Miller," Idun-Vecko Journalen, May 13, 1966, 20-26.
Ruuth records discussion between Ollee Lansberg and Miller on sex, life, and humanity. (In Swedish.)

E3510   Mitchell, Edward B. "Artists and Artists: The 'Aesthetics' of Henry Miller," Texas Studies in Literature and Language, VIII (Spring 1966), 103-115.
Discusses Miller's view of artist as creative "seer." For the great artists like Dostoyevsky, Whitman, Baudelaire, Hamsun, Blake, and Lautremont have gone beyond fragmentation to attain a new vision of life.

E3511   Smithline, Arnold. "Henry Miller and the Transcendental Spirit," Emerson Society Quarterly, II (Quarter 1966), 50-56.
Miller's novels depict raw personal experience like most transcendentalists, which Miller follows further through his moralistic and prophetic words.

E3512   "Henry Miller: Henry Miller Letters to Anaïs Nin," Choice, III (June 1966), 310.
Letters form Miller's autobiography from 1931 to 1945.

E3513   Ueno, K. "Henry Miller," New Bound, II (July 1966), 1-4.
A look at Miller's paintings in oil. (In Japanese.)

E3514   "[Henry Miller and 'The Cool World'], " Hon no Techô, VI (August 1966), 29-34.
The world has not been receptive to Miller's writing. (In Japanese.)

E3515   Hirokazu, Koto. "[Henry Miller and Lawrence Durrell]," Hon no Techô, VI (August 1966), 50-56.
Miller-Durrell Correspondence favorably reviewed. (In Japanese.)

E3516   Koichim, Irsima. "[Is Henry Miller a Burlesque?]," Hon no Techô, VI (August 1966), 61-65.
Exploration of Capricorn and Plexus. (In Japanese.)

E3517   Koji, Nishimura. "[Mythology and a Strayed Dog: Henry Miller's Essay on Greece]," Hon no Techô, VI (August 1966), 6-13.
Review of Colossus of Maroussi and of Miller's impressions on Greece. (In Japanese.)

E3518   Kojo, Nakada. "[Memoranda of Henry Miller]," Hon no
        Techô, VI (August 1966), 35-38.
        Look at Miller's stories and essays in The Cosmologi-
        cal Eye. (In Japanese.)

E3519   Masahito, Ara. "[Henry Miller and Dostoevsky]," Hon no
        Techô, VI (August 1966), 45-49.
        Miller's writing compared to Dostoevsky's. (In Japa-
        nese.)

E3520   Seiju, Narita. "[Tropic of Capricorn]," Hon no Techô,
        VI (August 1966), 19-23.
        Exploration of Capricorn. (In Japanese.)

E3521   Shinichiro, Nakamura. "[The Method of Novel in Henry
        Miller]," Hon no Techô, VI (August 1966), 57-60.
        Review of Remember to Remember as autobiographical
        novel. (In Japanese.)

E3522   Shoichi, Saeki. "[American Imagination--Miller and Poe],"
        Hon no Techô, VI (August 1966), 39-44.
        Miller's Big Sur compared to the writings of Poe.
        (In Japanese.)

E3523   Yasuo, Okubo. "[Memoranda of Henry Miller]," Hon no
        Techô, VI (August 1966), 24-28.
        Miller recalls moments and books from his past that
        have meant a great deal to him. (In Japanese.)

E3524   Yokichi, Miyamoto. "[Revolution of Sex Done by Henry
        Miller]," Hon no Techô, VI (August 1966), 14-18.
        Look at the ways Miller has freed literature. (In
        Japanese.)

E3525   Traschen, Isadore. "Henry Miller: The Ego and I,"
        South Atlantic Quarterly, LXV (Summer 1966), 345-354.
        Article looking at Miller's disintegration in his works
        following Cancer and ending with utter failure in Black
        Spring. Yet Miller's sexual freedom and literary
        freedom admired.

E3526   Zinnes, Harriet. "The Two Selves in Letters," Prairie
        Schooner, XL (Summer 1966), 172-174.
        Review of Miller's Letters to Anaïs Nin that sees
        Miller's devotion to the self as a devotion to truth.

E3527   Allen, James L. "Miller, Henry," Twentieth Century
        Literature, XII (October 1966), 164.
        Isadore Traschen's "Henry Miller" depicts a man
        whose life is without consequence.

E3528   Ueno, K. "Henry Miller as the Writer," New Bound, II
        (October 1966), 12-38.

A look at the uniqueness of Miller's writing.   (In Japanese.)

E3529   Roth, Gerhard.   "Über Henry Miller," Impuls, October-November-December 1966, 16-19.
Review of Sexus and other Miller works that compares him to Rimbaud, Céline, and D. H. Lawrence.   (In German.)

E3530   "[Henry Miller Proposes to Hoki Tokuda]," Josei Jishin, IX (November 1966), 115-117.
Article dealing with Miller's fifth marriage.   (In Japanese.)

E3531   "Lays of Ancient Paris," Times Literary Supplement, LXV (November 10, 1966), 1017.
Quiet Days in Clichy a book about Miller's sexual encounters in the Tropic world of Paris.

E3532   "[The Great American Writer, Henry Miller, Proposed to Hoki Tokuda]," Josei Jishin, IX (November 14, 1966), 115-117.
Miller proposes to woman who will be fifth bride.   (In Japanese.)

E3533   "Henry Miller May Wed Japanese Entertainer," Asahi Evening News, November 16, 1966, 6.
Miller asks Hoki Tokuda to marry him.   (In English.)

E3534   Ruuth, Marianne.   "Henry Milleristä ja elämästä," Me Naiset, November 16, 1966), 42-45.
(In Swedish.)

E3535   Beljon, J. J.   "Henry Miller Krijgt een Kwast," Podium, XX (December 1966), 10-16.
Biography of Miller which pays special attention to time he spent in U.S. after the War and to his painting.   (In Dutch.)

E3536   Dury, David.   "Henry Miller's Real Woman," Mademoiselle, LXIV (December 1966), 90-91, 150-151.
The central aspect of Miller's life is woman, a being who needs to be self-sufficient but not a man. Through gaining a sense of self, instead of imitating man, the woman is able to "be submissive [because] she's receptive and responsive and giving," because she is whole and has nothing to fear (p. 91).

E3537   Miller, Tony.   "Henry Miller: jours tranquilles à Clichy," Arcanes, 1967.
Quiet Days in Clichy described as humorous, sexy book depicting Miller's early years in Paris.   (In French.)

E3538   Hassan, Ihab.   "The Literature of Silence: From Henry

Miller to Beckett & Burroughs," Encounter, XXVIII (January 1967), 74-82.
Miller seen as writer who leaves readers with emptiness that makes one feel uncomfortable so he must dismiss this nothingness and death in life philosophy.

E3539   Katz, Joseph. "Henry Miller's Beauford DeLaney: A Correction," American Notes and Queries, LXVIII (January 1967).

E3540   Lund, Mary Graham. "Henry Miller: A Fierce Oracle," North American Review, CCLII (January 1967), 18-21.
Review of Sexus that sees Miller's acceptance of the moment, conflict, and America thus creating a many sided Bergsonian world.

E3541   Viereck, Peter. "The Muse and the Machine: Impact of Industrialism on Poets--and on Humanity," Etudes Anglaises, XX (January-March 1967), 38-46.
Miller a prophet who wants to defend natural primitive impulses against artificiality, rationalism, and all other corruptions of modern life.

E3542   Ikeda, Masuo. "Henry Miller and 'Henry'," Bungei, VI (February 1967), 224-229.
The two Henry Millers, the writer and the painter explored. (In Japanese.)

E3543   Pavillard, Dan. "Henry Miller Book in the Works," Tucson Daily Citizen, XCV (February 1967), 20.
Notes publication of Miller's Order and Chaos Chez Hans Reichel.

E3544   Sackett, S. J. "Vlaamse Gids," Abstracts of English Studies, X (February 1967), 131.
Article by Hugo Raes dealing with Tropic's effect on erotic literature.

E3545   Tonoyama, Taiji. "Seibungaku no Kyoshô Henri Mirâ Kaihimoku," Town, I (February 1967), 48-56.
Interview with Miller. (In Japanese.)

E3546   Anh, Tran thi Phuong. "Trois Messages," Synthèses, XXII (February-March 1967), 55.
Miller the humanitarian being who started the revolution of the sixties. (In French.)

E3547   Bose, Buddhadeva. "Visite à Big Sur," Synthèses, XXII (February-March 1967), 42-47.
Bose talks about his visit with Miller at Big Sur and the exchange of letters that resulted. (In French.)

E3548   Brassaï, Pauline. "Conversation avec Henry Miller," Synthèses, XXII (February-March 1967), 38-41.

Miller calls the American stupid and enjoys the
remoteness of Big Sur. (In French.)

E3549 Delaney, Beauford. "Trois Messages," Synthèses, XXII
(February-March 1967), 55.
Miller a spirit with a cosmic vision; his transcendent
philosophy based on the beauty and uplifting of here
and now. (In French.)

E3550 Delteil, Joseph. "L'Enfant Henry Miller," Synthèses,
XXII (February-March 1967), 30-31.
Miller's youth in New York explored. (In French.)

E3551 Denat, Antoine. "De Montaigne à Miller," Synthèses,
XXII (February-March 1967), 56-62.
Both Miller and Montaigne seen as disciples of Berg-
son. (In French.)

E3552 Durrell, Lawrence. "Le Souffle du dragon," Synthèses,
XXII (February-March 1967), 30-33.
Miller writes about his many lives in Tropic in a
realistic manner that rivals Joyce and Lawrence. (In
French.)

E3553 Gelre, Henk van. "Le Langage de la vie," Synthèses,
XXII (February-March 1967), 96-100.
Miller captures life in the Tropics, Black Spring,
Rosy Crucifixion, and Quiet Days in Clichy. (In
French.)

E3554 Gertz, Elmer. "Mon Client, Henry Miller," Synthèses,
XXII (February-March 1967), 51-53.
Gertz talks about his 1961 defense of Tropic in Illinois.
(In French.)

E3555 Hubin, Jean-Paul. "Bibliographie," Synthèses, XXII (Feb-
ruary-March 1967), 115-116.
Short unannotated primary source bibliography of
Miller's work in French. (In French.)

E3556 Hubin, Jean-Paul. "Miller raconte sa vie," Synthèses,
XXII (February-March 1967), 104-114.
Brief biography of Miller dating from 1891-1966. (In
French.)

E3557 Lambilliotte, Maurice. "Editorial," Synthèses, XXII
(February-March 1967), 7.
Miller's greatness and love for France discussed. (In
French.)

E3558 Lesdain, Pierre. "Le Colosse de Big Sur," Synthèses,
XXII (February-March 1967), 8-14.
Miller viewed as religious writer because of his con-
cern with life, rebirth, and God. (In French.)

E3559   Nin, Anaïs. "Pages de Journal," Synthèses, XXII (Febru-
        ary-March 1967), 18-29.
                Pieces from The Diary of Anaïs Nin presented as she
                discusses her relationship with Miller, the flamboyant
                revolutionary who wrote Tropic. (In French.)

E3560   Okumura, Osamu. "Miller et le moi authentique,"
        Synthèses, XXII (February-March 1967), 89-95.
                Miller compared to Emerson, Thoreau, Whitman,
                Lawrence. He is seen as naturalist, transcendentalist,
                and existentialist. (In French.)

E3561   Perlès, Alfred. "Encore une lettre d'anniversaire,"
        Synthèses, XXII (February-March 1967), 34-37.
                Perlès writes Miller letter of commemoration of life
                spent together in Paris. (In French.)

E3562   Prévélakis, Pandélis. "Prospéro le jeune," Synthèses,
        XXII (February-March 1967), 32-33.
                Miller an artist trying to reform society through
                heavenly creations. (In French.)

E3563   Ruuth, Marianne. "Pacific Palisades," Synthèses, XXII
        (February-March 1967), 48-50.
                Look at secluded life Big Sur affords Miller. (In
                French.)

E3564   Simenon, George. "Trois Messages," Synthèses, XXII
        (February-March 1967), 55.
                Miller changed a generation through a revolution in
                morality. (In French.)

E3565   Temple, F. J. "L'Oncle d'Amérique," Synthèses, XXII
        (February-March 1967), 32-35.
                Miller an artist, a pornographer, and a religious
                thinker. (In French.)

E3566   Wulff, Wilh Th. H. "Henry Miller, 75 ans...," Synthèses,
        XXII (February-March 1967), 101-103.
                Miller a prophet of life with apocalyptic vision. (In
                French.)

E3567   Fujishima, Taisuke. "[Henry Miller, Suffering from
        Love]," Asahi Gurafu, March 1967, 30-33.
                To Miller, love the same in every language except
                Japanese. (In Japanese.)

E3568   Fujishima, Taisuke. "[The Passion of 76-year-old Henry
        Miller]," Bungeishunju, XLV (April 1967), 316-322.
                Description of Miller's courtship of Hoki. (In Japa-
                nese.)

E3569   Ueno, K. "[Henry Miller and Hamsun]," New Bound, III

(April 1967), 13-54.
Miller compared to his idol, Knut Hamsun.   (In Japanese.)

E3570   Schwartz, Edward P.   "Henry Miller's Self-Liberation,"
Minneapolis Tribune, C (April 30, 1967), E7.
Review of William Gordon's The Mind and Art of Henry
Miller which Schwartz calls the first fine full-length
study of this author's belief in individualism and free-
dom.

E3571   Abe, Yasushi.   "[A Japanese Lady Who Rejected Henry
Miller's Love]," Mademoiselle [Tokyo], VIII (May 1967),
214-219.
Miller's courtship of Hoki recounted.   (In Japanese.)

E3572   "The End of Love," Shūkan-shinchō, XII (June 1967), 108-
110.
Miller's love affair with Hoki described.   (In Japanese.)

E3573   "International Love: Henry Miller Fell in Love with Hoki
Tokuda," Playboy, XIV (June 1967), 22-26.
Discussion of the Miller-Hoki love relationship.

E3574   Smith, Marcus.   "South Atlantic Quarterly," Abstracts of
English Studies, X (June 1967), 390.
Analysis of Traschen's "Henry Miller"; shows Miller's
lack of interest in sex.

E3575   Pavillard, Don.   "Henry Miller Book in the Works,"
Tucson Daily Citizen, XCV (July 1967), 20.
Loujon Press announces publication of Miller's Order
and Chaos Chez Hans Reichel.

E3576   Thomas, Bob.   "Henry Miller Annoyed by Belated Recognition," Tucson Star, July 6, 1967, 14.
Miller feels recognition came too late, yet early success might have been his ruin.

E3577   "[Love Letters Sent to Hoki Tokuda by Henry Miller],"
Shūkan Sanhei, XVI (July 10, 1967), 14-19.
Story about Miller's love for singer, Hoki Tokuda.
(In Japanese.)

E3578   Loper, Mary Lou.   "A Splashy Tribute to Henry Miller,"
Los Angeles Times, LXXXVI (August 1, 1967), IV 1.
Westwood Art Association honored author-painter
Miller who donated 60 paintings and 10 etchings to the
group.

E3579   Slotnikoff, Will.   "The Existentialist Ordeal of Michael
Fraenkel," Trace, XVI (Summer 1967), 175-184.
Discussion of the Miller-Fraenkel philosophy of death.

E3580   Dawson, Lawrence R.   "Encounter," Abstracts of English
        Studies, X (September 1967), 428.
             Review of Hassan's "Literature of Silence" which sees
        Miller's work as social outrage.

E3581   Gold, William E.   "Henry Miller, 75, to Wed Singer, 29,"
        Los Angeles Herald Examiner, XCVI (September 6, 1967),
        1.
             Miller to marry for fifth time.

E3582   "Henry Miller's Fiancee," West Los Angeles Independent,
        XXXVIII (September 7, 1967), 1.
             Miller to marry Hoki Tokuda.

E3583   "Wedding in the Offing," Los Angeles Times, LXXXVI
        (September 7, 1967), 3.
             Miller to marry Tokuda.

E3584   Windeler, Robert.   "Henry Miller Taking Art and Bride
        to Paris," New York Times, CXVI (September 8, 1967),
        36.
             Miller to marry Hoki Tokuda and travel to Paris with
        bride and paintings.

E3585   Gold, William E.   "Author Henry Miller Will Wed Japa-
        nese Actress," Los Angeles Herald Examiner, XCVII
        (September 9, 1967), 3.
             Miller to wed Hoki.

E3586   "Henry Miller, 75, and Singer Get License," Los Angeles
        Times, LXXXVI (September 9, 1967), 2.
             Miller and Hoki get marriage license.

E3587   Blackburn, Cliff.   "Henry Miller, Japanese Bride Plan
        Europe Trip," Los Angeles Herald Examiner, XCVI
        (September 11, 1967), 1.
             Miller and Hoki played ping pong following marriage.

E3588   "Henry Miller, 75, Marries Japanese Entertainer, 28,"
        New York Times, CXVI (September 11, 1967), 91.
             On September 10, Miller married Hoki.

E3589   Carroll, Jerry.   "Miller Begins 'Last Adventure' in SM,"
        Roberts News, September 14, 1967, 6.
             Miller's getting marriage license last great adventure.

E3590   "Henry Miller and Bride to Leave for Europe," Los Ange-
        les Times, LXXXVI (September 17, 1967), 2.
             Miller and Hoki leave for Europe on honeymoon trip.

E3591   "Henry Miller Escapes Crowd at His Art Show," New York
        Times, CXVII (September 23, 1967), 27.
             Exhibition of Miller watercolors and etchings interests

few, as many come to pay homage to Miller.

E3592   Phalle, Thérèse de Saint.   "Henry Miller à Paris,"
Le Figaro Littéraire, September 25-October 1, 1967, 44.
Miller discusses his love for Paris as he returns to
the streets where Tropic was written.   (In French.)

E3593   Bory, Jean-Louis.   "Voyage au bout du jour," Le Nouvel
Observateur, October 11-17, 1967, 36-37.
Miller praised for Letters to Anaïs Nin and Quiet
Days in Clichy.   (In French.)

E3594   Baxter, Annette K.   "A Singular Talent," New York Times,
CXVII (October 15, 1967), VII 46-47.
Review of Gordon's The Mind and Art of Henry Miller
sees Miller's writing as his attempt to discover the
self as artist and man.

E3595   Roche, Denis.   "Le Dernier des grands Américains," La
Quinzaine Littéraire, October 15, 1967, 12-13.
Noted is the friendship in this preface to selected
letters from Miller to Nin.   (In French.)

E3596   Djwa, Sandra.   "Leonard Cohen: Black Romantic," Canadian Literature, Autumn 1967, 32-42.
Cohen compared to American "Romantic" Miller.

E3597   Levitt, Morton P.   "Art and Correspondences: Durrell,
Miller, and the Alexandria Quartet," Modern Fiction
Studies, XIII (Autumn 1967), 299-318.
Article based on the Durrell-Miller Correspondence
which sees Durrell rising in the world of arts and
letters while Miller sinks.

E3598   Morcos, Mona Louis.   "Elements of the Autobiographical
in The Alexandria Quartet," Modern Fiction Studies, XIII
(Autumn 1967), 343-359.
Mentions the Durrell-Miller correspondence.

E3599   Phillips, William.   "Writing About Sex," Partisan Review,
XXIV (Fall 1967), 552-563.
Discusses Miller and Mailer and their feelings about
sex.

E3600   Phillipson, John S.   "Aryan Path," Abstracts of English
Studies, X (November 1967), 549-550.
Evaluation of Sylvia Norman's "Claude Houghton and
Texas" where it is noted that Miller was one of few
men to value Houghton.

E3601   "Henry Miller: Order and Chaos Chez Hans Reichel,"
Choice, IV (December 1967), 1117.
Essential work in Miller canon about artist Reichel.

E3602   Lund, Mary Graham.   "Paper Boats or the Hydra-Headed
         Woe," Trace, XVII (1968), 27-32.
         Miller uses dirty words for shock effect and to make
         reader aware of himself.

E3603   Slotnikoff, Will.   "The Existentialist Ordeal of Michael
         Fraenkel--II," Trace, XVII (1968), 353-364.
         Fraenkel seen as publisher of Miller.

E3604   Hoffman, Frederick J.   "The Mind and Art of Henry
         Miller," American Literature, XXXIX (January 1968), 580-
         582.
         Hoffman calls Gordon's treatment of Miller one of first
         movements in the direction of serious and fresh criti-
         cism of this author.

E3605   Stoddard, F. A.   "Paris Review," Abstracts of English
         Studies, XI (January 1968), 44.
         Review of interview between George Wickes and Miller
         where Miller discusses writing techniques and life
         before and after Tropic's publication.

E3606   Matthews, Frank M.   "Patriotic Justice: Down with Henry
         Miller--and Senator Joe Clark," New Republic, CLVIII
         (February 3, 1968), 13-14.
         Miller the dirty writer of filthy book called Tropic.

E3607   Cameron, Kenneth Walter.   "Emerson Society Quarterly,"
         Abstracts of English Studies, XI (March 1968), 132.
         Miller reflects admiration for Emerson and Whitman
         through his belief in potential divinity of man.

E3608   Pontual, Roberto.   "Fontes--Roteiro de Henry Miller,"
         Revista Civilização Brasileira, IV (March-April 1968), 153-
         168.
         Discussion of Rosy Crucifixion that sees work as revo-
         lutionary, consciousness expanding, erotic, and sur-
         realistic.   (In Portuguese.)

E3609   Eulert, Donald.   "East-West Review," Abstracts of Eng-
         lish Studies, XI (April 1968).
         Richard Bedford's "Full of the Old Harry" sees play
         as religious, an allegory of a Coney Island world,
         and a statement on self.

E3610   Matilla-Rivas, Alfredo.   "Notas sobre Naked Lunch de
         William S. Burroughs," Asomante, XXIV (April-June 1968),
         42-44.
         Burroughs continues the sexual explicitness of Miller.
         (In Spanish.)

E3611   Fujishima, Taisuke.   "[Mr. and Mrs. Henry Miller and
         I]," Asahi Gurafu, May 1968, 20-21.

Henry and Hoki Miller and Taisuke Fujishima are seen at Miller's home in Los Angeles.   (In Japanese.)

E3612   Kimio, Nakayama.   "[Henry Miller Exhibition]," Geijutsu Shinchô, XIX (May 1968), 112-116.
Exhibition of Miller's art in Tokyo.   (In Japanese.)

E3613   "The Millers and Exhibition," Asahi Gurafu, May 1968, 16-19.
Discussion of Henry, Hoki, and Henry's watercolors. (In Japanese.)

E3614   Tokuda, Hoki.   "[Please Look at the Paintings of My Husband, Henry Miller]," Asahi Graph, May 1968, 15-21.
On the showing of Miller's paintings in Tokyo, Hoki wrote this piece explaining importance of Miller's art. (Included are seven watercolors.)   (In Japanese.)

E3615   Nin, Anaïs.   "Novel of the Future," Studies in the Twentieth Century, Spring 1968, 79-108.
Miller a man of action and adventure who used the language of the man on the streets and then enriched this world through surreal flights of language.

E3616   Williams, John.   "Henry Miller: The Success of Failure," Virginia Quarterly Review, XLIV (Spring 1968), 225-245.
Concern for money and its rejection form the dual stands on which Miller's character is explored.   Miller repr⌣sents a man steeped in personal depression who turned inward and then turned his back on monetary success.

E3617   Iida, Yoshikuni.   "Around Henry Miller," Shusaku Bigutsu, June 1968, 10-20.
The world of Miller the artist explored.   (In Japanese.)

E3618   Weigel, John A.   "Lawrence Durrell's First Novel," Twentieth Century Literature, XIV (July 1968), 75-83.
Durrell, in the tradition of Miller, has insisted on certain human rights in his writing.

E3619   "Big Believers," Times Literary Supplement, LXVII (August 29, 1968), 922.
Gordon's The Mind and Art of Henry Miller called explication, not criticism.

E3620   Erzgraber, Willi.   "Modern Fiction Studies," Abstracts of English Studies, XI (September 1968), 365.
Mona Louis Morcos notes that the correspondence between Miller and Durrell is autobiography.

E3621   Erzgraber, Willi.   "Modern Fiction Studies," Abstracts of English Studies, XI (September 1968), 365.

Morton Levitt notes that Miller taught Durrell that no distinction can be made between artist and his art.

E3622   Paulson, Barbara A.   "Partisan Review," Abstracts of English Studies, XI (September 1968), 378.
In William Phillips' "Writing About Sex" he discusses Miller and Mailer and their feelings about sex.

E3623   Ruuth, Marianne. "O amor em questão," Cruzeiro, XL (September 21, 1968), 186-188.
Discussion of merits of Miller's marriage at 76 to Hoki.   Noted is fact that love can happen at any time. (In Portuguese.)

E3624   Allaback, Stephen.   "Miller, Henry," Twentieth Century Literature, XIV (October 1968), 176-177.
Miller has achieved Horatio Alger myth according to John Williams' "Henry Miller: The Success of Failure."

E3625   Bode, Elroy.   "The World on Its Own Terms: A Brief for Steinbeck, Miller, and Simenon," Southwest Review, LIII (Autumn 1968), 406-409.
Miller ignored because of the sexual stigma, and because he does not fit into the categories of essayist, novelist, or short story writer, and because Miller deals with the self (a part of one's being that most people are trying to escape).

E3626   Brodin, Pierre.   "Henry Miller," Studies in the Twentieth Century, Fall 1968, 61-68.
French biography of Miller where he is seen as bohemian and moralist in tradition of Thoreau, Emerson, and Whitman.   Also presented is a chronology of novels from 1934 to 1965.

E3627   Hauser, Marianne.   "Anaïs Nin: Myth and Reality," Studies in the Twentieth Century, Fall 1968, 45-50.
Miller, as early as 1937, saw the value of Nin's Diary.

E3628   McEvilly, Wayne.   "Portrait of Anaïs Nin as a Bodhisattva: Reflections on the Diary, 1934-39," Studies in the Twentieth Century, Fall 1968, 51-60.
Miller compared Nin's Diary to Confessions of St. Augustine.

E3629   Stern, Daniel.   "The Diary of Anaïs Nin," Studies in the Twentieth Century, Fall 1968, 39-43.
Nin seen as having influenced Miller and having been part of his bohemian circle.

E3630   Crunden, Patricia.   "Nouvelle Review Française," Abstracts

of English Studies, XI (November 1968), 486.
　　Jerome Peignot calls Miller a natural poet who glorifies life, like Gertrude Stein.

E3631   Pietralunga, Mario.   "Henry Miller il punto sul mondo,"
Executive, I (November 1968), 46-52.
　　Interview with Miller in the Pacific Palisades where
sex, Cancer, individualism, the writer, nudity, New
York, Hollywood, Colossus of Maroussi, Communism,
Italy, and other topics discussed.   (In Italian.)

E3632   Hochman, Sandra.   "Henry Miller: A World of Joy,"
New York Times, CXVIII (November 3, 1968), II 33.
　　Interview dealing with watercolor painting, Hoki, war,
California, insomnia, and self as clown.

E3633   "France Lifts Its Long Ban on Henry Miller's 'Sexus',"
New York Times, CXVIII (November 20, 1968), 51.
　　Sexus free to be sold to Frenchmen over age 17.

E3634   Meacham, Harry M.   "Collection of Letters: Corres-
pondence Adds to Miller Canon," Richmond News Leader,
XI (November 20, 1968).
　　Review of the Miller-Childs correspondence entitled
Collector's Quest, where Childs sees Miller as con-
temporary of Restif de la Bretonne.

E3635   Durrell, Lawrence.   "On Creativity," Playboy, XV (December 1968), 138.
　　Miller encouraged Durrell to be himself and display
his talent.

E3636   Patton, John J.   "Canadian Literature," Abstracts of English Studies, XI (December 1968), 512.
　　Leonard Cohen compared to Miller by Sandra Djwa.

E3637   Wieche, R. E.   "Virginia Quarterly Review," Abstracts of
English Studies, XI (December 1968), 557.
　　John Williams sees Miller's success as the failure of
his monetary ethic.

E3638   Cabau, Jacques.   "La Libération par la débauche,"
L'Express, December 16-22, 1968, 119-121.
　　Review of Sexus where Miller autobiographically de-
scribes his sexual liberation.   (In French.)

E3639   Detro, Gene.   "Patchen Interviewed," Outsider, II (Winter
1968-1969), 115-126.
　　Detro feels that Miller's prose has taken a back seat
to his painting.

E3640   Honda, Yasunari.   "Henry Miller," Waseda Review, VIII
(1969), 1-13.

Essay on Miller's early work, the Tropics and The Rosy Crucifixion where Miller talks about society's sterility.

E3641   Jackson, Paul R. "Henry Miller's Pregnancies," Literature and Psychology, XIX (1969), 35-49.
Miller uses the theme of rebirth and creates a cultural myth through the use of energy and feeling.

E3642   O'Dell, Jerry Clinton. "Miller, Henry," Twentieth Century Literature, XIV (January 1969), 251.
Review of Elroy Bode's "The World on Its Own Terms."

E3643   Ruuth, Marianne. "Sex Profeten med den Vackra Själen," Hemmets Journal, January 13, 1969, 8-9.
Marriage between Miller and Hoki shows great age difference yet a unity of love.   (In Swedish.)

E3644   Pauwels, Louis. "Louis Pauwels parle de Henry Miller," Le Nouveau Planète, February 1969, 151.
Publication of Sexus in France allowed Louis Pauwels to question Miller about the life force found in his Rosy Crucifixion.   (In French.)

E3645   Stoddard, F. G. "Paris Review," Abstracts of English Studies, XII (February 1969), 81.
Discussion of Miller's A Letter on Céline which basically consists of praise yet Miller's unwillingness to finish work.

E3646   Cotton, John. "Review: 'Collector's Quest...'," Private Library, II (Winter 1969), 190-191.
Collector's Quest a record of Child's Miller collection and of correspondence between these two men.

E3647   Balakian, Anna. "Anaïs Nin," American Literature, XLI (March 1969), 130-133.
Nin a friend of such experimental writers as Durrell and Miller.

E3648   "The Henry Miller Odyssey," Performing Arts at UCLA, April 1969, 17-18.
A look at Miller in Brooklyn and Paris.

E3649   " 'Henry Miller Odyssey' Set," Los Angeles Times, LXXXVIII (April 6, 1969), Cal 51.
Odyssey to premiere at UCLA's Royce Hall on April 12.

E3650   "Henry Miller's Plädoyer für die Liebe," Sieter, April 10, 1969, 79-80.
(In German.)

E3651   "Due Verfolgung; kurz Geschichte von Henry Miller,"
Twen, XI (May 1969), 53-58.
 Miller a mysterious man.   (In German.)

E3652   " 'Tropic of Cancer' in Production in France," Los Angeles
Times, LXXXVIII (May 23, 1969), IV 18.
 Tropic film directed by Joseph Strick being shot in
Paris.

E3653   Katz, Al.   "The Tropic of Cancer Trials: The Problem
of Relevant Moral and Artistic Controversy," Midway, IX
(Spring 1969), 99-125.
 Katz views eight court cases to suppress Cancer.

E3654   Hansen, Earl.   "Reflections on What We Can't Seem to
Stop," Seattle Post-Intelligencer, (June 21, 1969), S9.
 Review of television interview with Miller, who is
seen as the first prophet of American doom.

E3655   Thomas, Bob.   "Henry Miller Is Appalled at His Offspring,"
Richmond Times-Dispatch, CXIX (June 29, 1969), F5.
 Miller looks at America, her youth, and sees only deterioration: "This country is going through a process
of deterioration and disintegration."

E3656   Brassaï, Gyula Halász.   "Inédit: Paris en 1930 vu,"
Photo, VIII (July 1969), 24-33, 79.
 Brassaï remembers Miller, his works Tropic, Black
Spring, and Max, and their importance.   (In French.)

E3657   Thomas, Bob.   "The Novel Died 30 Years Ago," Shreveport Times, CXXXI (July 6, 1969), F13.
 Appraisal of Miller at age 77 where he is seen changing the course of literature.

E3658   Conger, Lesley.   "Other People's Bookshelves," Writer,
LXXXII (August 1969), 9-10.
 Salute to Miller's The Books in My Life.

E3659   "Tropic Revisited," Newsweek, LXVII (August 18, 1969),
10.
 Interview in 1969 in Paris as Miller watches filming
of Tropic, where he wishes he could return to the
past when writing the book.

E3660   Belmont, Georges.   "Le Vieil Homme et l'amour," Le
Nouvel Observateur, VII (August 25-31, 1969), 26-28.
 Look at Miller's rise from Tropic to best-seller
Sexus.   (In French.)

E3661   Davis, William V.   "Literary Theory," Abstracts of English Studies, XIII (September 1969), 3.
 Abstract of Nin's Novel of the Future where Nin sees

Miller as one of progressive writers attempting to link
unconscious to conscious mind.

E3662   Aba, Marika.   "Henry Miller Without the Horns," Los
Angeles Times, LXXXVIII (September 28, 1969), 1, 22, 43.
Miller a gentle, knowing man where Tropic readers
expect monster.

E3663   DeFalco, Joseph M.   "Miller, Henry," Twentieth Century
Literature, XV (October 1969), 183.
Summary of Paul Jackson's "Henry Miller's Literary
Pregnancies," where Jackson sees literary creation
involving transformation of personal doubt to myth of
personal regeneration.

E3664   Polley, George Warren.   "The Art of Religious Writing:
Henry Miller as Religious Writer," South Dakota Review,
VII (Autumn 1969), 61-73.
Miller's writing explores meaning of human existence,
which to Polley constitutes religious writing.   He
deals with rebirth, man's struggle to fulfill himself.

E3665   Almansi, G.   "Interview with Leslie A. Fiedler," 20th
Century Studies, I (November 1969), 56-67.
Fiedler sees Miller as writer attempting to write in
pleasure tradition and make sex a comic experience.

E3666   Almansi, G.   "Three Versions of an Article on Henry
Miller," 20th Century Studies, I (November 1969), 41-55.
Tropic helped return sex to literature in a passionate,
real-life manner.

E3667   Calvino, Italo.   "Considerations on Sex and Laughter,"
20th Century Studies, I (November 1969), 103-105.
Miller combines both grotesque and apocalyptic aspects
of erotic writer.

E3668   Cassola, Carlo.   "The Professional Viewpoint," 20th Century Studies, I (November 1969), 111-112.
Miller's work judged obscene.

E3669   "Henry Miller: Collector's Quest," Choice, VI (November
1969), 1223.
Letters provide more information about Miller.

E3670   Lodge, David.   "The Professional Viewpoint," 20th Century
Studies, I (November 1969), 118-120.
Miller a major contributor in battle for free expres-
sion.

E3671   Purdy, James.   "The Professional Viewpoint," 20th Century Studies, I (November 1969), 123.
Miller's ideas considered queer and inhuman like those

of the characters of The Scarlet Letter.

E3672   Granz, Norman.   "Letter to M. Georges Pompidou,"
L'Express, November 2, 1969, 87.
Miller mentioned.   (In French.)

E3673   Matthews, Jack.   "The Time and Place Were Special,"
New York Times, CXIX (November 16, 1969), 69.
In George Wickes' Americans in Paris, Miller feels
no artificial stimulus necessary to create.

E3674   Davis, William V.   "Anaïs Nin," Abstracts of English
Studies, XIII (December 1969), 255-256.
Review of Wayne McEvilly's "Portrait of Anaïs Nin"
where Miller compares her Diary to writing of St.
Augustine.

E3675   "Entretien avec Miller," Chroniques de l'Art Vivant, December 1969, 26-29.
Interview with Miller where he calls writing surrealistic.   (In French.)

E3676   Jackson, Paul R.   "The Balconies of Henry Miller," University Review, XXXVI (December 1969), 155-160.
Jackson views the detachment of the autobiographical
hero of Cancer through the balcony motif the book
presents.

E3677   Kallich, Martin.   "Henry Miller," Abstracts of English
Studies, XIII (December 1969), 255.
Abstract of Paul Jackson's 'Henry Miller's Pregnancies" where Miller uses archetypal images of rebirth
and recreation.

E3678   Thomas, Kevin.   " 'Miller Odyssey' on Screen at Caltech,"
Los Angeles Times, LXXXIX (December 5, 1969), IV 28.
Odyssey leaves one with liking of and knowledge of
Miller.

E3679   Schlesinger, Marian C.   "Anaïs Nin: An Era Recalled,"
Boston Globe, CXCVI (December 7, 1969), 20.
Nin attended screening of Henry Miller Odyssey at
Harvard.

E3680   Arbois, Janick.   "Bibliothèque de poche: Henry Miller,"
Le Monde, December 12, 1969, 3.
Miller will read from Nexus and will be photographed
walking through Paris with friends.

E3681   Sims, John F.   " 'Tropic' Not a Sex Movie," Los Angeles
Times, LXXXIX (January 3, 1970), II 7.
Joseph Strick sees Tropic as funny book, not primarily
sex story.

E3682   "An Afternoon with Anaïs Nin, an Evening with Henry
        Miller," Harvard Advocate, CIII (February 1970), 2-3.
        Discussion of Miller by Nin and viewing of Henry
        Miller Odyssey. The conclusion is that Miller one of
        great surrealists and originals to write in America.

E3683   Robillard, Douglas J. "Henry Miller," Abstracts of Eng-
        lish Studies, XIII (February 1970), 394.
        Summary of Emile Capouya's "Henry Miller" in which
        Miller is called a prophet.

E3684   Greenwood, Leonard. "Sex, Samba Disputes Cloud Carni-
        val for Rio," Los Angeles Times, LXXXIX (February 8,
        1970), B4.
        Theme of festival in Rio De Janeiro is "Sexus, Nexus,
        Plexus" for the Miller paintings entered.

E3685   Thompson, Howard. "Rip Torn Portrays Miller in 'Tropic
        of Cancer' Adaptation," New York Times, CXIX (February
        20, 1970), 31.
        Tropic movie much like book, a comic, sexual adven-
        ture.

E3686   Simon, John. "This 'Road' Is a Dead End," New York
        Times, CXIX (February 22, 1970), II 1, 11.
        Tropic film does not work as outpouring of Miller's
        lust and as documentary of American "lost generation"
        in Paris.

E3687   "Producer of 'Cancer' Raps Film's Rating," Los Angeles
        Times, LXXXIX (February 23, 1970), IV 20.
        Tropic film producer, Joseph Stark, considers anti-
        trust action against Motion Picture Association on
        grounds its rating system restricts trade.

E3688   Centing, Richard and Benjamin Franklin V. "The Henry
        Miller Odyssey," Under the Sign of Pisces: Anaïs Nin and
        Her Circle, I (Winter 1970), 3-6.
        Discussion of and quotes from The Henry Miller Odys-
        sey.

E3689   Centing, Richard. "Review of the Diary of Anaïs Nin,
        Volume Three, 1939-1944," Under the Sign of Pisces:
        Anaïs Nin and Her Circle, I (Winter 1970), 6-11.
        Miller writes to Nin describing devastation in Ameri-
        ca: "Imagine an area fifty square miles ... poisoned
        by the fumes [so] that everything is killed off ... "
        (p. 7).

E3690   Franklin, Benjamin. "Reprint of The Booster Now Avail-
        able," Under the Sign of Pisces: Anaïs Nin and Her
        Circle, I (Winter 1970), 11-12.
        Miller, Durrell, Perlès, Nin, and Saroyan formed

editorial board of The Booster.   Miller contributed
excerpts from Hamlet and Capricorn to magazine.

E3691   Jackson, Paul R.   "The Balconies of Henry Miller: Part
II, " University Review, XXXVI (March 1970), 221-225.
The balcony looked at as major metaphor in the two
Tropics where both the balcony and Brooklyn Bridge
afford Miller's protagonists a detachment from society.

E3692   Morton, Richard.   "John Cowper Powys, " Abstracts of
English Studies, XIII (March 1970), 442.
Review of Michel Gresset's "Les Rites matinaux de
John Cowper Powys" that compares the daily accounts
of Powys to those of Miller.

E3693   M. , J.   "Mixed Miller, " Newsweek, LXVIII (March 2,
1970), 57.
Review of movie Tropic that sees the horrible change
from Miller's 1930's people to Strick's 1960's milieu.

E3694   " 'Tropic of Capricorn' Ruled Obscene by Athens Court, "
New York Times, CXIX (March 8, 1970), 26.
Athens court ruled Tropic of Capricorn obscene and
ordered burning of 600 copies.

E3695   Weiler, A. H.   "Producer with 'X' Sues Over Rating, "
New York Times, CXIX (March 10, 1970), 51.
Strick challenged movie industry's rating system in
court for giving Tropic an 'X. "

E3696   "Suit on 'Tropic of Cancer' Called 'Baseless' by Valenti, "
New York Times, CXIX (March 11, 1970), 42.
Suit by Strick over Cancer rating called absurd by
Jack Valenti, president of Motion Picture Association.

E3697   Canby, Vincent.   "Will They Censor the Teenybopper? "
New York Times, CXIX (March 22, 1970), II 1, 22.
Tropic's "X" rating limits distribution capacity says
Strick.

E3698   Parbs, John R.   "Henry Miller, " Abstracts of English
Studies, XIII (April 1970), 530.
Review of Almansi's "Three Versions of Article on
Miller" where three different conceptions of this
artist are discussed.

E3699   Piche, Sister Robert Louise.   "Henry Miller, " Abstracts
of English Studies, XIII (April 1970), 530.
Review of Polley's "Art of Religious Writing" that
sees Miller as moral man caught in struggle with
evil.

E3700   Burns, Julie.   "Henry Miller: "There Are So Many Idiots

Among My Fans That I Wonder Who the Hell I'm Writing For," <u>Mademoiselle</u>, LXXI (May 1970), 162-163, 198-202. Interview where Miller sees life as everything and learning how to live together as essential.

E3701   "Henry Miller, Literary Dissident," <u>M. D.</u>, XIV (May 1970), 165-171.
Miller seen as man outside bounds of society.

E3702   Sachett, S. J. "Henry Miller," <u>Abstracts of English Studies</u>, XIII (May 1970), 593.
Evaluation of Esta Lou Riley's bibliography of Miller.

E3703   "Tropic of Cancer," <u>M. D.</u>, XIV (May 1970), 256.
Review of film <u>Tropic</u> that calls it uninhibited and funny.

E3704   Centing, Richard. "AN: A Selected Current Checklist," <u>Under the Sign of Pisces: Anaïs Nin and Her Circle</u>, I (Spring 1970), 15.
Centing suggests that Nin was much impressed with film on Miller, <u>The Henry Miller Odyssey</u>.

E3705   Centing, Richard. "The Henry Miller Odyssey," <u>Under the Sign of Pisces: Anaïs Nin and Her Circle</u>, I (Spring 1970), 9-11.
Miller and Nin discuss concept of universal love.

E3706   Centing, Richard. "Phoenix Rising," <u>Under the Sign of Pisces: Anaïs Nin and Her Circle</u>, I (Spring 1970), 14.
Miller first European editor of <u>Phoenix</u>. He wrote first major essay on Nin, "Un Être étoilique," concerning unpublished <u>Diary</u>.

E3707   Moore, Harry T. "Memorial Service for Caresse," <u>Under the Sign of Pisces: Anaïs Nin and Her Circle</u>, I (Spring 1970), 3-5.
Miller sent tape recording of remembrances to funeral.

E3708   Belmont, Georges. "Comment devenir vivant," <u>Planète</u>, XVI (June 1970), 21-27.
Miller depicts reality in <u>Tropics</u>, <u>Rosy Crucifixion</u>, <u>Colossus of Maroussi</u>. (In French.)

E3709   Beucler, Serge. "Truculence de la vérité," <u>Planète</u>, XVI (June 1970), 95-100.
Miller's work a series of contradictions. (In French.)

E3710   Bouyeure, Claude. "Miller et les autres," <u>Planète</u>, XVI (June 1970), 103-109.
<u>Sexus</u> viewed as tragedy-comedy. (In French.)

E3711   Desanti, Dominique. "La Faune et la femme nénuphar:

Henry Miller et Anaïs Nin," Planète, XVI (June 1970), 134-136.
> Unique love between Miller and Nin seen through the way one helps other. (In French.)

E3712   Durrell, Lawrence. "Le Souffle du dragon," Planète, XVI (June 1970), 53-55.
> Miller's work confirms value of life, like Joyce and Lawrence in his love for real world. (In French.)

E3713   Frère, J. C. "Connaissance de l'Orient," Planète, XVI (June 1970), 140-141.
> Miller compared to immortal sages of orient. (In French.)

E3714   Gennari, Bernard Thomas. "Les Rêves d'un rêve," Planète, XVI (June 1970), 119-125.
> Miller's Rosy Crucifixion seen as positive assessment of life. (In French.)

E3715   Hendache, Gilbert. "La Nouvelle Littérature Américaine," Planète, XVI (June 1970), 137-139.
> Miller one of first psycho-novelists to study American culture. (In French.)

E3716   Hordequin, Paul. "Les Pavés du Cancer," Planète, XVI (June 1970), 111-113.
> Miller's life one of misery when a member of Paris avant-garde. (In French.)

E3717   Lancelot, Patrick. "Just Wild About Harry," Planète, XVI (June 1970), 130-131.
> Just Wild About Harry a rhythmic, humorous piece for theatre quite different from O'Neill, Beckett, or Ionesco. (In French.)

E3718   Meirieu, Philippe. 'Dionysos: altérité et dualité," Planète, XVI (June 1970), 142-143.
> Miller shows nostalgia for Greek god, Dionysis. (In French.)

E3719   Odier, Daniel. "L'Instant comme extase," Planète, XVI (June 1970), 41-51.
> Miller a writer of symphonies about life. (In French.)

E3720   Parbs, John R. "Fiction," Abstracts of English Studies, XIII (June 1970), 659.
> Review of Almansi's "Interview with Fiedler" where Miller called greatest sex novelist we have.

E3721   Pauwels, Louis. "Lettre à Miller," Planète, XVI (June 1970), 7-11.
> Pauwels sends Miller love and admiration in letter

comparing Miller to Lawrence. (In French.)

E3722 "Quelques Thèmes...," Planète, XVI (June 1970), 57-80.
Authors look at certain themes in Miller's work: religion, sex, naturalism, women, the machine, fatalism,
freedom, the concept of place, and history. (In
French.)

E3723 Reumaux, Patrick. "Un Ciel sans images," Planète, XVI
(June 1970), 83-91.
Wholeness to life for Miller constantly in flux leading
to revolution. (In French.)

E3724 Smedt, Marc de. "Le Vagabond," Planète, XVI (June
1970), 13-19.
Biography of Miller traveling from his birth to early
years at Big Sur. His early works mentioned along
with belief he's a revolutionary. (In French.)

E3725 Smedt, Marc de. "Miller et la peinture de l'art naïf,"
Planète, XVI (June 1970), 129-130.
Miller the painter sees scope of life and captures its
spirit. (In French.)

E3726 Tees, Arthur T. "Henry Miller," Abstracts of English
Studies, XIII (June 1970), 655.
Review of Jackson's "Balconies of Henry Miller" that
sees detachment of autobiographical hero.

E3727 Tees, Arthur T. "Henry Miller," Abstracts of English
Studies, XIII (June 1970), 655.
Review of second part of Jackson article that sees
balcony as metaphor for Brooklyn Bridge that afforded
Miller detachment from society.

E3728 Thivolet, Marc. "Comment être tout et un," Planète, XVI
(June 1970), 29-39.
Miller has changed society through his violently real
picture of life. He has liberated sex and shown it for
what it is. (In French.)

E3729 Vos, Nelvin. "Norman Mailer," Abstracts of English
Studies, XIII (June 1970), 654-655.
Review of Millet's Sexual Politics where Miller's pro-
tagonist mocked.

E3730 Torn, Rip. "Brainwashed?" New York Times, CXIX
(June 7, 1970), II 6.
Torn disputes critic John Simon's saying he's goat-
like and has Texas accent in Tropic film.

E3731 "Henry Miller at 28 (and 77)," Gambit, June 9, 1970, 11.
Miller on TV in Encounter where he meets Buckminster

Fuller.

E3732   Champlin, Charles.   "Rip Torn Stars in 'Tropic of Cancer'," Los Angeles Times, LXXXIX (June 19, 1970), IV
17.
  Tropic film exploits sex yet misses Miller's freedom
and joy.

E3733   Champlin, Charles.   "Breakthrough or Breakdown in Film
Standards?" Los Angeles Times, LXXXIX (July 5, 1970),
Cal 1, 22.
  Miller's Tropic viewed as failure for film failed to
capture Miller during thirties in Paris.

E3734   "Federal Court Here Rejects Challenge to Film Ratings,"
New York Times, CXIX (August 1, 1970), 13.
  Judge Morris Lasker refused preliminary injunction
sought by Tropic Film Corporation and Joseph Strick,
producer of film.

E3735   "France Bans Movie Based on Miller Book," Los Angeles
Times, LXXXIX (August 15, 1970), II 8.
  Quiet Days in Clichy movie too sexy for French.

E3736   "France, His Literary Birthplace, Bans Film of Henry
Miller Book," New York Times, CXIX (August 15, 1970),
16.
  Miller calls film version of Quiet Days true to book
and cannot understand ban in France.

E3737   "Controversial Sculptor Bufano Found Dead in His S.F.
Studio," Los Angeles Times, LXXXIX (August 19, 1970),
3, 30.
  Miller called Bufano the poorest and richest artist in
America.

E3738   Centing, Richard and Benjamin Franklin V.   "A Less Academic Miller," Under the Sign of Pisces: Anaïs Nin and
Her Circle, I (Summer 1970), 14.
  Far from academic side of Miller presented in May
1970 Mademoiselle and June 1970 Playboy.

E3739   Centing, Richard.   "Anna Kavan's Shout of Red," Under
the Sign of Pisces: Anaïs Nin and Her Circle, I (Summer
1970), 1-8.
  Miller's Books in My Life considered one of best
reading lists.

E3740   Centing, Richard and Benjamin Franklin V.   "The Film of
Henry Miller's Tropic of Cancer," Under the Sign of Pi-
sces: Anaïs Nin and Her Circle, I (Summer 1970), 15.
  Miller's film of Tropic got horrible reviews.

E3741 Centing, Richard and Benjamin Franklin V. "Form and
Image in the Fiction of Henry Miller," Under the Sign of
Pisces: Anaïs Nin and Her Circle, I (Summer 1970), 14.
Jane A. Nelson's Form and Image in Fiction of Miller
study of allegorical patterns.

E3742 Centing, Richard and Benjamin Franklin V. "News of
Henry Miller," Under the Sign of Pisces: Anaïs Nin and
Her Circle, I (Summer 1970), 13-14.
Edward Schwartz presented University of Minnesota Li-
brary with gift of 350 volumes by and about Miller.

E3743 Centing, Richard. "Poverty Playhouse," Under the Sign
of Pisces: Anaïs Nin and Her Circle, I (Summer 1970),
12-13.
John McLean has produced play based on Diary of
Anaïs Nin, Volume I, where Mike Lane plays Miller.

E3744 Hoffman, Michael J. "Yesterday's Rebel," Western Hu-
manities Review, XXIV (Summer 1970), 271-274.
Miller a part of past, yesterday's rebel. This is the
fate of an author who has become a social, monetary,
and sexual success.

E3745 Nin, Anaïs. "Fünf von vier Millionen," Merian, XXIII
(September 1970), 80-82.
New York the city where Miller grew up. (In German.)

E3746 Thompson, Howard. "The Screen 'Quiet Days in Clichy',"
New York Times, CXX (September 22, 1970), 37.
Quiet Days in Clichy called pallid, poorly directed,
badly acted.

E3747 Attmore, Marie. "New Henry Miller Edition Is First
Albuquerque Venture," Albuquerque Journal, C (October 11,
1970), 1.
Discussion of Insomnia or the Devil at Large as both
collection of watercolors and book about Miller's
courtship of Hoki.

E3748 Champlin, Charles. "Critic at Large," Los Angeles
Times, LXXXIX (October 14, 1970), IV 1.
Announcement of opening of Quiet Days in Clichy in
Los Angeles. In film, sex seen as life force.

E3749 Centing, Richard. "News of Henry Miller," Under the
Sign of Pisces: Anaïs Nin and Her Circle, I (Fall 1970),
6-7.
Centing discusses first meeting with Miller on August
30, 1970, and talks about Insomnia.

E3750 Franklin, Benjamin. "Frances Steloff," Under the Sign
of Pisces: Anaïs Nin and Her Circle, I (Fall 1970), 1-6.

Frances Steloff, proprietress of Gotham Book Mart, helped make Miller's writing available in America.

E3751   Meredith, Tax.   "Sexual Politics," Ramparts Magazine, IX (November 1970), 51-52.
Miller attacked as dominant male in article that fails to perceive the man, his work, or anything else.

E3752   " 'Henry Miller' to Return," Los Angeles Times, LXXXIX (November 27, 1970), IV 24.
Henry Miller Odyssey a reminiscence about Miller's life in New York and Paris.

E3753   Phillipson, John S.   "Criticism," Abstracts of English Studies, XIV (January 1971), 334.
Look at Agostino Lombardo's "Italian Criticism of American Literature" where one essay focuses on Miller.

E3754   Phillipson, John S.   "Truman Capote," Abstracts of English Studies, XIV (January 1971), 324.
Abstract of Moravia's "Two American Writers" where Miller is seen destroying Puritan morality.

E3755   Robson, William J.   "Inside the Egg," Southern California Lit Scene, I (January 1971), 1-2.
"Miller has labored to bring genuine revelation to the enigma of life ... " (p. 1).

E3756   "Australia Lifts Ban on 'Tropic of Cancer'," New York Times, CXX (January 26, 1971), 25.
First time in 36 years it's legal to read Tropic in Australia.

E3757   Sattler, Virginia R.   "Subjects," Abstracts of English Studies, XIV (February 1971), 347.
Review of Meredith Tax's "Sexual Politics" in which Miller's women function primarily as sex objects.

E3758   Shepard, Richard.   "The Brooklyn Crowd on Mount Parnassus," New York Times, CXX (February 21, 1971), 75, 94.
Miller talks of love for Williamsburg, Brooklyn.

E3759   Centing, Richard.   "Bern Porter," Under the Sign of Pisces: Anaïs Nin and Her Circle, II (Winter 1971), 16.
Bern Porter published much Miller, including Murder the Murderer, The Plight of the Creative Artist in the United States of America, and Semblances of a Devoted Past.

E3760   Evans, Oliver.   "An Interview With Paul Bowles," Mediterranean Review, I (Winter 1971), 3-15.

Bowles feels that Henry Miller does not like thinking in his writing.

E3761   Mailer, Norman. "The Prisoner of Sex," Harper's, CCXLII (March 1971), 41-92.
Mailer feels Kate Millett's book blasts Miller in a way that shows her failure to read him in context.

E3762   Murphy, Mary B. "Gimpel, Miller: A Responsive Chord," Los Angeles Times, XC (April 13, 1971), IV 1, 6.
Pianist Gimpel credited with teaching Miller how to listen to self and others.

E3763   Jackson, Paul R. "Henry Miller, Emerson, and the Divided Self," American Literature, XLIII (May 1971), 231-241.
Miller's work discussed as product of Emerson's autobiographical tradition. They are divided because both are dreamers and realists caught in conflict.

E3764   Oringer, Judy. "Anaïs Nin on Women," Ramparts Magazine, IX (May 1971), 44-45.
Nin notes that Miller influenced and helped her writing.

E3765   Franklin, Benjamin, V. "Book That Includes Nin Circle," Under the Sign of Pisces: Anaïs Nin and Her Circle, II (Spring 1971), 12-13.
George Wickes' Americans in Paris focuses on six individuals, one Henry Miller.

E3766   Franklin, Benjamin, V. "Varda," Under the Sign of Pisces: Anaïs Nin and Her Circle, II (Spring 1971), 6-8.
Jean Varda first introduced Miller to Big Sur.

E3767   MacDonald, Edgar E. "The Childs Collection of Henry Miller at Randolph-Macon College," Resources for American Literary Study, I (Spring 1971), 121-125.
Listing of Miller collection at Walter Hines Page Library at Randolph-Macon College. Collection consists of many first editions plus periodicals, book reviews, and other items by and about Miller.

E3768   Greenway, John. "Norman Mailer Meets the Butch Brigade," National Review, XXIII (July 27, 1971), 815.
Review of Mailer's The Prisoner of Sex where Miller is defended against Kate Millett.

E3769   Ford, Hugh. "Michael Fraenkel," Under the Sign of Pisces: Anaïs Nin and Her Circle, II (Summer 1971), 3-4.
Fraenkel and Miller's correspondence comprises Hamlet.

E3770   Goulianos, Joan. "A Conversation with Lawrence Durrell About Art, Analysis, and Politics," Modern Fiction Studies, XVII (Summer 1971), 159-166.
        Miller a prophet who wrote about rejection of his technological culture years before this idea was popular.

E3771   Lowenfels, Walter. "Extracts From My Many Lives, Part One, The Paris Years, 1926-1934," Expatriate Review, Summer 1971, 4-25.
        Discusses Miller's circle of "Death Philosophers" and Miller's early books--Cancer, Black Spring, and Hamlet.

E3772   "Women's Place," Times Literary Supplement, LXX (September 17, 1971), 1114.
        Review of Mailer's The Prisoner of Sex that calls the book's sections on Henry Miller and D. H. Lawrence its best parts.

E3773   French, Warren G. "Henry Miller," Twentieth Century Literature, XVII (October 1971), 293.
        French reviews Jackson's "Henry Miller, Emerson, and the Divided Self" and McCarthy's "Henry Miller's Democratic Vistas."

E3774   Centing, Richard. "News of Henry Miller," Under the Sign of Pisces: Anaïs Nin and Her Circle, II (Fall 1971), 12.
        Miller views himself as a liberated being in "Henry Miller Talks to Henry Miller on Sex."

E3775   Franklin, Benjamin. "AN's Films," Under the Sign of Pisces: Anaïs Nin and Her Circle, II (Fall 1971), 10.
        Nin and Miller appear together in Henry Miller Odyssey.

E3776   Hays, Peter L. "The Dangers of Henry Miller," Arizona Quarterly, XXVII (Autumn 1971), 251-258.
        Anti-Miller appraisal of Tropic based on Hays' inability to see the dual nature of Miller's first book. He cannot understand the way Miller praises life while depicting its filth and disease.

E3777   Farzan, Massud. "Henry Miller," American Literature, XLIII (November 1971), 479-480.
        Walter Schmiele's book called first "bonafide biography of Miller in book length ..." (p. 479).

E3778   Ohashi, Kenzaburo. "Anaïs Nin's Diary: The Inner World and the Outer World," Gakuto, LXVIII (November 5, 1971), 12-15.
        Miller seen as Nin's ever-changing mirror. (In English.)

E3779   Kirby, Judy Kates.   "Literature and Society," Abstracts of
English Studies, XV (December 1971), 210.
Review of Peter Viereck's "The Muse and the Machine" that calls Miller one of the artists who scorns
social progress.

E3780   DeMott, Benjamin.   "Henry Miller: Rebel-Clown at
Eighty," Saturday Review, LIV (December 11, 1971), 29-
32.
Review of Henry Miller: Three Decades of Criticism
by Edward B. Mitchell and Miller's My Life and
Times. DeMott endorses Miller's plea for writers to
awaken the masses and show love for America.

E3781   Martuis, Justino.   "As Pessoas," Manchete, XX (December 25, 1971), 3.
Miller knows how to live.   (In Portuguese.)

E3782   Mendes, Lucas.   "Henry Miller: falou de disse," Manchete, XX (December 25, 1971), 60-66.
Interview with 80-year-old Miller where he is called
a true human being.   (In Portuguese.)

E3783   Ditsky, John.   "Carried Away by Numbers: The Rhapsodic
Mode in Modern Fiction," Ohioana Quarterly, LXXIX
(1972), 79-84.
Discussion of the use of "catalog" technique associated
with Homer, Whitman, and Miller's Black Spring.

E3784   Egor, Gvozden.   "Erotiska pikareska Henrija Milera,"
Knjizernost, LVI (1972), 92-100.
(In Serbo-Croatian.)

E3785   Hida, Shigeo.   "Dokeski Henry Miller," Eigo Seinen,
CXIX (1972), 330-331.
Miller as clown.   (In Japanese.)

E3786   Kubo, Tijiro.   "Watercolor Painting of Henry Miller,"
Geijutsu Seikatsu, 1972, 76-80.
Miller's brushwork called dynamic.   Depicted are
four paintings, two in color called "Lovers" and
"Morning Erection."

E3787   Lorenzana, Salvador.   "Henry Miller: O 'enfant terrible'
norteamericano," Grial, XXXVII (1972), 267-280.
(In Portuguese.)

E3788   C., S. T.   "Miller, Henry," Twentieth Century Literature,
XVIII (January 1972), 73.
Miller called anarchist by Peter Hays in "The Danger
of Henry Miller."

E3789   Saegeman, Elie.   "Het Parijs van Henry Miller," Snoecks,

XLVIII (January 1972), 90-102.
Miller's Paris of Tropic days is viewed.   (In Dutch.)

E3790   Spivey, Herman E.   "Henry Miller," Abstracts of English
Studies, XV (January 1972), 326.
    Abstract of Hoffman's "Yesterday's Rebel" who sees
Miller dated.

E3791   Burgess, Anthony.   "My Life and Times," New York
Times, CXXI (January 2, 1972), VII 1, 10-11.
    "All that the 'Tropics' and 'The Rosy Crucifixion' try
to do in the erotic arena is to convey the simple
gross pleasures of straight-forward heterosexual coi-
tion" (p. 1).

E3792   Diehl, Digby.   "Henry Miller Turns 80 at UCLA Center,"
Los Angeles Times, XCI (January 2, 1972), C41.
    UCLA plans birthday celebration for Miller with Dur-
rell, Powell, Nin, and the films, The Henry Miller
Odyssey and Henry Miller: Reflections on Writing.

E3793   Diehl, Digby.   "Q & A Henry Miller," Los Angeles Times,
XCI (January 23, 1972), W18-23.
    Biography of Miller followed by interview dealing with
Miller as saint, The World of Sex, Tropic film, Hitler, the theme of search as method for getting through
life, writing as therapy, becoming oneself, and first
publishing.

E3794   Baro, Gene.   "Henry Miller: Out on the Coffee Table,"
Washington Post, XCV (January 28, 1972), D1, 4.
    Review of My Life and Times that calls Miller the
best study of arrested development through autobiography.

E3795   Lambilliotte, Maurice.   "Europe et civilisation," Synthèses,
XXVII (January-February 1972), 10-11.
    Miller a very human being.   (In French.)

E3796   Robitaille, Gérald.   "Tête de vache ou vengéance indienne,"
Synthèses, XXVII (January-February 1972), 32-36.
    Miller's preface to Haniel Long's The Power Within
favorably discussed.   (In French.)

E3797   Schrank, Joseph.   "Henry Miller," New York Times,
CXXI (February 27, 1972), VII 22.
    Mockery of the Burgess article on Miller's My Life
and Times.

E3798   Centing, Richard.   "Anaïs Nin Today," Under the Sign of
Pisces: Anaïs Nin and Her Circle, III (Winter 1972), 1-6.
    Reference to Miller's 80th birthday and his book, Re-
member to Remember.

E3799   Centing, Richard. "News of Daisy Alden," Under the Sign
          of Pisces: Anaïs Nin and Her Circle, III (Winter 1972),
          16.
              Benjamin Franklin V teaching seminar on Nin and
              Miller at University of Michigan.

E3800   Franklin, Benjamin, V. "AN and the Rare Book Trade,"
          Under the Sign of Pisces: Anaïs Nin and Her Circle, III
          (Winter 1972), 11-16.
              William Young, owner of largest Nin collection, does
              not have copy of Henry Miller Letters to Anaïs Nin.

E3801   Lowenfels, Walter. "The Paris Years, 1926-1934: Part
          2," Expatriate Review, (Winter-Spring 1972), 10-20.
              "What brought Miller, Fraenkel, and myself together
              was a complete rejection of the going social world"
              (p. 16).

E3802   "International Soundtrack," Variety, CCLXVI (March 1,
          1972), 30.
              Longest film running in Munich is Miller's Quiet Days
              in Clichy.

E3803   H., J. "Tapes Tell Miller Story," New Orleans Times-
          Picayune, CXXXVI (March 26, 1972), III 4.
              My Life and Times a visual autobiography.

E3804   "Henry Miller: My Life and Times," Choice, IX (April
          1972), 215.
              Superbly edited taped conversations are next to best
              thing to actual visit with Miller.

E3805   Ness, Verna M. "Norman Mailer," Abstracts of English
          Studies, XV (April 1972), 533.
              Review of John Greenway's "Mailer Meets Butch Bri-
              gade" where Mailer shows deep appreciation for Miller.

E3806   Powell, Lawrence Clark. "Henry Miller at Eighty,"
          Westways, LXIV (April 1972), 26-29, 58-60.
              Miller far from pornographer, he's a moralist whose
              humor fulfills his reader.

E3807   "[Review of] My Life and Times," Playboy's Choice, April
          1972, 2-3.
              Miller a prophet of today's sexual revolution because
              his books Sexus and the Tropics began the war.

E3808   Ritterband, Molly. "An Interview with Lawrence Durrell,"
          Westways, LXIV (April 1972), 59.
              Durrell says he writes like Miller.

E3809   "Whose Turn to Serve?" Times Literary Supplement, LXXI
          (April 14, 1972), 408.

Review of <u>My Life and Times</u> that feels the book does
a fine job of showing the many sides of Henry Miller.

E3810   Erzgraber, Willi.   "Lawrence Durrell," <u>Abstracts of Eng-</u>
<u>lish Studies</u>, XV (May 1972), 577.
Abstract of Joan Goulianos' "A Conversation with Durrell" where Durrell calls self-liberation his real aim
much like work of Miller.

E3811   Snow, Joseph T.   "William Burroughs," <u>Abstracts of Eng-</u>
<u>lish Studies</u>, XV (May 1972), 585-586.
Alfredo Matilla-Rivas' "Notas sobre Naked Lunch"
sees Burroughs in the sexual tradition of Miller.

E3812   Zee, Nancy Scholar.   "A Checklist of Nin Materials at
Northwestern University Library," <u>Under the Sign of</u>
<u>Pisces: Anaïs Nin and Her Circle</u>, III (Spring 1972), 3-
11.
Miller proofread much of the unpublished Nin material
in Northwestern University Collection.

E3813   Brierly, Wendy.   "Review of O Mundo de Henry Miller,"
<u>Under the Sign of Pisces: Anaïs Nin and Her Circle</u>, III
(Summer 1972), 2-4.
Collection of writing by and about Miller translated
into Portuguese and edited by Sa Cavalcante.

E3814   Centing, Richard and Benjamin Franklin V.   "Henry Miller,"
<u>Under the Sign of Pisces: Anaïs Nin and Her Circle</u>, III
(Summer 1972).
Entire issue dedicated to Miller in celebration of his
eightieth birthday, December 26, 1971.

E3815   Centing, Richard R.   "Expatriate déjà vu," <u>Under the Sign</u>
<u>of Pisces: Anaïs Nin and Her Circle</u>, III (Summer 1972),
10-13.
Note on Miller's eightieth birthday and list of articles
and books by and about Miller.

E3816   Centing, Richard R.   "Miller on D. H. Lawrence," <u>Under</u>
<u>the Sign of Pisces: Anaïs Nin and Her Circle</u>, III (Summer
1972), 15.
Discussion of Miller's unpublished "The World of
Lawrence," a 600 page manuscript written about
Lawrence during Miller's greatest period.

E3817   Centing, Richard R.   "Viva Beniamino!" <u>Under the Sign</u>
<u>of Pisces: Anaïs Nin and Her Circle</u>, III (Summer 1972),
14-15.
Sculptor Bufano lauded by Miller in <u>Remember to Re-</u>
<u>member</u>.

E3818   Franklin, Benjamin, V.   "On Teaching Henry Miller,"

Under the Sign of Pisces: Anaïs Nin and Her Circle, III
(Summer 1972), 4-7.
Viewing of Miller as individual honest with himself to
the extent to which he affirms life.

E3819   Laughlin, James. "A Note from James Laughlin," Under
the Sign of Pisces: Anaïs Nin and Her Circle, III (Summer
1972), 16.
Laughlin, president of New Directions, has published
Miller since 1939.

E3820   Woods, Bruce. "On the Question of Miller's Anarchy,"
Under the Sign of Pisces: Anaïs Nin and Her Circle, III
(Summer 1972), 7-10.
Refutation of Hays' "The Danger of Henry Miller" that
calls Miller an anarchist who wants love, brotherhood,
and peace.

E3821   Griffin, L. W. "Henry Miller in Conversation...," Library
Journal, XCVII (October 1, 1972), 3160.
Miller called a thoughtful, opinionated man.

E3822   Hinz, Evelyn J. " 'No Puedo Mas': The Paradox of a
Pisces," Under the Sign of Pisces: Anaïs Nin and Her
Circle, III (Fall 1972), 6-10.
Nin notes a lack of insight on the part of Miller.

E3823   "Bibliographie," Magazine Littéraire, November 1972, 34-
35.
Unannotated bibliography of Miller work.   (In French.)

E3824   Bidaud, Anne-Marie. "Le Zarathoustra de Brooklyn,"
Magazine Littéraire, November 1972, 11-13.
Miller seen in great tradition of American individualism. He is called expressionistic for his use of cancer and deprivation, yet he exhibits a hope for future
through apocalypse.   (In French.)

E3825   Cendrars, Blaise. "Un Ecrivain américain nous est né,"
Magazine Littéraire, November 1972, 24.
Cendrars looks at vagabonding Miller of Tropic days.
(In French.)

E3826   "Der alte Mann--wie sehrer Liebebraucht," Magazine
Littéraire, November 1972, 166-172.

E3827   Durrell, Lawrence. "Le Roc heureux," Magazine Littéraire, November 1972, 25-27.
French translation of Durrell's article on Miller in
Porter's The Happy Rock: A Book About Henry Miller
where Miller is seen as one of the great American
writers, a social critic and moralist.   (In French.)

E3828 "Les Jours tranquilles d'Henry Miller," Magazine Litté-
raire, November 1972, 10.
Background on Miller's life in Clichy, Big Sur, the
Far East, and information on his work. (In French.)

E3829 Louit, Robert. "Miller ou l'écriture du désir," Magazine
Littéraire, November 1972, 17-18.
Miller a realist who has brilliant control of language.
He is compared to Joyce, Lawrence, Proust and Whit-
man. (In French.)

E3830 Maigret, Arnaud de. "Henry Miller et le Villa Seurat,"
Magazine Littéraire, November 1972, 14-16.
The Villa Seurat is the world that Miller inhabited in
Paris in the thirties where Cancer and Black Spring
were written. (In French.)

E3831 Steloff, Frances. "Gotham Book Mart," Intellectual Digest,
III (December 1972), 92-93.
Steloff recalls her first encounters with Miller, the
first dealing with the Booster and Delta, and the se-
cond concerned with her purchase of Cancer and Black
Spring.

E3832 Raaberg, Gwendolyn. "Surrealism in the Works of Henry
Miller and Anaïs Nin," International Comparative Litera-
ture Association, VII (1973).
Miller and Nin seen as surrealists.

E3833 Wüstenhagen, Heinz. "Die Dekadenz Henry Millers,"
Zeitschrift für Anglistik und Amerikanistik, XXII (1973),
41-65.
(In German.)

E3834 "Henry Miller in Conversation with Georges Belmont,"
Choice, IX (January 1973), 1447.
Miller called a brilliant conversationalist.

E3835 Centing, Richard. "Frances Steloff at 85," Under the Sign
of Pisces: Anaïs Nin and Her Circle, IV (Winter 1973),
13-14.
Article in Intellectual Digest (December 1972), that
mentions Nin's involvement with Miller.

E3836 Centing, Richard R. "Nin at Northern Illinois University,
De Kalb," Under the Sign of Pisces: Anaïs Nin and Her
Circle, IV (Winter 1973), 12.
Nin refused to deal with Kate Millett's criticism of
Miller's attitude toward women.

E3837 Schneider, Duane. "The Duane Schneider Press and Anaïs
Nin," Under the Sign of Pisces: Anaïs Nin and Her Circle,
IV (Winter 1973), 5-9.

Miller's enthusiasm caused Schneider to read Nin.

E3838   Skipsna, Alvin. "Anaïs Nin at Skidmore College," Under the Sign of Pisces: Anaïs Nin and Her Circle, IV (Winter 1973), 13.
In the Frances Steloff Collection of rare books at Skidmore are dedications by Miller.

E3839   Centing, Richard R. "Anaïs Nin at the University of Michigan," Under the Sign of Pisces: Anaïs Nin and Her Circle, IV (Spring 1973), 6-8.
Nin read from Diary an excerpt concerning Miller, Durrell, and herself.

E3840   Centing, Richard R. "Henry Miller on Pablo Picasso," Under the Sign of Pisces: Anaïs Nin and Her Circle, IV (Spring 1973), 16.
Miller views Picasso the man, not the legend.

E3841   Centing, Richard R. "Miller and the Capra Press," Under the Sign of Pisces: Anaïs Nin and Her Circle, IV (Spring 1973), 15-16.
Miller has published On Turning Eighty and Reflections on the Death of Mishima.

E3842   Clarity, James F. "Notes on People," New York Times, CXXII (June 13, 1973), 53.
At American Booksellers' Association Convention, Miller discussed his lack of interest in pornography.

E3843   "More or Less?" Washington Post, XCVI (June 14, 1973), B18.
At National Booksellers' Convention Miller told people to read less and less.

E3844   "From 'Chaos' to 'No Effect'," Washington Post, XCVI (June 22, 1973), B9.
Supreme Court decision to return obscenity rulings to states shocks Miller.

E3845   Feiffer, Jules. " 'Art for Court's Sake?'," New York Times, CXXII (August 5, 1973), II 1, 11, 16.
Miller angered at Supreme Court's returning obscenity rulings to states.

E3846   Polley, George. "Japanese Book on Henry Miller," Under the Sign of Pisces: Anaïs Nin and Her Circle, IV (Fall 1973), 13-14.
K. Ueno's Tropiques en voyageur shares Miller's deep spiritual insight about life as lived through the basic man.

E3847   Raaberg, Gwendolyn. "Raaberg on Surrealism in Miller

and Nin," Under the Sign of Pisces: Anaïs Nin and Her
Circle, IV (Fall 1973), 18.
    Miller considered a surrealist.

E3848   Krebs, Albin. "Notes on People," New York Times,
CXXIII (November 13, 1973), 18.
    Miller home after treatment to correct circulatory
disturbance.

E3849   Chaddah, R. P. "Henry Miller," Thought, XXV (November 17, 1973), 15-18.

E3850   Blockmans, Alex. "Henry Miller's Tropic of Cancer and
Knut Hamsun's Sult," Scandinavica, XIV (1974), 115-126.
    A comparison of Miller's first person narrator of
Tropic to Hamsun's narrator in Mysteries. Hamsun
is seen as a direct influence on Miller.

E3851   Traba, Martha. "The Monumental 'I' of Anaïs Nin,"
Dialogos, 1974, 27-29.
    Miller considered a person who also writes about the
self.

E3852   Broderick, Catherine. "The Reception of Anaïs Nin in
Japan," Under the Sign of Pisces: Anaïs Nin and Her
Circle, V (Winter 1974), 5-11.
    Miller stimulated Nin to write.

E3853   "People," Time, CIII (May 20, 1974), 58.
    Miller and Durrell chat in Miller's bed as he recovers
from surgery. They discuss the days of Tropic and
present notions of sexual equality.

E3854   Centing, Richard R. "Elmer Gertz and Henry Miller,"
Under the Sign of Pisces: Anaïs Nin and Her Circle, V
(Spring 1974), 15-16.
    Gertz defended Miller and constructed an exhibition of
Miller's writing and art at Southern Illinois University.

E3855   Christom, Lawrence. " 'I Believe in Life': Singing Soul
of Henry Miller," Los Angeles Times, XCIII (July 24,
1974), IV 11.
    Miller talks at Actors and Directors Laboratory in
Hollywood about the importance of feeling and restated
his belief in life and the individual.

E3856   Centing, Richard R. "Henry Miller's Not So Quiet Days,"
Under the Sign of Pisces: Anaïs Nin and Her Circle, V
(Summer 1974), 1-2.
    Miller's Quiet Days in Clichy film boring.

E3857   Centing, Richard R. "News From Eddie Schwartz," Under
the Sign of Pisces: Anaïs Nin and Her Circle, V (Summer

1974), 15-16.
Noted that Schwartz founded Miller Literary Society.

E3858   Martineau, Barbara Halpern.   "Nin's Films," Under the
Sign of Pisces: Anaïs Nin and Her Circle, V (Summer
1974), 7-10.
In Anaïs Nin Observed, Nin sits with Miller and
Frances Steloff.

E3859   "Playbill," Playboy, XXI (September 1974), 3.
Miller lives with and fights the demons of insomnia.

E3860   Jong, Erica.   "Two Writers in Praise of Rabelais and
Each Other," New York Times, CXXIII (September 7,
1974), 27.
Miller called "our modern American Rabelais."

E3861   Sayre, Norma.   'Screen: 'Miller Odyssey'," New York
Times, CXXIII (September 13, 1974), 31.
"The movie jumps most skillfully between past and
present, between California and France," and shows
the composite nature of Miller the sage.

E3862   Gilliatt, Penelope.   "The Current Cinema," New Yorker,
L (September 16, 1974), 95-98.
Discussion of the film, The Henry Miller Odyssey,
that sees Miller as an important author who perceived
his times.

E3863   Bald, Wambly.   "I Remember Miller," Lost Generation
Journal, II (Fall 1974), 38-41.
Bald discusses the Miller of the Left Bank of Paris
in the early 1930's.

E3864   Haber, Joyce.   "The Devil in Henry Miller," Los Angeles
Times, XCIV (December 8, 1974), Cal 45.
Interview where Miller states his philosophy to live
life to the full with no principles, ideologies, or
morality.

E3865   Allen, Bruce.   "Henry Miller: Insomnia; or, The Devil
at Large," Library Journal, XCIX (December 15, 1974),
3197.
Account of a 75-year-old author's love.

E3866   Porter, Bern.   "Two Maine Men," Observations from the
Treadmill RFD #1, I (1975), 7-10.
Porter looks at Miller from publishing him to letter
writing to his relationships with Anaïs Nin and Gertrude Stein.

E3867   Diehl, Digby.   "Endless Energy of Henry Miller," Los
Angeles Times, XCIV (January 12, 1975), Cal 49.

Miller continues to write, paint, play ping-pong, and drink in his life-embracing manner, as seen in <u>Insomnia</u> and <u>This Is Henry</u>.

E3868   O'Hara, T.   "Henry Miller: Insomnia; or, The Devil at Large," <u>Best Sellers</u>, XXXIV (January 15, 1975), 461.
Miller's anguish over a love affair with Hoki Tokuda.

E3869   Sayre, Norma.   "Screen: Documentary on Henry Miller," <u>New York Times</u>, CXXIV (February 16, 1975), 65.
Review of Tom Schiller's <u>Henry Miller Asleep and Awake</u>, a film where Miller takes his audience on a tour of his bathroom and the mind of Henry Miller.

E3870   Cott, Jonathan.   "Reflections of a Cosmic Tourist: An Afternoon with Henry Miller," <u>Rolling Stone</u>, (February 27, 1975), 38-46, 57.
Interview with 83-year-old Miller which contains excerpts of Miller's writing.   Cott calls Miller's major contribution his prose.

E3871   "Documentary Pins Henry Miller Down," <u>New Orleans Times-Picayune</u>, CXXXIX (May 1, 1975), III 6.
Snyder's <u>This Is Henry, Henry Miller from Brooklyn</u> allows one to know and understand Miller.

E3872   Centing, Richard R.   "More About Henry Miller," <u>Under the Sign of Pisces: Anaïs Nin and Her Circle</u>, VI (Spring 1975), 19-20.
Mentions two publications dealing with Miller in <u>Rolling Stone</u> (February 27, 1975) and Robert Snyder's <u>This Is Henry, Henry Miller From Brooklyn</u>.

E3873   Diehl, Digby.   "Lawrence Durrell at Caltech: An Interview by Digby Diehl," <u>Under the Sign of Pisces: Anaïs Nin and Her Circle</u>, VI (Spring 1975), 13-19.
Durrell excited that "Henry is blooming again, writing and in good health at 82" (p. 17).

E3874   Whiting, Brooke.   "Fragments of Conversation Between Lawrence Durrell, Henry Miller, and others," <u>Under the Sign of Pisces: Anaïs Nin and Her Circle</u>, VI (Spring 1975), 10-13.
Durrell, Miller, and others look at Durrell's first book, <u>Quaint Fragment</u>.

E3875   Whiting, Brooke.   "Register to the Lawrence Durrell Collection...," <u>Under the Sign of Pisces: Anaïs Nin and Her Circle</u>, VI (Spring 1975), 1-10.
Noted are Miller items in Durrell Collection at UCLA, including letters to Miller, drawings and watercolors, and discussions of Miller's <u>Hamlet</u>.

E3876   "This Is Henry...," Choice, XII (June 1975), 537.
        "Henry Miller's recognition as a significant American
        author has fully arrived."

E3877   Corwin, Phillip. "Letters of Henry Miller and Wallace
        Fowlie," Commonweal, CII (August 29, 1975), 377-378.
        The frequence of the Miller-Fowlie Correspondence
        makes it valuable.

E3878   Smith, Craig. "Harold Norse Reflects on Anaïs Nin,"
        Under the Sign of Pisces: Anaïs Nin and Her Circle, VI
        (Summer 1975), 8, 10.
        In Sunday After the War, Miller printed the first
        known article dealing with Nin.

E3879   "Playboy Interview: Erica Jong," Playboy, XXII (Septem-
        ber 1975), 61-78, 202.
        Jong praises Miller whom she credits as her inspira-
        tion.

E3880   Powell, Lawrence Clark. "Letter From the Southwest,"
        Westways, LXVII (September 1975), 32-34, 79.
        Powell sees Miller at 84, and they discuss old times.

E3881   Boyle, Kay. "Published in Paris," New York Times,
        CXXIV (September 14, 1975), VII 6.
        "Henry Miller was the Paris Tribune's most famous
        proofreader...."

E3882   Martin, Jay. "The Nightmare Notebook," New York Times,
        CXXIV (September 14, 1975), VII 7.
        Review of The Nightmare Notebook and Letters of
        Henry Miller and Wallace Fowlie where Miller's battle
        and acceptance of life are discussed: "Though the
        record of a failure, 'The Nightmare Notebook' itself
        is not a failure at all. Indeed, it beautifully ... ex-
        hibits Miller exposed to violent sensations and experi-
        encing blatant contradictions...."

E3883   Crossman, Sylvie. "Henry Miller ou la jouissance,"
        Cahiers du Chemin, XXV (October 15, 1975), 148-152.
        Miller viewed as the romantic clown who lives life.
        (In French.)

E3884   Lyon, Melvin. "Miscellaneous Miller," Prairie Schooner,
        XLIX (Fall 1975), 271-272.
        Review of Insomnia: "Usually the book is a powerful
        reminder of just how bad a writer Henry Miller can
        be upon occasion" (p. 272).

E3885   Pearson, Norman Holmes. "A Double Sense of Vision,"
        Yale Alumni Magazine, XXXIX (December 1975), 8-
        17.

Contains Miller's "Self Portrait."

E3886   "Book of Friends," Kirkus, XLIII (December 1, 1975), 1367.
         "[Miller's] memoir of his old friends continues the
         autobiographical romance he first published in Paris
         in the Thirties...."

E3887   "Book of Friends," Publishers Weekly, CCVIII (December
         15, 1975), 43.
         Review of Book of Friends: "Now 84, Henry Miller
         begins in this nostalgic and only moderately ribald
         memoir a project he says will be his last."

E3888   Lefebvre, Jacques. "Jeux et masques dans l'oeuvre
         d'Henri Miller," Les Langues Modernes, LXX (1976), 189-
         195.
         (In French.)

E3889   Mathieu, Bertrand. "Henry Miller and the Symboliste Be-
         lief in a Universal Language," Antigonish Review, XXVII
         (1976), 49-57.

E3890   Richard, Hughes. "Quatre Inédits de Cendrars," Europe,
         DLXVI (1976), 208-216.
         (In French.)

E3891   Powell, Lawrence Clark. "To Visit Monterey," Westways,
         LXVIII (January 1976), 23-26.
         Mentions the steep road to Miller's home at Partington
         Ridge, Big Sur.

E3892   Nin, Anaïs. "From Diary VI: Summer 1965," Under the
         Sign of Pisces: Anaïs Nin and Her Circle, VII (Winter
         1976), 1-5.
         Nin notes that she risked all in her preface to Tropic.

E3893   Traba, Martha. "The Monumental 'I' of Anaïs Nin,"
         Under the Sign of Pisces: Anaïs Nin and Her Circle, VII
         (Winter 1976), 8-14.
         Noted is the fact that Miller ranks Nin's Diary along-
         side St. Augustine, Rousseau, and Proust. In the
         Diary, Miller is Nin's literary contradiction.

E3894   Kirsch, Robert. "Henry Miller Among Friends," Los
         Angeles Times, XCV (March 4, 1976), IV 18.
         Review of Miller's Book of Friends that sees his
         companions as "special kinds of mirrors and as he
         looks back at them and into them, seeing himself...."

E3895   Bernd, Lois Arenz. "Love and the Man with Nine Wives,"
         Los Angeles Times, XCV (March 6, 1976), II 4.
         Letter to Miller that says that one can grow and
         change in a relationship with one person.

E3896   Fischkin, R.   "Love and the Man with Nine Wives," Los
         Angeles Times, XCV (March 6, 1976), II 4.
         Refutes Miller's article "Love and the Man with Nine
         Wives" by rejecting polygamy.

E3897   McKenna, John.   "Love and the Man with Nine Wives,"
         Los Angeles Times, XCV (March 6, 1976), II 4.
         Letter to Miller telling him that Jesus is the only way
         to freedom.

E3898   Mairesse, Michelle.   "Love and the Man with Nine Wives,"
         Los Angeles Times, XCV (March 6, 1976), II 4.
         Refutes Miller's essay, "Love and the Man with Nine
         Wives," for failing to understand the need for freedom
         on both man's and woman's parts.

E3899   Merrill, Patricia.   "Love and the Man with Nine Wives,"
         Los Angeles Times, XCV (March 6, 1976), II 4.
         Refutes Miller for calling Christ "meek."

E3900   Harmon, Ginger.   "Henry Miller," Publishers Weekly,
         CCIX (March 8, 1976), 10-11.
         Interview with Miller where he talks about Book of
         Friends and notes that he worked on it two hours a
         day.

E3901   Mailer, Norman.   "Henry Miller: Celebrating a Cause
         Celebre," Los Angeles Times, XCV (March 28, 1976),
         Cal 1, 3.
         Mailer explores the difficulty in evaluating Miller, a
         writer who is either too complex or too straightforward
         and harsh for readers to accept.

E3902   Mailer, Norman.   "Henry Miller: Genius and Lust, Narcis-
         sism," American Review, XXIV (April 1976), 1-40.
         Mailer looks at Miller's history and sees a cold, dis-
         tant mother as the basis for Miller's sexual rebellion
         in this psychological study.

E3903   Ward, Robert.   "Out of the Attic," Camera, XX (April
         1976), 40-45, 72.
         "Henry Miller dropped by ... in the 40's.   ... He
         wrote something about me ... in the Air-Conditioned
         Nightmare" (p. 72).

E3904   "Henry Miller's Book of Friends," Booklist, LXXII (April
         1, 1976), 1084.
         Review of Book of Friends: "Miller's unflagging en-
         thusiasms for sex and literature are revealed to be
         early preoccupations as he recalls some friendships
         and experiences from his younger years.

E3905   Reuven, Ben.   "Miller Recollects in Tranquility," Los

Angeles Times, XCV (April 4, 1976), Cal 3.
Miller feels the purpose of Book of Friends is to pay
tribute to his real friends and companions.

E3906   Smith, Jack.   "Bugging the Question," Los Angeles Times,
XCV (April 28, 1976), IV 1.
A note from Miller on bedbugs leads Smith to recall
the Los Angeles Tropic trials of the sixties.

E3907   Smith, Jack.   "... And Don't Let the Bedbugs Bite," Los
Angeles Times, XCV (April 29, 1976), IV 1.
Smith publishes Miller's piece, "The Cockroach and
the Bedbug," and humorously responds to Miller's
spoof.

E3908   Fremont-Smith, Eliot.   "Do Writers Ride in Cadillacs:
American Review 24," Village Voice, XXI (May 3, 1976),
47.
"The essay turns brilliant on the subject of Miller's
'Rosy Crucifixion' obsession with his second wife June,
and the nature--and effects of love, lust, and literary
genius--of narcissism, which Mailer defines ... as a
kind of wrenching inner dialogue in which part of oneself is constantly absorbed in the study of another."

E3909   Lewis, Leon.   "Henry Miller's Portrait of Walter Lowenfels," Lost Generation Journal, IV (Spring-Summer 1976),
16-17, 20.
Study of Miller's Jabberwhorl Cronstadt (Walter Lowenfels) as a man alive in a dead world.

E3910   Lant, Jeffrey L.   "Book of Friends," Best Sellers, XXXVI
(June 1976), 83.
"The real purpose of this book, then, is not so much
to pay tribute to them but to taunt them for not having
succeeded as Miller succeeded and for not sufficiently
helping or believing in him."

E3911   Loynd, Ray.   "Henry Miller: Jaunty, Irascible at 84,"
Los Angeles Herald Examiner, CVI (June 8, 1976), B 4.
Miller viewed as "the last of the great American ro-
mantics" as he appears before the Actors and Directors
Lab in Beverly Hills.

E3912   Kirsch, Jonathan.   "Henry Miller at 84: The Prisoner of
Pacific Palisades," Los Angeles Free Press, XIII (July
30-August 5, 1976), 1, 6-7.
Miller is a man who hates intellectual writing, as he
discusses writing, Erica Jong, his home, and father-
hood.

E3913   "Genius and Lust," Kirkus, XLIV (August 1, 1976), 901.
Review of Genius and Lust that notes Mailer's fine

comparisons between Miller and Hemingway.

E3914   Dangaard, Colin. "The Angry Old Sex Revolutionist," San
         Francisco Examiner, MCMLXXVI (August 15, 1976), TW
         29.
             A look at Miller at 84, still a lady's man, interested,
             but not in marriage anymore.

E3915   Auchincloss, Eve. "Window on the Fall," Washington Post,
         XCIX (August 29, 1976), M 1-2.
             Review of Genius and Lust that feels that Mailer
             "gives a real feel for [Miller] who was a major lite-
             rary influence ... " (p. M2).

E3916   Graham, P. "A Response to Under the Sign of Pisces,"
         Under the Sign of Pisces: Anaïs Nin and Her Circle, VII
         (Summer 1976), 1-4.
             Miller and Nin's relationship discussed. One benefitted
             the other.

E3917   Shifreen, Lawrence. "An Autobiography of Friends," Sun
         & Moon, III (Summer 1976), 94-97.
             Study of Miller's autobiographical style in Book of
             Friends that views Miller's need to keep psychoanalyz-
             ing himself to get to the roots of his own being as
             stemming from an insecurity.

E3918   Gertz, Elmer. "Censorship in Chicago: Tropic of Can-
         cer," Icarbs, III (Summer-Fall 1976), 49-59.
             Gertz talks about his involvement with Miller through
             the Chicago Tropic trials. Included are two letters
             from Miller.

E3919   Styron, William. "The Seduction of Leslie," Esquire,
         LXXXVI (September 1976), 92-97, 126-138.
             "[Leslie] is extremely bright, reinforcing Henry
             Miller's observation ... that sex is all in the head"
             (p. 126).

E3920   Crossman, Sylvie. "An Interview with Henry Miller,"
         Paris Metro, I (September 1, 1976), 1, 4-5.
             Interview where Miller talks about his maturity, paint-
             ing, the Orient, and France.

E3921   "Genius and Lust: A Journey Through the Major Writings
         of Henry Miller," Publishers Weekly, CCX (September 6,
         1976), 61.
             Mailer edits and writes an introduction to this study
             of Miller's work. The book blends the excellence of
             Mailer's critical commentary with Miller's finest
             works.

E3922   "Notes on People: Henry Miller," New York Times,

CXXVI (September 25, 1976), 44.
"Henry Miller ... has now written a book in French, a 60 page monologue ... entitled 'I'm Not Stupider Than Anyone Else.' "

E3923   Kernan, Michael.   "Personalities," Washington Post, XCIX (September 27, 1976), B2.
Notice about Miller's I'm Not Stupider Than Anyone Else.

E3924   Gilman, Richard.   "Norman Mailer Searches the Tropics-- 'Mr. Miller, I Presume?'," Village Voice, XXI (October 4, 1976), 43-44.
Review of Genius and Lust that sees the work as "Miller's peculiar and exemplary struggle to create something 'objective' out of his personal data" (p. 43).

E3925   Cushman, Keith.   "Genius and Lust," Library Journal, CI (October 15, 1976), 2178.
Review of Genius and Lust that calls Miller a "funky latter-day Whitman as he embraces all experience, ... a Whitman with a sense of humor."

E3926   Cabau, Jacques.   "Saint Miller," L'Express, XI (October 20-21, 1976).

E3927   Ridley, Clifford A.   "Capra Press: The Corner Grocery of Publishers," National Observer, XV (October 23, 1976), 21.
"Henry Miller's Book of Friends is a gentle look back at the old master's boyhood chums...."

E3928   Gass, William H.   "The Essential Henry Miller, According to Norman Mailer," New York Times, CXXVI (October 24, 1976), VII 1-3.
Review of Genius and Lust where Miller's work is called "shapeless, repetitious, and shamelessly self-indulgent." His work is described as expanding without depth as his psyche remains adolescent.

E3929   Holt, Rochelle.   "Stars In My Sky," Under the Sign of Pisces: Anaïs Nin and Her Circle, VII (Fall 1976), 13-15.
Frances Steloff has portraits of Henry Miller at Gothem Book Mart.

E3930   McMurtry, Larry.   "Mailer's View of Miller," Washington Post, XCIX (November 8, 1976), C2.
Review of Genius and Lust where McMurtry feels that "Mailer has taken his role of anthologist seriously and has made a careful effort to present a chunk of Henry Miller's best writing sufficient to get Miller taken seriously as one of the century's great writers."

E3931   Aldridge, John W.   "Godhead Revisited," Saturday Review,
        IV (November 13, 1976), 25-27.
> Review of Genius and Lust that sees a bond between
> Mailer and Miller: "Mailer and Miller resemble each
> other in several ... ways--in their shared outrage at
> the totalitarianism of modern machine society. [These]
> two ... major writers [see] that an alternative to
> [technology] ... may yet exist, that the frontier of
> sexual adventure ... remains open to exploration"
> (p. 27).

E3932   Kamentz, Roger.   "Paris When It Dazzles," Baltimore Sun,
        LXXVI (November 14, 1976), D5.
> Review of Brassaï's The Secret Paris of the Thirties
> where it is noted that Miller called Brassaï the "eye
> of Paris."

E3933   Prescott, Peter S.   "In the Torrid Zone," Newsweek,
        LXXIV (November 15, 1976), 109.
> "Norman Mailer has written a stylish, acute essay
> about Miller and has assembled a less than acute [se-
> lection] of Miller's writing."

E3934   McCardle, Dorothy, and Jacqueline Trescott.   "Personali-
        ties," Washington Post, XCIX (November 22, 1976), D3.
> "Henry Miller ... says he is 'very proud' to receive
> the French Legion of Honor..."

E3935   Bird, David.   "Notes on People," New York Times,
        CXXVI (November 23, 1976), 66.
> Miller receives the French Legion of Honor and says
> he owes all to the French.

E3936   Duberman, Martin.   "Genius and Lust by Norman Mailer
        and Henry Miller," New Republic, CLXXV (November 27,
        1976), 33-34.
> "However much Mailer identifies with Miller, ... he
> is himself the likelier candidate for literary greatness"
> (p. 34).

E3937   "Genius and Lust," Christian Century, XCIII (December 8,
        1976), 1108.
> "Miller, long a forbidden author because of his violent
> sexual writing, has lost some of his appeal now that
> anything goes.... These writings show that Miller
> was the best at the business--if you like the business."

E3938   Kirsch, Robert.   "Mailer on Miller Strikes Sparks," Los
        Angeles Times, XCVI (December 8, 1976), IV 1, 8.
> Review of Genius and Lust that considers the work
> important because "Miller and Mailer have something
> very much in common: Both are confessional writers
> above everything."

E3939   "Genius and Lust...," Booklist, LXXIII (December 15,
1976), 582.
"The lengthy extracts of Tropic of Cancer, Sexus, and
other Miller classics outweigh quantitatively and quali-
tatively Mailer's wildly individualistic and punchy ex-
plications."

E3940   Braunlich, Phyllis. "Air-Conditioned Nightmare," Lost
Generation Journal, IV (Winter 1976-1977), 26.
Study of Miller's wrath in The Air-Conditioned Night-
mare.

E3941   Braunlich, Phyllis. "Book of Friends," Lost Generation
Journal, IV (Winter 1976-1977), 26.
Review of Book of Friends that sees Miller's view of
women as one-dimensional.

E3942   Braunlich, Phyllis. "Sanctuary for a Tough Old Rascal,"
Lost Generation Journal, IV (Winter 1976-1977), 1-3.
Describes an attempt to meet Henry Miller.

E3943   Braunlich, Phyllis. "The Smile at the Foot of the Ladder," Lost Generation Journal, IV (Winter 1976-1977), 28.
Review of The Smile at the Foot of the Ladder calling
the book an "interesting vignette" about the clown in
each of us.

E3944   Glenn, Jack. "Reeling Round the World, Chapter II:
Stolen Thunder," Lost Generation Journal, IV (Winter 1976-
1977), 12-13, 21, 27.

E3945   Gordon, William A. "The Zen Mind of Henry Miller,"
Lost Generation Journal, IV (Winter 1976-1977), 6-7, 22-
24.
Gordon relates Miller's singleness to the Zen mind.

E3946   Hoffman, Michael J. "Miller & the Apocalypses of Transcendentalism," Lost Generation Journal, IV (Winter 1976-
1977), 18-21.
Miller viewed as a man in quest of primal energies
within the self in the true tradition of American Transcendentalism.

E3947   Jackson, Paul R. "Catching the Sleeper Awake," Lost
Generation Journal, IV (Winter 1976-1977), 8-11.
Painting seen as affording Miller a wholeness.

E3948   Moore, Harry T. "I Remember to Remember Henry
Miller," Lost Generation Journal, IV (Winter 1976-1977),
4-5.
Moore recalls his first meeting with Miller at Evans-
ton, Ill.

E3949   Wood, Tom. "Hooray for Henry Miller: The Dirty Old
        Man," Lost Generation Journal, IV (Winter 1976-1977),
        14-17, 24-25.
        A look at the importance of the four-letter word in
        the writing of Henry Miller.

E3950   "Two Brooklyn Egos," Lost Generation Journal, IV (Winter
        1976-1977), 3.
        Description of the Miller-Mailer meeting on the NBC
        Today Show in December.

E3951   Mathieu, Bertrand. "Henry Miller and the Symboliste Re-
        jection of the Quotidian," Under the Sign of Pisces: Anaïs
        Nin and Her Circle, VIII (Winter 1977), 15-24.
        "Like a true Symboliste, Miller expects all 'reality'
        to bestow a greater measure of awareness, of ecstacy,
        on its beholder ... " (p. 22).

E3952   Curnow, Wystan. "We're All Narcissists," Nation,
        CCXXIV (January 29, 1977), 117-118.
        Review of Genius and Lust that sees Miller's greatness
        coming as the result of his opening an unchartered
        area of the modern psyche.

E3953   "Genius and Lust...," Choice, XIII (February 1977), 1597.
        Review of Genius and Lust that views the comparison
        between the writing of Miller and Mailer.

E3954   Quinn, Brian. "Genius and Lust...," Best Sellers, XXXVI
        (March 1977), 401-402.
        Review of Genius and Lust that agrees with Mailer:
        "Miller is strange ... because he is both [a sexual
        gangster] and its opposite. He is sinner, ... but he
        is also saint.... "

E3955   Crews, Frederick. "Stuttering Giant," New York Review
        of Books, XXIV (March 3, 1977), 7-9.
        Review of Genius and Lust: "in Miller at his earliest
        and best we meet a liberator, one of those eccentrics
        of literature who, like Whitman, breaks every law and
        becomes a law.... We will have to learn to read
        [Miller] as he reads 'the great and imperfect ones' "
        (p. 9).

E3956   Sisk, John P. "The Obscene and Pornographic as Tools
        for American Writers," Baltimore Sun, CCLXXX (March
        28, 1977), B2.
        "Twentieth Century readers ... are likely to think
        [shock and outrage] appropriate for Henry Miller's
        'Tropic of Cancer'. "

E3957   Clark, Michael J. "Howard, Open to Latitude, Avoids
        'Tropic of Cancer' for Milder Zones," Baltimore Sun,

CCLXXX (May 8, 1977), B 12.
"For different reasons, the fictional works of Henry
Miller ... cannot be found on the shelves of the
Howard County library...."

E3958   Lewis, Leon. "Henry Miller's Portrait of Walter Lowenfels," Lost Generation Journal, IV (Spring 1977), 16-17,
20.

E3959   Pritchard, William H. "Merely Fiction," Hudson Review,
XXX (Spring 1977), 147-160.
Review of Genius and Lust that feels Miller is not in-
tellectually interesting.

E3960   "Genius and Lust," Publishers Weekly, CCXII (July 25,
1977), 70.
Superb sampling of Miller with excellent critical commentary by Mailer found in Genius and Lust.

E3961   Centing, Richard. "International College Tribute to Anaïs
Nin," Under the Sign of Pisces: Anaïs Nin and Her Circle,
VIII (Summer 1977), 3-6.
Miller mentioned.

E3962   "Paperbacks: New and Noteworthy," New York Times,
CXXVI (September 4, 1977), VII 23.
"A bountiful anthology of the writing of Henry Miller"
is found in Genius and Lust.

E3963   Turan, Kenneth. "A Mad Gaiety, a Verve, a Gusto:
Henry Miller Now," Washington Post, C (October 23, 1977),
H1, 6-8.
Miller discusses his past and present life and calls his
writing a distortion that is reality.

E3964   Campos, Julieta. "Anaïs Nin (1903-1977)," Under the Sign
of Pisces: Anaïs Nin and Her Circle, VIII (Fall 1977), 1-
5.
Miller sees Nin's Diary beside the revelations of St.
Augustine, Abelard, Rousseau, and Proust.

E3965   Harty, John. "Genius and Lust: A Journey Through the
Major Writings of Henry Miller," Under the Sign of Pisces:
Anaïs Nin and Her Circle, VIII (Fall 1977), 11-14.
Nin's importance in creating Miller the writer is dis-
cussed.

E3966   Martin, Jay. " 'The King of Smut': Henry Miller's Tragi-
cal History," Antioch Review, XXXV (Fall 1977), 342-367.
Excerpt from a biography dealing with the early years
in Miller's writing that covers his finding his voice in
the Tropics and his movement through the trials to the
publication of the "pornographic" Sexus.

E3967 Williams, Larry. "Miller: The Best and Worst of Lust,"
       Diamondback (University of Maryland), LXX (November 4,
       1977), 12.
              Review of Genius and Lust that sees the work con-
              cerned with sex and little else.

ANNEX: ARTICLES FOR WHICH DATES ARE UNAVAILABLE
(Arranged Alphabetically)

E3968 Adams, Donald. "Speaking of Books," n.p.
              New York State Court of Appeals, by vote of 4 to 3,
              called Tropic flagrantly obscene.

E3969 Aranda, Joanquin. "Henry Miller en castellano," Nuestro
       Tiempo, n.d., 465-468.
              Miller seen as complete writer--a fine story teller
              with a good sense of humor, a mystic. Compared to
              Hemingway and Faulkner. (In Spanish.)

E3970 Arion. "Ilya Ehrenbourg ou le materialiste contre la
       maternelle," n.p.
              Air-Conditioned Nightmare an important social com-
              ment. (In French.)

E3971 Arland, Marcel. "L'Epopée du cholera," Lettres.

E3972 Audiberti. "Les Médecins ne sont pas des plombaers,"
       Volonte, n.d., 4.
              Miller's "Preface" to Haniel Long's The Power Within
              Us considered excellent.

E3973 Beaudoin, Kenneth Lawrence. "What Henry Miller Said
       and Why It Is Important," n.p.
              Bern Porter feels sex is normal and natural in his
              assessment of Miller called What Henry Miller Said
              and Why It Is Important.

E3974 Billy, Andre. "Miller condamné une fois de plus les
       Etats-unis," n.p.
              Air-Conditioned Nightmare and Remember to Remem-
              ber both damning statements about America. (In
              French.)

E3975 Blancpain, Marc. "Maturité," Volonte, n.d., 4.
              Miller called courageous and profound in review of
              World of Sex. (In French.)

E3976 Bourdrel, Anne. "Henry Miller a Paris," n.p.
              Miller left Big Sur to see Paris once more. (In
              French.)

E3977 Bouvier, Emile. "Romans historiques," n.p.

Miller's "Preface" to Haniel Long's Cabaza de Vaca
mentioned.   (In French.)

E3978   Brady, Mildred Edie.   "The New Cult of Sex and Anarchy,"
Harper's, n.d., 312-322.
Miller's settlement in Big Sur has led many to make
pilgrimages to see this surrealist and anarchist.

E3979   Bufano, Beniamino.   "Genesis of the Night Life," What's
Doing, n.d., 26-27.
Miller sees night life as being only true life.

E3980   Burnett, James.   "Mixed Marriages," n.p., 7-8.
Durrell-Miller Correspondence called a fascinating relationship.

E3981   "Le Cabinet De Lecture," Cahiers du Sud, n.d., 327-328.
Black Spring called the story of paranoia.   (In French.)

E3982   Calas, Andre.   "Bribes littéraires...," Nord-Littoral
Calais.
List of members of Committee for Defense of Miller.
(In French.)

E3983   "Les Caprices de Themis," Courrier de l'Ouest.
Tropic called single most important novel written.   (In
French.)

E3984   "Ceux de l'Enfer," La France es Combat.
Miller a naturalistic writer.   (In French.)

E3985   Chadourne, Paul.   "Ecrivain maudit de l'Amérique, Henry
Miller," n.p.
Miller feels that if society cannot take his criticism,
it has no right to endure.   (In French.)

E3986   Chisholm, Hugh.   "A Man-Sized World," n.p., 149-155.
Letter to Miller in Big Sur, from Hugh Chisholm in
Athens, Greece, admiring the writing of Colossus of
Maroussi enough to tell Miller he lives and experiences
Greece.

E3987   "Club Attacks Ban on Miller Book as 'Outrageous'," Montgomery County Sentinel.
Kensington-Wheaton Democratic Club protested banning
of Tropic.

E3988   Conant, T. A.   "Tropic of Cancer," Star-Bulletin.
Police should ban Miller.

E3989   "Court Action over Best-Seller--'Injures Purity of
Thought'," Evening Standard.
French publishers of Capricorn being sued.

E3990   Courtney, Robert.   "The Four Letter World of Henry
        Miller," Rogue, 34-36, 73-76.
        Miller seen as most censored man in America, yet a
        major literary force in Europe.

E3991   De Pedrolo, Manuel.   "Cop d'Ull a l'Obra d'Henry Miller,"
        El Ponte, IX (n.d.), 21-27.
        Miller credited with having influenced a generation of
        sixties writers.   (In Italian.)

E3992   "Der Fall Miller," Bücher und Zeitschriften, 380-381.
        Miller's books not for Puritans.   (In German.)

E3993   Derleth, August.   "The Big Sur...," n.p., 14-15.
        Big Sur an account of Miller's 13 years in the moun-
        tains of California.

E3994   Derleth, August.   "Two by Henry Miller," Chicago Times.
        Black Spring a song about life and freedom, while
        Just Wild About Harry a bore.

E3995   "Dernières Fausses nouvelles," Le Herisson, no. 50.
        Miller compared to Picasso.   (In French.)

E3996   Domnergues, Pierre.   " 'Big Sur,' de Jack Kerouac,"
        n.p.
        Kerouac went to Big Sur to meet the father of the
        Beat Generation, Miller.

E3997   Donnelly, Tom.   "So 'Malone Dies'--Or Does He Really?"
        n.p.
        Tropic Miller's best book.

E3998   Durrell, Vernon.   "On Censorship," Star-Bulletin.
        Instead of censoring Tropic one should teach children
        its facts at home.

E3999   "Editor's Note," Herald.
        The Herald withholds judgment on Tropic until it gets
        copy.

E4000   Engberg, Harald.   "[Henry Miller]," n.p.
        Miller's Sexus trial in Norway discussed.   (In Nor-
        wegian.)

E4001   "L'Exposition Internationale du Surréalists," Les Deux
        Soeurs, no. 3, n.d.
        Miller attends International Surrealist Exposition.   (In
        French.)

E4002   Faure, Maurice.   "Miller, ou l'amour éperdu de la vie,"
        n.p.
        Miller's sense of love of life comes forth in Sexus.

(In French.)

E4003   Ferber, Christian.   "So mancher Ware gerne Henry
Miller," Die Welt.
Review of Nights of Love and Laughter.   (In German.)

E4004   "First Revise," Playboy.
Mailer sees Miller as honest and realistic, not a pornographer.

E4005   "4. 8 Million Is Asked in Banning 'Tropic'," n. p.
Publisher and author of Tropic sue for damages.

E4006   Frederiksen, Emil.   "Upaakraevet Oversaettelse," n. p.
Review of Cancer which compares it with Knut Hamsun's Hunger.   (In Norwegian.)

E4007   Fukuzawa, Ichiro.   "[Water Paintings of Henry Miller],"
n. p.
A look at Miller's watercolors.   (In Japanese.)

E4008   Gall, Michel.   "Henry Miller," Vous en Dit Plus Sept
Jours, 24.
Miller and Faulkner seen as the two great American
writers.   (In French.)

E4009   Garnier, Robert.   "Littérature, Morale & Revolution,"
L'Age Nouveau, 36-40.
Miller feels life is worth giving one's all to attain.
(In French.)

E4010   Gelre, Henk van.   "Het fenomeen Henry Miller," n. p. ,
15-18.
Miller's writing seen as continuous phenomenon in this
review of Big Sur.   (In Dutch.)

E4011   Germershausen, W. J.   "Editor," Star-Bulletin.
Tropic called slop.

E4012   Glanville, Brian.   "Banned Author Looks at Life," n. p.
Reunion in Barcelona and Reunion in Big Sur are
touching expressions of the Miller-Perlès friendship.

E4013   Gold, Mike.   "Literary Magazines of the Old School and
the New," n. p.
Review of Air-Conditioned Nightmare that feels Miller
dislikes democracy and favors Old South of slavery
times.

E4014   Gorn, Lester.   "Obscenity Issue," San Francisco Examiner.
Gorn feels the U. S. too puritanical about Tropic, yet
still calls book a bore.

E4015   Griffin, David W. "The Possibility of Joy. Henry Miller's
        Place in the American Tradition," n. p.
                Miller a man outside the bounds of a sick society that
                will not accept him.

E4016   Guardino, Joseph. "Editor," Herald.
                Everyone has the right to read Miller and discover that
                he's a boy who never grew up.

E4017   "Henry Miller," El Hogar, 77.
                Miller's story, "My Friend Stanley," gives the reader
                the perspective of being an adolescent in New York.
                (In Spanish.)

E4018   "Henry Miller academicien aux U.S.A. ou ses livres son
        interdits," France Soir.
                Miller joins American Institute of Letters.   (In French.)

E4019   "Henry Miller, Censored Writer, Marries Again," San
        Francisco Chronicle.
                On December 6, in Carmel, California, Miller mar-
                ried Evelyn Byrd McClure.

E4020   "Henry Miller Exhibition," Bridgestone Art Gallery, Tokyo.
                Miller's exhibit is a display of 40 fantasies.

E4021   "Henry Miller's Poem," Book Collecting & Library Month-
        ly, 13.
                Miller's prose seen as concise poetry that is first
                rate.

E4022   Horton, Michael. "Mostly About People," n. p.
                Rosy Crucifixion called a trilogy dealing with sex.

E4023   Inner. "Nobelpriset till Henry Miller," Aftonbladet.
                Writer feels Miller should be given the Prize.   (In
                Swedish.)

E4024   Javan, Minoo. "Henry Miller," Sakham, 719-739.
                Miller interviewed.

E4025   Kirsch, Robert R. "Miller Tales That Boston Didn't
        Ban," n. p.
                Reviews of Cosmological Eye, Remember to Remember,
                and Sunday After the War, three works that are better
                than Tropic and not banned.

E4026   Kitamura, Taro. "Comment on Henry Miller's 'Into the
        Night Life'," Cendre, no. 6-7, 28-29.
                This piece of writing from Black Spring considered to be
                Miller at his best.   (In Japanese.)

E4027   L., R. "Henry Miller," Quartier Latin, 1.

Miller a revolutionary. (In French.)

E4028 Laborde, Jean. "L'Auteur du 'Tropic du Cancer'," n.p.
Tropic called brutal. (In French.)

E4029 Laplayne, Jean-Rene. "Avec Miller contre ses detrae-
teurs," n.p.
Miller's works considered grotesques. (In French.)

E4030 Laprade, Jacques de. "Notes sur Miller," n.p.
The spiritual man of principle appears in Miller's
Rosy Crucifixion. (In French.)

E4031 Lauter, Hans. "Der Kampf für eine realistische Kunst
ist eine nationale Aufgabe," n.p.
Reference made to Miller. (In German.)

E4032 Lesdain, Pierre. "Chronique des livres," Volonte, 4.
Miller's writing involves meditation and apocalypse.
(In French.)

E4033 Lesdain, Pierre. "Liberté, o vain mot!" n.p.
Ridgely Cummings wants to expand circulation of
Miller in California. (In French.)

E4034 Lesdain, Pierre, and Jean Giono. "Les Âmes fortes,"
n.p.
Miller sees homage and goodness as man's only defense in life. (In French.)

E4035 Lyons, Eddie. "Eddie Lyons' Column," New York Post,
n.d., 23.
Nexus, the final book in The Rosy Crucifixion, in
print.

E4036 McCulloch, Alan. "Noted Scribe Takes Look at Local
Artists," Monterey Peninsula Herald.
Story about Miller at Big Sur.

E4037 McPhaul, Jack. "Is It Pornography?" n.p.
Whether Tropic is art or pornography depends on the
reader.

E4038 Madrid, Francisco. "Henry Miller: el novelista maldito,"
Revista de América, n.d., 33-34.
Miller's autobiographical literature the best way a
man can deal with his own life. (In Spanish.)

E4039 Marais, Noel. "Avez-vous Lu?" Conquêtes.
Both Tropics seen as pathetic autobiographies. (In
French.)

E4040 Marchand, Jean-Jose. "Mademoiselle Coeur-Brise," Le

Magasin du Spectacle, no. 3, 165-168.
Miller America's greatest Naturalistic writer.   (In French.)

E4041   Maulnier, Thierry.   "Ou va la littérature americaine?"
Variété, no. 3, 55-56.
Tropic called romantic, humorous, and realistic.   (In French.)

E4042   Mauriac, Claude.   "Henry Miller ange gardien, " n. p.
Miller celebrated in France.   (In French.)

E4043   Mauriac, Claude.   "Henry Miller l'homme fou d'écriture, "
n. p.
Rosy Crucifixion concerns itself with Miller's early years and his sexual expressions during this time.
(In French.)

E4044   Mavity, Nancy Barr.   "Our United States as Seen by
Three Persons, " Oakland Tribune.
Miller never liked America so it seems only natural that The Air-Conditioned Nightmare would be hostile.

E4045   Micha, Rene.   "Temps de la poésie, " L'Arche, no. 25,
31-41.
Miller called a dadist.   (In French.)

E4046   "The Miller Case, " Socialist Party Newspaper of Stras-
bourg.
Miller's books all about search for source of life.

E4047   Mitry, Jean.   "Le Corbeau juge par..., " Travelling.
Miller a realist.   (In French.)

E4048   Nicolareizis, D.   "The Colossus of Maroussi, " Athene,
n. d. , 62-63.
Review of Colossus of Maroussi calling it a prophetic book.

E4049   Norris, Hoke.   "Cancer in Chicago (Reprinted from Evergreen Review), " n. p.

E4050   Novales, R. Gil.   "El coloso de Marusi, " n. p. , 8.
Colossus of Maroussi depicts Miller's journey through Greece, the cultural cradle.   (In Spanish.)

E4051   Ohff, Heinz.   "Henry Millers Protest gengen die Tabus, "
n. p. , n. d.
Review of Nexus.   (In German.)

E4052   "126 exemplaires de 'Sexus' ont échappé à la police, "
Paris-Match.
The violence and sex in Sexus beyond compare.   (In

French.)

E4053   O'Neill, Frank. "Henry Miller in Paradise, No?" n.p.
        Big Sur a book about humanity and kindness.

E4054   "ORT See Film on Scholarship," New Jersey-Milner.
        Talk on Tropic's censorship at Jewish Community
        Center.

E4055   Pauwels, Louis. "Les Idées et les lettres l'affaire
        Miller," n.p.
        Miller's writing seen as immoral, yet society viewed
        as hypocritic. (In French.)

E4056   Pavillard, Don. "Downpour Swamps Webb Printery,"
        Tucson Daily Citizen, 2.
        Many of Webb's copies of Miller's Order and Chaos
        Chez Hans Reichel destroyed in flood.

E4057   Petit, Henri. "Le Monde du sexe," Libéré Parisien, IX
        (March 15).
        Miller's fundamental confessions about sex appear in
        The World of Sex. (In French.)

E4058   "Plumes au vent," Gavroche.
        Capricorn no more lewd than ancient Greece and
        Aphrodite. (In French.)

E4059   "Police Turn Over to Court 75 'Tropic of Cancer' Copies,"
        Danbury (Conn.) News-Times.
        Court given Tropic to read.

E4060   Potter, Kelly. "Naughty Books That Defied the Censors,"
        Rare Collections, 98-102.
        Capricorn banned in U.S.

E4061   Price, R. G. G. "Henry Miller," New English Review,
        368-369.
        Cosmological Eye viewed as fine introduction to Miller.

E4062   Pryce-Jones, David. "One By One," n.p.
        Miller enjoyed Bates' Seven by Five because of the
        author's pain and humor.

E4063   R., A. "Nous les élus," Arts Lettres, no. 8-9.
        Ban against Miller's sexist literature continues. (In
        French.)

E4064   Rexroth, Kenneth. "Henry Miller's Myth of Himself as
        Pariah," n.p.
        Stand Still Like the Hummingbird another anti-society
        piece.

E4065   Rieux, J.   "Deoartrez-Maus," Echos de France.
        Radio reading of Cancer reported upon.   (In French.)

E4066   Rolarvdael.   "Rue Marthe Richard," n. p.
        Cartoon of Miller and prostitute.   (In French.)

E4067   Rosen, Arthur.   "Sexus-Plexus-Nexus," n. p.
        Review of Rosy Crucifixion.   (In German.)

E4068   Rosseaux, Andre.   "Miller entre l'Amérique et la France,"
        Les Livres.
        Look at Remember to Remember where Miller's friend-
        ship for artists, his dislike for America, and his love
        for France are all noted.   (In French.)

E4069   Rougeul, Jean and Leo Sauvage.   "La Plaisanterie à assez
        dure," n. p. , n. d.
        Miller's belief in freedom noted.   (In French.)

E4070   S. , W. H.   "Miller as Playwright," Weekly.
        Just Wild About Harry a new form of drama.

E4071   Schleppey, Bloor.   "The Furrow," n. p.
        Air-Conditioned Nightmare a discovery of America.

E4072   Seco.   "El coloso de Marusi," Del Monte de Castilla.
        Miller's interest in Greece and the past not typically
        American.   (In Spanish.)

E4073   Simmons, Richard M.   "Uninformed Articles Fill Editorial
        Page," Dallas Times-Herald, n. d.
        Banning of morally objectionable books like Tropic
        lowers crime rate.

E4074   Smith, Miles A.   "Henry Miller Writes Book Dealing with
        Watercolors," n. p. , n. d.
        Miller writes and talks about his watercolors.

E4075   "Les Spectacles," Nouvelles Etudiantes.
        Miller a writer of fantasy.   (In French.)

E4076   Stangerup, Hakon.   "Eksplosion eller Onvendelse?" Dagens
        Nyheder.
        Capricorn may cause explosion in Denmark because it
        is too realistic for some people to accept.   (In Danish.)

E4077   Steiner, Rudolph.   "Henry Miller--A Debt," Span, no. 2,
        n. d. , 4-5.
        Miller viewed as one of greatest literary nonconform-
        ists.

E4078   Storm, Ole.   "Kunstneren som klovn," Carl Werner
        Skogholm, n. d. , 17-18.

Smile at Foot of Ladder the story about a child much
like Black Spring, only more of a fairy tale. (In
Danish.)

E4079   "Tage des Lesens im Zeichen des Spektrums," Der Bahn-
hofs-Buchhandel, 1137-1138.
German review of Miller's The Books in My Life.

E4080   Tank, K. L.   'Der Mensch kennt kein Ende," n. p.
Exploration of Plexus. (In German.)

E4081   Taylor, Barney L.   'Henry Miller," Herald.
Miller sounds his own horn.

E4082   " 'Tropic' Novel Trial Delayed," Hackensack Bergen Record, n. d.
Superior Court Judge Leyden defers Tropic action
pending result of District Court suit.

E4083   " 'Tropic' Publisher Gets Postponement," Hackensack Bergen Record, n. d.
Judge Wallace Leyder postponed Tropic trial.

E4084   " 'Tropic' Seller Is Fined $50," Fort Lauderdale Daily
News, n. d.
Sale of Tropic costs Mrs. Irene Walker of Fort Laua-
erdale $50.

E4085   "Vital Tropic," International Herald Tribune, 13.
Note that Joseph Strick will shoot next picture based
on Tropic.

E4086   Webster, Harvey Curtis.   "Fascinating, If You Survive the
Shock," n. p.
Sunday After the War excellent if one can take the
shocking social criticism of America.

E4087   Welch, Douglas.   " 'Tropic of Cancer'--It's 'Tame,' Now,"
n. p.
Tropic tame by American standards of the sixties.

E4088   White, William.   'SIU Press Crosscurrents," American
Book Collector, 3-4.
Wickes's Henry Miller and the Critics a representative
viewing of the author of Tropic.

E4089   Whitfield, Mark.   "Meeting with Henry," Cavalier, 6.
Miller a writer who is so many different people.

E4090   Winchell, Walter.   '[Tropic of Cancer]," n. p.
Cancer one of France's best-sellers.

E4091   Wood, Richard C.   "A Note About a Notable Correspondence,"

<u>Randolph-Macon College Magazine</u>, XXXVIII (n. d.), 8-11.
Miller's letters to J. Rives Childs discussed.   Childs
sees Miller in tradition of Restif de la Bretonne, not
as pornographer.

E4092   Wylie, Philip.   "Misadventures of an Heiress," n. p. , 14.
Miller called saint of an era for his <u>Air-Conditioned</u>
<u>Nightmare</u>.

E4093   Ye Olde Witch Hunter.   "Editor," <u>Star-Bulletin</u>.
<u>Tropic</u> should be outlawed.

INDEX OF AUTHORS, EDITORS, ET AL.

451

452   Index

INDEX OF MILLER'S WORKS*

The Air-Conditioned Nightmare A27, A73-4, B43, B53-4, B210,
B259, B315, B335, C79, C84, C105, E127, E183-5, E191-4,
E196, E199, E201-2, E207, E221, E350, E805, E936,
E1044-5, E1047, E1052, E1069, E1071, E1636, E1681,
E2008, E2639, E3031, E3073, E3120, E3134, E3373, E3481,
E3903, E3940, E3970, E3974, E4013, E4044, E4071, E4092

Aller Retour New York B57, C10, E10, E3055

The Angel Is My Water Mark C16, E1664, E1867, E2635

Art and Outrage A16, B135, E1438, E1445, E1451, E1484, E1495,
E1524, E1529, E1554, E1644, E1663

Beauford DeLaney E3539

The Best of Henry Miller E1559, E1596-8, E1600-16, E1618-22,
E1630-2, E1634, E1637, E1643, E1663, E1680, E1699,
E3337, E3445

Big Sur and the Oranges of Hieronymus Bosch A73-4, D3, E1130,
E1134, E1214, E1216, E1218-9, E1221-7, E1229, E1232,
E1234-5, E1239-40, E1251, E1257-65, E1267-71, E1274-82,
E1285-6, E1288-9, E1296-7, E1299-313, E1315-24, E1330,
E1332, E1339, E1341-3, E1345-6, E1348-51, E1353, E1357,
E1360-1, E1409, E1411-2, E1420-2, E1425, E1427, E1436-7,
E1441, E1443-4, E1461, E2774, E3522, E3558, E3993, E4010,
E4053

Black Spring A1, A27, A45, A73-4, B15, B30, B45, B200, B214,
B218, B230, B285, B291, B303, C16, C61, E7-9, E13, E15,
E93, E204-5, E215, E230, E256, E311, E352, E377, E382,
E452, E471, E609, E927, E982, E1515-6, E1532, E1539,
E1562, E1564, E1592, E1623, E1681, E2008, E2840, E3164,
E3191, E3193, E3196-7, E3208, E3214, E3248, E3313, E3449,
E3481-2, E3525, E3553, E3656, E3771, E3783, E3830-1,
E3909, E3981, E3994, E4026, E4078

---

*At well over 1700 citations, the entry for Tropic of Cancer is
omitted in the interests of practicality.